HUMAN RESOURCE MANAGEMENT

HUMAN RESOURCE MANAGEMENT

Bibhuti Bhusan Mahapatro
Reader
P.G. Department of Business Management
Fakir Mohan University, Vyasa Vihar
Balasore, Orissa

NEW AGE
MANAGEMENT

An Imprint of

NEW AGE INTERNATIONAL (P) LIMITED, PUBLISHERS

New Delhi • Bangalore • Chennai • Cochin • Guwahati • Hyderabad
Jalandhar • Kolkata • Lucknow • Mumbai • Ranchi
Visit us at **www.newagepublishers.com**

Published by New Age International (P) Ltd., Publishers
First Edition: 2010
Reprint: 2014

BRANCHES

•Bangalore 37/10, 8th Cross (Near Hanuman Temple), Azad Nagar, Chamarajpet, Bangalore-560 018
Tel.: (080) 26756823, Telefax: 26756820, **E-mail: bangalore@newagepublishers.com**

•Chennai 26, Damodaran Street, T. Nagar, Chennai-600 017
Tel.: (044) 24353401, Telefax: 24351463, **E-mail: chennai@newagepublishers.com**

•Cochin CC-39/1016, Carrier Station Road, Ernakulam South, Cochin-682 016
Tel.: (0484) 2377004, Telefax: 4051303, **E-mail: cochin@newagepublishers.com**

•Guwahati Hemsen Complex, Mohd. Shah Road, Paltan Bazar, Near Starline Hotel, Guwahati-781 008
Tel.: (0361) 2513881, Telefax: 2543669, **E-mail: guwahati@newagepublishers.com**

•Hyderabad 105, 1st Floor, Madhiray Kaveri Tower, 3-2-19, Azam Jahi Road, Near Kumar Theater Nimboliadda, Kachiguda, Hyderabad-500 027, Tel.: (040) 24652456, Telefax: 24652457
E-mail: hyderabad@newagepublishers.com

•Kolkata RDB Chambers (Formerly Lotus Cinema) 106A, 1st Floor, S.N. Banerjee Road, Kolkata-700 014
Tel.: (033) 22273773, Telefax: 22275247, **E-mail: kolkata@newagepublishers.com**

•Lucknow 16-A, Jopling Road, Lucknow-226 001
Tel.: (0522) 2209578, 4045297, Telefax: 2204098, **E-mail:lucknow@newagepublishers.com**

•Mumbai 142C, Victor House, Ground Floor, N.M. Joshi Marg, Lower Parel, Mumbai-400 013
Tel.: (022) 24927869, Telefax: 24915415, **E-mail: mumbai@newagepublishers.com**

•New Delhi 22, Golden House, Daryaganj, New Delhi-110 002

ISBN: 978-81-224-2673-1

Rs. 250.00

C-14-04-7525

Printed in India at Ram Printograph, Delhi.
Typeset at Subham Computers, Delhi.

PUBLISHING GLOBALLY
NEW AGE INTERNATIONAL (P) LIMITED, PUBLISHERS
7/30 A, Daryaganj, New Delhi-110002
Visit us at **www.newagepublishers.com**

Preface

All organizations, be these business, educational or Governmental are basically social system. The people run these. The functioning of these organizations depends on upon how people work or be have in the organization. The human behavior is caused and highly unpredictable. People in organizations need to lead in directions that accomplish organizational goals successfully. The human resources of an organization constitute its entire work force. Human resources management is responsible for identifying, selecting and inducting the competent people, train them, facilitating and motivating them to perform at the high level of efficiency and providing mechanism to ensure that they maintain their affiliation with their organization.

Human resources management is also an art of developing people and their potentialities for their personnel and the growth of the organization. It is the process of integrating the HR and organization together to ensure that their individual and collective goals are closely aligned. People have always been considered as critical factor in an organizational set up. Unlike other resources, such as technology, finance, materials, this can be purchased, human resources are critical and it needs to be handled with care. Often, organizations are concerned not only about the employees' productivity but also about the employee commitment and nurturing their capabilities for the maximum utilization and growth.

Since, which constitute the cornerstone of the organization, HRM assumes central importance in the organization. Any decision and/or process of an organization must be implemented by the people. In a competitive scenario, it is the ingenuity, zeal, enthusiasm and commitment of its HR that makes all the differences for an organization. So, the study of the HRM forms important aspects of the study of any management discipline.

The concept and practice of employee-employer relationships have also undergone a change over the last decade. In the globally competitive economy, efforts to boost productivity and quality are a continuous process. To be more responsive, the businesses are increasingly adopting the new approaches to HRM that emphasize on the redistribution of power, greater participation by the individuals, and team work. It has been observed that, the only sustainable competitive advantage on organization can have in today's environment is its people. Effective management of human resources is not an issue of survival. Therefore, the establishing practices of HRM must also be able to understand and apply innovative techniques successfully in managing human resources. In the years ahead, the importance of HRM will become more crucial.

The large scale production and the contribution of Industrial Revolution in the eighteenth and nineteenth century gave rise to the practice of "Personnel Management", which started as the voluntary movement in the US and UK. Traditionally, the role of HR manager was to maintain the records and administration and act as liaison executive between the employee and employer. The HR manager should apply the concept and convert it into practice. Recognizing that the human beings are the most important asset in the organization, the term personnel is replaced by the Human Resources Management. The development of human resource management is very crucial for quality productivity and growth. It is now increasingly used in development functions.

More now than ever, companies today want to deliver products better, faster and cheaper. At the same time, in high technology environment of the 21st century, nearly all organizations have found themselves building more and more complex products. HR manager is responsible for the human resources in your organization. Your continual mission is to seek ways of improving the return on investment in these human assets. In this context, I think, this book is a humble attempt in this direction.

Author

Acknowledgements

This book has been made possible through the direct and indirect cooperation of various persons whom I wish to express my appreciation and gratitude. First and the foremost, my intellectual debt is to those academicians and practitioners who have contributed significantly to the emerging fields of human behavior and whose work has been quoted copiously and used extensively by me in my writings for this book.

My academic colleagues, earlier at SMIT, BIMIT, CMS Bhubaneswar and Fakir Mohan University, Balasore deserves my appreciation for extending to me their whole heartedness cooperation and support. To my students and research scholars, I owe a deep sense of obligation. without their inquisitiveness and helpful participation, I could not possibly have developed and sustained an abiding interest in learning this.

I am extremely grateful to my computer friends of F.M. University, Balasore and Mr. Deepak Bose for helping in the computer data entry work. He also complied in association with me the Internet resources relating to this area. Several Colleagues of different institutions other than where I work have constantly encouraged me with their words, appreciation and advice.

I am also grateful to the anonymous reviewers of the initial texts of this, who provided very useful comments, all of which proved to be of immense help in preparing this book in a particular shape.

I am beholden to my parents and other family members for their blessings and particularly my wife Sunita and son their sacrifices and encouragement.

I am indebted to New Age International (P) Ltd., Publishers for the efforts they have put in for making the book a reality and giving a shape.

Dr. Bibhuti B. Mahapatro

Contents

Preface *v*
Acknowledgements *vii*

1. Human Resources Management: Context, Concept and Boundaries **1**
1.1 Introduction 1
1.2 Human Factor and their Importance 2
1.3 Definition of Human Resources Management 3
1.4 A New Mandate for Human Resources 4
1.5 Changing Role of the Human Resource Management 5
1.6 Managing human resources in the emerging scenario 7
1.7 Evolution of Management of Human Resources: An Indian Perspective 10
References 16

2. The Concept, Scope and Function of Human Resource of Management **18**
2.1 Introduction 18
2.2 Concept and Challenges of HRM 18
2.3 Objectives of HRM 22
2.4 Human Resource Functions 24
2.5 Scope of HRM 29
References 35

3. Human Resources Planning **37**
3.1 Introduction 37
3.2 What is Human Resources Planning? 38
3.3 Objectives of the Human Resources Planning 38
3.4 Needs of HRP 40
3.5 Human Resource Planning Process 46
References 60

4. Attracting the Talent: The Recruitment and Selection **62**
4.1 Introduction 62
4.2 What is Recruiting? 63
4.3 Corporate Mission, Objectives, Strategies and Tactics (Most) And Recruitment 64
References 81

5. Socialization, Mobility and Separation **82**
5.1 Introduction 82
5.2 Promotions 84
5.3 Demotion 86

5.4	Transfer	87
5.5	Placement	88
5.6	Induction	90
5.7	Employee Separation	92
	References	100
6.	**Managing the Performances**	**101**
6.1	Introduction	101
	References	136
7.	**Competency Mapping**	**138**
7.1	Introduction	138
7.2	Competencies and HR	142
	References	164
8.	**Potential Appraisal, Assessment Center and Career Succession Planning**	**166**
8.1	Introduction	166
8.2	Performance	170
	References	201
9.	**HR Measurement and Audit**	**233**
9.1	Introduction	203
9.2	HR Audit	215
9.3	The Audit Process	223
9.4	Human Resource Information System (HRIS)	227
9.5	Human Resource Accounting	233
9.6	Lev and Schwartz Compensation Model	242
	References	249
10.	**Human Resource Development**	**251**
10.1	Introduction	251
10.2	Principles of Successful Organization	274
	References	280
11.	**Training and Development**	**281**
11.1	Introduction	281
11.2	Management Development	299
	References	322
12.	**Compensation Strategy and Structure**	**325**
12.1	Introduction	325
12.2	Compensation Issues	326
12.3	Objective of the Compensation	328
12.4	Compensation Functions	334
12.5	Compensation policy and Objectives	334
12.6	Determinants of Compensation	342
12.7	Compensation Structure	343

12.8 Job Evaluation Systems 346
12.9 Pay Equity 350
12.10 Executive Compensation 351
12.11 Compensation Trends 356
References 367

13. Labour-Management Relationships **369**

13.1 Introduction 369
13.2 Concept and Scope of Industrial Relations 370
13.3 Functions and Objectives of Industrial Relations 374
13.4 Approaches of Industrial Relations 379
13.5 Key Issues and Critical Challenges in Industrial Relations 385
13.6 Globalization and Industrial Relations-Its Emerging Trends 397
13.7 Conclusion 401
References 405

Index **407**

CHAPTER 1

HUMAN RESOURCES MANAGEMENT: CONTEXT, CONCEPT AND BOUNDARIES

1.1 INTRODUCTION

Modern organizational setting is characterized by constant changing relation to environmental factors and human resources. As regard to the environmental factors, we find changes in the operating organizational structure, the network of the working procedures, customs on norms and the economic, political and the social patterns in which organizations exist. Moreover, there is a constant change in human resources, the individuals are employed daily with new creativity, ideas and experiences, while the existing workforce is also continuously changing their ideas, attitudes and even values. These two dimensions reveal the following trends.

- Increased complexity of the organizations, employment and a clear hierarchy of owners, managers and workers.
- Increased the number of employers, self-employed and enlarged size of workforce.
- Enhance the need of training in view of increased requirements of specialized skills.
- Public interventions and legal complications in employee and employer relationships.
- Enhanced training and development of managers and professionalisation of management education.
- Possibility of employment explosion in view of ever increasing size of workforce.
- Rising the formal level of education of rank and file employees who becoming increasingly critical of management malpractice and errors.
- Rank and file employees rapidly growing demands in different employment situations.
- Recognizing of close relationships between profits and earnings and ability to manage human resources.

Indeed these trends manifest themselves in problem areas as identified by the managers in organizational settings. Although the change may provide solutions to some problems, it may create several new ones. There is an urgent need to understand these problems, anticipate them and to find solution to them. The responsibility to find out the solutions to these problems lies with every manager who has prepared to deal with different change effectively through educational and developmental programs. Obviously, every manager is responsible for management of human resources of course with the advice and help of personnel department. Management of human resources is the essence of being manager who has to get things done through the people without whom he can be a technician but not a manager. Thus, every manager has to develop and maintain his competency in managing human resources, which have assumed utmost significance in modern organizations.

1.2 HUMAN FACTOR AND THEIR IMPORTANCE

The macroeconomic and management issues facing the Indian economy are the removal of the twin evils of employment and poverty. How to remove these twin evils and more important, promote optimum utilization of human capacities would be a major concern of not only the State but also Indian business and management. In addition, the following major macro and micro issues pose the serious problems to management and it is time that Indian business and management face the challenges of these issues and make a contribution in solving these issues.

The macro and micro issues:

- Capacity utilization-machine as well as human.
- Combating the inflation and holding the price line.
- Population problem.
- Motivation, involvement and consultation.
- Meeting basic physiological and other needs.
- Reducing the absenteeism, accidents, loss and damage.
- Generating employment opportunities, almost to the level of full employment.
- Human assets accounting, profits and growth.
- Eliminating strikes and lockouts through voluntary measures.
- Job redesigning, enlargement, enrichment.
- Promoting the health, self-renewal and creativity.
- Promoting exports and economic growth.
- Conservation of resources (renewal and non-renewal.)
- Increase the productivity of finance.
- Waste and cost reduction.
- Promoting the arts and culture, religion, sports, leisure activities.
- Adoption of village and communities.
- Promoting entrepreneurship, barefoot entrepreneurs and managers.
- Eliminating discrimination of all types.
- Promoting a sense of national identity, awareness and contribution.
- Promoting industrial and national security.
- Eliminating poverty completely.
- Improving the quality of working life.
- Improving the quality of life.

The human resources (total sum of knowledge, skills, creative abilities, talents and attitudes obtained in the population: National point of view) have also been designed a human factors. According to Michael J. Jucious, "human factor refers to a whole consisting of inter-related, interdependent and interacting physiological, psychological, social, and ethical components". It has physiological needs (food, rest, environmental conditions, security etc.), psychological needs (autonomy, achievement, power, acquisitiveness) social needs (affiliation, status, approval, prestige etc.) and it has an ethical creature, it has concepts of right and working. It tends to do what it thinks right. Obviously, the human factor is dynamic in nature as is revealed in motivation and defense mechanism. It is the on going process involving the four sub-processes.

The human resources are assuming increasing significance in modern organizations. Obviously, majority of the problem in organizational setting are human and social rather than physical, technical or economic. The failure to recognize this fact causes immense loss to the nation, enterprise and the individual. It is a truism that productivity is associated markedly with the nature of human resources and their total environment consisting of interrelated, interdependent and interacting economic and non-economic (political, religious, cultural, sociological and psychological) factors. Thus, the significance of human resources can be examined from time to time.

1.3 DEFINITION OF HUMAN RESOURCES MANAGEMENT

"Personnel Management is that part of management concerned with people at work and their relationship within the organization. It seeks to bring together men and women who make up an enterprise, enabling each to make his own best contribution to its success is both as an individual and as a member of a working group". **— NIPM**

"It is planning, organizing, directing and controlling of the procurement, development compensation, integration, maintenance and separation of human resources to the end that individual, organizational and societal objectives are accomplished". **— Edwin B. Flippo**

"It is that field of management which has to do with planning, organizing and controlling the functions of procuring, developing, maintaining and utilizing a labor force such as that the : (a) objectives for which the company is established are effectively, (*b*) objectives of all levels of personnel are served to the highest possible degree, (*c*) objectives of society are dully considered and served". **— Michael J. Jucious**

Human resources management can be defined as that part of management concerned with:

- All the decisions, strategies, factors, principles, operations, practices, functions, activities and methods related to the management of people as employees in any type of organization.
- All the dimensions related to people in their employment relationships, and all the dynamics that flow from it; and
- Adding value to the delivery of goods and services and to the quality of work life for employees, hereby helping to ensure continuous organizational success in transformative environments (www.hrsgb.org.za/HR_scope_and_definition.html).

Human Resource Management (HRM) is a process of bringing people and organizations together so that the goals of each are met. It is part of the management process which is concerned with the management of human resources in an organization. It tries to secure the best from people by winning their wholehearted cooperation. In short, it may be defined as the art of procuring, developing and maintaining competent workforce to achieve the goals of an organization in an effective and efficient manner. According to the Invancevich and Glueck, "HRM is concerned with the most effective use of people to achieve organizational and individual goals. It is the way of managing people at work, so that they give their best to the organization".

1.4 A NEW MANDATE FOR HUMAN RESOURCES

Human resources have never been more necessary. The competitive forces that we face today and will continue to face in the future demand organizational excellence. To achieve this excellence by focusing on learning, quality, teamwork, and reengineering are driven by the way organizations get things done and how employees are treated. To achieve this excellence we look at the work of Human resources. By designing an entirely new role and agenda that results in enriching the organization's value to customers, investors and employees, HR can help deliver organizational excellence by helping line managers and seniors move planning from the conference room to the market place, by becoming an expert in the way work is organized and executed, they should be a representative for the employees and finally by helping the organization improve their capacity for change. The responsibility for transforming the role of HR belongs to the CEO and to every line manager. HR will help organizations meet competitive challenges such as globalization, profitability through growth, technology, intellectual capital, and the greatest competitive challenge companies face, adjusting to nonstop change. HR's new role would be able to quickly turn strategy into action; to manage processes intelligently and efficiently; to maximize employee contribution and commitment; and to create the conditions for seamless change. HR should also become a partner in strategy executions by impelling and guiding serious discussions of how the company should be organized to carry out its strategy. Creating the conditions for this discussion involves four steps. First HR would define an organizational architecture by identifying the company's way of doing business. Next HR must be accountable for conducting an organizational audit. The third role for HR as a strategic partner is to identify methods for renovating the parts of the organizational architecture that need it. Fourth and finally, HR must take stock of its own work and set clear priorities. In their new role as administrative experts they will need to shed their traditional image and still make sure all routine work for the company is done well. HR must be held accountable for ensuring that employees feel committed to the organization and contribute fully. They must take responsibility for orienting and training line management about the importance of high employee morale and how to achieve it. The new HR should be the voice of employees in management discussions. The new role for HR might also involve suggesting that more teams be used on some projects or that employees be given more control over their own work schedules.

The new HR must become a change agent, which is building the organization's capacity to embrace and capitalize on change. They don't execute change but they make sure it is carried out. The new mandate for HR requires dramatic change in how HR professionals think and behave. Investing in new HR practices is another way to let the organization know that HR is worthy of the company's money and attention. Finally, the most important thing managers can do to drive the new mandate for HR is to improve the quality of the HR staff itself. Senior executives must get beyond the stereotypes of HR professionals as incompetent support staff and unleash HR's full potential.

The new role for HR is evident at the company I work for. They are present at any team or company meeting to make sure any issues the employees have are taken care of. They are the voice of the employees. They are responsible for training the line managers in keeping up the morale of the employees. They take care of any changes that need to be made and we have changes every 6 months. Whether in scheduling or seating arrangements, they are there to help. Often the HR department where I work is very involved in aspects of everyday operations, that, traditionally, Human resources never involved themselves in. Specifically, HR and upper management hold training seminars on a regular basis for the middle management team. They discuss ways to improve employee attitudes and performance. They are very active in our daily operations and employees know that while HR is a tool of the company, they do serve the employees as well. We also hold sensing sessions, which gives the employees an opportunity to address concerns about the company and about personnel issues. Human resource management would also be to guide staff with their career path and researching certain courses and learning institutes best suited to their work to develop all the necessary skills to achieve high results in the workplace. Encouragement is a big factor in job training and career courses to stimulate staff in their current role or to further their career options within the company. With today's workforce becoming increasingly diverse and organizations doing more to maximize the benefits of the differences in employees. Human resource managers are evolving from the "old school" sideline player to the front-line fighters. Personally, every time I have had questions about my future in the company, HR was there to provide answers and guidance to me so that I better understood my full potential. I now understand, the amount of work the HR department has. It's not just the payroll.

1.5 CHANGING ROLE OF THE HUMAN RESOURCE MANAGEMENT

The times have changed and the role of human resources within the organization needs to change. We can no longer be keepers of the records; we must become keepers of the flame. It is human resources' responsibility to lead the organization in tapping the one remaining resource it has people. In today's global economy, everyone can have the latest computers and software. They can have identical products. What they cannot have are the same people. Each organization is made up of a unique group of people. It becomes the responsibility of human resources to mesh the people with varying backgrounds with its vision and goals to create a merger that will accomplish the objectives of both the organization and the individual. Management needs to realize that in the future, raw materials, finished products and money will not be the keys to organizational success. People will be that key. Future success will depend on how we use the things that do not appear on a balance sheet or a Profit and Loss Statement, the intellectual capital of the organization, the knowledge its people possess. A recent study of U.S. businesses showed that the best way to improve goods and services and become more competitive.

There has been considerable research on the issues of board-level representation by personnel/HR directors and senior HR managers' involvement in strategic decision-making. Since the early 1990s there has been a growing interest in international HRM, reflecting the growing recognition that the effective management of human resources internationally is a major determinant of success or failure in international business. There is also evidence that HR constraints often limit the effective implementation of international business strategies. More recently, it has been argued that the more rapid pace of internationalization and globalization leads to a more strategic role for HRM as well as changes in the content of HRM. Yet, while there have been some attempts to integrate international corporate strategy and human resource strategy, surprisingly, the role of the corporate human resources function has been neglected, particularly in the context of the international firm. This seeks to redress the balance. The question addressed is, what is the role of the corporate HR function in the international firm? We found an emerging agenda for corporate HR in international firms which focuses on senior management development, succession planning and developing a cadre of international managers. We conceptualize this as a strategic concern with developing the core management competences of the organization, and argue that it can be usefully analyzed from the perspective of the learning organization.

"The point is the difference in attention to each persons can maximize his or her potential, so that organizations can maximize their effectiveness and so that the society as a whole can make the wisest use of its human resources" (Cascio). The challenges of HR managers today is to recognize talent and nurture the same carefully and achieve significant productivity gains over period of time. The organization is nothing but people. Technological advances globalize competition, demographic changes, the information revolution and trends towards service society have changed the rules of the game significantly. "In this scenario, organizations with similar set of resources gain competitive advantage only through effective and efficient management of human resources" (Dessler). The role of HR manager is shifting from a protector and screener to the planner and change agent. In present day competitive world, highly trained and committed employees are often a firm's best bet. HR managers plays an important role in planning and implementing down sizing, restructuring and other cost-cutting activities. They make the organization into more responsive to innovations and technological changes. Employees are the assets of corporate success. HR professionals can help the organization in selecting and train the employees for any emerging situations and promote commitments of all employees at various levels. In this case the employees can work willingly and enthusiastically and thus a competitive advantage to the organization. Now, employees are seen as the sources of competitive advantages.

A companies human resources represents one of the most potent and valuable resources. Consequently, the extent to which a workforce is managed effectively is a critical element in improving and sustaining organizational performance. Managing people is one of the most difficult aspects of organizational management; it means dealing with people who differ physically and psychologically. Human Resources Management emerged as a practiced personnel function, promising flexibility, and responsiveness and marked increased in the value of the employee. The organizational context in which the human resources management finds itself currently is one of the rapid change and considerable uncertainty. Human resources management is also in the process of change with regard to the nature of the role performed. In the past, human resources management professionals performed many functions themselves. The role they are taking on now is one of consultant to line managers, where line managers perform many functions traditionally handled by human resources management professionals. Similarly, the trend is for business to shed all functions not directly related to core business.

The changes surrounding us are not mere trends but the working of large, unruly forces, globalization, which has opened enormous new markets and a necessary corollary, enormous numbers of new competitors; the spread of information technology and the growth of networks; the dismantling of the corporate hierarchy and the politically charged down sizing and job disruption that accompany it.

The new economy is moving away from being asset-intensive towards becoming more knowledge-intensive. The focus is thus moving from providing product to providing services. As most organizations have access to the Internet and the latest technology, the people within the organization provide the competitive advantage, not the product or the technology. In the new economy, people are an organizations greatest asset. It is the role of human resource management and the human resource professional to nurture this asset. The new sources of sustainable competitive advantage in the new economy have the people at the center-creativity and talent, their aspirations and hopes, their dreams and excitement. The companies that flourish in this decade will do so because they are able to provide meaning and purpose, a context and frame that encourage individual potential to flourish and grow. Thus human resources management has an important and essential role to play in organizations in the new economy. To fulfill this role, organizations will needs to evaluate their existing human resources functions and adapt them to suit the needs of the new economy and individuals working in organizations in the new economy.

1.6 MANAGING HUMAN RESOURCES IN THE EMERGING SCENARIO

"People are our greatest asset" is a mantra that companies have been chanting for years. But only a few companies have started putting Human Resources Management (HRM) systems in place that support this philosophy. There are a number of challenges in the Indian IT industry which require the serious attention of HR managers to 'find the right candidate' and build a 'conducive work environment' which will be beneficial for the employees, as well as the organization. The IT industry is already under stress on account of persistent problems such as attrition, confidentiality, and loyalty. Other problems are managing people, motivation to adopt new technology changes, recruitment and training, performance management, development, and compensation management. With these challenges, it is timely for organizations to rethink the ways they manage their people. Managing HR in the knowledge based industry is a significant challenge for HR managers as it involves a multi-task responsibility. In the present scenario, HR managers perform a variety of responsibilities. Earlier their role was confined to administrative functions like managing manpower requirements and maintaining rolls for the organisation. Now it is more strategic as per the demands of the industry.

Managing People

In view of the industry dynamics, in the current times, there is a greater demand for knowledge workers. Resumes abound, yet companies still fervently search for the people who can make a difference to the business. Often talented professionals enjoy high bargaining power due to their knowledge and skills in hand. The attitude is different for those who are taking up responsibilities at a lesser age and experience. These factors have resulted in the clear shift in approach to individualised career management from organisation career commitment.

Motivating the Workforce

As the competition is growing rapidly in the global IT market, a technological edge supported by a talent pool has become a crucial factor for survival in the market. Naturally, as a result every organisation gives top priority to technology advancement programs. HR managers are now performing the role of motivators for their knowledge workers to adopt new changes.

Competency Development

Human capital is the real asset for any organisation, and this makes the HR role important in recruiting, managing, and retaining the best. The HR department has a clear role in this process and determines the success tempo of any organisation. An urgent priority for most of the organisations is to have an innovative and competent HR pool; sound in HR management practices with strong business knowledge.

Recruitment and Training

Recruitment has become a major function from an imperative sub-system in HR, particularly in the IT industry. HR managers play a vital role in creating assets for the organisation in the form of quality manpower. Attracting new talent also is a top priority for software companies, but less so for smaller companies. Another challenge for HR managers is to put systems in place to make the people a perfect fit for the job. Skill redundancy is fast in the IT industry. To overcome this problem, organisations give the utmost priority to training and skill enhancement programs on a continuous basis. Many IT companies are providing technical training to the employees on a quarterly basis. These trainings are quite useful also in terms of providing security to the employees.

The Trust Factor

Low levels of trust inhibit tacit knowledge sharing in the knowledge based industry. It is essential that the IT industry takes more initiatives to improve the security levels of the employees.

Work Life Balance Factor

Another dimension to the challenges faced by IT Industry is the growing pace of talent acquisition. This aspect creates with it the challenge of a smoother assimilation and the cultural binding of the new comers into the organization fold. The pressure of delivering the best of quality services in a reduced time frame calls for ensuring that employees maintain a work life balance.

Attrition/Retention of the Talent Pool

One of the toughest challenges for the HR managers in the IT industry is to deal with the prevalent high attrition levels. Though there is an adequate supply of qualified staff at entry level, there are huge gaps in the middle and senior level management in the industry. Further, the salary growth plan for each employee is not well defined. This situation has resulted in increased levels of poaching and attrition between organisations. The industry average attrition rate is 30–35 per cent and could range up to 60 per cent.

Bridging the Demand Supply Gap

HR managers have to bridge the gap between the demand and supply of professionals. They have to maintain consistency in performance and have to keep the motivation levels of employees high, despite the monotonous nature of work. The same also leads to recurring training costs. Inconsistent performance directly affects revenues. Dwindling motivation levels lead to a loss of interest in the job and a higher number of errors.

In India, about the current challenges in the industry and the retention initiatives in their companies. More executives were surveyed expressed that the major challenges for the HR managers are recruiting the right people and retaining them for longer times. The next most important HR concerns listed were meeting the demand, supply requirements in the industry, expectations management of the resources and other stakeholders, efficiency in processes and HR policies. When asked to rank the best motivating factors, the most frequently expressed priority was the nature of the job and job satisfaction. The next most important aspects were salary and monetary benefits, good peer group, positive, motivating and interactive environment and company processes. More interestingly, working for the right boss and company was very appealing to the authors.

The motivating factors and retention initiatives taken by different companies were very thought provoking. The most frequently mentioned initiatives were those related to salary and monetary benefits. Good salaries, increments, performance based pay, and ESOPs are some of the aspects mentioned. Transparency in the system was another major point mentioned by the employees. The requirement for recognizing loyalty to the company and hard work was highlighted. Flexible work culture and freedom to shift to a more interesting work area were some of the other aspects. The Vice President of an MNC mentioned 'expectations matching using the Key Responsibility Areas (KRAs)' was one of the major retention initiatives in his company.

When asked for the major reasons for attrition in the industry, the response was diverse. Indeed, there were a breadth of responses with more emphasis on the monetary aspects, nature of job and administrative policies. Those surveyed felt that the high demand in the industry is augmenting job hopping. Also, the wide difference in the salaries offered by the companies is another reason for staff mobility. Some of the other reasons mentioned were lack of expectations management, counseling and mentoring, lack of professionalism in immediate supervisor as well as head of the relevant department or group, and lack of differentiation between performers and non-performers. One of the senior managers in HR opined that the current supply of ready to use manpower is lower than the demand, and the lead time in getting productive people is a major limitation in recruitment, which in turn leads to more attrition. Another reason mentioned was bad HR/organizational values and lack of ethics.

The Indian industries are facing considerable challenges. In order to maintain India's competitive advantage of technically skilled knowledge workers with the right mix of technical, business and functional skills, the workforce needs to increase by at least 10 fold to 2.2 million knowledge workers by 2008 (Nasscom 2003a). To cope with such complexities, HRM strategy must have at its centre a focus on peoples needs and requirements. The IT industry, like any other service industry, is people driven. At present, the emphasis should be more on improving the personalities and processes and help each individual come out as a winner. HR managers have to continuously evolve career paths, motivate their employees and create a culture of oneness, which will also act as retention tools. Since the recurring recruitment costs are detrimental, it is requisite that great emphasis is to be levied on starting specialised training institutes to guide employees to identify the right people at the right time who can keep pace with the unique work patterns in this industry. The managers should take more initiatives to improve employee retention by taking suitable initiatives. However, it is also to be understood that staff turnover is as unpredictable as technological uncertainty. However, with suitable HR strategies the measures of the attrition percentage could be kept low giving addition organizational benefit and in turn, to the outsourcing advantage.

The 21st century would see the following inter-related phenomena emerging, posing challenges to the corporate world and culminating in Olympian competition.

- Borderless world
- Diversity
- Knowledge power.

The cross-cultural, cross-border mingling has resulted in the creation of a new class of people, global citizens with global attitudes, taste and networks. Since it unleashes multiple variables, the borderless world precludes immense complexity, complexity in the environment, in inter-organizational relationships, in the modes of conducting business and in socio-cultural diversity. One of the most important duties of the modern HR manager is to get things done through people. He has to bring employees into contact with the organization in such a way that the objectives of both groups are achieved. He must be interested in people, the work and the achievement of assigned objectives. To be effective, he must balance his concern for people and work. In other words he must know how to utilize human as well as non-human resources while translating goals into action.

1.7 EVOLUTION OF MANAGEMENT OF HUMAN RESOURCES: AN INDIAN PERSPECTIVE

Kautilya's Period: Kautilya provides a systematic treatment of management of human resources as early as in the 4th Century B.C. in his treatise titled 'Arthashastra'.

- There prevailed logical procedures and principles in respect of labour organizations such as 'Shreni' or Guild system and the cooperative sector.
- The wages were paid strictly in terms of quantity and quality of work turned out, and punishments were imposed for unnecessary delaying the work or spoiling it.
- Kautilya provides an excellent discussion on staffing and personnel management embracing job descriptions, qualifications for job, selection procedure, and executive development, incentive systems (Carrot and Stick approach).

Varnasharm: There are several indications regarding the operations of principles of the divisions of labour. The concept of Varnashram or caste system was originally based on these principles:

- The individuals, who used to earn their livelihood by engaging themselves in activities such as teaching, sacrifice or state management, were designed as Brahmins.
- Individuals engaged in the areas of trade, business and agriculture were called 'Vaishyas' and those devoting themselves to manual work were known as 'Shudras'. Later on, these professions emerged to be heredity which facilitated the transfer of skills and training from one generation to another.

The Medieval: (As regard to Indian Economy in Medieval India):

Although there were a lull because of numerous foreign aggressions for around 700 years, during the Mughal Rule, the Indian trade and commerce were reviewed.

- Several 'Karkhanas' were established at Agra, Delhi, Lahore, Ahmedabad and various other places.
- A majority of the artisans and the craftsmen had extremely poor conditions of existences and lived on starvation level.
- The productivity of workers was very low, low wages, climatic conditions and poor physique were the major factors responsible for it.

British Period: There prevailed laissez-faire policy towards business.

- As it is evidenced in the report of the Indigo Commission, the working conditions were appalling, living conditions were subhuman, and several abuses prevailed in Indigo plantations.

Again, as regards tea plantation, several cases of inhuman cruelties caused to the workers are encountered.

- Even the Plantation Act of 1863 makes provisions that if the workers failed to complete their period of contract, they should be imprisoned for a period not exceeding three months.
- The labourers who attempted to run away were subjected to imprisonment whipping and allied extreme punishments.
- Accordingly, the workers were entirely helpless in the face of organized and powerful European Planters.

The above conditions prevailed till the enactment of the Factory Act of 1881. According to the Act; the workers employed in the factories were allowed a weekly off day, and provisions were also made for inspection as well as limiting the hours of work for women workers to 11 per day. The Act further provided that the minimum age of children for employment should be seven years and that the maximum working hours for them should not exceed seven hours a day and that too in the day shift. In 1890, the first labour organization designated as 'Bombay Mill Hands Association' was established. Subsequently, in 1905, the Printers Union at Calcutta and in 1907, the Postal Union at Bombay were established. The Madras Labour Union was organized thereafter in 1918. In 1920, the indentured labour system involving migration of Indian labour to other countries on contract basis, was abolished as a result of a strong national movement. In the same year, the Central Labour Board was established to federate the different unions in the Bombay city and the All India Trade Union Congress was organized.

In 1923, for the first time in the organized sector, Tata Steel appointed K.A. Naoroji as a labour or welfare officer to look after labour issues in the various departments of the steel work. The formal implementation of the Indian Trade Union Act, 1926 forms a landmark in the history of industrial relations in this country. The Royal Commission on Labour (1929–1931) recommended the appointment of labour officers or liaison officers to deal with recruitment as measures to prevent corrupt practices in Indian industry. They were considered a recruitment officers directly reporting to general manager. As the commission observed, 'No employee should be engaged except by the labour officer personally in consultation with the departmental head, and none should be dismissed without his consent except by the manager after hearing what the labour officer had to say' accordingly, the Bombay Mill Owners Association and the Indian Jute Mills Association appointed labour officers in 1935 and 1938, respectively. During World War II, the need for mobilizing labour support was felt and thus, several welfare officers were appointed to deal with working conditions, canteen, ration shops, recreations, medical facilities, worker's housing and allied fringe benefits.

Post-Independence Period: With the emergence of compulsory adjudication under the Industrial Disputes Act, 1947, the welfare officers were made responsible for handling the disputes and adjudication pertaining to the conditions of services including wages, leaves, retirement benefits and bonus. Thus, they became industrial relations officers and started performing industrial relations functions such as collective bargaining, conciliation, and adjudication.

Employment Exchange (Compulsory notification of vacancies) Act, 1959 and the Apprentices Act, 1961 were passed to regulate recruitment and training of workers, respectively.

In the view of growing labour legislation commencing with the right to hire and ending with right to fire, the employees tended to employ welfare or labour officers with a legal background.

21st session of standing Labour conference held in Dec.1963 recommended that the functions of welfare officer and personnel officers should be precisely demarcated and that the former should not be responsible for dealing with disciplinary cases against workers or appears in court on behalf of the management against the workers in labour dispute cases.

Personnel Management during 1970s: In the early seventies, as Punekar observes, the personnel field covered under three major areas of professional disciplines: (1) Labour welfare, (2) Industrial relations, and (3) Personnel administration. These three areas revealed the chronological order of the development of the personnel field. Immediately after industrialization, labour welfare, mainly social reformist in nature, came into the picture. The inevitable emergence of trade unions resistance organizations to employers opened the field of industrial (or Union-Management) relations. Lastly, with the development of scientific management of industry, personnel administration took root. The three areas of labour welfare, industrial relations and personnel administration were being looked after the three professional functionaries: (1) Welfare officer, (2) Labour officer, and (3) Personnel officer. However, in the early 80s, the area of labour officer largely merged with personnel administration and refers to as personnel management.

Personnel Management during 1980s: In 1980s HRM was regarded as a specialized profession such as that of other professional functions. In addition to industrial relations functions (although sometimes the industrial relations formed a separate branch), the personnel branch was responsible for varied functions *i.e.,* employment, safety training, wages and salary administration and research and development. Indeed, the activities involved in the personnel department were akin to those performed in this department in other western countries. Specially, where the personnel, industrial relations and welfare functions were combined in one department, three categories of activities relating to these functions were obtained. The personnel department involves in technical and allied services. Thus, industrial relation activities including contract negotiations, grievance handling, preparation and presentation of arbitration cases and research in labour problems; for educational activities including employee training, supervisory training, organizational planning and management development, communication programs etc.; for wage and salary administration, including preparation of job descriptions, job evaluations, incentive and profits sharing systems and executive compensation; for employment activities, such as recruiting, psychological testing, medical examination, interviewing, and employee record keeping; and technical services: health and welfare measures. The personnel manager's role is to advice. Usually, advise the line and top management in respect of legal matters regarding the termination of services and transfer, human relations problems confronting the line managers and technical procedures in areas, such as wages and salary administration. In some instances, the personnel manager was required to advise management regarding the improvement of human climate in the organization.

Human Resource Management during 1990s: During 1990s a new human resources management has emerged, especially as a result of the globalization and liberalization. The economy and the policy of India is fast changing in the wake of liberalization policies mooted in year 1990. Consequently the form and content of capitalist relations between the various factors of production are undergoing a change. What has emerged a new era of HR Management? As a result of liberalization and globalization the human resources management and industrial relations have acquired strategic importance. The success of the new policies mostly depends on to a large extent, on the introduction of new industrial relations and human resources policies at the national and the organizational levels. The pressure of change is already visible in the economy and witnessed in the industrial relations and HRM areas. The world economic order is also changing rapidly. Evolutionary changes are taking place at revolutionary pace, largely influenced by the external forces, arising out of a desire to increase competitiveness and efficiency. Centrally planned economics are opening up to have their tryst with counterpart of free market economy. Structural adjustments and reforms are holding sway establishing primary of economic imperatives over dogmatic political compulsions. Organization today working in a commercially competitive global economic environment are struggling for their own survival and growth. The liberalizations and bold economic reforms by Government have thrown out many challenges and opportunities to the Indian industry. With explosion of the Information and communication technology, increased global competition, fast changing market conditions, the deregulations etc. organizations have to redesign their strategies and outlook to HRM.

Managing human resources to achieve better knowledge-related outcomes means "retaining personnel, building their expertise into the organizational routines through learning processes, and establishing mechanisms for the distribution of benefits arising from the utilization of this expertise" (Kamoche and Mueller, 1998, p. 1036). To identify which HRM practices could be employed to help organizations to achieve knowledge-related outcomes, a brief review of representative case-based and existing empirical studies undertaken by scholars from different research fields (international HRM, innovation, strategy, international business, etc.) on the link between HRM practices and various knowledge-related outcomes is necessary. The purpose is to determine what HRM practices organizations could employ to enhance knowledge-related outcomes, otherwise known as knowledge-driven HRM practices.

1. Human resource planning, which includes creating venture teams with a balanced skill-mix, recruiting the right people, and voluntary team assignment. This strategy analyzes and determines personnel needs in order to create effective innovation teams.
2. Performance appraisal, which includes encouraging risk taking, demanding innovation, generating or adopting new tasks, peer evaluation, frequent evaluations, and auditing innovation processes. This strategy appraises individual and team performance so that there is a link between individual innovativeness and company profitability. Which tasks should be appraised and who should assess employees' performance are also taken into account.
3. Reward systems, which include freedom to do research, freedom to fail, freedom to form teams, freedom to run businesses, balancing pay and pride, noticeable pay raises, dual career tracks, promoting from within, recognition rewards, and balancing team and individual rewards. This strategy uses rewards to motivate personnel to achieve an organization's goals of productivity, innovation and profitability.
4. Career management, which includes empowering people, leading by example, and continued education. This strategy matches employees' long-term career goals with organizational goals through continuing education and training. Recently, international business researchers have identified the role of HRM practices in the organizational learning as one subject of inquiry to investigate the link between new HRM practices and innovation performance, arguing that HRM practices are "most conducive to innovation performance when adopted, not in isolation, but as a system of mutually reinforcing practices". Applying principal component analysis, they identify two HRM systems that influence innovation performance. The first consists of HRM practices, which is knowledge transfer affect employees' ability to innovate. They are interdisciplinary workgroups, quality circles, systems for the collection of employee proposals, planned job rotation, delegation of responsibility, integration of functions, and performance-related pay. The second system is dominated by internal and external training. The overall conclusion is that "while the adoption of individual HRM practices may be expected to

influence innovation performance positively, the adoption of a package of complementary HRM practices could be expected to affect innovation performance much more strongly" (Laursen and Foss, 2003, p. 257). From the reviewed articles we learned that there are certain knowledge-driven HRM practices, the extensive use of which enhances knowledge-related outcomes. We also learned that the existing empirical work on the relations between HRM practices and knowledge-related outcomes has exclusively focused on the individual HRM practices and their isolated effect. That could become a serious limitation since HRM is defined as "a set of distinct but interrelated activities, functions, and processes that are directed at attracting, developing and maintaining (or disposing of) a firm's human resources". While HRM stands for competence, commitment and culture building in the organization. While in the past the HR practices of a number of Indian companies might not have proved to be excellent, the future certainly holds much more promise for effective HR function. As traditional sources of competitive advantage for companies have become less potent today, a strategic approach to HR becomes critical for creating and sustaining HR based competitive advantage. Today, employees are recognized as the key to building a world class organization. Thus, progressive Indian companies have started linking the human resources policies and practices with organizations overall business goals.

CASE STUDY–I

M/s Forex Pharmaceuticals is a reputed company in the country, known for its proactive HR policies and practices. The vision and the mission statements of the company also categorically enunciate the corporate social responsibility of undertaking environment-friendly manufacturing activities. Some of the innovative HR practices of the company are :

- Change management for preparing the company in the GATT scenario.
- Culture building exercise that support self initiation, openers, honesty and integrity, team work, etc.
- Career planning for good performs.
- Challenging and learning assignments for grooming future leaders.
- Sharing of knowledge management infrastructure, such as Intranet, which nurture and support shared learning.

The CMD of the company received a show cause notice from the Pollution Control Board on account of pollution created by one of the manufacturing units. The notice was well publicized in the print as well as electronic media and the company's image of being socially responsible was tainted. The PR managers carried out extensive campaigns clarifying the company's concern for the environment. The employees of the company were perplexed with the external information and started doubting the company's holy vision and mission statements and also the credibility of the top management. The Head, HR, met with the PR Manager and decided the course of action. He also held personal meetings of the CMD and top executives with the employees in the corporate office as well as the manufacturing locations, apart from interviews to the media. The Head, HR, in consultation with the PR Manager, created Employee Awareness Groups (EAGs), which were empowered to inspect the pollution control mechanism being implemented by the company. The members of EAG were counseled to tour the neighbouring villagers to create awareness among them about the responsive actions taken by the company.

QUESTIONS

1. Do you think that the company believes in practicing what it preaches?
2. Is the HR department proactive and does it display leadership capabilities in the crisis situation?
3. Do you suggest any additional steps by the HR department to address the challenges?
4. What steps should the HR department adopt to reinforce 'the value-based management'?

CASE STUDY–2

Managing the turnover of key employees with non-compete agreements: HRM practices

Companies in high-technology and creative industries (such as publishing and advertising) often worry about the turnover of high-potential employees. High-potential employees (sometimes called key employees) are people who have rare and special talents and who provide valuable contributions that can directly affect the firm's performance. Some well-known examples of high-potential people are film director Steven Spielberg (whose films are more profitable than those of any other director) and baseball stars Mark McGuire of the St. Louis Cardinals and Sammy Sosa of the Chicago Cubs, both of whom set records for home runs in baseball. Because most organizations have only a few high-potential employees, retaining these employees has important strategic implications for the business.

To protect themselves against the loss of high-potential employees and the intellectual property (such as trade secrets) that they may take with them, some companies are requiring all employees to sign non-compete agreements that restrict their freedom to work for a competitor after quitting the organization. For example, Career Track, a Colorado company that provides professional training seminars on business-related topics, took a former star trainer and workshop developer to court to enforce a non-compete agreement after this high-potential employee quit to work for competitor in California. The company wanted to avoid losing business to a competitor; it also wanted to let other high-potential employees know that the company is prepared to defend its rights if someone decides to challenge the non-compete agreement.

QUESTIONS

1. Do you think non-compete agreements are ethical? Should a company require all employees to sign them ore only high-potential employees? What problems could arise from the use of non-compete agreements?
2. Are there other HRM practices that could be substituted for non-compete agreements that would be likely to improve the retention of high-potential employees? Which ones would you recommend?

CASE STUDY–3

ROLE OF PERSONNEL MANAGER

In a company called Agro-Product Ltd., the following incident took place in the personnel department. There was a supervisor who had risen to his position by way of his hard work and sincerity. In his good old days, when he worked as a clerk in this company for fifteen years, before becoming a supervisor, he had been a staunch active and dynamic unionist.

After becoming a supervisor, in response to change in his responsibility, he was forced to drift away from union activities. However, it must be noted here, that his being promoted to a supervisory job was not a buy off. He was promoted because he really deserved that. But the union leaders, for reasons best known to them didn't like the clerk's promotion to the supervisory post.

Although with excellent inter-personal skills that the supervisor had, he could somehow manage to do his work satisfactorily. On one fine morning, he assigned some work to the peon of the department, but the peon refused to do the same. There was exchange of heated arguments, a lot of people gathered around and at a certain point of time, the supervisor offensively gesticulated towards the peon.

The basic issue remained aside and every one around started accusing the supervisor for apologized for this behaviour and the trade union was also brought into the picture.

QUESTIONS

1. Analyze the situation.
2. Discuss the role, the personnel manager is supposed to play in this situation.
   If you were the personnel manager, how could you resolve the problem?

REFERENCES

1. Apte, U., Sobol, M., Hanaoka, S., Shimada, T., Saarinen, T., Salmela, T., and Vepsalainen, A. (1997). *IS outsourcing practices in the USA, Japan and Finland: A comparative study.* Journal of Information Technology, **12 (4),** 289–304.
2. Bryce, D.J., and Useem, M. (1998), *The impact of corporate outsourcing on company value.* European Management Journal, **16(6),** 635–643.
3. Currie, W.L. (2003), *A knowledge-based risk assessment framework for evaluating web-enabled applications outsourcing projects.* International Journal of Project Management, **21(3),** 207–217.
4. DiRomualdo, A., and Gurbaxani, V. (1998), *Strategic intent for IT outsourcing.* Sloan Management Review, **39(4),** 67–80.
5. Elizabeth, S. (2004), *IT outsourcing: Current trends and future possibilities.* Available http://www.bcs.org/review04/articles/itservices/outsourcing.htm [2005, February 16th].
6. Ghemawat, P. (2000, July 31), *The Indian software industry at the millennium.* Harvard Business Case, Harvard Business School, Case No. 9–700–036.
7. Gopal, A.M.T., and Krishnan, M.S. (2002), *The role of software processes and communication in offshore software development.* Communications of the ACM, **45(1),** 193–200.
8. Hatch, P.J. (2004), *Offshore 2005 research: Preliminary findings and conclusions.* Ventoro (October 11, 2004) Report.
9. Kern, T., Willcocks. L.P., and Lacity, M.C. (2002), *Application service provision: Risk assessment and mitigation.* MIS Quarterly, **1(2),** 113–126.
10. Lacity, M.C., and Hirschheim, R.A. (1993), *Information systems outsourcing: Myths, metaphors and realities,* New York: Wiley Series in Information Systems.
11. Lacity, M.C., and Hirschheim, R.A. (1995), *Beyond the information systems outsourcing bandwagon: The insourcing response.* Chichester; New York: Wiley.

12. Lane, S. (2001), *Offshore software development: Localisation, globalisation and best practices in the evolving industry.* Aberdeen IT Services Practice: Aberdeen Group.
13. Loh, L., and Venkatraman, N. (1992), *Determinants of information technology outsourcing: A cross-sectional analysis.* Journal of Management Information Systems, **9(1),** 7–24.
14. Nasscom (2002), *Report on the IT industry in India: Strategic review 2002.* National Association of Software and Service Companies (NAASCOM): India.
15. Nasscom (2003a), *Knowledge Professionals Report.* National Association of Software and Service Companies (NAASCOM), India. Available http://www.nasscom.org/artdisplay.asp?cat_id=303 [2005, August 5th].
16. Nasscom (2003b), *Competitive Costs Report.* National Association of Software and Service Companies (NASSCOM), India. Available http://www.nasscom.org/artdisplay.asp?cat_id=31 [2005, August 5th].
17. Naureen, K., Currie, W. Weerakkody, V. and Desai, B. (2003), *Evaluating offshore IT outsourcing in India: Supplier and customer scenarios.* Paper presented at Hawaii International Conference on System Sciences (HICSS), The Big Island, Hawaii.
18. Porter, M.E. (1985), *Competitive advantage: Creating and sustaining superior performance.* The Free Press: New York.
19. Rajkumar, T.M., and Mani, R.V.S. (2001), *Offshore software development: The view from Indian suppliers.* Information Systems Management, **1(1)** 63–73.
20. Ravichandran, R., and Ahmed, N. (1993), *Offshore systems development.* Information and Management, **24(1),** 24–40.
21. Smith, M.A., Mitra, S., and Narasimhan, S. (1996), *Offshore outsourcing of software development and maintenance.* Information and Management, **31(2),** 165–175.
22. Terdiman, R., and Karamouzis, F. (2002), *Going offshore to globally sources IT services.* Gartner Research, **17.**
23. Vivek, A., Diana, F., and Jaana, K.R. (2003), *Offshoring and beyond.* The McKinsey Quarterly, Special Edition, 24–35.
24. Werner, K., Dieter, R., and Raymond, L.F. (2001), *Outsourcing in India.* IEEE Software, **18(2),** 78–85.

2

CHAPTER

THE CONCEPT, SCOPE AND FUNCTION OF HUMAN RESOURCE OF MANAGEMENT

2.1 INTRODUCTION

Organizations are not mere bricks, mortars, machineries or inventories. It is the people who staff and manage the organization. The objectives of an organization can be achieved on their own despite the best possible accumulation of technological, financial, human efforts working as a highly motivated team to achieve the short-term and long-term objectives of an organization.

Human resources are human wealth or means that can be drawn on. Human wealth or human capital of an organization can be treated as its human resources. There has been a greater appreciation of the fact that the more an organization invests in its human resources, the greater the return from the investment is likely to be.

In the contemporary business world any system which does not add real quantifiable value to the functions of business organization has no right to exist within the organization. The same also applies to the human resources function. This functional department of the business organization should try to make real value addition to overall functioning of the organization.

The globalizations, profitability through growth technology, intellectual capital, and continues change bring in significant changes in the role and requirements of HR. In a globalize market where there is increased competition to gain larger market share, every organization needs to adapt quickly to the international culture, a learning organization is the need of the hour.

To function effectively the organization needs to have employees who are highly skilled in their particular area, the knowledge workers. The intellectual capital, the knowledge, is the sole determiner of competitive advantage.

2.2 CONCEPT AND CHALLENGES OF HRM

According to Gunnigle *et.al.*, people are the life blood of organizations. A company's workforce represents one of its most potent and valuable resources. Consequently, the extent to which a workforce is managed effectively is a critical element in improving and sustaining organizational performance. Managing people is one of the most difficult aspects of organizational management: it means dealing with people who differ physically and psychologically. The essence of personnel management is that aspect of organizational management concerned with the management of an organization's workforce.

The term 'human resource management' has been commonly used for about the last ten to fifteen years. Prior to that, the field was generally known as 'personnel administration'. The name change is not merely comestic. Personnel administration, which emerged as a clearly defined field by the 1920s (at least in the US), was largely concerned the technical aspects of hiring, evaluating, training, and compensating employees and was very much of 'staff' function in most organizations. The field did not normally focus on the relationship of disparate employment practices on overall organizational performance or on the systematic relationships among such practices. The field also lacked a unifying paradigm. HRM developed in response to the substantial increase in competitive pressures. American business organizations began experiencing by the late 1970s as a result of such factors as globalization, deregulation, and rapid technological change. These pressures gave rise to an enhanced concern on the part of firms to engage in strategic planning—a process of anticipating future changes in the environment conditions (the nature as well as level of the market) and aligning the various components of the organization in such a way as to promote organizational effectiveness. Although the technical aspects of traditional personnel administration are still an integral component of HRM, strategy formulation and implementation has become its dominant and integrating paradigm. Human Resource (HR) managers are concerned with designing overall employment systems that are internal complementary and ultimately contribute to the firm's attainment of its principal goals. The function is also seen to be much closer to the strategic apex of the firm than personnel administration. The Strategic Human Resource Management (SHRM) literature envisions HR managers as utilizing, in effect, a kind of toolkit of HRM methods that can be crafted into an overall organizational HR system.

HRM is a strategic approach to the acquisition, motivation and development and the management of human resources. It is a specialized field that attempt to developing organizational corporate culture, implements the programs which reflect values of the organization and ensure its success. HRM is proactive rather than reactive *i.e.*, looking forward what to what needs to be done and then doing it, rather than waiting to be told what to do about recruiting, paying and training people, or dealing with employee relations problems as they arise. The techniques for the application of HRM will include many familiar functions of personnel managers, such as man-power planning, selection, performance appraisal, salary administration, training and management development and to improve communication systems, involvement, commitment and productivity. Broadly, there are three meaning attached to the concept of HRM. In the first place, persons working in an organization are regarded as a valuable source, implying that there is a need to invest time and effort in their development. Secondly, human resources have their special characteristics cannot be treated like other resources. And thirdly, human resources do not really focus on employees as individual, but also on other social realities, units and processes in the organizations.

In its essence, HRM is the qualitative improvement of human beings who considered as valuable assets of an organization—the source, resources and the end user of all products and services. HRM is clearly an out growth of older process and approach but it is much more than the parent disciplines *i.e.*, personnel management and behavioral sciences. It is also deep rooted than training and development and approach is multi-disciplinary. It is the scientific process of continuously enabling the employees to improve their competencies. The competencies of human resources play a major role in shaping the present and future expected roles so that the goals of the organization are achieved and the saine time the needs of the employees are also met. Some basic assumptions about human resources are also different from the traditional approach:

- The members of an organization are reservoirs of untapped resources.
- There is scope for unlimited development of these resources.
- It is more in the nature of self-development that development thrust from outside.
- The organization also undergoes development with overall benefits along with the development of its members.
- The organization further develops as a culture in which utmost emphasis is placed on harmonious relationships between superior-subordinate, team-work, collaboration of individuals, open communication, integration of overall goals of the organization.
- Top management takes the initiative for HRM, in the forms of plans, strategies and creates the overall climate and support mechanism for its implementation.

Traditional Personnel Functions (TPF) and Human Resources Development (HRD)

Traditional personnel functions (TPF)	*Human resources development (HRD)*
1. TPF is an independent functions.	1. HRD is a sub-system of a larger system (organization).
2. There are several sub-functions under TPF.	2. HRD is an organic whole; all the parts are interlinked.
3. The main task of TPF is to respond effectively to the demands.	3. The main task of HRD is to develop enabling capabilities.
4. TPF has the main responsibilities for their personnel matter.	4. All managers irrespective of functions share the responsibilities of human resources functions.
5. The main responsibilities of TPF relate to salary and job administration, and management of people and their development.	5. The responsibilities of HRS relate to HRS, people, system and the process of the total organization.
6. The major attention of TPF is on personnel administration or management.	6. The major attention of HRS is on developing people and their competencies.
7. Personnel system and procedures should be designed to achieve maximum efficiency.	7. HR systems and procedures should be designed on the basis of process values to reduce human wastage.
8. People in an organization are motivated mainly by salary and rewards.	8. People are primarily motivated by challenges and opportunities for development and creativity.

According to Gunnigle *etal.* (1997:9) the core activities of personnel management includes:

1. **Strategy and organization:** Contributing to organizational strategy, organization structure and process; influencing culture and values and developing personnel strategies and policies.
2. **Employee resourcing:** Incorporating human resource planning, recruitment and selection, deployment and termination of employment.
3. **Employee development:** Incorporating training and development, management development, career development and performance management.
4. **Reward management:** Incorporating the selection of reward strategies and the administration of payment and benefits systems.

5. **Employee relations:** Incorporating industrial relations, employee involvement and participation, communication, health safety and welfare and employee services.
6. **Employment and personnel administration:** Incorporating the administration of employee records, employment policies and practices, working conditions and personnel information systems.

HR Challenges

The organizations have to face lots of challenges in the present scenario. These challenges may be categorized according to their primary focus; the environment, the organization, or the individual.

Environmental Challenges

The environmental challenges are the forces external to the firm which influences the performances beyond management control. The strategist has to monitor the external environment constantly for opportunities and threats. The organization has to prosper and survive in a volatile environment of change. The rapid change can put employees under a great deal of stress, unless the firm has to develop a support mechanism to keep it manageable both the organization and employees may have to face a heavy price. The growth of internet in recent years represents the most important factor of affecting organization and their human resource practices. The internet makes the world open and disturb the effective labour market by loosing their talent to competitors. Which leads the workforce diversity? These trends are likely to accelerate in the future. Globalization is one of the most important challenges facing by the organizations by competing against foreign firms, both domestically and abroad. The organizations are always in the trouble with the international laws. The effectiveness of human resources largely depends on how effectively deals with international laws. Expansion of service sector employment is linked to a number of factors, including changes in consumer tastes and preferences, legal, regulatory changes in the way business are organized and managed.

Organizational Challenges

Organizational challenges are concerned or internal to a firm and is the byproduct of environmental forces because the organizations cannot run in a vacuum. The challenges include the need for competitive position and flexibility, the problems of down sizing and organizational restructuring, the use of self managed work teams, the rise of small business, the need to create a strong culture, the role of technology and the rise of outsourcing. The transferring the responsibility and decision-making authority from central office to the people and locations closer to the situation that demands attention. Downsizing creates an emotional dis-equilibrium. Which has to create and convert a new set of challenges for employees competing in the labour market, as well as government agencies that must deal with the social problems associated with employment insecurity? The dramatic transformations are witnessed in the firms regarding the organizational restructuring is concerned. The mergers and accusations are the common practices in this decade. A newer and rapidly growing form inter-organizational bonding comes in the form of joint ventures, alliances collaborations among firms that remain independent, yet work together on specific products to spread costs and risks. Flattening the organizations requires careful appraisal of staffing, workflows, communication channels, training needs, and their successful blending. The days of bosses are numbered. The firm has to develop self-managed teams. In the system employees are assigned to a group of peers and, together responsible for a particular area or task. The technological advances are being introduced to organizations at ever-increasing pace. The rise of telecommunications, information technology has a greater impact on overall working mechanism of the organization. Outsourcing now becomes a fade in modern firms. Their motivation is very simple; Outsourcing saves money. It creates several HR challenges for firms. The employees may face layoff and also the firm should remain accountable for the actions of its subcontractors. The subcontractors have to be evaluated and watched carefully.

Individual Challenges

Human resource issues at the individual level address the decisions most important to the organizations competitive position, which is likely to be affected to the most of the employees. It has much impact on the environment. The most important individual challenges today involve matching people and organizations, ethics and social responsibility, productivity, empowerment, brain drain and job security. This can contribute to firm performance most when the firm uses these strategies to attract and retain the potential employees who can best fit with the company culture and overall business objectives. The employees expect that the organization has to behave in the best possible behave ethically are increasing. HR strategies should make a balance between employees' expectation of ethical behaviour from the employer and in the business. Concept of social responsibility has been frequently exhibited as the counterpart to ethics. It attempts to create a balance its commitment towards not only to its investors, employees, customers, other businesses, and the communities in which it works. We consider that greater the productivity per individual, the higher the organizations productivity. In the knowledge based economy which driven by technology, the success of organizations depend more and more on the value of intangible human capital. The employee's ability, competence in performing a job, the persons desire to do the best possible job is to maintain in the firm. Now-a-days the employees retention mostly depends how the firm providing the quality of work life. High quality of work life is related to job satisfaction which has to be nurtured by firm providing. The workers with the skill and authority to make decisions. The firm has to develop committed, enthusiastic workforce by implementing the process of empowerment. This encourages employees to be creative, risk taking, which acts as the organizations competitive edge in a fast changing environment. The brain drain, job insecurity are the common phenomenon in the present organizational scenario.

The long-term challenges facing most of the HR professionals have to do with the strategic role of the human resource. This is what is known as the role of "Strategic Partner". The HR function needs to have a complete understanding of the various functions and business objectives. So also the business strategies, according to HR strategies should be formulated which will help in achieving the business objectives through the existing corporate strategy. Considering these points, it can be stated that the HR strategies has a significant role to play in the competitive positioning of the organization.

2.3 OBJECTIVES OF HRM

Objectives are pre-determined goals to which individual or group activity in an organization is directed. Objectives of personnel management are influenced by organizational objectives and individual and social goals. Institutions are instituted to attain certain specific objectives. The objectives of the economic institutions are mostly to earn profits, and of the educational institutions are mostly to impart education and/or conduct research so on and so forth. However, the fundamental objective of any organization is survival. Organizations are not just satisfied with this goal. Further, the goal of most of the organizations is growth and/or profits.

Institutions procure and manage various resources including human to attain the specified objectives. Thus, human resources are managed to divert and utilize their resources towards and for the accomplishment of organizational objectives. Therefore, basically the objectives of HRM are drawn from and to contribute to the accomplishment of the organizational objectives. The other objectives of HRM are to meet the needs, aspirations, values and dignity of individual employees and having due concern for the socio-economic problems of the community and the country.

The objectives of HRM may be as follows:

1. To create and utilize an able and motivated workforce, to accomplish the basic organizational goals.
2. To establish and maintain sound organizational structure and desirable working relationships among all the members of the organization.
3. To secure the integration of individual or groups within the organization by co-ordination of the individual and group goals with those of the organization.
4. To create facilities and opportunities for individual or group development so as to match it with the growth of the organization.
5. To attain an effective utilization of human resources in the achievement of organizational goals.
6. To identify and satisfy individual and group needs by providing adequate and equitable wages, incentives, employee benefits and social security and measures for challenging work, prestige, recognition, security, status.
7. To maintain high employees morale and sound human relations by sustaining and improving the various conditions and facilities.
8. To strengthen and appreciate the human assets continuously by providing training and development programs.
9. To consider and contribute to the minimization of socio-economic evils such as unemployment, under-employment, inequalities in the distribution of income and wealth and to improve the welfare of the society by providing employment opportunities to women and disadvantaged sections of the society.
10. To provide an opportunity for expression and voice management.
11. To provide fair, acceptable and efficient leadership.
12. To provide facilities and conditions of work and creation of favourable atmosphere for maintaining stability of employment.

Management has to create conductive environment and provide necessary prerequisites for the attainment of the personnel management objectives after formulating them. The primary objectives of HRM are to ensure the availability of competent and willing workforce to an organization. Apart from this, there are other objectives too. Specifically, HRM objectives are of four fold: societal, organizational, functional and personal.

Societal Objectives

The Societal Objectives are socially and ethically responsible for the needs and challenges of society. While doing so, they have to minimize the negative impact of such demands upon the organization. The failure of the organizations to use their resources for society may limit human resources decisions to laws that enforce reservation in hiring and laws that address discrimination, safety or other such areas of societal concern.

Organizational Objectives

The Organizational Objectives recognizes the role of human resources management in bring about organizational effectiveness. Human resource management is not an end itself; it is only a mean to assist the organizations with primary objectives.

Functional Objectives

Functional Objectives try to maintain the departments' contribution at a level appropriate to the organizational needs. Human resources is to be adjusted to suit the organizational demands. The department's level of service must be tailored to fit the organization it serves.

Personal Objectives

Personal objectives assist employees in achieving their personal goals, at least in so far as these goals enhance the individuals' contribution to the organization. Personal objectives of employees must be met if they are to be maintained, retained and motivated. Otherwise, employees' performance and satisfaction may decline giving rise to employee turnover.

HRM Objectives and Functions

HRM objectives	*Supporting functions*
1. Societal Objectives	1. Legal Compliances 2. Benefits 3. Union-management Relations
2. Organizational Objectives	1. Human Resource Planning 2. Employee Relations 3. Selection 4. Training and Development 5. Appraisal 6. Placement 7. Assessment
3. Functional Objectives	1. Appraisal 2. Placement 3. Assessment
4. Personal Objectives	1. Training and Development 2. Appraisal 3. Placement 4. Assessment

Source: William B. Werther, Jr. and Keith Davis, Human Resource and Personnel Management, p. 15.

2.4 HUMAN RESOURCE FUNCTIONS

Human Resources management has an important role to play in equipping organizations to meet the challenges of an expanding and increasingly competitive sector. Increase in staff numbers, contractual diversification and changes in demographic profile which compel the HR managers to reconfigure the role and significance of human resources management. The functions are responsive to current staffing needs, but can be proactive in reshaping organizational objectives.

Managing human resources to achieve better knowledge related outcomes means "Retaining personnel, building their expertise into the organizational routines through learning processes, and establishing mechanisms for the distribution of benefits arising from the utilization of this expertise" (Kamoche and Mueller, 1998, p. 1036). To identify which HRM practices could be employed to help organizations to achieve knowledge related outcomes, a brief review of representative case-based and existing empirical studies undertaken by scholars from different research fields (international HRM, innovation, strategy, international business, etc.) on the link between HRM practices and various knowledge related outcomes is necessary. The purpose is to determine what HRM practices organizations could employ to enhance knowledge related outcomes, otherwise known as knowledge-driven HRM practices.

1. Human resource planning, which includes creating venture teams with a balanced skill-mix, recruiting the right people, and voluntary team assignment. This strategy analyzes and determines personnel needs in order to create effective innovation teams.
2. Performance appraisal, which includes encouraging risk taking, demanding innovation, generating or adopting new tasks, peer evaluation, frequent evaluations, and auditing innovation processes. This strategy appraises individual and team performance so, that there is a link between individual innovativeness and company profitability. Which tasks should be appraised and who should assess employees' performance are also taken into account.
3. Reward systems, which includes freedom to do research, freedom to fail, freedom to form teams, freedom to run businesses, balancing pay and pride, noticeable pay raises, dual career tracks, promoting from within, recognition rewards, and balancing team and individual rewards. This strategy uses rewards to motivate personnel to achieve an organization's goals of productivity, innovation and profitability.
4. Career management, which includes empowering people, leading by example, and continued education. This strategy matches employees' long-term career goals with organizational goals through continuing education and training. Recently, international business researchers have identified the role of HRM practices in the organizational learning as one subject of inquiry to investigate the link between new HRM practices and innovation performance, arguing that HRM practices are "most conducive to innovation performance when adopted, not in isolation, but as a system of mutually reinforcing practices". Applying principal component analysis, they identify two HRM systems that influence innovation performance. The first consists of HRM practices, which is knowledge transfer affect employees' ability to innovate. They are interdisciplinary work groups, quality circles, systems for the collection of employee proposals, planned job rotation, delegation of responsibility, integration of functions, and performance-related pay. The second system is dominated by internal and external training. The overall conclusion is that "while the adoption of individual HRM practices may be expected to influence innovation performance positively, the adoption of a package of complementary HRM practices could be expected to affect innovation performance much more strongly" (Laursen and Foss, 2003, p. 257). From the reviewed articles we learned that there are certain knowledge-driven HRM practices, the extensive use of which enhances knowledge related outcomes. We also learned that the existing empirical work on the relations between HRM practices and knowledge related outcomes has exclusively focused on the individual HRM practices and their isolated effect. That could become a serious limitation since HRM is defined as "a set of distinct but interrelated activities, functions, and processes that are directed at attracting, developing and maintaining (or disposing of) a firm's human resources".

5. *Training and Development:* The managerial training is a challenge for organization to equip the managerial personnel to meet the ever advancing Technology and other Socio-economic and Political factors. It enriches and experiences of the managerial personnel to get maximum productivity in an organization. Managers should explore the policies, procedures, and structures used to guide the work of nonprofit organizations. They learn how to effectively develop transparent organizational structures and policies, identify and describe appropriate roles for staff and board members, methods of effective communication, and how to monitor and respond to change. Training and Development programs provide useful means of assuring that the employees are capable of performing their jobs at acceptable level and also more than that.

The role of HRM is to plan, develop and administer policies and programs designed to make expedious use of an organizations human resources. It is that part of management which is concerned with the people at work and with their relationship within enterprises. Its objectives are: (*a*) effective utilization of human resources, (*b*) desirable working relationships among all members of the organizations, and (*c*) maximum individual development.

HR Function: From Professional to Strategic Partner

Recent decades have witnessed dramatic shifts in the role of HR. Traditionally, managers saw the human resources function as primarily administrative and professional. HR staff focused on administering benefits and other payroll and operational functions and didn't think of themselves as playing a part in the firm's overall strategy.

Efforts to measure HR's influence on the firm's performance reflected this mindset. Specifically, theorists examined methodologies and practices that are focused at the level of the individual employee, the individual job, and the individual practice (such as employee selection, incentive compensation, and so forth). The idea was that improvements in individual employee performance would automatically enhance the organization's performance.

Although such research attempted to extend the range of HR's influence, it did little to advance HR as a new source of competitive advantage. It provided scant insight into the complexities of a strategic HR architecture. And simply put, it didn't encourage HR managers to think differently about their role.

In the 1990s, a new emphasis on strategy and the importance of HR systems emerged. Researchers and practitioners alike began to recognize the impact of aligning those systems with the company's larger strategy implementation effort and assessing the quality of that fit. Indeed, although many kinds of HR models are in use today, we can think of them as representing the following evolution of human resources as a strategic asset:

The personnel perspective: The firm hires and pays people but doesn't focus on hiring the very best or developing exceptional employees.

The compensation perspective: The firm uses bonuses, incentive pay, and meaningful distinctions in pay to reward high and low performers. This is a first step toward relying on people as a source of competitive advantage, but it doesn't fully exploit the benefits of HR as a strategic asset.

The alignment perspective: Senior managers see employees as strategic assets, but they don't invest in overhauling HR's capabilities. Therefore, the HR system can't leverage management's perspective.

The high-performance perspective: HR and other executives view HR as a system embedded within the larger system of the firm's strategy implementation. The firm manages and measures the relationship between these two systems and firm performance.

We're living in a time when a new economic paradigm—characterized by speed, innovation, short cycle times, quality, and customer satisfaction—is highlighting the importance of intangible assets, such as brand recognition, knowledge, innovation, and particularly human capital. This new paradigm can mark the beginning of a golden age for HR. Yet even when human resource professionals and senior line managers grasp this potential, many of them don't know how to take the first steps toward realizing it.

In our view, the most potent action HR managers can take to ensure their strategic contribution is to develop a measurement system that convincingly showcases HR's impact on business performance. To design such a measurement system, HR managers must adopt a dramatically different perspective, one that focuses on how human resources can play a central role in *implementing* the firm's strategy. With a properly developed strategic HR architecture, managers throughout the firm can understand exactly *how people can create value* and *how to measure the value-creation process.*

Learning to serve as strategic partners isn't just a way for HR practitioners to justify their existence or defend their turf. It has implications for the very survival of the firm as a whole. If the HR function can't show that it adds value, it risks being outsourced. In itself, this isn't necessarily a bad thing; outsourcing inefficient functions can actually enhance a firm's overall bottom line. However, it can waste much-needed potential. With the right mindset and measurement tools, the HR architecture can mean the difference between a company that's just keeping pace with the competition and one that is surging ahead.

We have all along heard that "time moves on steadily and relentlessly". Then how is it that especially in the new millennium, we need to review the challenges for the HR function in organizations? Has it taken a dramatic turn, or is it because the start of the century is a very convenient milestone to take stock? After all, such milestones not only show how far and in what direction we are progressing, but also give the distance to our destination, and are often excellent anchors to take time off to re-examine the future course of action. Be what it may, this article will try to touch on some of the major concerns that need to be tackled for success by the corporate leaders in India now, and in particular by the HR functionaries. I will be covering the background, discuss some of the major reasons and needs initially on a somewhat conceptual plane and finally, the challenges at a practical level that are simpler to understand, but still may be vital for future success. Needless to state that nothing is easy to achieve without careful planning and appropriate actions. Therefore, the very first benchmark to tackle is: *"If others can do it, so can we!"*

The threats facing managements have been changing with time, and what was a fine solution yesterday may no longer be valid tomorrow! We all know that the world is moving at an extremely fast pace, and that the rate of change is continuing to accelerate, as Alvin Toffler stated so aptly many years ago in "Future Shock". It can now be said that we have moved to the era of not just change, but an accelerated rate of change. This demands that corrective steps too need to be taken fast without a long drawn wait and see attitude. As compared to the past, the twenty-first century corporations are getting to be globally market driven ones with 'invest anywhere and share everywhere' concept. The impact of e-commerce with rapidly changing Information Technology (IT) will similarly transform conventional business structures dramatically—even smaller organisations will not be immune. These will demand a totally different type of HR strategy and intervention.

Amongst other issues, the paper highlighted the four stages of growth and evolution process of the Human Resource Management (HRM) function as follows:

The Reactive HRM Function

Where the main purpose is seen as maintenance of industrial harmony, and avoiding disruption through strikes etc. and exists generally where organizations are operating in near monopoly situations with assured growth—the interactions between HR and operating managers being minimal under normal situations at this stage.

The Independent HRM Function

Where the function is recognized as an independent entity. In this stage, while HR is involved in setting up industrial systems and procedures for operating managers, but is not fully responsible for the monitoring or correcting the problems in the system—only being marginally involved in various processes and other functions or results. Other functions would mostly seek HR's help in administrative or on few specific issues, and line managers do not see HR as a repository of expertise.

The Supportive HRM Function

It has its own direction with a distinct status within the organization, and actively contributes to the efforts of other functions in producing results. Organizations requiring product or technology changes rapidly in a competitive scenario generally need such HR involvement with high demands for qualified and competent manpower, often in a high turnover or mobility situation. Emphasis on people development and motivation generation comes from such HR, but their understanding or involvement in total business perspective remains limited or inadequate, even with higher functional participation.

The Integrative HRM Function

It is the stage when the competitive success of the organisation involves HRM significantly in an integrated manner, and demands such capabilities from the HR specialists. Their roles shift from a facilitator to a functional peer with competencies in other functions, and are recognised as an equal partner by the others. The typical HRM in this case is geared to contribute to organisational objectives of profitability and customer satisfaction, and is seen as a vehicle for implementation of quality processes. The department has a responsibility for monitoring employee satisfaction, since it is seen as surrogate to customer satisfaction.

They went on to state that "catalyst for such alignment" was evident from McKinsey's 7-S framework model. According to this framework, effective organisation change is a complex relationship between seven S's. HRM is a total matching process between the three Hard S's (Strategy, Structure and Systems) and the four Soft S's (Style, Staff, Skills and Super-ordinate Goals). Clearly, all the S's have to complement each other and have to be aligned towards a single corporate vision for the organization to be effective. It has to be realized that most of the S's are determined directly or indirectly by the way Human Resources are managed, and therefore, *HRM must be a part of the total business strategy.*

There are four roles which HR play, according to Dave Ulrich. The first, strategic partner role-turning strategy into results by building organizations that create value; second, a change agent role—

making change happen, and in particular, help it happen fast; the third, an employees champion role—managing the talent or the intellectual capital within a firm; and the fourth, an administrative role—trying to get things to happen better, faster and cheaper.

HRM has received a tremendous attention in recent years. Its role in organizations has also undergone a substantial change and many organizations have gradually oriented themselves from the traditional personnel management to a human resources management approach, although many see it as the "old wine in new bottle". The basic approach of HRM is to perceive the organizations in its totality. Its emphasis is not on production and productivity but also on the quality of life. It seeks to achieve the fullest development of human resource and the fullest possible socio-economic development.

2.5 SCOPE OF HRM

Scope of Human Resources Management was very limited in the beginning. Their activities were confined to administration, arranging little parties and picnics. This was the ancient time when Adam Smith saw 'factors of production' as land, labour and capital. Things have changed since then. The scope of the management in general and personnel in particular has changed considerably, covering more areas and responsibilities. It is the fact that there is no general agreement among the authors as to the scope of HRM. However, American Society for Training and Development (ASTD), conducted fairly an exhaustive study in this field and identified nine broad areas of activities of HRM. These are given below:

- Human Resource Planning
- Design of the Organization and Job
- Selection and Staffing
- Training and Development
- Organizational Development
- Compensation and Benefits
- Employee Assistance
- Union/Labour Relations
- Personnel Research and Information System.

Human Resource Planning: The objectives of HR Planning are to ensure the organization has the right types of persons at the right time at the right place. It must prepare human resources Inventory with a view to assess present and future needs, availability and possible shortages. Thereupon, HR Planning must forecast demand and supplies and identify sources. Last but not the least, HR Planning must develop strategies long-term and short-term meet the man-power requirement.

Design of Organization and Job: This is the task of laying down organization structure, authority, relationship and responsibilities. This will also mean definition of work contents for each position in the organization. This is done by "job description". Another important step is "Job specification". We shall go into the details of these terms shortly. Job specification identify attributes of persons most suitable for each job which is defined by job description.

Selection and Staffing: This is the process of recruitment and selection to staff. This involves matching people and their expectations with which the job specifications and career path available within the organization.

Training and Development: This involves an organized attempt to find out training needs of the individuals to meet the knowledge and skill which is needed not only to perform current job but the future needs of the organization.

Organizational Development: This is an important aspect whereby developing healthy inter-personal and inter-group relationship "Synergetic effect" is generated in an organization.

Compensation and Benefits: This is the area of wages and salaries administration where wages and compensations are fixed scientifically to meet fairness and equity criteria. In addition labour welfare measures are involved which include benefits and services.

Employee Assistance: Each employee is unique in character, personality, expectation and temperament. By and large each one of them faces problems everyday. Some are personal some are official. In their case he or she remains worried. Such worries must be removed to make him or her more productive and happy.

Union-Labour Relations: Healthy Industrial and Labour relations are very important for enhancing peace and productivity in an organization. This is one of the areas of HRM.

Personnel Research and Information System: Knowledge on behavioural science and industrial psychology throws better insight into the workers expectations, aspirations and behaviour. Advancement of technology of product and production methods have created working environment which are much different from the past. Globalization of economy has increased competition many fold. Science of ergonomics gives better ideas of doing a work more conveniently by an employee. Thus, continuous research in HR areas is an inescapable requirement. It must also take special care for improving exchange of information through effective communication systems on a continuous basis especially on moral and motivation.

HRM as a Business Partner

All these changes have led to the notion of the HR system as a strategic asset. Strategic assets are "... the set of difficult to trade and imitate, scarce, appropriable, and specialized resources and capabilities that bestow the firm's competitive advantage." (Amit and Shoemaker 1993: 36). This ideal is delineated by Becker, *etal.* (2001) who assert that the development of HRM practices can be represented by four evolutionary processes. These processes are identified as: (1) The personnel perspective, (2) The compensation perspective, (3) The alignment perspective, and (4) The high performance perspective. According to Becker and colleagues the personnel perspective focuses on practices employed by firms which hire and pay people, but does not emphasise the very best practices for developing exceptional employees. These authors also claim the compensation perspective is revealed in firms that use bonuses, incentive pay, and meaningful distinctions in pay to reward high and low performers. A further contention is that the alignment perspective is represented by senior managers who see employees as strategic assets, but do not encourage investment in overhauling personnel capabilities, despite the fact that such negligence or indifference results in the inability of the company HR system to leverage the management's perspective. Finally, the high performance perspective is illustrated when senior executives view HR as a system embedded within the larger system of the firm's strategy implementation. The firm manages and measures the relationship between these two systems and firm performance.

The increasingly significant role of HRM in achieving management objectives is reflected in the transformation of the personnel management function (Silva 2002). Over the last two decades, this function was often marginalised in terms of its importance in management activities and hierarchy. It has evolved from a concentration on employee welfare to one of managing people for the best possible productivity of the employee. In Thailand, the former approach has been emphasised in the Buddhist context as it is embedded in family values and management values such as compassion and kindness. One of the many principles of management taught in Buddhism is termed 'Brahmvihaara 4'. This principle advances a notion that those who are the leaders of others, either in the household or in the workplace, should practise four central tenets. These are: (1) Met-taa (compassion), (2) Garunaa (kindness), (3) Mudhitaa (Sharing the joy of success of others), and (4) Ubekkhaa (Let go and accept that it is up to the other's karma, when one cannot be of any further help to others even they have already tried very hard to do so) (Siengthai and Bechter 2004).

The changing management approach emphasises productivity enhancement through methods that provide employees with both intrinsic and extrinsic rewards. Therefore, today, far from being marginalised, the HRM function becomes recognised as a central business concern. In practice, performance and delivery are integrated into line management for the aims shift from merely securing compliance to more ambitious ideals of winning commitment. Human resource investment has become one of the main business strategies of firms in creating their competitive advantage. These initiatives are associated with, and perhaps are even predicated upon, a tendency to shift from a collectivist orientation to an individualist workforce. Accordingly, management inspects for 'flexibility' and seeks to reward performance differentially.

An assessment of these notions was recently undertaken (Siengthai and Bechter 2001). The survey was conducted during 1999–2000 with a number of Thai firms that had cadres of 200 employees or more. A regression analysis revealed that bundles of HRM practices were significantly and positively related to the level of innovation in the industry (Siengthai and Bechter 2001). When the data base was used to investigate HRM business partnerships between the studied firms it was generally revealed by the respondents (who were mostly human resource directors, some functional managers and some managing directors) that the top management in their organisation thought that the HR strategy was an important component of an innovation strategy (Siengthai and Bechter 2004). However, most of the respondents were reluctant to say that: (1) their top management valued HR more than other resources, (2) their top management believed human resource policies were a source of competitive advantage, or (3) their top management considered the HR manager a strategic partner in formulating and implementing business strategy (Siengthai and Bechter 2004). Arguably, it can be concluded that most of the HR departments or divisions are still not regarded as being a significant business partner in many firms' business strategies and change implementation. In reflection, in the case of Thailand, it may be claimed that the development of the HRM function and the perception of the other departments in the majority of firms have developed to the second stage, or that of a compensation perspective. However, the globalisation process has brought about changes and the image of HRM is being perceived more as a business partner in large organisations in the 2000s.

Globalization and Key HRM Challenges and Opportunities

Globalization has elevated the importance of HRM development in firms operating in Thailand. Investment in international markets has been viewed as a way to increase returns and decrease risks, but these business engagements also entertain substantial macro and micro level adjustments. Among the changes at the macro level are the deregulation policy or privatization initiatives decreed by the government as a response to external environmental changes. Hence, firms have incorporated restructuring or downsizing policies to take advantage of the new information and communications technology and thus create new competitive business strategies. Consequently, many corporations are now confronting labour market issues created by technological developments, rising prosperity and market realignment. The radical transformations have created numerous challenges for HRM practitioners who have to deal with the shift from low wage to high wage and high skilled labour as well as the need for management development to cope with these changes, the workforce diversity which comes with the globalisation process and the regionalisation process which allows free flow of products, capital and labour. At the micro level of firm operation managers have to balance the link between the HRM functions and the financial performance of the company, organisational innovation and productivity improvement, the empowerment of employees, project based contracts, the management of workforce redundancy, as well as bipartite labour management relations. These are but a few societal expectations, for regional level industrialisation and globalisation has been predicated to bring about the convergence of HRM/IR systems and practices (Lee 2002). In short, the management of change compels HRM function to be a proactive and innovative business partner.

Balancing business economic efficiency with social equity is an emerging dilemma for Thailand society. There is a need for Thailand to move away from the notion of low wages as a source of competitiveness and to begin to invest more in the development of a skilled workforce, which calls for far reaching reforms in the educational system (Kamoche 2000). Such efforts are perceived to be hindered by existing cultural norms. For example, the hierarchical 'nakrian ajarn' (student teacher) relationship turns the student into a passive recipient of knowledge and probably creates a culture of dependence in which the student (or in this case the employee) is taught that it is impolite or inappropriate to question the 'ajarn' (supervisor or employer). If the HR component is to make a significant contribution to economic recovery and industrial development, it will be important to institute change that creates more inquisitiveness and a willingness to challenge conventional wisdom in education, and allow more scope for management and employees to engage in constructive dialogue as to how best to tackle their difficulties. This will entail reviewing the sustainability of existing patterns in organisational paternalism.

The impact of the financial crisis is still prevalent. The government as well as private sector organisations are still working on the recovery of the economy. Together with the fierce competitive environment, it is foreseen that organisations will keep on shredding the redundant workforce that has resulted from bringing in more labour saving technology such as information technology and the automation of certain services functions. Even though the introduction of such technology will create the need for some certain skilled labour, the size of the workforce needed will not be equivalent to the earlier period of economic development. Another implication is that the increase in overhead costs as higher skilled employees will also receive a higher level of wages and salaries in organisations which cannot maintain a redundant workforce as slack resources. This can only be offset by an increase in organisational productivity. Hence, the need for organisational restructuring to become flatter organisations for those that are now large corporations will be the on going movement to enhance customer responsiveness, and hence, innovation and productivity. The dual economy in Thailand will become more evident as there will be a digital divide between organisations which now take advantage of the new (ICTs), and those which are still run by traditional management approach and are basically small scale family business enterprises with an absence of formal HRM system. For those companies, which are now moving into more high technology led operations, the new competitive landscape will necessitate that they resort to more of the individualised terms and conditions of employment for higher skilled and scarce employees.

It has been observed that many organisations, in both private and public sectors, have currently made used of the new ICTs to enhance the efficiency and effectiveness of their HRM practices. Many have started to have the so called 'e-HR' of which the most popular function seems to be 'e-learning' programs. Other institutions, and particularly the large sized organisations, are adopting similar courses of action after initial attempts to restructure their organisations by implementing combinations of the four more popular HRM strategies, which have been referred to under the following terms:

- Early retirement program
- Redeployment program
- More effective performance management
- Core competencies appraisal program

In contrast to the period before the financial crisis, one positive aspect for firms is that the phenomenon of job hopping has decreased significantly. However, an accompanying caveat is that for people with poor employment related skills their job opportunity will remain low while their job mobility will remain relatively high.

The dramatic and discontinuous changes that are taking place in the global environment have contributed to the evolution of traditional multinational corporations (MNCs) into global organisations that are more of a network nature (Gimeno and Woo 1996, Wolf 1997, Galunic and Rodan, 1998). The global network form of organising roles and activities infuses into the firm a heightened need for cross functional interdependence, which in turn, can increase role ambiguity for a human resource manager (Grimm and Smith 1997).

In Thailand, many corporations are now trying to maintain the core work force and outsourcing of some activities has become more common. In fact, casual observations suggest that many large corporations have started to divest some units into other legal entities that serve the core unit operations of the company, such as the customer relationship management unit, marketing unit, the HRM unit, the auditing unit, and the legal unit. This results in both downsizing and increased efficiency of operations due to a higher level of autonomy of decision-making and speed to market services. The divestiture is more, to some extent, a creation of the network organisations. Most of the projects or bidding will be granted to the divested unit. When the latter becomes better organised, both in term of services and human resources, a greater variety of services can then be offered to the market in general (Huws and Flecker 2004). This means that the HRM function also will be separated from the parent organisation. It usually has its own autonomy in terms of business formulation and implementation as the nature of the business may not be the same as that of its parent organisation. This is an advantage in terms of HRM and the recent trend of outsourcing management of particularly large corporations.

Conclusion

There is greater awareness in The companies for integrating strategic HRM with national, social, economic and environmental exigencies. Major shifts in the global marketplace, escalating demographic changes, the rapid technological advancements, as well as the changing role of women in contemporary industrial society has pressured managers to rethink fundamental organisational practices and policies. A notable conclusion is that these discontinuities have been imposed by both external and internal environmental factors. On one hand, the external environmental factors include globalisation of market or economic situations, government policies or politics, growth of the foreign or the joint venture sectors, stages of industrial relations development, and other significant changes in the domains of firms. Consequently, there has been a call for HRM to have a more strategic role.

In this chapter, the forces that have led to the role transition of HRM have been traced. Specifically, a historical perspective of HRM development in Thailand has been delineated into the period before 1990s and after 1990s, and particularly when Thailand experienced the Asian financial crisis. Within the globalisation process in which the business operations become borderless, the need for a speedy reaction to market volatility has led to many organisational restructuring and change programs. The availability of information technology has demanded changes to the skill composition of employees, and coupled with an increased participation of females in the work place, has compelled Thai organisations to transform their structures and work practices. Consequently, resource planning and work related initiatives have become central in HRM functions to improve corporate productivity and employee enterprise.

CASE STUDY–1: MANAGING PEOPLE: BEING NICE TO PEOPLE

Nawal graduated from a reputed management institute last year and joined his father's business, which employed 2 supervisors, 10 skilled workers and 28 semi-skilled workers. After one month, his father, a retired government officer, called him and said, "Nawal, I have had a change to observe your working with the men and women for the past few days. Although I hate to, I must say something. You are just too nice to people. I know they taught you human relations stuff at the management institute, but it just does not work here. I remember, when the Hawthorne studies were first reported, every one in the academic field got excited about them. But, believe me, there is more to managing people than just being nice to them."

QUESTIONS

1. Do you think, Nawal's father understood and interpreted the Hawthorne studies correctly?
2. If you were Nawal, what would your reaction be to your father's comments?
   (Adopted from C.A., Nov. 1995)

CASE STUDY–2: HRM PRACTICES

Companies in high-technology and creative industries (such as publishing and advertising) often worry about the turnover of high-potential employees. High-potential employees (sometimes called key employees) are people who have rare and special talents and who provide valuable contributions that can directly affect the firm's performance. Some well-known examples of high-potential people are film director Steven Spielberg (whose films are more profitable than those of any other director) and baseball stars Mark McGuire of the St. Louis Cardinals and Sammy Sosa of the Chicago Cubs–both of whom set records for home runs in baseball. Because most organizations have only a few high-potential employees, retaining these employees has important strategic implications for the business.

To protect themselves against the loss of high-potential employees and the intellectual property (such as trade secrets) that they may take with them, some companies are requiring all employees to sign non-compete agreements that restrict their freedom to work for a competitor after quitting the organization. For example, Career Track, a Colorado company that provides professional training seminars on business-related topics, took a former star trainer and workshop developer to court to enforce a non-compete agreement after this high-potential employee quit to work for competitor in California. The company wanted to avoid losing business to a competitor; it also wanted to let other high-potential employees know that the company is prepared to defend its rights if someone decides to challenge the non-compete agreement.

QUESTIONS

1. Do you think non-compete agreements are ethical ? Should a company require all employees to sign them or only high-potential employees ? What problems could arise from the use of non-compete agreements ?
2. Are there other HRM practices that could be substituted for non-compete agreements that would be likely to improve the retention of high-potential employees ? Which ones would you recommend?

REFERENCES

1. Amit R., and Shoemaker, P. (1993), *Strategic assets and organisational rent.* Strategic Management Journal, **14(1),** 33–46.
2. Becker, B.E., Huselid, M.A., and Ulrich, D. (2001), *The HR scorecard: Linking people, strategy, and performance.* Boston, MA: Harvard Business School Press.
3. Bothidaht, P. (2001), *Preparing for organisation change: A case study of TOT.* A research study in partial fulfilment for the degree of Master of Business Administration (Executive Program), School of Management, Asian Institute of Technology, Thailand.
4. Chaweewattanasakul, N. (1998), *Human resource development in the 21st century of C.P.* Dissertation Master's Degree of Public Administration, Chulalongkorn University, Thailand.
5. Galunic, D.C., and Rodan, S. (1998), *Resource recombinations in the firm: Knowledge structures and the potential for Schumpetarian innovation.* Strategic Management Journal, **19(12),** 1193–1201.
6. Gimeno, J., and Woo, C.Y. (1996), *Hyper-competition in a multi-market environment: The role of strategic similarity and multi-market contact in competitive de-escalation.* Organization Science, **7(3),** 322–341.
7. Grimm, C.M., and Smith, K.G. (1997), *Strategy as action: Industry rivalry and coordination.* Cincinnati, OH: South-Western College Publishing.
8. Huws, U., and Flecker, J. (2004), *Asian emergence: The world's back office*? IES Report 409, Institute for Employment Studies: Brighton, United Kingdom.
9. Kamoche, K. (2000), *From boom to bust: The challenges of managing people in Thailand.* International of Human Resource Management, **11(2),** 452–468.
10. Kongchant, A. (2001), *Human resource management in Thai firms and multinational corporations in Thailand.* A Research Report, Chulalongkorn University, Thailand.
11. Kongsanchai, T. (2001), '*Creating competencies for strategic TOT Services.*' A research study in partial fulfilment of the requirements for the degree of Master of Business Administration, Chulalongkorn University, Thailand.

12. Laohathanakul, V. (1999), *Human resource management during the economic crisis*. Dissertation Master's Degree of Public Administration, Chulalongkorn University, Thailand.
13. Lawler, J., and Siengthai, S. (1997), *Human resource management strategy in Thailand: A case study of the banking industry*, Research and Practice in Human Resource Management, **5(1),** 73–88.
14. Lawler, J., Siengthai, S., and Atmiyananda, V. (1997), *Human resource management in Thailand: Eroding traditions*. In C. Rowley (Ed.), Human Resource Management in the Asia-Pacific Region, (170–196) London: Frank Class Publishers.
15. Lee, J.S. (2002), *Asia in the 21st century: Challenges and opportunities in work and labour*. A rapporteur's report (Track 5). In T. Hanami (Ed.) Universal Wisdom Through Globalisation, (277–286) Selected Papers from 12th IIRA World Congress, Tokyo.
16. Siengthai, S. (1993), *Tripartism and industrialization of Thailand*. A Research Paper Prepared For The ILO, December, ESCAP, Thailand.
17. Siengthai, S., and Bechter, C. (2001), *Strategic human resource management and firm innovation*. Research and Practice in Human Resource Management, **9(1),** 35–57.
18. Siengthai, S., and Bechter, C. (2004), *Human resource management in Thailand*. In P. Budhwar (Ed.) HRM in Southeast Asia and the Pacific Rim (141–172), London: Routledge.
19. Silva, S.R. (2002), *Human resource management, industrial relations and achieving management objectives*. Paper Prepared for East Asia multi-disciplinary advisory team, ILO, Bangkok.
20. Suehiro, A., and Wailerdsak, N. (2004), *Family business in Thailand: Its management, governance, and future challenges*, ASEAN Economic Bulletin, **21(1),** 81–93.
21. Vorapongse, V. (2001), *Human resource management in economic recovery: A case study of real estates business*. Master's Degree Thesis, Chulalongkorn University, Thailand.
22. Wailerdsak, N. (2003), *Retaining and developing managers and professionals in a Thai telecommunications firm*. Journal of Asian Business, **19(1),** 67–87.
23. Wolf, J. (1997), *From 'starworks' to networks and heterarchies*? Management International Review, Special Issue, **37(1),** 145–169.

3

CHAPTER

HUMAN RESOURCES PLANNING

3.1 INTRODUCTION

Human Resources Planning have been a function of management since the origins of the modern industrial organization. Economist Alfred Marshall observed in 1890 that the head of a business must assume himself that his managers, clerks and foremen division of labour, specialization, organization of management into levels, work simplification, and application of standards for selecting employees and measuring their performance were all principles applied early in industrial management. They were also applied in large non-industrial organizations, including religious, governmental and military organization.

Planning for the staff for work is not a recent notion. During the first part of the century, the focus in the manpower planning was upon the hourly production worker. The aim of improving efficiency through work engineering and early industrial psychology application was consistent with the need to improve productivity and introduce greater objectivity to personnel practices. During the World War II and the past war years the HRM focus intensified on employee productivity and on the availability of the competent managerial personnel. These needs resulted from a civilian talent shortage in combination with an increasing demand for the goods and services. New technologies and a new awareness of and interest in behavioural aspects of work also complicated and the manpower-planning task. The expanded demand for high potential personnel in the 1960 resulted from high technology programs and rapid corporate expansion and diversification. In response, human resources planning practices attempted to balances supply and demand, particularly for managerial, professional and technical personal.

Human Resources planning mean different means to different organizations. To some companies, human resources planning mean management development. It involve helping executives to make better decisions, communicate more effectively, and know more about the firm. The purpose to make men and women better managers. The emphasis is having current managers who are sucked in there function and reasonably qualified for promotions. Too frequently the acquisition and development of the skills and knowledge needed for the future are lacking. The goal is often only to make the manager a better manager today.

3.2 WHAT IS HUMAN RESOURCES PLANNING?

In the other firms, the approach to human resources planning is reserved. Here the problem in defined as estimating future manpower needs. The goal is to make the person into the future requirements. The qualitative aspects of the development are some how to be met by a natural development process, even though future knowledge and skill requirements are ignored in the planning efforts.

Human Resources planning is a process by which management determine how the organization should move from its current manpower position to its desired manpower position. Through planning, management strives to have the right number and the right kinds of people, at the right place, at the right time, doing things, which result in both organization and the individual receiving maximum long-run benefits.

It is four-phased process. The first phase involves the gathering and analysis of data through manpower inventories and forecasts, the second phase consist of establishing manpower objectives and policies and gaining top management approval of these. The third phase involves designing and implementing plans promotions to enable the organization to achieve its manpower objectives. The fourth phase in consumed with control and evaluation of manpower plans sent programs to facilitate progress to benefits both the organization and the individual. The long run view means that gains may be sacrificed in the short run for the future grounds. The planning process enables the organization to identify what its manpower needs is and what potential manpower problems required current action. This leads too more effectively and efficient performance.

3.3 OBJECTIVES OF THE HUMAN RESOURCES PLANNING

1. To ensure optimum use of human resources current employees.
2. To assess or forecast future skill requirement.
3. To provide control measures to ensure that necessary resources are available as when required.
4. A number of specified reasons for attaching importance to manpower planning and forecasting exercises are:
    - To link manpower planning with the organizational planning
    - To determine recruitment levels.
    - To anticipate redundancies.
    - To determine optimum training levels.
    - To provide a basis for management development programs.
    - To cost the manpower.
    - To assist productivity bargaining.
    - To assess future accommodation requirement.
    - To study the cost of overheads and value of service functions.
    - To decide whether certain activity needs to be subcontracted, etc.

The HR forecasts in responsible for estimating number of people and the jobs needed by an organization to achieve its objectives and realize its plans are time in the most efficient and effective manner possible in the simplest sources, HR needs are computed by subtracting HR supplies or numbers of the people available from expected HR demands or number of people required to produce at a desired level. It is a strategy for acquisition, utilization, improvement and preservation of the human resources of an enterprise. The objective is to provide right personnel for the right work and optimum utilization of the existing human resources. HRP exists as the part of planning process of business. This is the activity aims to coordinating requirements for the availability of the different types of employers. The major activities are include the forecasting, (future requirements), inventorying (present strength), anticipating (comparison of present and future requirements) and planning (necessary program to meet the requirements).

The objectives of human resource planning may be summarized as below:

- ***Forecasting Human Resources Requirements:*** HRP is essential to determine the future needs of HR in an organization. In the absence of this plan it is very difficult to provide the right kind of people at the right time.
- ***Effective Management of Change:*** Proper planning is required to cope with changes in the different aspects which affect the organization. These change needs continuation of allocation/ reallocation and effective utilization of HR in organization.
- ***Realizing the Organizational Goals:*** In order to meet the expansion and other organizational activities the organizational HR planning is essential.
- ***Promoting Employees:*** HRP gives the feedback in the form of employee data which can be used in decision-making in promotional opportunities to be made available for the organization.
- ***Effective Utilization of HR:*** The data base will provide the useful information in identifying surplus and deficiency in human resources.

The objectives of HRP is to maintain and improve the organizational capacity to reach its goals by developing appropriate strategies that will result in the maximum contribution of HR. HR planning should involve in the following areas:

- They should collect, maintain, improve and interpret the relevant information regarding human resources.
- They should report periodically human resource objective and requirements, existing employees, and allied features of human resources.
- They should develop procedures and techniques to determine the requirements of different types of human resources over period of time from the standpoint of organizational goals.
- They should develop the measures of HR utilization as components of forecast of human resources requirements along with independent validation.
- They should employ suitable techniques leading to effective allocation of work with a view to improving human resources utilization.
- They should conduct research to determine the factors hampering the contribution of the individuals groups to the organization with a view to modifying or removing these handicaps.
- They should develop and employ methods of economic assessment of human resources to reflect its features as income generator and cost and accordingly improve the quality of decisions affecting the human resources.
- They should evaluate the procurement, promotion, and retention of the effective human resources.
- They should analysis the dynamic process of recruitment, promotion, and the loss to the organization and control these process with a view to maximizing the individual and the group performances without involving high cost.

It is usually the top management that formulates the vision and translates the vision into the objectives. Further, these objectives get translated into strategy and long-range plans. These plans usually form the guidelines for the human resources department to plan for the human resources requirements. The HR department should coordinate the above information and prepares the human resources plan.

3.4 NEEDS OF HRP

Major reasons for the emphasis on HRP at the Macro level:

Employment-Unemployment Situation: Though in general the number of educated unemployment is on the rise, there is acute shortage for a variety of skills. This emphasis is the need for more effective recruitment and retaining people.

Technological Change: The myriad changes in production technologies, marketing methods and management techniques have been extensive and rapid. Their effect has been profound on the job contents and job contexts. These changes cause problems relating to redundancies, retaining and redeployment. All these suggest the need to plan manpower needs intensively and systematically.

Organizational Change: In the turbulence environment marked by cyclical fluctuations and discontinuities, the nature and pace of changes in organizational environment, activities and structures affect manpower requirements and require strategic considerations.

Demographic Change: The changing profile of the work force in terms of age, sex, literacy, technical inputs and social background has implications for HRP.

Skill Shortage: Unemployment does not mean that the labour market is a buyer's market. Organizations generally become more complex and require a wide range of specialist skills that are rare and scare. Problems arise when such employees leave.

Governmental Influences: Government control and changes in legislation with regard to affirmative action for disadvantages groups, working conditions and hours of work, restrictions on women and child employment, causal and contract labour, etc. have stimulated the organizations to be become involved in systematic HRP.

Legislative Control: The policies of "hire and fire" have gone. Now the legislation makes it difficult to reduce the size of an organization quickly and cheaply. It is easy to increase but difficult to shed the fat in terms of the numbers employed because of recent changes in labour law relating to lay-offs and closures. Those responsible for managing manpower must look far ahead and thus attempt to foresee manpower problems.

Impact of the Pressure Group: Pressure groups such as unions, politicians and persons displaced from land by location of giant enterprises have been raising contradictory pressure on enterprise management such as internal recruitment and promotion, preference to employees' children, displace person, sons of soil etc.

Systems Approach: The spread of system thinking and advent of the macro computer as the part of the on-going revolution in information technology which emphasis planning and newer ways of handling voluminous personnel records.

Lead Time: The log lead time is necessary in the selection process and training and deployment of the employee to handle new knowledge and skills successfully.

Approaches to Human Resources Planning

On the theoretical plane there are three options to any educational planner. The first option is to treat the education as consumption goods and demand for education as an aggregate of individual consumer's demand schooling, and to provide the facilities for education and training according. The second option is to view education an investment goods, evaluate the investments in education at par with investment in education with the rate of return on investment in physical capital. The third option is to considered skilled manpower as basic inputs to the production goods and services within the economy; assess the skill requirements to achieve any predetermined economic growth target, and to gear the expansion of educational system to provide the needed education and training.

There are three approaches to educational planning:

- **Social demand approach**
- **Rate of return approach, and**
- **Manpower requirement approaches.**

Social Demand Approach: The social demand approach lies on the assessment of society's requirement for education. In principles, it is an aggregate of individuals demand for education in respect of all individuals within the society. It is not always possible particularly in large societies, to assess individual demand for education. In practice, therefore, social demand approach relies on a projection of past trends in demographic aspects of population and the enrollment at the different levels of education.

Social demand approach is thus capable of revealing the number of students with differently types of professional preparations that may be a given target date, based on past experiences. Projections of social demand for education are contingent upon given levels of:

- Income of educated people,
- Taste and references of household for education,
- Demographic characteristics such as fertility and mortality,
- Direct costs of education,
- Student grants, and
- Existing standard of admission to various levels of education.

Added to these constraints, there are the perennial problems associated with the data base on demographic aspects at disaggregated levels such as districts, blocks and villages and data on wastage and stagnation in education, and intensity of utilization of existing educational facilities.

Social demand approach thus suffers from the difficulties associated with any futurological exercise.

Rate of Return Approaches: Critics of social demand approach argue that the decision to choose more or less of education, beyond a legal school-learning age, is made by an individual who attaches a positive value to the present and the future benefits of education. Aggregate of individuals demand for education, which is constructed the social demand for education, should then be based exaggerate of individuals assessment of benefits of education-reflecting the social benefits.

This brings us the rate of return approach to education:

Rate of return approach looks upon education as a contributor to productivity and this sense, it is expected to facilitate investment decisions in education whether or not the students should undergo more schooling, or whether or not the state should invest more and expand educational facilities.

Like in the rate of return on investment analysis, rate of return on investment in education is used to expand educational facilities until schooling equalizes.

- On the one hand yield of investment in different types of education, and
- On the other hand yield of investment in education vis-à-vis other sectors of economy.

The analysis, however, is confined to formal education only.

Estimation of rate of return involves the calculation of internal rate of return which equates the present value of returns earned throughout the future active life with cost incurred soon after investment decision is made. There are thus three parameters involved in the estimation of rate of return.

- Costs of Education,
- Return on education, and
- Discounted rate (Used in discounting future returns to arrive at present value).

Variety of conceptual issues are involved in the estimation of these three parameters.

Costs of Education: Economic analysis of investment in education has a simple two element taxonomy of cost:

(*i*) Direct Costs and (*ii*) Indirect Costs

Direct Costs: The direct costs again have the **two elements:**

(1) Private expenditure on education, and (2) Public expenditure on education.

Private expenditure on education is the expenditure incurred by the individuals pursuing education which includes items such as tuition fees, cost of the books, extra room and board expenses and out-of-pocket expenses. It is relatively easier expenditure on these items.

Public expenditure on education is what the Government spends on creating, expanding and maintaining educational facilities. Public expenditures may be divided into recurring and non-recurring items of expenditure. Recurring expenditure consist of items such as salaries of teaching and non-teaching staff, maintains expenditure, office expenditure including the contingencies and the expenditure on student welfare. Non-recurring expenditure comprises costs of building, plant and equipment, library and sports complex. In the case of recurring expenditure, apportioning salaries of teaching staffs lecturing so students in more than one discipline is a problem, as it requires an assessment of workload distribution which is not uniform among the various educational institutions. Non-recurring expenditure poses two sets of problems; one imputing costs to any particular cohort of students. Second, appropriating costs imputed to any cohort among students belonging to various disciplines, as all students may not use each and every facility in an accidental manner. For example, social sciences students do not use laboratories.

Indirect Costs: Indirect costs may be viewed from both private and social angles. From the private angle it is the earning foregone by individual students while attending schools. There are a variety of conceptual issues involved in estimating earnings and in attributing it to a particular level of education. Estimation of foregone earnings is even more difficult, as it calls for identification of all possible avenues of employment and possible earnings there from, and assessment of money value of foregone leisure. This necessitates subjective valuation of earning and leisure.

The social view of Indirect Costs involves estimation of opportunity costs of public expenditure on education. There are no standard procedures in the estimation of social indirect costs.

Return to Education: Direct monetary benefits to educations are the extra life-time earnings received that can be attributed to schooling.

Observed earnings differentials of any education program, say college education, can at best constitute a first approximation to the true earnings differentials attributable to college education. This is because intelligence, family wealth, parents' education and earnings and the motivation play an important role—more than education *per se* isolating the effect of all such factors and estimating the true earnings differential between differential attributable to any given level of education is a difficult task.

As for earning data on only on the past and present returns are available. To estimate future returns it calls for intelligent guess regarding productivity and growth in incomes. Any assumptions on the secular rate of growth of earnings differential between high school and college students may have a crucial effect on the rate of return to college education.

Computation of the life time earning also necessitates adjustment for education specific unemployment and mortality rates, which is a difficult task as no data exist in this regard. This apart, monetary gain to an individual over his life time should be measured by his disposable income—income net of taxes. Anticipating future tax structures for different streams of life time income is not an easy job.

Indirect Monetary Benefits: Education definitely influences the earnings from the first job. Earnings from the subsequent jobs are not all dependent on initial education. Rather, they are dependent on the skills acquired through on-the-job training and other in service training. Additional earnings attributes to such training are thus indirect to initial education. Such training, however, is dependent on initial level of education, although the nature of on-the-job/in service training received need not necessarily be the same for all individuals with identical initial education. Isolating effect of such training on the future earnings from the life time earnings to a given initial education, in computing returns to a given level of education, is a difficult job.

Human capital in educated workers is often used to increase the productivity of co-workers. For example, an educated worker may improve production techniques and the office procedures which may improve the efficiency of all other workers and lead to an increase in the overall productivity. Corrections should therefore be made to add productivity related earnings gain of all the lesser educated who may benefit from the education and skill of the workers who causes improvement in production, as other workers are indirect by products of education and such benefits are not captured by the recipients of education.

If the earnings of the private returns is extended to include all benefits received by the recipients family, then there are other forms of indirect monetary benefits such as:

- *Child care services*—During the period of child is at the school the parents have free time to further their economic interests, and
- *Generational transmission of education*—Educated parents facilitates inherited aptitude for schooling among their children and effective home instructions which save expenditure on the private tuitions.

It is easier to visualize numerous such miscellaneous indirect benefits. The problem, however, is that of quantifying monetary gains from such benefits.

Non-Monetary Benefits: There are some non-monetary benefits accrue to the individual pursuing education. Education may, for instance, alter and modify taste, preferences and outlook leading to cultural up gradation. Likewise the education may facilitate individuals to take up more satisfying job with higher prestige and greater independence and less of stress and strain. In fact, the attraction of such psychological returns as compared with the monetary returns of white collared jobs which swells the number seeking them among the educated.

More other non-monetary benefits of education are not captured by the educated individual. Rather, they benefit the society. These benefits are categorized as 'externalities'. The educated mind is trained to inquire and questions, and to accept authority by default. This aspect of education is expected to strengthen democratic principles, and reduce the chances of losing collective and individual freedom of the society. Likewise, education causes better understanding and appreciation of the importance of health and hygiene thus leading to improved health standards of the society at large. Proponents of education even argue that schooling improves social order.

Education causes quality improvement in labour. Given other factors of production, including the physical capital endowments, growth of the economy can come about only through the improvement in the quality of labour. Education this contributes to economic growth.

Non-monetary benefits of education are all qualitative in nature. They are not amenable to quantitative measurement.

Discount Rate: While the cost of the education are included at the beginning, return to education accrue over the life time. In the computation of the internal rate of return which is used as a criteria for making investment decision on education, there is a need to discount future returns to arrive at their present value. Rate of return to education thus depends on the discount rate used for discounting future returns.

In case of private returns the discount rate could be:

- Either the rate of interest which an individual borrow for financing education.
- Or the rate of return from the best possible alternatively to investment in education.

Here aging there is no. of possible alternatives and there is no objectives criterion for making choice among the alternatives.

Choosing a discount rate in respect to the social returns is even more complicated. This is because, apart from the economic criteria, welfare consideration also enters the calculus to the determination of an acceptable social rate of discount.

Limitations of Rate of Return Approach: Apart from the conceptual issues associate with parameters involved in the estimation of rate of education and difficulties associated with the availability of data, there is a no. of other limitations associated with this approach.

The primary limitation is the indeterminacy of the signal it generates for the educational planning. Rate of return analysis is only indicative of relative policies. It does not facilities value judgment among the different projects in the priorities ordering. In particular, when it comes to making a choice among non-among comparable projects, rate of return approach is an extremely defective tool. Even within the education, because of sequential hierarchical linkages, it is difficult to make decision on how much to invest at the each level purely based on rate of return analysis and without any references to backward and forward linkage of the level of education concerned.

Rate of return analysis does not take cognizance of supply and demand of skills in the labour market. Excess supply (or excess demand) is likely to cause distortions in the occupation education profiles and hence affect the life-time earnings profile. These distortions are likely to vitiate the signals made available by the rate of return analysis which may ultimately lead to a wrong set of choice in education.

To an economist, education is the only a screening device in analyzing the process of human capital formation. Even there is no unanimity among scholars with regard to the filtration function of the education. In the view of this, it is doubtful whether rate of return to education could be used as an effective tool in making investment decision within education sector as well as among the different sectors of economy with education included as a sector.

Manpower Requirement Approach: The fundamental axioms of manpower requirements approach is that there is a definite link between the education and economic growth and that lack of skilled manpower in required number impedes growth.

In this approach an attempt is made to forecast future requirements of educated manpower to fulfill a future target of Gross National Product (GNP) or specified targets of industrial production. Based on the forecasts of educated manpower requirement over a specified period, the planners would then indicate the directions of development of the educational sector over the same specific period.

The basic steps involved in this exercise are as under:

- Anticipating the directions and the magnitude of development of each individual sectors of the economy.
- Evolving norms of the employing manpower in each individual sector keeping the view the technological options—Present as well as future—for each sector of the economy.
- Translating the physical targets for the development of each individual sector into the manpower requirement using the sector specific manpower norms.
- Estimating the educational; equivalents of the manpower requirement.
- Analyzing the implications of estimates of educated manpower requirements for educational development, based on assumptions regarding the enrollment rates, transitions probability and wastage and the stagnation rates at the each level of education.

Limitations of the Manpower Requirement Approach: The first limitation assumes that the educated manpower of different types are used in fixed proportions and that there no substitutions possibilities among the various categories of educated manpower.

The second limitation is that it postulates a definite link between an industrial task and an educational level. Prices, either in terms of cost of producing educated manpower or in terms of salaries and wages of educational people do not play any role in matching demand with supplies of educated manpower in this brand of educational planning. This makes the good sense if formal education and training is the only means of producing educated manpower. If there are alternative ways of producing a given category of skilled manpower, then prices play a significant role and the manpower requirements approach fails to take cognizance of this respect. In the Indian context, even in the case of highly skilled occupation where graduate level engineers are required, it has been observed that over 30 per cent of the manpower do not have the basic minimum qualification. They have reached these levels through on-the-job training and such other informal training, in the requisite skills. Such persons are categorized as "practical" and these practical are to be found in every occupation.

The crucial information in all forecasting exercises is the assumptions about the distant unknown future. Any error in judgment, in this regard, will seriously affect manpower balances at a later date resulting in either excess supply or excess demand. In the context of educational planning, excess demand is relatively easier to manage. Excess supply, on the other hand, leads to serious economic and sociological problems which are often difficult to deal with.

3.5 HUMAN RESOURCE PLANNING PROCESS

Often we express that the most important asset in organization is our people. Without the right people, it is unlikely that even the most comprehensive and business plans/strategies will deliver negative performances. The vast majority of organization comes when the right people with right knowledge, skills and behaviour are deployed throughout an organization.

HR planning is how to achieve that match of skills, knowledge and behaviours. It is about:

- Developing an understanding of everything possible about the internal and external environment and how these will affect our current and future workforce. It is about understanding the make up of our current workforce and the necessary skills, capabilities and aptitudes that will be required to achieve business outcomes in our current and changing environment.
- It is about assuring that we link our human resources strategies with business outcomes and that our workforce plans reflect those initiative/strategies and provide our managers with a framework for making informed decisions in line with our managers with a framework for making informed decisions in the line with our mission, strategies plan and financial resources.
- Also, it provides the opportunity for longer term thinking about future service pressures and needs, and what you need to do now to get workable strategies in place not only for the employees development, but for strategies financial and human capital management.

HR planning has a critical role to play in delivering improved services and is an important issue for an organization.

At its simplest, HR Planning is a planning process and analytical capability to measure and compare the current workforce (supply or faces) with the future workforce (demand or space). This planning process provides insight into the best policies and initiative needed to improve the overall human resources system. It has a critical role in developing personnel requirements/data elements, which should be linked to strategic organizational planning, budgeting processes and all recurring recruitment needs, training recruitments and planning activities.

There is no one set of model of workforce planning but the underlying concepts are similar. All models are concerned about analyzing your current workforce, and then extending that analysis to identify the future skills and competencies needed to deliver new and improved services that are aligned with achieving the organizational mission. (Demand and supply analysis) The comparison between the present workforce and desired future workforce will highlight your shortages, surpluses and competency gaps, whether due to external pressure or internal factors. (Gap Analysis) These gaps become the focus of each detailed workforce plan in identifying and implementing strategies that will build the relevant skills and capacity needed for organizational success.

An ideal Human Resources Planning System should be:

- Holistic in its approach linked with strategies planning and budget process.
- Built around our service needs and skills required to deliver quality service.
- Responsive to change variables *i.e.*, economic, technological, political, environmental mandate.
- Supportive of continual learning and development concepts.
- Data driven that allow for scenario building because of changing assumptions for different desired outcomes.

Process of an Integrated Workforce Planning System Uses Future Requirements and Current Workforce Information

Fig. 3.1 Human Resources Planning

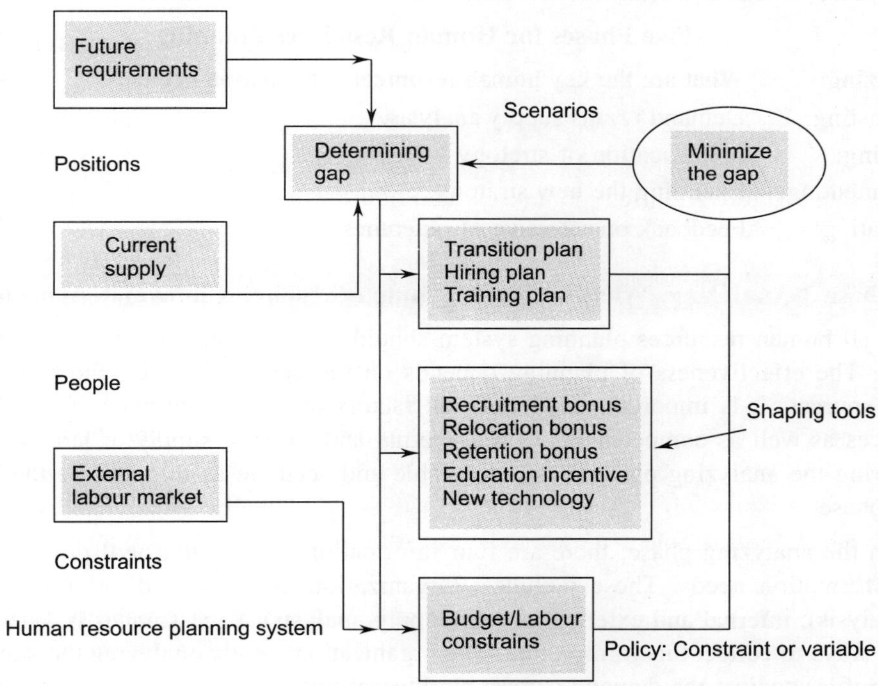

Before beginning the human resources planning process, you have to need to have a firm grasp on main drivers for workplace planning and any influence of those drivers on the human resources planning exercise being done. These drivers set the context for everything you will be looking at throughout this process. The four main drivers for any human resources planning are:

Organization Directions: Includes the organizational plans, budget forecasts new technology, working practices, organizational culture and reward systems.

Internal labour: Which includes a determination of human resources profile by multidimensions (gender, age, grade, occupations, length of services etc.); identification of any internal management issues like retention, separation, promotion patterns, etc. identify potential area of our workplace that are vulnerable to current or future skills gaps imbalances and look at geographical issues that could be the cause of issues identified. All of these factors have implications for recruitment and retention of our workforce across the organization.

External Labour: Demographic change in our potential workforce is affecting both the demand for services and workforce supply to fill our vacancies.

Business Change: Technological changes are leading to changes in service/information delivery, way of working and the skills needed in the workforce. Consequently, this will change the competencies for positions and how we need to recruit, hire and engage our current and future workforce.

The scope of human resources planning is to build a longer term context within which short-term staffing decisions can be made. Human resources planning is a living process and needs to be periodically reviewed in order to respond to changing circumstances. Regular monitoring will ensure that organizational element will avoid strategic drift and ensure that organization's human resource planning remain current. This process is still about the ensuring that sufficient people with the right skills are in place to deliver a seamless service to the internal and external stakeholders.

Five Phases for Human Resources Planning

1. Analyzing: What are the key human resources information needed?
2. Forecasting: Demand *versus* supply analysis.
3. Planning: Identification of stretogy
4. Implementing: Exemling the new stratogy
5. Evaluating: Feedback on effective of outcomes.

Phase 3-Analyzing: What are the key human resources information needed?

The over all human resources planning system should be well thought out, systematic and well documented. The effectiveness of planning depends on the detail, accuracy and reliability of the information sources. It is important to identify all factors that could influence future demand for output/services as well as competencies of the internal and external supply of labour. Information gathered during the analyzing phase must be reliable and accurate as this will be the basis of the forecasting phase.

The begin the analyzing phase; there are four information sources that will provide key human resources information needs. These includes; Organization direction and environmental factors (demand analysis); internal and external labour (supply analysis). Each sources is listed below and provides the ways to collect this information. The organization simply analyzing the supply (current workforce profile) against the demand (future workforce profile).

Suggested checklist for organization information:

- Demand Analysis.
- Strategic plan/Business priorities.
- Internal or External reports that could affects business outcomes.
- Budget Estimates (Short-Term and Long-Term).
- Plans for New Technology.
- Employee Survey Information.
- External Contract Services.
- Organization Culture.
- Changing Competencies.

Suggested checklist for organization's environmental factors information:

Political expectations

Demographic changes

Influence of technology on work

Changes in economic forecasting

Analysis current and future level of accountability

Suggested checklist for organization's internal and external labour profile information:

Supply Analysis

Internal

- Age and gender distribution
- Retirement rates
- Location of the workplace
- Diversity characteristics
- Length of service
- Resignation rates
- Internal career paths

External

- Labour trends
- Internal vs. External acceptance rates

Phase 3-Forecasting: Demand versus Supply analysis

Forecasting is considering the future needs of organization. One of the most useful outcomes of this phase is the identification of potential problems or issues facing your organization. This analysis will be based on the data collected from the information sources in the analyzing phase. The result of this phase will help to develop the gap analysis and emergent strategies to manage the future. It involves the identification of any predicted changes and/or developments that may result from demand and analysis. Business elements may have varying issues identified based on needs of their organizations. The aim is to create necessary resources/strategies to optimize the future position of organization. There are four steps in forecasting phase; identifying key workforce assumptions, validating assumptions, utilizing assumptions for scenario building and performing the gap analysis.

The first step is to identify key workforce assumptions/issues for the elements based on the data/information collected from the information sources during the analyzing phase. Ensure that all of these forecasting assumptions describe the potential impact on business element, any inherent risks and any likelihood of occurrence based on element culture.

The second step is to validate these assumptions by utilizing focus groups or administrating questionnaires/interviews to various leaders in the organization. The feedback provided will ensure that gathered assumptions are valid and based on the basic data available. Additionally, feedback should provide insight in the reasoning behind the assumptions.

The third step is utilizing these assumptions in scenario buildings. Scenarios are a way to develop alternative futures based on different combinations of assumptions, facts and trends that will help the organization's forecasting goals mentioned earlier. Scenarios are generally descriptive statements presenting a particular picture of the future that includes comments on the probability of certain events occurring. Moreover, scenarios are usually accompanied by qualitative or quantitative information.

The next step after outlining best, worst and most likely scenarios is to create a preferred scenario detailing what organization wants as an outcome taking into account the assumptions previously identified. Additionally use the information from any warning indicators above which should be used to monitor changes consistent with preferred outcome.

It will be useful to apply SWOT or PESTLE analysis to help through this phase. SWOT is an acronym for Strength, Weakness, Opportunities and Treats. Strengths and Weaknesses are **internal** factors. Opportunities and Treats are **external** factors. It is a simple technique as it uses four perspectives for decision-making and summarization. For example what are the strengths, weakness, opportunities and threats of your scenario? This would be done for each scenario suggesting the best, worst and most likely outcomes. PESTLE is essentially the same technique but is useful for examining the external factors affecting a problem. The acronym stand for Political, Economic, Sociological, Technological, Legal and Environmental.

Fig. 3.2 SWOT Analysis Model

Strength	Weaknesses
Opportunities	Treats

PESTLE Analysis

Political Issues Accountability Equal Opportunities Diversity Partnership working	**Economic Issues** Skill Shortage Cost of Living
Social Issues Changing customer expectations and needs Changing Demographics Changing employee expectations and needs *i.e.*, work-life balance issues Inequalities and deprivation Qualifications, skills and competencies	**Technological Issues** Innovation Communication New Way of working
Legal Issues Service obligations Employment legislation Environmental	**Environmental Issues** Increased awareness and expectations

The tools (SWOT and PESTLE) are useful for handling the qualitative data. Either tool will help to organize and promote thinking about issues or problems that are facing the organization. It will help to clarify/identify the organizations future trends and to apply to those trends to the organization to help explicitly identify any underlying assumptions and to set priorities. The using the SWOT analysis, step one is to identify organizations assumptions and utilize the matrix using the demands and supply information obtained in the analysis phase. Step two is to identify organizations assumptions/key workforce issues from step one and take into account the potential impact on your business elements, potential impact on assumptions, risk inherent in the assumptions and the likelihood of its occurrence.

The final phase of forecasting is performing Gap Analysis. After completing your preferred scenario the organization need to look back at your current workforce and your future demands to identify any gaps in skills, people needed to meet preferred scenarios etc. Demand is based on the preferred scenario and competencies/skills need to meet demand requirements. The Gap Analysis should indicate the skills gap, surplus any recruitment issues and retentions issues to meet the demand etc. Organization should continue this exercise for each scenario until you have developed your suggested strategy/initiative/action to deal with the preferred outcomes to meet organizations needs.

Techniques of Forecasting

The HRP must lead an organization through the process of determining how many employees the organization needs and the characteristics that those employees should have to facilitate the accomplishment of organizational. Human Resources Planning is the process of determining how to staff the organization with the right employees at the right time and in the right place. HR planning is increasingly indistinguishable from organizational strategic planning in those organizations where human capital is the critical factor in organizational success. For the purposes of discussion and explanation in this section, it is assumed that organization has completed its strategic-planning process and determined its strategic goals and objectives.

The purpose of workforce planning then becomes to determine the characteristics needed in the organization's workforce to facilitate achievement of those objectives. In this scenario, workforce planning is strategic planning at the HR level and involves similar processes, including a SWOT analysis, which occurs at the organizational level. In simplistic terms, the HR function must determine the numbers and types of employees needed and evaluate the availability of both internal and external individuals having the correct characteristics. Based on these analyses, a determination can be made as to the proper HR programmatic activities required to achieve the correct workforce composition. Workforce planning then involves three stages: forecasting workforce needs, determining internal and external supply of employees, and developing appropriate strategies to achieve forecasted needs in relationship to projected supply. These three processes are discussed in the following sections.

Forecasting Workforce Needs

The organization's strategic plan and allied business plan provide guidance as to the number and type of employees that the organization needs during the planning period. Expansion, retrenchment, new products or services, introduction of new technology, entrance of new competitors in the market, economic conditions, employee retirements, workforce turnover, and so forth must be considered when forecasting workforce needs. *Forecasting* is the process of using both historical data and predicted scenarios to determine workforce needs during a stated planning period. Following is a discussion of several forecasting methods that are often used.

Trend Analysis

Trend analysis involves studying historical organizational employment levels to predict future employment levels. For example: If, on average, employment levels in the organization have increase

5% per year, it might be logical to forecast a 5% increase for the next planning period. A more accurate forecast using this method might be to evaluate trends in separate departments or other organizational subentities and then aggregate the increases (or, potentially, decreases) at the organizational level. Doing so provides more specificity as to not only the numbers of employees but also the types of employees needed.

Trend analysis assumes that history will repeat itself. In today's more volatile times that might not be the case. However, trend analysis provides some data on which a final forecast can be made.

Ratio Analysis

Ratio analysis is a forecasting technique that assumes a set relationship between one variable and another, and that the relationship allows for the prediction of workforce needs. Assuming no increases in productivity, an organization might be able to predict total workforce requirements based on predicted total sales or total productivity. For example: If, historically, it takes five employees for each 100,000 unit of product produced, a projected increase of 1,000,000 units per year will require an additional 50 employees.

Organizations often have standard staff tables that can be used in ratio analysis. As an example, a restaurant chain would know how many servers, cooks, managers, and so forth are needed to staff a restaurant. Based on a projected expansion in terms of number of restaurants, increase in workforce needs can be forecast.

Turnover

Analysis of historical turnover—in reality a type of trend analysis—provides additional data for forecasts. Average turnover rates provide an indication of the number of new employees required just to maintain current employment levels. Obviously, turnover is affected by many environmental factors, most notably unemployment rates, so other variables must be considered when using these data for forecasting.

Nominal Group Technique

The *nominal group technique* is a group-forecasting and decision-making method that requires each member of the group to make an independent forecast prior to discussion of any forecasts. Members of the group meet and independently develop a forecast. Each member must present his or her forecast before any of the forecasts are discussed. After all presentations are made and clarifying questions addressed, the group works to come up with a final forecast.

Delphi Technique

The Delphi technique is another group forecasting method in which experts independently develop forecasts that are shared with each other, but in this approach the experts never actually meet. Each of the members refines his or her forecasts until a group consensus is reached.

Group Think

The nominal group and Delphi techniques are used to avoid the phenomenon known as group think. Group think occurs when group members, in the interest of developing group cohesiveness, reach consensus without fully considering what might be divergent forecasts.

Managerial Judgment

Managers and executives are asked, based on their experience and knowledge, to develop forecasts. Forecasts, like budgets, can be a top-level overall estimate or a bottom-up aggregation of multiple departmental estimates. Top-level forecasts provide a gross indicator of needed employment levels, but do not indicate where those employees should be allocated in the organization. Bottom-up forecasts, provided by managers in the various departments, provide a better idea of allocation of the workforce and the types of employees that are needed. However, bottom-up forecasts tend to overestimate workforce needs as each manager tries to increase staff size.

Statistical Forecasts

Statistical analysis was discussed in Chapter 2 in the section on research. Various statistical procedures, including regression analyses, can be used to develop forecasts based on scenarios or theorized relationships between variables.

Computer Modelling

Many organizations use sophisticated forecasting software. This permits the organizations to evaluate workforce needs under various scenarios.

Multiple Methods

In the final analysis, no single forecasting method is likely to be accurate every time. Most organizations use multiple methods to develop different forecasts. Ultimately, it is likely to be a top-level manager, using intuition based on accumulated knowledge and years of experience, that makes the final determination of the most likely forecast.

Determining Internal and External Supply of Employees

Not only must the demand for employees be determined, but workforce planning must include an analysis of the potential supply. Forecasts must be made of the supply of candidates for jobs within the organization and the supply external to the organization in the relevant labour market. Methods of forecasting supply, internally and externally, are discussed in the following section.

Internal Supply

The internal supply of candidates can be determined using a number of methods, such as replacement charts, succession plans, human resource management information systems, and departmental estimates. A brief discussion of each of these methods follows.

Replacement Charts

Replacement charts are manual or automated records indicating which employees are currently ready for promotion to a specific position. If needs are forecasted for a particular job, replacement charts provide data with which to determine the supply of internal candidates to fill the openings.

Succession Planning

The concept of succession planning is similar to replacement charting except the time perspective is different. *Succession planning* is the process of identifying candidates for future openings. It is a longer-term plan for developing candidates to fill positions. Traditionally, succession planning has been reserved for only high-level positions. However, because of the increased importance of human capital in many organizations, succession plans are being developed for the orderly replacement of lower-level employees.

Human Resource Management Information Systems

Many human resource management information systems frequently contain data on qualifications or skills of current employees. After workforce demand is forecast, the database can be queried regarding the supply of potential internal candidates that possess the necessary qualifications or skills.

Departmental Estimates

Organizations are not static. Most organizations and their component departments experience constant flows of employees both in and out. Analysis of this movement provides valuable information to forecast internal supply. Fig. 3.3 provides the formula used to forecast internal supply within a particular department in the organization and common sources of employee movement in and out.

Fig. 3.3 Estimated Internal Labour Supply for a Department

Current Staffing Level – Outflows + Inflows = Internal Supply

Inflows	Outflows
Transfers from other departments	Retirements
Hires from the external labour market	Resignations
Recalls from lay-offs	Death
Returns from leaves of absence and sabbaticals	Promotions to other departments
	Transfers to other departments
	Terminations

External Supply

There is a huge amount of information available to assist in the forecasting external supplies of labour. State and local economic and workforce development agencies typically can provide data on the labour supply availability. The department of labour has data available for virtually any location and publishes annual forecasts of labour supply by occupation, and the Bureau of Labour Statistics provides a wide variety of labour force information that is available online. In addition, various professional organizations regularly analyze labour availability within their respective professions. The availability of external candidates is affected by:

- Economic conditions.
- Unemployment rates.
- College and high school graduation rates in the relevant labour market.
- Net migration in or out of the area.
- Relative skill levels of potential candidates in the labour market.
- Competition for labour in the labour market.
- Changes in the skill requirements of the organization's potential job openings.

You should be familiar with the various methods of forecasting both demand for and supply of employees and candidates.

Determination of Strategies

The analysis of demand and supply for labour leads the SPHR to develop appropriate strategies to achieve the planned level of employment. The result of the analysis can result in one of three conditions:

- **Equality:** In which case the strategy becomes one of retaining current employees.
- **Insufficient number of employees:** In which case the strategy becomes recruitment.
- **Too many employees:** In which case the strategy becomes decruitment.

Retention of employees involves strategies designed to maintain or improve job satisfaction and organizational commitment. They are discussed throughout this entire book as they apply to a particular program area. For example, retention strategies involve creating pay equity and providing desired benefits when compensation and benefits strategies are being developed. Both recruitment and decruitment (organizational exit) are discussed later in this chapter.

It would be very similar if the analysis reveals that only one of the conditions from the preceding list exists. However, that is not often the case and the SPHR frequently finds that some departments are currently staffed appropriately for future needs during the planning period, whereas some departments have too many employees and others too few. Thus, strategies of recruitment, decruitment, and retention must be developed simultaneously and interdependently because the recruitment objectives of one department can often serve to fulfill the decruitment objectives of another.

It provides a basis for understanding two major programmatic activities that are discussed later in this chapter: recruitment and selection. Assuming that an expansion of the workforce is required, strategy determination is affected by the forecasts of yield rates and the timeframes required for each step in the recruitment and selection process. *Yield rates* are a comparison of the number of applicants or potential applicants at one stage in the recruitment/selection process with the number of applicants that remain available at the next stage. To determine programmatic activities and action plans, the SPHR must work backward from the total number and types of employees that will be needed, including dates on which they will be needed. Based on experience, moderated by any projected changes in timeframes or yield rates, the planning process must incorporate an evaluation of the scope and timing of activities to produce the desired results.

Phase 3-Planning: (Identification of Strategy)

After completing the surplus/demand analysis, gap analysis, scenario building exercise, SWOT etc. you will begin the planning phase. Strategies, initiatives and programs and policies should be developed to address the gaps identified in the analyzing phase. This will ensure that your element will recruit, develop and retain the critical staff needed for a successful workforce plan. A few factors should be considered when deciding upon strategies to address a workforce gap.

Human resources planning should include a wide range of strategies around staff development, succession planning, redeployment, recruitment, technology improvement, competitive sourcing, changes in work practices *etc.* The organizational HR plans should be flexible to address workforce but it must be quite realistic.

Phase 4-Implementating: Executing the New Strategies

After organization have analyzed, forecasted and planned, it is critically important to put together an implementation plan to carry out the planned activities included in the human resources plan. This will be the process of using all the information gathered in the previous phases and devising a plan to execute the new strategies. There are a few basic considerations that should be addressed before beginning the implementation plan. These includes organization support, allocating the different resources required, clarifying the roles and responsibilities, identifying who is involved in implementing what and where coordination among different parts of the organization or with different agencies is needed, establishing timeliness, determining performances measures and communicating the plans.

Phase-5 Evaluating: Feedback on Effectiveness of Outcomes

Evaluation of organizations human resources plan is imperative in determining if the devised strategies are address the gaps specified. It is important to obtain feedback concerning the effectiveness of outcomes. There are several methods in getting feedback such as surveys, focus groups, meetings etc. regardless of the methods, effectiveness of strategies.

CASE STUDY–I

Keeping Good People: Staffing

Given the current labour market, the costs of recruiting and hiring are becoming more apparent than ever to organizations. After going through the difficulty of attracting and hiring talented people, business do not want to lose them to competitions. Difficulty is staffing has created an emphasis on retaining human resources.

Applied Industrial Technologies, a Cleveland-based business, has taken steps to reduce turnover. Specifically, they have made self-fulfillment—the process of helping each person reach their full potential—a central value in the organization. According to CEO John Dannemiller, the company views its self-fulfillment mission as important as salary and benefits in motivating talented employees. He attributes a doubling in revenues over the past eight years and a turnover rate below the industry average to the self-fulfillment program. Here is a summary of Applied Industrial's self-fulfillment strategy:

- The company commits to 40 hours of training each year–a significant amount.
- Applied Industrial conducts regular leadership and personality testing. The test results are used to identify areas for personal improvement and to measure growth.
- The company offers reading lists of management books.
- Employees are reimbursed for education expenses.

QUESTIONS

1. What other actions could Applied Industrial Technologies take to improve this program?
2. Now assume that you are an Applied Industrial Technologies manager working to orient and hire new employees.
   (*a*) How would you orient an employee who accepts a position at applied but does not care about the self improvement program? So far, the employee has met but does not exceed the job requirements.
   (*b*) What steps could you take in selection to assess whether prospects would respond effectively to the self-fulfillment program? (*Hint:* As a start, consider individual characteristics that might affect a prospect's response to this type of program).

3. Applied Industrial views its self-fulfillment program as a retention effort. Is it also a recruitment tool ? What, if any, do you think are the differences between tactics designed to improve retention versus those designed to improve attraction and recruitment?
4. Now let us assume that the labour market shift toward an increase in supply. Should Applied Industrial continue to invest in its human resources with the self-fulfillment program? Explain your recommendation.

Source: Dannemiller, J.C. (1998). How we keep good people. Across the Board, 35, 21.

CASE STUDY–2

Management Skills Builder: (Staffing) Issues and Exercises

The Grade 1 Company manufactures hand tools—from screwdrivers to hammer to all types of wrenches. The company takes pride in producing the highest-quality tools for crafts people worldwide and has exacting specifications for both mass and customized tool production. However, Grade 1 realizes that the time is takes to fulfill an order is problematic because it is not fast enough to satisfy customers. Timing is so crucial in this industry that Grade 1 is losing clients.

A study of the issue quickly revealed the source of the problem: The Company still used a labour intensive production system that is not computerized. Other tool companies have switched to computerized production systems and production control systems that deliver comparable quality in shorter times. Furthermore, those companies can give definite promises about product delivery dates, whereas Grade 1 can only offer educated guesses that are often incorrect.

As a result of the study, Grade 1 has made a commitment to computerized its operations. Over the past six months the production control system has been computerized, and everyone at Grade 1 is excited about the potential benefits. Production and scheduling are now done by computer, and software accurately forecast delivery dates. However, management's excitement is tempered by the realization that to use the system effectively employees must learn a new set of skills. Grade 1 has offered an early retirement option to its workforce, and a number of workers have taken it. There is now room in the production area to hire a significant number of new employees.

Consider the Issues

1. How large a role do you think personality or "fit" issues should play in Grade 1's selection system? How much of a role should tool production experience play? Explain your answers.
2. The Grade 1's workers who did not take or were not eligible for early retirement may or may not be acceptable employees under the new system. How should the company determine what to do with its current employees?
3. How should Grade 1 assess the validity of the selection measures used to hire new employee to work with the computerized production system?

Take Action

1. With a partner or small group, identify the characteristics that might be most important to job performance in Grade 1's computerized production area. Prepare a list of the best ideas and present these to the class.

Do It Together

2. With a partner or small group, identify the characteristics that might be most important to job performance in Grade 1's computerized production area. Prepare a list of the best ideas and present these to the class.
   (*i*) Which selection tools should Grade 1 use in its staffing process? Consider the possibilities with your partner or team and present your conclusions to the class. If more than one predictor should be used, should they be ranked in order of importance?

Questions

1. After eight as a marketing assistant for the New York office of a large French Bank, Sarah Schiffler was told that her job, in a non-revenue-producing department, was being eliminated. Her choices: She could either be laid off (with eight months' severance pay) or stay on and train for the position of credit analyst, a career route she had turned down in the past. Nervous about making mortgage payments on her new condo, Sarah agreed to stay, but after six months of feeling miserable in her new position, she quit. Was her separation from the bank voluntary or involuntary? Can you think of situations in which a voluntary separation is really an involuntary separation? What are the managerial implications of such situations?
2. What are the advantages and disadvantages or using seniority as the basis for lay off? What alternatives to seniority are available as lay off criteria?
3. Would an employer ever want to increase the rate of employee turnover in a company? Why or why not?
4. What role does the HR department play in employee separations and outplacement?
5. In an age when more and more companies are down sizing, an increasingly important concept is "the virtual corporation." The idea is that a company should have a core of owners and managers, but that, to the greatest degree possible, workers should be contingent—temporary, part-time, or on short-term contracts. This gives the corporation maximum flexibility to shift vendors, cut costs, and avoid long-term labour commitments. What are the advantages and disadvantages of the virtual corporation from the point of view of both employers and workers?
6. Under what circumstances might a company's managers prefer to use lay offs instead of early retirements or voluntary severance plans as a way to down size the workforce?
7. Under what set of conditions should a company lay off employees without giving them advance notice?
8. "The people who actually have the face-to-face contact with the person who is being laid off are not the ones who made the decision. They often did not have any input into which of their people would go." says a technician at a firm that experienced large-scale lay offs. What role should managers—who have the "face-to-face" contact with employees—play in implementing a lay off? Do you think managers and HR staff members always agree on how employee separations should be handled? Why or why not?
9. Managing survivors in a lay off is important. As a manager, what concerns would you have about the surviving workforce after a lay off? How can the HR management staff be of assistance in providing support for the survivors to a lay off?
10. Why should management be concerned with helping employees retire from their organization successfully?

Problems of the Human Resource Planning

Man power planning is not always successful, the main problems are described below:

1. *Accuracy of Forecasting:* Human Resource planning involves the forecasting the demand and supply of human resources. Thus the effectiveness of planning depends on the accuracy of forecasts. If the forecast is not correct planning will be defective. Inaccuracy depends when departmental forecasts are merely prepare with out critical review.
2. *Identity Crisis:* Many of the organization's human resources do not the whole process of human resource planning. Because of this, there is generally an identity crisis. Till the specialist are developed a strong sense of purpose, planning will be effective.
3. *Support of the Top Management:* HR Planning requires full and wholeheartedness support from the top management. In the absence of this support and commitment, it would not be possible to ensure the necessary resources, cooperation and support for the success of human resources planning.
4. *Resistance from the Employees:* Employees and the Trade Unions resist manpower planning. They feel that this planning increases their overall workload and regulates them through productivity bargaining. They are also feel that it would lead to wide spread unemployment, especially of unskilled workers.
5. *Insufficient Initial Efforts:* Successful HR Planning flourishes slowly and gradually. Sometimes sophisticated technologies are forcefully introduced just because competitors have adopted them. These may not be possible unless matched with the needs and environment of the particular enterprises.
6. *Management Information System:* Effectiveness of planning depends on the reliability of the information system. In the most of Indian industries, HR Information System has not fully developed. In the absence of reliable data it would not be possible to have effective planning.
7. *Uncertainties:* It is the risky to depend on general estimates of manpower in the face of rapid changes in the environment. Absenteeism, turnovers, seasonal employments, technological changes and market conditions are the factors of major uncertainties which serve as constraints to manpower planning. Although discounts are made for these factors while preparing the plan, but these factors cannot be estimated correctly.
8. *Expensive and Time Consuming:* HR planning is an expensive and time consuming process. Employers may resist manpower planning feeling that it increases the cost of manpower.
9. *Coordination with other Managerial Functions:* There is general tendency of manpower planners to remain aloof from the other operating managers and become totally absorbed in their own world. To be effective man power planning must be integrated with other management functions.
10. *Unbalanced Approach:* Many human resources experts give more importance on the quantitive aspects of manpower to ensure that there is adequate flow of people in and out of the organization. The over look the qualitative aspects like career development and planning, skill development, morale etc. are overlooked by them. Such unbalanced approach affects the effectiveness of the human resources planning.

Thus the human resources planning suffer from above problems while implementing HR planning in the respective organizations.

Conclusions

The quality and effectiveness of the organization is determined by the quality of the people that are employed. Success for most organizations depends on finding the employees with the skills to successfully perform the tasks required to attain the company's strategic goals. Management decisions and processes for dealing with employees are critical to ensure that the organization gets and keeps the right staff.

In order to get the most out of staff, human resource management integrates all processes, programs, and systems in an organization designed to ensure that employees are acquired and used in an effective way. These are the key HR processes in an organization. You will note that these processes do not function in isolation: HR management functions within the culture of the organization. And of course; the organization is impacted by its environment. By paying careful attention to these facts, an organization can recruit competent, high-performing employees who are capable of sustaining their performance over the long-term.

HR planning is the strategy for the acquisition, utilization, improvement and preservation of an organization's human resources. It relates to the establishment of job specifications or the qualitative requirement of the jobs, determining the number of personnel required and the developing the sources of supply of manpower. The objectives of the HR planning is to maintain and improve the organization's ability to attain its goals by developing the strategic purporting to magnify the contributions of human resources regularly in the foreseeable future. In addition, the manpower strategist should take into account the considerations including the organizations objectives demanding specific type of manpower required for the market situations, and the features of existing human resources in the organizations. As these factors are constantly changing, the human resources strategy has to be constantly reviewed and modified if necessary. Considering HR Planning in this concern, this is seems to be very dynamic and continuous process. HR Planning is not considered as isolation. It is an integrated strategy which involves long-term as well as short-term decisions. This is an integral part of the process of setting and meeting corporate objectives.

HR Planning not only can be a strategic tool, it can also help establish an organization's sustainable competitive advantage. Retaining good workers has become even more important as it is projected that there will be a shortage of nearly a million workers in near future. Achieving competitive success through people requires a fundamental change in how managers think about their employees and how they view the work relationship. It involves seeing employees as "partners" not just as costs to be minimized or avoided.

REFERENCES

1. Armstrong, M. A, *handbook of personnel management practices,* London: Kogan Press, 1995, 79.
2. Cascio W.F. (1991), "*Applied psychology in personnel management*", New York: Prentice Hall.
3. Cascio W.F. (1991), "*Managing human resources*", New York: McGraw Hill, 1995; 142.
4. Yoder D., *Personnel management and industrial relations*, New Delhi, Prentice Hall of India, 1972.
5. Miller E.C., *Personnel Policies–Framework of management decisions*, The Management Review **49(1)** January 1960: 20–26.
6. Kempner T., *A handbook of management*, London Weidenfield and Nicolson, 1973, 310.
7. Odiorne G.S., *Personnel administration by objectives*, Homewood, IIlinois, Richard Irwin Inc 1971; 69–89.

8. Beach D., *Personnel–The management of people at work*, New York: McMillan 1975; 69–70.
9. Kalsi B.S., "Purposeful personnel policy" in Bhonsle Y. B. (Ed) *Personnel Management–The Indian Scene*, New Delhi, S. Chnad and Company; 1977; 21–27.
10. Kudchedkar L.S., "*Purposeful personnel policy*", in Bhonsle Y. B. (Ed) *Ibid*, 17–20.
11. Davar R.S., *Personnel Management and Industrial Relations*, New Delhi, Vikas Publications, 1983, p. 41.
12. Geisler E.B., *Manpower planning: An emerging staff functions*; New York, American Management Association, 1967.
13. Beastty R.W., and Schneider C.E.: *Personnel administration: An experimental skill building approach*, Massachusetts; Addition Wesley, 1981, 31.
14. Stainer G., *Man power planning, london,* William Heinemann, 1971, 3.
15. Kempner T, *op. cit.,* p. 217.
16. Seth T., *A survey of research in management and industrial relations–A trend report,* in Dayal I A survey in research in Management, Vol. I, New Delhi : Vikas Publication House, 1973, 295.
17. Armstrong M. A. handbook of personnel management practices, london: Kogan Press, 1995, 403–04.
18. Decenzo, David A. and Stephen P. Robbin, (1989), "*Personnel/human resources management*" New Delhi, Printice Hall of India.
19. Edwin Flippo (1984), "*Personnel management*", New York, McGraw Hill.
20. Wether William B. and Keith Devis (1993), "*Human resources and personnel management*", New York, McGraw Hill.
21. Anthony, Williams P. (1993), "*Startegic human resources management*", New York, Dryden Press.
22. Mathis and Jackson (1982), "*Personnel–contemporary perspectives and application*", New York; West Publishing Co.

4

CHAPTER

ATTRACTING THE TALENT: THE RECRUITMENT AND SELECTION

4.1 INTRODUCTION

In the present business environment, organizations are faced with the pressure to produce more with fewer resources. Employees, on whom an organization's profitability depends, comprise the largest fixed cost that an organization incurs. In the past, individuals used to work with one or two organizations during their entire working life (averaging between 20–30 years). Organizations too used to believe in the lifetime employment concept. However, such concepts are being eroded as a result of the unpredictable business environment. Hence, organizations have to evolve methods not only to improve productivity but to also keep the costs down.

On the human resources front, productivity can be improved by ensuring that the organization attracts the best talent at the lowest possible cost. This objective translates into the adoption of the best recruitment and selection methods and instituting measures to retain and develop them. Further, a quantitative measurement of recruitment and selection effectiveness has to be conducted to prove one's point. With respect to quantitative measures to improve HR effectiveness, the field is still in its nascent stages. Nevertheless, a few approaches and metrics have been developed and applied among several organizations.

This book provides insights on some of the recruitment and selection methods, which have been found to have a greater correlation with employee suitability and performance levels with the organization's needs. It also provides an overview of survey results conducted in different parts of the world to reveal the most popular and effective methods of recruitment and selection being applied along with requisite analysis. For a comprehensive account of hiring strategies, it is suggested that this book may be read in conjunction with the other volume titled, *Effective Recruitment: Concepts and Cases* (also published by ICFAI University Press), which includes a suite of articles pertaining to hiring metrics. These two books, read together, can provide a number of innovative ideas, in addition to conceptual articles and cases for developing a coherent recruitment strategy to fit the needs of organizations. Leading a corporate recruitment or staffing function is not easy. Maneuvering through corporate politics, planning processes, strategy development, managing relationships with internal and external constituencies, designing and implementing effective metrics, as well as leading, motivating, and managing a team of recruiting and staffing experts is a very significant task. Planning and managing an effective recruiting function depends upon your ability to plan and manage against demand...using the concept of workforce planning you will be able to more effectively plan, organize, and manage your organization's recruiting and staffing systems. The basis of all great recruiting and staffing excellence is the understanding that recruiting is really about building and cultivating relationships. As recruiting and staffing leaders, we have to build and cultivate relationships with many different constituencies.

A strong international economy has raised competitive pressures on companies to hire and retain quality employees. Employers may be tempted to make recruiting statements that are less than fully accurate or complete; many companies still face a continuing unmet demand for skilled workers. "Indeed, in the service sectors experiencing the most intense expansion—construction, health care, consulting, engineering, finance, and education—the fight for talent continues". Employers needing to compete for service professionals face pressure to describe their current and potential financial health as favourably as possible when trying to recruit and retain quality workers.

People are the assets on which competitive advantage is built, whether in the public or private sector, whether in the corporate world or in the world of education. In the words of the latest theory on human resource management, people are an "inimitable" asset. People and their skills is the one thing that competitor organizations cannot imitate. So human resource management and the practices associated with it have become accepted by managers in all forms of organizations as one of the most important strategic levels to ensure continuing success. The most valuable asset of any large organization is high-caliber employees. Finding right people and putting them at right jobs is the most important challenge for any organization. At the stage of Human Resource planning, as we have already discussed in the previous chapter, the human resource requirement is forecasted, keeping in the mind the forecast the function of attracting the best available talent is carried out by an organization. It involves functions like, recruitment, selection, *in*duction etc.

4.2 WHAT IS RECRUITING?

Once the required number and kind of human resources are determined, the management has to find the places where required human resources are or will be available and also find the means of attracting them towards the organization before selecting suitable candidates for jobs. All this process is generally known as recruitment.

Some people use the term 'recruitment' for employment. Recruitment is only one of the steps in the entire employment process. Some others use the term recruitment for selection. These two terms are not one and the same either.

Technically speaking the function of recruitment precedes the selection function and it includes only finding, developing the sources of prospective employees and attracting them to apply for jobs in an organization, whereas the selection is the process of finding out the most suitable candidate to the job out of the candidates attracted. Formal definition of recruitment would give clear cut idea about the function of recruitment.

Recruitment is defined as, "a process to discover the sources of manpower to meet the requirements of the staffing schedule and to employ effective measures for attracting that manpower in adequate numbers to facilitate effective selection of an efficient workforce." Edwin B. Flippo defined recruitment as "process of searching for prospective employees and stimulating them to apply for jobs in the organization."

Those definitions can be analyzed by discussing the processes of recruitment through systems approach.

Objectives of Recruitment

1. To attract people with multi-dimensional skills and experiences that suits the present and future organizational strategies.
2. To induct outsiders with a new perspective to lead the company.
3. To infuse fresh blood at all levels of the organization.
4. To develop an organizational culture that attracts competent people to the company.
5. To search or head hunt people whose skills fit the company's values.
6. To devise methodologies for assessing psychological traits.
7. To seek out non-conventional development grounds of talent.
8. To search for talent globally and not just within the company.
9. To design entry salary that competes on quality but not on quantum.
10. To anticipate and find people for positions that does not exist yet.

Sub-systems of Recruitment

The recruitment consists of the following sub-functions:

1. Finding out and developing the sources where the required number and kind of employees will be available.
2. Developing suitable techniques to attract the desirable candidates.
3. Employing the techniques to attract candidates.
4. Stimulating as many candidates as possible and asking them to apply for jobs irrespective of number of candidates required.

Management has to attract more candidates in order to increase selection ratio (*i.e.*, number of applications per one job vacancy) in order to select the most suitable candidates out of the total candidates. Recruitment is positive as it aims at increasing the number of applicants and selection is somewhat negative as it selects the suitable candidates in which process the unsuitable are automatically eliminated. Though, the function of recruitment seems to be easy, a number of factors make performance of recruitment a complex one.

4.3 CORPORATE MISSION, OBJECTIVES, STRATEGIES AND TACTICS (MOST) AND RECRUITMENT

Corporations have started linking their Mission, Objectives, Strategies and Tactics (MOST) to the functions of recruitment and selection. The economic liberalizations and consequent competition through quality and services necessitated the companies to search for and attract competent human resources. Corporations focusing on new business development will have to seek entrepreneurial abilities. Companies chasing growth alliances should employ people comfortable in different cultural backgrounds. Above all, companies must hire for the future, anticipating jobs that may not be in existence yet. Recruitment managers must focus for attitudes and approaches that fit the corporate goals and culture.

Recruitment Policy

Recruitment policy of any organization is derived from the personnel policy of the same organization. In other words, the former is a part of the latter. However, recruitment policy by itself should take into consideration the government's reservation policy, policy regarding sons of soil etc. Personnel policies of other organizations regarding merit, internal sources, social responsibility in absorbing minority sections, women etc.

Recruitment policy should commit itself to the organization's personnel policy like enriching the organization's human and handicapped people of the society. The policy must incorporate motivating the employees through internal promotions, improving the employee loyalty to the organization by absorbing the retrenched or laid off employees or casual/temporary employees or dependents of present/former employees etc. subject to their capabilities.

The following factors should be taken into consideration in formulating recruitment policy. They are:

1. Government policies;
2. Personnel policies of other competing organizations;
3. Organization's personnel policies;
4. Recruitment sources;
5. Recruitment needs;
6. Recruitment cost;
7. Selection criteria and preference etc.

Impact of Personnel Policies on Recruitment Policies

Recruitment policies are mostly drawn from personnel policies of the organization. According to Dale Yodar and Paul D. Standohar general personnel policies provide a variety of guidelines to be spelt out in recruitment policy. After formulation of the recruitment policies, the management has to decide whether to centralize or decentralize the recruitment function.

Centralized vs. Decentralized Recruitment

Recruitment practices vary from one organization to another. Some organizations like commercial banks resort to centralized recruitment while some organizations like the Indian Railways (for junior level positions) resort to decentralized recruitment practices. Personnel department at the central office performs all the functions of recruitment in case of centralized recruitment and personnel departments at unit level/zonal level perform all the functions of recruitment concerning to the jobs of the respective unit or zone.

Merits of Centralized Recruitment

1. Average cost of recruitment per candidate/unit should be relatively less due to economies of scale.

2. It would have more expertise available to it.
3. It can ensure broad uniformly among human resources of various units/zones in respect of education, skill, knowledge, talent etc.
4. It would generally be above malpractices, abuse of powers, favourites, bias etc.
5. It would facilitate interchangeability of staff among various units/zones.
6. It enables the line managers of various units and zones to concentrate on their operational activities by relieving them from the recruitment functions.
7. It enables the organizations to have centralized selection procedures, promotional and transfer procedure etc.
8. It ensures the most effective and suitable placement to candidates.
9. It enables centralized training programs which further brings uniformity and minimizes average cost of staff.

Despite these advantages of centralized recruitment some organizations resort to decentralized recruitment for the following reasons:

Merits of Decentralized Recruitment

1. The unit concerned concentrates only on those sources/places where it normally gets the suitable candidates. As such the cost of recruitment would be relatively less.
2. The unit gets most suitable candidates as it is well aware of the requirements of the jobs regarding cultural, traditional, family background aspects, local factors, social factors etc.
3. Units can recruit candidates as and when they are required without any delay.
4. The units would enjoy freedom in finding out, developing the sources, in selecting and employing the techniques to stimulate the candidates.
5. The unit would relatively enjoy advantage about the availability of information, control and feedback and various functions/processes of recruitment.
6. The unit would enjoy better familiarity and control over the employees it recruits rather than on employees selected by the central recruitment agency.

Both the systems of recruitment would suffer from their own demerits. Hence, the management has to weigh both the merits and demerits of each system before making a final decision about centralizing or de-centralizing the recruitment. Alternatively management may centralize the recruitment of certain categories of employees preferably middle and top level managerial personnel and decentralize the recruitment of other categories of employees' preferably lower level positions in view of the nature of the jobs and suitability of those systems for those categories of positions. The management has to find out and develop the sources of recruitment after deciding upon centralizing or decentralizing the recruitment function.

In conclusion there is no hard and fast rule what type of recruitment is to be followed. The organization can be international, multinational, government or private each of them follows the methodology what they consider it as effective.

Factors Affecting Recruitment

Both internal and external factors affect recruitment. The external factors include supply of and demand for human resources, employment opportunities and/or unemployment rate, labour market conditions, political, legal requirement and government policies, social factors, information systems etc.

The internal factors include the company's pay package including salary, fringe benefits and incentives, quality of work life, organizational culture, career planning and growth opportunities, size of the company, company's product/services, geographical spread of the company's operations *viz.*, local, national or global, company's growth rate, role of Trade Unions and cost of recruitment.

Recruiting process: Recruiting is the process of generating a pool of qualified candidates for a particular job. It is a set of activities an organization uses to attract candidates who have the abilities and the attitudes needed to help the organization achieve its objectives. Some essential groundwork including the internal factors and external factors need to be laid before the recruiting process can begin.

Internal Factors

Preparing a detailed job description must complement the initial step of identifying specific human resource needs. The job description is a legal requirement and assists the HR manager in screening candidates. The direction the company goes from there will depend greatly on the corporate philosophy:

- Will the company look internally or externally to fill its employment needs?
- Does the company believe in hiring the most qualified candidates, regardless of background, or does it aspire to be an industry leader when it comes to workforce diversity?
- Will the firm try to sell itself as a high wage, high search, or high training as identified by Stigler?

Meshing this philosophy with existing company policies and practices gives the recruiter the necessary base from which to proceed to the external environment.

External Factors

For legal, ethical, and practical reasons, it is critical for the recruiter to be acutely aware of the organization's external environment. All of these factors will play a hand in the recruiter's strategy:

- ***Legal:*** The legal environment is constantly changing, as new laws and regulations are passed affecting all aspects of Human Resource Management. The recruiter must abide by the rules to avoid unpleasant government actions.
- ***Ethical:*** In keeping with the corporate philosophy identified internally, the recruiter has a moral obligation to follow the guidelines that facilitate and further the company's positive corporate image.
- ***Practical:*** A wide array of avenues is open for the recruiter in seeking appropriate job candidates. Having updated information on the composition of the labour market and economy on both a national and local level will improve the efficiency of the effort.

All of the above considerations will lead to an efficient and effective recruiting effort for the HR professional. The purpose of this website is to offer one of the many tools available to the recruiter: the Internet. Although its popularity increases daily, it is by no means the end-all recruiting tool. Many of the tried and true methods are as effective as ever, as each situation requires a thorough analysis and a detailed plan.

Internal vs. External Recruiting

Internal recruiting is the search for in-house employees who have the abilities and the attitudes to fulfill the requirements needed and to help the organization achieve its objectives.

Although internal recruiting is often neglected, and the Internet hardly offers any useful discussions for this recruiting strategy, it is crucial not to overlook this strategy. The discussion of internal recruiting provides the advantages and disadvantages of this recruiting technique in comparison to the external method.

Advantages of Internal Recruiting

- ***Recruiting costs:*** Since the recruiting machinery is focused on an already existing pool of employees to fill a vacant position, and therefore selection and socializing processes are less time and energy consuming, internal recruiting tends to be less expensive than external recruiting.
- ***Motivation:*** The prospect of potential promotion or transfers provides a clear sign to the current work force that the organization offers room for advancement. This addresses the employee's need for self-achievement.
- ***Familiarity:*** The familiarity of the employee has a two-side effect: On the one hand the employee is familiar with the organization's policies, procedures, and customs. At the same time, the organization has established an employment history showing the workers formal and informal skills and abilities.

Why do organizations prefer internal sources for recruitment?

Internal sources include: (*a*) present permanent employees, (*b*) present temporary/casual employees, (*c*) retrenched or retired employees, (*d*) dependents of deceased, disabled, retired and present employees.

(*a*) **Present Permanent Employees**

Organizations consider the candidates from this source for higher level jobs due to:

1. Availability of most suitable candidates for jobs relatively or equally to the external source.
2. To meet the trade union demands.
3. To the policy of the organization to motivate the present employees.

(*b*) **Present Temporary or Casual Employees**

Organizations find this source to fill the vacancies relatively at the lower level owing to the availability of suitable candidates or trade and pressure or in order to motivate them on the present job.

(*c*) **Retrenched or Retired Employees**

Generally a particular organization retrenches the employee due to lay off. The organization takes the candidates for employment from the retrenched from the retrenched employees due to obligation, trade union pressure and the like. Sometimes the organizations prefer to re-employ their retired employees as a token of their loyalty to the organization or to postpone some interpersonal conflicts for promotion etc.

(*d*) **Dependents of Deceased, Disabled, Retired and Present Employees**

Some organizations with a view to developing the commitment and loyalty of not only the employee but also his family members and to build up an image to provide employment to the dependents of deceased, disabled and present employees. Such organizations find this source as an effective source of recruitment.

Why Do Organizations Prefer Internal Sources?

Organizations prefer this source to external source to some extent for the following reasons:

(*a*) Internal recruitment can be used as a technique of motivation.

(*b*) Morale of the employees can be improved.

(*c*) Suitability of the internal candidates can be judged better than the external candidates as "known devils are better than unknown angels."

(*d*) Loyalty, commitment, a sense of belongingness, and security of the present employees can be enhanced.

(*e*) Employees' psychological needs can be met by providing an opportunity for advancement.

(*f*) Employees' economic needs for promotion, higher income can be satisfied.

(*g*) Cost of selection can be minimized.

(*h*) Cost of training, induction, orientation, period of adaptability to the organization can be reduced.

(*i*) Trade unions can be satisfied.

(*j*) Social responsibility towards employees may be discharged.

(*k*) Stability of employment can be ensured.

But organizations do not excessively rely on internal source as too much consumption of even sugar tastes bitter. The excessive dependence on this source results in inbreeding, discourages flow of new blood into the organization, organization would become dull and back number without innovations, new ideas, excellence and expertise. Hence, organizations depend on internal source to the extent of motivating and then depend on external sources.

Where are suitable candidates available in required number? How can they be informed about the availability of jobs and about the jobs and organization? Now, we deal with first question as the answer to it deals with the sources of recruitment and answer to the second question deals with the techniques of stimulating the prospective candidates (or techniques of recruitment).

Generally, the learners of human resources management may feel that sources and techniques of recruitment are one and the same. But they are different. Sources are those where prospective employees are available like employment exchanges while techniques are those which stimulate the prospective employees to apply for jobs like nomination by employees, advertising, promotion etc. Management has to find out and develop sources of recruitment as early as possible because of high rate of time-lapse.

Disadvantages of Internal Recruiting

- ***Inbreeding:*** One drawback of extensive internal recruiting is the reduced likelihood of innovation and new perspectives. A lack of new employees from the outsides leads to a lack of new ideas and approaches.
- ***EEO Criteria:*** A use of the internal pool for the consideration of vacant positions can lead to conflicts with the Equal Employment Opportunity Commission. The organization has to ensure and continuously check its balance of a diverse workforce. This has to relate to the organization's legal, political and geographical environment.
- ***More training:*** Internal recruiting demands a higher degree of employee training. In order to develop the skills needed to train the current workforce in new processes and technologies, the organization has to provide a more expensive training program.

External Sources of Recruitment for Organization

External Sources Include: (*a*) Campus Recruitment, (*b*) Private Employment Agencies/Consultants, (*c*) Public Employment Exchanges, (*d*) Professional Associations, (*e*) Data Banks, (*f*) Casual Applicants, (*g*) Similar Organizations, (*h*) Trade Union.

Campus Recruitment: Different types of organizations like industries, business firms, service organizations, social or religious organizations can get inexperienced candidates of different types from various educational institutions like Colleges and Universities imparting education in Science, Commerce, Arts, Engineering and Technology, Agriculture, Medicine, Management Studies etc.

Trained candidates are recruited with different specialization in subjects, like engineering, medicine from the training institutes of State Government or National Industrial Training Institutes for Engineers or Vocational Training Centers.

Most of the Universities and Institutes imparting technical education in various disciplines like engineering technology, management studies provide facilities for campus recruitment and selection. They maintain the bio-data and performance required of the candidates. Organizations seeking to recruit the candidates from this source can directly contact the institutes either in person or by post and stimulate the candidates to apply for jobs. Most of the organizations using the source perform the function of selection after completing recruitment in the campus of the Institute itself with a view to minimizing time lapse and to securing the cream before it is attracted by some other organizations.

Campus Recruitment Techniques: Companies realize that campus recruitment is one of the best sources for recruiting the cream of the new blood. The techniques of campus recruitment include:

1. Short listing the institutes based on the quality of students intake, faculty facilities and past track record.
2. Selecting the recruiting team carefully.
3. Offering the smart pay rather than high pay package.
4. Presenting a clear image of the company and the corporate culture.
5. Present the company but do not oversell the company.
6. Getting in early. Make early bird flu.
7. Focusing on career growth opportunities that the company offers to the recruits.
8. Include young line managers and business school (B-school) and engineering School (B-school) alumni in the recruiting team.
9. Build the relationships with the faculty, administrators and students to grab them before the rivals do.

Private Employment Agencies/Consultants: Public employment agencies or consultants like ABC. Consultants in India perform the recruitment functions on behalf of a client company by charging fee. Line managers are relieved from recruitment functions so that they can concentrate on their operational activities and recruitment functions is entrusted to a private agency or consultants. But due to limitations of high cost, ineffectiveness in performance, confidential nature of this function managements sometimes do not depend on this source. However, these agencies function effectively in the recruitment of executives. Hence, they are also called executive search agencies. Most of the organizations depend on this source for highly specialized positions and executive positions.

Public Employment Exchange: The Government set-up Public Employment Exchanges in the country to provide information about vacancies to the candidates and to help the organizations in finding out suitable candidates. The Employment Exchange (Compulsory Notification or Vacancies) Act, 1959 makes it obligatory for public sector and private sector enterprises in India to fill certain types of vacancies through public employment exchanges. These industries have to depend on public employment for the specified vacancies.

Professional Organizations: Professional organizations or associations maintain complete bio-data of their members and provide the same to various organizations on requisition. They also act as an exchange between their members and recruiting firms in exchanging information, clarifying doubts etc. Organizations find this source more useful to recruit the experienced and professional employees like executives, managers, engineers.

Data Banks: The Management can collect the bio-data of the candidates from different sources like Employment Exchange, Educational Training Institutes, Candidates etc. and feed them in the computer. It will become another source and the company can get the particulars as and when it needs to recruit.

Casual Applicants: Depending upon the image of the organization, its prompt response, participation of the organization in the local activities, level of unemployment, candidates apply casually for jobs through mail or handover the applications in Personnel Department. This would be a suitable source for temporary and lower level jobs.

Similar Organizations: Generally, experienced candidates are available in organizations producing similar products or engaged in similar business. The management can get most suitable candidates from this source. This would be the most effective source for executive positions and for newly established organization or diversified or expended organizations.

Trade Unions: Generally, unemployed or underemployed persons or employees seeking change in employment put a word to the trade union leaders with a view to getting suitable employment due to latter's intimacy with management. As such the trade union leaders are aware of the availability of candidates. In view of this fact and in order to satisfy the trade union leaders, management enquires with trade unions for suitable candidates. Management decides about the sources depending upon the type of candidates needed, time lapse period, etc. It has to select the recruitment technique(s) after deciding upon source.

The Recruitment Process

Interviews are a crucial part of the recruitment process for most organisations. Their purpose is to give the selector a chance to assess you and for you to demonstrate your abilities and personality. It's also an opportunity for you to assess them and to make sure the organisation and position are right for you.

The recruitment process for most organizations follows a common theme: applications/CVs are received, either online or by post; and candidates are short-listed and invited for interview. The interview format can vary considerably and may include an assessment centre and/or tests. The number of interviews also varies. Some companies are satisfied after one interview, whereas others will want to recall a further shortlist of candidates for more. If successful at the final interview stage, you will receive an official job offer.

Interview format

Interview format is determined by the nature of the organization, but there are various standard formats.

Chronological interviews

These work chronologically through your life to date and are usually based on your CV or a completed application form.

Competency-based interviews

These are structured to reflect the competencies that an employer is seeking for a particular job (often detailed in the recruitment information). The chances are you will have focused on these in your application form. This is the most common type of interview for graduate positions today.

Technical interviews

If you have applied for a job or course that requires technical knowledge (*e.g.*, positions in engineering or IT) it is likely, at some stage in the selection process, that you will be asked technical questions or have a separate technical interview to test your knowledge. Questions may focus on your final year project and your choice of approach to it or on real/hypothetical technical problems. You should be prepared to prove yourself but also to admit to what you don't know (stress that you are keen to learn).

Case study interviews

Used largely by consulting firms, these can range from a straightforward brainteaser to the analysis of a hypothetical business problem. You will be evaluated on your analysis of the problem, how you identify the key issues, how you pursue a particular line of thinking and whether you can develop and present an appropriate framework for organizing your thoughts. There is no perfect way to solve each problem and how you reach your solution is often more important than the solution itself.

The Generic Overview

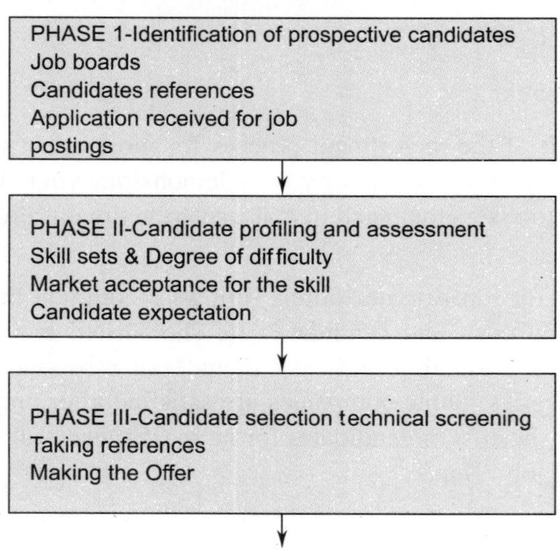

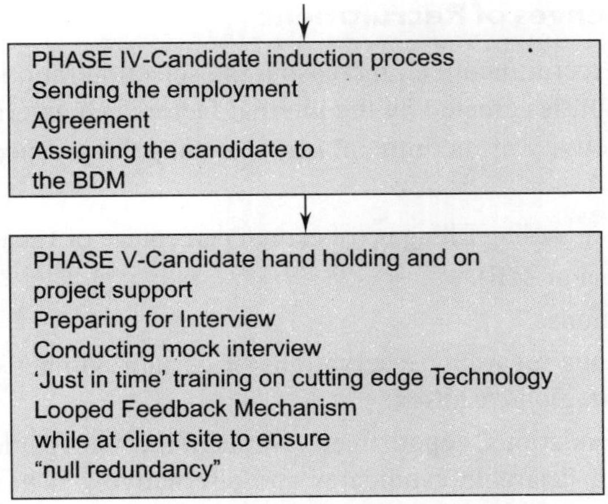
PHASE IV-Candidate induction process
Sending the employment
Agreement
Assigning the candidate to
the BDM
PHASE V-Candidate hand holding and on
project support
Preparing for Interview
Conducting mock interview
'Just in time' training on cutting edge Technology
Looped Feedback Mechanism
while at client site to ensure
"null redundancy"

Fig. 4.1

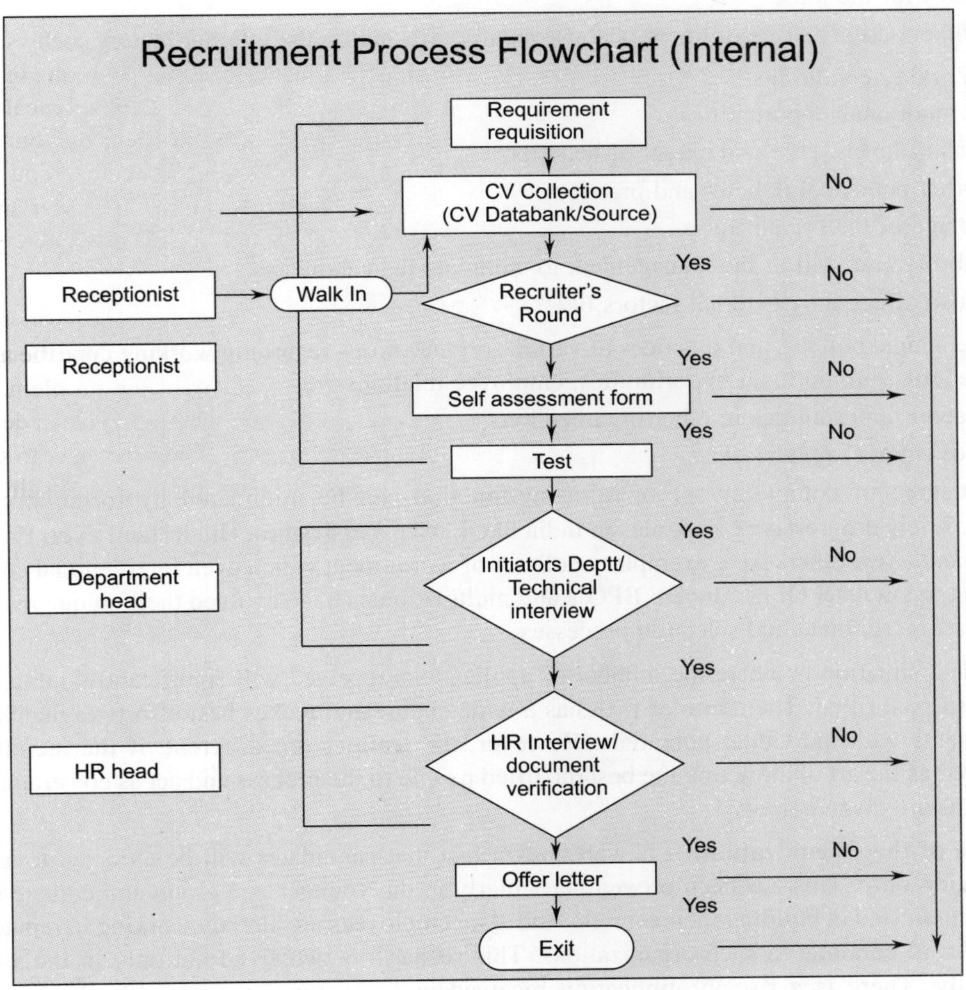
Recruitment Process Flowchart (Internal)
Requirement requisition
CV Collection (CV Databank/Source)
Receptionist
Walk In
Recruiter's Round
Receptionist
Self assessment form
Test
Department head
Initiators Deptt/ Technical interview
HR head
HR Interview/ document verification
Offer letter
Exit
Yes
No

Fig. 4.2

Complexity and Challenges of Recruitment

Performing the function of recruitment *i.e.*, increasing the selection ratio is not as easy as it seems to be. This is because of the hurdles created by the internal factors and external factors which influence an organization. The first activity of recruitment *i.e.*, searching for prospective employees is affected by many factors like:

1. Organizational policy regarding filling up of certain percentage of vacancies by internal candidates.
2. Local candidates (sons of soil).
3. Influence of trade unions.
4. Government regulations regarding reservations of certain number of vacancies to candidates based on community/region/caste/sex.
5. Influence of recommendations, nepotism etc. As such, the management is not free to find out or develop the source of desirable candidates and alternatively it has to divert its energies for developing the sources within the limits of those factors though it cannot find suitable candidates for the jobs.

The other activity of recruitment is consequently affected by the internal factors such as:

1. Working conditions.
2. Promotional opportunities.
3. Salary levels, type and extent of benefits.
4. Other personnel policies and practices.
5. Image of the organization.
6. Ability and skill of the management to stimulate the candidates.

It is also affected by external factors like:

1. Personnel policies and practices of various organizations regarding working conditions, salary, benefits, promotional opportunities, employee relations etc.
2. Career opportunities in other organizations.
3. Government regulations.

The degree of complexity of recruitment function can be minimized by formulating sound policies. A few progressive companies in India like Larsen and Toubro, Hindustan Lever, Procter and Gamble and a few others have exemplary policies of recruitment which even International companies are trying to emulate. Of late Indian BPO's and multinationals have evolved their unique methodologies in fast recruitment and selection processes.

An ideal situation is where the number of applications received will significantly outnumber the number of post filled. The recruiter than has a wide choice and makes best efforts to match the job requirements with individual potentials. However, the realities are different. If the recruitment is considered as the art of attracting the best qualified people to the process and act as constraints. Some constraints are given below:

Image of the Organization: It is well known fact that candidates will be attracted to a reputed organization only. This has been proved particularly in the younger age group and college students who are interested in building their careers. And also, employees are already working in reputed firms would like to continue in such organizations. This scenario is perceived not only in India but also universally. There is a rise in application received in IT sector companies like Infosys, Wipro Technologies, etc. These companies enjoy the positive image in the eyes of public at large. Microsoft too enjoys a positive image to the point where the company receives more applications for recruitment. However, not all companies enjoy such reputations. This image of a company may be perceived as low because of its non-performances, low turnover, policies and practices that pollute the environment, poor quality products, unsafe or inadequate working conditions etc.

Attractiveness of the Job: If the job is unattractive, recruiting a large and qualified pool of candidates will be difficult. In the recent past it has been observed that employers find it difficult to get suitable candidates for the jobs that are considered as routine, boring, physically hazardous, wrongly scheduled, low salary structure, lack of promotional potential etc.

Organizational Policies: Promotional policies of the organization will definitely attract the potential applicants at the initial level but not at the higher positions. Although this is promising, once one is hired, it may reduce the number of applications for higher positions.

Legislation: Organization should comply the existing rules and regulations governing the recruitment process and cannot make any discrimination on the ground of age, religion, race, sex etc. relating to the organizational recruitments.

Cost of the Recruitment: The cost of the recruitment is always expensive. This continuing search for best applicants may be limited by many factors to it.

Ethical standards and manpower recruitment

The problem of regressive practices in headhunting, recruiters say, assumes the form of a vicious circle. The challenge of acquiring large volumes of employable candidates is so immense that organizations prefer to pass on this task to a recruitment agency. These agencies are faced with their own share of troubles.

Some of the challenges they face are

1. Most candidates lie to varying degrees on their CVs. When recruiting in large numbers, this leads to a real screening near impossible task. Candidates may consider their CVs to be advertisements of their skills and achievements, and they project all sorts of unbelievable information. This may be acceptable to a marginal extent but not in excess when the information crosses the line to become absolute lying. Databases at educational institutes are also not available which makes it difficult to trace candidates' academic records. This is especially true of older candidates being considered for higher positions.
2. The rapidly multiplying of job websites is something of a problem. Corporate companies often cut out of costs by pointing out that the resumes received from the Recruiting agency are already available on the websites and are not genuinely compiled data base.

The manpower recruiting consultancies quickly became competitive and the instinct to survive and deliver results much faster led to some unethical operators indulging in business malpractices. These led to candidates being shown the door by IT majors Wipro, IBM, for manipulating their resumes.

Experts are saying that such incidents are commonplace and sometimes take place with the knowledge, and even the active connivance of the recruitment agency. Confidentiality and respecting the clients' interests must be the priority of the headhunting organizations. Some of the methods that recruitment agencies are currently using are questionable. The recruitment industry has been coming up in a big way but of late the ethical problems are coming into focus.

Headhunters and search agencies in the West have long been grappling with the malaise of unethical recruitment practices. This has percolated into the Indian recruiting industry. However, there is a growing realization among organizations and industry bodies in India which are confident of coming out with some sort of systematic reforms.

Recruiting agencies need to realize that while wrong practices might help in the short-term, flash in the plan operators will not be able to do well in the long-term. But recent incidents have created mistrust of reputed organizations in some of the headhunters because of their unreliable work. However, the experts refuse to participate and waste time in finding out cunning recruiters. They attribute the current problems to declining standards of ethics concerning three parties namely candidates, the agencies and organizations.

Some CEOs of reputed recruiting organizations expressed the opinion that there needs to be a good system to address complaints strictly. The relevant associations are working some methodology to ensure that all its members are completely 'above board' and do not indulge in professional malpractices. Organizations need to be careful about the consultants that they work with and be careful about hard bargaining or going for low cost recruiters.

The realistic reason for the problem is that there is a skilled manpower shortage particularly in a booming economy of some developing countries like India.

Organizations and recruiters must put in fair practices act to eliminate unethical practices which is not going to be possible overnight. However, with a little initiative and a strong commitment to the cause, it is absolutely possible to reduce the recent occurrences to rare occurrences.

Recruiters to maintain ethical standards must follow:

- Maintain high moral standards and deliver full value for money to the clients.
- Candidate's confidentiality is really kept confidential.
- Avoid cutting service levels to get assignments at cut prices.
- Keep away from corrupting clients' HR people for more assignments.

Get assignments from clients by proven track record in recruitments.

Recruiting in the Internet Age

The Information Age has drastically changed the way companies recruit employees. The Internet makes huge numbers of job seekers available to any firm with access to the Web. At the same time, many companies increasingly rely on executive search firms to locate good candidates for important posts. But traditional recruitment methods—from word-of-mouth to newspaper advertisements—still work best for some firms. Here's the low-down on each recruitment method and how you can make it work for your business:

The Internet. Learn to love the Internet—it's probably the greatest recruitment resource around. By 2001, an estimated 96 per cent of U.S. companies will be recruiting on the Web. Already, more than two-thirds of human resources professionals use the Internet to recruit.

Millions of job seekers surf the Web each week, post their resumes, fill out online applications and even conduct email interviews. One online search firm reports that computer-assisted applicant searches take one-third the time of traditional searches. Moreover, some evidence indicates that applicants are more truthful over the Internet.

But figuring out how to recruit over the Internet can be daunting. A recent search on the phrase "employee recruitment" found more than 1 million Web pages.

Executive search firms. The executive search industry has grown rapidly in recent years, thanks to our booming economy and the resulting labour shortage. Large corporations make up most of the search firms' business. But small companies, which lack the resources or recruiting expertise of larger competitors, stand to gain even more by hiring a search firm. Since startup and emerging businesses have fewer employees than large corporations, a bad hire hurts a growing business more than it does a big, established company.

Executive search firms come in two varieties: retainer firms and contingency firms. Retainer firms act as ongoing consultants to your business. They are more expensive than contingency firms, but they commit more time and effort to your firm. Retainer search firms are generally used to find applicants for senior management positions. Contingency firms are paid only after filling your position. They're more appropriate for filling mid-level openings.

Traditional recruiting methods. Don't be so wowed by fancy technology and premium-priced headhunters that you ignore time-tested ways of finding good talent. Often, the best prospective employees are people you hear about from trusted friends or associates.

Likewise, an inexpensive advertisement in a trade publication or the classified pages of your paper might draw qualified candidates to your door. Be sure that your advertisement details the work you need to be done and the qualifications you require.

Conclusion

The main relationships between culture and recruiting are associated with employee attraction, selection and retention. From an attraction standpoint, culture is primarily about the brand image a company projects. Companies that take culture seriously actively market their culture to candidates. This attracts people who will thrive in the organization and repels people who would be more effective working elsewhere. Such efforts pay off directly and indirectly. People appeared to join the company expecting a certain culture, and if their expectations were not met, they left. Another reason to recruit around culture is that while job demands and requirements constantly shift, a defining characteristic of culture is that it remains constant in the face of change. A person hired based partly on his fit with an organization's culture is more likely to continue on as a valuable company resource, even if the position he was originally hired for ceases to exist. In fact, an effective organizational culture actually helps people work together to adapt to business changes.

The challenges of attracting and retaining talented manpower exists in all sectors of business activity, be it consultancy, manufacturer or the service sector, with each sector developing its own perspectives based on its experiences. A sharing experience from the companies in the engineering, chemicals, pharmaceuticals, consumer goods, consultancy and information technology sectors revealed that though the challenges of attracting and retaining talent in such a range of companies differed in the intensity and type, a common thread seemed to link the divergent spectrum. The impact of the attraction/retention strategies could be presented in the form of eight vertices *i.e.*, work culture, job/career, team, compensation, titles, golden handcuffs, individual, values etc. There is no mantra to retain the talent. It is important to capture the knowledge and talent in the organization by having the systems of documenting. The organization must have to leverage the urge of employees to learn as a powerful retention tool. Compensation is not issue always in retentions terminology values, work culture, career planning and job design have a key role to play in attracting and retain the employees in the organization. The work place should mean fun and joy to the employee—not a place that will squeeze out of an employee all that an employer can get, for the least possible returns. It is very much important to distinguish between high performers, high potentials, and high effort, while designing the strategies to attract and retain the employees. The strategies mapped and followed by the each of the companies for retaining and attracting talent would also depends on the stages of development and growth of the company.

CASE STUDY–I

Recruitment and Selection

Wanted: Enthusiastic Employees to Grow with Growing Minds. Inc.

Growing Minds, Inc. is a national chain of retail outlets specializing in creative toys and innovative learning materials for children. The company caters to the upper end of the market and focuses on customer service for a competitive advantage. It provides workshops for parents and children on topics such as learning with the computer and indoor gardening and offers crafts classes ranging from papier-mache to pottery.

Growing Minds plans to expand and to open five new retail outlets in the coming quarter. This may mean up to 200 new hires, and the executive team wants to make sure that the best people are hired and retained. It has issued a challenge to its retail management personnel to design a staffing process that will accomplish these goals.

The children's market in which Growing Minds operates demands service personnel who are endlessly patient; knowledgeable about children, toys, and learning; and, perhaps most important, sociable, enthusiastic, and engaging. Excellent customer service is the top priority at Growing Minds, and obtaining the desired performance from personnels has meant a major investment in training. Unfortunately, new workers often leave within a year of being hired. This means that the company barely gets an adequate return on the training it has invested in its new hires. Apparently, turnover is due (at least in part) to the demanding nature of the job. Recently, Growing Minds has been emphasizing the establishment of work teams to improve the quality of its services, identify and fix any problems in service delivery and brainstorm new opportunities. This approach has yielded better than anticipated results, so the team concept will be central to the new outlets.

Critical Thinking Question

1. How can Growing Minds attract the best applicants for jobs at its new retail outlets? On what groups, if any, should be company's recruiting effort focus? How should the recruiting be done?
2. How should Growing Minds select the best candidates? What type of characteristics and measures should be used? Why?
3. How might Growing Minds socialize its employees so that they are attuned to the firm's culture and plans for the future?
4. How might Growing Minds address its retention problems?

5. Students who have worked in a result setting, particularly one focusing on children and/or excellent customer service, share with the class the worker characteristics they found most important in that experience.

Divide into groups of three or four to identify possible sources of Growing Minds' employee retention problem. What could be done in the staffing process to address this problem ? Each person in the group should list at least one possibility. Compile the best ideas produced by the group and present them to the class

CASE STUDY–2

Recruitment and Retention

A medium-sized company with turnover of around Rs. 1000 crore is into manufacture of semiconductors and has a plant each in Pune and Goa, respectively. The corporate office is located at Mumbai. The company is a private limited company and the promoters hold the majority of the stake. The organization has recently recruited a new Head-HR, Mr. Stanley Joseph, to revamp the HR strategies. Mr. Joseph after reviewing the existing status decided to focus on the recruitment policy, since he rightly identified that attracting the right manpower is the first step towards building competent human assets for the organization.

The new HR policy is as follows:

- ***Purpose:*** The purpose is to ensure availability of adequate resources to attain better productivity and profitability.
- ***Coverage:*** It covers all levels in the organization for recruitment of permanent and temporary employees.
- ***Policy:***
  - Recruitment of permanent staff of XYZ shall be made as per the manpower budget prepared every year or employee requisition duly approved by the Chief Executive Officers (CEO).
  - An annual plan has to be prepared by a departments and units and sent to the HR department in the corporate office.
  - The respective project leaders, in coordination with the HR department, would procure the resources required for various projects in accordance with the annual plan.
  - For any requirement that is not a part of the formal plan, the concerned project leader has to forward the additional requirements to the HR-Head, who would then submit it will his inputs to the CEO for approval.
  - As regards recruitment for any position, the order of priority would be as under:
    - Experienced people within the organization (internal resources).
    - Candidates referred by the employees, employee referred (in case of recruitment employees concerned would be given monetary rewards, after three months joining of the new recruit, as motivational.
    - Open recruitment, *i.e.* recruitment through advertisement, etc.

The policy guidelines regarding recruitment of temporary staff are as under:

- The CEO would authorize the recruitment of staff on temporary basis.

- ➢ The period of recruitment of temporary staff cannot exceed six months or the duration of project, whichever is earlier. However, on a case-to-case basis.
- ➢ A committee consisting of the concerned departmental head or Project Leader, Head-HR, and Vice President (Operations) would conduct the selection process to carry on the recruitment.

All employees with prior work experience will be on probation for a period of one year, while new recruits will be on probation for a period of one and half years. Probationary experience of employees will be considered for the purposes of performance appraisal and promotion. The probation period can be extended, based on the recommendations of the appraising and reviewing authorities. Employees would be confirmed in the service of the company after successful completion of the probation period.

The company's recruitment policy aims at attracting and retaining the best available talent in the industry so that the appropriate quality and number of employees are available at the right time.

Objectives: The objectives of the recruitment policy are:

- To ensure that all positions identified in the organization are staffed by persons with the skills, knowledge, experience, and qualifications required to perform them effectively.
- To provide career opportunities for deserving personnel in line with their skills and potential.
- To infuse fresh talent, skills, and competencies in the organization to help enhance its capabilities.

Manpower planning: Manpower plans will be prepared annually for each department by respective department heads along with the budgeting process. The budget year for the purpose would be the company's financial year. The parameters to be considered for compilation of manpower include:

- Level of business operations.
- Staffing requirements in terms of quality and numbers.
- Existing staffing strength.
- Planned promotions/transfers.

The CEO will approve the final manpower plan, while the Head-HR will be responsible for monitoring and implementation of the approved plan.

Manpower sources: For each of the positions identified and depending on the type of vacancy and skills required, the appropriate source of suitable personnel required for the position will be determined. The recruitment sources include:

Direct recruitment

Advertisement in newspapers, magazines, etc.

Universities and educational institutions for entry-level professional positions where no experience is necessary.

- Display on company notice board (if considered appropriate).
- ***Placement consultants:*** The placement consultants should counduct personality development programs for the potential applicants. They should focus & is to evable the participants to identify their strength, build thir confidence, develop thir personality and develop thir analytical skills.
- ***Employee gets employee scheme:*** The existing employee can refer names of candidates for various positions being displayed on the notice board. If the candidate is selected, he or she will get rewarded with a one-time cash award of Rs. 2,500.

CONCEPT REVIEW QUESTIONS

1. Explain the term placement. And discuss its importance in the organizations.
2. Define induction discussing in detail the components of an employee induction programme.
3. What measures should be taken to make the induction programme a success in the organization?
4. What are the advantages and disadvantages of promoting employees from within the company?
5. Why do employers transfer employees?
6. What is the voluntary retirement scheme? Write a note on it.
7. Bring out the differences between lay off and retrenchment.
8. Give a note on conditions that prompt the dismissal of an employee.

REFERENCES

1. Beach D.S. (1985), "*Personnel management*", New York: McMillan.
2. Casey, Thomas E. (1990), "*Making the most of a selection interview*", Personnel Sept.
3. Cascio W.F. (1991), "*Applied psychology in personnel management*", New York: Prentice Hall.
4. Dessler Gary (1994), "*Personnel/Human resource management*" New York: Prentice Hall.
5. Gatewood R. and H. Field (1994), "*Human resource selection*", Fourth Edition: Dryden.
6. Lath rop, Richard (1976), "*Who is hiring who*", Reston Publishing: Reston.
7. Miner, Jhon B. (1992), "*Industrial psychology*", New York: McGraw Hill.
8. Pell, Arthur, (1969), "*Recruiting and selecting personnel*", New York, Regents.
9. Sur, M. *et.al.* (1970), "*Personnel management in India*", Mumbai, Asia Publishing House.
10. Lord J.S., *External and internal recruitment.* In Cascio W.F. (Ed); *Human resources planning, Employment and placement,* D.C. Bureau of National Affairs 1989; 2–73 to 2–102.
11. Heneman III H.G *et.al.;* "*Personnel/Human resources management*", New Delhi; University Book Stall 1989; 248.
12. Yoder D, Heneman H.G., Turnbull J.G. and Stone C.H. ; *Handbook of personnel management and labour relations*, New York : McGraw Hill 1958;7:2.
13. Kempner T., *A Handbook of management*, London Weidenfield and Nicholson, 1973, 310.
14. Famularo J.J., *Personnel Recruitment*, In Maynard H B (Ed); Handbook of business administration, New York; McGraw Hill 1970; II, 49.
15. Jucious M.J., *Personnel management, Homewood,* IIlinois, Richard Irwin Inc 1971; 310.
16. Dunn J.D., Stephens E.C., *Management of personnel:* New York: McGraw Hill 1972: 121.
17. Yoder D., Heneman H.G., Turnbull J.G. and Stone C.H.; *op. cit.*, p. 7, 26.
18. Armstrong M., *A Handbook of personnel management practices,* London: Kogan Press, 1995, pp. 403–04.
19. Yoder D. *et al.*, *op.cit.*, p.-7–30.
20. Report of the Royal Commission on Labour in India, pp.10–12.
21. Labour Investigation Committees. Main Report print, 1958; 68–80.
22. Report on National Commission on Labour, 1969; 69.
23. Das R.P., *Handbook of managerial recruitment and selection,* New Delhi, Kaniska Publishing House, 1992, 303–08.
24. Arora S., *How to hire for a Fit: Business today,* January 7–21, 1996, 68–73.
25. Sreenivasan S.; *How to hire the best CEO,* Business Today, January 7–21, 1996, 74–79.

5
CHAPTER

SOCIALIZATION, MOBILITY AND SEPARATION

5.1 INTRODUCTION

Socialization is the process by which an individual learns to appreciate the values, abilities, expected behaviours and the social knowledge essential for assuming an organizational role and for participating as a member of the organization. Socialization is commonly treated as one of the learning process. By which an individual can learn how to behave in explicit (policies and procedures) and implicit (cultural) expressed environments. It takes place over the period of time, not as a discrete event. Actual and anticipatory socialization are vitally important in all our lives. Eventually, as the managers and professionals, the person will be responsible for the socialization of the new comers and subordinates in his/her organization.

The individual joining in any new organization develops new values, attitudes and behaviour appropriate for membership. The problems associated with entrances into and adaptation to work organizations is issues of the adult socialization. One of the most important periods of adult socialization is on the boundary of as new organization ready to become a member. Organizational socialization is the process of becoming accepted members is a reciprocal process; individual adapts, but so does the organization.

Fig. 5.1 The Socialization Process

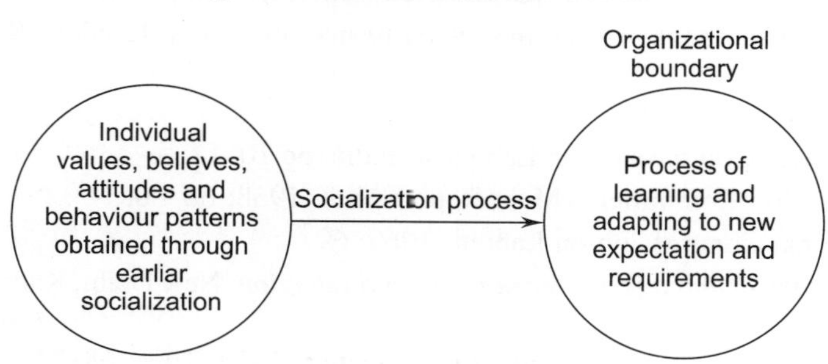

Individual with certain image of themselves when entering the organization. This, undergo changes and they interact with organization and learn new tasks and roles. Organizational life gives opportunities to test her knowledge and skills and to assess his/her own strengths and weakness. Members often require the development of new values appropriate to the position. To become successful members, the individual must accommodate, at least to some degree, the goals, value and practices of the organization. It is very important to establish the individual's values, expectation, behaviour patterns and achievement orientation. The member has to adjust about the personal characteristics, behaviour and performance of the individual. Frequently both the individual and the organizations have some influences in the selection process with more effective socialization and integration. socialization is a two-way process. It continuously modifying the individual's behaviour based on the degree of change effected in the organization and in their agents of socialization is directly related to the new situation with which individuals are exposed.

Socialization leads to higher expectations on the part of the individuals about their organizational roles than can be fulfilled. The individuals should be realistic in recognizing that entering into any organization may lead to some gain and some losses. The socialization process requires the abandonment of certain past values, attitudes and behaviour patterns that may have been part of the self-image cultivated by the individual. The organizational socialization can be underdone, appropriately done, or over done. If it is underdone, appropriately done, rebellion and alienation on the part of individual who rejects all the norms and values of the organization. The rebellious individual is dissatisfied with both himself and with the organization; where the individual totally confirms to the organizations, unquestionably perpetuating and demanding acceptance of the exciting goals, values and practices. The goal of the appropriate socialization should develop creative individualism where the person generally accepts the key goals, values, and norms of the organization but also retains the desire to seek changes and improvement.

Concept of Mobility

Mobility is an organizational activity to cope with the changing organizational requirements like change in organizational structure, fluctuation in requirement of the organizational products, introduction to new methods of work etc. Mobility in an organizational context includes mainly "promotion" and "transfer'. A sometimes demotion also comes under mobility. Thus the promotion, transfer and separation functions provide workforce flexibility, mobility required in view of the normal "life-cycle" as well as the varying needs of functioning of the organization. There may be the numerous factors responsible for frequent adjustment of or shifting of workforce. This may occur because of the changes in the boundaries of the department and relocation of individuals, jobs and departments'. Moreover, the increase and decline in the volume of production and employment cause an adjustment of workforce. Basically internal mobility is necessary to match the employees' skill and requirements with the requirements of the job and those of the organization continuously. Internal mobility is needed because of the these reasons *i.e.*, (Change in job structure, job design, change in technology, mechanization, expansion, diversification of production/operation, change in employee skills, knowledge, abilities, aptitude, values etc. changing government roles and social and religious conditions of the employees or the region). The external mobility refers to movement of employees from one organization to another seeking better employment based on his skills and the requirements and the needs of the various organizations. Employees resort to external mobility techniques and the organizations resort to external candidates when the chances of the suitable placement on the either side or both the sides are non-existence within an organization. An employee prefers internal mobility as long as he is sure of getting suitable placement/employment within the organization. Similarly, organizations may resort to internal mobility until they find suitable candidate to different jobs.

Purpose of Mobility

Mobility serves the following purposes:

- To improve organizational effectiveness,
- To maximize employees efficiency,
- To cope with changes in operation, and
- To ensure discipline.

5.2 PROMOTIONS

The employees are given the promotions to higher posts and positions as and when vacancies are available or when new posts are created at the higher levels. It is quite common in all types of organizations. It is the product of internal mobility of the employees due to change in organizational processes, structure etc. It is better ten direct recruitment which satisfy many human resources problems of the organization and helps in achieving organizational objectives. Promotion means higher position to an employee who carries higher status, more responsibilities and higher salary. The higher status and salary is the two most important ingredient of any promotion. It is an advancement of employee to a higher post with greater responsibilities and higher salary, better service conditions and thus higher status.

Purpose of Promotion

- To motivate employees to higher productivity.
- To attract and retain the services of qualified and competent people to recognize and reward the efficiency of an employee.
- To increase the effectiveness of the employee and the organization.
- To fill up higher vacancies from the within the organization.
- To built loyalty, morale and the sense of belongingness in the employee.
- To impress upon others that opportunities are available to them too in the organization, if they perform well.

Promotion Policy

We have seen policy is the guideline for action. Policy varies with organization. So the promotion is very sensitive to employees, it is very essential. The promotion policy should clearly stated, widely circulated, and fully explained to their employees. The promotion policy which influences the number of factor of the organization such as, morale, motivation, turnover of the personnel in the organization. The personnel department of the organization must develop an effective promotion policy. This should be in written, flexible subject to situations. In order to make the promotion policy successful, it is necessary that the employees' assessment and confidential reporting system should be objective as far as possible so that every employee has faith in promotion policy and hence induced for better performance to get promotion.

The promotion policy should consider merit, potential and seniority of the employees. The merit factor requires a good procedure for evaluating the performance of the employee. The performance of the each employee should be appraised periodically and should form the part of personal record.

Principles of Promotion

Promotion is a double edged weapon. If handled carefully, promotion is a double edged weapon. If handled carefully, it contributes to employee satisfaction and motivation. If it is mishandled, it leads to discontentment, frustration, skepticism, bickering among the employees and culminates in a high rate of employee turn over, HR department has taken the responsibility of designing, implementing the total promotion policy in an organization. The policy of promotion should be clear in the following matters:

- The management must take it clear where to fill-up higher positions by internal promotions or recruit people from outsides. Generally speaking, top positions by external recruitment. The lower positions should however, are filled up by promotions from within.
- When it has been decided to fill-up higher positions with promotions, further decisions on determining the basis of promotion should be made by the management. The basis of promotion may be seniority or merit or both.

The merit's are:

- It is easy to administer.
- There is less scope for subjectivity or arbitrariness in fixing seniority.
- Labor Unions welcome seniority based promotions.
- Seniority and experience go hand in hand; therefore, it is right and proper to make promotions on this basis.
- Subordinates are willing to work under an older boss who are given many years of service to the company.
- Loyalty is rewarded.

Demerits are:

- Seniority is no indication of competence.
- In spite of judicial pronouncement, there are no single criteria for fixing the seniority of an employee.
- Young and competent people get frustrated and might leave the organization.

If the competency is the basis for promotion, an employee whose performance is the best, as revealed by performance appraisal, is promoted. He or She beats all others by his or her merit is rewarded.

The merits of promotion by competency:

- Efficiency is encouraged, recognized and rewarded.
- Competent people are retained because better prospects are open to them.
- Productivity increases.

The disadvantages of promotion by merit are:

- Discontentment among senior employees.

- Scope for favouritism.
- Loyalty and length of service are not rewarded.
- Opposition from union leaders.

5.3 DEMOTION

Demotion is the opposite of promotion. It is a downward movement of employees in the organizational hierarchy with lower status and lower salary. It is the downwarding process and is insulating to an employee. Demotion is the punishment for incompetence or mistake of serious nature on the part of the employee. It is serious types of the penalty or punishment and should be given rarely and only under exceptional circumstances and tactfully. Demotions may be necessary under the following conditions:

- When the organization reduces activities, officer occupying certain posts are demoted.
- Errors in the promotions already made are corrected through demotions.
- It may be necessary to use demotions as a tool of disciplinary action against erring employees.

The tool of demotion should be used only when it is absolutely necessary. However, there should not be any injustice to any of employees in this regard. Demotions should be made for genuine reasons. Promotions are easily as they affect their status, career and position. Demotion usually treated as an insult and naturally resented by the employees in one way or the other. It is, therefore, desirable to avoid demotions as far as possible. Demotions should be an exception but not the normal rule of the organization.

Demotion Policy

Demotion is very harmful for the employee's morale. It is an extremely painful action, impairing the relationships between people permanently. While effecting the demotions, managers should extremely careful not to place himself on the wrong side of the fence. It is therefore, very necessary to formulate a demotion policy so that there may be no grievances on the part of the unions and the employee concerned.

Yoder, Henemann, Turnbull and Stone has suggested a five fold strategy relating to the demotion of the employees in an organization.

1. A clear list of rules along with the punishable offences be made available to all the employees.
2. Any violation be investigated thoroughly by a competent authority.
3. In case of violation, it is better to state the reasons for taking such punitive actions clearly and elaborately.
4. Once violation is proved, there should be a consistent and equitable application of the penalty.
5. There should be enough room for review.

Demotions should have serious impact on need fulfillment. Needs for esteem and belongingness are get frustrate leading to a defensive behaviour on the part of the person demoted. There may be complaints, emotional turmoil, inefficiency or resignations. Hence, demotions are very rarely resorted to by managers. Manager prefers to discharge the employees rather than face the problems arising from the demotions.

5.4 TRANSFER

One of the internal mobility of the employee is transfer. It is lateral movement of employee in an organization by the employee. Dale Yoder has defined transfer as "A transfer involves the shifting of an employee from one job to another without changing the responsibilities or compensation". Transfers of employees are quite common in all organizations. This can also be defined as a change in job within the organization where the new job is substantially equal to the old in terms of pay, status and responsibilities. Transfers of employees can possible from one department to another from one plant to another. Transfer may be initiated by the organization or by the employees with the approval of the organization. It can be also due to changes in organizational structure or change in volume of work, it is also necessary due to variety of reasons. But broadly can be done either to suit the conveniences of organization and to suit the convenience of employees.

The purposes of the Transfer: The transfer are generally affected to build up a more satisfactory work team and to achieve the following purposes:

- To increase the effectiveness of the organization.
- To increase the versatility and competency of key positions.
- To deal with fluctuations in work requirements.
- To correct incompatibilities in employee relations.
- To correct, erroneous placement.
- To relieve monotony.
- To adjust workforce.
- To punish employees.

Types of Transfers most of the transfers generally carried out four types of transfers which are discussed below:

Production Transfer: Such transfers are resorted to when there is a need of manpower in one department and surplus manpower in other department. Such transfers are made to meet the company requirements. The surplus employees in one department/section might be observed in other place where there is a requirement.

Replacement Transfers: This takes place to replace a new employee who has been in the organization for a long time and there by giving some relief to an old employee from the heavy pressure of work.

Remedial Transfers: As the name suggest, these transfers are made to rectify the situation caused by faulty selection and placement procedures. Such transfers are made to rectify mistakes in placement and recruitments. If the initial placement of an individual is faulty or has not adjusted to work/job, his transfer to a more appropriate job is desirable.

Versatility Transfer: Such transfers are made to increase versatility of the employees from one job to another and one department to another department. Transfer (Job Rotation) are the tool to train the employees. Each employee should provide a varied and broader job experiences by moving from one department to another. This is for preparing the employee for promotion, this will definitely help the employee to have job enrichment.

Transfer Policy

Every organization should have a fair and impartial transfer policy which should be known to each employee. The responsibility for effecting transfers is generally entrusted to an executive with power to prescribe the conditions under which requests for transferred are approved. Care should be taken to ensure that frequent or large scale transfers are avoided by laying down adequate selection and placement procedures for the purpose. A good transfer policy should:

- Specifically clarify the types of transfers and the conditions under which these will be made.
- Locate the authority in some officer who may initiate and implement transfers.
- Indicate whether transfers, *i.e.*, whether it will be based on seniority or on the skill and competency or any other factor.
- Decide the rate of pay to be given to the transfere.
- Intimate the fact of the transfer to the person concerned well in advance.
- Be in writing and duly communicated to all concerned.
- Not be made frequently and for sake of transfer only.

A sound, just and impartial transfer policy should be evolved in the organization to govern all types of transfers. This policy should be clearly specified so that the superiors cannot transfer their subordinates arbitrarily and subordinates may not request for transfers even for the small issues. The management must frame policy on transfers and apply it to all the transfers instead of treating each case on its merit. Such a policy must be based on the following principles:

1. Transfer policy must be in writing and be made known to all the employees of the organization.
2. The policy must very clearly specify the types and the circumstances under which company initiated the transfer will be made.
3. Basis of the transfer should be clearly mentioned in the policy, whether it will be based seniority or on the skill and the competency or any other factors.
4. It should indicate the executives who will be responsible for initiating and approving the transfers.
5. The policy should specify the region or unit of the organization within which transfers will be administered.
6. The effect of the transfer on the pay and seniority of the transferred employee may be clearly evaluated.
7. It should be prescribed in the policy whether the training or retraining is required on the new job.
8. Transfer should be clearly defined as temporary or permanent.
9. The interest of the organization are not to be forgotten in framing a policy of transfer.
10. Reasons for the mutual transfer of employees or reasons to be considered for the personal transfers should be specified.
11. The fact of the transfer should be intimated to the person concerned well in advance.
12. Transfer should not be made frequent and not for the sake of transfer only.

5.5 PLACEMENT

After the employee is hired and oriented, he/she must be placed in his/her right job. Placement is understood as the allocation of people to the job. It is assignment or re-assignment of an employee to a new or different job. Placement includes initial assignment of new employees and promotion, transfer or demotion of present employees. The placement is arising out of promotion, transfer, demotion. Assignment of new employee to a job apparently seems to be simple task. The employer advertises inviting applications from candidates for a specific post. The advertisement contains job description and job specifications in detail. When a candidate has selected, it is logical that individual is placed in a position that was advertised earlier. But the task of placement is not that simple it appears. Times are changing. Changes in the work ethics reflecting the demand for meaningful work. All these factors are causing organizations and individuals to determine the placement process more closely. We are entering the age when applicants must be considered for several jobs rather than one.

From the managerial perspective, the task is to understand and capitalize on each person's individually. Since, human attributes vary along many relatively independent ability, interest, biographical sketch and the personality dimensions, a person's individuality is best viewed as his/her unique profile of scores on a variety of individual measures. Once we establish the unique profile for each individual, people and jobs can be matched optimally within the constraints set by available jobs and available people. If the number of individuals is large in relation to the available jobs, only the best qualified persons can be selected and placed. On the other hand, when more jobs are available, optimal placement is possible. Thus the number of people and the number of jobs determine the placement process in any organization.

Placement Problems

The difficulty with placement is that we tend to look at the individual but not at the job. Often, the individual does not work independent of others. Whether the employee works independent of others or is dependent depends on the types of jobs. Jobs in this context can be classified into the three categories:

- Independent (in such activities of one worker have little bearing on the activities of the other workers, here the placement is simple to conduct).
- Sequential (activities of the workers are dependent on activities of a fellow worker example assembly line sequential jobs).
- Pooled (where the job are high degree of interdependence among activities. The final output of is the result of contribution of all workers. It is team work which matters. Placement for this is quite difficult).

Fig. 5.2 Assessment-Classification Model and Employee Placement

Collect details of the employee

↓

Construct his/her profile

↓

Which sub-group profile to job family profile?

↓

Which job family profile does subgroup profile best fit?

↓

Assign the individual to job family

↓

Assign the individual to specific job after further counseling and assessment

Source: Wayne F. Cascio and Elios M. Awad, Human Resources Management, p. 265.

Principles of Placement

A few basic principles should be followed at the time of placement of a workers on the job. This is elaborated below:

1. Man should be placed on the job according to the requirements of the job. The job should not be adjusted according to the qualifications or requirements of the man. Job first, man next, should be the principle of the placement.
2. The job should be offered to the person according to his qualification. This should neither the higher nor the lower than the qualification.
3. The employee should be made conversant with the working conditions prevailing in the organization and all things relating to the job. He should also be made aware of the penalties if he commits the wrong.
4. While introducing the job to the new employees, an effort should be made to develop a sense of loyalty and cooperation in him so that he may realize his responsibility better towards the job and the organization.
5. The placement should be ready before the joining date of the newly selected person.
6. The placement in the initial period may be temporary as changes are likely after the completion of training. The employee may be later transferred to the job where he can do better.

Proper placement helps to improve the employees' morale. The capacity of the employees can be utilized fully. The right placement also reduces labour turnover, absenteeism and also the accident rate. Than the employee can adjust to the required environment of the organization effectively and the performance of the employee will not be hampered.

Problems of the Placement

The main problem of placement arises when the recruiters look at the individuals but not the job. Often the individual does not work independent of the others. Jobs in this context are classified into the three categories:

1. ***Independent Jobs:*** In the independent jobs the non-overlapping territories are allocated to each employee *e.g.*, in the sales. In such situations, the activities of the one employee have little bearing on the activities of the other workers. The independent jobs do not pose great problems in placement. Each employee has to be evaluated between his capabilities and the interests and those required on the job. The objective of the placement will be:

   To fill the job with people who have at least the minimum required qualifications. People should be placed on the job that will make the best possible use of their talents, given available job or HR constraints.
2. The dependent jobs may be sequential or pooled. In sequential jobs, the activities of the one employee are dependent on the activities of the fellow employee *e.g.*, assembly lines are the best example of such job.
3. In the pooled jobs, there is a high interdependence among the jobs. The final output is the result of the contribution of all the workers.

5.6 INDUCTION

Socialization is the process by which an individual learns to appreciate the values, abilities, expected behaviours and the social knowledge essential for assuming an organizational role and for participating as a member of the organization. Socialization is commonly treated as one of the learning process. Induction is a learning process. Induction is a process through which a new employee is introduced to the organization. It refers to the process of welcoming and socializing the individual into an organization. It is a process where an individual is made to feel comfortable and feel at home in the organization. Induction is a process of integration attempted by the organization with the new employee. The new employee can be handed over a rule book or documents of the policy procedures, which are quite impersonal in nature, however, the employee feels the sense of belongings when communicated personally. It is the responsibility of personnel department to execute the induction program.

The main objectives of Induction Program:

- Reduce Insecurity,
- Reduced Anxiety,
- Reduced Cultural Shock, and
- Reduced Exploitation.

Steps of the new Induction Program

- Welcomes the new comer to the organization.
- Explain the over all objectives of the company and the department.
- Explain the employees' role in achieving the objectives.
- Show the location or place of work.
- Handover the rules and job descriptions.
- Give detail the training opportunities and promotional advancement.
- Discuss the working conditions.
- Furnish all details regarding salary and benefits.
- Guide the employees through a tour of entire of the organization.
- The induction program usually done either by formal induction program and or by informal induction program. Some large organizations follow the formal induction program, which carefully planned induction-orientation training program helps a new employee to quickly adjust to the new surroundings, assimilate the new culture, and Reduce Insecurity, Reduced Anxiety, Reduced Cultural Shock, and Reduced Exploitation. In some medium and small organizations informal induction program is carried out either by Supervisor system and or Buddy or Sponsor system.

Elements of good Induction Programme

A good induction programme has three main elements which is described below:

1. **Introductory Information:** Introductory information regarding the history of the company and company's products, its organizational structure, policies, rules and regulations etc. should be given informally or in group session in the personnel department. It will help the candidates to understand the company and the organizational policies and standards well.
2. **On the Job Information:** Further information should be given to the new employee by the department supervisor in the department concerned where he is placed on the job about

departmental facilities and requirements such as nature of the job, the extent of his liability and the employee activities such as recreational facilities, safety measures, job routine etc.

3. **Follow up Interviews:** A follow up interview should be arranged several weeks after the employee has been on the job by the supervisor or a representative of the personnel department to answer the problems that are a new employee may have on the job.

5.7 EMPLOYEE SEPARATION

Employees separate from the campus in a variety of ways. Some separations are voluntary and initiated by the employee, such as resignation or retirement. Others are involuntary and initiated by management, such as lay off or medical separation. The death of an employee or dismissal for cause creates unique challenges. Each type of separation requires specific, different actions by you, though some processes are common to all. Your common sense and good judgment will serve you well in response to the special circumstances that arise with each employee's separation. Whatever the circumstances, every employee leaving the campus, whether voluntarily or involuntarily, should feel they were treated with respect. Keep this goal in mind as you review the guidelines for different types of separations in this chapter.

- Death of an Employee
- Dismissal
- Exit Interviews
- Job Abandonment
- Lay off
- Medical Separation
- Resignation
- Retirement

Death of an Employee: When an employee dies, the surviving family members or named beneficiaries may be eligible for certain benefits. You should report the death immediately so notifications can be made and paperwork started. It's also important to maintain contact with the family and offer assistance.

Retirement benefits may be due to the family and if the employee retired with a disability, additional insurance may be due. The beneficiaries will be contacted by the offices involved.

Dismissal: Dismissal is the ultimate disciplinary action, normally used when other methods employed to correct performance or behavioural problems have not been successful. Dismissal is usually preceded by coaching, performance appraisal, and progressive disciplinary action. Under circumstances of extreme misconduct, dismissal without prior warning may be warranted. Dismissal or discharge involves separating an employee from the payroll for violation of company rules or for inadequate performances. Discharge is often called as capital punishment for the employees and so is considered a drastic step. This must be dealt with utmost care. Since, this leads to traumatic experience of the employees, most of the managers should reluctant to undertake such actions. Discharge due to unsatisfactory performance refers to persistence failure on the part of the employee to perform his assigned job/work/duties to meet the standard for his job. It is willful violation of organization rules and regulations by the employees. Which include indiscipline, insubordination and dishonesty and so constitutes the major cause of dismissal.

Separation: After a dismissal letter has been delivered, you may prepare separation documents and start recruiting for your vacancy. Remember that discharge is the capital punishment of employment, which results in no further opportunities for correction. Be sure it is the appropriate action to take.

Exit Interviews: Employees terminating from the campus are valuable resources. Through hearing their feelings, concerns, and impressions, you collect data relevant to your department and the campus. A meeting with employees before they leave is an opportune time to get their candid and honest reactions to policies, systems, management, and overall working conditions.

As soon as you know an employee is leaving, schedule an exit interview meeting. Exit interviews are used primarily for voluntary separations. During this meeting, talk about the employee's reasons for leaving, and how the employee feels about the job and supervision. Ask for specific suggestions the employee may have for you and the department. Take note of anything you may want to change. Look for trends as you receive feedback from several employees.

The exit interview process provides you and the campus with data which might not normally be collected from employees. Use this time to your advantage and make this process a worthwhile one for you and the employee.

Job Abandonment: An employee who does not report to work when expected or call into report their absence for five consecutive days or more may be considered to have abandoned their position, and may be subject to dismissal without prior discipline, as noted in the *Dismissal section of this chapter*. To help you decide whether dismissal is warranted, consult with your L/ER Analyst and consider the following:

Lay off: The purpose of the lay off is to reduce the financial burden on the organization in the event that human resources cannot be utilized profitably. Lay off involves temporary removal from the payroll of the people with surplus skills. According to the Industrial Act, 1947, lay off means the failure, refusal or inability of employer on account of shortage of power, raw material or accumulation of stocks, breakdown of machinery or by any reason to give employment to a workmen whose names appear to be in master roll. The organization's lay off policy and procedures fairly and attempting to minimize the effects of lay offs. Implementation of a staff reduction program may be one of the most difficult challenges you face. Therefore, the following guidelines are intended to provide you with general information and suggestions to be used along with direct services offered by Human Resources.

Medical Separation: When an employee becomes unable to perform essential, assigned duties of a position as a result of a disability or medical condition, the campus is committed to providing services to assist the employee, including efforts at reasonable accommodation. If accommodation efforts are unsuccessful, the employee may be medically separated.

Resignation: When the separation is initiated by the employee himself, it is termed as resignation. Although some resignation to rectify the mistakes in the procurement of personnel or to bring new blood into the affected unit, but excessive turnover may prove costly to the organization. It is a fact that, the investment in the recruitment, selection and training of the employees is lost due to resignation. Employees who voluntarily separate from employment are considered to have resigned their from employment. Requirements for the amount of notice vary, depending on the personnel program.

Retirement: When an employee separates service from the organization at the *superannuation* age, refer the employee to the benefits staff for information on options for retirement and savings plans. Majority of the separations are from retirements. The organizations should have the clear cut policy regarding retirement. Employees who have rendered services to the organization for a number of years expect the organization to provide for their future, when they have retired. Retirement of an employee is an important event in his life also has an important impact on the organization, where the employee worked for a major portion of his life. Therefore at the time of parting or separation there must be an exit interview to know the improvements he wanted to be introduced in the organization.

Conducts efficient and effective employee separation programs that assist employees in transitioning to non-Federal employment; facilitates the removal of unproductive, non-performing employees; and assists employees in transitioning to retirement. Laying off people from work is one of the hardest part and responsibility of being the immediate supervisor in business organizations. Reasons may vary, like poor individual performance or simply the lack of justification for operations to help sustain its finances. Proper protocol is however needed, such as verbal warnings and memorandums prior to actual execution of the decision to part ways. For the professional people who take pride in their work and are clearly educated in the actual performance of a company, they offer a more rational understanding of why such an occurrence would eventually get to this point. Being in the organization itself, the employees can more or less assess overall performance and of course the usual rumours and gossips that would get around for informal ways of gathering information. While gossip may not be a good sign within an organization, it simply cannot be avoided. Gossip becomes one of the more common expected components in a work place, and a place without it may seem awkward for most organizations. Usually, this would be concentrated towards the rank and file employees. Having it include the managers and upper managing personnel is not a good sign, and professionalism is definitely absent. While each organization has different ways of management styles, the usual employee would barely last in such a scenario. Organization should employ professional procedures to ensure that professional work ethics are held to minimize such unwanted practices. While there will still be some present, containing it a level where it will not resort to a full blown issue is something that will help allow most companies focus more on functional operations rather than petty issues, something that most companies would surely want to see in their daily operations.

Conclusion

Once the offer of employment is made after the selection process, and such offer has been accepted, the next logical step is to place the individual on to the job. We have seen it in previous sections that only those candidates who have successfully come out of all hurdles in the selection process are finally offered the jobs. Practice of placing has become a general policy because the attrition rate in the early stages are more. Placement play an important role, so that the new recruits are recognized, acknowledged and welcome by the existing workers. This improve the chances of building rapport with his colleagues and strengthen his bond with the organization. Both these go a long way of reducing attrition rate in the initial stages of employment.

Induction is the welcoming of the new employees (processes) to make the new employee feel at home and generate in him a feeling of belongingness to the organization. It is concerned with the problem of introducing or orienting a new employee to his work group, supervisor and the organization. It is the fusion of organizational goal and personal goals of the new employee. Induction can be viewed as the socialization process. It is the indoctrination of new employee into the organizational culture. And helps the employees to adopt in basic values, norms and customs for becoming the accepted member of organization and assuming organizational roles.

CASE STUDY–I

DRS Industries Ltd. is a large scale manufacturing enterprise with a staff strength of 900 operative employees and 125 executives. The staffing policy of the company is to employ trainees at the lowest intake level and absorb them after successful completion of training. Higher posts are normally filled by promotion and such posts are advertised only if suitable internal candidates are not available.

The electrical division of the company was created in 1992 and seven Junior Engineers (electricals) joined as Management Trainees in July 1992 and were absorbed after completion of six months' training. The J.Es. were put under the charge of an Assistance Engineer (AE) who in turn reported to the Project Manager. As per Board decision, an executive must have at least four years' experience on his job to be considered for promotion to the higher job.

Because of increase in workload of the electrical division, the company advertised a post of J.E. (Electricals) seeking application from those with at least 2 years' experience as J.E. One Mr. Bharat Bhushan who had 3.5 years' experience in another firm applied and got selected for the said job. He joined the company in August 1993. After two years, the Asst. Engineer left his job and the company inserted an advertisement in a leading paper in Oct. 1995 inviting applications from candidates with at least four years' experience as Junior Engineer. Mr. Bharat Bhushan who fulfilled this requirement applied for the post through proper channel. He was called for the interview along with ten other external candidates.

Mr. Bhushan's performance at the interview was outstanding and he was congratulated by the General Manager who was the Chairman of the Selection Committee. The Selection Committee forwarded it recommendation on Mr. Bhushan's selection to the Human Resource Department. But the next day, three of the other Junior Engineers met the G.M. and threatened to resign if Mr. Bharat Bhushan becomes their boss. The G.M. asked the Human Resource Manager not to issue the appointment letter to Mr. Bharat Bhushan because of the following reasons:

(*i*) Mr. Bharat Bhushan can't be promoted to a higher post without completing four years' service in the organization.

(*ii*) Mr. Bharat Bhushan who is junior to the seven J.Es. in the electrical division would supersede them all which might lead to frictions in the division. Moreover, the G.M. did not want to lose any of the J.Es.

QUESTIONS

1. If Mr. Bharat Bhushan had been an external candidate, would he have got the job of Assistant Engineer? Why?
2. In an open vacancy, is it justified to treat the internal and external candidates differently?
3. How far do you agree with the employment/promotion policies of the company?

[MHROD, Delhi, 1997]

CASE STUDY–2

Induction in Industry

A global company with its headquarters in the United States and business divisions all over the world is very people oriented, and the parent company is keen to implement as many global processes as possible, with customization to meet country-and business-specific needs. There is, for example, a global performance and development planning scheme (appraisal) which occurs annually at the same time across the branches worldwide. Other processes have local (country and division) components. The aim is to make management processes as easy as possible; most of the support material and process tracking is available online. Across the board, the responsibility for managing and developing staff is very much vested in local managers: the HR departments do not have a 'policing' role. All activity is based on objectives (organizational and divisional objectives cascaded down the management to individuals). Individuals are also responsible for their own development as much as their managers are and there is a wide range of internal and external development opportunities for those who want them (where they are relevant to the job).

Levels of Induction

The company's induction practice in the UK is about to change, partly due to feedback from staff about induction and partly through a need to communicate coherently at the organizational (global) level following a merger. Induction has three tiers. There is a global, online, Web-based induction programme for all employees, which is just about to be released following a period of piloting. This has four elements: company strategies, structure and process, values and behavior, reward, and other 'individual' issues. At the country (UK) level, a new induction day has also started recently. This is particularly in response to staff feedback. Although new starters understood their role and place in the local organization, they were less clear about how the different UK businesses fitted together and how their role contributed to the UK-wide business as a whole. New induction day is observed every 2-3 months to bring together new recruits from across the country along with the UK Director and Senior Managers from the range of UK businesses. It is called a Business and Networking Orientation Event. An interesting component is the 'interview': new recruits divide into small groups, each of which interviews one of the senior managers and then provides feedback to the rest (in front of the managers) regarding what they have learned from the interview. There is also a quiz (unchecked) that aims to reinforce some of the learning from the day.

At the local level, each manager has a checklist (available through the company intranet) which they are prompted to use as soon as an appointment has been accepted. The recruitment and induction processes are therefore linked. The checklist highlights things to do before the new recruit arrives, such as ordering equipment, setting up voicemail, what to do on the first day and subsequently. This includes booking new staff on the local health and safety induction, which is the only part of the local induction not conducted by the managers. New starters are also sent an email confirming their automatic booking on the UK induction and highlighting things they must do as in the first few weeks. It is very much the manager's responsibility to make sure that induction is done effectively. There is no central policing of whether the checklist is being compiled with. There is a very strong philosophy in the company that staffs are manager's responsibility. HR will check attendance at the

UK induction (but there is no check on effectiveness). This is expected to come through in performance monitoring processes (the performance planning process). Managers will set objectives for new staff usually for a six month period, with regular reviews. Any issues arising from an ineffective induction should be highlighted as part of this. Any senior manager can see the performance plans and ratings of the managers and staff in their divisions.

Performance planning process (appraisal)

There is no probation process as such, but short-term objectives are set for the new staff, which are fed into regular reviews and the annual performance planning process at the same time across the entire organization. The scheme is objective-oriented and results in a 'rating' which indicates to managers what salary increase might be applicable for the staff. The system is automated, so that the previous year's objectives and development actions are brought forward for review. If no progress has been made, the manger has to explain this. Development actions in particular are the responsibility of both the manager and the employee. Training or development needs identified are taken forward within the context of company-wide training and development programmes.

There are core programmes, many of which are delivered over the Web, and specific business-related programmes, which are available for all staff and supported by the central budget. Any job-specific needs not covered by core programmes are met by courses or other activities paid for from the manager's budget. The company uses a system of 'job families' with a guide to the development needed for each: there is an expectation (but no compulsion) that employees will undertake the recommended training or development prior to moving up to a new level. Again, feedback and evaluation on the effectiveness of the performance planning process is left to individuals and managers rather than being part of any centrally driven activity. There is an employee comments section on each appraisal form, which is recorded. An open door policy is also followed, allowing any member of staff to refer to a senior manager if they are dissatisfied. Many of the Web-based programs have initiated by staff who have highlighted gaps in their own and their teams' knowledge or understanding.

Although a global company with global process, the company's philosophy is very much one of management responsibility for people and development. Supporting frameworks, materials, and processes are available—largely accessible via the company intranet—and are expected to be used. Trust must play a significant part. The online induction is interesting and it would be good to revisit this in a few months to see what, if any, feedback there has been on its success. Similarly, the 'interview' component of the UK-wide induction is worth nothing, particularly the commitment that this requires from senior managers to attend and participate effectively. What is most interesting is what, whilst many apparently robust processes exist to support people management, it is the bottom line that is evaluated and measured (*i.e.*, the success of the business and how well people meet their objectives and contribute to business success) rather than the processes themselves; implementation of processes may sometimes become an end in itself in other organizations. Finally, the company does not have any external accreditations for people management and does not follow any external quality frameworks such as Investors in People or EPQM, at least in the UK.

QUESTIONS

1. Critically examine the induction process and its role in placement of employers.
2. Do you think the three-tier induction would be enough for successful placement of employees?
3. Can the localization of placement be improved? If so, how?
4. Does the performance planning have a role in placement?

Critically examine the individualization of performance planning vis-à-vis centralization and its effectiveness in the organization

CASE STUDY–3

Promotion Criteria

Mr. Ramchandran is the President of ABC Limited. Recently, it was decided by the Board of Directors that it would be profitable for the corporation to open its own Marketing Department. Mr. Ramchandran has been directed to pick up a person who he feels in capable of heading the department, and then putting this person in-charge of getting the department on its feet. After considering a number of good men, Mr. Ramchandran has narrowed the field down to two possible choices: Rajesh Mehta and Pramod Kumar.

Rajesh Mehta has a good track record with the company. He was hired eight year ago, and through the years he has shown a good ideal of drive and initiative in all of his endeavors. He is an aggressive young man, and has received the nickname of go-getter in his department. Although Mehta seems to be more concerned at times with ends rather than means, he is very efficient and he is considered a good leader by those who work under him. As one worker stated, "Although he can get rough with you at times, you always know where you stand with him, and when you have done a good job, he lets you know it." Mehta is also credited with accepting full responsibility, in all cases, and making quick decisions when action is called for.

Pramod Kumar has been with the company for eleven years. He is well liked by all in his department, and his work is first rate. Kumar's leadership style differs from Mehta's in that Kumar is not as aggressive and quick to act as Mehta. Before Kumar makes a decision, he generally consults others who he feels can contribute further information on a given subject. This often includes those who work under him. Those who work under Kumar consider him a good leader, and state that the atmosphere of participation produced by Kumar really encourages their utmost individual output while on the job. This can be seen by the production increase which soon occurred when Kumar became the head of his work-force.

QUESTIONS

1. If you were Mr. Ramchandran, whom would you select as the head of the Marketing Department? Why?
2. Will you give any weightage to the length of service in the organization? Why?

(Chhabra, T.N., Principles and Practice of Management, Dhanpat Rai & Co., Delhi, 1999)

CASE STUDY–4

Managing Outplacement at Rockey Mountain Oil

Rockey Mountain Oil has announced that it will reduce the scale of its U.S. operations and eliminate several hundred administrative positions at its Denver headquarters. The organization wants to provide outplacement assistance to the employees who will lose their jobs. However, it does not want to spend much money on outplacement.

The company had formed an outplacement committee consisting of top managers, most of the business. The committee has provided a recommendation for an outplacement program that has been accepted by Rockey Mountain's CEO, Barbara Robinson. This program consists of two parts. First, each laid-off employee's immediate supervisor will provide counseling and emotional support to his or her laid-off employees. All supervisors will receive an outplacement counseling packet that includes the recent article, "Ten Easy Steps to Help Employees Deal With Losing Their Jobs." Trailers will be placed at the far end of the company parking lot to serve as temporary offices for former employees, who can use them while searching for jobs and receiving counseling from their former supervisors.

Second, the outplacement program will help former employees develop job-search skills. Each employee will be given a copy of the book, What Color is Your Parachute ? Which provides tips on how to conduct a job search. In addition, each employee will be offered the opportunity to take a course at nearby Black Rock Junior College called "Introduction to Personnel Management."

QUESTIONS

1. At ARCO Transportation, a $1 billion division of Atlantic Richfield, employees are hired, promoted, and apprised according to how they fulfill the performance dimensions most valued by the company. One of these performance dimensions is "communication"—specifically, "listens and observe attentively, allowing an exchange of information" and "speaks and writes clearly and concisely, with an appropriate awareness of the intended audience." Would you say that ARCO apprises performance based on personality traits, job behaviour, or outcome achieved? On which of these aspects of performance do you think workers should be appraised?
2. Superficially, it seems preferable to use objective performance data (such as productivity figures), when available, rather than subjective supervisory ratings to assess employees. Why might objective data be less effective performance measures than subjective ratings?
3. How important are rating formats to the quality of performance ratings? What is the most important influence on rating quality?
4. What is comparability? How can it be maximized in performance appraisal?
5. "Occasionally an employee comes along who needs to be reminded who the boss is, and the appraisal is an appropriate place for such a reminder." Would the manager quoted here be likely to use a rational or a political approach to appraisal? Contrast the rational and political approaches. To what extent is possible to separate the two?
6. Do you think performance appraisal should still be done in quality-oriented organizations ? If so, what should be measured and how ?
7. What criteria do you think should be used to measure team performance ? What sources should be used for the appraisal ? Should individual performance still be measured ? Why or why not?

You're the owner of a 25-employee company that has just had a fantastic year. Everyone pulled together and worked hard to achieve the boost in company profits. Unfortunately, you need to sink most of those profits into paying your suppliers. All you can afford to give your workers is a 3 per cent pay raise across the board. At appraisal time, how would you communicate praise for a job well done coupled with your very limited ability to reward such outstanding performance? Now assume you can afford to hand out some handsome bonuses or raises. What would be the best way to evaluate employees when everyone has done exceptional work?

REFERENCES

1. Kenneth Blanchard and Spencer Johnson, *The one minute manager*, Morrow Publications, New York, 1982.
2. Donald l. Kirkpatrick, *Evaluating an house training programme, training and development journal,* 32 September, 1979.
3. Edgar H. Schein, "*The individual, The organization and career—A conceptual scheme*", Journal of Applied Behavioral Science, 1971.
4. Silver Gerald, *A Introduction to management*, West Publishing House, New York, 1981.
5. C.B. Memoria, *Personnel management*, Himalaya Publishing House, New Delhi, 1995.
6. Decenzo, David A, and Stephen P. Robbin, (1989), "*Personnel/human resources management*", New Delhi, Prentice Hall of India.
7. Yoder D., *Personnel management and industrial relations*, New Delhi, Prentice Hall of India, 1972.
8. Chris Agyris, *personality and development*, Harper, New York, 1957 and "*Future of laboratory education*", Journal of Applied Behavioral Science, Vol. 3.; No. 2, April 1967.
9. Tripathy P.C., and P.N. Reddy, *Principles of management*, Tata-McGraw Hill, New Delhi, 1994.
10. Beach D., *Personnel-The management of people at work*, New York: McMillan 1975; 56–59.
11. Armstrong M., *A Handbook of Personnel management practices*, London: Kogan Press, 1995.
12. Rudrabasavaraj M.N., *Dynamic personnel administration*, Himalaya Publishing House, New Delhi, 1991.
13. De Berlew and D.T., Hall: "*Socialization of managers; Effects of expectations on performances*", Administrative Science Quarterly, 11, New York, Jhon Wiley, 1966.
14. Yoder D. Henemann, H.G. Turnbull. G.J. and Stone C.H., *Hand book of personnel management and labor relations*, McGraw Hill Book Company, New York, 1958.
15. Shasi K. Gupta and Rosy joshi, *Human resource management*, Kalyani Publishers, New Delhi, India.
16. Chabaria T.N., *Human resource management: Concepts and issues*, Dhanpat Rai & Co, New Delhi, India.
17. Dwivedi R.S., *Management of human resources: A behavioral approach to personnel*, Oxford & IBH Publishing Co. New Delhi, India.
18. Mirza S. Saiyadain, *Human resource management*, Tata-McGraw Hill, New Delhi, 1996.
19. Yoder D., Heneman H.G., Turnbull J.G. and Stone C.H.; op. cit., p. 7, 31.
20. Heneman III H.G. *et.al.*, "*Personnel/Human resources management*", New Delhi; University Book Stall 1989; 248.
21. Yoder D., Heneman H.G., Turnbull J.G. and Stone C.H., *Handbook of personnel management and labour relations*, new york: McGraw Hill, 1958; 7:2.
22. Kempner T., *A handbook of management*, London Weidenfield and Nicolson, 1973, 310.
23. Harris O. Jeff, *Managing people at work concepts and cases in interpersonal behaviour*, Jhon Wiley & Sons, New York, 1976.

6

CHAPTER

MANAGING THE PERFORMANCES

6.1 INTRODUCTION

Evaluating employee performance is a key responsibility of managers. Performance appraisals, a powerful tool, provide to documented feedback on an employee's level of performance. They help determine continued employment, promotion, transfer, bonuses, and pay raises, and allow for improved communications between managers and employees. The actual performance appraisal documents become part of an employee's permanent record and can greatly influence lives and careers.

A poorly-managed evaluation system can be used against an employer in court. Managers must recognize the potential ramifications of failing to adequately manage employees' performance. They must be ready, willing, and able to communicate clear expectations, provide support to achieve those expectations, and develop and professionally present a factual and well-documented performance evaluation to ensure effectiveness of their review process and safeguard the company/organization from legal liability. Simply put, performance management helps organizations achieve their strategic goals. Rather than discarding the data accessibility previous systems fostered, performance management harnesses it to help ensure that an organization's data works in service to organizational goals to provide information that is actually useful in achieving them. And focus on the Operational Networking Processes between that performance levels.

All organizations currently apply a system of individual performance appraisal, although it does not apply uniformly to all levels of staff members. In the majority of organizations, the performance appraisal system applies either to all levels of staff members. Performance review which provides a formal opportunity for a manager to assess the staff member his/her progress towards agreed objectives. In most organizations, the annual performance appraisal process is initiated by the directors or heads of department in order to remind them of the appraisal requirements and the deadline for completion. Based on the information provided by the organizations on their performance appraisal systems, it can be concluded that most of the organizations have initiated changes in their performance management systems in order to improve service delivery and organizational efficiency. In particular, the setting of individual goals that are aligned with the objectives of the organization has been developed in most organizations. However, this practice can be improved or further developed in some of them. The present distribution of ratings in organizations does not allow for the implementation of an effective performance-related pay system. However, in the context of cultural change and on the basis of a robust performance appraisal system, this issue should be overcome. Related to this is the broadening of the appraisal base and the move to multiple assessor appraisals and committee reviews in a number of organizations, which would provide staff members with the opportunity to respond in case of disagreement. The idea that competencies are the foundation for effective performance in any job or position is widespread in all the organizations of the common system. Accordingly, an increasing number of organizations have recently developed competency frameworks, including core and functional competencies. Client orientation, with a few exceptions, has not been widely developed. Here again, the issue would be overcome if cultural change is effective and the leadership role of managers strengthened. A few organizations of the common system have included the accountability of managers as a key element of the new performance culture. In these organizations, all managers and staff with supervisory responsibility are held accountable for the effective use of the performance appraisal system as a management tool. In practice, the manager is responsible for matching performance at the department/unit and individual levels, and for the measurement and interpretation of goal achievement and related corrective actions. An exemplary performance agreement should lie at the heart of the rigorous management of individual performance. The development of this agreement would be based on dialogue between the manager and staff member. It would draw its coherence from the work plans and budget of the department or unit, the job description of the staff member and the competency framework of the organization. It would identify objectives that are specific, measurable, agreed, realistic and time-bound. A range of organizations have taken the necessary steps to move towards linking pay to performance, regardless of the related pay system *i.e.,* broad banding system or the current salary structure. However, it is clear that the need for cultural change is a major imperative. Organizations are conscious of this prerequisite and have worked (or are working) towards changing organizational cultures at all levels to emphasize results, performance and competitiveness.

The History

The history of performance appraisal is quite brief. Its roots in the early 20th century can be traced to Taylor's pioneering Time and Motion studies. But this is not very helpful, for the same may be said about almost everything in the field of modern human resources management. As a formal management procedure used in the evaluation of work performance; appraisal really dates from the time of the Second World War, not more than 60 years ago. In a broader sense, the practice of appraisal is a very ancient art. In the scale of things historical, it might well lay claim to being the world's second oldest profession. There is, says Dulewicz (1989), "... a basic human tendency to make judgments about those one is working with, as well as about oneself." Appraisal, it seems, is both inevitable and universal. In the absence of a carefully structured system of appraisal, people will tend to judge the work performance of others, including subordinates, naturally, informally and arbitrarily. The human inclination to judge can create serious motivational, ethical and legal problems in the workplace. Without a structured appraisal system, there is little chance of ensuring that the judgments made will be lawful, fair, defensible and accurate. Performance appraisal systems began as simple methods of income justification. That is, appraisal was used to decide whether or not the salary or wage of an individual employee was justified. The process was firmly linked to material outcomes. If an employee's performance was found to be less than ideal, a cut in pay would follow. On the other hand, if their performance was better than the supervisor expected, a pay rise was in order. Little consideration, if any, was given to the developmental possibilities of appraisal. If was felt that a cut in pay, or a rise, should provide the only required impetus for an employee to either improve or continue to perform well. Sometimes this basic system succeeded in getting the results that were intended; but more often than not, it failed. For example, early motivational researchers were aware that different people with roughly equal work abilities could be paid the same amount of money and yet have quite different levels of motivation and performance. It was found that other issues, such as morale and self-esteem, could also have a major influence. As a result, the traditional emphasis on reward outcomes was progressively rejected. In the 1950s in the United States, the potential usefulness of appraisal as tool for motivation and development was gradually recognized. The general model of performance appraisal, as it is known today, began from that time.

The Concept

Evaluating employee performance is a key responsibility of managers. Performance appraisals, a powerful tool, provide documented feedback on an employee's level of performance. They help determine continued employment, promotion, transfer, bonuses, and pay raises, and allow for improved communications between managers and employees. The actual performance appraisal documents become part of an employee's permanent record and can greatly influence lives and careers. A poorly-managed evaluation system can be used against an employer in court. Managers must recognize the potential ramifications of failing to adequately manage employees' performance. They must be ready, willing, and able to communicate clear expectations, provide support to achieve those expectations, and develop and professionally present a factual and well-documented performance evaluation to ensure effectiveness of their review process and safeguard the company/organization from legal liability. The aim of this training is to assist supervisors to understand how to properly manage and document the performance of those who report to them for employee motivation, performance, and productivity.

After employee selection, performance appraisal is arguably the most important management tool a farm employer has at his disposal. The performance appraisal, when properly carried out, can help to fine tune and reward the performance of present employees. In this chapter, we : (1) discuss the purpose for the performance appraisal, O.C. (2) introduce the *negotiated performance appraisal* approach, and (3) talk about the steps to achieving a worthwhile *traditional performance appraisal.*

Strengths of the negotiated performance appraisal are its ability to promote candid two-way communication between the supervisor and the person being appraised and to help the latter take more responsibility for improving performance. In contrast, in the traditional performance appraisal, the supervisor acts more as a judge of employee performance than as a coach. By so doing, unfortunately, the focus is on blame rather than on helping the employee assume responsibility for improvement.

Does that mean that the traditional performance appraisal approach should be discarded? Not at all. Experts in the field have often suggested that the performance appraisal should not be tied to decisions about pay raises. When appraisals are tied to pay raises, they argue, employees are more defensive and less open to change. So how should pay raise decisions be made, then, if not through the performance appraisal? I would suggest that the traditional performance appraisal can still play a critical role in management and is ideal for making pay raise decisions. But it is in the negotiated approach where employees can truly come to grips with what it is that they need to do to maximize performance, potential career advancement and earnings.

For the employee to have enough time to respond and improve, the negotiated performance appraisal should take place at least 9 to 12 months before the traditional one. There are no such strict time requirements when the traditional approach (used to make decisions about pay) precedes the negotiated one (used as a coaching tool).

Modern Appraisal

Performance appraisal may be defined as a structured formal interaction between a subordinate and supervisor, that usually takes the form of a periodic interview (annual or semi-annual), in which the work performance of the subordinate is examined and discussed, with a view to identifying weaknesses and strengths as well as opportunities for improvement and skills development. In many organizations but not all appraisal results are used, either directly or indirectly, to help determine reward outcomes. That is, the appraisal results are used to identify the better performing employees who should get the majority of available merit pay increases, bonuses, and promotions. By the same token, appraisal results are used to identify the poorer performers who may require some form of counseling, or in extreme cases, demotion, dismissal or decreases in pay. (Organizations need to be aware of laws in their country that might restrict their capacity to dismiss employees or decrease pay). Whether this is an appropriate use of performance appraisal—the assignment and justification of rewards and penalties—is a very uncertain and contentious matter.

Controversy, Controversy

Few issues in management stir up more controversy than performance appraisal. There are many reputable sources—researchers, management commentators, psychometricians—who have expressed doubts about the validity and reliability of the performance appraisal process. Some have even suggested that the process is so inherently flawed that it may be impossible to perfect it (see *Derven, 1990,* for example). At the other extreme, there are many strong advocates of performance appraisal. Some view it as potentially "... the most crucial aspect of organizational life" (*Lawrie,* 1990). Between these two extremes lie various schools of belief. While all endorse the use of performance appraisal, there are many different opinions on how and when to apply it. There are those, for instance, who believe that performance appraisal has many important employee development uses, but scorn any attempt to link the process to reward outcomes such as pay rises and promotions. This believes that the linkage to reward outcomes reduces or eliminates the developmental value of appraisals. Rather than an opportunity for constructive review and encouragement, the reward-linked process is perceived as judgmental, punitive and harrowing.

Neither is the desire to distort nor deny the truth confined to the person being appraised. Many appraisers feel uncomfortable with the combined role of judge and executioner.

Such reluctance is not difficult to understand. Appraisers often know their appraisees well, and are typically in a direct subordinate-supervisor relationship. They work together on a daily basis and may, at times, mix socially. Suggesting that a subordinate needs to brush up on certain work skills is one thing; giving an appraisal result that has the direct effect of negating a promotion is another. The result can be resentment and serious morale damage, leading to workplace disruption, soured relationships and productivity declines. On the other hand, there is a strong rivalries which claims that performance appraisal must unequivocally be linked to reward outcomes. The advocates of this approach say that organizations must have a process by which rewards—which are not an unlimited resource—may be openly and fairly distributed to those most deserving on the basis of merit, effort and results.

There is a critical need for remunerative justice in organizations. Performance appraisal—whatever its practical flaws—is the only process available to help achieve fair, decent and consistent reward outcomes. It has also been claimed that appraises themselves are inclined to believe that appraisal results should be linked directly to reward outcomes—and are suspicious and disappointed when told this is not the case. Rather than feeling relieved, appraises may suspect that they are not being told the whole truth, or that the appraisal process is a shame and waste of time.

This fact sheet gives introductory guidance. It:

- considers the performance management process and how it works.
- outlines the tools used in performance management.

Fully realized, performance management is a holistic process, bringing together many of the elements which go to make up the successful practice of people management, including in particular learning and development. But for this very reason, it is complex and capable of being misunderstood. This fact sheet cannot go into all the details, but it gives an overview so that readers will have a better understanding of the fundamentals when they undertake the necessary further readings.

What is Performance Management?

In their definitive text upon which this factsheet is based, Armstrong and Baron define performance management as 'a process which contributes to the effective management of individuals and teams in order to achieve high levels of organisational performance. As such, it establishes shared understanding about what is to be achieved and an approach to leading and developing people which will ensure that it is achieved'. They go on to stress that it is 'a strategy which relates to every activity of the organisation set in the context of its human resource policies, culture, style and communications systems. The nature of the strategy depends on the organisational context and can vary from organisation to organisation.'

In other words performance management should be:

- ***Strategic:*** It is about broader issues and longer-term goals.
- ***Integrated:*** It should link various aspects of the business, people management. and individuals and teams.

It should incorporate:

- ***Performance improvement:*** Throughout the organisation, for individual, team and organisational effectiveness.
- ***Development:*** Unless there is continuous development of individuals and teams, performance will not improve.
- ***Managing behaviour:*** Ensuring that individuals are encouraged to behave in a way that allows and fosters better working relationships.

Armstrong and Baron stress that at its best performance management is a tool to ensure that managers manage effectively; that they ensure the people or teams they manage:

- know and understand what is expected of them.
- have the skills and ability to deliver on these expectations.

- are supported by the organisation to develop the capacity to meet these expectations are given feedback on their performance.
- have the opportunity to discuss and contribute to individual and team aims and objectives.

It is also about ensuring that managers themselves are aware of the impact of their own behaviour on the people they manage and are encouraged to identify and exhibit positive behaviours.

Performance management may mean:

Performance measurement is the process of assessing progress toward achieving predetermined goals, while performance management is building on that process adding the relevant communication and action on the progress achieved against these predetermined goals (Bourne, M., Franco, M. and Wilkes, J. (2003). Corporate performance management. Measuring Business Excellence; 2003; 7, 3; p. 15).

- In *network performance management,* (*a*) A set of functions that evaluate and report the behaviour of telecommunications equipment and the effectiveness of the network or *network element,* and (*b*) A set of various subfunctions, such as gathering statistical *information,* maintaining and examining historical logs, determining *system performance* under natural and artificial conditions, and altering system modes of operation.

Source: From *Federal Standard 1037C* and from *MIL-STD-188.*

- In *organizational development* (OD), **performance** can be thought of as Actual Results vs. Desired Results. Any discrepancy, where Actual is less than Desired, could constitute the performance improvement zone. Performance management and improvement can be thought of as a cycle:

1. *Performance planning* where goals and objectives are established.
2. *Performance coaching* where a manager intervenes to give feedback and adjust performance.
3. "Performance appraisal is an organizational system comprising deliberate processes for determining staff accomplishments to improve staff effectiveness."

Performance appraisal is a formal, structured system that compares employee performance to established standards. Assessment of job performance is shared with employees being appraised through one of several primary *methods* of performance appraisals. Elements in performance appraisal methods are tailored to the organization's employees, jobs, and structure. They include objective criteria for measuring employee performance and ratings that summarize how well the employee is doing. Successful appraisal methods have clearly defined and explicitly communicated standards or expectations of employee performance on the job.

Performance appraisals, performance evaluation and assessment of job skills, personality and behaviour and tips for '360 degree feedback', '360° appraisals', 'skill-set' assessment and training needs analysis tips and tools.

This has several implications for performance appraisals, documents used, and the training of people who conduct staff appraisals. For example, while not unlawful, the inclusion of age and date-of-birth sections on appraisal forms is not recommended (as for all other documentation used in assessing people). For further guidance about the effects of Age Equality and Discrimination on performance appraisals, and other aspects of managing people.

Performance appraisals are essential for the effective management and evaluation of staff. Appraisals help develop individuals, improve organizational performance, and feed into business planning. Formal performance appraisals are generally conducted annually for all staff in the organization. Each staff member is appraised by their line manager.

Appraisals, Social responsibility and whole-person development

There is increasingly a need for performance appraisals of staff and especially managers, directors and CEO's, to include accountabilities relating to **corporate responsibility,** represented by various converging corporate responsibility concepts including: the 'Triple Bottom Line' ('Profit People Planet'); Corporate Social Responsibility (CSR); Sustainability; Corporate Integrity and Ethics; Fair Trade, etc. The organisation must decide the extent to which these accountabilities are reflected in job responsibilities, which would then naturally feature accordingly in performance appraisals. More about this aspect of responsibility is in the director's job descriptions section.

Significantly also, while this appraisal outline is necessarily a formal structure this does not mean that the development discussed with the appraisee must be formal and constrained. In fact the opposite applies. **Appraisals must address 'whole person' development**—not just job skills or the skills required for the next promotion.

Appraisals must not discriminate against anyone on the grounds of age, gender, sexual orientation, race, religion, disability, etc.

Performance Management and Organizational Development

When personnel are subjected to individually oriented training and development programs, the personnel performed well in the work environment. But this did not always mean that it impacted the general organizational functioning in any way.

Organizational Development was born in order that the organization's culture also gets impacted. Organizational development can be defined as a complex educational strategy intended to change the beliefs, attitudes, values and structure of organizations so that they can better adapt to new technologies, markets and challenges, and the rate of change itself. The output from performance management can be used as an input to Organizational Development. Continuous and Continual improvement can also be used in improving the Quality of Human resources in any scenario. While both are complementary they are not exactly the same, while continuous improvement gives a time frame for checks and improvement. Continual improvement means checking after each process. To become a firm using continual improvement, the organization should be a learning organization.

So performance management is about establishing a **culture** in which individuals and groups take responsibility for the continuous improvement of business processes and of their own skills, behaviour and contributions. It is about **sharing** expectations. Managers can clarify what they expect individual and teams to do; likewise individuals and teams can communicate their expectations of how they should be managed and what they need to do their jobs. It follows that performance management is about **interrelationships** and about improving the quality of relationships between managers and individuals, between managers and teams, between members of teams and so on, and is therefore a **joint** process. It is also about **planning**—defining expectations expressed as objectives and in business plans and about **measurement;** the old dictum is 'If you can't measure it, you can't manage it'. It should apply to **all employees,** not just managers, and to **teams** as much as individuals. It is a **continuous** process, not a one-off event. Last but not least, it is **holistic** and should pervade every aspect of running an organisation.

How does performance management work?

Because performance management is (or should be) so all-pervasive, it needs structures to support it. These should provide a framework to help people operate, and to help them to help others to operate. But it should not be a rigid system; there needs to be a reasonable degree of flexibility to allow people freedom to operate.

Performance management is a process, not an event. It operates as a continuous cycle. Corporate strategic goals provide the starting point for business and departmental goals, followed by agreement on performance and development, leading to the drawing up of plans between individuals and managers, with continuous monitoring and feedback supported by formal reviews.

Tools of Performance Management: It is impossible to go into details of each of the tools used by performance management, so the following paragraphs simply provide an outline.

Performance and development reviews

Many organisations without performance management systems operate 'appraisals' (see our factsheet on *Performance appraisal* for more information on this topic), in which an individual's manager regularly, usually annually, records performance, potential and development needs in a top-down process. It can be argued that the perceived defects of appraisal systems (that line managers regarded them as irrelevant, involving form-filling to keep the personnel department happy, and not as a normal process of management) led to the development of more rounded concepts of performance management. Nevertheless, organisations with performance management systems need to provide those involved with the opportunity to reflect on past performance as a basis for making development and improvement plans, and the performance and development review meeting (note the terminology; it is not appraisal) provides this chance. The meeting must be constructive, and various techniques can be used to conduct the sort of open, free-flowing and honest meeting needed, with the reviewee doing most of the talking.

Learning and development

Employee development is the main route followed by most organisations to improved organisational performance, which in turn requires an understanding of the processes and techniques of organisational, team and individual learning. Performance reviews can be regarded as learning events, in which individuals can be encouraged to think about how and in which ways they want to develop. This can lead to the drawing up of a Personal Development Plan (PDP) setting out the actions they propose to take (with the help of others, not least their managers) to develop themselves. To keep development separate from performance and salary discussions, development reviews may be held at other times *e.g.*, anniversary of joining an organization.

Increasing emphasis on talent management also means that many organizations are re-defining performance management to align it to the need to identify, nurture and retain talent. Development programmes are reflecting the needs of succession plans and seeking to foster leadership skills. However, too much of an emphasis on talent management may be damaging to overall development needs and every effort needs to be made to ensure that development is inclusive, accessible and focused on developing organizational capability.

Coaching

Coaching is an important tool in learning and development. Coaching is developing a person's skills and knowledge so that their job performance improves, leading to the achievement of organisational objectives. Coaching is increasingly recognised as a significant responsibility of line managers, and can play an important part in a PDP. They will take place during the review meetings, but also and more importantly should be carried out throughout the year. For some managers coaching comes naturally, but for many they may not and training may be needed to improve their skills. See our factsheet on *Coaching* for more information.

Objectives and performance standards

Objectives (some organisations prefer to use 'goals') describe something to be accomplished by individuals, departments and organizations over a period of time. They can be expressed as targets to be met (such as sales) and tasks to be completed by specified dates. They can be work-related, referring to the results to be attained, or personal, taking the form of developmental objectives for individuals. Objectives need to be defined and agreed. They will relate to the overall purpose of the job and define performance areas—all the aspects of the job that contribute to achieving its overall purpose. Targets then need to be set for each performance area, for example, increase 'sales by x per cent', 'reduce wastage by y per cent' ...

Along side objectives are performance standards. They are used when it is not possible to set time-based targets, or when there is a continuing objective which does not change significantly from one review period to the next and is a standing feature of the job. These should be spelled out in quantitative terms if possible, for example, speed of response to requests or meeting defined standards of accuracy.

Competences and competencies

Some organisations, but by no means all, use competences and competencies as components of performance management. Competences describe what people need to be able to do to perform a job well (the descriptions in National Vocational Qualifications are examples of competences). Competencies (more helpfully, 'behavioural competencies') are defined as the dimensions of behaviour that lie behind competent performance. Though the language used does not help in making the distinction, to perform well it is necessary both to be able to do a job at a technically competent level and to have behaviours that reinforce those technical skills; an obvious example of behaviour is the surgeon who needs a good bedside manner and to be able to communicate with colleagues, in addition to surgical skills. There are various techniques for measuring competence (some organisations prefer to use 'capability') and once an analysis has been made, it provides a tool for measuring performance and, of course, for providing development activities to help people meet the required standards.

Measurement

To improve performance, you need to know what current performance is. Measurement provides the basis for providing and generating feedback, and thus can build the platform for further success or identify where things are going less well so that corrective action can be taken. But what gets measured? Measure the wrong things, perhaps simply because they are easy to measure, and an entire performance management system can fall into disrepute. Use too many measures and you can't see the wood for the trees. For measuring performance, the achievement of objectives, levels of competency, standards of performance, and work outputs are used but the emphasis varies according to categories of staff—for example, a senior manager would be mainly measured by meeting objectives, but a production worker mainly by achieving outputs. Increasingly organizations are using more sophisticated measuring techniques such as balanced scorecards or ROI (return on investment).

Individual and team performance needs to be capable of being linked in an understandable manner to organisational performance, and there are various approaches to this. They include the 'balanced scorecard', a set of measures that looks at the business from customer, internal, learning and financial perspectives; the European Foundation for Quality Management, which indicates that customer satisfaction, employee satisfaction, and impact on society are achieved through leadership; and other economic measures, including traditional financial measures. Measures used will depend on the organisation; for example, public service organisations are likely to use different measures from private companies.

Pay

Performance management is often linked with **performance-related pay** (PRP), although by no means all organisations claiming to use performance management have PRP. Nevertheless, PRP is an important element in many performance management schemes because it is believed to motivate; it is said to deliver the message that performance and competence are important, and it is thought to be fair to reward people according to their performance, contribution or competence. Others, though, believe that other factors are more important than PRP in motivation; that it is usually based on subjective assessments of performance, that it inhibits teamwork because of its individualistic nature, and that it leads to 'short-termism'. An alternative to PRP is **competence-related pay,** which provides for pay progression to be linked to levels of competence that people have achieved, using a competence profile or framework. The difficulty here is measuring competence, and some organisations use a mix of PRP and competence-related pay. Further possible pay systems are **team-based pay,** a kind of PRP for teams; and **contribution-related pay** which means paying for results plus competence, and for past performance and future success.

Performance may be used to determine all or some aspects of pay. In many instances only non-consolidated bonus payments are linked to performance which tend to reflect organisational, team and individual performance whilst salary progression is linked to service, market rates and pay scales.

Many organisations believe that when performance management is linked to pay the quality of performance discussions will inevitably deteriorate.

Teams

Team working has become an important part of life in many organisations, and where teams are permanent or for long-standing projects, measures can be based on team performance. They will mainly be concerned with output, activity levels (*e.g.*, speed of servicing), customer service and satisfaction, and financial results. Indeed, team measures are not very different from those for individuals, and of course team members need to agree their objectives and receive feedback in the same way as if they were not part of a team. Other team members can contribute towards this, in a process of peer review.

360-degree feedback

360-degree feedback became increasingly talked about in the 1990s, if not widely used. It consists of performance data generated from a number of sources, who can include the person to whom the individual being assessed reports, people who report to them, peers (team colleagues or others in the organisation), and internal and external customers. It can also include self-assessment. 360-degree feedback is used mainly as part of a self-development or management development programme, and is felt to provide a more rounded view of people, with less bias than if an assessment is conducted by one individual.

Performance problem solving

Performance management is a positive process, and good systems will create a culture in which success is applauded. Nevertheless, poor performance will exist. It may be a result of inadequate leadership, bad management or defective systems of work, and if so, remedies (often involving learning and development) can be put in place. But individuals may under-perform and improvements can be achieved through continuing feedback and joint discussion between them and their managers, involving analysing and identifying the problem, establishing the reasons for the shortfall, and deciding and agreeing the action to be taken. If all this fails, disciplinary action may need to be taken, as in any of performance management is difficult to implement. It is about ownership by everyone in the organisation, and especially line managers—it is emphatically not about guardianship by personnel departments. Surveys suggest that individuals and managers in organisations with performance management systems quite like it, and especially its emphasis on personal development, although performance-rating (often linked to PRP) often provokes hostility. Schemes can be over-detailed and require too much form-filling, and there can be a lack of definition in terms of what is meant by performance and how to achieve it. Schemes can be less successful than they might be because of lack of training, especially at the beginning.

The keys to the successful introduction and application of performance management are:

- being clear about what is meant by performance.
- understanding what the organisation is and needs to be in its performance culture.
- being very focused on how individual employees will benefit and play their part in the process.
- understanding that it is a tool for line managers and its success will depend on their ability to use it effectively organisation.

Effective approaches to performance management operate at two levels:

- The organizational level, for example through the use of service or business planning and the cascading of organizational objectives.
- The individual and team level, for example through the use of appraisals and training and development needs analysis and plans.

Managing the performance of people at work is about linking service and wider organisational plans and objectives to individual jobs and members of staff. Effective performance management requires an ongoing dialogue with employees and this, in turn, needs continual reinforcement. This is because people may not make the link between their day-to-day roles and achieving objectives.

Fig: 6.1 The Steps Involved in Managing People's Performance

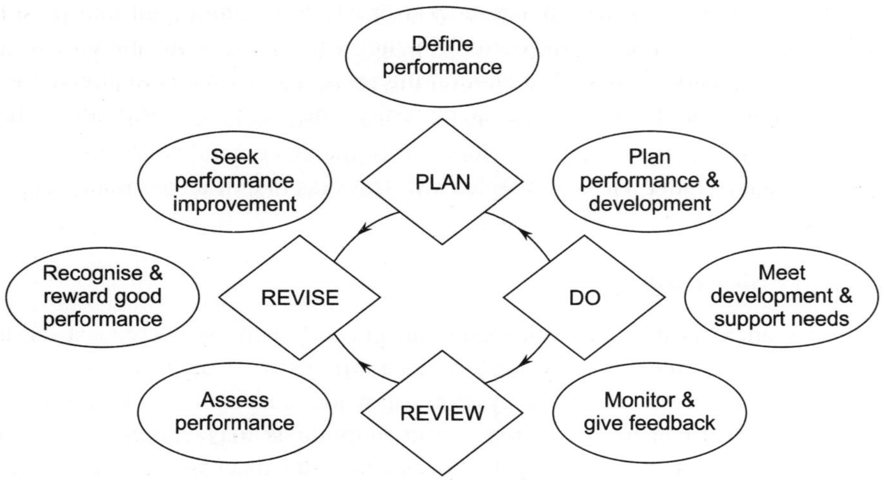

Source: ARMSTRONG, M. and BARON, A. (2004) Managing performance: Performance management in action. London: Chartered Institute of Personnel and Development.

PERFORMANCE EVALUATION

Would you study differently or exert a different level of effort for a college course graded on a pass-fail basis than for one in which letter grades from A to F are used? When I ask that question of students, I usually get an affirmative answer. Students typically tell me that they study harder when letter grades are at stake. Additionally, they tell me that when they take a course on a pass-fail basis, they tend to do just enough to ensure a passing grade.

This finding illustrates how performance evaluation systems influence behaviour. Major determinants of your in-class behaviour and out-of-class studying effort in college are the criteria and techniques your instructor uses to evaluate your performance. Of course, what applies in the college context also applies to employees at work. In this section, we show how the choice of a performance evaluation system and the way it's administered can be an important force influencing employee behaviour.

In many organizations, this inconsistency is aggravated by the practice of having separate wage and salary reviews, in which merit rises and bonuses are decided arbitrarily, and often secretly, by supervisors and managers.

Why Performance Appraisal?

Performance appraisal is a vehicle to: (1) validate and refine organizational actions (*e.g.*, selection, training); and (2) provide feedback to employees with an eye on improving future performance.

Validating and refining organizational action

Employee selection, training and just about any cultural or management practice—such as the introduction of a new pruning method or an incentive pay program—may be evaluated in part by obtaining worker performance data.

The evaluation may provide ideas for refining established practices or instituting new ones. For instance, appraisal data may show that a farm supervisor has had a number of interpersonal conflicts with other managers and employees. Some options include: (1) Paying more attention to interpersonal skills when selecting new supervisors, (2) Encouraging present supervisors to attend communication or conflict management classes at the local community college, or (3) Providing the supervisor one-on-one counseling.

Data from performance appraisals can also help farmers: (1) Plan for long-term staffing and worker development, (2) Give pay raises or other rewards, (3) Set up an employee counseling session, or (4) Institute discipline or discharge procedures.

For validation purposes (Chapter 3), it is easier to evaluate performance data when large numbers of workers are involved. Useful performance data may still be collected when workers are evaluated singly, but it may take years to obtain significant data trends.

Employee need for feedback

Although employees vary in their desire for improvement, generally workers want to know how well they are performing. A successful people need positive feedback and validation on a regular basis. Once an employee has been selected, few management actions can have as positive an effect on worker performance as encouraging affirmation. These are, in effect, good-will deposits, without which withdrawls cannot be made. This does not mean you should gloss over areas needing improvement. When presented in a constructive fashion, workers will often be grateful for information on how to improve shortcomings. Such constructive feedback, however, "can happen only within the context of listening to and caring about the person". In general, supervisors who tend to look for worker's positive behaviours—and do so in a sincere, non-manipulative way—will have less difficulty giving constructive feedback or suggestions. Furthermore, in the negotiated approach, the burden for performance analysis does not fall on the supervisor alone, but requires introspection on the part of the individual being evaluated.

Feedback may be *qualitative* or *quantitative*. Qualitative comments are descriptive, such as telling the shop mechanic you appreciate the timeliness and quality of his repairs. In contrast, quantitative feedback is based on numerical figures, such as the percentage of plant grafts that have taken. Some researchers feel feedback is particularly useful when workers have an achievement objective. Performance improved substantially in a number of settings when workers were given specific goals to achieve and received performance feedback. Next to employee discipline, performance appraisal interviews are probably the most dreaded management activity. Traditional performance appraisals put the supervisor in a position of being the expert on the employee's performance. Although the appraisal process can take place between supervisor and employee alone, the use of a third party can greatly facilitate the success of the approach. The message is thus clearly sent to all involved that this process is important to the farm organization.

Appraisals, social responsibility and whole-person development

There is increasingly a need for performance appraisals of staff and especially managers, directors and CEO's, to include accountabilities relating to **corporate responsibility,** represented by various converging *corporate responsibility concepts* including: the 'Triple Bottom Line' ('Profit People Planet'); Corporate Social Responsibility (CSR); Sustainability; Corporate Integrity and Ethics; Fair

Trade, etc. The organisation must decide the extent to which these accountabilities are reflected in job responsibilities, which would then naturally feature accordingly in performance appraisals. More about this aspect of responsibility is in the *directors job descriptions section*.

Significantly also, while this appraisal outline is necessarily a formal structure this does not mean that the development discussed with the appraise, must be formal and constrained. In fact the opposite applies. **Appraisals must address 'whole person' development** not just job skills or the skills required for the next promotion.

Appraisals must not discriminate against anyone on the grounds of age, gender, sexual orientation, race, religion, disability, etc.

PURPOSES OF PERFORMANCE EVALUATION

Performance evaluation serves a number of purposes in organizations (see Exhibit 16-3 for survey results on primary uses of evaluations). Management uses evaluations for general human resource decisions. Evaluations provide in put into such important decisions as promotions, transfers, and terminations. Evaluations identify training and development needs. They pinpoint employee skills and competencies that are currently inadequate but for which programs can be developed to remedy. Performance evaluations can be used as a criterion against which selection and development programs are validated. Newly hired employees who perform poorly can be identified through performance evaluation. Similarly, the effectiveness of training and development programs can be determined by assessing how well those employees who have participated do on their performance evaluation. Evaluations also fulfill the purpose of providing feedback to employees on how the organization views their performance. Furthermore, performance evaluations are used as the basis for reward allocations. Decisions as to who gets merit pay increases and other rewards are frequently determined by performance evaluations.

Each of these functions of performance evaluation is important. Yet their importance to us depends on the perspective we are taking. Several are clearly relevant to human resource management decisions. But our interest is in organizational behaviour. As a result, we shall be emphasizing performance evaluation in its role as a mechanism for providing feedback and as a determinant of reward allocations.

Performance appraisals seek to meet specific objectives. They include tell and sell, tell and listen, problem solving, and mixed model. *Tell and sell* is evaluative in nature. It is used for purely evaluative purposes. The supervisor coaches by telling the employee the evaluation and then persuading the employee to follow recommendations for improvement. *Tell and listen* is evaluative in nature. The supervisor coaches by telling the employee the evaluation and then listens to the employee's reactions to the evaluation in a nonjudgmental manner. *Problem solving* is developmental in nature and involves counseling. It is used for employee development purposes. The supervisor does not offer evaluation but lets the employee decide his or her weak areas and works with the employee to develop an action plan for improvement. The *mixed model* combines coaching and counseling. It is used for both evaluative and development purposes. The supervisor begins the appraisal with a problem-solving session and concludes with a more directive tell and sell approach.

Performance appraisals can achieve and contribute to when they are properly managed, for example:

- Performance measurement—transparent, short, medium and long-term.

- Clarifying, defining, redefining priorities and objectives.
- Motivation through agreeing helpful aims and targets.
- Motivation through achievement and feedback.
- Training needs and learning desires–assessment and agreement.
- Identification of personal strengths and direction–including unused hidden strengths.
- Career and succession planning–personal and organizational.
- Team roles clarification and team building.
- Organizational training needs assessment and analysis.
- Appraisee and manager mutual awareness, understanding and relationship.
- Resolving confusions and misunderstandings.
- Reinforcing and cascading organizational philosophies, values, aims, strategies, priorities, etc.
- Delegation, additional responsibilities, employee growth and development.
- Counseling and feedback.
- Manager development—all good managers should be able to conduct appraisals well—it's a fundamental process.
- The list goes on.

Performance Evaluation and Motivation: In this Chapter 7, considerable attention was given to the expectancy model of motivation. We argued that this model currently offers one of the best explanations of what influences the amount of effort an individual will exert on his or her job. A vital component of this model is performance, specifically the effort–performance and performance–reward linkages.

But what defines performance? In the expectancy model, it's the individual's performance evaluation. To maximize motivation, people need to perceive that the effort they exert leads to a favourable performance evaluation and that the favourable evaluation will lead to the rewards that the value.

Following the expectancy model of motivation, if the objectives that employees are expected to achieve are unclear, if the criteria for measuring those objectives are vague, and if the employees lack confidence that their efforts will lead to a satisfactory appraisal of their performance or believe that there will be an unsatisfactory payoff by the organization when their performance objectives are achieved, we can expect individuals to work considerably below their potential.

What do we Evaluate?

The criteria or criterion that management chooses to evaluate, when appraising employee performance, will have a major influence on what employees do. Two examples illustrate this.

In a public employment agency, which served workers seeking employment and employers seeking workers, employment interviewers were appraised by the number of interviews they conducted. Consistent with the thesis that the evaluating criteria influence behaviour, interviewers emphasized the number of inter placements client in jobs.

A management consultant specializing in police research noticed that, in one community, officers would come on duty for their shift, proceed to get into their police cars, drive to the highway that cut through the town, and speed back and forth along this highway for their entire shift. Clearly this fast cruising had little to do with good police work, but this behaviour made considerably more sense once the consultant learned that the community's city council used mileage on police vehicles as an evaluative measure of police effectiveness.

These examples demonstrate the importance of criteria in performance evaluation. This, of course, begs the question: What should management evaluate? The three most popular sets of criteria are individual task outcomes, behaviours, and traits.

Individual Task Outcomes if ends count rather than means, then management should evaluate an employee's task outcomes. Using task outcomes, a plant manager could be judged on criteria such as quantity produced, scrap generated, and cost per unit of production. Similarly, a salesperson could be assessed on overall sales volume in his or her territory, dollar increase in sales, and number of new accounts established.

Behaviours in many cases, it is difficult to identify specific outcomes that can be directly attributable to an employee's actions. This is particularly true of personnel in staff positions and individuals whose work assignments are intrinsically part of a group effort. In the latter case, the group's performance may be readily evaluated, but the contribution of each group member may be difficult or impossible to identify clearly. In such instances, it is not unusual for management to evaluate the employee's behaviour. Using the previous examples, behaviours of a plant manager that could be used for performance evaluation purposes might include promptness in submitting his or her monthly reports or the leadership style that the manager exhibits. *Pertinent* salesperson behaviours could be average number of contact calls made per day or sick days used per year.

Note that these behaviours needn't be limited to those directly related to individual productivity. As we pointed out in our previous discussion on organizational citizenship behaviour (see specifically Chapters 1 and 4), helping others, making suggestions for improvements, and volunteering for extra duties make work groups and organizations more effective. So including subjective or contextual factors in a performance evaluation—as long as these factors contribute to organizational effectiveness—may not only make sense; they may also improve coordination, teamwork, cooperation, and overall organizational performance.

Traits the weakest set of criteria, yet one that is still widely used by organizations, is individual traits. We say they are weaker than either task outcomes or behaviours because they are farthest removed from the actual performance of the job itself. Traits such as having "a good attitude," showing "confidence," being "dependable," "looking busy," or possessing "a wealth of experience" may or may not be highly correlated with positive task outcomes, but only the native would ignore the reality that such traits are frequently used in organizations as criteria for assessing an employee's level of performance.

Who should Do the Evaluating?

Who should evaluate an employee's performance? The obvious answer would seem to be his or her immediate boss! By tradition, a manager's authority typically has included appraising sub-ordinates' performance. The logic behind this tradition seems to be that since managers are held responsible for their employees' performance, it only makes sense that these managers do the evaluating of their performance. But that logic may be flawed. Others may actually be able to do the job better.

Immediate Superior: As we implied, about 95 per cent of all performance evaluations at the lower and middle levels of the organization are conducted by the employee's immediate boss. Yet a number of organizations are recognizing the drawbacks to using this source of evaluation. For instance, many bosses feel unqualified to evaluate the unique contributions of each of their employees. Others resent being asked to "play God" with their employees' careers. Additionally, with many of today's organizations using self-managed teams, and other organizing devices that distance bosses from their employees, an employee's immediate superior may not be a reliable judge of that employee's performance.

Peers: Peer evaluations are one of the most reliable sources of appraisal data. Why? First, peers are close to the action. Daily interactions provide them with a comprehensive view of an employee's job performance. Second, using peers as raters results in a number of independent judgments. A boss can offer only a single but peers can provide multiple appraisals. And the average of several ratings is often more reliable than a single evaluation. On the downside, peer evaluations can suffer from co-workers' unwillingness to evaluate one another and from biases based on friendship or animosity.

Self-evaluation: Having employees evaluate their own performance is consistent with values such as self-management and empowerment. Self-evaluations get high marks from employees themselves; they tend to lessen employees' defensiveness about the appraisal process; and they make excellent vehicles for stimulating job performance discussions between employees and their superiors. However, as you might guess, they suffer from over inflated assessment and self-serving bias. Moreover, self-evaluations are often low in agreement with superiors' ratings. Because of these serious drawbacks, self-evaluations are probably better suited to developmental uses than evaluative purposes.

Immediate subordinates: A fourth judgment source is an employee's immediate subordinates. For instance, Datatec Industries, a maker of in-store to computer systems, uses this form of appraisal. The company's president says it's consistent with the firm's core values of honesty, openness, and employee empowerment.

Immediate subordinates' evaluations can provide accurate and detailed in formation about a manager's behaviour because the evaluators typically have frequent contact with the evaluate. The obvious problem with this form of rating is fear of reprisal from bosses given unfavorable evaluations. Therefore, respondent anonymity is crucial if these evaluations are to be accurate.

360-Degree evaluations: The latest approach to performance evaluation is the use of 360-degree evaluations. It provides for performance feedback from the full circle of daily contacts that an employee might have, ranging from mailroom personnel to customers to bosses to peers (see Exhibit 16-4, page 119). The number of appraisals can be as few as three or four evaluations or as many as 25; with most organizations collecting five to ten per employee.

A recent survey shows that about 12 per cent of American organizations are using full 360-degree programs but the trend is growing. Companies currently using this approach include Alcoa, Du Pont, Levi Strauss, Honeywell, UPS, Sprint, Amoco, AT & T, and W.L. Gore & Associates.

What's the appeal of 360-degree evaluations? They fit well into organizations that have introduced teams, employee involvement, and TQM programs. By relying on feedback from co-workers, customers, and subordinates, these organizations are hoping to give everyone more of a sense of participation in the review process and gain more accurate readings on employee performance.

Fig. 6.2

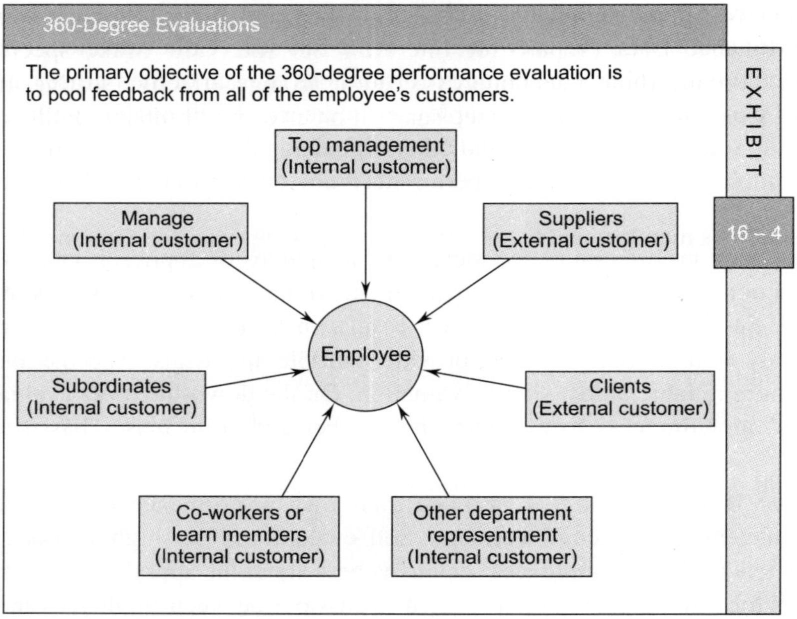

Source: Adapted from *Personal journal,* November 1994, p. 100.

METHODS AND PROCESS OF PERFORMANCE EVALUATION

Steps in a Performance Review Do **Background** work for the Performance Review:

- Clarify job description and responsibilities.
- Clarify employee development interests and needs.
- List specific development areas for concentration.
- Review performance objectives and performance standards.
- Review progress toward objectives through ongoing feedback and periodic discussions.
- Decide on Purpose(s) Typically the purposes include.
- Giving employees answers to:
  - What am I expected to do?
  - How well am I doing?
  - What are my strengths and weaknesses?
  - How can I do a better job? How can I contribute more?

Other purposes include providing information about work performance judgmental-provide basis for reward allocation, promotions, transfers, lay offs; identify high potential employees developmental-foster work improvement, identify training and development opportunities, develop ways to overcome obstacles, barriers; establish supervisor employee agreement on expectations sometimes these two don't mix well translating organizational goals into individual job objectives communicating expectations regarding employee. performance providing feedback; coach on how to achieve objectives diagnosing strengths and weaknesses of employees determining a development plan for improving job performance. Define the behavioural aspects of performance and analyze performance; Identify specific problem to be solved identify specific levels of performance communicate all data to individuals about performance, Gather Performance Data Develop specific, measurable, reasonable goals for each worker-make sure the worker accepts the goal, Choose Performance Review Approach (*e.g.*, Tell and sell, Tell and listen, Problem-solving), Evaluate (Interpret), Performance Data Prepare for Interview Set Interview Make specific appointment (at least an hour), Private (hold telephone calls, etc.); arrange effective seating arrangement Use Characteristics of Constructive Feedback (see handout on effective feedback) Follow-up Action Plan for Future.

General:

- Ideally PA allows management to specify what employee must do; combines feedback and goal setting.
- Everyone involved needs to recognize that performance appraisal involves human judgment and information processing; can never be totally objective or infallible.
- System should aim to be easy to operate, easy to explain, easy to maintain, easy to administer.
- System should be job related, relevant, sensitive, reliable, acceptable, practical, open, fair, and useful.
- Ratee should participate in the development.
- Need to take legal issues into account.

This explained what we evaluate and who should do the evaluating. Now we ask: How do we evaluate an employee's performance? That is, what are the specific techniques for evaluation? This section reviews the major performance evaluation methods.

Written Essays Probably the simplest method of evaluation is to write a narrative describing an employee's strengths, weaknesses, past performance, potential, and suggestions for improvement. The written essay requires no complex forms or extensive training to complete. But the results often reflect the ability of the writer. A good or bad appraisal may be determined as much by the evaluator's writing skill as by the employee's actual level of performance.

Critical Incidents focus the evaluator's attention on those behaviours that are key in making the difference between executing a job effectively and executing it ineffectively. That is, the appraiser writes down anecdotes that describe what the employee did that was especially effective or ineffective.

The key here is that only specific behaviours, not vaguely defined personality traits, are cited. A list of critical incidents provides a rich set of examples from which the employee can be shown those behaviours that are desirable and those that call for improvement.

Graphic Rating Scales one of the oldest and most popular methods of evaluation is the use of graphic rating scales. In this method, a set of performance factors, such as quantity and quality of work, depth of knowledge, cooperation, loyalty, attendance, honesty, and initiative, is listed. The evaluator then goes down the list and rates each on incremental scales. The scales typically specify five points, so a factor such as job knowledge might be rated 1 ("poorly informed about work duties") to 5 ("has complete mastery of all phases of the job").

Why graphic ratings are scales so popular? Though they don't provide the depth of information that essays or critical incidents do, they are less time consuming to develop and administer. They also allow for quantitative analysis and comparison.

Behaviourally Anchored Rating Scales behaviourally anchored rating scales (BARS) combine major elements from the critical incident and graphic rating scale approaches: The appraiser rates the employees based on items along a continuum, but the points are examples of actual behaviour on the given job rather than general descriptions or traits.

BARS specify definite, observable, and measurable job behaviour. Examples of job-related behaviour and performance dimensions are found by asking participants to give specific illustrations of effective and ineffective behaviour regarding each performance dimension. These behavioural examples are then translated into a set of performance dimensions, each dimension having varying levels of performance. The results of this process are behavioural descriptions, such as anticipates, plans, executes, solves immediate problems, carries out orders, and handles emergency situations.

Multi-person Comparisons evaluate one individual's performance against the performance of one or more others. It is a relative rather than an absolute measuring device. The three most popular comparisons are group order ranking, individual ranking, and paired comparisons.

The group order ranking requires the evaluator to place employees into a particular classification, such as top one-fifth or second one-fifth. This method is often used in recommending students to graduate schools. Evaluators are asked whether the student ranks in the top 5 per cent of the class, the next 5 per cent, the next 5 per cent, and so forth. But when used by managers to appraise employees, managers deal with all their subordinates. Therefore, if a rater has 20 employees, only four can be in the top fifth and, of course, four must also be relegated to the bottom fifth.

The individual ranking approach rank-orders employees from best to worst. If the manager is required to appraise 30 employees, this approach assumes that the difference between the first and second employee is the same as that between the twenty-first and twenty-second. Even though some of the employees may be closely grouped, this approach allows for no ties. The result is a clear ordering of employees, from the highest performer down to the lowest.

The paired comparison approach compares each employee with every other employee and rates each as either the superior or the weaker member of the pair. After all paired comparisons are made, each employee is assigned a summary ranking based on the number of superior scores he or she achieved. This approach ensures that each employee is compared against every other, but it can obviously become unwieldy when many employees are being compared.

Multiperson comparisons can be combined with one of the other methods to blend the best from both absolute and relative standards. For example, in an effort to deal with grade inflation, Dartmouth College a few years back changed its transcripts to include not only a letter grade but also class size and class average. So a prospective employer or graduate school can now look at two students who each got a B in their physical geology courses and draw considerably different conclusions about each because next to one grade it says the average grade was a C, while next to the other it says the average grade was a B+. Obviously, the former student performed relatively better than did the latter.

Practical Approaches to Performance Appraisal

According to the Creamer and Janosik that performance appraisal is not about a single event, such as completing a standard review form, but rather a process that is ongoing. Appraisal activities, as an ongoing process, should connect the process to organizational functioning and have as their focus staff improvement, not simply salary adjustment and/or disciplinary action. Davis (2001) proposed a model of performance appraisal for use in student affairs that includes three phases: Getting started/renewal, Achievement, and Evaluation. The model includes detailed suggestions for conducting an appraisal interview.

Creamer and Janosik outline several approaches to performance appraisal, including behaviour based approaches, results-focused approaches, and appraisals of team performance.

Behaviour-Based Approaches: These approaches tend to use specific performance factors to evaluate staff. Measures of performance can be either quantitative or qualitative.

One approach is the *conventional rating scale*. These scales use words or phrases to describe the degree to which certain behaviours or characteristics are displayed. Categories for behaviourally anchored scales can be created from job descriptions. If there are no appropriate behaviours or characteristics within job descriptions, supervisors should work with staff to determine what behaviours and characteristics would be most useful in an appraisal setting.

Another way of approaching this type of appraisal is the *behaviourally anchored scale*. In this approach, broad categories of practice are identified, ideally through collaborations between supervisors and staff. Specific job behaviours are then linked to the categories. Measures of staff member behaviour are rated on a scale in relation to specific behaviour items, such as "understands department functions."

Henderson (1980) notes that job-dimensions usually yield similar broad categories, such as planning, setting priorities, and responsiveness to supervision. Categories such as these may be useful in framing evaluation criteria in this approach to appraisal.

Another means of approaching behaviour-based appraisal is the *behavioural frequency scale*. Here, desired behaviours are described and the staff member is evaluated on how often those behaviours occur.

The *weighted checklist* is another way of approaching behaviour-based appraisal. This method provides a list of performance related statements that are weighted. Staff members are judged on a scale indicating the degree to which the statement accurately describes performance.

A final approach to behaviour-based appraisal is the forced-choice method. Here, a list of performance related statements about job performance are evaluated on how well they discriminate among staff and how important they are to unit or institutional performance. Discrimination and desirability statements are placed on a grid in clusters that differ on discrimination but are closely related in desirability. Discrimination and desirability are multiplied to yield a total scale score.

Results-Focused Approaches: *Creamer and Janosik* (in press) note that there are both advantages and disadvantages to results-based performance appraisal approaches. On the positive side, they produce short and long-term results in the context of original performance and organizational objectives, are generally perceived as fair, tend to generate high levels of commitment to the organization, and they encourage a high level of participation and are thus defensible. On the negative side, they can be overly results oriented especially in educational organizations, and they may be inflexible.

If supervisors determine that the advantages outweigh disadvantages, results-focused approaches may be incorporated. There are two general techniques of enacting results-focused approaches: Management by Objectives (MBO) and Accountabilities and Measures (*Grote, 1996*).

MBO emphasizes participation by all organization members. Grote identifies the following core elements in MBO:

- Formation of trusting and open communication throughout the organization.
- Mutual problem solving and negotiations in the establishment of objectives.
- Creation of win-win relationships.

- Organizational rewards and punishments based on job-related performance and achievement.
- Minimal uses of political games, forces, and fear.
- Development of a positive, proactive, and challenging organizational climate.

Additionally, Grote defines eight steps in the MBO process:

1. Formulate long-range goals and strategic plans.
2. Develop overall organizational objectives.
3. Establish derivative objectives for major operating units.
4. Set realistic and challenging objectives and standards of performance for members of the organization.
5. Formulate action plans for achieving the stated objectives.
6. Implement the action plans and take corrective action when required to ensure the attainment of objectives.
7. Periodically review performance against established goals and objectives.
8. Appraise overall performance, reinforce behaviour, and strengthen motivation.

Supervisors need to ensure that appraisal processes are congruent with objectives and goals. An *MBO rating form* needs to provide space to list staff member objectives in order of importance, as well as space for the evaluator to describe staff member performance using a mutually agreed upon scale. Categories of performance can include: distinguished performance, competent performance, provisional performance, and inadequate performance.

Accountabilities and Measures approaches involve the supervisor and staff member agreeing on accountability and performance factors and including them in the job description. Performance is then forecast for each factor to enable quantifiable measures for each factor. An *Accountabilities and Measures form* can be created, with performance factor categories.

Performance Appraisals Process

- ***Prepare:*** Prepare all materials, notes agreed tasks and records of performance, achievements, incidents, reports etc. anything pertaining to performance and achievement—obviously include the previous performance appraisal documents and a current job description. A good appraisal form will provide a good natural order for proceedings, so use one. If your organization doesn't have a standard appraisal form then locate one, or use the template below to create one, or download and/or adapt the appraisal forms from this page. Whatever you use, ensure you have the necessary approval from your organization, and understand how it works. Organize your paperwork to reflect the order of the appraisal and write down the sequence of items to be covered. If the appraisal form includes a self-assessment section and/or feedback section (good ones do) ensure this is passed to the appraisee suitably in advance of the appraisal with relevant guidance for completion. A sample performance appraisal template is available free below, which you can adapt and use to create your own form. Part of your preparation should also consider 'whole-person' development—beyond and outside of the job skill-set—as might inspire and appeal to the appraisees. Many people are not particularly interested in job skills training, but will be very interested, stimulated and motivated by other learning and development experiences. Get to know what your people are good at outside of their work. People's natural talents and passions often contain significant overlaps with the attributes, behaviours and maturity that are required and valued in the workplace. Use your imagination in identifying these opportunities to encourage 'whole-person' development and you will find appraisals can become very positive and enjoyable activities. Appraisals are not just about job performance and job skills training. Appraisals should focus on helping the 'whole person' to grow and attain fulfillment.

- ***Inform:*** Inform the appraisee—ensure the appraisee is informed of a suitable time and place (change it if necessary), and clarify purpose and type of appraisal—give the appraisee the chance to assemble data and relevant performance and achievement records and materials. If the appraisal form does not imply a natural order for the discussion then provide an agenda of items to be covered.
- ***Venue:*** Ensure a suitable venue is planned and available—private and free from interruptions —observe the same rules as with recruitment interviewing—avoid hotel lobbies, public lounges, canteens—privacy is absolutely essential (it follows also that planes, trains and automobiles are entirely unsuitable venues for performance appraisals......).
- ***Layout*:** Room layout and seating are important elements to prepare also - don't simply accept whatever layout happens to exist in a borrowed or hired room - layout has a huge influence on atmosphere and mood—irrespective of content, the atmosphere and mood must be relaxed and informal—remove barriers—don't sit in the boss's chair with the other person positioned humbly on the other side of the desk; you must create a relaxed situation, preferably at a meeting table or in easy chairs—sit at an angle to each other, 90 degrees ideally—avoid face to face, it's confrontational.
- ***Introduction:*** Relax the appraisee—open with a positive statement, smile, be warm and friendly—the appraisee may well be terrified; it's your responsibility to create a calm and non-threatening atmosphere. Set the scene—simply explain what will happen—encourage a discussion and as much input as possible from the appraisee—tell them it's their meeting not yours. Confirm the timings, especially finishing time. If helpful and appropriate begin with some general discussion about how things have been going, but avoid getting into specifics, which are covered next (and you can say so). Ask if there are any additional points to cover and note them down so as to include them when appropriate.
- ***Review and measure*:** Review the activities, tasks, objectives and achievements one by one, keeping to distinct separate items one by one—avoid going off on tangents or vague unspecific views. If you've done your preparation correctly you will have an order to follow. If something off-subject comes up then note it down and say you'll return to it later (and ensure you do). Concentrate on hard facts and figures, solid evidence—avoid conjecture, anecdotal or non-specific opinions, especially about the appraisee. Being objective is one of the greatest challenges for the appraiser—as with interviewing, resist judging the appraisee in your own image, according to your own style and approach—facts and figures are the acid test and provide a good neutral basis for the discussion, free of bias and personal views. For each item agree a measure of competence or achievement as relevant, and according to whatever measure or scoring system is built into the appraisal system. This might be simply a yes or no, or it might be a percentage or a mark out of ten, or an A, B, C. Reliable review and measurement requires reliable data—if you don't have the reliable data you can't review and you might as well re-arrange the appraisal meeting. If a point of dispute arises, you must get the facts straightened out before making an important decision or judgment, and if necessary defer to a later date.

- ***Agree an action plan*****:** An overall plan should be agreed with the appraisee, which should take account of the job responsibilities, the appraisee's career aspirations, the departmental and whole organization's priorities, and the reviewed strengths and weaknesses. The plan can be staged if necessary with short, medium and long-term aspects, but importantly it must be agreed and realistic.
- ***Agree specific objectives*****:** These are the specific actions and targets that together form the action plan. As with any delegated task or agreed objective these must adhere to the SMARTER rules—specific, measurable, agreed, realistic, time-bound, enjoyable, recorded. If not, don't bother. The objectives can be anything that will benefit the individual, and that the person is happy to commit to. When helping people to develop, you are not restricted to job-related objectives, although typically most objectives will be.
- ***Agree necessary support*****:** This is the support required for the appraisee to achieve the objectives, and can include training of various sorts (external courses and seminars, internal courses, coaching, mentoring, shadowing, distance-learning, reading, watching videos, attending meetings and workshops, workbooks, manuals and guides; anything relevant and helpful that will help the person develop towards the standard and agreed task. Also consider training and development that relates to 'whole-person development' outside of job skills. This might be a hobby or a talent that the person wants to develop. Developing the whole person in this way will bring benefits to their role, and will increase motivation and loyalty. The best employers understand the value of helping the whole person to develop. Be careful to avoid committing to training expenditure before suitable approval, permission or availability has been confirmed—if necessary discuss likely training requirements with the relevant authority before the appraisal to check. Raising false hopes is not helpful to the process.
- ***Invite any other points or questions*****:** Make sure you capture any other concerns.
- ***Close positively*****:** Thank the appraisee for their contribution to the meeting and their effort through the year, and commit to helping in any way you can.
- ***Record main points, agreed actions and follow-up*****:** Swiftly follow-up the meeting with all necessary copies and confirmations, and ensure documents are filed and copied to relevant departments, (HR, and your own line manager typically).

SUGGESTIONS FOR IMPROVING PERFORMANCE EVALUATIONS

The performance evaluation process is a potential mine field of problems. For instance, evaluators can make leniency, *halo*, and similarity errors, or use the process for political purposes. They can unconsciously inflate evaluations (positive leniency), understate performance (negative leniency), or allow the assessment of one characteristic to unduly influence the assessment of other characteristics (the *halo* error). Some appraisers bias their evaluations by unconsciously favouring people who have qualities and traits similar to themselves (the similarity error). And, of course, some evaluators see the evaluation process as a political opportunity to overtly reward or punish employees they like or dislike. While there are no protections that will guarantee accurate performance evaluations, the following suggestions can significantly help to make the process more objective and fair.

Emphasize Behaviours Rather Than Traits Many traits often considered to be related to good performance may, in fact, have little or no performance relationship. For example, traits such as loyalty, initiative, courage, reliability, and self-expression are intuitively appealing as desirable characteristics in employees. But the relevant question is: Are individuals who are evaluated as high on those traits higher performers than those who rate low? We can't answer this question easily. We know that there are employees who rate high on these characteristics and are poor performers. We can find others who are excellent performers but do not score well on traits such as these. Our conclusion is that traits such as loyalty and initiative may be prized by managers, but there is no evidence to support that certain traits will be adequate synonyms for performance in a large cross-section of jobs.

Another weakness of trait evaluation is the judgment itself. What is "loyalty"? When is an employee "reliable"? What you consider "loyalty," I may not. So traits suffer from weak interrater agreement.

Document Performance Behaviours in a Diary Diaries help evaluators to better organize information in their memory. The evidence indicates that by keeping a diary of specific critical incidents for each employee, evaluations tend to be more accurate and less prone to rating errors. Diaries, for instance, tend to reduce leniency and halo errors because they encourage the evaluator to focus on performance-related behaviours rather than traits.

Use Multiple Evaluators as the number of evaluators increases, the probability of attaining more accurate information increases. If rater error tends to follow a normal curve, an increase in the number of appraisers will tend to find the majority congregating about the middle. You see this approach being used in athletic competitions in such sports as diving and gymnastics. A set of evaluators judges a performance, the highest and lowest scores are dropped, and the final performance evaluation is made up from the cumulative scores of those remaining. The logic of multiple evaluators applies to organizations as well.

If an employee has had ten supervisors, nine having rated there excellent and one poor, we can discount the value of the one poor evaluation. Therefore, by moving employees about within the organization so as to gain a number of evaluations or by using multiple assessors (as provided in 360-degree appraisals), we increase the probability of achieving more valid and reliable evaluations.

Evaluate Selectively Appraisers should evaluate in only those areas in which they have some expertise. If raters make evaluations on only those dimensions on which they are in a good position to rate, we increase the interrater agreement and make the evaluation a more valid process. This approach also recognizes that different organizational levels often have different orientations toward ratees and observe them in different settings. In general, therefore, we would recommend that appraisers should be as close as possible, in terms of organizational level, to the individual being evaluated. Conversely, the more levels that separate the evaluator and evaluate, the less opportunity the evaluator has to observe the individual's behaviour and, not surprisingly, the greater the possibility for inaccuracies.

Train Evaluators**:** If you can't find good evaluators, the alternative is to make good evaluators. There is substantial evidence that training evaluators can make them more accurate raters.

Common errors such as halo and leniency have been minimized or eliminated in workshops in which managers practice observing and rating behaviours. These workshops typically run from one to three days, but allocating many hours to training may not always be necessary. One case has been cited in which both halo and leniency errors were decreased immediately after exposing evaluators to explanatory training sessions lasting only five minutes. But the effects of training do appear to diminish over time. This suggests the need for regular refresher sessions.

Provide Employees with Due Process**:** The concept of due process can be applied to appraisals to increase the perception that employees are treated fairly. Three features characterize due process systems: 1. Individuals are provided with adequate notice of what is expected of them; 2. All relevant evidence to a proposed violation is aired in a fair hearing so individuals affected can respond; and 3. The final decision is based on the evidence and free from bias.

There is considerable evidence that evaluation systems often violate employees' due process by providing them with infrequent and relatively general performance feedback, allowing them little input into the appraisal process, and knowingly introducing bias into performance ratings. However, when due process has been part of the evaluation system, employees report positive reactions to the appraisal process, perceive the evaluation results as more accurate, and express in creased intent to remain with the organization.

Performance Development Plan

Developing employee performance furthers the mission of the organization and enhances the overall quality of the workforce within the Organisation by promoting a climate of continuous learning and professional growth; helping to sustain employee performance at a level which meets or exceeds expectations; enhancing job or career-related skills, knowledge and experience; enabling employees to keep abreast of changes in their fields; promoting affirmative action objectives; and motivating employees. Performance development plans may be considered at each stage of the performance management process.

An important component of the performance management process is development of employees' work-related skills, knowledge and experience. The development process offers another opportunity for you and your employee to work collaboratively to improve or build on his or her performance and to contribute to organizational effectiveness.

Continuous Learning

Development of employee skills, knowledge and experience is essential in today's rapidly changing workplace. In order for the organization to remain competitive and to retain its reputation for excellence, employees should have *up-to-the-minute* information and the ability to use new technologies, adapt to organizational change, work in flatter organizations in which cross-functional skills and knowledge are required, and work effectively in teams and other collaborative situations. Employees, too, recognize that it is essential for them to continue to learn so that they will be effective in their current jobs and able to move into other positions or accept new responsibilities as circumstances demand.

Preparing the Plan

There are four principal occasions when preparation of a performance development plan might be considered: 1. After definition or review of performance standards, 2. As a part of the ongoing process of observation and feedback, 3. As the final element of the performance appraisal process, 4. When an employee initiates a request for education or development opportunities. At any of these points in the performance management process, you may discuss training, education or development opportunities with your employee. Identify the specific steps to be taken and document a strategy for accomplishing these objectives. That documentation should include:

- A description of the specific steps to be taken.
- The names of those who will assist the employee.

- End dates for the completion of the plan's objectives.
- A statement of how successful completion of the plan's objectives will be appraised.

BEST PRACTICES: PERFORMANCE APPRAISAL

A New Paradigm

Performance appraisal has finally caught up with 21st century management practices. In the old model, performance appraisal tended to be one-way, adversarial, oriented toward the past and universally despised by all. In the new model, performance appraisal:

- Involves an ongoing process of planning, goal-setting, feedback and performance review.
- Is an ongoing series of discussions between supervisor and employee rather than an annual event?
- Focuses on the future more than the past.
- Focuses on improving employee performance and career development rather than employees' mistakes.
- Is used as a tool to build trust, open communication and better supervisor/employee relationships at all levels of the organization.

Performance Appraisal Best Practices

Companies with world-class performance appraisal systems generally engage in the following practices:

- Make performance appraisal part of the culture.
- Walk the talk. (The CEO must model the right performance appraisal behaviour with his or her direct reports).
- Link performance appraisal to organizational objectives.
- Invest in training and education.
- Design the system for the unique needs of the organization.
- Use performance appraisal to build relationships between supervisors and employees.
- Use flexible, customized appraisal forms.
- Separate the compensation conversation from performance review.

Implementing a Performance Management System

Implementing an effective performance management system requires four basic steps:

1. **The planning session:** Supervisor and employee mutually agree on the job responsibilities and goals and the measurement criteria.
2. **Regular performance reviews:** Supervisor and employee meet every one to two months to track progress against the goals.
3. **Ongoing coaching for improvement:** Supervisor and employee identify areas for improvement and supervisor provides additional coaching and resources.
4. **A formal, year-end performance review:** Supervisor and employee agree on performance *versus* expectations and plan for the next year.

Preparing for the Performance Review Session

Experts recommend a five-step process:

1. **Review the objectives of the session:** The primary objectives are to review performance over that previous period, discuss any "leftover" issues and plan the future.'
2. **Dual preparation:** Both supervisor and employee should prepare a rough draft evaluation as well as lists of any questions or issues to be discussed.
3. **Plan your approach:** Identify what you want to learn from and convey to the employee. Create a list of open-ended questions to keep the employee talking during the session.
4. **Check your attitude:** Are you doing the review because you feel obligated or because your view it as part of the performance management process?
5. **Select the right time and place:** Plan at least one hour of uninterrupted time preferably outside your office, with no distractions or interruptions.

Creating a Customized Appraisal Form

Avoid standardized performance appraisal forms. Instead, create your own customized form that:

- Fits the unique needs of your organization and your performance appraisal system.
- Properly documents job-based understandings that develop between supervisor and employee.
- Provides easy-to-reference information to properly guide the future development of the employee.
- Is highly flexible.
- Focuses more on the future than the past.

Conclusion

Evaluating individual work performance is a form of control because it ties performance feedback to rewards and corrective actions. Employee evaluation is an on-going process; taking place informally every day in the organization performance appraisal is a formal, structured system that compares employee performance to established standards. Assessment of job performance is shared with employees being appraised through one of several primary methods of performance appraisals. Elements in performance appraisal methods are tailored to the organization's employees, jobs, and structure. They include objective criteria for measuring employee performance and ratings that summarize how well the employee is doing. Successful appraisal methods have clearly defined and explicitly communicated standards or expectations of employee performance on the job. Performance appraisals seek to meet specific objectives. They include tell and sell, tell and listen, problem solving, and mixed model. It is used for employee development purposes. The supervisor does not offer evaluation but lets the employee decide his or her weak areas and works with the employee to develop an action plan for improvement. Performance appraisals are essential for the effective management and evaluation of staff. Appraisals help develop individuals, improve organizational performance, and feed into business planning. Formal performance appraisals are generally conducted annually for all staff in the organization. Aside from formal traditional (annual, six-monthly, quarterly, or monthly) performance appraisals, there are many different methods of performance evaluation. The use of any of these methods depends on the purpose of the evaluation, the individual, the assessor, and the environment.

After employee selection, performance appraisal is arguably the most important management tool a *farm employer* has at his disposal. The performance appraisal, when properly carried out, can help to fine tune and reward the performance of present employees. In this chapter we: 1. discuss the purpose for the performance appraisal, 2. introduce the *negotiated performance appraisal* approach, and 3. talk about the steps to achieving a worthwhile *traditional performance appraisal.*

Base on the information provided by the organizations on their performance appraisal systems, it can be concluded that the most of the organizations have initiated changes in their performance management systems in order to improve service delivery and organizational efficiency. In particular, the setting of the individual goals that are aligned with the objectives of the organization has been developed in the most organizations. However, this practice can be improved or further developed in some of them. Key objectives of performance appraisals include: 1. validating selection and other management or cultural practices; 2. helping employees understand and take responsibility for their performance; and 3. making decisions about pay or promotions.

Important steps to obtaining useful traditional appraisals include determining the type of data to be collected as well as who will conduct the appraisal, establishing a rating philosophy, overcoming typical rating deficiencies, creating a rating instrument, and engaging the employee in making decisions on future performance changes.

An effective negotiated performance appraisal helps the employee take additional ownership for both continuing effective performance and improving weak areas. Employee goals set through performance appraisals should be difficult but achievable, as goals that are overly ambitious are doomed for failure. Some employees tend to boycott their own progress by setting impossible goals to achieve. Finally, employees *want to know* what you think of their work. *Letting* workers know that you have noticed their efforts goes a long way towards having a more motivated workforce. Performance appraisal is concerned with setting objectives for individuals, monitoring progress towards these objectives on a regular basis in our atmosphere of trust and cooperation between the appraiser and the apprise. Well designed appraisal systems benefit the organization, managers and the individuals in different ways and the needs to fulfill certain key objectives if they are to be successful. Appraisal systems should be designed to focus employees on the both of their short and long-term objectives and career goals. It is also important to be awareness of the problems associated with the performances appraisal system.

However, in the context of cultural change and on the basis of a robust performance appraisal system, this issue should be overcome. Related to this is the broadening of the appraisal base and the move to multiple assessor appraisals and committee reviews in a number of organizations, which would provide staff members with the opportunity to respond in case of disagreement. The idea that competencies are the foundation for effective performance in any job or position is widespread in all the organizations of the common system. Accordingly, an increasing number of organizations have recently developed competency frameworks, including core and functional competencies. Client orientation, with a few exceptions, has not been widely developed. Here again, the issue would be overcome if cultural change is effective and the leadership role of managers strengthened. A few organizations of the common system have included the accountability of managers as a key element of the new performance culture. In these organizations, all managers and staff with supervisory responsibility are held accountable for the effective use of the performance appraisal system as a management tool. In practice, the manager is responsible for matching performance at the department/unit and individual levels, and for the measurement and interpretation of goal achievement and related corrective actions. An exemplary performance agreement should lie at the heart of the rigorous management of individual performance. The development of this agreement would be based on dialogue between the manager and staff member. It would draw its coherence from the work plans and budget of the department or unit, the job description of the staff member and the competency framework of the organization. It would identify objectives that are specific, measurable, agreed, realistic and time-bound. A range of organizations have taken the necessary steps to move towards linking pay to performance, regardless of the related pay system (*i.e.*, broad banding system or the current salary structure). However, it is clear that the need for cultural change is a major imperative. Organizations are conscious of this prerequisite and have worked (or are working) towards changing organizational cultures at all levels to emphasize results, performance and competitiveness.

CASE STUDY–I

Performance Appraisal System in the Cyprus Civil Service Problems

The aims of the performance appraisal system currently being used in the civil service, as provided in the relevant regulations of 1990 and 1993, are the following:

(*a*) To decide whether employees on probation should be permanent,

(*b*) To identify employees' readiness to be promoted to higher posts,

(*c*) To help employees develop their abilities, and

(*d*) To promote a better functioning and management of the civil service.

Unfortunately, there are no signs that the system is being used for the latter two [(*c*) and (*d*)] purposes, and if it is used, it is done very rarely and not systematically. Since, also, without exception, all the employees on probation are considered fit to become permanent, the system is, in practice, used for promotion purposes only. But ironically, even for promotion purposes, the system is, in practice, used for promotion purpose only. But ironically, even for promotion purposes, the system is not effective it all, because of the widespread overestimation prevailing—97% of employees are appraised as having outstanding performance. As a result, outstanding and bad performers are equalized, and therefore, promotion is basically based on seniority alone, despite the fact that is should officially (according to public service law) be based on merit, qualification and seniority.

The Public Administration and Personnel Department, which is the central government agency responsible for all human resource matters in the whole public service, is, since a long time, examining ways to overcome or minimize this problem, and ultimately, boost the morale of the employees and the productivity of the public service.

This case study describes the problems of the appraisal system currently being used in the civil service, their significance to the performance of the public service, and possible ways to address the problem in the most efficient manner.

The problem described in the paragraph above, and other problems of the system can be attributed to two main categories of reasons–those arising from the system itself, and those arising from the way it is implemented.

Problems arising from the system are described below:

- Only one appraisal form is used for all civil servants, without taking into consideration the duties and responsibilities of each post.

- The evaluation scale of four ratings (outstanding, very satisfactory, satisfactory and non satisfactory) is inadequate to accurately measure employee's performance. These ratings have a reflection on 'personality' rather than performance–something which should be avoided.
- The description of duties on the appraisal form is completely inadequate.
- The criteria contained in the appraisal form are subject to different interpretation by appraises.
- No common standards of appraising exist throughout the whole civil service.
- No appeal mechanism exists in case of disagreement between the appraiser and the appraisee.
- No provision for appraisal interviews exist for setting common targets to be attained by the employee during the next year.

Problems related to its implementation are as follows:

- Performance appraisal system is not considered as an ongoing yearly cycle process, but as a mechanistic, one a year obligation ('filling of a form').
- There is a lack of dialogue between the appraiser and the appraisee.
- Criteria are not used as they were supposed to be used, and there is a lack of specific objectives and agreed targets to be achieved, either at the departmental or the individual level.
- There is a lack of commitment by Civil Service Managers and no leadership from the very top to make the system work.
- The appraisers seem reluctant to fair/evaluate employees, so as to avoid negative reactions and conflicts.
- Employees themselves are not willing to accept 'criticism' and comparison with their colleagues.
- There is a perception, among some employees, that appraisers are unable to appraisers in a fair manner.
- Both appraisers and appraisees are not trained to a satisfactory extent.
- External interference and influences exist in the system.
- The system is quite vulnerable to problems related to human nature, such as subjectivity and to pressures related to family and other relationships.
- There is a tendency for appraisers to appraise in a more lenient manner, in cases where promotions are imminent.

The Cyprus Public Service

It would be impossible for a performance appraisal system to operate in isolation. In order for such system to serve its purpose, and to be an effective management tool, it must be designed bearing in mind the environment in which it operates, and in correlation with the organization's missions and strategies. It must also be closely linked to all other human resource management policies.

Some negative situational factors are discussed below:

- The structure of the public service is basically bureaucratic, with a high degree of centralization, and inflexible organizational structure and procedures.
- Objectives and targets, both at the department and individual level, are either absent or vague.
- The current payment system in the civil service is a very competitive one and a vast different exists between the level of public service pay and that of private sector pay, especially with regard to the entry-level posts (pay in the private sector is lower than that in government) addition, it does not contain any incentives elements; on the contrary, the majority of civil servants are entitled to uninterrupted salary acceleration irrespective of actual performance.

- The civil service is highly unionized, with one powerful union: PASYDY.
- Cyprus is a small country; it citizens are inevitably close to each other and this may lead, to some extent, to a culture of favouritism.

Some promising changes in the recent years are as follows:

- Some years ago, the Council of Ministers approved a 'comprehensive plan for reforming the entire civil service', most of the provisions of which are at the implementation stage. The plan includes measures for controlling the size of the public service and improving its productivity. Among others, it provides for:
  - Reforming the existing payment system, in order to make it more realistic, fair, and flexible.
  - Improving the public service performance appraisal system.
  - Restructuring departments and moving towards decentralization.
  - Improving the schemes of service (job descriptions) with a view to re-designing and enriching jobs and adhering to European Union requirements.
  - Enhancing mobility of staff within the civil service.
  - Improving the selection and recruitment procedure.
  - Simplifying procedure.
  - Introducing new technology.
- The House of Parliament, political parties and the new government, elected in 2003, support the plan for reforming the civil service, and, especially, the introduction of a new performance appraisal system.
- The civil service trade union, PASYDY, seems to agree with the public service plan to improve the appraisal system.

Addressing the Problem

Early in the previous decade, it was made clear that the performance appraisal system was not succeeding in its goals; therefore, a decision had to be made to either partly change the current system, or introduce a new one. Because of the complexity of the subject and its importance with regards to the productivity of the civil service, it was decided to design and implement a new appraisal system.

To achieve that, first, it should be made clear what went wrong with the current system and how the mistakes of the past could be avoided. The methodology of redesigning a new system should involve:

- Collection of data from all interested parties (*e.g.*, top-level management, PASYDY, political parties, etc.) via personal interview and questionnaires.
- Careful examination of appraisal systems used in other countries, with a view to incorporating any useful elements into the new system, always taking into consideration the Cypriot civil service culture.

After a comprehensive evaluation of the data collected, as described above, a suggestion should be prepared for a new appraisal system and presented to the decision-makers to approve its implementation. Decision-makers are: (*i*) The Minister of Finance who is responsible for the civil service human resource matters, (*ii*) The Council of Ministers, and (*iii*) The House of Representatives. Top civil service managers (permanent secretaries of ministries and heads of departments) and

PASYDY, the public service trade union, should be consulted, and they should agree on all the provisions of the proposed system.

The Public Administration and Personnel Department, in cooperation with a private consulting firm, conducted a survey and came up with a preliminary suggestion that includes, among others, the following:

- Separation of the appraisal process conducted for promotion purposes, from the conducted for development purposes, in an effort to eliminate the pressure, on behalf of appraisers, to overrate employees so that they will be promoted to the next level.
- At this stage, the 'criteria' for appraisal should include competencies (performance indicators). Assessment on the basis of targets 'objectives may be incorporated into the system at a later stage, when the necessary culture prevails.
- Detailed definitions of criteria for appraisal, taking into account the duties and responsibilities of each post, and setting up of departmental committees that will ensure homogeneous evaluation.
- Training of appraisers to equip them with the skills, knowledge, and specially, attitudes needed for effectively appraising employees.
- Incorporation of the 'appraisal interview' into the system, so as to enhance communication between the appraiser and the appraisee.
- Introduction of the 'self-appraisal process' in an effort to foster critical self-examination of one's performance and areas that one needs to develop.

The next step/challenge is to finalize the suggestion for a new performance appraisal system. It should be done by taking into account the views of the Attorney General of the Republic regarding the legality of certain provisions, presenting it to the Council of Ministers and the rest of the decision makers, gaining the support of all influenced parties including trade unions, and then proceeding with its implementation.

QUESTIONS

1. Critically analyze the performance appraisal system of the civil service in Cyprus.
2. Suggest method for improving the use of the performance appraisal system for the two key factor–employee development, and improving the functional efficiency of civil services in Cyprus.
3. Analyze the problems arising out of the implementation of the performance appraisal system and suggest improvements to overcome them.
4. Do you think that designing a performance appraisal system in isolation, without addressing the negative situational factors, would lead to the desired results in this case? If not, suggest an action plan.

CASE STUDY–2

Developing appraisal to align performance contributions with organizational goals performance appraisal

A College of Business at a large university (we will not name it, but this is a description of a real project) is currently implementing a new professor teaching appraisal system that is linked directly to college goals. Some of the college goals include teaching international aspects of business, providing team skills and sensitivity to ethical issues, and encouraging collaborative learning. The dean formed a committee to develop ways to measure how well professors meet each of these goals. For example, the committee proposed that student give feedback about how much they developed team collaboration skills in a course or how much they improved their ability to make ethical decisions.

With this type of appraisal system, the college goals are the dimensions on which professor performance levels are measured. Because the major purpose of the new appraisal system is to encourage professors to contribute to the college goals in their teaching efforts, merit pay is tied to well professors rate in the categories.

QUESTIONS

1. A number of professors are concerned that their courses do not contribute to all the goals. For instance, a course might address the international but not the ethical goal. How do you think this problem should be dealt with in the appraisal system ?
2. Do you think students should be the rates in this appraisal system ? What other sources of appraisal would you concerned ?
3. A number of faculty are concerned that student ratings are only a popularity contest and do not indicate teaching quality or amount of learning. Do you agree ?

EXERCISES

1. In small groups design a faculty evaluation system for your college. Here are some key issues to address:
   - What should be the criteria?
   - How should performance be measured (what items, or outcomes, and so on)?
   - Who should be the raters?
   - Should faculty set weights on criteria or choose criteria to be evaluated on?
   - Should customers be involved in developing the system? Who are the customers?
2. The college goals promote teamwork and a collaborative learning environment. However, some faculty are gifted presenters and may not perform as well if forced into a different mode of instruction.
   (*a*) Form small groups of two to six people and discuss this issue. The problem described here has been characterized as a less than optimal use of the human resource. Describe what you think this statement means.
   (*b*) What should be done about the problem? Should all faculties be forced into the same mode of instruction? If not, what should be measured in the appraisal?

CASE STUDY–3

Performance Appraisal

Unique Funds Ltd. is a reputed finance company having 10 branches in different parts of the country. Its staff includes 290 operative employees and 70 executives. The company has a performance rating plan under which the staff members are rated at the end of each financial year by a committee of two executives by means of graphic scale. The qualities considered are: Responsibilities, initiative, dependability, leadership potential, cooperative attitude and community service. After the performance is evaluated, the ratings are discussed with the concerned employees by their immediate boss and are used to counsel them and arrange further training for them. The ratings are also used for granting or with holding of increments and promoting or meritorious staff.

Recently, two employees working at the Head Office have been denied annual increments due to comparatively low ratings. They have made a representation to the Chief Executive of the company expressing their dissatisfaction with the appraisal system and insisting that community service is not a part of their job and it should not influence their ratings. The employees seem to organize a union and demand that annual increments should be granted automatically.

The Chief Executive feels that performance appraised is a dangerous source of friction and so it should be discontinued altogether.

QUESTIONS

1. If you were the Human Resource Manager, how would you defuse the problem?
2. How far do you agree with the Chief Executive's view that performance appraisal should be discontinued?
3. On what lines would you recommend modifications in the performance appraisal system of the company?

CASE STUDY–4

Internal appraisal and goal setting at FedEx: performance appraisal

Appraisal ratings from multiple sources can provide a rich source of feedback to employees. However, translating this feedback into concrete objectives that will guide and improve performance in the next appraisal period may be difficult. To improve its internal operations, FedEx is shifting to a future oriented approach and a 360 degree "goal-setting system."

How does this system work? Departments at FedEx assess how well other departments are providing needed inputs to their internal customers. Based on the ratings it receives, each department summarizes the goals of its internal customers and then provides those customers with a service guarantee. For example, FedEx HR department has provided the following guarantee to its internal customers:

- Timely response.
- A 24-hour turnaround for feedback on important requests.
- Two-hour response time to emergency call.
- Critical feedback on equal employment opportunity and employee grievances.
- Semi-annual training sessions on topical subjects.
- Updates on employee relations issues.
- Meetings with managers to review recruitment, plants, goals, and results.
- Bimonthly meetings with employees.

- These goals set a clear foundation for future customer assessment of how well HR employees are performing.

QUESTIONS

1. A potential problem with 360 degree goal setting is that various internal customers may have unrealistic and conflicting performance expectations. What actions could managers take to avoid this problem?
2. It is possible for a business to be overly concerned with satisfying customers. For example, giving away products for free might delight customers but would put the company out of business. How could a company use customer-driven goal setting to avoid this problem?

REFERENCES

1. Kubo, H. (1990, February 14–16). *Improving Employee Communications.* Presented at Pacific North West Orchard Business short course. Washington State University and Oregon State University.
2. Scholtes, P.R., (1988), *The Team Handbook: How to Use Teams to Improve Quality* (p. 6–25). Joiner Associates.
3. Latham, G.P., & Locke, E.A., (1983). Goal Setting-A Motivational Technique That Works. In *Contemporary Problems in Personnel* (3rd Ed.) (pp. 313–324). Edited by Pearlman, K., Schmidt, F.L., & Hamner, W.C. New York: John Wiley & Sons.
4. I refined this approach working with an agribusiness firm during a VOCA/US AID labour management mission to Uganda, East Africa, in 1996. While one of the top managers suggested that I was wasting my time with this approach, after she met with her boss for a performance appraisal using this list approach, she thanked me explaining that she had never had a more productive meeting with the owner/operator
5. Carroll, S.J., & Schneier, C.E. (1982), *Performance Appraisal and Review Systems: The Identification, Measurement, and Development of Performance in Organizations* (p. 40). Glenview, Illinois: Scott, Foresman, and Company; Strauss, G., & Sayles, L.R. (1980). *Personnel: The Human Problems of Management* (4th ed.) (pp. 522–23). New Jersey: Prentice-Hall; and Kujawski, C.J., & Young, D.M. (1979). "Appraisals of 'People' Resources." *In ASPA Handbook of Personnel and Industrial Relations* (pp. 4–193). Washington D.C.: The Bureau of National Affairs.
6. Schlei, B. L., & Grossman, P. (1983), *Employment Discrimination Law* (p. 531). Bureau of National Affairs.
7. Dion, K.; Berscheild, E., & Walster, E. (1986), "What Is Beautiful Is Good," *Journal of Personality and Social Psychology*, (24: 285–290).; and Bull, R. (1986), In Brown, Roger. *Social Psychology: The Second Edition* (p. 391–393). New York: The Free Press.
8. Landy, D., & Sigall, H. (1974), "Beauty Is Talent: Task Evaluation as a Function of the Performer's Physical Attractiveness," Journal of Personality and Social Psychology (29: 299–304). In Brown, Roger (1986). Social Psychology: The Second Edition (p. 393–394). New York: The Free Press.
9. Carroll, S.J., & Schneier, C.E. (1982), *Performance Appraisal and Review Systems: The Identification, Measurement, and Development of Performance in Organizations* (p. 121). Illinois: Scott, Foresman, and Company.
10. One popular performance appraisal approach of the "descriptive" type is the behaviorally anchored rating scale (or BARS). These scales are anchored with descriptive alternative behaviours. For every given category of behaviour or performance, statement are ordered in an ascending or descending

order of excellence. One challenge to BARS is the great number of descriptive category areas needed. Another difficulty is ordering observations so each statement of higher performance excellence subsumes the others.

11. ARMSTRONG, M and BARON, A. (2004), *Managing performance: performance management in action*. London: Chartered Institute of Personnel and Development.
12. Rupp, D.E. (2005), Assessment centers, competencies, and Integrated HR Systems. *Human Capital Management* (Korean), 24, 16–17.
13. W.F. Cascio, Applied Psychology in Personnel Management (Reston, Virginia: Reston Publishing Co., Inc. 1982).
14. Task Force on Assessment Center Standards, Standards and Ethical Consideration for Assessment Center Operations (New Orleans, Louisiana: June 1979.
15. K. McNutt, "Behavioral Consistency and Assessment Centers: A Reconciliation of the Literature, "Journal of Assessment Center Technology, II (1979), 1–6.
16. C.L. Jaffee and J.T. Sefcik, "What is an Assessment Center?" Personnel Administrator (February 1980, 40–43 abd Joseph Kwarteng, Assessment Center Validity and Reliability; An Evaluation of The Ohio * State University, Columbus, 1986).
17. W.C. Byham, "Assessment Centers for Spotting Future Managers" in Perspectives on Employees, Staffing, and Selection, G.F. Dreher and P.R. Sackett, eds. (Homewood, Illinois; Irwin, 1983), pp. 229–47.
18. Byham, "Assessment Centers"; J.R. Hinricks and S. Haanpera, "Reliability of Measurement in Situational Exercises: An Assessment of the Assessment Center Method," Personnel Psychology, XXIX (1976), 31–40; and Leslie Bart, The Role of Assessee Involvement in Development Assessment Center (Ph.D. dissertation, The Ohio State University, Columbus, 1986).
19. Bart, Role of Assessee and W.C. Byham, "The Assessment Center as an Aid in Management Development," in Contemporary Problems in Personnel, rev. ed., W.C. Hamner and F.L. Smidt, eds. (Chicago, Illinois: St. Clair, 1977).

7

CHAPTER

COMPETENCY MAPPING

7.1 INTRODUCTION

Competency-based HR is considered the best HR. In India, however, competency development and mapping still remains an unexplored process in most IT organizations despite the growing level of awareness. The underlying principle of competency mapping just about finding the right people for the right job. The issue is much more complex than it appears, and most HR departments have been struggling to formulate the right framework for their organization. Competency mapping is a process of identifying key competencies for a particular position in an organization, and then using it for job-evaluation, recruitment, training and development, performance management, succession planning, etc. "The competency framework serves as the bedrock for all HR applications. As a result of competency mapping, all the HR processes like talent induction, management development, appraisals and training yield much better results," however points out that the competency movement has caught on much better in the non-IT sector than the IT sector. Only a few IT organizations which are at the higher end of the HR value chain are known to be doing some work in this area; most are more busy handling recruitment and compensation-related matters. "Unless managements and HR heads have holistic expectations from their HR departments, the competency movement is unlikely to succeed as it requires lot of time, dedication and money," pointing out that before an organization embarks on this journey it has to be very clear about the business goals, capability-building imperatives and core competencies of the organization. The competency mapping process needs to be strongly integrated with these aspects.

Best organizations succeed not because they have right people. A person may be capable of doing things, which may be, bring in a paradigm shift in the industry and make you a leader but only if they are provided an opportunity. Being capable alone does not have any significance unless one can prove it. It is surprising what a man can do when he has to and how little most of the men do when they don't have to companies usually design the job descriptions and then search for the best people mainly on the basis of qualifications. Scanning the competencies of the applicants will provide the company a pool of employees with grate potential for performance excellences.

What is Competency?

Competency is an underlying skill, potential characteristics, or motive demonstrates by a various observable behaviours that contribute to outstanding performance in a job. Competencies exist at different levels of personality. The various levels are:

- ***Knowledge:*** Information that an individual has in a particular area.
- ***Skills:*** An individual's ability to do something well.
- ***Behaviour:*** Action of a person in a given situation.
- ***Personal Characteristics:***

  Traits: A typical way of behaving such as taking initiatives.

  Motives: A fundamental and often unconscious driver of thoughts and behaviour for example concern for excellence. Personal characteristics are hard to develop and it is more cost effective to select people having the desired personality traits. Knowledge and skills are easy to develop so training is cost effective.

What is Competency Mapping?

In this work we adopt the definition of *competence* as "effective performance within a domain/context at different levels of proficiency", as given in (Cheetam and Chivers, 2005). Note that there exists some confusion on the term *competency* in the literature. (IEEE RCD, 2005; IMS RDCEO, 2002) define the stricter term of competency as "any form of knowledge, skill, attitude, ability, or learning objective that can be described in a context of learning, education or training". In fact, if that information becomes part of the competency definition, its reusability is drastically reduced (with the consequence of, *e.g.*, having different competency definitions for each context in which a competency is applied, and for any proficiency. "A specific, identifiable, definable, and measurable knowledge, skill, ability and/or other deployment related characteristic (*e.g.*, attitude, behaviour, physical ability) which a human resource may possess and which is necessary for, or material to, the performance of an activity within a specific business context". In this case, "measurable" indicates a relationship with a specific proficiency level and competency now applies only to the business context.

As stated above, current approaches to modeling competencies do not explicitly address proficiency level and context. On the contrary, we believe that competency, proficiency level and context are three different dimensions that should be modeled separately in order to maximize their reuse.

It is about identifying preferred behaviours and personal skills which distinguish excellent and outstanding performance from the average. A Competency is something that describes how a job might be done, excellently; a Competence only describes what has to be done, not how. So the Competences might describe the duties of a Sales Manager for example, such as manage the sales office and its staff, prepare quotations and sales order processing, manage Key Accounts and supervise and motivate the field sales force. The Competencies which might determine excellence in this role could include Problem Solving and Judgment; Drive and Determination; Commercial Awareness; Inter-personal skills etc. all of which might be described further by Behavioural Indicators relating specifically to that post in that organization. The broad concept might be said to be based on the frequently quoted adage: people get hired for what they know but fired for how they behave!

Competency Mapping is a process of identifies key competencies for an organization and/or a job and incorporating those competencies throughout the various processes (*i.e.*, job evaluation, training, recruitment) of the organization. To ensure we are both on the same page, we would define a competency as a behaviour (*i.e.*, communication, leadership) rather than a skill or ability. The steps involved in competency mapping with an end result of job evaluation include the following: 1. Conduct a job analysis by asking incumbents to complete a position information questionnaire (PIQ). This can be provided for incumbents to complete, or you can conduct one-on-one interviews using the PIQ as a guide. A sample PIQ that we use when conducting this step with our clients was provided to this client. The primary goal is to gather from incumbents what they feel are the key behaviours necessary to perform their respective jobs. 2. Using the results of the job analysis, you are ready to develop a competency based job description.

When the technique is applied this way, it is not strictly correct to call it "concept mapping". The term implies that what is being measured is purely conceptual, but no assessment method captures pure conceptual understanding: there is always a practical element. Furthermore, computer programming is not in itself a pure theory subject. The ability to write useful, efficient and correct programs is more of a craft than a science. Because practical abilities such as proficiency with the compiler are likely to affect students' marks, it is to be expected that they should show up on the map—indeed, for some tasks they might dominate the clustering pattern. "Competency mapping" is a better phrase. A competency is a practical ability that is informed to some degree by theoretical understanding: this is a much better model for assessment than any purely conceptual model. Although the aim of the assessment may be to work out the students' grasp of a concept, what is measured is of necessity the result of some practical process.

Fig: 7.1 Competence is the combination of Context, Competency and Proficiency Level

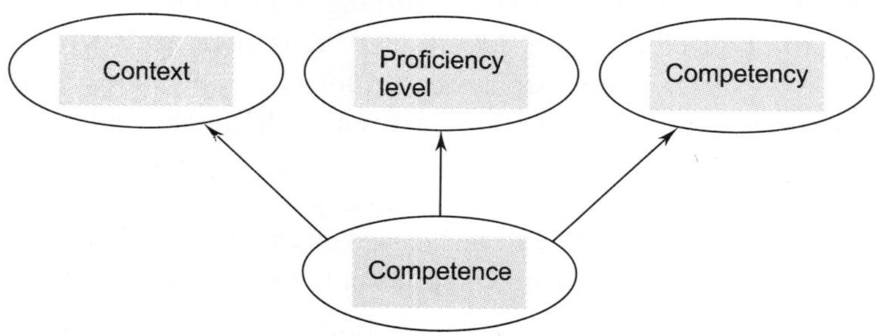

History of Competencies

A team of Educationists lead by Benjamin Bloom in the USA in mid fifties laid the foundation for identifying educational objectives and there by defining the knowledge attitudes and skills needed to be developed in education. The task force lead by Bloom took several years to make an exhaustive classification of the educational objectives that were grouped under the cognitive domain.

David McClelland the famous Harvard Psychologist has pioneered the competency movement across the world. His classic books on "Talent and Society", "Achievement Motive", "The Achieving Society", "Motivating Economic Achievement" and "Power the Inner Experience" brought out several new dimensions of the competencies. These competencies exposed by McClelland dealt with the affective domain in Bloom's terminology. The turning point for competency movement is the article published in American Psychologist in 1973 by McClelland titled where in he presented data that traditional achievement and intelligence scores may not be able to predict job success and what is required is to profile the exact competencies required to perform a given job effectively and measure them using a variety of tests. As Douglas Brey and his associates at AT and T in the US where in they presented evidence that competencies can be assessed through assessment centers an on the job success can be predicted to some extent by the same has laid foundation for popularization of the competency movement.

Latter McBer a Consulting Firm founded by David McClelland and his associate Berlew have specialized in mapping the competencies of entrepreneurs and managers across the world. They even developed a new and yet simple methodology called the Behaviour Event Interviewing (BEI) to map the competencies. With increased recognition of the limitations performance appraisal in predicting future performance potential appraisal got focused. And assessment centers became popular in seventies. The setting up an assessment center was in integral part of the HRD plan given to L & T by the IIMA professors as early as in 1975. L & T did competency mapping and could not start assessment centers until much latter as it was not perceived as a priority area.

Competency mapping is the process of identification of the competencies required to perform successfully a given job or role or a set of tasks at a given point of time. It consists of breaking a given role or job into its constituent tasks or activities and identifying the competencies (technical, managerial, behavioural, conceptual knowledge, an attitudes, skills, etc.) needed to perform the same successfully. Competency assessment is the assessment of the extent to which a given individual or a set of individuals possess these competencies required by a given role or set of roles or levels of roles. Assessment centers use multiple methods and multiple assessors to assess the competencies of a given individual or a group of individuals. In order to enhance objectivity they use trained assessors and multiple methods including psychometric tests, simulation exercise, presentations, in-basket exercises, interviews, role-plays, group discussions etc. The methods to be used depend on the nature of competencies.

Who Identifies Competencies?

Competencies can be identified by one of more of the following category of people: Experts, HR Specialists, Job Analysts, Psychologists, Industrial Engineers etc. in consultation with: Line Managers, Current and Past Role Holders, Supervising Seniors, Reporting and Reviewing Officers, Internal Customers, Subordinates of the role holders and other role set members of the role (those who have expectations from the role holder and who interact with him/her).

Benefits of Competency Mapping

Competency maps have many potential benefits for students and teaching staff. Of course, because staff and students share many goals, these benefits are not entirely divisible; some aspects of competency mapping will benefit both staff and students. A partial list of potential uses for competency mapping follows. It is likely that more benefits will be discovered as the technique matures.

Benefits for Staff

If competency mapping can actually give a picture of the structure of the course as the students experience it, teaching staff will be able to use that picture as the basis for course refinement. The identification of key concepts is the first step towards designing a syllabus. The information gained can also be published to the students, for example by including it in the subject information handout that students usually receive in their first lecture, or by putting it on the courseware web page.

Of course, it is quite possible that the structure revealed by analysis of student results does not match the lecturer's idea of the conceptual structure of the course. In this case, the revealed structure may suggest ways in which the course can be improved. For example, if two competencies that should be related (for example, C pointers and passing by reference) are not clustered together, it could indicate a need to make the connection more explicit to the students. If the competency map uses all the coursework marks as input, this will not help the students of that year; however, it may well help teaching staff to refine the coursework for the next delivery of the course. It would also be useful to staff who are teaching follow-on courses, as they would gain a better idea of which topics need revision.

There are different approaches to competency analysis. While some competency studies take months to complete and result in the vague statements that have little relevance to the people in the organization but if done well they provide the following benefits of the organizations:

- Increased productivity.
- Improved work performances.
- Training that focused on organizational objectives.
- Employees know up front what is expected of them.
- Employees are empowered to partners in their own performance development.
- The approach builds trust between employees and the managers.

7.2 COMPETENCIES AND HR

In the struggle to rethink new approaches to HR, many private businesses and government entities are moving toward competencies and competency-based systems as the answer to meeting organizational needs. But, what do we mean by competencies and how do they actually relate to HR? For the purpose of this study, the following definition was chosen for the word "competency": "An underlying characteristic of an employee (*i.e.*, a motive, trait, skill, aspects of one's self-image, social role, or a body of knowledge) which results in effective and/or superior performance (Boyatzis, 1982)." Competencies may be grouped as follows (Tucker and Cofsky, 1994):

Skills: The demonstration of expertise (*e.g.*, the ability to make effective presentations, or to negotiate successfully);

Knowledge: Information accumulated in a particular area of expertise (*e.g.*, Accounting, Human resources management);

Self-concepts: Attitudes, values and self-image;

Traits: A general disposition to behave in certain ways (*e.g.*, flexibility); and

Motives: Recurrent thoughts driving behaviours (*e.g.*, drive for achievement, affiliation).

Organizations that have used competencies tend to define these competencies in their own terms, tailored to their own unique situations. The National Park Service, for example, defines its competencies as a combination of knowledge, skills, and abilities in a particular career field which when acquired, allows a person to perform a task or function at a specifically defined level of proficiency. Competencies can be further broken down into different categories that distinguish different purposes and/or uses:

Essential Competencies serve as the foundation of knowledge and skills needed by everyone. (Spencer *etal.,* 1990). These can be developed through training and are relatively easy to identify.

Differentiating Competencies distinguish superior performance from average performance (Spencer *etal.,* 1990). These include self-concepts, traits and motives and although hard to develop, can determine long-term success on the job. With a valid competency-development methodology, one can define, measure and reward these competencies.

Strategic Competencies include those that are "core" competencies of the organization. These tend to focus on organizational capability and include competencies that create a competitive advantage (*e.g.*, innovation, speed, service, technology).

Why Competencies?

Competencies can be used to facilitate change in Human Resources: There is recognition that the role of HR is moving from an emphasis on rules to a focus on results. To help facilitate this paradigm shift, a variety of organizations, both public and private, are identifying new competencies. Competencies are being used as a way to refocus the organization on what is really important and what it takes for the workforce to be successful. In addition, competencies provide the mechanism to zero in on the technical aspects of a particular job and devise a critical path through regulations and laws to the results desired by management. Furthermore, competency models highlight competencies needed by the organization and serve as vehicles for change.

Competencies can be used to "raise the bar" on employee performance: According to a 1996 American Compensation Association (ACA) study focusing on competency applications in HR, Organizations are using competencies to integrate selection, training, appraisal, and compensation. In staffing, competencies are used to select and promote employees. In human resources development, competencies are used to identify and close the gaps in individuals' capabilities. In performance management, competencies and results are appraised to connect how a job was done to the results achieved. In compensation, pay can be based on the certified skills and competencies used on the job.

Many hope that competencies will also help their organizations communicate desired behaviours, control costs and increase customer satisfaction.

Competencies are also being used in the following ways to support the new role of Human Resources

- As a strategy to strengthen the link with organizational culture, results, and individual.
- Performance by emphasizing competencies that are needed across occupational specialties.
- As a tool to help describe work and what is required from employees in jobs in a broader, more comprehensive way.
- As a method to align individual and team performance with organization, vision, strategies, and the external environment.

How Do Competencies Relate to KSAs?

Traditionally knowledge's, skills, and abilities (KSAs) have been used in the organization is currently exploring the use of competencies as the basis for establishing qualifications for employment. **Knowledge, skills and abilities (KSAs) and competencies are not mutually exclusive, but can complement and build upon each other to reinforce desired behaviours.** Determine an applicant's qualifications for selection or promotion. Such KSAs serve as the foundation for competency models. Competencies can be used to assess and train employees for future needs, while KSAs focus typically on what is needed to do the job today. Competencies build upon the same KSAs used under the current Federal system but are more inclusive in that they also include traits, motives, and behaviours. Additionally, key knowledge, skills and abilities can be clustered to form a set of competencies that determine superior, not just basic, performance. Competencies can then be linked to a set of behaviours that answer the question, "How do we know good performance when we see it?" And they can serve as the foundation to hire, train and develop employees and ultimately to set their pay. The ease of integrating all HR applications and communicating these linkages to stakeholders appears to be an attractive feature of competencies and serves as the compelling reason for their increasing popularity over traditional HR methods.

WHAT IS A COMPETENCY MODEL?

In the book, *Human Resource Champions,* David Ulrich speaks of a new vision for HR, "that it is defined not by what it does, but by what it delivers—results that enrich the organization's value to customers, investors (taxpayers), and employees." He believes HR needs to shed "Old Myths" and take on "New Realities" and adopt competencies and redefine roles focused on results in order to evolve into a true profession that makes a difference for the organization.

OLD MYTHS	NEW REALITIES
People go into HR because they like HR	HR departments are not designed to provide corporate therapy or social or people. Health-and-happiness retreats. HR professionals must create the practices that make employees more compe-titive, not more comfortable.
Anyone can do HR	HR activities are based on theory and research. HR professionals must master both theory and practice.
HR deals with the soft side of a business. The impact of HR practices on business results can and must be measured, and is therefore not accountable	HR professionals must learn how to translate their work into financial performance.
HR focuses on costs, which must be controlled	HR practices must create value by increasing the intellectual capital within the firm HR professionals must add value, not reduce costs.
HR's job is to be the policy police health-and-happiness patrol	The HR function does not own compliance managers do. HR practices do not exist to make employees happy but to help them become committed. HR professionals must help managers commit employees and Administer policies.
HR is full of fads	HR practices have evolved over time. HR professionals must see their current work as part of an evolutionary chain and explain their work with less jargon and more authority.
HR is staffed by nice people	At times, HR practices should force vigorous debates. HR professionals should be confrontational and challenging as well as supportive.
HR is HR's job	HR work is as important to line managers as are finance, strategy, and other business domains. HR professionals should join with managers in Cham-pioning HR issues.

Source: Ulrich, Dave, *Human Resource Champions,* Harvard Business School Press, Boston, MA, 1997, p. 18.

Ulrich's vision of the "New Realities" of HR is applicable to all sectors. With HR changes occurring in Government related to HR processes, structures, and delivery of HR services, HR professionals are taking on new roles to perform effectively in this changing environment.

Fig: 7.2 Making Competencies Work ...

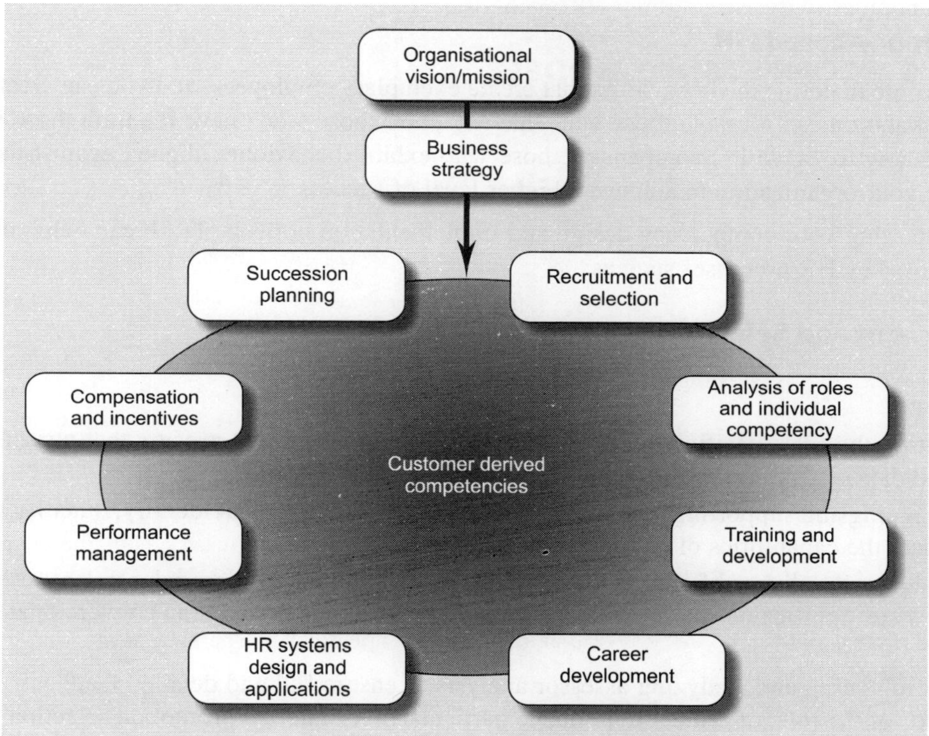

Competency Research and Development

Using best in class processes:

- Develops competency models with leveled behavioural indicators.
- Updates, and/or validates existing models.
- Globalizes models.

Creating Job Family Competency Models

Companies that have a wide variety of job titles often find there are just a few actual job families. ITAP can help define those jobs that are related enough to fit into "job families." Then the development of competency models is easier to manage and less expensive.

Creating Themed Competency Models

Rather than provide competency models for entire organizations, ITAP recommends a focus on mission critical positions, such as leadership, call center agents, sales professionals, and global branding themes. Investing in defining effective and exemplar behaviour in just a few of these areas creates the opportunity for a significant return on investment.

Competency-based HR

If it is possible to define the behaviours that create exemplary employees, and you can create a model to codify that, you can promote those who "have it", hire those who "have it", train those who don't have it on how to "have it", compensate those who exhibit behaviours aligned against the model... thus drive your organization to achieve a higher level of success.

By supporting your competency design and implementation projects, ITAP can help your organization across key HR processes such as:

Recruitment and Selection

Services

- Getting the role specification right and designing a recruitment process that attracts the right candidates.
- Designing and supporting assessment and selection processes that identify, quantify and differentiate the capabilities of good candidates.
- Design and delivery of 'Behavioural' interview techniques, which independent research indicates are significantly more effective at predicting success in role than conventional interviewing.
- Consolidating and analyzing assessor analysis to ensure full and detailed feedback against the needs of the role, of critical importance particularly for internal promotion selection processes.
- Training internal assessors in the process skills necessary for effective, high-quality and non-discriminatory selection.

Benefits

- Reduce staff turnover
- Reduce recruitment costs
- Reduce training costs
- Improve new staff productivity
- Improve long-term performance
- Improve the return on training and development investment.

Performance Management

Services

- Integrating competencies into existing or new performance management processes.
- Designing or integrating with 360° or other multi-rater processes.

- Validating, calibrating and assuring the quality of performance management process output.
- Creating effective links between capability, performance and compensation.

Benefits

- Improve the accuracy, consistency and reliability of performance data, within cultures and across multiple cultures for international organizations.
- Capture and integrate behavioural measures with quantitative measures of performance.
- Improve the performance and capability development output from your process.
- Accurately target rewards and incentives effectively across the international business environment.

Training and Development

Services

- Identifying training and development needs accurately and methodically across key behavioural and technical competencies.
- Enabling accurate 'gap analysis' between the capability of the individual and the requirements of current or future roles.
- Facilitating reality-based assessment and valuable feedback through 'critical incident' focus.
- Identifying and quantifying T and D needs across teams, functions, locations and organizations, translating into comprehensive T and D plans.

Benefits

- Radically improve the accuracy of T and D needs analysis.
- Deliver comprehensive T and D plans for individuals, teams, functions, organizations.
- Create T and D processes that identify and deliver the most effective interventions, sensitive to the cultural norms of international staff.
- Radically improve the return on T and D investment and build the 'human capital' of the organization.

Succession Planning and Capability Mapping

Services

- Building succession-planning processes that focus on and deliver the competencies the organization needs for its current and future roles, not to match job-descriptions and boxes on organization charts that will be out-of-date by the time the position is available.
- Enabling the identification and accessibility of competency anywhere in the organization, when it is needed: ITAP's 'Real Time Succession' process.
- Enabling organizations to build accurate 'maps' of capability across teams, functions, business units, locations, countries and regions.

Benefits

- Identify the capabilities the organization needs for its future, not its past.

- Quantify and analyze capability gaps at organization level, against the strategic requirements of the business, internationally.
- Identify capability surpluses that can be utilized in other parts of the organization.

Assessment Center Design and Delivery

Services

- Designing and building assessment center processes that can be delivered on flexible platforms.
- As events, in modular form, in 'virtual' form, in self-assessment formats, in tight or extended time-scales.
- Utilizing behavioural-event assessment focused against competency-based role profiles, in selection and/or development scenarios.
- Ensuring accurate and appropriate use of psychometrics, capability measures and other methodologies.
- Ensuring effective assessor training and consistent evaluation of capability.
- Delivering design that ensures applicability and fair assessment across multiple cultures.

Benefits

- Significantly improve the credibility of assessment feedback.
- Develop assessment processes that are genuinely effective across multiple cultures—not just in the home-country of the organization—so that the international strategic needs of the business can be met.
- Enable flexible delivery that engages individuals and delivers the information and capability the organization needs.

Competency approach to the job depends on the competency mapping. Competency mapping is a process to identify key competencies for an organization and/or a job and incorporating those competencies throughout the various processes (*i.e.*, job evaluation, training, recruitment) of the organization. A competency is defined as a behaviour (*i.e.*, communication, leadership) rather than a skill or ability.

Competency mapping is a process of identifying key competencies for a company or institution and the jobs and functions within it.

To make it even clearer, we could say that a competency is a behaviour (*i.e.*, communication, leadership) rather than a skill or ability although it sometimes includes these steps:

Step 1: Find and locate relevant competency resources

The first action here must be to identify what types of competencies the individual most needs to focus on. The individual may be employed by or seeking employment with an organization that uses any one of the four ways of categorizing competencies that were identified earlier in the article: Organization-Wide Core Competencies, Job Family or Business Unit, Position-Specific, or by Levels of Contribution (*i.e.*, Individual Contributor, Manager, or Organizational Leader).

Then, of course, the next action is to find a resource that covers the types of competencies the individual is focusing on.

Some primary options for competency resources would include

1. A variety of competency listings and corresponding materials such as card sorts, are immediately available on the Internet. (Competency card sorts are decks of cards with individual competencies described on each card. They are useful for individuals during the sorting process, in determining the competencies that are part of their map). Some of these resources are in the public domain while others are not. Some are available at no charge, and some must be purchased from private consulting organizations.
2. Numerous books on the subject of competency identification, available on the Internet, directly from publishers, and sometimes at bookstores. On-line booksellers are an immediate source of these items.
3. Local career coaches who are experienced in identifying competencies.
   (*Note:* The International Association of Career Management Professionals has an "Experts Section" on its website, www.iacmp.org <http://www.iacmp.org> that would be a good resource).
4. Informational interviews with known experts in an occupational field, and within key organizations the individual is targeting in his/her career search. In order to increase the effectiveness of discussing the individual's competencies during informational interviews, there is one suggestion to make. Many subject-matter experts, both inside and outside of the human resource field, have little direct knowledge or experience with the language of competencies or behavioural science. Therefore, it is found beneficial for the individual to take a sample list of easily understood competencies, including their own top competencies, to their informational interviews. Such a visual aid will provide an example of how the person being interviewed can best support to meet the individual's needs for information.

Step 2: Identify one's competencies and determine their top competencies

As noted in Step 1 above, the individual can identify current competencies directly by using a card sort. Competencies can also be identified with the assistance of an experienced coach, either organically through sample interview questions, standardized assessments, answer and writing exercises, or through the use of a 360-degree feedback process (*i.e.*, a full-circle multi-rater evaluation) where one is assessed by one's supervisor, subordinates, peers, customers, clients, or others.

No matter which method is used, the individual should do a quick validation of the list of competencies that emerge to establish their face validity—in other words, a "reality check." (A validation of this sort need not be scientifically done to add important value to the process.) Next, the individual should identify the four to seven Top Competencies that they believe are the most important to success at this point in their career. As described in the definition of a "Top Competency" and "Importance" from the individual's perspective is an intuitive decision based on a combination of three factors: 1. Past demonstrated excellence in using the competency; 2. Internal passion for using the competency; and, 3. The current or likely future demand for the competency in the individual's current position or targeted career field.

Three primary ways of validating one's competencies, and then determining the top competencies, include:

- A review of the list by an experienced coach who knows the client well, in comparison to an established list of competencies.
- The inclusion of the individual's competencies in a 360-feedback or multi-rater evaluation process, if feedback is sought from others as part of the coaching process.
- Feedback from one or more trusted, experienced mentors.

Step 3: Define the top competencies using behaviours the individual has demonstrated through past performance

Career or performance coaches who have expertise in resume writing often are ideally suited to assist with this task. It can be a somewhat time-intensive task, made easier by the use of competency development resource materials (see Step 1). One caution is to ensure that behaviours are worded to include specific, concrete action verbs (*e.g.*, "Helps others see the personal benefits of doing their job well") instead of vague, cliche-oriented wording (*e.g.*, "Inspires others to go the extra mile"). Another suggestion is to limit the number of behaviours per competency to no more than seven, since the human mind starts to lose its focus once a list exceeds seven items in length.

Step 4: List performance examples of each key behaviour

This is one of the most crucial steps in preparing individuals for competency-based self-presentation. In addition, it's a step for which the individual owns the bulk of the initial responsibility, since the coach does not have easy access the individual's library of all past experiences. Individuals should compose a list of their prior work experiences, projects, and volunteer roles. Then, under each entry, they should spend "quiet time" thinking of one or two concrete behavioural examples—times when they had positive results from their effort. More recent examples are most advantageous, as they tend to have greater "selling value."

Most career coaches have probably encountered many scenarios where individuals state some difficulty and/or discomfort with coming up with specific examples of accomplishments for resume writing. A very useful technique for clients in envisioning their competency examples is to suggest categories of end results, and then ask the individual to brainstorm examples that fit under each category.

Step 5: Prepare verbal explanations of the examples, using the CAR Model

Many career development practitioners have had experience in preparing clients to develop and present CAR examples. Provided below are a few tips for coaching individuals to come up with examples when they are confronted with unexpected interview questions, or requests for unusual examples:

Have written notes, with condensed CAR examples organized by competency, in one's portfolio during an interview or performance discussion.

Take time to pause and think during the discussion—although silence at these times can be a painful experience to the candidate, when an example does not immediately come to mind. A quick glance at one's notes during these times will be a great help, as well. The pausing technique requires individuals to develop an inner reservoir of tolerance for silence. Becoming comfortable with these moments of silence requires practice on the part of the individual. Our mainstream Western culture does not tend to reward silence, as does Eastern thinking and culture.

Ask the questioner to rephrase the question, if the meaning is not clear. This allows the individual more time to think, and may also result in a more clearly worded question from the questioner.

Step 6: Use the top competencies and key behavioural examples to write or revise resumes

But there are at least four areas where a competency-based approach to writing a resume has impact:

1. In writing a chronological resume, the competency titles and some of the behavioural action verbs should be integrated into the descriptions of ongoing responsibilities for each position.
2. In writing a functional resume, the headings of the functional accomplishment sections should lie directly into the titles of the individual's most important competencies. This is especially true for self-employed consultants, whose functional experience headings should correlate with their most important consulting service offerings. Those service offerings should be ones that incorporate the consultants' top competencies.
3. In either version of a resume, accomplishment statements should form a solid core of information in the experience section. The verbal CAR statements previously developed can be condensed into ideal resume accomplishment statements.
4. The summary of qualifications section, usually found at the beginning of a resume, is an ideal place to list the titles of the individual's top competencies, almost verbatim.

What Challenges Do Individuals Face, Who Want to Map Their Competencies

Yes, there are some challenges that an individual will have to surmount in order to truly integrate competency mapping into his or her career management efforts. It is important to highlight some of those challenges here, and to make some suggestions for overcoming them.

The first challenge has to do with the fact that effective competency mapping calls for some insight into the requisite competencies for success in the individual's career field and in key positions of interest. It is often difficult to find competency-based position descriptions, or organizational lists of key competencies with effectively-worded behavioural definitions. And many of the key contacts the individual might seek out for informational interviews will not be used to describing success in an organization or position in competency terminology. So, the individual's questions to their contacts about essential competencies for success in a position or organization may not be answered well or accurately. These factors will require the individual to do some guessing as to the most desired or required competencies.

This raises the second challenge. It will be a bit difficult for many individuals to create their own competency maps, given limited experience with competencies and their behavioural definitions, as well as some "blind spots" about their own prior accomplishments. The apparent solution is for the individual to find and hire an experienced career coach, as mentioned earlier. If this option is taken, the individual should use "due diligence" in selecting their coach by conducting thorough investigations of candidate coaches' credentials and experience in working with the design, development and application of competencies in organizational settings. Many career coaches are experienced in working with their clients to identify knowledge and skills, but they may not be experienced in the more substantial practice of identifying competencies as they are used in organizations today. The major reason for this is that competencies include, in addition to knowledge and skills, other attributes such as traits, thought patterns, self-esteem, mindsets, and other characteristics that extend beyond one's knowledge and skills alone. (This would be a good time for the reader to pause and review my earlier definition of a competency).

A third challenge has been mentioned earlier. A common occurrence for many career consultants is encountering individuals who are less than comfortable putting the extra effort into: (*a*) writing their examples, and (*b*) focusing so much on accomplishments, since this activity often feels to them like self-congratulatory back-patting. The value of working with an experienced career coach to overcome these two barriers cannot be overestimated.

Fourth and finally, there is an issue also mentioned earlier that, based on the Gallup Organization's research, many competencies may not be "trainable" or, cannot be developed by an individual, no matter their level of personal effort. Suffice it to say here that a good career coach will do a great service to individual career clients by seriously focusing on the idea of position or career field "fit" in light of their current competencies, while advising them to be cautious about attempting to develop competencies that might not be developable.

Methods of Competency Mapping

The competency mapping process is a way of identifying competencies that are required to meet or exceed customer requirements. It charts the critical competencies that a person must have and the desired competencies that would be an added advantage, if the person has them. Competency mapping aids in both, the recruitment of new staff and in the training requirements of existing staff. For example, in recruitment, candidates with more of the desired competencies can be recruited, from among those who have the critical competencies required.

It is not easy to identify all the competencies required to fulfill the job requirements. However, a number of methods and approaches have been developed and successfully tried out. These methods have helped managers to a large extent, to identify and reinforce and/or develop these competencies both for the growth of the individual and the growth of the organization. In the following discussions, some major approaches of competency mapping have been presented:

Assessment Centre

Before World War II, the German army implemented a multiple-assessment procedure they believed would greatly help in selecting military officers. The Germans knew that paper and pencil tests alone didn't give a proper or total picture of a person's potential as an officer and wanted to be able to observe the behaviour of potential candidates under different situations. England and the United States soon followed Germany's technique, using a similar procedure to select spies. Since, this wartime effort, American and European businesses have used and improved the multiple-assessment concept, now using these centers for staff development and promotional purposes.

An assessment centre is one of the most sophisticated selection methods available. It is a process incorporating group and individual exercises, tests and interviews for the measurement of performance against key criteria, which have been identified (by job analysis research) as critical to the success of a particular position, or level of management. Research has shown assessment centres to be a much more accurate and cost effective way of selecting individuals than a standard interview. They work on the principle of multi-trait multi-method assessment. Any single assessment method may give misleading results; some people interview well, while others are good at tests, whereas a well designed assessment process is based on a criteria/assessment grid and allows multiple assessments of each criteria.

Why use them?

Many major business, government and non-profit organisations are now using assessment centres to assist them in selecting their future employees, due to the wide range of benefits they offer.

Assessment centers can

- Improve the accuracy of selection decisions by providing the opportunity to observe candidates actually handling the types of tasks and situations with which they will be faced on the job.
- Produce a far higher capacity for predicting job performance than that of an unstructured interview.
- Save time and money by combining selection, assessment and the identification of training needs in the same procedure.
- Allow group testing; saving time and staff resources when compared to one-to-one testing.
- Create group dynamics, allowing aspects of the individual to be studied that cannot be measured by other means.
- Allow one to obtain a more accurate impression of candidates' true qualities.
- Help an organization in the early identification of management potential and in the diagnosis of individual management development. Thus, training and development effort can be invested more cost effectively.
- Provide valuable training for those managers used as assessors, particularly in the areas of performance appraisal, counseling and interviewing skills.

In short, assessment centers are a good way of predicting how a candidate is likely to behave on a job.

How can competency models be used to integrate all HR functions?

A competency model, when developed and constructed appropriately, is a beautiful thing. For example, if a thoroughout job analysis is conducted, the job analyst should have a plethora of information about the job of interest. These data should alert the HR team which competencies should be required upon hiring (*i.e.*, the competencies for selection) and which competencies could be learned on the job (*i.e.*, the competencies for training and development). In addition, since the job analysis will make very clear that the competencies are absolutely required for effective job performance, it should also be these same competencies that are used to design compensation systems, develop incentive programs, and should be the exact criteria on which a performance appraisal system is based. In other words, the competency model is the mechanism by which all HR functions are linked together. It is the umbrella. It is the circulatory system. It is the anchor. There are a striking number of organizations that have yet to discover this truth. However, it is my colleagues and my hope that HR practitioners will come to understand that this is the best way to develop HR systems that are effective (valid), fair, and legally defendable.

Why are assessment centers well suited for integrated HR systems?

Several global companies are beginning to discover that an effective tool for linking HR practices together through competencies is the assessment center method. Assessment Centers (ACs) refer to a method by which applicants or employees participate in several assessments, some of which are behavioural simulation exercises, which are observed and rated by multiple trained assessors. The AC method allows for multiple competencies to be assessed across multiple assessment formats. Research has shown that the method is quite valid for both selecting/promoting employees as well as for diagnosing training needs. In addition, because behavioural simulation exercises are used, and feedback can be incorporated at multiple points in the assessment process, ACs have also been shown to be successful in training and development interventions. We refer to such centers as DACs (Developmental Assessment Centers) because they are for the purpose of assessment, diagnosis, and development. If the job analysis/competency modelling process is carried out appropriately, information collected about the job can be used to develop behavioural definitions for each competency, and can also be used to develop high fidelity assessments (*e.g.*, behavioural simulation exercises).

Assessment Center Process

Three trained assessors evaluate participants, in groups of six, on their performance in eight individual and group exercises. A candidate's overall evaluation is based on a pooling of information from the assessors. Performance on the eight exercises rate according to 16 job-related dimensions that were identified by a team of county chairs at a special job-analysis workshop. The dimensions, with abbreviated definitions, the exercises, and how the exercises relate to the different roling dimensions. Here's a brief description of the eight exercises:

Inbasket: Assesses are given an adequate period of time to respond to a number of actual letter, memos, etc. taken from county chair inbaskets.

Inbasket: Interview. Assesses explain their handling of these items to assessors.

1. **Leaderless Group (Assigned Roles):** Assesses are assigned an issue that will require a verbal report. Adequate preparation time is given. After the report, the balance of the allotted time is used by the six assesses to come to a consensus on the issue.
2. **Leaderless Group (Unassigned Roles):** Assesses are each given a description of the same typical county problem. The group is then charged with coming to a consensus on how to handle the problem in an allotted time period.
3. **Case-Study Analysis:** Assesses are given a typical county budget problem and an adequate amount of time to provide a written solution.
4. **Background Interview:** Assessor's interview assesses one-on-one to determine leadership qualities, communication skills, and ability to work with committees or small groups.
5. **Fact Finding:** Assesses are given an overview of a conflict in a county office. They then question the resource person (assessor) for additional facts that would help solve the problem. After a short period provided to organize their thoughts, they explain to the assessor how they'd handle the conflict.
6. **Interview Simulation:** Assesses are given some background information on a "typical" county agent (either agriculture, or home economics) for overnight perusal. The next day, they interview this agent (actor) in a performance appraisal setting.

The assessment planning, implementing and continually evaluating such a program worth it? We've discovered, as others have, that the center:

1. Has greater validity for promotion and selection than traditional techniques.
2. Having been developed on the basis of a job analysis is inherently content-valid.
3. Has shown itself to be a better indicator of future success than any other tool yet devised.
4. Is relatively objective, provides uniform standards for judgment by trained observers, is valid, and can serve as a developmental experience for the participants.
5. Could aid an organization in the early identification of management potential and in the diagnosis of individual management development needs so that training and development efforts can be invested more efficiently.

We are particularly concerned with numbers 4 and 5, in that we're trying to provide a valid developmental activity that not only will aid current chairs, but help administration choose competent agents for future chair positions. Plans are to continue to help administration select county chairs and help agents with developmental plans that will aid them in sharpening specific skills needed to be effectively utilized by the organization.

Critical Incident Technique Method

The critical incident method of performance appraisal involved identifying and describing specific events (or incidents) where the employee did something really well or something that needs improvement. It's a technique based on the description of the event, and does not rely on the assignment of ratings or rankings, although it is occasionally coupled with a ratings type system.

The use of critical incidents is more demanding of the manager since it requires more than ticking off things on a form—the manager must actually write things out. On the other hand critical incidents can be exceedingly useful in helping employees improve since the information in them is more detailed and specific than in methods that involve rating employees.

Some managers encourage employees to record their own critical incidents (where the employee excelled, situations that did not go well). That's an interesting variation that places more responsibility with the employee, and also does not require the manager to have been present when the incident occurred.

Generally, it's important that incidents be recorded AS THEY OCCUR, and not written at or around the annual performance review. Delaying the recording of critical incident reports (either good incidents or not so good) means a loss of detail and accuracy.

Critical incident technique is a method of gathering facts (incidents) from domain experts or less experienced users of the existing system to gain knowledge of how to improve the performance of the individuals involved:

- Basic Description
- How To
- Special Considerations

The Critical Incident Technique (CIT) is used to look for the cause of human-system (or product) problems to minimize loss to person, property, money or data. The investigator looks for information on the performance of activities (*e.g.*, tasks in the workplace) and the user-system interface. Both operators and records (*e.g.*, documented events or recorded telephone calls) can provide such information. The investigator may focus on a particular incident or set of incidents which caused serious loss. Critical events are recorded and stored in a database or on a spreadsheet. Analysis may show how clusters of difficulties are related to a certain aspect of the system or human practice. Investigators then develop possible explanations for the source of the difficulty.

Despite numerous variations in procedures for gathering and analyzing critical incidents researchers and practitioners agree about the definition of what Critical Incident Technique (CIT) analysis should do:

The critical incidents technique can be defined as *a set of procedures for systematically identifying behaviours that contribute to success or failure of individuals or organizations in specific situations.*

In real world task performance, users are perhaps in the best position to recognize critical incidents caused by usability problems and design flaws in the user interface. Critical incident identification is arguably the single most important kind of information associated with task performance in usability oriented context.

Several methods have been developed for conducting usability evaluation without direct observation of a user by an evaluator. However, contrary to the modern—'user reported critical incident method', none of the existing remote evaluation methods (nor even traditional laboratory-based evaluation) meets all the following criteria for a successful CIT analysis:

Data are centred around real critical incidents that occur during a task performance.

Tasks are performed by real users.

Users are located in their normal working environment.

Data are captured in normal task situations, not contrived laboratory settings.

Users self report their own critical incidents after they have happened.

No direct interaction takes place between user and evaluator during the description of the incident(s).

Quality data can be captured at low cost to the user.

Typical application areas

Useful for obtaining in-depth data about a particular role or set of tasks. Also extremely useful to obtain detailed feedback on a design option.

The basic steps involved are:

Gather facts (incidents) about what actually happened

- Before
- During
- After the incident

Analyse the content of the verbal report.

Infer how to improve performance based on the above feedback.

Step 1: Gathering facts

The methodology usually employed is an open-ended questionnaire, gathering retrospective data. The events should have happened fairly recently: the longer the time period between the events and their gathering, the greater the danger that the users may reply with imagined stereotypical responses. Interviews can also be used, but these must be handled with extreme care not to bias the user.

CIT generates a list of good and bad behaviours, which can then be used for performance appraisal.

Vague, generic answers suggest:

- Poor focus of study to begin with.
- Inaccurate perceptions/memory in users.
- Response bias or cultural norm responding.

Step 2: Content analysis

Subsequent steps in the CIT consist of identifying the content or themes represented by clusters of incidents and conducting "retranslation" exercises during which the analyst or other respondents sort the incidents into content dimensions or categories. These steps help to identify incidents that are judged to represent dimensions of the behaviour being considered.

This can be done using a simple spreadsheet. Every item is entered as a separate incident to start with, and then each of the incidents is compiled into categories. Category membership is marked as:

- Identical
- Quite similar
- Could be similar.

This continues until each item is assigned to a category on at least a 'quite similar' basis.

Each category is then given a name and the numbers of the responses in the category are counted. These are in turn converted into percentages (of total number of responses) and a report is formulated.

Step 3: Creating feedback

It is important to consider not only the bad (negative) features of the report, but also the positive ones, so as not to undo good work, or to make destructive recommendations.

The poor features should be arranged in order of frequency, using the number of responses per category. Same with the good features.

Go back to the software and examine the circumstances that led up to each category of critical incident. Identify what aspect of the interface was responsible for the incident. Sometimes one finds that there is not one, but several aspects of an interaction that lead to a critical incident; it is their conjunction together that makes it critical and it would be an error to focus on one salient aspect for instance, to focus on the very last event before the incident when a litany of errors has preceded it.

Drawbacks of the method

1. It focuses on critical incidents therefore routine incidents will not be reported. It is therefore poor as a tool for routine task analysis.
2. Respondents may still reply with stereotypes, not actual events. Using more structure in the form improves this but not always.
3. Success of the user reported critical incident method depends on the ability of typical end users to recognize and report critical incidents effectively, but there is no reason to believe that all users have this ability naturally.

Interview Techniques

Almost every organization uses the interview techniques in some shape or form, as the part of competency mapping. Enormous amounts of research have been conducted into interviews and the numerous books have been written on the subject. There are however, a few general guidelines, the observation of which should aid the use of an interview for competency mapping.

An interview is a face-to-face situation. The applicant is on guard and careful to present the best face possible. At the same time, he or she is in tense, nervous and possibly frightened. Therefore, during the interview, tact and sensitivity can be very useful. The fundamental step is establishing 'rapport' putting the interview at ease, conveying the impression that the interview is a conversation between two friends, and not a confrontation of employees and employers. Once the interviewee is put at ease the interviewer starts asking questions, of seeking information related to the job. It is advisable to follow the simple to the complex sequence while asking questions. Leading questions should be avoided because they give the impression that the interviewer is seeking certain kinds of answers. Finally, the interviewer should discuss the interview, identify areas of disagreement, and make a tentative decision about the candidate.

- Before the actual interviews begin, the critical areas in which questions will be asked must be identified for judging ability and skills. It is advisable to write down these critical areas with examples, and form a scale to rate responses. If there is more than one interviewer, some practice and mock interviews will help calibrate variations in individual interviews rating.
- The second step is to scrutinize the information provided skills, incidences and experiences in the career of the candidate, which may answer questions raised around the critical areas. This procedure will make interviews less defferent from the reality and the applicant will be more comfortable because the discussion will focus on his experiences.
- An interview is a face-to-face situation. Therefore, during the interview, tact and sensitivity can be very useful. The interviewer can get the better response if he creates a sense of ease and informally and hence uncover clues to the interviewee's motivation, attitudes, feelings temperament, etc. which are otherwise difficult to comprehend.
- The fundamental step is to establishing the "rapport" by putting the interviewee at ease; conveying the impression that the interview is conversation between two friends and not the confrontation between the employee and the employer. One way is to achieve this by initially asking questions not directly related to the job, *i.e.*, chatting casually about the weather and journey etc.
- Once the interview is put to ease the interviewer starts asking the questions, or seeking information related to the job. Here, again it is extremely important to lead up to complex questions gradually. Thus, it is advisable to follow the pattern of simple-to-complex sequence.
- Showing the surprises or disapproval of speech, clothes, or answers to questions can also inhibit the candidate. The interviewee is over-sensitive to such questions. Hence, an effort to try and understand the interviewee's point of view and orientation can go long way in getting to know the applicant.
- Leading question should be avoided because they give the impression that the interview is seeking certain kind of answers. This may create a conflict in the interview, if he has strong views on the subjects. Nor should the interviewer allow the interview to get out of the hand. He should be alert and check the interviewee if he tries to lead the discussion in the areas where he feels extremely competent, if it is likely to stray fro the relevant areas.
- The interview should be prepare with precise questions, and not take too much of time in framing them.

Once this phase is over, the interviewers should discuss the interviewees, identify areas of agreement and disagreement, and make tentative decisions about the candidate. It will be helpful if, in addition to rating the applicants, interviewers made short notes on their impression of candidates' behaviour responses. Which can then be discussed later? If the interview is to continue for many days and evaluation of the days work, content of the questions and general pattern of response should be made for possible. In addition, large number of methods have been developed to measure and map competencies. Most of them are of recent origin and are designed to identify those skills, attitudes and knowledge that are suited for most for specific job.

Questionnaires

Questionnaires are written list of questions that users fill out questionnaires and return. You begin questions about your product based on the type of information you want to know. The questionnaires sources below provide more information on designing effective questions. These techniques can be used at any point of time of development, depending on the questions that are asked in the questionnaires. Often questionnaires are used after products are shipped to assess customer satisfaction with the product. Such questionnaires often identify usability issues that should have been caught in house before the product was released.

(*a*) ***Common Matric Questionnaire (CMQ):*** They examine some of the competencies to work performances and have five such sections *i.e.*, Background, contact with the people, decision-making, physical and mechanical activities and work setting.

(*b*) ***Functional Job Analysis:*** The most recent version of Functional Job Analysis uses seven scales to describe what worker does in their jobs. These are: Things, Data, People, Worker Instructions, Reasoning, Mathematics and Proficiency of the languages.

(*c*) ***Multipurpose Occupational System Analysis Inventory (MOSAI):*** The job analysis inventory collects data from the office of the personal management system through a variety of descriptors. There are two major descriptors such as the task and competencies. Tasks are rated on importance and competencies are rated on several scales including importance and requirements for performing the task.

(*d*) ***Occupational Inventory Analysis:*** The major analysis is based on five folds: Information Received, Mental Activities, Work Behaviour, Work Goals, and Work Context. Then the matching is done between competencies and work requirements.

(*e*) ***Position Analysis Questionnaire (PAQ):*** It is the instrument for measuring the job characteristics that fall into five categories: Information input, mental processes, work output, relationship with other persons and job context.

(*f*) ***Work Profiling System (WPS):*** It helps employers to accomplish the human resources functions. The competency approach is designed to yield reports targeted towards various human resource functions such as individual development planning, employee selection, and the job description which covers all types of functions of an organization. This is consisting of structured questionnaires which measures ability and personality attributes.

Psychometric Tests

Most of the organizations are using the psychometric evaluation as the part of their selection and other related functions in HR. This is a prospect for some people towards the understanding about the unknown. It is a standardized measurement of sample behaviour. Most of the psychometric tests are classified in two broad categories *i.e.*, Aptitude Tests and Achievement Tests.

Some of the methods that can be used to map competencies are

- Identification and Analysis of Tasks/Jobs
- Analyze Recruitment Strategies
- Interviews
- Questionnaires

- Performance Appraisals: Assessment Centre
- Group feedback

Following is a step-by-step process of creating a competency map

- Profile, a particular job or a role.
- Work out competencies with the help of a job specialist; interviewing past members who have been successful in that role or current members successful in that role, will additionally help.
- Point out knowledge, skills, attitudes, values etc.
- Competencies are then further broken down into results *i.e.*, what has to be achieved, behavioural indicators etc.
- Once done, the same process can then be repeated for other roles too.

More on SWOT analysis

A SWOT analysis is a strategic planning tool used to identify the strengths, weaknesses, opportunities and threats involved in a project or venture. It audits both an organization and its environment. SWOT gives a good snapshot of an individual's approach as well as his competencies by indicating internal factors such as the individual's strengths and weaknesses, and the external factors in the environment that serve as opportunities and threats to the individual's strengths and weaknesses as well as to the company.

SWOT is highly recommended because of its ease of use and its ability to scope the entire setting (playing field) *i.e.*, both internal and external factors (environments), its ability to match between the two and because of its ability to chart out sound strategies thereafter.

How to fill capability gaps?

Once the capability gaps have been identified, they can be filled by:

- Moving to technologies which are recent and the need of the hour.
- Obtaining appropriate capabilities.
- Training available resources through workshops and seminars.
- Coaching and mentoring existing team.

How to avoid capability gaps?

Capability gaps can be avoided by incorporating an integrated strategic planning process to facilitate development of cohesive planning options that anticipates and identifies potential gaps, so that timely and cost-effective solutions can be formulated. This planning process, then needs to be integrated to a smart decision-making process that will seek to implement the outcome of the planning process.

Capability gaps are closely tied with customer needs and requirements. It is crucial then to:

- Constantly define customer needs.
- Constantly review, evaluate solutions and people capabilities. It is pivotal that an organization keeps pace with the best solutions that the market offers.
- Constantly evaluate to see if customer requirements are met, else identify the discrepancy and re-run the same process.

Conclusion

Competence refers to an individual's knowledge, skills, abilities, or personality characteristics that directly influence his or her job performance. The concept of individual competence has a long tradition in the managerial field. Most of this work has focused on leaders and general managers. Other research has sought to specify HR competencies through interviews with executives within a single firm or from a limited set of firms. Many companies have tried to identify HR competencies by asking line managers within the company what they expect from HR and the kinds of competencies HR professionals should exemplify (*e.g.*, what line managers need from HR). This approach assumes that each company may have unique expectations of its human resources professionals and that, as clients, line managers play a central role in defining those expectations.

Defining HR competencies company by company through executive interviews has some advantages. For one thing, it anchors the findings in behaviours, because the questions asked in the interviews can target actual cases in which HR professionals within the company demonstrated competence. It also tailors the process to the specific needs of the companies in question. However, the danger is that executives may not know what they don't know. That is, they may identify only those competencies they have seen, when in fact other HR competences may have more importance for their firm if they only knew about them. This approach may also lead to biased results, depending on the sample of executives chosen for interviews. Executives' managerial orientation, rather than the actual needs of the business, may influence their expectations of HR. The line managers that have never seen HR professionals in a strategic role may not be able to think of HR as anything other than administrative overhead.

In the years ahead, agencies will likely be given new authorities to design unique pay systems tailored to their agency mission. HR professionals will be relied upon by managers to use their HR technical competencies to help design and implement these new pay systems and to meet other challenges that arise in aligning HR systems to agency mission. In addition to HR technical expertise which will be a continuing requirement, competencies in the areas of system design, organizational culture, business strategy, change, consensus building, consultation, communication, and marketing skills will be even more important than they are now. A cross-functional team of HR experts and agency managers and based on the experience, managers will be willing to bring HR "to the table" once HR has proven its worth. The most credible HR professionals in the eyes of the managers are those who serve in the role of business partner by providing a variety of options and solutions. Instead of just saying "no" to some perhaps ill-conceived idea, HR experts say "yes" and help managers design systems tailored to their agencies within the framework of the Merit System Principles. With increased flexibility in pay, performance-based organizations and higher expectations on the part of 16 line managers for strategic HR programs, HR will also be relied upon to a greater extent to serve in the role of change agent. That is, they will be called upon not only to design new HR systems and processes, but also to facilitate and manage the change process. Knowing that these changes are necessary is a major step on the road to transforming HR. To begin moving forward, agencies need to know where they stand in terms of the necessary HR competencies that are required for organizational effectiveness. As mentioned earlier, the next report in this study will provide findings and insights on which competencies are currently possessed by Federal HR professionals. These will be compared to those competencies which experts in both the private and Federal sectors say are needed now and in the future. Based on this analysis, competency gaps will be identified and practical recommendations will be made so that each agency can assess its own situation, take corrective actions, and better prepare to meet the future challenges of our dynamic HR community-based organizations.

CASE STUDY–I Management skills builder: Issue and exercise

Ron Moore has worked for Assessment System, Inc., for five years. In his third year with the company, he was recognized as a top performer because of his outstanding enthusiasm and reliability, his team orientation, and his dedication to charitable activities. Don Madison, his manager, was very proud of Moore's performance and often held him up as a model employee. A little over a year ago, Madison left to direct an overseas arm of Assessment Systems, Inc., and another manager, Paul Adams, took his place. Shortly afterward, Moore's performance began to decline.

When Adams arrived, Madison told him that Moore was an excellent performer. Adams met with Moore and told him that he felt fortunate to have such a good performer under his direction.

At first, things went well. Adams found he could even count on Moore to take responsibility when Adams was called away for meetings and other duties. Then Adams started to notice a dip in Moore's performance. At first this consisted of avoiding responsibility in Adams's absence and responding to other employees' requests by telling them to wait for Adams to deal with the issue. Then Moore started calling in sick and showing up late for work. This pattern was unprecedented in Moore's work record, and Adams thought that Moore might be having some personal problems. He decided not to confront him about the change in his performance, but rather to cut his some slack so he could work out whatever problems he was having.

When the performance problems continued for more than a months, Adams felt compelled to confront Moore. The following conversation occurred at Moore's workstation after he arrived late yet again.

Adams: About time you rolled in, Ron. I've been waiting for you since 8 A.M., and it's now 12 minutes after. I don't have time for this and you, award-winning performance or not, have no business showing up here late.

Moore: Well, good morning, Paul. It's nice to see you.

Adams: Listen; don't give me that nonchalant stuff. Your whole attitude has become too nonchalant. It's time you turned things around.

Moore: Hey, what's the big deal? Other people come in late and don't have you jumping on them for it.

Adams: I know what you're capable of, Ron. You owe it to yourself and the company to perform to the best of your potential. I'm going to be watching you closely from now on, and another string of absences or late arrivals in going to get you a verbal warning.

Adams walked away. He hated making threats, and the confrontation had gone even worse than he had anticipated. But, he told himself, he couldn't just let things go on as they were. He hoped he would see Moore's performance jump back to what it had been when he first arrived at the unit.

Two weeks later, Adams was examining performance records and noticed that Moore was today only one day. "What an improvement," he thought, "I guess our little talk did some good after all. "But this positive feeling soon disappeared when he noticed Moore's productivity. Although Moore had routinely performed at or near the top, he was now in the average range. Another talk with Moore was definitely in order.

Adams: Ron, your performance over the past few weeks hasn't been up to pay. You can do better if you apply yourself. I know you can.

Moore: What do you mean; My performance hasn't been up to par?

Adams: It looks like you've locked the problem of getting here on time, but your productivity is off. You're only hitting the average for your group.

Moore: So, what's so bad about average?

Adams: You know the answer to that. You're capable of doing better. Let me give you some advice. I've had rough periods, too. The key is to just knuckle down and do it. When the going gets tough, the tough get going, and all that sort of thing. OK?

Moore: Yeah, I'll see what I can do.

Moore's performance problems continued and so did Adam's frustration. Every performance record gave Adam's a reason to confront Moore. The confrontations accomplished nothing and Adams was feeling increasingly frustrated. The annual appraisal was coming around, and Adams was considering giving Moore a low rating so that he would get the message that his performance was unacceptable.

Consider the Issue

1. What is wrong with Adams's approach to managing Moore's performance problem?
2. Do you agree with Adams's decision to give Moore a low rating to send him a message? Why or why not?

Take Action

1. How would you try to identify the causes(s) of Moore's performance difficulties?
2. How would you approach the issue of improving Moore's performance?

Do It Together

1. Form groups of three students each. One student in each group takes the role of Ron Moore and the other two play Ron's coworkers. The role-play begins with Ron describing his recent run-ins with Paul Adams, perhaps over lunch. The coworkers should react as they think coworkers would react in such a situation.
2. Form pairs of students. One student takes the role of Paul Adams, the second the role of Don Madison. Paul has placed on overseas call to Ron Moore's former boss because he is very frustrated by his inability to reach Ron. Role-play the resulting phone conversation.
3. Form into groups of four students each. One student assumes the role of Ron and another plays Paul Adams. The situation is the performance review session that has followed the interactions described in the case. As the two students role-play that session, the other two students observe and then critique the interaction. What alternate approaches might Adams take?

CASE STUDY–2 Performance contributions with organizational goals

A College of Business at a large university (we will not name it, but this is a description of a real project) is currently implementing a new professor teaching appraisal system that is linked directly to college goals. Some of the college goals include teaching international aspects of business, providing team skills and sensitivity to ethical issues, and encouraging collaborative learning. The dean formed a committee to develop ways to measure how well professors meet each of these goals. For example, the committee proposed that student give feedback about how much they developed team collaboration skills in a course or how much they improved their ability to make ethical decisions.

With this type of appraisal system, the college goals are the dimensions on which professor performance levels are measured. Because the major purpose of the new appraisal system is to encourage professors to contribute to the college goals in their teaching efforts, merit pay is tied to well professors rate in the categories.

QUESTIONS

1. A number of professors are concerned that their courses do not contribute to all the goals. For instance, a course might address the international but not the ethical goal. How do you think this problem should be dealt within the appraisal system?
2. Do you think students should be the rates in this appraisal system? What other sources of appraisal would you concerned?
3. A number of faculty are concerned that student ratings are only a popularity contest and do not indicate teaching quality or amount of learning. Do you agree?

GROUP LEARNING EXERCISES

1. In small groups design a faculty evaluation system for your college. Here are some key issues to address:
    - What should be the criteria?
    - How should performance be measured (what items, or outcomes, and so on)?
    - Who should be the raters?
    - Should faculty set weights on criteria or choose criteria to be evaluated on?
    - Should customers be involved in developing the system? Who are the customers?
2. The college goals promote teamwork and a collaborative learning environment. However, some faculties are gifted presenters and may not perform as well if forced into a different mode of instruction.
    (*a*) Form small groups of two to six people and discuss this issue. The problem described here has been characterized as a less than optimal use of the human resource. Describe what you think this statement means.
    (*b*) What should be done about the problem? Should all faculties be forced into the same mode of instruction? If not, what should be measured in the appraisal?

REFERENCES

1. American Compensation Association, *Raising the bar: Using competencies to enhance employee performance,* May 1996.
2. American Compensation Association's Competencies Research Team, "The role of competencies in an integrated HR strategy" *ACA Journal,* Summer 1996. pp. 5–21.
3. Cofsky, Kathryn M. "Critical Keys to Competency-Based Pay," *Compensation and Benefits Review,* November-December 1993. pp. 46–52.

4. Corporate Leadership Council, *Developing individual competencies for HR professionals.* April 1998. pp. 1–13. Washington: The Advisory Board Company.
5. Corporate Leadership Council, *Developing a strategic HR function: Aligning individual.*
6. *Competencies,* January 1997, Washington: The Advisory Board Company.
7. Laabs, Jennifer, "Why HR can't win today." *Workforce,* May 1998, pp. 62–74.
8. National Academy of Public Administration. *A Competency model for human resources.*
9. *Professionals,* June 1996, Schoonver, Stephen C., Phd. *Human resource competencies for the year 2000: The wake-up call.* Society for Human Resource Management. 1998.
10. Spencer, Lyle M., David C. McClelland, and Signe M. Spencer, *Competency assessment methods: History and state of the art.* Boston: Hay/McBer Research Press, 1990.
11. Spencer, Lyle M., and Signe M. Spencer, *Competence at work: Models for superior performance.* New York: J. Wiley and Sons, 1993.
12. Tucker, Sharon A., and Kathryn M. Cofsky, "Competency-based pay on a banding platform." *ACA Journal,* Spring 1994, Volume 3, Number 1.
13. Ulrich, Dave, "The future calls for change." *Workforce,* January 1998. pp. 87–91.
14. Ulrich, Dave, *Human resource champions.* Harvard Business School, Boston, MA, 1997, pp. 1–281.
15. Ulrich, Dave, "A new mandate for human resources," *Harvard Business Review,* 1998.
16. USDA Graduate School, *Competency based training task force report,* October 1998.
17. U.S. Merit Systems Protection Board, *Federal personnel offices: Time for change?* 1993, p. 18
18. Yeung, Arthur, Patricia Woolcock, and John Sullivan, "Identifying and developing HR competencies for the future: Keys to sustaining the transformation of HR functions." *Human Resource Planning.* 1996, Volume 19, Number 4, pp 48–58.
19. W.F. Cascio, Applied psychology in personnel management, (Reston, Virginia: Reston Publishing Co., Inc., 1982).
20. Task Force on Assessment Center Standards, Standards and Ethical Considerations for Assessment Center Operations, (New Orleans, Louisiana: June 1979).
21. K. McNutt, "Behavioural Consistency and Assessment Centers: A Reconciliation of the literature," Journal of Assessment Center Technology, II (1979), 1–6.
22. C.L. Jaffee and J.T. Sefcik, "What Is an Assessment Center?", Personnel Administrator (February 1980), 40–43 and Joseph Kwarteng, Assessment Center Validity and Reliability: An Evaluation of The Ohio Cooperative Extension Service Assessment Center (Ph.D. dissertation, The Ohio State University, Columbus, 1986).
23. W.C. Byham, "Assessment Centers for Spotting Future Managers," in Perspectives on Employees, Staffing, and Selection, G.F. Dreher and P.R. Sackett, eds. (Homewood, Illinois: Irwin, 1983), pp. 229–47.
24. Byham, "Assessment Centers"; J.R. Hinricks and S. Haanpera, "Reliability of Measurement in Situational Exercises: An Assessment of the Assessment Center Method," Personnel Psychology, XXIX (1976), 31–40; and Leslie Bart, The Role of Assessee Involvement in Development Assessment Center (Ph.D. dissertation, The Ohio State University, Columbus, 1986).
25. Bart, Role of Assessee and W.C. Byham, "The Assessment Center as an Aid in Management Development," in Contemporary Problems in Personnel, rev. ed., W.C. Hamner and F.L. Schmidt, eds. (Chicago, Illinois: St. Clair, 1977).

8 CHAPTER

POTENTIAL APPRAISAL, ASSESSMENT CENTER AND CAREER SUCCESSION PLANNING

8.1 INTRODUCTION

Commitment to the 'People, Process, and Technology' (PP and T) concept has never been more prevalent among businesses. Large firms, small firms, service firms, product firms, global firms, and regional firms alike—all, it seems, have adopted the potentials of human resources. But given the ease with which "people, process, and technology" rolls off the tongue, it can be easy to begin to continuously group them together as three equal and homogeneous concepts. In reality, the most successful businesses consider each element—and its proper weighting and role in organizational execution—individually and carefully. Increasingly, organizations are realizing that people, process, and technology do not carry equal weight in organizational design. People, process, and technology do not require the same type or degree of attention and interaction in order to succeed. Unfortunately, not every company has recognized that lesson. Given the importance of the employee in reaching organizational goals, it is surprising how little is invested in human capital management, best companies to work for demonstrates the importance of training to companies committed to attract the best human capital. On and on the human capital theme go down Fortune's list; investment in training and the establishment of strong goal-oriented reward systems to attract and maintain the best possible personnel. Combine the improved workflow of a well-trained employee with the reduction in the 'hidden cost' of employee turnover by engaging, incentivizing and retaining key employees, and the dividends begin to stack higher and higher. But one key component is still crucial to realizing those financial returns: ensuring that employees are focused and directed toward achieving the company's goals.

The employees aspire to grow and expect this growth to take place at frequent intervals. Achievements of organizational goal, increased productivity and fulfillment of corporate objectives can be possible if the employees are feeling satisfaction and achievement. To achieve this, there must be a well thought system of career planning and also the succession planning in an organization. This chapter deals with the growth opportunities as provided by the organization.

Human capital is one of the most challenging strategic assets to manage for many firms. It can often seem easier to choose exciting new technology products or revisit existing business processes with the latest management textbook thinking than to carefully and objectively develop a plan for maximizing the value of human capital. But as shown in this document, the ultimate source of maximum enterprise value for an organization is seated at desks and around conference room tables, not located in the data center or the process transformation 'war room.' Investing in human capital provides a true 'force multiplier' for the other elements of the people, process, and technology equation; such investment does not just improve the efficiency of good processes and state-of-the-art technology, but amplifies their effectiveness by orders of magnitude. We, the people are committed to the success of the process in order to:

1. Fully develop employee potential and improve communication relating to performance.
2. Provide a method to reward employees on a merit basis.
3. Improve productivity and the performance of the organization.
4. Reinforce mission, value and culture.

The success of the process depends on your understanding and use of the performance appraisal process as an opportunity to improve your productivity and develop your full potential. Understanding expectations is an important element of the appraisal process. Defining the expectations is the joint responsibility of you and your supervisor. Using the job description as a starting point, employees and supervisors must develop a mutual understanding of the roles, responsibilities and expectations of the position. The objectives of the performance appraisal are to provide feedback on your past performance, to agree on standards for future performance, and to develop goals and objectives for your personal and professional growth. For these objectives to be achieved, both you and your manager must have a good understanding of the process and fully support it. In addition to your annual performance appraisal, supervisors should conduct reviews regularly during the year in order to discuss the employee's progress toward accomplishing desired results and to address ongoing issues. Good employee relations are built upon fair and equitable treatment. We must base our treatment of employees on definite standards, applied fairly and without discrimination. The performance appraisal is a tool to honestly and objectively evaluate performance.

Maximizing the People Potential

Most employees now-a-days expect to be appraised as part of their job. But now can appraisals be used to add real value and meet the strategic needs of the organization. A performance appraisal is a discussion between two people (normally line manager and employee) which sets out to achieve the following:

- Confirms the progress of the individual.
- Highlights the strengths and development areas of the person against previously agreed objectives.
- Examines ways to develop strengths and overcome weaknesses.
- Identifies training and development needs.
- Ensures that both manager and employee are involved in and committed to further performance improvement.
- Raised performance levels.

- Identification of potential.
- Feedback.
- Increased motivation.

People designated as leaders because of their actions, rather than title alone, know that their success is measured by the success of their employees. Such leaders know that if they foster an inhospitable environment, only the hardiest of employees—like the determined Cops will grow despite the harsh conditions. The most skillful leaders uncover and help nurture individuals' potential, using missteps or mistakes as opportunities to augment and build on strengths. This approach elevates the performance of the group, and thus, supports and reflects well on the leader.

However, many evaluation methods, such as performance reviews, focus too heavily on identifying areas of low performance or weakness. Concentrating on these weaknesses, without highlighting strengths and emphasizing how weak areas might be strengthened, may result in a self-fulfilling prophecy, where you build a poor image of the employee and he performs "down to" his potential. Or it can lead to waste of resources, where you get a minimal level of performance from an employee with star potential.

Some results of under-expecting the performance potential of employees are guaranteed, in comparison to what's possible: Low morale, unsatisfactory performance and higher degrees of employee turnover.

How can you unearth and nurture an employee's strengths?

Make time for positive recognition: Whether in casual conversation or a formal performance review, think about and genuinely express positive feedback for the employee. Be specific about what she or he is doing well, and share examples. The benefit is two-fold: The employee knows what behaviours are most valued, and what help shift your thinking from "can't do" to "there's potential here."

Identify ways to apply existing strengths in new ways: Thomas Edison saw sewing-thread as a light bulb filament. What qualities has your employee demonstrated, and how can they translate to needed skills.

Ask the employee what he/she likes to do: There's a funny equation applied to many promotions: People who excel at a specific job are promoted to management level. Often, you've taken the person out of the exact environment in which he or she succeeds and likes—possibly reducing his or her success in the new position. Also, you cannot fully uncover a person's strengths without his or her input. Tap into what he or she discerns as his or her strengths by asking what he or she enjoys most, and why, and in what role he or she believes she or he of most value to the organization.

Get co-workers' thoughts: As the business leader, you work with employees in different ways than they work with each other. "Fertilize" your assessment about an employee's strengths with co-workers' thoughts. However, implementing a 360-degree feedback or sharing thank-you's at staff meetings can provide insight into traits and behaviours that suit and benefit the entire team.

Turn a weakness on its head: Physicists know that every action has an equal an opposite reaction. Applied to employees, consider, "What's the opposite of this weakness?" To unearth possible strengths. For instance, if an employee inconsistently completes projects that he or she developed in the first place, perhaps his or her strength is in generating ideas, not executing them.

Allow the employee to test-drive a new role: May be you' re seeing the employee in his or her specific role, yet more of his or her strengths would blossom in another role. This test-drive might spark new ideas about increased value from the employee, and allow you to see where a role-shift may make sense for the company.

These may be areas where the employee has not had a real opportunity to demonstrate the potential ability and there may be areas with which you, as the appraisers are not familiar. There are few indicators of potential which may be considered.

Fig: 8.1 Indicators of Potential

A sense of reality:	This is the extent to which a person thinks and acts objectively, resisting purely emotional pressures but pursuing realistic projects with enthusiasm.
Imagination:	The ability to let the mind range over a wide variety of possible causes of action, going beyond conventional approaches to situations and not being confined to, "This is the way it is always being done".
Power of Analysis:	The capacity to breakdown, reformulate or transform a complicated situation into manageable terms.
Breadth of Vision:	The ability to examine a problem in the context of much broader framework of reference; being able to detect, within a specific situation, relationships with those aspects which could be affecting the situation.
Persuasiveness:	The ability to sell ideas to other people and gain a continuing commitment, particularly when the individual is using personal influence rather than "management authority".

Sources: Adopted from Philip, Tom (1983). Making Performance Appraisal Work, McGraw Hill Ltd., UK.

Like the performance appraisal, potential appraisal is also done by the employees' supervisor who has had the opportunity to observe the employee for some time. Potential appraisal may be done either regularly or as and when required. The feed-back that you get from the appraisal should be constructive so that it can be used to help them progress as an individual by rectifying their weaknesses. It is important that you comment on their better aspects instead of just identifying their areas of concern. By doing so, it will give them the sense that they can perform and therefore will have the motivation to act upon any actions suggested. Once the feed-back has been acknowledged and an action plan has been created, you should have a follow up assessment to check up on the progress of the employee.

How to Appraise Potential

It is a tough practice, but it has tremendous potential. Measuring an employees potential in order to gauge today what he could achieve tomorrow may be the stiffest challenges ever posed to the science of performance appraisal and it is already worrying corporate India.

"People are like icebergs, what you see above the surface (Performance) is only a small part. A large part of the attributes needed to perform excellently in a future job which people call potential, is not immediately visible. It is hidden below the surface". Unleashing the iceberg may be the difficult, but it is also critical for corporate survival. Not only does potential appraisal help in catching high fliers but snapshot of breeding CEOs for the corporate.

The recent organizations are now redesigning their system by shifting from pure performance orientations-potential-cum-performance-based appraisal system.

"The potential to adapt to changing market conditions and the potential to assume responsibility for complex tasks and decisions have to be assessed early and continuously watched" .

In the matrix model, the vertical axis measure potential whiles the horizontal, performance. Both are further subdivided into two major parameter *i.e.*, low and high resulting the four quadrants of classification.

The Two-by-two Fig: 8.2 Matrix Model: The Philip Model

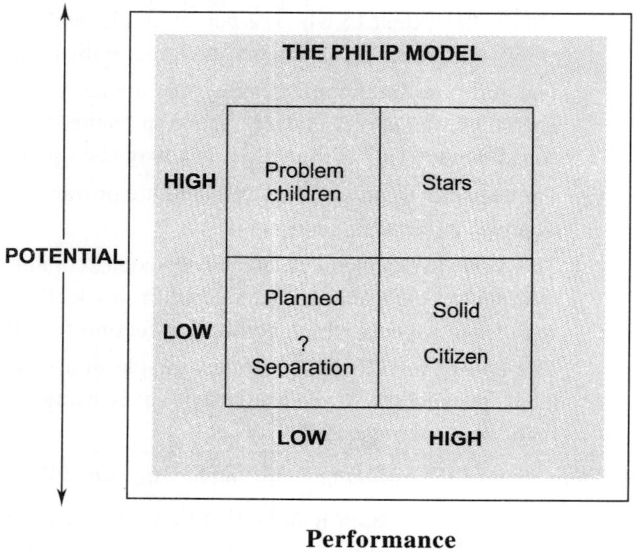

8.2 PERFORMANCE

Low potential-low performance: It defines these employees as question marks. The company asks such employees to improve their performance levels. If those efforts fail, it works towards a planned separation.

High potential–low performance: These are the problem children, in 8 out of 10 cases, if location, boss, or job profile changes, they groom to become star performers. To tap their potential such employees are given a new scenario to work in and are closely monitored. However, if the performance levels still remain low, they are reclassified as question marks and the separation process is initiated.

High potential–high performance: These are the star performers. These are the race horses. They are to be kept engaged with complex assignments all the time and groomed to take up the top positions in the organization. Or they will leave.

Low potential–high performance: Defined as the solid citizens'. High skilled but limited capability to grow beyond their current job–profile they constitute 70 to 75% of the companies employees. The company constantly recognizes their limitations and look after their needs. The potential appraisal system use a five point grading scale—excellent, very good, good/adequate, weak and insufficient—to evaluate employees on the four broad attributes of conceptual effectiveness operational effectiveness, impersonal effectiveness and achievement motivation.

Fig: 8.3 Potential Appraisal Criteria

Conceptual effectiveness	**Interpersonal effectiveness**
* Vision * Business orientation * Entrepreneural orientation * Sense of reality	* Network directedness * Negotiating power * Personal influences * Verbal behavior
Operational effectiveness	**Achievement motivation**
* Result orientation * Individual effectiveness * Risk-taking * Control	* Drive * Professional ambition * Innovativeness * Stability

Potential appraisal is the critical for succession planning. As it is encourages employees to grow from within the organization, the company already identified the potential candidates for the important positions of the company. As the informal cross-reference, the company also asks supervisors to fill out a small section in the performance appraisal form on employee potential by listing the attributes *i.e.*, accountability, attitudes, commitment, initiative, drive, judgment, leadership and ethics. To further assess its manager's potential, the company sets up task-forces to tackle minor and major emergencies. But some companies rate their employees on the basis of their generic competencies *i.e.*, Job Knowledge, Thinking Clearly, Goal-Setting and the Planning, Relationships, Leadership Innovation etc. "These competencies which are scored on a five point numerical rating scale, with five for outstanding performance and one for unsatisfactory performances. We believe that a potentially good manager must display certain behavioural characteristics which transcend his job". But for an accurate picture, a structured approach will be necessary. The company has able to measure the quantitatively measure the qualitative potential of their managers.

The Best Practices

- Build the appraisal and reward of potential into your assessment system.
- Clearly separate reward for potential from reward for past performances.
- Start evaluating potential as early as possible to identify the best talent.
- Factors used to evaluate potential must be explained to every employee.
- Communicate potential assessment to each individual at a regular interval.

Most businesses have invested in an arsenal of strategic and operational tools to deliver sustained corporate productivity. Their investments in structure, process and systems have yielded benefits in the short-term but for the some of the leading companies; this has leveled off fairly quickly and often, does not give a competitive edge any longer. Clearly the organizations need a new engagement model to build business agility and sustain productivity. An insight what constitutes the true value of organization's work force may possibly be the enduring driver of corporate growth; that companies need to recognize, cultivate and channel the inner potential of the individual workers as a source of organizational creativity, innovation.

Recognizing its managing energy, not Just People

The effective management of the strategic workforce extends beyond mapping their "hard skills and competencies" rationally and then deploying them to key initiatives. A holistic understanding of the individual, the acknowledgement of the emotional drivers of the employee potential, and the capacity to use this knowledge towards organizational goals are a powerful and strategic HR opportunity.

Unlocking individual potential and raising the organizational adrenalin can spur corporate growth even in the face of constrains in process, capital or other extrinsic factors. This built-in resistance to otherwise crippling issues that organizations have a sustainable road map to productivity. Cultivating the organizational energy is not easy.

Channeling the potential to Corporate Productivity

The management of rational extrinsic factors, like structure, process and subsystem needs to be matched to the effective management of intrinsic factors, like clarity, catalysts development and recognition. However, employees must always be recognized to perform in a manner and direction that is aligned to organizational goals that are well-defined, mutually accepted and transparent.

Fig: 8.4 Aligning HR with Business Strategy: Gartner's Four-Step Approach

Know strategy/goals	**Know intangible assets**	**Align assets and strategy: Drive performances**	**Measure and Reinvest**
Revenue growth, operational excellence, Innovation, Customer Satisfaction/ loyalty, Employee enrichment, Talent development.	Customer knowledge, Employee knowledge, Core competencies, Digitized information, Operational excellence, Networks, diversity, Experts, relationships	Work force Analysis Performance Management E-Learning E-Recruiting Knowledge Management Career/Succession Planning Talent Management	Financial return, Key performance indicators Economic value-added balanced scorecard Intellectual assets Balance sheet SBU scorecard.

Source: Gartner

Gartner research in a 2003 study recommended a four step approach to aligning with business strategy. Step three highlights specific systems that play a role in alignment of HR strategy to corporate goals. Further, according to a recent industry research, workforce management strategies that are disconnected from business needs will be unable to keep pace with shifting operational models in a volatile economy. To thrive, companies will need adaptive workforce management, which Forrester defines as "relentlessly aligning the supply of talent with changing business needs" .

However, without actively engaging the intrinsic potential of the workforce, an organization cannot expect its drive to corporate productivity to be optimal.

The enormity of human capital and its pivotal role in corporate productivity cannot be overstated. While the most of the organization have employed comprehensive process and rationale-driven metrics to drive performance, only a more holistic view of individual engagement in the workplace can raise organizational energy level and deliver a sustained boost in individual productivity.

Organizational energy can be recognized, cultivated and aligned to corporate goals simply when HR plans expand their scope of what constitutes individual engagement to the professional tasks. There are four basic sources—Clarity, Catalyst, Development and Recognition—must be tapped in a structured and transparent manner organization who thus optimize the investments in their people and find the organization gets the 'soft benefits' in the form of quicker response to the business events and opportunities, better deployment of capable resources to key initiatives, qualitative superiority and innovation in the work practices and a satisfied workforce that actually optimize the competitive advantage of the company.

Assessment center

We have a wealth of experience in assessment and development center design, delivery and management, role and competency profiling and are also able to design, and offer independent advice on, assessment tests and exercises. In 2003, we assessed over 150,000 people and ran over 5,000 assessment events.

What are they?

An assessment centre is one of the most sophisticated selection methods available. It is a process incorporating group and individual exercises, tests and interviews for the measurement of performance against key criteria, which have been identified (by job analysis research) as critical to the success of a particular position, or level of management.

Research has shown assessment centres to be a much more accurate and cost effective way of selecting individuals than a standard interview. They work on the principle of multi-trait multi-method assessment. Any single assessment method may give misleading results; some people interview well, while others are good at tests, whereas a well designed assessment process is based on a criteria/assessment grid and allows multiple assessments of each criteria.

Why use them?

Many major business, government and non-profit organizations are now using assessment centres to assist them in selecting their future employees.

Assessment centers can

- Improve the accuracy of selection decisions by providing the opportunity to observe candidates actually handling the types of tasks and situations with which they will be faced on the job.
- Produce a far higher capacity for predicting job performance than that of an unstructured interview.
- Save time and money by combining selection, assessment and the identification of training needs in the same procedure.
- Allow group testing; saving time and staff resources when compared to one-to-one testing.
- Create group dynamics, allowing aspects of the individual to be studied that cannot be measured by other means.
- Allow one to obtain a more accurate impression of candidates' true qualities.
- Help an organization in the early identification of management potential and in the diagnosis of individual management development. Thus, training and development effort can be invested more cost effectively.
- Provide valuable training for those managers used as assessors, particularly in the areas of performance appraisal, counseling and interviewing skills.

In short, assessment centers are a good way of predicting how a candidate is likely to behave on a job.

The most important and precious resource in company is its employees. The results are produced thanks to technologies, capital, and also well prepared and trained team. We believe in potential of every person, and the potential of organization. The organizations want to help managers and staff members work effectively on the market. The organization has recruitment, selection, and assessment services constructed to build, and maintain, stable, and flexible, and creative structures. The most efficient and successful method helping to assess human potential at work is Assessment Centre Method.

Our approach is based on four major components of Human Resources Management: recruitment and selection of personnel, assessment of an employee potential, remuneration and development. The most strategic of it is: long-term criteria for selection, assessment for an employee potential, career planning, and alternative remuneration systems The most efficient and successful method helping to assess human potential at work is Assessment Centre Method.

Assessment Center Defined

An assessment center consists of a standardized evaluation of behaviour based on multiple inputs. Multiple trained observers and techniques are used. Judgments about behaviours are made, in major part, from specifically developed assessment simulations. These judgments are pooled in a meeting among the assessors or by a statistical integration process.

Candidate: A managerial candidate, a person assessed, someone who has applied for a managerial job.

Dimensions: Aspects of people that are assessed, such as leadership and decision-making. The dimensions are managerial skills that come from a job analysis.

Exercises: Activities or tasks given to the candidates. These are used to elicit behaviours used in judging the candidates relative standings on the dimensions.

Assessors: Judges trained in the assessment center method. The judges record candidate behaviour and evaluate candidate standings on the dimensions.

Assessment Centre Method enables to assess effectively assess the potential of individual growth and development of an employee. Thanks to it, the organization has possibility to allocate its resources in the most optimal way, due to organization's growth. The aim of Assessment Centre is to define critical success factors for specific position, and their systematical evaluation. The criteria are defined. Their choice is the result of job analysis.

The most important for the job analysis are:

- the results of functioning of the position;
- tasks and the responsibilities;
- other activities on the position;
- environment of the position (ex. market, clients);
- internal environment of the position;
- critical success factors;
- skills and knowledge.

History

The origins of the Assessment Centre lie in the period before Second World War, when it was used for selection of British and German officers. There are also some, who believe Cesar Hadrian has started it; recruiting officers for his army through simulations.

The method began to get off the ground in the forties, primarily in United States, and by the late fifties was being further developed by the business community, in particular by the American Telephone and Telegraph Company (AT and T). Since 1970, the Assessment Centre Method has grown into a force to be reckoned with in the United States and in Europe.

Early Roots ("Pre-history")

- Early psychometricians (Galton, Binet, Cattell) tended to use rather complex responses in their tests. First tests for selection were of "performance" variety (manipulative, dexterity, mechanical, visual/perceptual):
- Early "work samples"
- World War I
- Efficiency in screening/selection became critical
- Group paper-and-pencil tests became dominant

German Officer Selection (1920's to 1942)

- Emphasized naturalistic and "Gestalt" measurement
- Used complex job simulations as well as "tests"
- Goal was to measure "leadership," not separate abilities or skills
- Assessment staff (psychologists, physicians, officers) prepared advisory report for superior officer

- No research built-in
- Multiple measurement techniques, multiple observers, complex behaviours

British War Office Selection Boards (1942...)

- Sir Andrew Thorne had observed German programs
- WOSBs replaced a crude and ineffective selection system for WW II officers
- Clear conception of leadership characteristics to be evaluated
- Level of function
- Group cohesiveness
- Stability
- Psychiatric interviews, tests, many realistic group and individual simulations
- Psychologists and psychiatrists on assessment team—in charge was a senior officer who made final suitability decision.
- Lots of research criterion-related validity incremental validity over previous method
- Spread to Australian and Canadian military with minor modifications

British Civil Service Assessment (1945...)

- British Civil Service Commission—first non-military use
- Part of a multi-stage selection process
- Screening tests and interviews
- 2–3 days of assessment (CSSB)
- Final Selection Board (FSB) interview and decision
- Criterion-related validity evidence
- See Anstey (1971) for follow-up

Harvard Psychological Clinic Study (1938)

- Henry Murray's theory of personality
- Sought understanding of life history, person "in totality"
- Studied 50 college-age subjects
- Methods relevant to later AC developments
- Multiple measurement procedures
- Grounded in observed behaviour
- Observations across different tasks and conditions
- Multiple observers (5 judges)
- Discussion to reduce rating errors of any single judge

OSS Program: World War II

- Goal: Improved intelligence agent selection
- Extremely varied target jobs and candidates

- Key players: Murray, McKinnon, Gardner
- Needed a practical program, quick!
- Best attempts made at analysis of job requirements
- Simulations developed as rough work samples
- No time for pretesting
- Changes made as experience gained
- 3 day program, candidates required to live a cover story throughout
- Used interviews, tests, situational exercises
- Brook exercise
- Wall exercise
- Construction exercise ("behind the barn")
- Obstacle exercise
- Group discussions
- Map test
- Stress interview
- A number of personality/behavioural variables were assessed
- Professional staff used (many leading psychologists)
- Rating process
- Staff made ratings on each candidate after each exercise
- Periodic reviews and discussions during assessment process
- Interviewer developed and presented preliminary report
- Discussion to modify report
- Rating of suitability, placement recommendations
- Spread quickly. over 7,000 candidates assessed
- *Assessment of Men* published in 1948 by OSS Assessment Staff
- Some evidence of validity (later re-analyses showed a more positive picture)
- Numerous suggestions for improvement

AT and T Management Progress Study (1956...)

- Designed and directed by Douglas Bray
- Longitudinal study of manager development
- Results not used operationally (!)
- Sample of new managers (all male)
- 274 recent college graduates
- 148 non-college graduates who had moved up from non-management jobs
- 25 characteristics of successful managers selected for study
- Based upon research literature and staff judgments, not a formal job analysis
- Professionals as assessors (I/O and clinical psychologists)

Assessment Techniques

- Interview
- In-basket exercise
- Business game
- Leaderless group discussion (assigned role)
- Projective tests (Thematic Appreciation Test)
- Paper and pencil tests (cognitive and personality)
- Personal history questionnaire
- Autobiographical sketch
- Evaluation of participants
- Written reports/ratings after each exercise or test
- Multiple observers for LGD and business game
- Specialization of assessors by technique
- Peer ratings and rankings after group exercises
- Extensive consideration of each candidate
- Presentation and discussion of all data
- Independent ratings on each of the 25 characteristics
- Discussion, with opportunity for rating adjustments
- Rating profile of average scores
- Two overall ratings: *would* and/or *should* make middle management
- Michigan Bell Personnel Assessment Program (1958)
- First industrial application: Select 1st-line supervisors from craft population
- Staffed by internal company managers, not psychologists
- Extensive training
- Removed motivational and personality tests (kept cognitive)
- Behavioural simulations played even larger role
- Dimensions based upon job analysis
- Focus upon behaviour predicting behaviour
- Standardized rating and consensus process
- Model spread rapidly throughout the Bell System

Use expands slowly in the 60's

- Informal sharing of methods and results by AT and T staff
- Use spread to a small number of large organizations
- IBM
- Sears
- Standard Oil (Ohio)

- General Electric
- J.C. Penney
- Bray and Grant (1966) article in *Psychological Monographs*
- By 1969, 12 organizations using assessment centre method
- Closely modeled on AT and T
- Included research component
- 1969: two key conferences held

Explosion in the '70's

- 1970: Byham article in *Harvard Business Review*
- 1973: 1st International Congress on the Assessment Centre Method
- Consulting firms established (DDI, ADI, etc.)
- 1975: First set of guidelines and ethical standards published
- By end of decade, over 1,000 organizations established AC programs
- Expansion of use:
- Early identification of potential
- Other job levels (mid- and upper management) and types (sales)
- US model spreads internationally

We offer a human resource management system incorporating various aspects of personnel management. The heart of this system is formed by the Assessment Centre Method. It's a modern method for determining job requirements and evaluating human capacities in terms of objectively observable behaviour.

Underlying Assumptions

- Employees are a valuable asset.
- Selecting the right people makes a difference.
- Corporate culture should be managed to achieve compatibility between individual development and corporate objectives.
- Committed employees are more valuable than those who are merely complaint.
- Commitment is achieved through mutuality.
- Appraisal processes are one aspect of managing the corporate culture to achieve mutuality.

Aims of Assessment and Appraisal

- Selecting qualified and talented people.
- Highlighting potential/succession planning.
- Identification of training and development needs.
- Providing individuals with feedback on their personal strengths and weaknesses.
- Creating a dialogue between superiors and subordinates about performance.

- Encouraging the (formal) exchange of performance information.
- Validating previous recruitment, selection and training decisions.
- Motivating and rewarding employees by providing data for Performance Related Pay (PRP).
- Setting up a performance management system.

Characteristic of the method

The following elements are characteristic of the method:

- behaviour is central: behaviour predicts behaviour,
- the qualities of the various candidates are determined with the aid of various techniques, such as interviews, psychological tests and exercises,
- most of the exercises take the form of simulations of tasks and situations which arise in the future job,
- the exercises can also be carried on in a group, so that the candidates' interaction and co-operation can be observed,
- the candidates are observed by a number of different appraisers, preferably senior managers from their own organizations,
- the observed behaviour is evaluated on the basis of previously defined criteria derived from job analysis,
- the final evaluation is the outcome of synthesis of the judgments of the different appraisers.

Many methods base the evaluation of an individual's aptitude for a new job primarily on performance in previous jobs. This is quite possible when the new job does not appreciably differ from the old. When it does differ, however, trying to predict future performance on the basis of present can be fairly risky business. The fact, that someone is an outstanding salesman, for example, does not guarantee that he will be a good sales manager. In such cases, the Assessment Centre method can be a real boon.

Managing for Results

The human resource management system incorporating various aspects of personnel management. The heart of this system is formed by the Assessment Centre Method. It's a modern method for determining job requirements and evaluating human capacities in terms of objectively observable behaviour.

Assessment Centre Method has a bearing on the following aspects of personnel management:

- Staffing: Decision-making on selection, promotion, turnover and dismissal;
- Staff development: Determining educational and training requirements;
- Improving performance in the management/staff relationship;
- Bringing compensation policy in line with general policy objectives.

Fig: 8.5 Assessment Centre: An Integrated Evaluation.

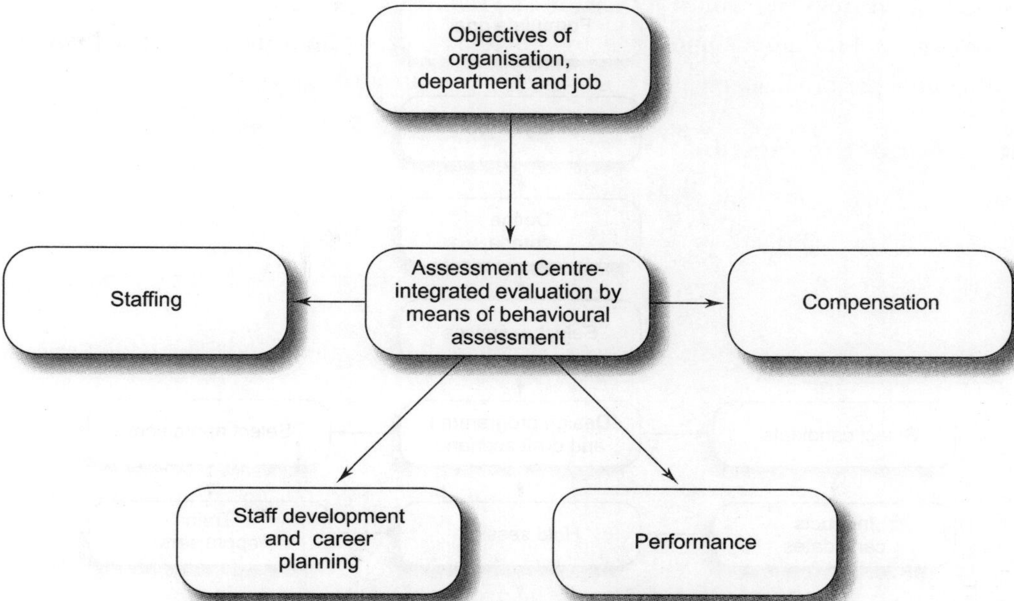

The Assessment Centre Programme

The average Assessment Centre Programme involves six to eight candidates over a one to two day period. The participant takes part in interviews, tests, and exercises designed to bring the light on the particular behavioural criteria considered to be significant for a given position. During the assessment session, the candidates are observed, and interviewed by two to four appraisers who make notes concerning their behaviour. Each appraiser changes candidates with each new exercise, or interview. When the participants depart at the end of the session, the appraisers meet to discuss their findings and come to unanimous opinion. A final report is then drawn up for each participant. The information contained in this report is made available to both the candidate and the company.

In today's competitive business world, making sure that having the right knowledge, skills and abilities (KSAs) among people are important for an organization to stay afloat in the industry. Competencies are the KSAs that will lead to successful performance. Competency assessment is the process of assessing those defined competencies. Selection of competencies, methods to assess competencies, applications of competencies in the organization, and validity and reliability of competency assessment are discussed. Competencies form the foundation for many human resource functions (*e.g.*, selection) and are an integral part in maintaining a competitive advantage.

Assessment Centre Process

The Assessment Centre is a very systematic, step-by-step approach, which produces results at every phase and thus has a wide range of possible applications. The method consists of the following:

Fig: 8.6 Assessment Process

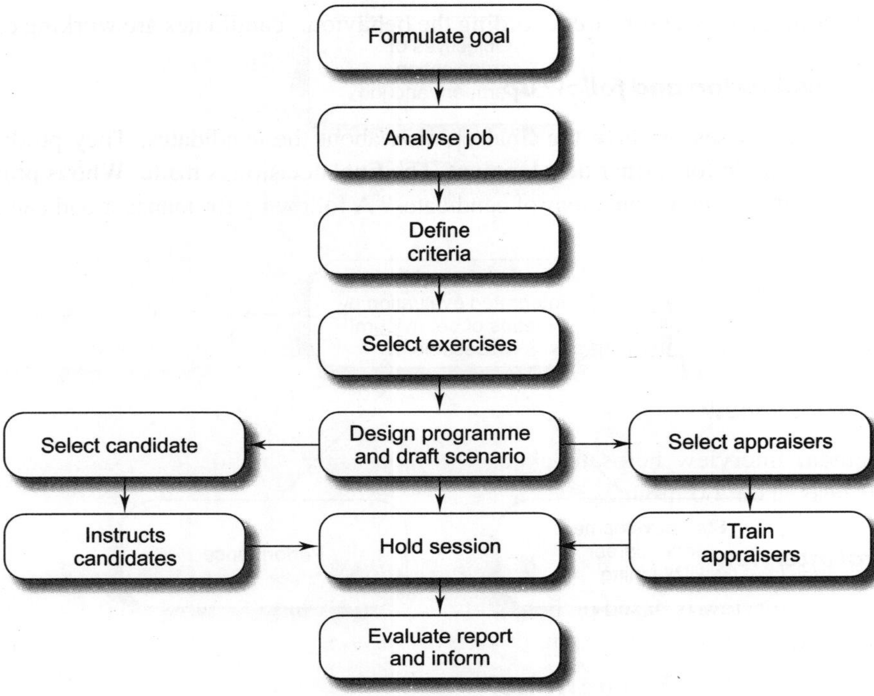

Stages of the Assessment process

Formulate goal

For which purpose is the Assessment Centre Method to be used? For selection? Management development? Evaluation? Schooling and training? Each purpose demands its own particular approach and methodology.

Target jobs

What is the target group? Sales personnel, trainees, specialists, managers?

Analyse jobs and establish criteria

How are the target jobs structured? What are their key characteristics? What does the appraiser need to know about: leadership, organizational ability, planning, communicating skills, stress tolerance?

Choose the methodology

Which tools to use and why? Which simulations, interview questions and/or psychological tests will be employed?

Draft scenario for the session

How is the programme to be carried out in practice, how long will it last and where and when will the session be held?

Assessment Centre session

The session is going, the assessors are recording the behaviour, candidates are working on simulations.

Final report, evaluation and follow up

After the session the assessors give the final opinion about the candidates. They produce the report, constructed to be a guide for further development. The final decision is made: Who is promoted, who is accepted, what are the development areas of candidates? A follow up for manager and candidate is made.

THE EXERCISES

Many kinds of exercises are used in assessment centre session. The examples are:

Biographical interview

The biographical interview helps to check the meritorical knowledge, experience and skills of candidate. It lasts about 60 minutes.

Behavioural interview

The behavioural interview is based on behavioural criteria. The questions and the interview process is build on the critical behavioural criteria chosen during the job analysis. The interview lasts 90–120 minutes.

The simulation interview

The simulation interview—role playing depends on the individual characteristic of the exercise. It takes, together with preparation phase 60 minutes. During this stage the candidate faces an interpersonal problem to be solved.

"In-basket" exercise

The candidate has to handle several written problems concerning some situation in a company. It takes 90–240 minutes.

Group exercise

The participants are working in a group. They have roles to play. Together they must solve a problem. Created situations are similar to their everyday responsibilities. The group exercises take 30–120 minutes.

Presentations

The participant obtains a description of an situation and problem. His job is to show his opinion about the problem. Average time takes 120 minutes.

Fact-finding

This kind of exercise bases on decision-making. The candidate has to make decision about the situation. He/she has to ask questions to obtain enough information to make decision. This kind of exercise takes 60 minutes.

Benefits

Proper job analysis

The construction of job analysis bases on the results the position should generate for the company, and the function it holds. The responsibilities need special behaviour of an employee. On this basis critical success criteria are defined and chosen. Job analysis is systematic: starts a from responsibility, than to activities, and finally to behavioural criteria.

Exact and completed information on the potential of an employee

Thanks to Assessment Centre a company can obtain completed information about an employee possibilities, and potential, his strengths, and developmental area.

Understandable report

All the information concerning the process and the opinion are placed in the final report. The report is a tool to the candidate's development. The report is written in clear and understandable way. It consists of the information about the criteria, their levels, and information concerning future work on the development of an employee.

Assessment Centre Method and its wide range of activities

Assessment Centre Method is used on many occasions in personal policy management. Thanks to information gained by Assessment Centre one can plan careers for staff, promotions, trainings, remuneration systems, performance appraisal. Thanks to it Assessment 360° can also be constructed.

Competency Assessment

In the corporate world, identifying characteristics for successful performance is more important than ever, given the growing competition among industries. Recognizing the different components and behaviours leading to success helps the organization grow and become more competitive in its industry. These behaviours are labeled competencies. Competencies are distinguishing characteristics of successful performance within an established role (Wolfe, 1998, p. 228). The characteristics may include any combination of the following: knowledge, skill, traits, values/beliefs, motives, and physical ability (Wolfe, 1998, p. 228).

By extension, competency assessment is the process of identifying the competencies among a group of employees, typically by department, job category, or hierarchical structure (McNerney and Briggins, 1995). About one-third of organizations use competency assessment today (Armstrong and Baron, 1998). A success profile is usually created to describe the behaviours relevant to success at a company; the success profile is usually called a competency model. A competency model lists the competencies associated with exemplary performers and ties to a corporate culture (McNerney and Briggins, 1995).

McNerney and Briggins (1995) distinguish between competency assessment and task analysis in the following way: task analysis bases training on what people do, whereas competency assessment bases training on who the successful performers are. Task analysis typically focuses on jobs with an emphasis on manual labour and psychomotor skills, whereas competency assessment conducts training for workers who perform decision-making and knowledge work such as managers and professionals (McNerney and Briggins, 1995).

Competencies are used in many different human resources (HR) functions. Primarily, competency assessment and modelling are used heavily in performance management, compensation, developmental purposes (*i.e.*, to improve in areas where one is weak), and training. Applications of competencies used in HR functions will be discussed later in the chapter.

McNerney and Briggins (1995) state several reasons for the increasing use of competency assessment in corporations today. First, the speed of change in today's business environment is sparking interest in assessment because of the dated nature of task analysis; competency assessment is much more flexible and does not date itself as quickly. Second, the nature of work is changing. Hourly workers are beginning to make more decisions these days, relying less on psychomotor skills than before. Employees are becoming more empowered. As stated before, competency assessment is used more as more decisions are made in job responsibilities. Third, widespread corporate downsizing requires training and development professionals to move away from tightly constructed and bureaucratic jobs to more flexible definitions of work. Finally, competency assessment can become the basis for an entire corporate HR department's activities such as those mentioned before and more. Recruitment, selection, orientation, training, work design, compensation, performance appraisal, career paths, and succession planning all use competency assessment as the centerpiece of the function.

Selection of Competencies

Companies that assess companies use different methods in how to select competencies. However, most companies assess competencies based upon previous research models in academia, such as Industrial/Organizational psychology and management. Also, many companies use surveys to better understand what is happening in their organization. Data from previous research in the company is used. For example, at American Airlines, in an attempt to define the competencies that will fit the desired culture for a rollout of multi-rater feedback for managers, two other project leads and use a combination of research methods. First, data from employee opinion surveys and organizational culture surveys mould the initial competencies. We developed verbiage around the competencies using research from consulting firms and other companies. Existing job analyses helped in further defining the behaviours associated with successful performance.

Transamerica Life Companies identified competencies using a five-step process. The first step was strategy. They asked the question of how they wanted to achieve their goals. Secondly, they wanted to know their capabilities—what must they do well. The third step is processes—how do they work. Structure is the fourth step asking how do they organize. Lastly, competencies were developed asking what skills, knowledge, and behaviours they needed in order to perform successfully (Wolfe, 1998, p. 237).

Another way to select competencies is using job analysis. HR Zone defines job analysis as the research and analysis of all aspects of work and all its aspects; job analysis is the systematic analysis of an existing or proposed position or group of positions within an organization (cited in Harris, 1998). Defining the skills needed to perform a job help in identifying the competencies, which include skills.

Methods Used in Assessing Competencies

Competency tests are often used in assessing competencies. Pharmacists use testing as a way to assess whether or not they still possess the professional skills necessary for relicensure (Ukens, 1996). The National Association of Boards of Pharmacy authorized a study for the development of a Pharmacist

Competency Assessment (PCA) mechanism. Mostly, the program would be to help pinpoint some practice deficiencies and may be send them to continuing education programs in order to help them develop and improve; no punishment is meant for the pharmacists. In other words, PCA is a developmental tool for pharmacists. An expert panel of practitioners, pharmacy board members, and academics will set the areas of competence. The panel would first have to define continuing competence and how that differs from beginning competence. That is, what knowledge, skills, and abilities (KSAs) are necessary for those who have been working for a while as opposed to those who have just entered the field. The panel of experts would also have to determine how continuing competence can be assessed in a practical way (Ukens, 1996).

Assessment centres are another method used in assessing competencies. Assessment centres use situational tests to observe specific behaviours of the participants (Thornton, 1992, p. 2). Individuals are evaluated based upon the behaviours exhibited throughout in the tests. Competencies are the foundation of the assessment centre process. The behaviours being assessed are determined from the competencies. Assessment centres are valuable in that there appears to be a high correlation between assessment centre scores on high-performance competencies and actual performance in jobs (Sparrow, 1996).

One approach suggests six modules to assessing core competencies (Gallon *etal.,* 1995). The first module is the planning stage where everyone involved has a common language and knowledge base from which to work. In the second module, inventories of capabilities are developed in order to determine the categories needed to be assessed. Then, using questions developed by experts then assesses core competencies in the third module; for example, does it translate into customer-perceived value? In the fourth module, candidate competencies are selected from those that were assessed as being better than the other competencies. The fifth module tests those candidate competencies, and in the sixth module are evaluated to see which ones are finally selected.

Strategic approaches to competency assessment have also been investigated. The premise behind competency assessment is that if an organization's managers are equipped with the right competencies to carry out their jobs effectively, corporate success should, all things being equal, not only be improved, but accelerated (Tovey, 1993-a). The link between management development and corporate strategy are growing these days for several reasons: the emergence of new organizational structures and designs to cope with the pressures and competition of the 1990s. Human resource departments are now being seen as being able to enable a deeper understanding of business objectives and the actions that need to be taken in order to achieve them. Therefore, competency assessment is the bridge between strategy and management development (Tovey, 1993-a).

Before beginning competency assessment, some questions, taken verbatim from Tovey (1993-a), are worth asking:

1. What is the nature of the organization? Is it structured and hierarchical, operating in a relatively stable industry or is it fast-moving and in an industry which is "high-tech" related?
2. What is the purpose of competency assessment? Will it serve as a basis for all activities in the management development cycle: selection, assessment, development, and/or succession? Is it required for a specific element described above for a competency-based performance management system?
3. For which levels of the organization do you want to identify competencies? All levels, non-managerial, supervisory/junior management, middle/senior management?
4. How can competencies be defined so that they are meaningful to the organization in question?

This method of assessment is a popular option for companies who want to maintain a competitive advantage. There are many uses for competencies such as selection, assessment, training and development, succession planning, and supporting organizational change efforts. In all of these areas, competencies are forming the foundation of these efforts. The company will gain an advantage if it decides to invest in using and assessing competencies.

Career Development

Introduction: IT IS HOT HOLD-THEM-BACK STRATEGY. Realizing that they can expect to retain their top talent—and get the best out of them—only by the offering the prospect of unhampered growth, corporate are beginning to plan, design and mould their employees' careers. But just how should you manage your employees' growth? Should the company have out a clear career path for each, simply taking care to match ability and prowess to the job? Or should it leave every executive to plan his own career, accommodating all individual aspirations somehow? Or is it a better idea to make the process an effort, fitting the employees' goals to those of the corporations and thus evolve an optimum fit? Actually, there cannot be one approach for all the problems.

Career development and succession planning go hand in hand. When they are linked to the organization's vision, employees can align their personal aspirations to the organization's current and future needs, creating a mutually beneficial environment. Career development and succession planning synergy creates happier and more productive employees in a growth-oriented company. The organization experiences positive bottom-line results while preparing for future business needs based on mutual corporate and individual growth. The ongoing business strategy incorporates retention and succession planning as part of the systemic structure. Internal career development, training initiatives, mentoring, coaching, evaluations, annual reviews, and orientation programs are meaningfully connected to organizational goals. The result is a workable process that consistently addresses the corporate requirements for finding, keeping, and placing talent in key positions as needed. Internal career development programs are proving critical in keeping valued employees while concurrently ensuring greater control over the succession planning process. Retention research indicates that individuals tend to stay longer where they are experiencing personal and professional growth. Employers who actively partner with their employees to align career direction with company goals are realizing better retention rates. Employees actively involved in their personal development more satisfaction with their work and tend to stay longer with the organization.

The business environment today is highly competitive and complex and there is a certain degree of ambiguity and uncertainty about the career development. Consequently, employees are also confused about their career development. Earlier the employees are enjoyed the job security by taking up a position in an organization. It is a psychological contract between the employee and the employer. In the then time, the loyalty and devotion, commitments were the factors for higher position in an organization. Now, contrastingly, career planning for an employee is very difficult. Career growth has already crossed the boundaries and has undergone a great change. Switching organizations and ideas are now the common phenomenon in the present situation. The need of the employees are also has gone sea of changes and the trainers are experiencing difficult times in organizing and developing programs to suit their needs. In addition to it, restructuring, downsizing, rightsizing and layoffs have become common practices in the organizations. Hence, the need of the hour is enhancing or increasing the employability of individuals in an organization. So attempts to differentiate between career and job, identify steps in career planning, and analyze the steps require by an employee for success in the career.

The traditional career paths of yesterday defined a point-to-point progression that targeted a select few for specific leadership positions. Career-management pathing programs generally worked because the environment was more static, jobs more stable, and employees were loyal and more connected to their organization. These conditions do not describe today's world of work. Job jumping, career changing, volatile industries, and shifting work environments are now a way of organizational life. The contracts between employer and employee have significantly changed.

Organizations wanting to effectively manage the career expectations and progression of their employees are working in an environment radically different from that of a few years ago. Current career planning challenges include:

- Operating in a hyper-competitive business environment in which resources are scarce.
- Attracting and retaining highly skilled and capable people within an aging workforce.
- Factoring in a greater proportion of contract and casual employees with no long-term allegiance to the organization.
- Engaging the talents, motivations and creativities of people whilst aligning to business requirements.
- Managing employee expectations in an environment in which there are fewer opportunities for promotion.
- Supporting marginal performers in increasing their discretionary effort and contribution to the role.
- Encouraging poor performers to move on in a respectful way.

Career Planning and Development Defined: A Career is a general course that a person chooses to pursue through out his/her working life. Historically, a career was a sequence of work-related positions an individual has occupied during a lifetime, although not always with the same company. However, there are a few relatively static jobs that require infrequent training and virtually no development for maintaining acceptable productivity levels. This may satisfy the objective perspective of career. The subjective viewpoint is more or less held together by a self-concept that consists of perceived inclinations and abilities, basic values, career motives and needs. In the both the perspectives we assume that individuals control their destiny and that available opportunities need to be manipulated to maximize the success and satisfaction in their careers. So, career planning is very important because the consequence of the career success or failure is linked closely to each individual's self-concept, identity, and satisfaction with career and life.

Career Planning is an ongoing process whereby an individual sets career goals and identifies the means to achieve them. Career planning should not concentrate only on advancement opportunities since the present work environment has reduced many of these opportunities. At some point of time, career planning should focus on achieving success that does not necessarily entail promotions.

Organizational Career Planning is the planned succession of the jobs worked out by afirm to develop its employees. With organizational career planning, the organizations identifies paths and activities for the individual employees as they develop. A career path is a flexible line of movement through which an employee may move during employment with a company. Following an established career path, the employee can undertake career development with the firm's assistance. From the workers prospective, following a career path may involve weaving from the company to company and from position to positions he/she obtain greater and experience.

Career Development is a formal approach used by the organization to ensure that the people with the proper qualifications and experiences are available when needed. Formal career development is important to maintain a motivated and committed workforce. Career development tools, which are specified during career planning and utilized in the career development program, most notably include various types of training and the application of organizational development techniques. Career planning and development benefit both the individual and the organization and must therefore be carefully considered by the both.

Individual Career Planning: The self-assessment: Through the career planning, a person continuously evaluates his/her abilities and interests, considers the alternative career opportunities, establishes the career goals and plans practical developmental activities. Individual career planning must begin with self-understanding or self-assessment. Then, the person is in a position to establish realistic goals and determine what to do to achieve these goals. This action also lets the person know whether his or her goals are realistic.

Self-assessment is the process of learning about oneself. Anything that could affect one's performance in a future job should be considered. Realistic self-assessment may help a person avoid the mistakes that could affect his or her entire career progression. Often an individual accepts a job without considering whether it matches his or her interests and abilities. Some useful tools are including a strength/weakness balance-sheet and likes and dislikes surveys. However, any reasonable approach that assists self-understanding is helpful. A self-evaluation procedure, developed originally by Benjamin Franklin, that assist people in becoming aware of their strengths and weaknesses by the strength/weakness balance-sheet. Employees who understand their strengths can use them to maximum advantage. By recognizing their weaknesses, they are in a better position to overcome them. The mechanics of preparing the balance-sheet are quite simple. A person should take minimum devote sufficient time to the project to obtain a fairly clear understanding of his or her strengths and weaknesses. Typically, the process should take minimum of one week. The balance-sheet may not give the answer to all questions regarding strength and weaknesses, but many people have gained out of it. You can determine the means to react to your findings and perhaps, overcome a weakness after you have conducted the self-assessment.

Likes and Dislikes Survey: An individual should also considered Likes and Dislikes as the part of a self-assessment. Likes and Dislikes Survey assists individual in recognizing restrictions they place on themselves. A self-assessment such as this one helps a person understand his or her basic motives and sets the stage for pursuing a career. People who know themselves can make more easily make the decisions necessary for successful career planning many people get sidetracked as they choose careers based on haphazard plans or wishes of others rather than on what they believe to be the best for them.

Organizational career Planning: The process of establishing career paths and activities for individuals within a firm is referred to as organizational planning. Organizational career planning should begin with person's job placement and initial orientation. Management then observes the persons job performances and compares it to job standards. At this stage, strengths and weaknesses will be noted, enabling management to assist the employee in making a tentative career decision. Naturally, this decision can be altered later as the process continues. This tentative career decision is based on a number of factors, including personal needs, abilities and aspirations and the organizations needs. Management can then schedule development program that relate to employees specific needs. Career Planning, is an on going process. It takes into consideration the changes that occur in people, in organizations and in the environment. This type of flexibility is absolutely necessary in today's dynamic organizational environment. Not only do the firm's requirements change, but individuals may also choose to revise their career expectations.

Although the primary responsibility for career planning rests with the individual, organizational career planning must closely parallel individual career planning if the firm is to retain its best and brightest workers. Employees must see that the firms' organizational career planning efforts is directed toward furthering their specific career objectives. Organizational career planning must begin with a virtual redefinition of the way work is done. Creativity, resourcefulness, flexibility, innovation and adaptability are becoming much more important than the ability to perform a precisely specific job. Through the effective organizational planning a pool of men and women can be developed who can thrive in any number of organizational structures in the future. Firms should undertake organizational career planning (varies from organizations to organizations) programs only when the programs contribute to achieving current and future organizational goals. This rationale is more important in today's environment. Career planning programs are expected to achieve one or more of the following objectives; Effective development of available talent.

- Self-appraisal opportunities for employees considering new or non-traditional career paths.
- Development of career paths that cut across divisions and geographic locations.
- A demonstration of a tangible commitment to CEO and affirmative action.
- Satisfaction of the employees' specific development needs.
- Improvement of performances.
- Increased employee loyalty and motivation, leading to decreased turnover.
- A method of determining training and development needs.

Successful career planning depends on firm's ability to satisfy those that it considers most crucial to employee development and the achievement of the organizational goals.

Career Development: Career development is a formal approach taken by the organization to ensure the people with the proper qualifications and experiences are available when needed. Career development benefits both the organization and also the employee because properly developed employees are better prepared to add value both to themselves and to the company. Thus career development includes exposure to any and all activities that prepare a person for satisfying the present and future needs of the firm. Career development tools consist of skills, education, and experiences, as well as behavioural modification and refinement techniques that allow individuals to work better and add value. Therefore, the need for organizational development is often essential. Organizational development is important because it helps develop total units behaviour. Organizational development efforts include number interventions such as survey feedback, quality circles, sensitivity training and team building. The career development methods are: discussion with the knowledgeable individuals, company materials, performance appraisal system, workshops, and personal development plans etc.

Succession planning: In today's highly competitive global environment, human capital is an organization's most important asset, often differentiating highly successful businesses from those that struggle. Yet, in the ongoing effort to develop a strong and capable workforce, many organizations focus almost entirely on hiring and training. They neglect succession planning—perhaps the most essential ingredient in building an organization that is capable of achieving its strategic goals.

Today, succession planning requires more than just an organizational chart showing who holds what job within the enterprise. Best practice organizations use succession planning to develop and maintain strong leadership and to ensure that they address all the skills and competencies required for today's business environment. Succession planning can also be an extremely powerful tool in motivating and retaining top leadership.

Succession planning is an ongoing, dynamic process that helps an organization to align its business goals and its human capital needs. It also ensures that an enterprise can keep pace with changes to the business, industry, and overall marketplace. To achieve outstanding results using succession planning, an organization must develop an effective and highly focused strategy that centres on organizational excellence.

Understanding the need: In most cases, succession planning focuses on three main areas. First, it addresses the needs of the organization as senior management ages. During that time, business practices and procedures become increasingly entrenched and daily issues take precedence. Too often, the enterprise neglects succession planning and does not have people available who are fully prepared to assume the top posts at many businesses, having little or no succession planning wreaks havoc when the organization's leader retires. Nobody is fully prepared to assume the top post. Second, succession planning helps an organization to prepare for an unexpected event. It is often difficult to plan for the unimaginable. Yet, the sudden eventualities (Unfortunately, diseases, automobile accidents, plane crashes, and other disasters) are an ongoing reality. It can reverberate throughout an organization, paralyzing both management and staff and impeding the organization's ability to execute its business plan, recent world events illustrate how important succession planning. Finally, succession planning ensures that an organization has the right personnel to function at peak efficiency. Today, many organizations strive to identify key objectives and business goals and shape a work-force accordingly. Although executives and senior managers play a crucial role in defining such organizations, there is a need for specific skills and competencies throughout the enterprise. Not only does succession planning serve as a way to create an organizational hierarchy, but it can also help organizations conduct an inventory of human capital and better understand gaps. It can also help organizations manage change in a more holistic way.

A strategic approach: Although successful organizations usually focus on training to develop leadership from within the executive circle, they also understand that it is sometimes wise to look outside for particular skills and knowledge. Of course, the more prominent a position within an organization, the tougher it is to find a suitable candidate. Thus, some turn to outside consultants to manage recruiting and, sometimes, the entire succession planning process. Consultants can provide objectivity and help develop a strategic plan that encompasses all levels of the enterprise. This approach is useful to a wide range of organizations.

Succession Planning: The Concept and Definition

In organizational development, succession planning is the process of identifying and preparing suitable employees through mentoring, training and job rotation, to replace key players—such as the Chief Executive Officer (CEO)—within an organization as their terms expire. From the risk management aspect, provisions are made in case no suitable internal candidates are available to replace the loss of any key person. It is usual for an organization to insure the key person so that funds are available if she or he dies and these funds can be used by the business to cope with the problems before a suitable replacement is found or developed.

Definition: Succession planning can be broadly defined as identifying future potential leaders to fill key positions. Wendy Hirsh[1] defines succession planning as 'a process by which one or more successors are identified for key posts (or groups of similar key posts), and career moves and/or development activities are planned for these successors. Successors may be fairly ready to do the job (short-term successors) or seen as having longer-term potential (long-term successors).'

According to Hirsh, succession planning sits inside a very much wider set of resourcing and development processes called 'succession management', encompassing management resourcing strategy, aggregate analysis of demand/supply (human resource planning and auditing), skills analysis, the job filling process, and management development (including graduate and high-flyer programmes).

Succession planning involves having senior executives periodically review their top executives and those in the next-lower level to determine several backups for each senior position. This is important because it often takes years of grooming to develop effective senior managers. There is a critical shortage in companies of middle and top leaders for the next five years. Organizations will need to create pools of candidates with high leadership potential.

Succession planning is a process whereby an organization ensures that employees are recruited and developed to fill each key role within the company. Through your succession planning process, you recruit superior employees, develop their knowledge, skills, and abilities, and prepare them for advancement or promotion into ever more challenging roles.

Through your succession planning process, you also retain superior employees because they appreciate the time, attention, and development that you are investing in them. To effectively do succession planning in your organization, you must identify the organization's long-term goals. You must hire superior staff.

You need to identify and understand the developmental needs of your employees. You must ensure that all key employees understand their career paths and the roles they are being developed to fill. Succession planning is seen as an important process by most large businesses but what does it mean?

Some of the confusion surrounding succession planning is due to people using the term in many different ways. Succession planning is best described as a process where one or more **'successors'** are identified for key jobs, and career moves and/or employee development activities are planned for these successors. Successors may be fairly ready to do the job (short-term successors) or seen as having longer-term potential (long-term successors).

Objectives of Succession Planning: The main objectives (and advantages) of succession planning are:

- Improved job filling for key positions through broader candidate search, and faster decision-making.
- Active development of longer-term successors through ensuring their careers progress, and by making sure they get the range of work experiences they need for the future.
- Encouraging a culture of "progression" through developing employees who are seen as a 'business resource' and who share key skills, experiences and values seen as important to the future of the business.

Of the above objectives, it is the active development of a strong 'talent pool' for the future which is often viewed as the most important. Increasingly, this is also seen as vital to attraction and retention of the 'best' people (particularly in service businesses like the accountancy and legal professions).

All organisations, whether in the private or public sectors, need to be able to find people with the right skills to fill key and top leadership jobs. This process needs to be managed, and traditionally, large blue-chip companies ran highly-structured, mechanistic, secretive and top-down schemes aimed at identifying internal successors for key posts and planning their career paths to provide the necessary range of experience. These schemes worked reasonably well in a stable environment where structures were fixed and careers were long-term. But with growing uncertainty, increasing speed of change in the business environment, and flatter structures, succession planning of this sort declined in the 1990s. How could one plan ahead, it was argued, for jobs that might not exist next year? One apparent result was that more and more people came to be appointed to top jobs from outside organisations. A further problem with traditional succession planning was that it failed to take account of non-managerial roles—a brilliant scientist, for example, who might be crucial to the future of the organisation and who wanted to stay in a research role. In a climate of growing skills shortages and lack of confidence in the leadership potential of the existing workforce, interest in succession planning has revived. But the new succession planning looks quite different from the old version, with a broader vision and far closer links to wider talent management practices. This factsheet looks at the main features of modern succession planning and the role of the HR function in the process.

Main features of modern succession planning

Organisations differ in size, scope and type, so it is difficult to point to any single model of succession planning. However, it is most common for succession planning to cover only the most senior jobs in the organisation, plus short-term and longer-term successors for these posts. The latter group are in effect on a fast-track, and are developed through job moves within various parts of the business. This focus on the most senior posts—perhaps the top two or three levels of management—means that even in large organisations, only a few hundred people at any given time will be subject to the succession planning process. It also makes the process more manageable, because it is much easier to concentrate on a few hundred individuals rather than (say) several thousand. However, many large organisations attempt to operate devolved models in divisions, sites or countries where the same or similar processes are applied to a wider population.

Balance between individuals and organisations

The old succession planning was purely about organisational needs. The modern version takes account of the growing recognition that people—men as well as women—increasingly need to make their own career decisions and to balance career and family responsibilities. So the emphasis is about balancing the aspirations of individuals with those of their employing organizations, as far as possible customizing moves to meet the needs of employees, their families and the changing skill requirements of the organization.

Broadening experience by lateral moves

Traditionally, people would have gained experience by upward moves, with accompanying increases in status and salary. Now-a-days that may not be possible, because organisations are less hierarchical, with fewer management layers. A sideways move into a different job may be all that is available, without any extra cash. Traditional fast-tracking created expectations of upward progression, and if status and money are thought to be motivators, different methods of generating commitment may have to be found.

Roles, not jobs

In the past, people would move up to specific, often specialist, jobs. Now (although some jobs will always require specialists) the main focus is on identifying and developing groups of jobs to enable potential successors to be identified for a variety of roles. So jobs might be clustered by role, function and level so that the generic skills responsible for particular roles can be developed. The aim is to develop pools of talented people, each of whom is adaptable and capable of filling a number of roles. Because succession planning is concerned with developing longer-term successors as well as short-term replacements, each pool will be considerably larger than the range of posts it covers.

Competencies

Many organisations have developed frameworks for technical and generic competencies, which relate to a broad range of desired skills and behaviours. The assessment process attached to generic frameworks (especially for management competencies) can provide a useful starting point for evaluating an individual's potential for a senior role. Thus succession plans need to be integrated with existing competency frameworks. However, there should not be an over-reliance on competencies because they may be too limiting and mechanistic to assess skills such as leadership. Moreover, they relate to the past and present rather than to the future, which is where organisational leaders need to look).

Links with business planning

Those responsible for succession planning need to know as much as possible about the future of the business, how it is likely to change, and how such change might affect the numbers involved and the skills they need to possess. Of course this is not easy, but it does imply a close relationship at a senior level between top managers responsible for shaping the future of the business (including in particular the chief executive) and the HR function, which acts as a facilitator. (There is more on the role of HR below.

Openness, fairness and diversity

Greater openness and transparency have come with the greater emphasis on the individual and the focus on roles rather than jobs. (In the past it was felt that the motivation of those not on the fast track would be shaped by the knowledge that they were not on it). Secrecy is being gradually reduced, and advertising of internal jobs is increasing. It is now more widely believed that employees need to understand the succession process, the methods used to judge potential successors, and the kinds of jobs that are considered suitable for each individual.

With openness should go fairness; objective assessments of all available candidates need to be seen to be so they can be corrected made, and succession development committees (under a variety of names) exist in many large companies to review key talent and succession plans and to examine how to improve the process. Those covered by the process need to be able to make an input about their own career aspirations, preferences and constraints. They also need feedback about how they are perceived by their employers and the sorts of job moves for which they would be considered.

As a growing number of organisations recognise the business case for diversity, they are increasingly aware of the need to ensure that the talents of women and ethnic minorities are properly developed.

Insiders and outsiders

All organisations need a certain amount of new blood to bring in new ideas and approaches, and fill unanticipated roles. Many seem to rely either too much on outsiders or too much on insiders, suggesting that it is difficult to find the right balance. Some academic commentators suggest that a ratio of around 80:20 between insiders and outsiders is about right. Some also argue that outsiders should not be brought in at board level but somewhere below it, so that people with outside experience can become accustomed to the corporate culture and undergo development before making the next step up. Others, though, argue that if an objective business case can be made for bringing in outsiders at board level, it should be done (although not over-done), and in particular that a failing business needs to recruit from outside, and needs to be seen to be doing so to satisfy investors. Nevertheless, it is not difficult to make the case that many companies would be better served if they spent as much on developing their own talent through succession planning as they do on recruiting and paying off failed board members.

Deploying a Succession Management Process

- Best-practice organizations make succession planning an integral corporate process by exhibiting a link between succession planning and overall business strategy. This link gives succession planning the opportunity to affect the corporation's long-term goals and objectives.
- Human resources is typically responsible for the tools and processes associated with successful succession planning. Business or line units are generally responsible for the "deliverables" *i.e.*, they use the system to manage their own staffing needs. Together, these two groups produce a comprehensive process.
- Technology plays an essential role in the succession planning process. Ideally, technology serves to facilitate the process (make it shorter, simpler, or more flexible) rather than becoming the focus of the process or inhibiting it in any way.

Identifying the Talent Pool

- Best-practice organizations use a cyclical, continuous identification process to focus on future leaders.
- Best-practice organizations use a core set of leadership and succession management competencies.

Engaging Future Leaders

- Best-practice organizations emphasize the importance of specific, individualized development plans for each employee.
- Individual development plans identify which developmental activities are needed, and the "best practice" firms typically have a mechanism in place to make it simple for the employee to conduct the developmental activities. Typically, divisional human resource leaders will monitor employee follow-up in developmental activities.
- Best-practice partners rely on the fundamental developmental activities of coaching, training, and development most frequently and utilize all developmental activities to a much greater extent than the sponsor organizations.
- In addition to traditional executive education programs, best-practice partners increasingly use special assignments, action learning, and web-based development activities.

Monitoring and Assessing the Program

- Best-practice organizations develop methods of assessment to monitor the succession planning process. These methods vary according to business goals and company culture.

Recommendations for Success

When the firms who had been recognized as "best-practice organizations" were asked for any insights that might be helpful to other firms interested in improving their succession management, they responded with the following recommendations.

1. Keep the process simple. Most refinements to succession management systems involved making the process more logical and simple so that busy line executives would not feel that bureaucracy was burdensome.
2. Engage technology to support the process. Information technology makes it possible for managers throughout the world to monitor and update developmental needs and activities on a timely basis. Making information timely and reducing the time required to manage the system are major contributions of technology.
3. Align succession management within overall business strategy. Line executives are much more likely to support a system that clearly reinforces corporate goals and objectives.
4. Secure senior level support for the process. None of the best practice firms would have been as successful without top management endorsement and support.

The 'succession savvy' corporations possess several traits that characterize their winning approaches to succession management. First, their succession systems are easy to use. Winning systems are non-bureaucratic, uncomplicated processes—with a unified approach to ensure consistency and maintain objectivity across business units, organizational levels and geographic areas. The best systems are developmentally oriented, rather than simply replacement oriented. The system becomes a proactive vehicle for managers and executives to reflect on the progress of their talent and the opportunities they require for genuine development. Highly effective systems always actively involve the very top players in the organisation. Senior executives view effective succession management as a critical strategic tool for attracting and retaining talent. Best practice succession systems are also effective at spotting gaps in talent and identifying important lynchpin positions—the select set of jobs that are critical to the overall success of the organization. Succession planning does the job of monitoring the succession process, enabling the company to ensure that the right people are moving into the right jobs at the right time and that gaps are being spotted early on. The most successful systems are built around continual reinvention. Best practice companies continually refine and adjust their systems as they receive feedback, monitor developments in technology and learn from other leading organizations. Where old systems were characterized by complete confidentiality and secrecy, today's systems actually encourage involvement by individuals who are participants and candidates. Under older systems, few participants knew where they actually stood in terms of their potential for career opportunities ahead.

Conclusion

Succession planning is an effective tool which can be used by HR managers as a means of identifying critical management positions, starting at the supervisory levels and extending to the highest positions in the management, thus providing for a "second-in-line" trajectory towards these critical positions. In the current business scenario, the need to devise a succession plan for the key positions in the organizations has only multiplied. With varied market forces are at play, a well qualified, talented and experienced professional has the global economy beckoning him to participate in its growth, there is a need for the management to ensure that it making efforts for continuous effective performance by the departments or work groups in the organization by making provision for the development, replacement and strategic application of key people overtime.

Potential appraisal is another powerful tool of employee development. Whether managers realise it or not, they are accustomed to making potential assessments. Every time a manager recommends or fails to recommend an employee for a promotion, a potential assessment has, in fact, been made. The process of assessing the managerial potential of employees deals with the question of whether or not they have the ability to handle positions in the future which involve considerably more responsibility than what they have right now. As long as individuals are viewed as being able to handle increased or different responsibilities, they would be considered to have potential (either latent or visible). Potential appraisal may thus be defined as a process of determining an employee's strengths and weaknesses with a view to use this as a predictor of his future performance. This would help determine the promotability of an individual to a higher position and help chalk out his career plan. The fundamental difference between reviewing performance and assessing potential is in the criteria used. In reviewing performance, the criteria used is what goals the employee achieved and what skills he or she currently possesses that could be indicators of his or her ability to assume different or more advanced responsibilities. Managers cannot rely exclusively on past performance since a person's ability to adequately handle one level of responsibility does not necessarily mean that he or she can perform well in a position with a higher level or different responsibility. It is this that makes potential appraisal a very crucial and critical area. If an employee without requisite abilities is promoted to a higher position and does not perform as per expectations, then it becomes impossible to demote him. Thus, he is unable to perform at the higher level and becomes a 'passenger' in the system. It is rightfully assumed that every individual has potential, low or high. Many organizations have people whose potential being low; performance too is not up to the mark. Whilst the question in our minds comes that how such people got into the system, the fact remains that they do not contribute to the organization's performance. A major problem that companies face is tackling the problem children. They have the ability to perform but do not perform and do not contribute to the organization's performance. This is mainly seen as an attitudinal problem. Further, these problem children bask in the glory of their potential but are unable to contribute to their own jobs. Dealing with workhorses too could be tricky. They can perform very well on routine tasks but have limited potential. Hence, their promotability is difficult and this creates frustrations for the employees. If promoted, they are unable to perform higher level jobs and this too creates problems both for the individuals and the organization. We easily conclude that 'stars' are ideal people to have in organizations. But retaining these stars could be difficult. They have high potential backed by high levels of performance and could be always on the lookout for greener pastures. Thus, as we see, potential appraisal is more intricate and complex vis-à-vis performance appraisal.

Because of the nature of the potential assessment activity, its timing and frequently is left to the manager's discretion. In assessing potential, managers are asked to make predictions about the future. These predictions concern many unknown factors, namely whether the individual can handle new responsibilities in a different managerial capacity. In addition, the potential assessment criteria is based mostly on an employee's process skills, which may be difficult to measure in a precise way. Thus, the timing and frequency of conducting potential assessment can be quite different from the more predictable timing of a performance review. For example, the potential assessment might occur when an employee has been on the job for one year, when an employee reaches certain 'mile-stones' (*i.e.*, every three years), or in preparation for major organizational shifts brought about by changes in the business such as reorganizations, expansion or rationalization. It is recommended that the potential assessment process take place at least over a six-month period, with a manager-employee meeting at both the beginning and end of the process. To begin the process, the manager and employee should meet to identify the process skills and the technical and administrative skills required for the employee's future responsibilities. The manager explains why these skills are necessary and explores with the employee how these skills might be learned and utilized on the current job. This includes nominating employees for some specific training programmes, both skill-based and knowledge-based. Some organization may also organise such programmes on an in house basis. Further on-the-job training could also be incorporated for the employees. It is recommended that the manager observe the employee for at least three to six months to assess the extent to which the employee possesses and demonstrates the acquired skills. During the observation period, the manager should note specific behavioural examples of these skills and be prepared to discuss them with the employee at the concluding assessment meeting. The employee should also be prepared to discuss behavioural examples that demonstrate ability and need. At the assessment meeting, the manager and employee jointly review their observations. This discussion should include the identification of the employee's skill strengths and developmental needs. The manager then provides a written assessment in the form of 'summary statement'.

CASE STUDY–I

"There it is finished", thought Sanjiv Choudhary as he laid aside the last of 12 Performance forms. It had been a busy week for Sanjiv, who supervises a road maintenance crew for Department of Highways, Indiana Police.

In passing through the Sanjiv's districts a few days earlier, the governor had complained to the area Superintendent that the repairs were needed on several of high ways. Because of this, the Superintendent assigned Sanjiv crew an unusually heavy work load. In addition, Sanjiv received a call from the personnel office that week telling him that the performance appraisals were late. Sanjiv explained that his predicament, but the personnel specialist insisted that the forms be completed right way.

Looking over the appraisal again, sanjiv thought about the several of the workers. The performance appraisal from had places for marking quantity of work, quality of work, and cooperativeness. For each characteristic, the worker could be graded as outstanding, good, average, below average or unsatisfactory. As Sanjiv's crew had completed all the extra work assigned for that week,, he marked the every worker outstanding in quantity of work. He marks David average in cooperativeness because David had questioned one of is decisions that week. Sanjiv had decided to patch a pothole in one of the roads, and David thought the small section of the road surface ought to be broken out and replaced. Sanjiv did not include this in the remarks section of the form, though. As a matter of fact, he wrote no remarks on any of the forms.

Sanjiv felt a twinge of guilt as he thought about Robert. He knew that Robert had been sloughing off, and the other workers had been carrying him for quite some time. He also knew that Robert would be upset if the found that he had been marked lower that the other workers. Consequently, he marked Robert the same to avoid a confrontation.

"Anyway", Sanjiv thought," these things are a pain, and I really should not have to bother with them.

As Sanjiv folded up the performance appraisal and put them in the envelop for mailing, he smiled. He was glad he would not have to think about the performance appraisals for another six months.

QUESTIONS

1. What weaknesses do you see in Sanjiv's potential and performance?

CASE STUDY–2

As the production supervisor for Alex Electronics, Mike Mahoney' was generally well regarded by most of his subordinates. Mike was an easy-going individual who tried to help his employees in any way he could. If a worker needed to have a small loan until payday, he would dig into his pocket with no question asked. Should employees need some time off to attend to a personal problem? Mike would not dock the individual's pay; rather he would take up the slack himself until the worker returned.

Everything had been going smoothly, at least until the last performance appraisals period. One of the Mike's Workers Bill had been experiencing a large no. of problem for the past years. Bill's wife had been sick much of the time and her medical expenses were high. Bill's son had a speech impediment and the doctors had recommended a special clinic.

Bill, who had already borrowed the limit the bank would loan, had become upset and despondent over his general circumstances.

When it was time for Bill's annual performance appraisal, Mike decided he was going to do as much as possible to help him. Although Bill could not be considered more than an average worker, Mike rated him outstanding in virtually every category. Because the firm's compensation system was heavily tied to performance appraisal, Bill would be eligible for a merit increase of 10% in addition to a regular cost-of living raise.

Mike explained to Bill why he was going him such high rating, and Bill acknowledged that his performances had really been no better than average. Bill was very great full and expressed these performances to Mike. As Bill left the office, he was excitedly looking forward to telling his friends about what a wonderful boss he had. Seeing the Bill smile as he left gave Mike a warm feeling.

Keeping Good people

Given the current labour market, the costs of recruiting and hiring are becoming more apparent than ever to organizations. After going through the difficulty of attracting and hiring talented people, business do not want to lose them to competitions. Difficulty is staffing has created an emphasis on retaining human resources.

Applied Industrial Technologies, a Cleveland-based business, has taken steps to reduce turnover. Specifically, they have made self-fulfillment—the process of helping each person reach their full potential—a central value in the organization. According to CEO John Dannemiller, the company views its self-fulfillment mission as important as salary and benefits in motivating talented employees. He attributes a doubling in revenues over the past 8 years and a turnover rate below the industry average to the self-fulfillment program. Here is a summary of Applied Industrial's self-fulfillment strategy:

- The company commits to 40 hours of training each year—a significant amount.
- Applied Industrial conducts regular leadership and personality testing. The test results are used to identify areas for personal improvement and to measure growth.
- The company offers reading lists of management books.
- Employees are reimbursed for education expenses.

DISCUSSION QUESTIONS

1. What other actions could Applied Industrial Technologies take to improve this program?
2. Now assume that you are an Applied Industrial Technologies manager working to orient and hire new employees.
   (*a*) How would you orient an employee who accepts a position at applied but does not care about the self improvement program? So far, the employee has met but does not exceed the job requirements.
   (*b*) What steps could you take in selection to assess whether prospects would respond effectively to the self-fulfillment program? (Hint: as a start, consider individual characteristics that might affect a prospect's response to this type of program.)
3. Applied Industrial views its self-fulfillment program as a retention effort. Is it also a recruitment tool? What, if any, do you think are the differences between tactics designed to improve retention versus those designed to improve attraction and recruitment?
4. Now let us assume that the labour market shift toward an increase in supply. Should Applied Industrial continue to invest in its human resources with the self-fulfillment program? Explain your recommendation.

Source: Dannemiller, J.C. (1998). How we keep good people. Across the Board, 35, 21.

CASE STUDY–3 WANTED

Enthusiastic Employees to Grow with Growing Minds. Inc.

Growing Minds, Inc. is a national chain of retail outlets specializing in creative toys and innovative learning materials for children. The company caters to the upper end of the market and focuses on customer service for a competitive advantage. It provides workshops for parents and children on topics such as learning with the computer and indoor gardening and offers crafts classes ranging from papier-mache to pottery.

Growing Minds plans to expand and to open five new retail outlets in the coming quarter. This may mean up to 200 new hires, and the executive team wants to make sure that the best people are hired and retained. It has issued a challenge to its retail management personnel to design a staffing process that will accomplish these goals.

The children's market in which Growing Minds operates demands service personnel who are endlessly patient; knowledgeable about children, toys, and learning; and, perhaps most important, sociable, enthusiastic, and engaging. Excellent customer service is the top priority at Growing Minds, and obtaining the desired performance from personnels has meant a major investment in training. Unfortunately, new workers often leave within a year of being hired. This means that the company barely gets an adequate return on the training it has invested in its new hires. Apparently, turnover is due (at least in part) to the demanding nature of the job. Recently, Growing Minds has been emphasizing the establishment of work teams to improve the quality of its services, identify and fix any problems in service delivery and brainstorm new opportunities. This approach has yielded better than anticipated results, so the team concept will be central to the new outlets.

CRITICAL THINKING QUESTION

1. How can Growing Minds attract the best applicants for jobs at its new retail outlets? On what groups, if any, should be company's recruiting effort focus? How should the recruiting be done?
2. How should Growing Minds select the best candidates? What type of characteristics and measures should be used? Why?
3. How might Growing Minds socialize its employees so that they are attuned to the firm's culture and plans for the future?
4. How might Growing Minds address its retention problems?
5. Students who have worked in a result setting, particularly one focusing on children and / or excellent customer service, share with the class the worker characteristics they found most important in that experience.
6. Divide into groups of three or four to identify possible sources of Growing Minds' employee retention problem. What could be done in the staffing process to address this problem? Each person in the group should list at least one possibility. Compile the best ideas produced by the group and present them to the class.

REFERENCES

1. Armstrong, M., and Baron, A. (1998, July 23), *Out of the tick box.* People Management, 4(15), 38–41.
2. Custard, S. (1998, November 4), *Competency-based interviewing: Selecting the right employee for the right job.* Conference Proceedings of Linkage Incorporated, USA, 5, 519–536.
3. Dewey, B. (1997, March/April), *Six companies share their insights: The challenges in applying competencies.* Compensation and Benefits Review, 29(2), 64–75.
4. Gallon, M.R., Stillman, H.M., and Coates, D. (1995, May/June), *Putting core competency thinking into practice.* Research-Technology Management, 38(3), 20–28.
5. Harris, C. (1998). Major approaches to job analysis. Denton, TX: University of North Texas.
6. Klein, A.L. (1996, July/August), *Validity and reliability for competency-based systems: Reducing litigation risks.* Compensation and Benefits Review, 28(4), 31–37.
7. Kush, L.J. (1994), *Competency assessment: One step at a time.* Nursing Management, 25(8), 78–79.
8. McNerney, D.J., and Briggins, A. (1995), *Competency assessment gains favor among trainers.* Hr Focus, 72(6), 19.
9. Robinson, S.M., and Barberis-Ryan, C. (1995), *Competency assessment.* Nursing Management, 26(2), 40–44.
10. Scarbrough, J., and Trill, M. (1998, November 3), *Using competencies to enhance organizational change efforts.* Conference Proceedings of Linkage Incorporated, USA, 5, 95–114.

11. Smith, J. (1998, November 4), *Linking competencies to compensation at Toyota.* Conference Proceedings of Linkage Incorporated, USA, 5, 281–320.
12. Sparrow, P. (1996, December 5), *Too good to be true?* People Management, 2(24), 22–24.
13. Thornton, G.C., III. (1992), *Assessment centers in human resource management.* New York: Addison-Wesley.
14. Tovey, L. (1993-a), *Competency assessment: A strategic approach-Part 1.* Executive Development, 6(5), 26–27.
15. Tovey, L. (1993-b), *A strategy approach to competency assessment.* Journal of European Industrial Training, 17(10).
16. Ukens, C. (1996, June 10), *Boards to test how to assess pharmacists' competence.* Drug Topics, 140(11), 45.
17. Wolfe, M. (1998, November 4), *Transitioning to a competency for pay system.* Conference Proceedings of Linkage Incorporated, USA, 5, 203–279.
18. Anstey, E. (1971), *The Civil Service Administrative Class: A follow-up of post-war entrants. Occupational Psychology,* 45, 27–43.
19. Bray, D.W. and Grant, D.L. (1966), *The assessment center in the measurement of potential for business management. Psychological Monographs,* 80 (whole no. 625).
20. Gaugler, B.B. Rosenthal, D.B., Thornton, G.C., and Bentson, C. (1987), *Meta-analysis of assessment center validity. Journal of Applied Psychology,* 72, 493–511.
21. Cascio, W.F. and Silbey, V. (1979), *Utility of the assessment center as a selection device. Journal of Applied Psychology,* 64, 107–118.
22. Howard, A., and Bray, D.W. (1988), *Managerial lives in transition: Advancing age and changing times.* New York: Guilford Press.
23. Thornton, G.C. (1992), *Assessment centers in human resource management.* Reading, MA: Addison-Wesley. Thornton, G.C. and Byham, W.C. (1982). *Assessment centers and managerial performance.* New York: Academic Press.
24. " *IPD publication Urges Employers to Wise up to career development*", Management Services; 44 (April 2000): 4.
25. Joel Schettler, "*A new social contract*", Training 39 (April 2002): 62.
26. M.F. Wolff, "Despite Layoffs, *It's still tough to find and keep the best,*" Research Technology Management "45 (Nov.– Dec. 2002; 4–5.
27. Richard Ream, "*Changing jobs?*" *It's a changing market,*" Information Today17 (Feb. 2000): 18.
28. Kevin Voigt, "*The New Face of HR*", Far Eastern Economic Review, Sep. 5, 2002; 61.
29. Rob Yeung, "*Business managing your career–Goal and attack*", Accountancy 130. (Nov. 2002; 60).
30. Mark Morgan, "*Career building strategies*", Strategic Finance, 83, June 2002; 38–43.

9

CHAPTER

HR MEASUREMENT AND AUDIT

9.1 INTRODUCTION

'Our people are our greatest asset' is a common observation in high performance organizations, and the biggest single business expense in most organizations is the cost of the people doing the jobs—the organization's human resources. So, much of the performance of an organization depends on the motivation and commitment of its employees, as well as their knowledge and skill. Yet relatively few organizations make a systematic attempt to assess the initiatives and programs that are put in place to maximize the effectiveness of human resources or to measure improvements over time.

This factsheet aims to help your organization measure human resource outcomes. It includes ideas on how you might do this, as well as examples from other organizations where such measurement strategies have been successfully implemented. While there are some broad strategies that can be used to remember that each organization is different, so the specific tools and techniques that work may differ. You will need to tailor any ideas to your own unique situation.

However one thing is certain; any measurement strategy will need to be based on agreement and consensus between all those involved—managers, employees and any representative body such as a trade union.

Successfully measuring human resource outcomes requires a step-by-step approach and this factsheet sets out a three-stage process to help you. And although this factsheet focuses on measuring human resource outcomes, it must be seen in the context of the other strategies canvassed in related factsheets.

High performance organizations ensure they maximize all resources. This includes their key resource–their employees. They put in place programs and initiatives to ensure they get the best possible outcomes from and for their employees and they collect data to ensure they can measure the success of these programs and initiatives.

Each person in an organization has a role in human resource management, be it observing occupational health and safety requirements, or taking part in training to maintain their skills. Measurement of the human resources is basic to understanding the character of the organization: number of the employees, their location, skill base, length of time with the organization and views about the work place are some examples of data that can be used for measurement. There are several ways to measure the human resources outcomes. One is to simply measure the effectiveness of the function. Another way is to demonstrate the links between human resources strategies and organizational performances. One has to measure the effectiveness of all policies or programs that impact on the people in the organization.

HR become a major player in the organization's strategic thinking, HR must change the attitude of line managers who perceive HR to be merely a cost centre.

This report will show you how to:

- Improve the visibility of HRs business value.
- Define actionable HR measurements.
- Assess the value of your organization's human capital.
- Use the balanced scorecard to align HR measures with corporate goals.
- Link intangible measures to bottom-line performance.
- Develop custom metrics to demonstrate HRs contribution.
- Use measurements as a catalyst for performance improvement.
- Develop effective reporting and benchmarking.

The innovative companies with emerging best-practice principles to show you how to build indicators and measurement programs that support the development of a world-class HR capability. It includes practical guidelines for tracking key aspects of people performance.

HR is under unprecedented pressure to demonstrate the value of HR to the business. Senior managers, along with other stakeholders inside and outside the organization, are looking for hard evidence of HRs contribution to business development and bottom line performance.

The new HR measurement agenda is being driven by a number of companies in present new competitive contexts:

- Managers looking for a demonstration of HR's bottom line contribution.
- Government and regulatory bodies calling for companies to report on human capital and people performance issues.
- Investors, analysts, partners and other stakeholders who want greater understanding of HR's impact on the business.

And, not least of all, those HR wants to be accepted as equal partners by the business and know how vital it is to demonstrate incontrovertibly that HR is essential to the achievement of business goals.

For all these reasons, there is a new strategic HR measurement agenda in the making and this report demonstrates how forward-thinking HR management can take the lead in putting it into practice. Learn how to give your organization the capabilities it most needs to succeed: motivation, a shared mindset, customer consecutiveness, and the ability to innovate.

Develop customized metrics for any organization to measure:

- Human Capital
- Commitment
- Engagement
- Innovation
- Strategic Capabilities.

Creating a Human Resource Measurement Framework

All too often Human Resource (HR) professionals undertake detailed and lengthy measurement activities of a variety of human resource practices, outcomes and processes, present it with a flourish the management. So, we should redefine the human resource measurement intervention in the first place if all it is going to do is reinforce preconceived notions of the human resources function as a transactional, low value-adding component of the business. The reality is that measurement can be very powerful, both as a strategic tool and in challenging these perceptions. Three key elements must be clear and must be in place for HR measurement to become a strategic tool:

1. Define and articulate the business case for HR as a strategic asset (Firstly because by mapping your human capital requirements to organizational priorities you are both immediately prioritizing what is required to be measured (so that you are not measuring for measurement's sake) and aligning measurement so that when you measure, you will measure that which is most meaningful).
2. Ensure HR has the right competencies (the measurement framework should also include an indication of how human capital priorities will be operationalised. This creates both an expectation from the organization and accountability for the HR practitioner. For your HR measurement framework to succeed, HR must deliver on its outputs).
3. Ensure the right HR practices and systems are in place (the purpose of the measurement intervention is to ensure that the organization's human capital is aligned with and helps to drive organizational performance. In this regard measurement is bound to reveal areas of poor performance and indicate actions that need to be taken). Other measures that you could consider are:

- Absence rate
- Employee turnover
- Training hours per employee
- Remuneration/revenue
- Customers per employee
- Developmental training spend per employee.

The potential measures for use are considerable, but should always reflect and relate to the organizational priorities. The next step is to actually measure. Decide on how frequently you will want to measure and report (as you will want to demonstrate change over time), and determine at what organizational levels you will want to measure. Will you measure for the organization as a whole only, will you measure for individual business units, or will you measure for particular departments? As you cascade measurement down organizational levels remember that different business units or departments may have different human capital requirements and therefore may require a different measurement framework. Remember too, that the intention is not to overwhelm but to provide easily accessible and meaningful strategic information.

The most important part of the process is to interpret and action your measurement results; it is only by doing this and communicating the outcomes to the organization that you will move away from the trap of measuring for measurement's sake. Your interpretation should: consider the results from various benchmarks together in order to provide a more informed and holistic interpretation; consider previous measurement results so that you understand how performance has altered over time; and should consider—where possible—how compare externally, *i.e.*, how you stack up against others. Whilst other organizations or competitors may not have the same human capital and organizational priorities, by demonstrating external comparison and performance to your organization you are demonstrating an appreciation for how human capital drives your organization's performance relative to others, and what competitive advantage in human capital management means.

The HR function, today and in the future, need not be concerned about replacing the fundamentals of its trade with a focus on figures. Rather, the adoption of an HR measurement framework is about extending the credibility of HR on the one hand, and on the other placing human capital firmly and strategically on the organization's balance sheet. Measurement represents a powerful tool by which HR can change the way it works and the value the organization perceives it to create.

Proposes a method to assess the relative value of organizational human resource (HR) based on total performance. The total performance of the man-machine resource base of an organization includes its profitability together with how it affects the interests of consumers, the national economy and society (*i.e.*, other than profitability performance). Remember that measurement of human resource outcomes is not an end in itself. Its purpose is to improve work performance and organizational productivity. 'If you can't measure it, you can't manage it' is a truism that also applies when assessing human resource outcomes against the agreed goals and objectives within the organization. A comprehensive human resource strategy will include aims, objectives and indicators for measurement. It will also include links to the organizational business plan.

Studies in India and abroad have found relationship between the best HR practices and reduced turnover and increased employee productivity. Further, those practices enhanced profitability and market value of the organization. The data to evaluate performance and its relationship with HR practices comes from several sources, but five systems are the most often used to measure HR effectiveness. These are:

1. Benchmarking
2. HR Audit
3. HR Accounting
4. HR Information System, and
5. HR Research.

1. **Benchmarking:** There has been a progressive increase in the topic of benchmarking—but for all that there is still a great deal of ignorance about what it actually is. It has taken its place as a management buzzword alongwith BPR, TQM, change EVA and many others—but its true nature is poorly understood. Some see it as stealing (or 'borrowing') ideas; others as a mechanism for comparison with a competitor; whilst others view it as a form of industrial espionage. In fact it is all of these and none of these at the same time, but instead involves understanding strategic gaps; cooperation; hard work; a willingness to question and where necessary to change fundamental precepts (sacred cows) and complementation.

Benchmarking is rapidly becoming an indispensable tool for savvy finance executives. Used wisely, it can transform a company's vision and clarify decisions on performance, markets and internal efficiency. "**Benchmarking** is a tool to help you improve your business processes. Any business process can be benchmarked." "**Benchmarking** is the process of identifying, understanding, and adapting outstanding practices from organizations anywhere in the world to help your organization improve its performance." "**Benchmarking** is a highly respected practice in the business world. It is an activity that looks outward to find best practice and high performance and then measures actual business operations against those goals". One of the biggest mistakes people make when beginning their benchmarking endeavor is that they only look to benchmark someone within their own industry. The concept of discovering what is the best performance being achieved, whether in your company, by a competitor, or by an entirely different industry. Benchmarking is an improvement tool whereby a company measures its performance or process against other companies' best practices, determines how those companies achieved their performance levels, and uses the information to improve its own performance. Benchmarking is a continuous process whereby an enterprise measures and compares all its functions, systems and practices against strong competitors, identifying quality gaps in the organization, and striving to achieve competitive advantage locally and globally.

The benchmarking defines as a tool that "improves performance by identifying and applying best demonstrated practices" to operations and sales. "Managers compare the performance of their products or processes externally to those of competitors and best-in-class companies and internally to other operations within their own firms that perform similar activities," the carefully worded definition continues. "The objective of benchmarking is to find examples of superior performance and to understand the processes and practices driving that performance. Companies then improve their performance by tailoring and incorporating these best practices into their own operations—not by imitating, but by innovating."

What is benchmarking?

The term benchmark comes from surveying where it was used to denote a notch or mark representing a given altitude and against which other heights could be calibrated or 'benchmarked', since when it has come to mean any standard against which something is compared; and some of the leading exponents in business include Xerox and GE. In business terms there are numerous definitions of benchmarking, but essentially it involves learning, sharing information and adopting best practices to bring about step changes in performance. So, at its simplest, benchmarking means:

"Improving by learning from others *i.e.*, benchmarking is simply about making comparisons with other organizations and then learning the lessons that those comparisons throw up".

Another definition is:

Benchmarking is the continuous process of measuring products, services and practices against the toughest competitors or those companies recognized as industry leaders (best in the class)".

Robert Camp's definition:

"A positive, proactive process by which a company examines how another company performs a specific function in order to improve how it performs the same, or similar function. Operational processes must be comparative or analogous if the highest degree of knowledge transfer between benchmarking partners is to be achieved".

Benchmarking allows you to discover the gaps in your performance when compared with someone else. Nothing will happen, however, unless you actually do something to close the gap or surpass it. The real payback comes from changing what you do to improve your operations—and as we all know change is difficult. Once the gap has been identified the key questions is "How much of the gap do we wish to close? A little, a lot or become the best-in-class. Some areas will need greater efforts to change and what will be the cost? But all must be compared to probable benefit/return for that effort (*e.g.*, revenue, cost efficiency or customer satisfaction). It may not be cost effective to go the whole way and in some cases best-in-class may a step too far! But it may act as a stretch target to which you aspire or re-visit later.

In practice, benchmarking usually encompasses: regularly comparing aspects of performance (functions or processes) with others;

- identifying gaps in performance;
- developing performance improvements to close the gaps thus identified;
- implementing the improvements;
- monitoring progress; and
- reviewing the benefits.

The key questions on which successful benchmarking turns are:

- How do **we** do it? and
- How do **they** do it?

In other words a comparison of your processes with : (*a*) more successful organization(s) to establish exactly where the differences lie and then taking steps to use the knowledge to close the gaps. The underlying reason for benchmarking is to learn how to improve your business processes and thereby increase your competitiveness. Organisations choose to benchmark outstanding companies whose business processes are analogous to their own even if they are in different industries! Benchmarking allows you to identify those practices that have facilitated those successful companies' superior performance and that can be adapted to your own business. Accordingly, benchmarking is an operational process involving continuous learning and adaptation which enables you to improve your organization's competitive position.

Why Benchmark?

Although many organisations initiate benchmarking projects because of some dubious reasons; for practical purposes the only reason to benchmark is because you recognise that somewhere, somehow you are not as efficient or as capable of satisfying your customers as your competition—whether currently or because you have spotted a trend in the market that you need to exploit, follow or respond to.

There are two key drivers for an organisation—profitability and revenue growth (the former being a function of the latter after costs) and there are many variables that impact on these. The key to maximising both is to understand where competitors are better than you–where customers value it. It is of little value having the best process for selling insurance if what customers really want is an easy to use claims process and yours isn't! Similarly it is no good having an extremely slick sales process for commodities if the delivery is poor, patchy and unreliable.

Fig: 9.1 Drivers and contribution to growth/profit

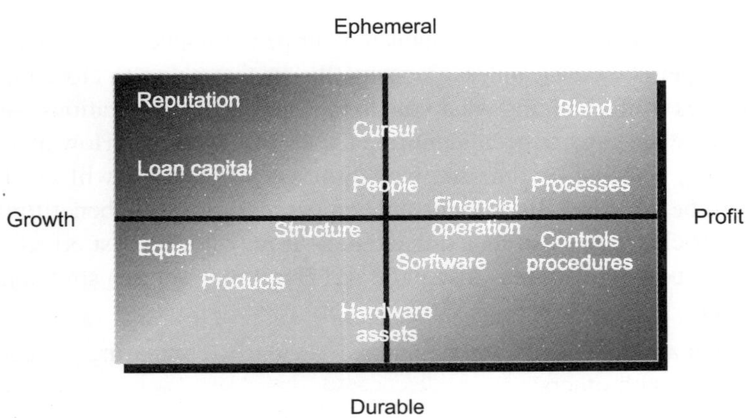

As the diagram shows, processes, although an ephemeral component of an organisation (as opposed to more durable items such as hardware and fixed assets) because they change easily, are critical for profitability as delivery of products/services is crucial to customer satisfaction, payments and ultimately profit. Similarly reputation (ephemeral) is critical to growth but can be lost all too easily—especially if processes/people do not deliver [c/f Arthur Andersen].

Although benchmarking is a measurement process and does generate comparative performance measures, it also about attaining exceptional performance. The practices that lead to exceptional performance are called enablers. Thus the process of benchmarking results in two types of outputs: benchmarks, or measures of superior performance, and enablers. Process enablers are developed to meet a specific business need within the context of a specific business environment and company culture. This is why it is of little value to 'steal' from others because you will not have explored whether and where their business practices are relevant or transferable to yours.

Benchmarking: The Metamorphosis

Watson (1993) suggests that benchmarking is an evolving concept that has developed since 1940s towards sophisticated forms. He proposes that it has undergone five generations:

The first one is entitled "Reverse Engineering" was product oriented, comparing the product characteristics, functionality and performance of the competitive offerings. The second generation "Competitive benchmarking" involves the comparisons of process with those of the competitors. The third Generation, the process benchmarking was based on the idea that learning can be made from companies outside their industry. Hence, sharing of the information become less restricted, non-competitive nature of intelligence gathering. But at the same time it requires more in-depth understanding and needed to understand similarities in the processes, which on the surface it looks different. Fourth Generation benchmarking, in 1990s, introduced strategic benchmarking, involves a systematic process for evaluating options, implementing strategies and improving performance by understanding and adopting successful strategies from the external partners. Typical to this perspective is continuous and long-term development and aim to make fundamental shift in the process. With Fifth Generation this was complemented by the global orientation. The basic philosophy behind the competency benchmarking is the idea that the foundation of organizational change processes lies in the change of action and behaviour of individuals and teams. Karlof and Ostblom (1995) use the term bench learning, which also refers to a cultural change in efforts to becoming a learning organization. Organization can improve their effectiveness by developing competencies and skills and by learning how to change attitudes and practices. The last indicate that benchmarking was a useful tool for interactive learning (1999). In the small business sector obtained the similar findings from generic success was the change in attitudes towards customers and how essential was the developing of collaborative learning and company culture through the Network Benchmarking.

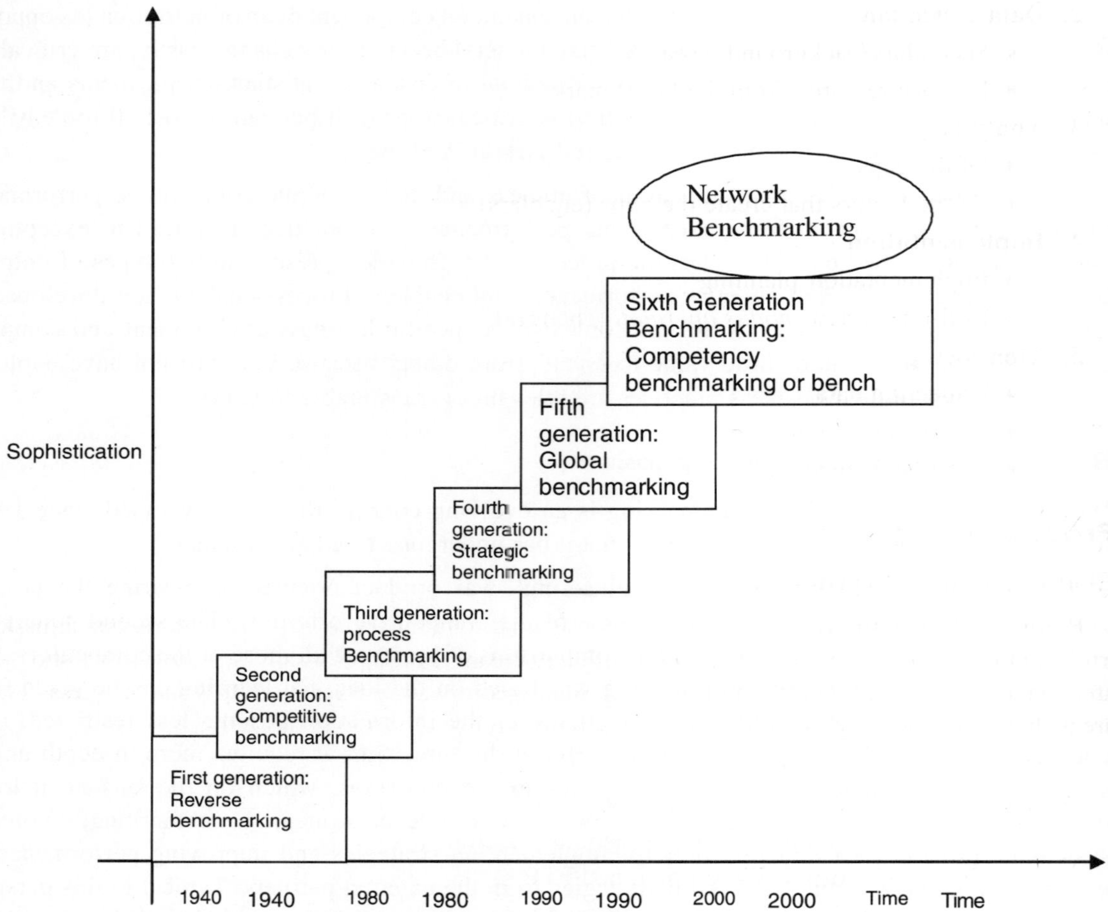

There are several 'types' of benchmarking including:

- Generic, *e.g.*, comparisons in a general sense—often using terms such as customer, strategic or operational
- Functional, *e.g.*, Finance, Sales or HR efficiency (*e.g.*, HR staff to total employees)
- Process, *e.g.*, insurance claims or delivery of buik commodities
- Global—across the world
- Cost—focusing on cost dynamics
- Performance—looking at revenue or growth

Steps in benchmarking—Five key stages

There are five key stages in benchmarking:

1. **Proto-planning**
    - Decide what you wish to benchmark
    - Decide against whom you need to benchmark
    - Identify outputs required
    - Determine data collection methodologies

2. **Data collection**
    - Secondary/background research
    - Primary research from the benchmark
3. **Analysis**
    - Of the gaps
    - Of the factors that create the gaps (enablers)
4. **Implementation**
    - Implementation planning
    - Roll-out of new *modus operandi* (changes)
5. **Monitoring**
    - Collecting data
    - Evaluating progress
    - Iterative change

Proto-planning

Choosing what to benchmark

Before starting a programme you must choose what to compare. It is of little value benchmarking irrelevant processes or activities [*e.g.*, how efficient cleaners or night watch men are]—they should be areas that have the potential to add real sustainable competitive advantage to your business. Those areas that you benchmark should be chosen with reference to key criteria such as:

- Core to you and your competition
- Important to you in terms of [some or all of]:
    - Volume (large number of transactions undertaken)
    - Cost (high costs-based on time and FTE's)
    - Value (significant in terms of revenue to you and/or benefit to the customer)
- Easy to measure and offering comparisons
- Risk inherent:
    - Processes that are difficult to control, thus presenting a risk to the business
    - Processes that vary in performance and impact profits and costs so that you can maximise the benefits from improvements.

NB–not every process needs to be world class, it is only those that will deliver sustainable competitive advantage. Similarly one process should not shine at the expense of the entire system or there will be an efficiency mis-match leading to ineffectiveness.

The company must understand its strategic intent, and identify core competencies, key business processes, and critical success factors. Then the particular process to be benchmarked must be documented and flowcharted, to determine its inherent capability.

Specific activities are:

- understand business strategic intent.
- identify core competencies, and map company capabilities.
- select the specific process to benchmark.
- select a benchmarking team leader and participants.

- identify the customer profiles and expectations.
- analyse process flow and performance measures.
- define process inputs and outputs.
- document and flow chart the process.
- identify, understand and measure critical success factors.
- select critical success factors to benchmark.
- develop the company selection criteria.
- establish the data collection method.
- develop a preliminary questionnaire.

Choosing your benchmark

Having decided what you want to benchmark the next question is: 'against whom will we benchmark?'—the choice of organisation is key and dependent on several factors as discussed above. Requirements must be established for selecting benchmarking partners, given the benchmarking objective, or for characterising the degree of relevance that any particular company may have as a potential benchmarking partner. At this stage you need to decide if it will be a one: one exercise or a peer group.

Deciding on outputs

Before collecting data it is vital that you decide on the format of the outputs. This will in turn shape both how you collect the data and the method you use for analysis. This should lead to developing benchmark metrics for use during the project.

Defining the data collection methods

This will be driven by:

- the outputs required.
- the form of the information.
- the nature of the exercise (group versus one: one) .
- time.
- process to be benchmarked.

Data collection

Data collection is based on 'secondary research, public background and primary research, directly from benchmarks.

Secondary: It is important to learn as much as possible before making any direct contact and this can be accomplished using 'desk research including publications and websites etc. This enables you to get a picture of the firm(s) that you might wish to benchmark and an understanding of what you can bring to them. From this you can develop a shortlist.

Primary: Direct data collection from the benchmark. If this is a one to one exercise then it will involve staff 'living' with the organisation to understand what it does and how; if it is part of a larger exercise say of peers/competitors then it will be a formal data collection programme in which you will participate. This will involve:

- planning the data collection.
- developing an interview guide/questionnaire.
- conducting primary research (telephone survey, mail survey, or individual interviews).
- monitoring process performance and analyse performance gaps.
- making on-site observations to clarify and verify previous observations.
- conducting a post-site-visit debriefing with team members, to record observations.
- preparation of a report.

Analysis: The analysis consists of two aspects

- Determining the magnitude of the performance gaps between you and the other companies, using the benchmarking metrics identified during the proto-planning step.
- Identifying the process enablers that facilitated the performance improvements at the leading companies.

The analysis step in the benchmarking process model consists of five phases:

1. data analysis.
2. data presentation.
3. root cause analysis.
4. results projection.
5. enabler identification.

The goal of this step is to identify adaptable process enablers for implementation.

The specific activities are:

- organise and graphically present the data for identification of performance gaps.
- normalise performance to a common measurement base.
- compare current performance against the benchmark.
- identify performance gaps and determine the root causes.
- project the performance 3 to 5 years into the future.
- develop scenarios case studies for discussion.
- isolate process enablers that correlate to process improvements.
- evaluate the nature of the process enablers to determine their relevance to your organisation.

Implementation

The objective of this phase is to make the changes to your processes to improve performance and this involves, implementation planning—*i.e.*, developing the how of the change; rolling out the new methods etc. and finalising measures for excellence. The main activities are:

- set goals to close, meet, and then exceed the performance gap.
- select best practices and enablers for consideration.
- modify process enablers to match the company culture and organizational structure.
- enhance these enablers based on team observations for integrating process improvements.
- develop a formal action plan for implementing improvements.
- obtain management buy-in and ownership of the required changes.

- commit resources.
- implement the plan-piloting where sensible.
- iterate changes based on pilot.
- roll-out elsewhere as appropriate

Monitoring

This is about ensuring that the new processes work and that any 'edge' created is sustained, and involves collecting data on the new process, evaluating progress and if necessary, iterating changes, monitoring and reporting improvement progress, identifying opportunities for future benchmarking and recalibrating the measure regularly.

Conclusion

Benchmarking is more than just a comparative analysis—this sort of analysis has been undertaken for many years with little benefits. What benchmarking contributes is that 'lessons are learned'. The difference with a benchmarking study is that a better way of doing things is analysed and then the key factors—the enablers—are then used to close the gap. NB techniques and enablers that were critical in recent past will not remain the same so the processes should be revisited periodically to see if they are still extant and if not to find out what needs to be done. There are a few key issues for organisations beginning benchmarking efforts:

- top management commitment and participation are necessary.
- sufficient time must be allowed for the project as it takes time.
- an able, well-trained team is critical—where appropriate get outside help (consultants) .
- it is heavy on resources: people, travel, research, consultants, and other factors are involved.
- process rigour is an absolute sine qua non for success—you cannot 'graze the surface'.
- quantitative data is often difficult and time consuming to obtain.

In addition there are some principles that have evolved over time which form a framework to such studies:

- legality—you must be open and honest.
- exchange—a quid pro quo.
- confidentiality—it remains between you and the benchmark.
- use—only for the purpose agreed.
- preparation—is essential to succeed.
- completion—of all tasks and implementation must be carried out.
- understanding—of your processes, gaps, enablers [and their relevance to you] and the action to close the gap are key to success.

Successful benchmarking requires three basic ingredients: a real problem with management willing to solve it; access to benchmarking partners who have previously resolved that problem; a knowledgeable benchmarking team with the ability to use quality tools and research practices to investigate process problems to their root cause. In most cases it is advisable to use external consultants who bring expertise and experience and can help you carry out a benchmarking exercise avoiding pitfalls and maximizing return from investment.

9.2 HR AUDIT

Introduction

The Human Resources (HR) Audit is a process of examining policies, procedures, documentation, systems, and practices with respect to an organization's HR functions. The purpose of the audit is to reveal the strengths and weaknesses in the nonprofit's human resources system, and any issues needing resolution. The audit works best when the focus is on analyzing and improving the HR function in the organization. The audit itself is a diagnostic tool, not a prescriptive instrument. It will help you identify what you are missing or need to improve, but it can't tell you what you need to do to address these issues. It is most useful when an organization is ready to act on the findings, and to evolve its HR function to a level where it's full potential to support the organization's mission and objectives can be realized. With this human resource audit, a company can tap the most exciting, inexpensive, readily available source of talent in the world–its own workforce. No search fees, no exhausting interviews, no great time lags in "finding that right person" need to be incurred. The right person is probably working for you right now, only perhaps not working at what they should be doing. Once this audit has been completed, and you have fully maximized the human resource completely available to you, a company can then look objectively at what lacks still exist and can then go about filling those needs from the outside, and fitting the new people appropriately into a team, the character of which are now well known. How the individual fits into the team is as much a key factor as the individual's own ability. In summary, Sigmund Freud, once said that life is all about **Lieb und Arbeit**. The important thing, given this, is that love and work wherever possible be combined. The truly successful person, who makes maximum contributions to a company, loves his or her work. An individual can perform at a mediocre level not loving their job, but never at a top level. To deal with change, a company must know those people and maximize the productivity of each of its precious employees. Only through a human resource audit and building future hiring around the team that current exists, can this be achieved.

Human Resources Audit

In order to provide useful information to managers, it is necessary to evaluate the results generated by the design and implementation of personnel policies. This is the goal of the HR audit that includes two different analyses and valuations: the HR policies and their level of fit with the strategy of the firm, and the characteristics of human capital. Several criteria have been used to assess different HR policies. Nevertheless, the measurement of the value that human capital brings to the firm is a very complex topic. Consequently, different models are being presented that aim to properly solve this challenge. This chapter will analyze the HR function from two perspectives: the evaluation of the implemented policies and the quality of human capital in relation to real competencies, and the capability to learn and develop new skills.

The human resource valuation system cannot be considered to be a complete system of accounting unless it is followed by an equally competent system of auditing. Application or use of human resource accounting, therefore, must also be followed by a separate HR audit to ascertain whether or not the performance of the managers has been true and fair in the overall interests of the organization they serve. The application and usefulness of human resource valuation depends on the future efforts and experiments to be made by practising managers, accountants and academicians. It also needs support from the professional bodies and government. In the absence of human resource valuation, the management may not realize the negative effects of certain programmes aimed at improving profits in the short run. Such programmes may result in decreased value of human assets due to a fall in productivity levels, high labour turnover and low morale. Audit of human resources could help in finding out the efficiency of every segment. Human resource audit could enable the appraisal of the performance of various managers. The basic function and management of human resources is also greatly facilitated. Hence, human resource valuation and audit activity could be helpful in improving the efficiency of human resources in the changing business scenario.

What is an HR audit?

Used optimally, a human resource audit helps senior management to:

- Ensure compliance with wage-and-hour laws and the myriad of other employment and benefits-related statues.
- Examine the effectiveness and costs of HR policies and practices and their role in the organization's strategic planning.
- Benchmark actual against desired performance and develop an action plan for addressing shortfalls.
- Save money by identifying and correcting inefficiencies and compliance problems.

Progressive organizations will embrace a well-executed HR audit as an important tool for creating, updating and executing HR strategies and best practices that will provide long-term support to the organization's big picture.

Audit: The Definition

- A systematic examination of the activities and status of an entity, based primarily on investigation and analysis of its systems, controls, and records.
- An examination in general; a judicial examination.
- An independent review and examination of records and activities to assess the adequacy of system controls, to ensure compliance with established policies and operational procedures, and to recommend necessary changes in controls, policies, or procedures.
- To conduct an independent review and examination of system records and activities in order to test the adequacy and effectiveness of data security and data integrity procedures, to ensure compliance with established policy and operational procedures, and to recommend any necessary changes.
- To attend an academic class on a not-for-academic-credit basis.

Audit (*noun*)

1. An inspection of the accounting procedures and records by a trained accountant. *synonyms*: audited account, audit.

Audit (*verb*)

1. The accounts and tax returns; with the intent to verify. *synonyms*: audit, scrutinize, inspect.
2. Attend academic courses without getting credit. *synonyms*: audit.

HR was previously a stand-alone function, and has now become more integrated into the rest of the organizational functions. The HR function needs to move away from performing transactions and towards forging strategic business partnerships in the organization. It needs to measure and demonstrate the value and contribution of HR to the business strategy.

- Thoroughly understand the overall corporate strategy.
- Examine your HR strategy to ensure that it is clearly aligned to your business strategy.
- Ensure executive buy-in for your HR strategy by engaging in discussions with key decision-makers in your organization.
- Evaluate the contribution of the HR function to the business strategy by determining and implementing effective measurements.

Your HR function needs to support your company's business strategy. Auditing your HR procedures will assist you in HR planning and forecasting for the success of your HR processes. Your organization will also attract the right people by gaining credibility as an Employer of Choice. Give your HR function structure and direction to save time and money and increase the quality of service by learning how to:

- Determine the scope of your internal HR audit.
- Analyse your HR procedures to ensure that they are fully documented to avoid incurring penalties and fines from the Department of Labour.
- Establish your employees' level of awareness of your company HR policies and procedures to avoid the instigation of CCMA cases.
- Ensure you conform with the Basic Conditions of Employment Act by verifying that your HR processes are properly practiced to ensure your credibility as an Employer of Choice.
- Review the company HR procedures at induction to ensure your new staff are informed and to validate your HR practices.
- Understand the recently released HR Draft Code of Good Practice and other Codes to ensure you are properly updated and conform to the requirements.

There has been a great deal of pressure on employers to formalize and improve the standard of their HR practices, policies and procedures, due to the various factors that influences their organizations.

Purpose of a Human Resources Audit

This document presents an audit procedure to assess whether the Human Resource (HR) Function at Business Unit (BU) level is delivering its mandate and roles.

The methodology that drives this audit is based on four key principles advocated by a leading HR consultant and teacher, Dave Ulrich and his associates in the USA.

Their cutting edge research and consulting work has shown time and again that worthy HR professionals ensure that:

(*a*) Line manager friendly systems, and procedures are available to help management execute their people management role (*i.e.*, the technical-professional and service role of HR).

(*b*) Line management are equipped to work within the various labour relations laws and codes of conduct that govern the relationship between labour and management in the workplace (the compliance role of HR).

(*c*) Each Business Unit has an overall people management (HR) strategy in place that increases the value of employees to the business (the strategic role of human resources).

(*d*) HR systems and procedures are run at optimal cost (financial management role of human resources). Please do not read optimal as lowest cost, but as the right price for the job on hand.

These assumptions can be translated into four critical roles that professional HR professionals must play if they wish to be seen to make a real contribution to a business' success.

Scope of the HR Audit

The best option, therefore, is to widen the scope of the HR audit so that it covers the corporate strategy, the human resource function, managerial compliance and employee satisfaction. (Werther and Davis, 2000)

HR has a definite role in meeting the organization's corporate strategy. Organizations are composed of people, and HR is entrusted with the responsibility of finding the best people for the jobs so that the organization can gain a competitive advantage in the marketplace. Understanding the firm's corporate strategy has strong implications for planning, staffing, compensation, employee relations and other HR activities. HR is effective only when it contributes to the firm's strategic goals. The HR department can learn about the firm's overall strategy through interviews with key executives, review of long range business plans, and systematic scanning of the environment to uncover changing trends. (Hooper, Catanello and Murray, 1987)

The HR audit is a logical review of the workings of the HR department. For the audit to be comprehensive, it must review all the major areas, such as HR Planning, Job Analysis, Compensation Administration, Affirmative Action, Recruiting, Selection, Training and Orientation, Career Development, Performance Appraisals and Labour Management Relations. Larger organizations perform HR Audits much in the same manner as financial audits, designating a team of experts who are likely to have the requisite functional experience in one or more specific areas, although based in another location. The best place to start the HR audit is on the basis of past audit reports, or on the basis of functions carried out by the department, the controls in place and the policies and procedures followed in each case. The audit team will seek to identify who is responsible for each activity, determine the objectives of each activity, review the policies and procedures used, sample the available records to find if the policies and procedures are being followed, prepare an audit report commending proper objectives, policies and procedures, develop an action plan to correct errors in objectives, policies and procedures, and follow up on the action plan at a later stage, to see if it solved the problems found through the audit. (Berry, 1967).

The focus on managerial compliance is to find out how well the managers in other departments comply with HR policies and procedures. The audit should preferably uncover instances where managers have ignored or abused policies and violated laws. Compliance with laws is especially important, as the Government would hold the company responsible. In ensuring compliance, the HR department improves its image, value and contribution to the company. Conversely, the HR department will earn the respect of operating managers if it seeks their views relating to HR needs in their respective areas. Acting on these discussions will increase its contribution to the organizational objectives, while also being seen as being more responsive to departmental needs.

The audit team/individuals will, in the process of the HR audit, gather data from workers to find out how well their needs are being met. Employee feedback and information is collected on wages, benefits, supervision, career planning, and performance appraisals. Employee actions like turnover, absenteeism and unionism are more likely to occur when their needs are not being met. The effectiveness of the HR department can be judged by its ability to meet the employee's needs while at the same time, serving the interests of the organization. Common Research Approaches to the HR Audit: Just as there is some value to scanning the environment in making note of trends and changing business practices, there is also some value in using a research based approach to evaluating HR activities. This falls in the realm of applied research.

(*a*) ***Comparative Approach:*** In this approach, another division or company that has better practices or results is chosen as the model. The audit team audits and compares the audited firm's results with the best practices of the model organization. This approach is commonly used to compare the results of specific activities or programs. This 'best practices' approach is often used with turnover, absence, salary data and staffing levels. It helps detect areas where improvement is needed. It also makes sense to compare where a procedure is being used for the first time.

(*b*) ***Outside Authority Approach:*** In this approach, standards set by a consultant or taken from published research findings serve as the benchmark for the audit team. The consultant or research findings may help diagnose the cause of problems.

(*c*) ***Statistical Approach:*** This approach relies on performance measures drawn from the company's existing information system. From existing records, the audit team generates the Statistical standards against which activities and programs are evaluated. With the mathematical standards as a base, the team may uncover errors while they are still minor. For example, by tracking and managing turnover and absenteeism rates from one period to another, the team can compare and analyze the data to see how well HR and operating managers control these problem areas. Often this approach is supplemented with comparative data from external sources such as other firms, or industry association surveys. The information is usually expressed in ratios or formulas that are easy to compute and use.

(*d*) ***Compliance Approach:*** This approach reviews past practices, to determine if actions taken followed legal requirements, company policies and procedures. The audit team here often examines a sample of employment, compensation, discipline and employee appraisal forms. The purpose of the review is to ensure that the field offices and the operating managers have complied with internal rules and legal regulations, such as minimum wages and equal employment opportunity laws. By sampling elements of the human resources information system, the audit team looks for deviations from laws and company policies and procedures. The team can then determine the degree of compliance achieved.

(*e*) **MBO Approach:** In this 'management by objectives' approach, managers and specialists set objectives in their area of responsibility. Then they create specific goals against which this performance can be measured. The audit team researches actual performance and compares it with the previously set objectives. They can then evaluate the trends in this area. (Werther and Davis, 2000)

In actual practice, audit teams commonly use several of the above strategies, depending on the specific activities under consideration. Feedback is then given to senior management, the operating managers and the employees. Unfavorable feedback leads to corrective action and improvement in the contribution of the HR department.

Tools of the HR Audit

The audit team uses a combination of several information-gathering tools to collect data about the firm's HR activities. These tools include interviews, surveys, historical analysis, external information, human resource experiments and international audits. Each tool provides partial insights into the firm's activities. By using these tools skillfully, the audit team can get an insight into the effectiveness of the organization's HR activities. (Werther and Davis, 2000)

Interviews of employees and managers often provide audit teams with a powerful tool for collecting information about HR activities and identifying areas that need improvement. Interviews can be conducted on both sides to determine the reasons for problems like turnover or absenteeism. Comments and criticisms from interviewees can help pinpoint perceptions and causes that will then form the basis for corrective action. Suggestions by interviewees may reveal ways of better dealing with the issues. Where criticisms are valid, changes should be made. Where the HR department is correct however, employees may have to be educated and trained by explaining the reasons for the procedures in place that are a cause for concern. Exit interviews are conducted with departing employees to learn their views and experiences with the organization. Questions asked along these lines are reviewed later to find out if there is a major cause for turnover, absenteeism, dissatisfaction etc. The HR department must take an active interest in exit interviews—some employees may be reluctant to criticize and speak their mind. Reasons must be studied to determine if trends exist among divisions, departments or managers.

The scope for taking interviews is however time consuming and limited, therefore there is a trend among HR departments to use questionnaires to broaden the scope of their research. Questionnaires may lead to more candid answers than face to face interviews. Attitude survey feedback can find answers to concerns. Trends revealed through the questionnaires can then be addressed, in order of importance to those surveyed.

An analysis of historical records can also reveal important trends. Compliance with laws and company policies and procedures can also be determined as well as the success of action plans to remove points of concern. Specific areas that may be covered include employee safety and health, grievances, compensation, affirmative action, programs and policies. There may be a conflict between these laws and the organization's practices, however a proper study and analysis is helpful to iron out these inconsistencies and meet the organizational goals.

External information can also be helpful in giving the audit team a perspective against which the firm's activities can be judged. Such information can be available from various public and private agencies and government departments. Examples include wages and salary surveys, employee turnover rates, workforce projections, future employment opportunities, and accident rates by professions that can serve as benchmarks for comparison purposes. Workforce demographics such as age, sex, education and racial composition are useful in evaluation of affirmative action programs. Some information may also be provided from consultant studies and research bureaus.

Another tool available to the HR audit team, especially in evaluating new programs and trends on which there is no available data for comparison purposes, is to themselves conduct a field experiment. In using the field experiment, the HR audit team compares an experimental group with a control group, under realistic conditions. Such experimentation is usually employed in researching absenteeism, turnover, compensation, job satisfaction and safety activities. For example, in checking the effectiveness of a job safety program, the audit team may implement a safety training program to half the supervisors (the experimental group). The other group (control group) contains supervisors that have not been given this training. The accident rates and safety records of both groups can be compared at a later stage, some months after the safety program has been concluded. If results reveal that the experimental group has a considerably lower accident rate and better safety record, there is evidence that the safety program was effective. A cost benefit analysis will also be conducted to compare the costs of the training program with the benefits to the workers and the company. However, the field experiment method can have some drawbacks. Managers may be reluctant to experiment with workers because of morale problems and potential dissatisfaction among those who were not selected. On the other hand, employees involved in the experiment may feel manipulated. The experiment itself may be confounded by changes in the work environment or simply by the two groups talking to each other about the experiment.

The HR audits of international organizations are more complex. Such complexity is due to differences in laws, languages, cultures, traditional practices, and expectations. There is a tendency for the audit team to use the standards and experiences from their home countries as a benchmark against which the evaluation is conducted. The auditors must make allowances for variations in standards and laws followed in the host country. Discrimination by sex, race, social status, caste or religion may be allowed and even encouraged in the lesser-developed nations, as a matter of national practice. This often will make it difficult for the auditors to distinguish and identify areas of variation from company practice that are not justified by the foreign context. Variations should be noted however, so that the policy makers can determine whether such differences may be allowed to continue. It is the probing into the reasons for the variations that can uncover either appropriate justification or poor management practices. Unless the necessities of business justify differences, the goal should be uniformity in policies, practices, and procedures throughout the organization. Such uniformity will facilitate ease of administration and re-assignment of personnel. It also makes research into intra-company comparisons easier and more accurate.

Benefits of HR Audit

Several benefits associated with HR audit are listed below. It reminds the members of HR department and others its contribution, creating a more professional image of the department among the managers and specialist. The audit helps clarify the department's role and leads to greater uniformity, especially in the geographically strategic plans in an action.

- Identifies the contribution of HR department to the organization.
- Improves the professional image of the HR department.
- Encourages greater responsibility and professionalism among the members of the HR department.
- Clarifies the duties and responsibilities.
- Stimulates uniformity of the HR policies.
- Finds critical HR problems.
- Ensures timely compliance with legal requirements.
- Reduce human resources cost through more effective HR procedures.
- Creates increased acceptance of needed change in the HR procedures.
- Requires through review of HR departments information system.

Besides ensuring the compliances, the audit can improve the department's image and contribution to the company. Operating managers may have more respect for the department when an audit team seeks their view. If the comments of the manager are acted on, the department will be seen as being more responsive to their needs. And since it is service department, these actions may improve its contribution to organizational objectives.

Immediate benefits of an HR audit

As with accounting audits, the findings and recommendations from HR audits are only as good as the information provided. If you are not entirely honest and objective, no purpose is served.

However, if staying on the right side of the law and reducing legal exposure are not enough incentive to launch your organization on the audit path today, consider the other benefits. Very typically, small to medium-size companies realize almost instant cost savings once an audit is complete and changes are implemented. For example:

- Correcting benefit premium errors and overpayments can generate many thousands of dollars in savings.
- Initiating a safety program can reduce workers compensation experience modification numbers, reducing annual premium costs by tens of thousands of dollars.
- Shopping benefit costs among alternative carriers and modifying employer/employee co-pay ratios can recoup dramatic savings.
- Examining the effectiveness of recruiting tools can spare the expense of filling positions.

A small or medium-size firm also may benefit from using an HR audit to:

- Study retention and turnover, employing a neutral party to solicit honest feedback from employees, and allowing the company to develop an action plan.
- Examine the company's foundation for its compensation philosophies and develop an objective method of grading jobs, with new ranges that are market-competitive and internally equitable.
- Create or enhance an employee-referral program or internal jobs board.
- Improve employee communication and ensure that the HR department is accessible.
- Identify opportunities to outsource areas within human resources that offer more value to the company.

Obviously, audits are time consuming. As results, small firms used an ad hoc arrangement that often limits the evaluation to selected areas. Very large organizations have audits teams similar to those used to conduct financial audits. These teams are especially useful when the department is decentralized into regional or field offices. Through the use of audits, the organization maintains consistency in its practice even through there is several offices in different location. And the mere existence of corporate audit team encourages compliances and self audits by the regional offices between visits.

Align corporate and HR strategies and establish legal compliance

Create cost-effective personnel policies and procedures

Prevent expensive litigations

Ten Step Plan for Auditing and Improving your Company's HR Function and Cost Effectiveness

Assess company's current and future HR needs and define the role of HR function within your overall business plan.

Process of HR Audit

The purpose of a Human Resources Audit is to provide a professional and objective perspective on a company's Human Resources efforts, identification of areas that can be improved and recommendations for changes, including the compliance. In an effort to address these complex issues both small and large companies are increasingly auditing their Human Resources functions in order to stay compliant. Regardless of the type of company or the size of your HR department, the HR Audit is a simple, yet comprehensive tool to analyze and improve your effectiveness as a function.

The audit is made up of four main steps:

1. Define desired HR practices for your organization.
2. Assess current practices against the criterion that you have established.
3. Analyze the results.
4. Establish improvement goals and take action.

This simple four-step approach can be repeated as the annual planning and goal setting process occurs within your company. Progress can be measured against goals and a continuous improvement cycle naturally unfolds.

Purpose(s) of an Audit

The audit can serve any of the following purposes:

To clarify desired practices of HR work and roles within the organization (HR Department, Line Managers).

To establish a baseline for future improvement.

To evaluate current effectiveness.

To standardize practices across multiple sites within a division or company.

To assess current knowledge and skills required of HR practitioners.

To improve performance levels to key customers within the organization.

9.3 THE AUDIT PROCESS

Step One—Defining Audit Statements

Definition of desired HR practices can occur through in a variety of ways.

A good starting point is to take some time and reflect on the legal requirements and programs that the department must administer. Simply listing them is a good first step.

Next, consider your areas of responsibility and traditional HR practices covered by your function. They may include HR Planning, Staffing, Performance Management, Employee Relations, Compensation and Benefits, Training and Development, Safety and Wellness,

Finally, other areas to consider are company initiatives that the HR function may be required to support, *i.e.*, internal customer requirements. Specifics are unique to your company, but examples could include supporting a Total Quality Management initiative, Team Based Work System, etc.

With this list in hand, a statement can be written about each major practice that you want to define. Typically, they are stated in the present tense and in a positive manner. The following examples illustrate these traits:

The staffing process is documented so that the responsibility of each person in the process is clear and understood.

Performance appraisals are completed for each employee in the organization.

There is a train-the-trainer program for each major training program within the company.

New employees complete a new hire orientation program of key company policies and procedures within the first 30 days of work.

There is an issue resolution process that is well understood and used by employees.

As you may notice, definitions can be as complete or detailed, as the developer desires. In starting out, it is better to make more general statements and improve from year to year in those areas that you choose to raise the level of performance.

Step Two—Assessing Current Practices

With the list of statements completed, the assessing current practices requires you to be objective. A good approach is to look for evidence that supports or refutes each statement made. Evidence may take the form of policies and procedures, output from employee surveys, interviews with key customers, data collection from a Human Resource Information System, reports issued to regulatory departments, statistics, etc.

The first time the assessment is made, it may become apparent that the definition in step one needs improvement or modification. These changes should be noted and made a part of the next "improvement cycle."

Step Three—Analyze the Results

It is important to recognize strengths and opportunities for improvement. As results are reviewed, themes will emerge around specific HR areas. For example, one company may be very strong in administration and managing legal requirements. On the other hand, it may need improvement in developing higher-level systems definition. Another company may be very strong in areas like Safety, Security, and Training, but need improvement in communication practices that run across the company.

Reviewing the data in a variety of perspectives is helpful to formulate a picture of overall HR performance against the audit. It can reflect the positive effect of actions taken in previous years as well as provide information for future actions.

It may become apparent that all definitions are "not equal in importance". The effort required to meet the definition is one factor to consider. For example, having performance appraisals for all employees may require significant effort. On the other hand, if you already have a good new hire orientation program in place, that definition is more easily met.

The contribution that meeting a definition may have to the organization is another factor to consider. For example, supporting a company initiative like Total Quality Management may be more meaningful to the organization at this point in time than other statements.

In summary, the purpose of analysis is to sort through the areas of strength and opportunities for improvement in order to take positive action steps to improve the effectiveness of the HR function.

Step Four—Establish Improvement Goals and Take Action

The ideal time to complete an audit is just prior to the annual planning process. With audit information in hand, you can be poised to take advantage of your insights into setting next year's goals.

There are two aspects of setting goals: maintenance of current good practices and development of improved practices. Knowing the capacity and capability of the HR department and system is critical in developing a realistic plan. Good practices need to become a part of the HR system and "baked in", so that they occur in a reliable, predictable fashion. Once a process or program has reached that level, then future development can occur more effectively. With little discretionary time available, it is prudent to review the analysis of step three and decide which one or two areas will provide the greatest overall improvement for the HR function, its customers and the organization. These need to be the areas that goals are established for the next year.

This is the point in the audit process, where definitions are reviewed and modified to create a new and improved vision of the HR system as you wish it to be. Doing this on an annual basis allows practices to be improved and benefits shared.

The HR audit can be a powerful lever of change in your department and organization. In one sense it is simple, in that each step can be completed fairly quickly and with ease. Also, the degree of detail and definition of performance is within the control of the audit developer. At time passes, the Audit enriches itself through better definition development and higher levels of performance expectations. It takes on a systems approach because it is comprehensive, inclusive of all traditional HR practices, yet accommodating to the uniqueness of company cultures and business initiatives. Finally, it moves HR professionals into an active state of defining their direction, making sense of their choices, and contributing to the business in a more definitive way.

The Result of an HR Audit: The Audit Report

Once the audit has been concluded, the HR audit team leader will compile the findings, concerns and recommendations of the audit team into the HR Audit Report. This report is a comprehensive definition of the HR activities and includes both commendations for effective practices and recommendations for improving practices that are less effective. Recognition of both good and bad practices is more balanced and makes room for wider acceptance of the report. It is an comprehensive description of HR activities that includes both commendation for effective practices and recommendations for improving practices that are less effective.

The HR audit report may address separately the concerns of the line managers, the functional managers and the overall HR head. For line managers, the report summarizes the HR objectives, responsibilities and duties. People problems are also highlighted, and poor management practices revealed. This information was given to the managers of training and development alongwith the recommendation for more programs to develop promising supervisors and managers. The report may also provide other feedback such as attitudes of operating managers about the HR specialist efforts.

The HR managers' reports contain all the information given to both operating managers and staff specialists. In addition, the manager gets feed back about:

(*a*) Attitude of operating managers and employees about the department's benefits and services.
(*b*) A review of the departments' objectives and plans to achieve them.
(*c*) HR problems and their implications.

(*d*) Recommendations for needed changes and the priority for the implementation.

With the information contained in the report, the HR manager can take a broad view of the function. Instead of solving the problem in a random manner, the manager can focus on those which have the greatest potential for improving the department's contribution to the organization. Perhaps the most important, the audit serves as the map of the future efforts and a references point for the future audits. With the knowledge off the department's current performances, the manager can make a long-term plans to upgrade crucial activities. These plans identify new goals for the department, which serve as standard for future audit.

Conclusion

Certainly, companies that complete an HR audit for compliance and cost reasons will enjoy an improved employment climate and a healthier bottom line. Organizations that opt to gain maximum benefit, however, also will use the HR audit to ensure that HR practices are linked to and play a vital role in the company's strategic planning and execution. Evaluate your current HR audit knowledge and skills within your work environment and general experiences. Based on the outcome, develop a set of personalized/organizational objectives.

HR was previously a stand-alone function, and has now become more integrated into the rest of the organizational functions. The HR function needs to move away from performing transactions and towards forging strategic business partnerships in the organization. It needs to measure and demonstrate the value and contribution of HR to the business strategy.

- Thoroughly understand the overall corporate strategy.
- Examine your HR strategy to ensure that it is clearly aligned to your business strategy.
- Ensure executive buy-in for your HR strategy by engaging in discussions with key decision-makers in your organization.
- Evaluate the contribution of the HR function to the business strategy by determining and implementing effective measurements.

HR function needs to support the company's business strategy. Auditing your HR procedures will assist you in HR planning and forecasting for the success of your HR processes. Your organization will also attract the right people by gaining credibility as an Employer of Choice. Give your HR function structure and direction to save time and money and increase the quality of service by learning how to:

- Determine the scope of your internal HR audit.
- Analyse your HR procedures to ensure that they are fully documented to avoid incurring penalties and fines from the Department of Labour.
- Establish your employees' level of awareness of your company HR policies and procedures to avoid the instigation of CCMA cases.
- Ensure you conform with the Basic Conditions of Employment Act by verifying that your HR processes are properly practiced to ensure your credibility as an Employer of Choice.
- Review the company HR procedures at induction to ensure your new staff are informed and to validate your HR practices.
- Understand the recently released HR Draft Code of Good Practice and other Codes to ensure you are properly updated and conform to the requirements.

As costs are involved, you need to ensure that training and development directly impact your company's bottom line through increased productivity. Continuous skills development will ensure the sustainability of your company as well as your status as an Employer of Choice. Audit the integrated use of organizational development, career development and training and development to improve individual, group and organizational effectiveness. The HR function to be efficient, you need to ensure you have HR information database in place that provides current, readily available HR management information. This is in compliance with good corporate governance as well as for the smooth running of your HR planning function. A review of your audit will provide valuable information on the true market value of your organization by evaluating the value of your people assets, and analyse how your company matches up against other players in the market. It will also ensure you utilize your HR processes efficiently because inefficiencies will lead to higher running costs in your organization.

The concept of the HR Audit Systems did emerged from the practice of yearly finance and accounting audit, which served as an examination of practices and systems for identifying problems and ensuring that sound accounting principles were followed. An audit is defined as a systematic process, which examines the important aspects of the function and its management, and is a means to identify strengths, weaknesses and areas where rectification may be warranted. The basic reason why organizations conduct an HR Audit Systems Review is to get a clear judgment about the overall status of the organization and also to find out whether certain systems put in place are yielding any results. HR Audit Systems also helps companies to figure out any gaps or lapses and the reason for the same. Since every company plans certain systems and targets, an HR Systems Review compares the plans to actual implementation. The HR Audit Review process is there to confirm whether the plans and policies of the organization have been implemented by the right processes and procedures, and that the information in the documented records shows that the system is working correctly, and further, that the gaps and variances are noted and future plans are improvised. HR Audit Reviews the starts with an understanding of the future business plans and corporate strategies, while always keeping business goals in focus. In keeping the business focus at the center, HR Systems Review attempts to evaluate HR strategies, structures, systems, staff, skills, style and shared values as well as their appropriateness in the organization.

9.4 HUMAN RESOURCE INFORMATION SYSTEM (HRIS)

Introduction

The belief that the people working for a firm are one of its main assets and one of the decisive factors in determining its results is one that leaves little room for argument. There is no question regarding the fact that workers' qualities, attitudes and behaviour in the workplace go a long way to accounting for a company's success or lack of it. While this type of resource is one over which companies do not have complete control, there do exist certain instruments to enable them to exert their influence on the quality and performance of the human capital on which they rely. The Human Resource Information Systems (HRIS) practices that they adopt will have a vital influence in this area and thereby on the results obtained by the firm. Driven by significant internal and external forces, HRIS has evolved from largely a maintenance function, to what many scholars and practitioners regard as a source of sustainable competitive advantage for organizations. HRIS has become a key vehicle for developing and improving organizational effectiveness.

In the information era, organizations are progressively incorporating ICT into their processes, using different tools and solutions. These tools are applied in a wide variety of ways (*i.e.*, manufacturing resource planning, office automation, computer-supported cooperative work, distributed teams, supply-chain, enterprise-wide resource planning, or virtual integration). ICT is transforming organizations and the way that people work, interact and, feel in knowledge-based organizations. To cope with these new human resources challenges, it is necessary to review and to transform organizational HRM practices. Those in the world of human resources management are often accused of living in an ivory tower, managing the human side of their organizations in ways that lack relevance in the new information era. The impetus for the HRM change comes from recognition of recent developments in the HRM profession and a realization that the current practices do not reflect those changes, especially those changes related with ITC strategies.

In the information society, HR/HRIS managers need to rethink how to deploy and mobilize the more valuable corporate resource: the human capital. HR management professionals are becoming strategic business partners in their organizations, capable of contributing to the improvement of the organization's competitive advantage. Whether human resources contribute to competitive advantage in the new business world depends critically on the chosen strategies. Given this strategic focus, practices needed to be revised in order to help HR professionals in their new role. Recognizing the need for substantive revision and greater emphasis on relevant human resources management, any HR manager should begin the process of policies change and adjustment. Towards that end, this Encyclopedia will focus on describing a collaborative effort between human resource management practitioners, HR faculty, and HR researchers. The effort will be focused on the revision of the human resource management practices in the knowledge era. In this process, a brief review of both personal and managerial competencies and abilities is also needed.

There is no question regarding the fact that workers' qualities, attitudes and behaviour in the workplace go a long way to accounting for a company's success or lack of it. While this type of resource is one over which companies do not have complete control, there do exist certain instruments to enable them to exert their influence on the quality and performance of the human capital on which they rely. The Human Resource Information Systems (HRIS) practices that they adopt will have a vital influence in this area and thereby on the results obtained by the firm. Driven by significant internal and external forces, HRIS has evolved from largely a maintenance function, to what many scholars and practitioners regard as a source of sustainable competitive advantage for organizations. HRIS has become a key vehicle for developing and improving organizational effectiveness.

Information as Resources

Information, defined as knowledge in communicable form, is recognized today as one of the main requirements for development. Indeed the ability to record and use data, information and knowledge is one of the most important human characteristics."—UNESCO/PGI.

"Information is data that has been processed into a form that is meaningful to the recipient and is of perceived value in current or prospective decisions".

This also provides a working definition which has been used in many organizations. "Information is some meaningful message transmitted from source to users. In this process information may be stored in information products and systems organised for providing a memory in numerical, sound and image forms. Information may also be communicated through interpersonal channels. The "source" may be documentary material, institutions or people."

Information is not homogenous and can be categorised into various types, leading to further problems of definition. The types may be distinguished by:

Role, *e.g.*, information for decision-makers.

Coverage, *e.g.*, in specialized subjects.

Level, *e.g.*, technical, popular.

Channel, *e.g.*, computerized services, mass media.

Accessibility, *e.g.*, public and classified.

It is also to be noted that information forms a part of a hierarchical relationship of Data; Information; Knowledge; Wisdom. As with any hierarchy the base is considerably more extensive than the apex, and we can suspect that quantity of wisdom that eventually develops from the basic data will be limited.

The Evolution of the HRIS

For the past 30 years, organizations of all sizes have been using technology to help them with human resource processes. These processes have ranged from maintaining databases by location to store employee information, to keeping a global, enterprise-wide data repository of employees, their skills and competencies, and their development plans. Most HR management system deployments today are, for the most part, transactional engines that focus on functionality, including:

- Core HR data, including name, address, department number and manager.
- Core benefits data.
- Payroll information.
- Transactional reporting on HR, benefits and payroll.

With the rise of the Internet and corporate intranets, organizations continue to look for opportunities to reduce HR transactional costs by deploying employee and manager self-service (or direct access) solutions to both increase availability of information to the workforce and decrease the focus on transactions. The typical types of transactions include:

- Creating a job requisition.
- Viewing an employee's paycheck.
- Changing an employee's address.
- Viewing and enrolling in benefits.
- Changing an employee's salary.

While these functions are important, most of the time HR information technology professionals have difficulty proving the value of these solutions to executives.

One of the most manual (or semi-automated) processes that still exists in organizations today is the performance review. Employees complete their reviews in a Word document and e-mail them to their manager. The manager might edit the reviews and send them on to HR. HR then enters the reviews into the HR system, and there they are kept. This process is in desperate need of an overhaul in most companies, and the right time to do it is now.

The historical development of information presents several phases. The earliest or oral phase is of considerable importance and traditionally most information would have been captured thus. This is still the case—witness meetings and gatherings such as this. The method however has its drawbacks in that the amount of information that can be stored by an individual or even collective memory is limited in quantity and by the lifespan of individuals. The second major phase emerges with the evolution of systems of writing and the associated tools and materials with which and on which to write. In the first few years of life and school a child can now reproduce the steps that took thousands of years of this evolutionary process.

Defining a "knowledge occupation" as "one that involves activities, gainful or costly, that are designed chiefly to aid in the generation, transmission or reception of knowledge of any type, sort or quality, including giving, directly or through instruments, visual, aural, or otherwise sensible signals, and ranging from carrying messages to creating new knowledge. Information forms the major base on which the growth of knowledge and so much else depends. Without information decisions will be random *ad hoc* choices, projects are unlikely to meet set objectives; reports will not adequately reflect situations. Imagine this situation occurring daily and then multiply it by the numbers of the population because information is used at all levels and everyone has information needs. In general we can suspect that these will not be met. There is need therefore for information to be used as one Papua New Guinea's natural resources capable of being exploited for personal advancement of all citizens and the good of society. In an atmosphere of almost constant change, however, new services, and new approaches and centers will need to be created if information is to contribute to national development.

Definition

Human Resource Information Systems (HRIS) have become a major MIS sub-function within the personnel areas of many large corporations. The development of HRIS as an entity independent of centralized MIS, assesses its current operation and technological base, and considers its future role in the firm, especially its relationship to the centralized MIS function.

The HRIS is a software or online solution for the data entry, data tracking, and data information needs of the Human Resources, payroll, management, and accounting functions within a business. Normally packaged as a data base, hundreds of companies sell some form of HRIS and every HRIS has different capabilities. Pick your HRIS carefully based on the capabilities you need in your company.

The Objectives of HRIS

Typically, the better the Human Resource Information Systems (HRIS) provide overall:

(*a*) Management of all employee information.

(*b*) Reporting and analysis of employee information.

(*c*) Company-related documents such as employee handbooks, emergency evacuation procedures, and safety guidelines.

(*d*) Benefits administration including enrollment, status changes, and personal information updating.

(*e*) Complete integration with payroll and other company financial software and accounting systems.

(*f*) Applicant and resume management.

The HRIS that most effectively serves companies tracks:

(*a*) attendance and PTO use,
(*b*) pay raises and history,
(*c*) pay grades and positions held,
(*d*) performance development plans,
(*e*) training received,
(*f*) disciplinary action received,
(*g*) personal employee information, and occasionally,
(*h*) management and key employee succession plans,
(*i*) high potential employee identification, and
(*j*) applicant tracking, interviewing, and selection.

The functions of HRIS

An effective HRIS provides information on just about anything the company needs to track and analyze about employees, former employees, and applicants. Your company will need to select a Human Resources Information System and customize it to meet your needs.

With an appropriate HRIS, Human Resources staff enables employees to do their own benefits updates and address changes, thus freeing HR staff for more strategic functions. Additionally, data necessary for employee management, knowledge development, career growth and development, and equal treatment is facilitated. Finally, managers can access the information they need to legally, ethically, and effectively support the success of their reporting employees.

An emerging human resources job is the human resources information system specialist, who develops and applies computer programs to process personnel information, match job seekers with job openings, and handle other personnel matters. Jobs of the human resources information system specialist can include developing Intranets, cooperating on the recruiting aspects of the company's website, developing organization weblogs (or blogs), developing online data bases of employee information, developing online searchable data bases of applicant resumes, training staff, training record maintenance, and any other aspect of human resources requiring information storage or computer software, hardware, and desktop support.

The world of performance management processes and performance reviews has changed drastically over the years, in both policy and principle. Best-of-breed companies are using the performance management process not only to manage compensation, but also to manage the performance of the workforce and drive it to new strategic levels.

In most companies, the performance management process can be integrated into the existing HRIS footprint through:

- ***Recruiting:*** This is one of the last places most organizations consider important for integration with performance, but it really is one of the most important. As talent becomes harder to find, recruiters look within their own house for the next applicant for that all-important job. Recruiters want the ability to understand internal applicants in greater detail than the external candidates, including a performance history and learning details to assess their fit for open positions. The integration of performance into the HRIS, where recruiting data often is housed, would open a new door for continued focus on internal mobility.

- ***Core HR Information:*** To manage the performance management process in the most effective and efficient manner possible, organizations must leverage the data that exists within their HR systems. This includes basic data, such as name, department and supervisor, but organizations do not often take advantage of other data that could be instrumental to the process. This data includes other employees in the department to support the 360-degree review process, the employees' matrix reporting structure that many organizations adopt today and the comparative data available based on the job code of the employees. The ability to compare and contrast performance of employees with like jobs gives managers and executives visibility and decision-making tools that they have never had in the past.
- ***Career and Succession Plans:*** Most existing HR solutions provide tools and technologies to store career and succession plans for the workforce. Integrating these plans with performance management processes is crucial to support employee growth and job satisfaction. Executives have requested this data for years, as retention is a top metric within most companies. Today, this data is not a request, but a requirement, and the need to automate a very manual process is crucial for success and keeping a competitive edge.
- ***Competency Management:*** Understanding the skills and abilities of the workforce continues to baffle most executives. Many organizations know more about their IT investments and expenses than about their people. On average, companies spend 8 per cent of their total expense line on IT and 70 per cent on labour. The fact that a company would know more about how much memory is in a computer, who sends e-mail to whom and what Web sites get visited most frequently than what their "most important asset" knows illustrates the need for a renewed critical focus on assessing the true value of the workforce.
- ***Compensation:*** For years, the purpose of the performance review has been to allocate annual salary increases. While this process has generally been handled manually, it also has seen a great deal of controversy and change. Compensation is truly the biggest driver of certain types of behaviour and works differently for various job groups. Incentive compensation is a great tool to drive sales and specific performance targets, whereas base compensation is a great tool for driving overall employee satisfaction and improving performance. What has been missing in all links from compensation to performance is measurement of year-over-year increases in performance and the impact that compensation has on performance. Organizations that take an interactive view of the performance management process and ensure that compensation is just one of many outcomes, which might also include promotion, new opportunities for learning and development, and other forms of recognition, understand the importance of integrating performance and HRIS to measure total compensation and rewards. Organizations that still rely on a manual, semi-automated process as a once-a-year, meet-the-requirement tool will soon realize that the war for talent and staffing shortages will make it necessary to approach pay-for-performance as an integrated process.
- ***Reporting and Metrics:*** Another missing link for the performance management process that HRIS technology can assist with is in the area of reporting and metrics. The two reports that managers traditionally focus on in this area are transactional: How many have been turned in, and how do we look compared to a typical performance bell curve? This information may be great to have, but does it drive business results? Executives want answers to strategic questions, such as: What revenue increases have resulted from a performance management process and allocation of compensation increases? How has customer satisfaction increased because of an increased investment in agents? And how has employee turnover decreased because of a

renewed focus on people? The sooner that those involved in the performance management process stop looking in the mirror at their performance throughout the process and put in place measures that explain how the process has impacted business results, the more value and attention performance management will receive from executives.

Future of HRIS

There will be access to that information through the HRIS. Other process changes will have the most effect on the human resource representatives in each department. The largest of those changes is probably electronic forms processing. Representatives will be able to submit forms on the web and access human resource and payroll data. Of course, those most seriously affected by this switch are the human resource employees in central administration who will use the new system daily. It's a major change in daily tasks for all of our staff. Major changes like this can be upsetting for dedicated employees who have devoted years to development and maintenance of one complex system only to have it replaced by a totally new one, complex in different ways. People will be learning how to process forms with the web-based system, and they will be learning how to get data that meet their needs out of the system. This will require new skills and in some cases will require people to adapt to new ways of doing things. The people we have working on this new system are extremely good, and have faith in HRIS. Productivity and efficiency can be expected to decline somewhat while we learn the new system. After we become comfortable with these new tools, the embedded software systems will allow us to achieve higher levels of productivity and efficiency than before. I think the best way to deal with change is to get comfortable with what is different. And hope the staffs will take full advantage of the new system. And they will practice with the new system as soon as it is available to achieve higher levels of productivity and efficiency than before.

9.5 HUMAN RESOURCE ACCOUNTING

Introduction

"People are the most important resource" has actually come to mean something. Today more than ever the management realizes that the most effective asset in an organization is its people. In fact, it is obsolete to say people are the most important asset; rather they are the only dynamic asset. Nothing happens without people—money, equipment, technology … nothing means anything without a human to act. Hence, the management has slowly realized the importance which in turn has edged Human Resources (HR) from the background into mainstream organizational strategies. Time and again, every manager has always stated 'You cannot manage what you cannot measure'. Efficiency in any industry stems from the human being and not the machines nor the technical processes. However, while the later tangible aspects can be measured, gauging the human resources for its worth is a difficult task which has to be handled with care.

"Employees are the most valuable resources of comparison in the service (software, banking, management consultancy, etc.) sector. Like all other resources of the company, the employees possess value because of providing future services".

"The significance of manpower management and the implications of human resource valuation from the point of view of management, investors and financiers, constitute the central theme of human resource accounting. It examines the worth-whileness of human resource accounting for internal management purposes and decision-making by investors and creditors. Accounting has always concerned itself with information production, processing and reporting while cost and management accounting has sought to provide managers with accounting techniques involved in the production of cost information. Cost and management accounting also describes the application of the techniques to a broad range of managerial decision-making, planning and control activities. The aim of the text is provide a thorough understanding of the basic theory and practice of cost and management accounting.

With the change in the business environment, the needs of the business change and increase and it becomes difficult for the HR professionals to manage and measure the employees' goals. The main objective of HR function is to attract, retain and motivate the best employees, make them feel that they are the leaders of their own company. The basic HR function involves a lot of activities recruiting, selecting, hiring, training, promoting, retention, separation and supporting of faculty, and staffing. It also includes all decisions, strategies, processes, principles and functions related to managing people in any organization. Organizations are increasingly finding it imperative to improve returns on investment, in order to stay competitive. Traditionally, accounting norms were viewed only from the financial perspective and were applied to all departments ranging from marketing, production distribution etc. HRM was limited to salary and administration and, while doing so, it was analyzed from the perspective of balancing performance management across all organizations.

Human Resource Accounting (HRA) is an information system that tells the management what changes have been occurring in the HR department of the business over a period of time. HRA also involves accounting for investment in people, their replacement costs, and the economic value of the people in an organization. The organization can assess how much they can earn from an individual as the intellectual assets of a company are often worth three or four times the tangible asset value. Human capital provides valuable experts services, such as consulting, financial planning and assurance services, which are in great demand.

The need to convert Human Resources Management (HRM) activities in economic terms has become vital in this competitive scenario. And truly enough HR has also evolved wherein its functions of the hiring, paying salaries, administration, benefits, developing and retaining employees etc. have been translated into quantitative terms in order to monitor results and facilitate changes. And today the data that is collected as such as being converted to monetary values and thus emergence of HR Accounting.

Definition

The American Accounting Association defined Human Resource Accounting as "the human resource identification and measuring process and also its communication to the interested parties'. In simple terms it is an extension of the accounting principles of matching costs and revenues and of organizing data to communicate relevant information in the financial terms. According to the theory of accounting for HR propounded by Flamholtz EG: (*i*) people are valuable resources of an enterprises, and (*ii*) information on the investment and value of human resources is useful for internal and/or external decision-making. According to the Brummet RL *et al.*, a firm has to capitalize on its expenditure on HRM's functions namely recruitment, selection, orientation, training and development of people and treat them as assets for the purpose of HRA. The amounts so capitalized can be shown in the balance-sheet as human assets as distinguished from physical assets.

"Human Resource Accounting as the activity denoted to attaching dollar estimates to the value of firm's human resources and its customers"—Likert.

"Human Resource Accounting is the measurement and quantification of human organizational inputs such as recruitment, training, experiences and communication".—Stephen Knauf.

"Human Resource Accounting is an attempt to identify and report investments made in human resources of an organization that are presently not accounted for in conventional accounting practice, basically it is an information system that tells the management what changes over time are occurring to the human resources of the business".—Wood Ruff.

"Accounting for people as organizational resources. It is the measurement of the cost and value of people for the organization."—Eric Flamholtz.

HRA is Human Resource Accounting which is used in knowing the potential of human assets in monetary terms. Until a few years back no importance was given to these human assets and it was also assumed that valuing these human assets was difficult and sometimes impossible as they had no specific metrics to measure.

Human resources are an important asset in the organization whose value goes on increasing with its right placement, application and development in the organization. In spite of vast physical resources with latest technology, an organization may quite often find itself in financial crisis if it does not have the right persons to mange its affairs. Thus human resources are a very valuable assets for the organization which aims to progress all directions amidst heavy competition.

Though the concept of Human Resources Accounting is very old. Organizations have not made any effort to assign any monetary value to his in their accounting practices till the recent past. The real efforts for viewing the human resources as an asset were till the recent past. The real efforts for viewing the human resources as an asset was started by behavioural scientist from 1960 onwards who try to develop appropriate methodology and procedure for finding out the cost and value of the people in the resources were identified as the value of the production capacity of an organization, and the value of the customer good will. There are many reasons why human resources accounting have been receiving so much attention in the recent years.

HR audit is defined as the systematic assessment of an organization's HR service excellence and help the organization to identify the HR programmes that are most important to achieve the organization's objectives.

Human Resource Accounting (HRA) is an information system that tells the management what changes have been occurring in the HR department of the business over a period of time. HRA also involves accounting for investment in people, their replacement costs and the economic value of the people in an organization. Issues and concepts:

1. Competency
2. Commitment, and
3. Culture.

Competency: It is not restricted to individuals, but can be spread through the teams, departments, processes and systems etc. They provide the competitive edge to the organization.

Commitment: The commitment of the employee is a complex factor, it dependent upon a host of factors *i.e.*, reward and recognition, developmental and learning opportunities, mentoring fault-tolerance level in the organization.

Culture: The value and norms articulated and practiced by the organization. It improves the motivational and commitment of the employees, help instilling the sense of pride.

HRA can be defined as the measurement and reporting of the economic cost and value of people as organizational resources. It involves accounting for investments in people, their replacement cost and for their economic value to organizations. This study focused on the aspect of HRA dealing with replacement cost and involved developing a computer based method to calculate the recruitment, selection, development (training) and separation costs associated with positional replacement cost. Replacement cost is defined as the sacrifice that would have to be incurred at the present time to replace human resources currently employed.

Need of HR Accounting

Accounting is now regarded as a service activity, a descriptive analytical discipline and an information system. The primary role of accounting is to provide an effective measurement and reporting system for decision-making. The human resources accounting is more concerned with this decision-making area of accounting. It is an effective tool for decision-making. The information generated through HRA can be utmost help for making decision in the following areas:

(*a*) Formulating the policies and programs for the development of human resources.

(*b*) Decisions regarding cost reduction programs.

(*c*) Training and Development.

(*d*) Recruitment and Selection.

(*e*) Manpower Planning and Control.

(*f*) Conservation and reward of human resources.

(*g*) Making the choices between various types of human investment and investment in other assets etc.

Human resources have certain distinct characteristics from physical assets like personality, self-control, devotion, quality, skill, talents loyalty and initiativeness. It is basic need of the present time to improve productivity that can be improved by the human force. Hence, to encourage, is necessary to account them and take progressive decision for them. The business organizations have now realized that no production and performance is possible without wiling participation and support of human skill of the concern. Therefore, it is essential to collect and report the human resources information which is useful for different types of users.

In the traditional accounting practices, HR a vital asset also did not find its place. The expense incurred in respect of selection, lay-off, training promotions etc. of employees are treated as revenue expenditure. It is argued that, such expenditure should be capitalized and shown in the balance-sheet.

The proponents like Likert, Johnson and Kaplan (1987) and others argued that, absence of human resources as an assets in the balance-sheet, violates the acturrial principles, discards matching principles, defies principles of disclosure, underrates the firm's net worth and current income and there by not reflect the true and fair view of the organization.

The antaonist also argued that whether the employers be allowed to earn their imputed salary. The knowledge of individual about the human resources could affect the employee's bargaining power within and outside the enterprise. Further published HRA figure could affect the employees bargaining power within and outside the enterprise having the less HR value which may affect the entire control system of the organization.

Thus, we may conclude that the information generated through human resources accounting is useful not only to management as a tool for decision-making, but also to the potential investors and others in analyzing and interpreting the financial statements of a firm. Human Resources Accounting has certain behavioural implications also.

With the change in the business environment, the needs of the business change and increase and it becomes difficult for the HR professionals to manage and measure the employees' goals. The main objective of HR function is to attract, retain and motivate the best employees, make them feel that they are the leaders of their own company. The basic HR function involves a lot of activities recruiting, selecting, hiring, training, promoting, retention, separation and supporting of faculty, and staffing. It also includes all decisions, strategies, processes, principles and functions related to managing people in any organization.

A history of human asset accounting

Human resources accounting was first started with simple measures of trying to convert output data into contributions. When an HR program had affected a change in the output especially for organizations operating on the profit basis, its value was determined by calculating the profit contribution. Rensis Likert in the 1960s was the first to research in HR and emphasized the importance of strong pressure on the HR's qualitative variables and on its benefits in the long-run. According to the Likerts model, human variables can be divided into three categories: (*i*) causal variable; (*ii*) intervening variable; and (*iii*) end result variables. The interaction between the causal and intervening variables affects the end-result variables by the way of job satisfaction, costs, productivity and earnings.

The modern search for a method to provide HR value information in external corporate reports has interested practicing HR professionals since the late 1960s. Since that time there have been repeated efforts to include HR value and other intangibles such as intellectual capital in corporate reports. Their arguments include the need for more corporate financial transparency, and concerns that the omission of the value of human, structural and intellectual capital as organization assets results in an under-valuation of the knowledge based companies that drive the new economy. Arguments generally are to demonstrate that human capital, intellectual capital and structural capital concepts are similar to other assets. It is argued that organizations acquire HR to generate future revenues, and therefore HR should be considered when valuing a company by capitalizing instead of expensing them in the current period. The crux of the argument is that human, intellectual, and structural capital should be treated in the same way as the things they are like; the things these advocates think they are most like are assets, and since assets are reported on the balance-sheet, these also should be reported along with the physical assets.

Formally accounting for HR's value, a type of intangible capital, on a balance-sheet is in the domain of HR accounting, a concept that has intrigued practicing HR professionals for almost 40 years. In my view, and it may only be my singular view, a review of this 40 years period can be divided roughly into three parts: the beginning, the mid-term and the recent.

Pyle, Flamholtz, and Brummet

Pyle's scholarly publications on HR accounting generally tend to be the co-authored articles written with Brummet and Flamholtz. While he reduced his emphasis on HR accounting, Pyle continued working with an association of companies on proprietary HR issues.

Of the three initial HR accounting proponents, Flamholtz has, by any standards, been the most prolific. There are two important conclusions that any reviewers of Flamholtz's work could feel secure in stating. First, in the years after the R.G. Barry project, he has been prolific and persistent in his publications on HR Accounting. And second, as evidenced by a lack of widespread adoption of his methods, his persistent efforts have not provided any acceptable HR accounting approach. Flamholtz has continued to maintain an active role in HR accounting and serves on the editorial board of the prestigious *Journal of Human Resource Costing and Accounting*.

Brummet's former service as president of the American Accounting Association gave these early HR accounting advocates great credibility and brought positive attention to the HR asset. One would also have to suspect that the involvement of Brummet, as well as the famous Rensis Likert, at the meetings that gave rise to *Human Resource Accounting, Development and Implementation in Industry*. By the mid-1970s, the only one who has remained active in HRA is Flamholtz.

More recent contributors to the HR valuation field include **Cascio** with the fourth edition of his book *Costing Human Resources* with their utility approach for valuing HR, and **Boudreau,** who has published multiple articles on the subject. These authors attempted to solve some of the application and conceptual problems that kept, and still keep, human assets off balance-sheets. An organization might use HRA asset models to reflect its investment in employees—models that assess the value of employees, treating them as capitalized resources. In contrast, an organization might use HRA expense models to measure the economic effects of employee's behaviour. The latter are particularly useful in attempts to account for intellectual capital.

Lev and Schwart

Lev's position on HR as assets is summarized the requirements, including the ownership requirement, for something to be considered an asset. He explains in a footnote that public corporations are required to report pension obligations, post-retirement benefits and stock and incentive payment plans, and states unequivocally that these disclosures do not convey the direct information relevant to the value of HR intangibles "systematic research on the measurement and valuation of HR intangibles is extremely lean". His definition of a HR asset commences with a declaration that companies spend money to affect employee knowledge and motivation, but that all such expenditures do not create assets. He contends that assets only arise "when the benefits from such expenditures—in the form of increased employee productivity—exceed costs". Lev concludes that for all the intangibles, the least systematic information exists for HR. He reports that it is not even clear what expenditures on HR create assets, and believes that more corporate disclosure will be needed to advance research on HR intangibles.

Common to all past HR accounting work is the effort to deal with the requirements of the Generally Accepted Accounting Practices. The cost benefit studies attempt to show that there was a flow of value as a result of some HR expenditure. Such a demonstration is often cited as a requirement to claim the HR activity is an asset. Other attempts have been directed at methods to determine and assign the value to HR. Demonstrations of an ability to assign such value in a reliable objective fashion and so that the determined values are material (significant enough to make some difference) are required to account for them as assets. Even if these approaches have dealt adequately with these two points (and as Lev and his reviewers write, there is still dispute over that), the ownership and/or control issue from the asset definition still needs to be met.

Objectives of Human Resources Accounting

In tracing the history of human resource accounting, most reviewers would agree that the topic is now experiencing something of a revival. This research set out to explore why HR accounting is regarded as important, to whom it is important and its links with organizational and HR strategies. Component analysis revealed two reasons why measuring human resources is perceived as being important. The first illustrates the view that 'measurement reflects the strategic and competitive importance of human resources', while the second suggests that, 'to earn credibility, HRM must be expressed in financial terms'. Further analysis highlighted the importance of senior management and financial managers' support for measuring human resources and drew attention to what may appear to be a 'hard view' of HRM held by HR managers in relation to why they consider this important.

HRA by arguing that its objectives are wider than appear to have been admitted. Such is the importance of HRA for problems as disparate as economic efficiency, organizational effectiveness, and social effectiveness that it must become a subject in its own right with its own methodology and measurements. Many conceptual and measurement problems have not yet been adequately treated. The immediate objective of research should be a rigorous testing of the validity of the assumptions that have hitherto been relied on.

The study of HR accounting is for two primary reasons. The first aim was to combine a human resources costing and accounting approach (HRCA) with a quantitative statistical approach in order to get an integrated model. The second aim was to apply this integrated model in a quasi-experimental study in order to investigate whether preventive intervention, affected sickness, absence costs at the company level. The intervention studied contained occupational organizational measures, competence development, physical and psychosocial working environmental measures and individual and rehabilitation measures on both an individual and a group basis.

"The significance of manpower management and the implications of human resource valuation from the point of view of management, investors and financiers, constitute the central theme of this work. It examines the worth-whileness of human resource accounting for internal management purposes and decision-making by investors and creditors. The desirability of public disclosure of human resource data in corporate annual reports has been proved by the author empirically on the basis of professional opinion obtained through questionnaire survey. In that process, the author has also assessed the practicability of applying in the Indian context some of the valuation models developed by western writers. Apart from the discussion on issues germane to the subject matter, the study provides an insight into the possible impact of human resource data on managerial decisions." The main objectives of Human Resource Accounting System are as follows:

- To furnish cost value information for making proper and effective management decision about acquiring, allocating, developing and maintaining human resources in order to achieve cost effective organizational objectives.
- To monitor effectively the use of human resources by the management.
- To have an analysis of the human asset *i.e.*, whether such assets are conserved, depleted or appreciated.
- To aid in the development of the management principles and proper decisions-making for the future by classifying financial consequences of various practices.
- In all, it facilitates valuation of human resources recording the valuation in the books of account and disclosure of the information in the financial statement.
- It helps the organization in decisions-making in the following areas. (Direct recruitment vs. promotion, transfer vs. retention, retrenchment vs. retention, impact on budget control of human relations and organization behaviour, decision on reallocation of plants closing down existing units and developing overseas subsidiaries).
- Improve management by analyzing investment in HR.
- Consider people as its asset.
- Attract and retain qualified people.
- Profile the organization in financial terms.

Advantage of Human Resource Accounting

Human resource accounting helps to know whether human asset is being built in the business or not. Human resources planning anticipate not only the required kind and number of employees but also determine the action plan. The major benefits of HR accounting are:

- It checks the corporate plans of the organization. The corporate plan aiming for expansion, diversification, changes in technology growth etc. has to be worked out with availability of human resources for such manpower placements or key positions. If such manpower is not likely to be available, HR accounting suggests modification of the entire corporate system.
- It offsets uncertainty and change, as it enables the organization to have the right person for the right job at the right point of time and place.
- It provides scope for advancement and development of the employees by effective training and development.
- It helps individual employees to aspire for promotion and better benefits.
- It aims to see that the human involvement in the organization is not wasted and bring high returns to the organization.
- It helps to take steps to improve employees' contribution in the form of increased productivity.
- It provides different methods of testing to be used, interview techniques to be adopted in the selection process based on the level of skill, qualifications and experiences of the future human resources.
- It can foresee the change in value, aptitude and attitude of human resources and accordingly change the techniques of interpersonal management.
- Human resources accounting will give the cost of developing human resource in the business.

- Investment on the development of human resources can be compared with the benefits and the result derived.
- The return on investment can be realistically be calculated only when investment on human resources is also taken into account. So ROI can give the accurate information about the investment made on human resources.
- It will help management in planning and execution of personnel policies.
- Human resources accounting will help in improving the efficiency of employees.

Limitations of Human Resource Accounting

Human Resources Accounting is the term use to describe the accounting methods, system and techniques, which coupled with special knowledge and ability, assist to HR management in the valuation of personal in financial terms. There are some produce more, understand faster and show efficiency in training as compared to others. HR accounting facilitates decision-making about the personal, either to keep or dispense with their services or to provide training. HR accounting development and application in different industries and organizations has not fully grown. There are many limitations which make the management reluctant to introduce HR accounting in their organizations. Some limitations are also given below:

- There are not particular and clear cut guidelines for determining cost and value of people of an organization. The existing human resources value systems have number of drawbacks.
- Human resources accounting may demoralize some of the employees having less value than the others having more value for the organization.
- Human resources are not capable of being obtained, retained and utilized like other physical assets. Hence, treating them assets in an organization may not be appropriate.
- Cultural differences and different attitudes may create problems in arriving at correct valuation of human resources.
- Human resources accounting suffers on account of accounting problems. The technical problems of cost based HRA may not so much as accounts deal with such aspects on regular intervals. Whereas some technical problem is being faced by accountants in value based HRA.
- There is a constant fear of criticism from the Trade Unions. They may bargain for more wages on account of basis of valuation made by the organization.
- Determination of amortization rate is also a main problem being faced by accountants.
- It has been found very difficult to change management's view of humans being from being an expense rather than assets.
- There is no universally accepted method of human resource valuation.
- In spite of its significance and necessity, tax laws do not recognize human beings as assets.

Concepts of Human Resources Accounting

Efficiency in any industry stems from the human being and not the machines nor the technical processes. However, while the later tangible aspects can be measured, gauging the human resources for its worth is a difficult task which has to be handled with acre. Human Resources Accounting is a method with which such task is sought to be achieved.

There has been a lot of research in the area of quantification of human resources. Prof. Flamholtz. Eric G. defines HRA as accounting for people an organizational resource. It involves measuring the cost incurred by the company to recruit, select, hire, train and develop human resources. It involves measuring the economic value of the people of the company. Rensis Likert, one of the leading proponents of HRA observes, "Human resources accounting refers to the activity devoted to attaching dollar estimates to the value of a firm's human organization and its customer's goodwill". Steps in HRA: what emerges is that HRA is the process of measurement of the value of the human resources of a company and its incorporation into books of accounts. It capitalizes the measured value in a significant manner for use by the management.

The above terminology necessitates the following:

- Identify the investment made in human resources (expenditure on recruitment, selection, training, and development).
- Measure the value of human resources.
- Record the investment in human resources through capitalization process.
- Amortize the investment like other relative assets.
- Report such investment in the account books.

The measurements of human resources value

The measurements of human resources value and its valuation approach have been suggested in the literature by the following proponents of HRA:

- Hermanson's adjusted Discounted Wages Model.
- Likerts Socio-Psychological Model; of Human Resources Valuation.
- Flamholtz's Model of Human Resources Valuation: A stochastic process with service rewards.
- Morse's Model of Human Resources Valuation as assets and capital.
- Jaggi and Lau's Model of Human Resources Valuation on career movements of the employees.
- Lev and Schwartz Compensation Model of Human Resources Valuation.
- Friedman and Lev measure for the firm's investment in Human Resources.
- Myres and Flower's five dimensional Model of Human Resources Valuation.
- Pekin Organ's model of Human Resources Valuation for professional services organizations.

9.6 LEV AND SCHWARTZ COMPENSATION MODEL

The most acceptable model to various organizations can be summarized in the Lev and Schwartz Model of Human Resources Valuation. The model of measurement of human capital suggested by Brauch Lev and Aba Schwartz is based on the economic concept of human capital. Capital is defined as a source of income over a period of time and its worth is present value of future income discounted by the certain rate.

Formula

According to Lev and Schwartz, the value of human capital represented by a person of age 'r' is the present value of his remaining future earnings from his employment. They have given in the following formula for calculating the value of an individual where, Vr = the value of an individual 'r' years old.

I (t) = An individual's annual earning up to the retirement.

T = Retirement age.

R = Discount rate specific to the person.

t = Active service (in years).

Lev and Schwartz are of the opinion that the determination of the total value of a firm's labour force is a straight forward extension of the measurement procedure of an individual to the organization. They have divided the whole labour force into certain homogeneous groups such as unskilled, technical staffs, managerial staffs, etc. and in accordance with different age groups.

$$\text{Vr} = \sum_{T-r}^{T} I(t)/(1+r) \wedge t - r$$

In brief, the model identifies an individual's expected economic value to the organization to his future earnings for his remaining active service life. His future expected income stream is discounted by appropriate rate to arrive at the present value of his service.

Limitations/Deficiencies

(*a*) It ignores the people's inherent qualities, mannerism traits and skills and the environment of an organization.

(*b*) The model also does not take into account the possibility and probability of an individual leaving the organization for reasons other than death or retirement.

(*c*) It also ignores the situation of transfer of the employee.

Formula

He gives the following formula for quantifying individual economic values:

Where,

Kkj = total adjusted net present value of human resources in a professional service organization.

Vqj = Certainty-equivalent net profit.

L = end of the estimated useful life of the employee for the organization.

J = jth individual; j = 1, 2, 3 ...... n.

r = a discount rate external to the organization (risk free assumed).

K = time periods in the future. Revenue and cost are assumed occur. At the end of kth time period.

t = some time period from 1 to L which is a point in the useful life of the employee to which the certainty-equivalent net benefits that occur after 't' are discounted.

$q = k + t$

$$\text{K}k\text{J} = \sum_{J=1}^{n} \sum_{k=t}^{L-t} 1/(1+r)\, k\, \text{V}q\text{J}.$$

Pekin Ogan's model presents a new concept of determination of certainty-equivalent net benefits stream from each employee in an organization, which consists of two elements: (*a*) his or her benefits and total costs; and (*b*) a certainty factor which is comprised of the employee's probability of continued employment and probability of survival.

He has presented his model of human resources valuation in the figure 9.3:

Fig. 9.3 Model of Human Resources

Certainty equivalent net Benefits	Discounting	Summation	Adjusted total net present value of HR for the organization.
		n L – t	
VqJ.	1		
	(1 + r) k		
		K = t J = 1	K k j

The model presented by the Pekin Ogan is certainly an improvement over the other models presented earlier. This model takes with accounts the cost generated by the employees for the organization, which the other models have ignored. It also makes use of the 'certainty factor 'designed to measure the probability of continued employment and the probability of survival.

Limitations/Deficiencies

A major shortcoming of this model is that it can be applied only in those where costs and benefits of the employees can be traced fairly objectively.

It can thus, be seen that using different models, accounting of human resources is a fairly simple affair. Since, we are dealing with HR; there will naturally be certain limitations and deficiencies in different models of HRA. A high turnover of the employees in every company also possesses problems for HRA. Notwithstanding these difficulties, HRA today is being implemented by most of the professionally managed companies in different countries as well.

CASE STUDY: 1 HR AUDIT

Skandia-Reporting on Intellectual Capital

Skandia is one of Sweden's largest service companies and is listed on the Stockholm Stock Exchange. The company does domestic and international business in insurance, real estate, and banking. The company has been recognized for developing a concept for measuring and reporting on intellectual capital since 1994.

Reporting to the public has taken place twice a year since 1984, basically as reports issued with annual or half-yearly financial reports.

Skandia's definitions of intellectural capital and connected terms and definitions are described in Skandia's reporting model, Navigator, is influenced by the concept of the balanced scorecard, which is an internal management tool.

Table 9.1 depicts the concept of Skandia's Reporting Model. For each of its business lines, Skandia reports on a number of focal points. For its subsidiary American Skandia, which provides variable annuities (unti-linked assurance) in the American market, was as shown in Table 9.1.

Table. 9.1 *The concept of Skandia's Reporting Model as of 30 June 1997*

Financial focus	1996	1995	1994	1993
Return on Capital	31.3	28.7	12.2	24.3
Operating Result	597	355	115	96
Value Added/employee	2206	1904	1666	1982
Return on capital employed	3103	28.7	12.2	24.3
Operating Result (MSKE)	597	355	115	96
Value Added/employee (SEK000s)	2206	1904	1666	1982
Customer Focus				
Number of Contracts	133641	87836	59089	31997
Savings/Contracts (SEK000s)	396	360	333	371
Surrender Ratio %	4.4	4.1	4.2	3.6
Point of Sale	33267	18012	11573	4805
Human Focus				
Numbers of employees Full time	418	300	220	133
Number of Managers	86	81	62	NA
Training Expenses/emp (SEK000s)	15.4	2.5	9.8	10.6
Change in company IT literacy %	NA	+2	+7	NA
Process Focus				
Number of Contracts/employee	320	293	296	241
IT expenses/administration %	12.5	13.1	8.8	4.7
Renewal and Development				
Share of Gross premiums written new	23.7	49.2	11.1	5.2
Increase in net premium written %	113.7	29.9	17.8	204.8
Development Expenses %	909	10.1	11.6	9.8
Proportion of staff under 40 years %	78	81	72	74

It can be seen that Skandia has developed a number of performance indicators for each of the five focal points and it reports consistently on these indicators every six month.

QUESTIONS

1. Critically analyze the concept of reporting on the intellectual capital systematized by the Swedish group Skandia?
2. Does the report of Skandia have similarities with the balanced scorecard of the Indian organization?

3. Can we fine tune the objective related to the human focus for achieving better results.
4. Do you think it is also necessary to conduct the HR audit in the wake of the implementation of the balanced scorecard? If yes, please explain.

CASE STUDY–2 Environmental Protection Agency-Agency Annual Report

In 1995, the Danish Government decided to launch projects designed to develop annual agency reports for a number of government agencies. The pilot scheme comprised 70 government agencies in 1996. Since 1997 the scheme has become compulsory for all government agencies meeting certain criteria of size and appropriation status. Annual agency of size and appropriation status. Annual agency reports should be closely linked to the budget for the year in question (the parliamentary appropriation).

The primary target group of the annual agency reports is the department of the relevant ministry, the Auditor General and the Public Accounts Committee as well as the Finance Committee and the Parliament. Secondary target groups include users of the services of the institution in question, the Ministry of Finance, the general public, labour market organizations, other interest groups, and private suppliers of competing services.

The annual agency reports are prepared with public availability in mind. Among other places, similar high-quality accounts are found in Norway and Sweden. The main contents of the annual reports are:

- A narrative description of the agency as a whole, including its objective and assignments, as well as its budgetary and financial situation, etc.
- Reliable reports on the financial and professional situation for the year, competition, etc. including:
  - A description of financial and professional achievements.
  - An explanation of the difference between budgeted and realized result.
  - A description of activities carried out compared with goals set.
  - A basis for the assessment of financial considerations.
  - A basis for benchmarking with other government institutions.

The standard contents of agency annual reports area as follows:

1. Statement of revenue and expenditure
2. Profit and loss analysis
3. Staff and organization
4. Grant statement
5. Construction statement
6. Environmental account (not required).

What is of interest for the purposes of this discussion paper is the requirement for a report on staff and organization. Such a report should cover all following:

- Staff time (in man-years) for the accounting year and the three previous years, and budget figures for the following year.
- Absences due to sickness for the accounting year and the three previous years.

- Staff turnover for the accounting year and the three previous years.
- Overtime and additional work for the accounting year and the three previous years.
- Description of organizational structure and organizational chart.
- Analysis and evaluation of development.

As and example of how a Danish government agency has chosen to present its staff relations, part of the relevant section of the Danish Environmental Production Agency's financial statements for 1996 is cited in the following.

Staff policy

The primary aim of the staff policy of Danish Environmental Protection Agency (DEPA) is to create a basis to ensure that the Agency, as part of a political and administrative system, can perform current and future work assignments at a highly professional and resource-efficient level. The key words are readiness for change, adaptability and flexibility. The Agency's main resource is its employees, and the staff policy is to recruit and keep qualified staff and to develop and enhance the motivation and qualifications of individual employees.

The staff policy is thus designed to ensure that the Agency's staff-mix and profiles are suitable for achieving the Agency's overall goals, strategies and visions. In addition, the staff policy must fulfill the broad spectrum of demands, which the very varies professional staff make from their workplace.

The pivotal point of the Agency's staff policy is the annual appraisal reviews. A number of minor adjustment were made to the staff review concept at the end of 1996, based in part on a very positive external evaluation during the year and discussions at the Agency's Staff Conference. The Agency has implemented its staff policy in a number of agreements in the following main areas: recruitment induction, skills development and career, mobility, working life and family life, working relations forums, working hours, work environment, etc.

Staff Categories of DEPA

Staff Category	*Distribution, end 95*	*Distribution, end 95*
Management Grade (37–39)	6.4%	6.2%
Consultant (35–36)	2.7%	3.5%
Middle Management	22.3%	24.5%
Academic Technicians (AC)	31.2%	28.6%
Administrative Staff	31.2%	28.6%
Others	5.7%	4.5%
Total	100.0%	100.0%

Middle management consists mainly of academics with a social science degree. AC technicians comprise academics with technical degree, that is, engineering, physics, agricultural science, pharmacy, veterinary science, etc. The category 'Other' comprises security staff, assistants, students workers, etc. The relative distribution of the Agency's employees at the end of 1996 shows the continuation of the long-term trend towards the expansion of the middle management and AC technician categories at the expense of the administrative staff.

Staff Turnover (Permanent Staff Only) at DEPA

	1995	*1996*
Engagement	60	69
Resignations	43	43
Gross Staff Turn Over	28%	28%

The table details the engagement and resignation of permanent staff during the period, including job rotation to and from other agencies within the ministerial area and to and from the Environmental Protection Agency.

The average number of days of absence due to sickness within the public sector in 1995 was 7.1 days per employee. In the above table, absence due to sickness is calculated in terms of man-years, and the average absence data is thus not immediately comparable. Using an estimated average number of employees with the Agency in 1995, the Agency' average number of days of absence due to sickness is approximately one days of absence due to sickness is approximately one day per employee above the public sector average for 1995, while the estimated average per employee in 1996 was reduced to approximately 6.8 days (that is, below the 1995 public sector average).

Skill development and supplementary training

The handling of day-to-day work assignments in the Danish Environmental Protection Agency places great demands on the staff. As mentioned earlier, one of the principal objectives of the staff policy is to develop and enhance the motivation and qualifications of each employee from a quality control perspective as well as with a view to securing and recruiting staff.

The most important skill development is in the form of in-house training for varying types of work. The Agency seeks to enhance the skill profiles of individual employees through diverse tasks that have professional and personal development potential. The Agency has a tradition of giving each employee personal responsibility and, as much as possible, of lettering employees follow a case from start to finish. In addition to workplace training, employees' skills are developed through various forms of supplementary training such as secondment, participation in courses, etc. The supplementary training of individual employees is set out at the appraisal reviews. The course-based supplementary training of the Environmental Protection Agency is planned and coordinated in the Central Supplementary Training Committee.

Supplementary training includes the Ministry's compulsory basic training course for new employees, as well as the selection of courses common to the ministerial area. In 1996, 313 of the Agency's employees attended 884 courses. In comparison, 267 Agency employees attended 606 courses in 1995. In 1996, an overhaul of the ministry's common supplementary training system was launched with a view to establishing a new basic training programme, technical courses, and a modular superstructure. Supplementary training activities within the Environmental Protection Agency in 1996 included:

- Implementation of a special supplementary training programme for employees on international assignments.
- Implementation of a specialized accounting course for a administrative staff.

- Continued implementation of a special supplementary training programme for IT super users.
- A special programme in connection with the Project Electronic Workplace for all employees.

The increasing number of international assignments undertaken by the Agency has necessitated the institution of a supplementary training programme for employees on internationals assignments. In addition to assignments under the auspices of the EU, the Scandinavian countries and other international forums, the Agency has since 1991 undertaken assignments under the auspices of the Danish Ministry of Foreign Affairs related to environmental assistance to Central and Eastern, Europe and certain developing countries. The international project work, in particular, places new demands on its employees, which the Agency seeks to address with the special programme for employees on international assignments.

In 1996, the Environmental Protection Agency continued its implementation of a staff administration system. This system rationalizes staff administration and helps achieve a more systematized staff development.

As the above demonstrates, the presentation is very open, incorporating policies and details from the staff interview programme, benchmarking on sickness, etc. The presentation includes a significant amount of specific data.

QUESTIONS

1. Critically analyze how the Danish Environmental Protection Agency has utilized legal requirements for reporting on 'staff and organization' to measure a number of HRA performance indicators and for benchmarking other agencies?
2. Do the main contents emphasized upon in the annual report have a close resemblance to the balanced scorecard?
3. Which approach do you think is more appropriate for the HR audit or the balanced scorecard?
4. Explain the relevance of the balanced scorecard to the organization.
5. Can an audit of HR projects reduce the turnover and absenteeism by identifying the causes for these issues and arriving at some solutions?

REFERENCES

1. Ahmed, P.K. and Rafiq, M. (1998), Integrated benchmarking: a holistic examination of select techniques for benchmarking analysis, *Benchmarking for quality management and technology*, Vol. 5 No. 3, pp. 225–42.
2. Ball, A. (2000), Benchmarking in local government under a central government agenda, *Benchmarking: An international journal*, Vol. 7, No. 1, pp. 20–34.
3. Bhutta, K.S. and Huq, F. (1999), Benchmarking ± best practices: an integrated approach, *Benchmarking: An International Journal*, Vol. 6, No. 3, pp. 254–68.
4. Bu¨yu¨ko¨zkan, G. and Maire, J.L. (1998), Benchmarking process formalization and a case study, *Benchmarking for Quality Management and Technology*, Vol. 5, No. 2, pp. 101–25.
5. Carpinetti, L.C.R. and de Melo, A.M. (2002), What to benchmark? A systematic approach and cases, *Benchmarking: An International Journal*, Vol. 9, No. 3, pp. 244–55.
6. Comm, C.L. and Mathaisel, D.F.X. (2000), A paradigm for benchmarking lean initiatives for quality improvement, *Benchmarking: An International Journal*, Vol. 7, No. 2, pp. 118–27.

7. Davis, P. (1998), The burgeoning of benchmarking in British local government, *Benchmarking for Quality Management and Technology*, Vol. 5, No. 4, pp. 260–70.
8. Dewey, J. (1951), *Experience and Education*, 13th ed., Macmillan, New York.
9. Elmuti, D. and Kathawala, Y. (1997), an overview of benchmarking process: a tool for continuous improvement and competitive advantage, *Benchmarking for Quality Management and Technology*, Vol. 4, No. 4, pp. 229–43.
10. Fernandez, P., McCarthy, P.F. and Rakotobe-Joel, T. (2001), An evolutionary approach to benchmarking, *Benchmarking: An international Journal*, Vol. 8, No. 4, pp. 281–305.
11. Hammer, M. and Champhy, J. (1993), *Re-engineering the Corporation: A Manifesto for Business Revolution*, Brealey, London.
12. James, W. (1913), *Pragmatismi*, Otava, Helsinki.
13. Jones, R. (1999), The role of benchmarking within the cultural reform journey of an awardwinning Australian local authority, *Benchmarking: An International Journal*, Vol. 6, No. 4, pp. 338–49.
14. Karlof, B. and O stblom, S. (1995), *Benchmarking: Tuottavuudella ja Laadulla Mestariksi*, Gummerus.
15. Kulmala, J. (1999), Benchmarking in ammatillisen aikuiskoulutuskeskuksen toiminnan kehitta¨misen va¨lineena¨, Acta Universitatis Tamperensis 663, Tampere. Longbottom, D. (2000), Benchmarking in the UK: an empirical study of practitioners and academics, *Benchmarking: An International Journal*, Vol. 7, No. 2, pp. 98–117.
16. Lamsa, A.M. And Takala T. (2001), Interpretative study of concepts, available at: www. metodix.com
17. McAdam, R. and Kelly, M. (2002), A business excellence approach to generic benchmarking in SMEs, *Benchmarking: An International Journal*, Vol. 9, No. 1, pp. 7–27.
18. Prado, J.C.P. (2001), Benchmarking for the development of quality assurance systems, *Benchmarking: An International Journal*, Vol. 8, No. 1, pp. 62–9.
19. Sarvimaki, A. (1988), *Knowledge in Interactive Practice Disciplines: An Analysis of Knowledge in Education and Health Care*, Research Bulletin 68, Department of Education, University of Helsinki, Helsinki.
20. Senge, P. (1990), *the Fifth Discipline: The Art and Practice of the Learning Organization*, Century Publishers, London.
21. Watson, G.H. (1993), *Strategic Benchmarking: How to Rate your Company's Performance against the World's Best*, John Wiley and Sons, Inc., New York.
22. Yasin, M.M. (2002), The theory and practice of benchmarking: then and now, *Benchmarking: An International Journal*, Vol. 9 No. 3, pp. 217–43.
23. Zairi, M. and Whymark, J. (2000a), the transfer of best practices: how to build a culture of benchmarking and continuous learning-part, *Benchmarking: An International Journal*, Vol. 7, No. 1, pp. 62–78.
24. Zairi, M. and Whymark, J. (2000b), The transfer of best practices: how to build a culture of benchmarking and continuous learning-part 2, *Benchmarking: An International Journal*, Vol. 7, No. 2, pp. 146–67.

10

CHAPTER

HUMAN RESOURCE DEVELOPMENT

10.1 INTRODUCTION

The human resources have been part of business and organizations since the first days of civilization, the modern concept of human resources began in reaction to the efficiency focus of Taylorism in the early 1900s. By 1920, psychologists and employment experts in the United States started the human relations movement, which viewed workers in terms of their psychology and fit with companies, rather than as interchangeable parts. This movement grew throughout the middle of the 20th century, placing emphasis on how leadership, cohesion, and loyalty played important roles in organizational success. Although this view was increasingly challenged by more quantitatively rigorous and less "soft" management techniques in the 1960s and beyond, human resources had gained a permanent role within the firm. Human resources development is a key aspect of enhancing service orientation, improving administrative cost-effectiveness and optimizing organizational procedures. A "modern state" needs motivated, performance-oriented employees who know and make the best of their own potential for growth. Strategic human resources development is an important element of any modern, efficient administration.

Human resource (or personnel) management, in the sense of getting things done through people. It's an essential part of every manager's responsibilities, but many organizations find it advantageous to establish a specialist division to provide an expert service dedicated to ensuring that the human resource function is performed efficiently.

"People are our most valuable asset" is a cliché which no member of any senior management team would disagree with. Yet, the reality for many organizations is that their people remain:

- under valued
- under trained
- under utilized

- poorly motivated, and consequently
- perform well below their true capability.

The rate of change facing organizations has never been greater and organizations must absorb and manage change at a much faster rate than in the past. In order to implement a successful business strategy to face this challenge, organizations, large or small, must ensure that they have the right people capable of delivering the strategy.

The market place for talented, skilled people is competitive and expensive. Taking on new staff can be disruptive to existing employees. Also, it takes time to develop 'cultural awareness', product/process/organization knowledge and experience for new staff members.

As organizations vary in size, aims, functions, complexity, construction, the physical nature of their product, and appeal as employers, so do the contributions of human resource management. But, in most the ultimate aim of the function is to: "ensure that at all times the business is correctly staffed by the right number of people with the skills relevant to the business needs", that is, neither overstaffed nor understaffed in total or in respect of any one discipline or work grade.

In general, development is the 'mind preparation' and carried out remote from the actual work area, training is the systematic development of the attitude, knowledge, skill pattern required by a person to perform a given task or job adequately and development is 'the growth of the individual in terms of ability, understanding and awareness'. Within an organization all are necessary in order to:

- Develop workers to undertake higher-grade tasks;
- Provide the conventional training of new and young workers (*e.g.*, as apprentices, clerks, etc.);
- Raise efficiency and standards of performance;
- Meet legislative requirements (*e.g.*, health and safety);
- Inform people (induction training, pre-retirement courses, etc.);

In order to know the business environment in which any organization operates, three major trends should be considered:

Demographics: The characteristics of a population/workforce, for example, age, gender or social class. This type of trend may have an effect in relation to pension offerings, insurance packages etc.

Diversity: The variation within the population/workplace. Changes in society now mean that a larger proportion of organizations are made up of female employees in comparison to thirty years ago. Also over recent years organizations have become more culturally diverse and have increased the number of working patterns (part-time, casual, seasonal positions) to cope with the changes in both society and the global market. It is important to note here that an organization must consider the ethical and legal implications of their decisions in relation to the HRM policies they enact to protect employees. Employers have to be acutely aware of the rise in discrimination, unfair dismissal and sexual/racial harassment cases in recent years and the detrimental effects this can have on the employees and the organization.

Skills and qualifications: As industries move from manual to more managerial professions so does the need for more highly skilled graduates. If the market is 'tight' *i.e.*, not enough staff for the jobs, employers will have to compete for employees by offering financial rewards, community investment etc. also the political issues

The human resource management function is changing-perhaps more radically than ever before. The HR function and its activities are being examined in microscopic detail in many large organizations.

Human resource processes, especially those involving the collection and dissemination of information, are being computerized and automated, potentially eliminating routine clerical activities. HR information and knowledge is being linked and integrated with other information systems, breaking down departmental barriers. As HR processes become more easily measurable, the need for justification and the means to do so become more obvious. Concepts such as the high performance organization and knowledge management offer HR specialists the chance to push HRM to the fore. HR processes and their outcomes are central to these concepts and the introduction of technology allows more exact methods of determining whether or not human resource initiatives do affect the 'bottom line' and shareholder value. The HRM function and HRD profession have undergone tremendous change over past 20–30 years. Many years ago, large organizations looked to the "Personnel Department," mostly to manage the paperwork around hiring and paying people. More recently, organizations consider the "HR Department" as playing a major role in staffing, training and helping to manage people so that people and the organization are performing at maximum capability in a highly fulfilling manner.

Development of human resources is essential for any organization that would like to be dynamic and growth oriented. Unlike other resources, human resources have rather unlimited potential capabilities. The potential can be used only by creating a climate that can continuously identify, bring to surface, nurture and use the capabilities of people. HRD system aims at creating such a climate. A number of HRD techniques have been developed in recent past years to perform the above task based on certain principles. This unit provides an understanding of the concept of HRD system, related mechanisms and the changing boundaries of the HRD.

The Concept and Definition of Human Resources Development

HRD (Human Resources Development) is a new concept that has evolved in the last decade. HRD in USA is identified with training and development and it is only in the recent years other components of human resources development are being included under the term HRD. In our country some organizations have taken the lead of evolving and implementing an integrated human resources development system. The HRDs consists of subsystems like performance appraisal, potential appraisal, career planning and development, feedback and counseling, training, OD and systems development and data storage for development decisions. This traces the history of HRD in USA as well as in India. In this chapter the author argues that the HRD concept evolved in India is for advanced than that in use in USA. HRD is not an old wine in a new bottle. It has its own developmental focus and deserves special attention by organizations including creation of separate roles of HRD managers.

Of all the resources, the 'human resources' is the most significant and the only active factor of production. All other factors like capital, materials, buildings, plant and machinery, etc. remain inactive unless there are competent people to utilize them for producing goods and services desired by the society. The goal of achieving the greater quality and higher productivity depends on the skills of people. Developing the human resources, upgrading their skills and extending their knowledge and the competencies would lead to organizational development. Therefore, human resources development is the key to enhancing and effective utilization of intellectual, technological and entrepreneurial skills of human resources. Increasingly more importance is given to "people" in the organization. This is because that human asset is the most important of all assets. People cannot be taken for granted any more. The concept of HRD is comparatively recent development and is now used at both macro and micro levels. At the macro level, HRD is described as the core of all developmental efforts in the sense of improvement of the quality of life of the people of a nation. At the micro or the organizational level, HRD connotes the improvement in the quality of managers and workers so as to achieve greater quality and higher levels of productivity. The concept of human resources system that human beings are a great asset to an organization. They are not merely evils to be reckoned with in fact they can contribute a great deal to the achievements of organizational goals. This positive view of the people working in the organizations as an asset with unlimited potential is the core of the concept of the human resources system. Investment for increasing the resources is important and the more an organization invests in its human resources, the greater the return from the investment is likely to be. The realization of continuous investment, and the possibility of substantial return, is an important concept of the human resources system. Human Resource Development is the framework for helping employees develops their personal and organizational skills, knowledge, and abilities. Human Resource Development includes such opportunities as employee training, employee career development, performance management and development, coaching, succession planning, key employee identification, tuition assistance, and organization development.

The focus of all aspects of Human Resource Development is on developing the most superior workforce so that the organization and individual employees can accomplish their work goals in service to customers.

Human Resource Development can be formal such as in classroom training, a college course, or an organizational planned change effort. Or, Human Resource Development can be informal as in employee coaching by a manager. Healthy organizations believe in Human Resource Development and cover all of these bases.

Definition of HRD

In the organizational context, human resources development may be defined as a continuous process to ensure the development of employee competencies, dynamism, motivation and effectiveness in a systematic and planned way. HRD is a process concerned with an organized series of learning activities designed to produce behavioural changes in the human resources in such a way that they acquire desired level of competence for present and future roles. In other words, HRD brings about 'all round development' of the people so that they can contribute their best to the organization society and nation.

According to the T.V. Rao, "HRD is a continuous planned process by which employees are helped to":

- To acquire or sharpen capabilities required to perform various functions associated with their present or expected future roles.
- Develop their general capabilities as individuals and discover and exploit their own inner potentials for their own or/and organizational development purposes.
- Develop an organizational culture in which supervisor-subordinates relationships, team work and collaboration among sub-units are strong and contribute to the professional well being, motivation and the pride of the employees.

Human Resources Development may be defined as development of people by providing the right environment where each individual may grow to fullest extent. Megginson viewed resources as 'the total knowledge, skills, creative abilities, talents and attitudes of an organization's workforce as well as the values, attitudes and beliefs of the individual involved".

According to the Ewsar Dayal, HRD involves:

- Ways to better adjust the individual to his job and the environment,
- The greatest involvement of an employee in various aspects of his work, and
- The greatest concern for enhancing the capabilities of the individual.

It's actually been around for some time under many different names. It's a broad field, encompassing many subject areas. But it's never been more important, more necessary.

A definition of HRD is "organized learning activities arranged within an organization in order to improve performance and/or personal growth for the purpose of improving the job, the individual, and/or the organization". HRD includes the areas of training and development, career development, and organization development. This is related to Human Resource Managementa field which includes HR research and information systems, union/labour relations, employee assistance, compensation/benefits, selection and s Human Resource Development (HRD) is the integrated use of training, organizational development, and career development efforts to improve individual, group, and organizational effectiveness.

Human resource development program is designed to develop ethical, competent professional leaders who can perform effectively in critical HRD roles, such as administrator of HRD programs, training manager or director, instructor, facilitator, trainer, management development specialist, organization change agent, program designer, or individual career development advisor, staffing, performance management systems, HR planning, and organization/job design etc.

The definition of HRD is limited to the organizational context. In the context of a state or the nation it would differ. HRD is a process, not merely a set of mechanism and techniques. The mechanism and techniques such as performance appraisal, counseling, training and organization development interventions are used to initiate, facilitate and promote this process in a continuous way. Because the process is no limit, the mechanisms may need to be examined periodically to see whether they are promoting or hindering the process. Organizations can facilitate this process of development by planning for fit, by allocating organizational resources for the purposes, and by exemplifying an HRD philosophy that values human beings and promotes their development.

To be successful in the current rapidly-changing world, we need to maximize the productivity of all of our resources—physical, financial, information, and human. How are we doing?

Physical resources: The organizations have made major investments in updating our physical equipment, so we can compete with state-of-the-art production tools and facilities.

Financial resources: Sure, we're really capital intensive. But that's the nature of our production businesses. The money will follow our ideas, our successes, and our productivity.

Information and knowledge resources: To continue attracting capital in competition with other industries, we need to be as good as they are in accessing the new world of information. It's time to join the Internet.

Human resources: This is the leverage point! Here's where we can make significant differences in our lives, our careers, and our organizations.

What is HRD? Evolution of the Field

In 1970 Len Nadler published his now-classic book Developing Human Resources, in which he coined the term "Human Resource Development" (HRD). The term HRD provided a conceptual umbrella under which the field began to unify, using the three-fold notion of training, education, and development. HRD provided purpose and direction for the continued growth of the field: organized learning to provide the possibility of performance change. It further identified a core discipline from which a field of study could develop: adult learning in the workplace. McLagans HRD studies in 1983 and 1989 reflected a shift taking place in HRD work. In 1983 the assumptions in the competency models focused on change in technology. In 1987 Patricia McLagan proposed the following narrative definition of HRD:

HRD is the integrated use of training and development, career, development, and organization development to improve individual effectiveness.

In 1989 there were signs of an emerging concern for economic impact. The field began to move from focusing to what is performed to what is produced. One of the forces in 1989 was an increased use of systems approaches in HRD. Another shift in the fields that took place was that the focus on individual learning was shifting to organizational learning as the primary activity and goal of the field. Patricia McLagan's role and competency study Models for HRD practice described in 1989 a broadened scope of various roles in the competency models. The definition of HRD expanded beyond training and organization development. The move was toward HRD responsiveness and relevance.

Arriving at the final count down to the 21st century HRD remains an important force for the future. In the article on HRD competencies and future trends in HRD Pat McLagan (1996) identified nine important roles for HRD practioners to perform. As HRD practitioners ctreate rather than just respond, they will seek leverage and ways to help managers, teams, and individuals take charge of their own human resouce practices. According to McLagan "HRD may be the only function in a clear position to represent human ethics and morality". It is in the following roles that the present HRD professionals are challenged to create new ways to address the human resource issues:

1. *HR strategic advisor:* In this role the issues and trends concernging an organization's external and internal people are brought to the attention of the strategic decision-makers.
2. *HR systems designer and developer:* This role involves designing and preparing HR systyems for implementation so that HR systems and actions are mutually reinforcing and have maximum impact on organizational performance, development and endurance.
3. *Organization change consultant:* This role means facilitating the development and implementaion of strategies for transforming organization.
4. *Organization design consultant:* This role involves identifying the work required to fulfill organizational strategies. It also involves organizing the work so that it makes efficient and effective use of resources.
5. *Learning program specialist:* In this role learning needs are identified to design and devlop structured learning programs and materials in a variety of media formats for self-study and workshop or electronic delivery.
6. *Instuctor/facilitator:* This is an increasingly difficult role. In it information is presented, structural learning experiences are lead and group discussions and group processes facilitated.
7. *Individual development and career consultant:* This role involves helping people assess their competencies, values and goals so they can identify, plan, and implement development actions.
8. *Performance consultant:* This role means assisting a group or individuals to add value in the workplace. It's a coaching and consulting role in which HRD people perform both analytical and systems design work.

9. *Researcher:* This role involves assessing HRD pracitces and programs and their impact empirically. It also means communicating results so that the organization and its people accelerate their change and development.

Objectives of HRD

Human Resources Development is a multipurpose. It has the following objectives:

- Provide the opportunity and comprehensive framework for the development of human resources in the organization full expression of their talents and manifest potentials.
- Develop the constructive mind and over all personality of each employee.
- Develop each individual's capabilities to perform the present job and to handle future roles.
- Develop and maintain high motivation level of employees.
- Strengthen superior-subordinate relationships.
- Develop the sense of team spirit, team work and inter team collaboration.
- Develop the organizational health, culture and climate.
- General systematic information about the human resources.

The relationships of the above goals will ultimately contribute to organizational effectiveness reflected through better quality, higher productivity, cost reduction, higher profits, and better public image. This explains the increased relevance of HRD for modern organizations operating in the uncertain social, political, economic, technological and international environment.

- To disseminate HRD knowledge and skills among HRD professionals and practitioners, and share information and experiences relating to HRD so as to learn and benefit from each other.
- To discover knowledge and skills relevant to HRD, its philosophy, processes, and implementation, through exploration and experimentation.
- To discover knowledge and skills relevant to HRD, its philosophy, processes, and implementation, through exploration and experimentation.
- To generate, acquire and continuously develop new knowledge and skills related to HRD through research and development.
- To build a storehouse of knowledge and skills pertaining to HRD.
- To strengthen the HRD movement by developing the imployee performance Quality & productivity.
- Drawing attention of chief executives of different organizations, agencies and Government departments to HRD philosophies and processes and their benefits.
- Assisting organizations and agencies in designing and implementing HRD systems, evaluating the impact of HRD systems and processes, and feeding back the results and improvement.
- To help systems and organizations develop innovative approaches and technologies based on national needs.
- To help develop professional expertise in HRD.
- To develop and maintain standards of professional excellence in HRD.
- To help stimulate positive forces for humanising systems and organizations in national life enabling persons working in them to make their best contribution.
- To act as a clearing-house for all referrals related to HRD activities in the State.

Need and Significance of HRD

It is very difficult to survive in the present environment unless the growth and development of the people. Keeping the fast developing changes, HRD must be viewed as the total system inter-related and interacting with other systems at work—the production, financial, marketing, with which a business system functions. Though the personnel policies can keep the morale and motivation of employees high, yet theses efforts are not enough to make the organization dynamic and take it to new heights. Employees capabilities must continuously be sharpened and used.

The need of the HRD is felt is to create a climate which will improve the work life by overcoming monotony, ensuring better communications and creation of familiar sort of work conditions where creativity of all the members comes into fullest utilization. The focus of HRD mainly is on.

The organizations and jobs will never be the same. Changes are based on the global economy, on changing technology, on our changing work force, on cultural and demographic changes, and on the changing nature of work itself. The changes are different this time. They are permanent, and will permanently affect the way our work and our lives are structured. HRD helps us to learn new skills and develop new abilities, to respond to these changes in our lives, our careers, and our organizations. We can deal with these constructively, using change for our competitive advantage and as opportunities for personal and organizational growth, or we can be overwhelmed by them. Who is affected by change—you are! With all the downsizing, outsourcing and team building, responsibility and accountability are being downloaded to individuals. So everyone is now a manager. Everyone will need to acquire and/or increase their skills, knowledge and abilities to perform their jobs (and now, to perform other people's jobs too!). The goal of HRD is to improve the performance of our organizations by maximizing the efficiency and performance of our people. We are going to develop our knowledge and skills, our actions and standards, our motivation, incentives, attitudes and work environment.

The Nature of the HRD

1. **System Perspective:** HRD is said to be core of a larger system known as Human Resource System. It is concerned with providing learning experience for the organizational members to develop their competencies. HRD is only a sub-system of the organization which is integrated with all other sub-systems such as production, finance, marketing etc.

   HRD is viewed as a system consisting of several interdependent and interrelated sub-systems. These include performance appraisal, potential appraisal, role analysis, training, job enrichment, communication etc. In designing a human resources development system enough attention should be paid to building linkages can be established in number of ways depending upon the companies of the system.
2. **Behavioural Science Knowledge:** Human Resources Development makes the use of the principles and concepts of behavioural science for the development of the people. It uses knowledge drawn from the psychology, sociology and anthropology for planning and implementing various programs for the development of individuals, groups and organization.
3. **Continuous Process:** As a dynamic and proactive process, HRD believes in and emphasize the need for "continuous development" of personnel to face the innumerable challenges in the functioning of an organization. However, HRD mechanisms, process, policies, etc. differ from organization to organization to suit the need of the situation. HRD sub-systems are deeply interlinked with social, cultural, economic and political factors.

4. **Quality of life:** In general, HRD has its relevance to the "quality of human life improvement". At the organizational level, it is concerned with improving the quality of work life so as to achieve greater satisfaction of employees and higher level of productivity.

Benefits of HRD

In general, HRD is 'mind preparation' and is carried out remote from the actual work area, training is the systematic development of the attitude, knowledge, skill pattern required by a person to perform a given task or job adequately and development is 'the growth of the individual in terms of ability, understanding and awareness'.

Within an organization all three are necessary in order to:

- Develop workers to undertake higher-grade tasks;
- Provide the conventional training of new and young workers (*e.g.*, as apprentices, clerks, etc.);
- Raise efficiency and standards of performance;
- Meet legislative requirements (*e.g.*, health and safety);
- Inform people (induction training, pre-retirement courses, etc.).

"The philosophy does not limit itself to direct employees of an organization. Therefore humans or people—as opposed to just employees—need to be managed in a way that is consistent with broad organizational requirements such as quality or efficiency. Personnel policies and organization structures have to be managed in a way that is congruent with organizational strategy and organizational effectiveness depends on there being a tight 'fit' between human resource and business strategies. HRM strategies are all about making business strategies work and so emphasis is placed on how to best match and develop 'appropriate' HRM systems." The human resource management function is changing perhaps more radically than ever before. The HR function and its activities are being examined in microscopic detail in many large organizations. Human resource processes, especially those involving the collection and dissemination of information, are being computerized and automated, potentially eliminating routine clerical activities. HR information and knowledge is being linked and integrated with other information systems, breaking down departmental barriers.

As HR processes become more easily measurable, the need for justification and the means to do so become more obvious. Concepts such as the high performance organization and knowledge management offer HR specialists the chance to push HRM to the fore. HR processes and their outcomes are central to these concepts and the introduction of technology allows more exact methods of determining whether or not human resource initiatives do affect the 'bottom line' and shareholder value.

"Varied across a number of dimensions and then (*they*) stipulated a set of hypotheses about the personnel and industrial relations practices that were needed. They identified the most important HRM practices about which strategic decisions had to be made and for each practice noted the dichotomous but logical alternatives that could be applied. HRM could be seen as a menu of strategic choices to be made by HR executives intended to promote the most effective role behaviours that are consistent with the organization strategy and are aligned with each other."

Human Resource Development in an organization can have the following benefits:

- It helps in the integrated growth of the employees.
- It helps employees to know their strengths and weaknesses and thus enable them to improve their performance and that of the organization.

- It facilitates the creation of an environment where opportunities are available for fuller utilization of the known potentials of the employees. The climate of such an organization is one of the mutually, trust, collaborations, openness etc.
- It generates valid data about employees for personal functions like training, placement, selection, promotion etc.
- It insists on provision of feedback and guidance by the superior to the employees for the improvement of their performance.
- It leads to greater organizational effectiveness.

HRD Culture

HRD helps in creating a common understanding of current corporate culture and change corporate culture to meet strategic objectives. Corporate culture is often defined as "the way we do things around here" and it can be a strategic advantage as well as a strategic disadvantage. In a constantly evolving business environment, culture should be monitored to determine current strategic impact. Oftentimes, organizations need more appreciation, not re-design. Appreciative Inquiry is a way of thinking, seeing, and acting for powerful, purposeful change in organizations. It is particularly useful in systems being overwhelmed by a constant demand for change. Appreciative Inquiry works on the assumption that whatever you want more of already exists in all organizations. While traditional problem-solving processes separate, dissect, and pull apart, Appreciative Inquiry generates affirming images that pull people together.

New Work Culture is an act of continuity. Phil Harris has combined and updated two of his seminal publications, prophetically written 1980's that brought to light the emerging norms, values and behaviours of organizations moving into the future. He updates and documents the progress that has been made in the transition from the industrial age organization to the current stage of meta-industrial management.

Predicting the future, even from what seem to be evident trends is often a risky process. This new volume shows, however, that Harris was largely spot-on a decade ago. Now he charts the learnings and challenges and provides advice from the perspective of the Human Resource Development field. The book has four units, discussing, respectively:

1. The HRD challenges that we face in making the transition to the new work culture.
2. What makes up the new work culture?
3. How this affects the day-to-day conduct of Human Resources Management.
4. Successful HRD strategies for the new work culture.

Not surprisingly, we find the impact of cultural factors on new ways of working. There are observations about international as well as corporate and professional cultural factors, and how these impel and give direction to changes in management and business practice. Information and brain power define the nature of work and the structure of activity in today's meta-industrial organization. Hence, it is critical to understand the nature of communication within and beyond the organization. Who manage and work in the emerging technological work culture. Unlike industrial age companies whose leadership defined and even dictated their purposes in terms of market strengths, the new organization is proactive and consciously self-defined.

The selection of the relevant dimensions of HRD in an organization would depend upon the requirements of the organization for developing its human resources. In the fast changing environment, the organizations have to develop and maintain an enabling culture to become dynamic and growth oriented. The purpose of HRD is to facilitate development of such a culture in the organization. An enabling culture is one where employees use their initiative, risk, experiment, innovate and make things happen. HRD culture is characterized by Openness, confrontation, trust, autonomy, proaction, authenticity and collaboration which are represented by the term 'OCTAPAC' consisting of first letter of each characteristics. All HRD interventions should be anchored within a comprehensive HRD plan that lays out the strategic thinking behind the interventions as well as the linkages between these. If such an HRD strategy is to be developed and implemented effectively, there has to be broad buy-in from a cross-section of the institution and there should be commitment from across the board to see the implementation through. Numerous HRD strategies and plans that have been externally driven have failed to be implemented because of the lack of involvement and buy in from institutional stakeholders.

HRD Climate

HRD climate is an integral part of general organizational climate. Organizational climate is the summery of perception which people have about the organization. It is the global expression of what the origination is. Organizational climate is the manifestation of the attitudes of the organizational members towards the organization itself. An organization tends to attract and keep people who fit its climate so that its patterns are perpetuated at least to some extent. Organization climate is a relatively enduring quality of the internal environment that is experienced by its members, influences their behaviour and can be described in term of values of a particular set of characteristics of the organization.

HRD climate may be defined as perceptions of the employees have of the developmental environment of an organization. HRD climate contributes to the organizations overall health and self-renewing capabilities which, in turn, increase the enabling capacities of individual, dyads, teams and the entire organization. HRD (Human Resources Development) is a new concept that has evolved in the last decade. HRD in USA is identified with training and development and it is only in the recent years other components of human resources development are being included under the term HRD. In our country some organizations have taken the lead of evolving and implementing an integrated human resources development system. The HRD is consists of sub-systems like performance appraisal, potential appraisal, career planning and development, feedback and counseling, training, OD and systems development and data storage for development decisions. This paper traces the history of HRD in USA as well as in India. HRD is not an old wine in a new bottle. It has its own developmental focus and deserves special attention by organizations including creation of separate roles of HRD managers. All HRD interventions should be anchored within a comprehensive HRD plan that lays out the strategic thinking behind the interventions as well as the linkages between these. If such an HRD strategy is to be developed and implemented effectively, there has to be broad buy-in from a cross-section of the institution and there should be commitment from across the board to see the implementation through. Numerous HRD strategies and plans that have been externally driven have failed to be implemented because of the lack of involvement and buy in from institutional stakeholders.

To facilities HRD, an optimal level of "developmental Climate" is essential. Some of the characteristics of such a climate are:

- A tendency at all levels and specially the top management to treat people as the most important resources.
- A perception that developing the competencies in the employees is the job of every manager/ supervisor.
- Faith in the capability of the people to change and acquire new competencies any stage of life.
- A tendency to be open in communication.
- A tendency to encourage risk taking.
- A tendency to help employees recognize their strengths and weaknesses.
- A tendency on the part of employees to be generally helpful to each other and collaborate.
- Team spirit.
- A general climate of trust.
- A tendency to discourage favouritism and biasness.
- Supportive personnel or human resources policies.
- Development-oriented appraisals, training rewards system, job rotation, career planning and potential appraisal.

Organizations differ in the extent to which they have these tendencies, some others may have only a few of these and a few may have most of these. It is possible to work out the profile of an organization on the basis of these tendencies.

Organizational climate is the human environment within which an organization's employees do their work. It may refer to the environment within a department, a major company unit such as branch, plant or an entire organization. Climate can influence motivation, performance and job satisfaction. It does this by creating certain kinds of expectancies about what will follow from different actions. Employees expect certain consequences will follow from different actions employees expect certain reward, satisfaction, and frustration on the basis of their perception of the organizational climate. These perceptions tend to motivation.

Organizational climate affects significantly the process of participative system of decision-making and is bound be ineffective in a climate in which is pre-dominantly characteristics by an autocratic style of management. Group decision-making without creating a proper organizational climate generates more cynicism among the group members. The group members normally perceive group decision-making system as a façade and an eye wash. It is, therefore, essential to democratize the organizational systems for successful decision-making. In other words, introduction of group decision-making process must be coupled with supportive and congenial organizational climate.

HRD Matrix

HRD matrix identifies the interrelationships between the HRD instruments, process, outcomes and organizational effectiveness as mentioned in the Fig.10.1. HRD instruments includes performance appraisal, counseling, role analysis, potential development, training, reward system, job enrichment etc. These mechanisms may vary depending upon the size of the organization, the commitment of the top management, the environment, the culture and climate, the perception off the people, technology used, methods employed by the competitors, etc. It is in the interest of the organization that the top management should give due weightage to these factors to keep the workforce motivated all the time providing challenging jobs and designing career planning and suitable compensation packages.

Fig. 10.1 Linkages between HRD instruments, process outcomes and organizational effectiveness.

These instruments lead to generation of HRD process like role clarity, developmental planning, developmental climate, risk-taking and dynamism in employees. Such HRD processes should result in more competent, satisfied and committed people who by their contributions, would make the organization grow. Such HRD outcome influences organizational effectiveness also depends on a number of other variables like environment, technology, competitors etc. on a number of other variables like environment, technology, competitors etc. However, together things being the same, an organization that has competent, satisfied, committed and dynamism people is likely to do better than an organization that scores low on the HRD outcome variables. Similarly, an organization that has better HRD climate and processes is likely to be more effective than an organization that does not have them.

HRD Subsystems (Mechanism or Instruments)

The dimensions/components/subsystems of the HRD is concerned, various thinkers and the professionals have given their views in different ways. This is the opinion of TV Rao that, HRD subsystem is consist of performance appraisal, potential appraisal, career planning, training, performance coaching, organization development, employee welfare, rewards, quality of work life and human resources information system. Udai Pareek view this as performance appraisal, career planning, potential appraisal, training as the dimension of HRD. A well structured HRD program should have the following subsystem:

Performance Appraisal: Performance appraisal is a formal, structured system that compares employee performance to established standards. Assessment of job performance is shared with employees being appraised through one of several primary methods of performance appraisals. Elements in performance appraisal methods are tailored to the organization's employees, jobs, and structure. They include objective criteria for measuring employee performance and ratings that summarize how well the employee is doing. Successful appraisal methods have clearly defined and explicitly communicated standards or expectations of employee performance on the job.

Evaluating employee performance is a key responsibility of managers. Performance appraisals, a powerful tool, provide documented feedback on an employee's level of performance. They help determine continued employment, promotion, transfer, bonuses, and pay raises, and allow for improved communications between managers and employees. The actual performance appraisal documents become part of an employee's permanent record and can greatly influence lives and careers. In other words performance management should be:

Strategic: It is about broader issues and longer-term goals.

Integrated: It should link various aspects of the business, people management, and individuals and teams.

It should incorporate:

Performance improvement: Throughout the organization, for individual, team and organizational effectiveness.

Development: Unless there is continuous development of individuals and teams, performance will not improve.

Managing behaviour: Ensuring that individuals are encouraged to behave in a way that allows and fosters better working relationships.

The process of performance appraisal consists of:

Setting Standards for performance.

Communicating the standards to the employees.

Measuring the performance.

Comparing the actual performance with standards set.

Potential Appraisal: Like the performance appraisal, potential appraisal is also done by the employees' supervisor who has had the opportunity to observe the employee for some time. Potential appraisal may be done either regularly or as and when required. The feed-back that you get from the appraisal should be constructive so that it can be used to help them progress as an individual by rectifying their weaknesses. It is important that you comment on their better aspects instead of just identifying their areas of concern. By doing so, it will give them the sense that they can perform and therefore will have the motivation to act upon any actions suggested. Once the feed-back has been acknowledged and an action plan has been created, you should have a follow up assessment to check up on the progress of the employee. The HRD function has a long way to go in introducing a streamlined potential appraisal system which ensures a good match between the employee and the job.

Feedback Counseling: Generating the data through the feedback of performance can be used in various way *i.e.,* career planning, training, and development of the employees, to identify the potential of employee etc. Counseling serves several purposes in any organization. It helps in strengthening the superior and subordinate relationship, helps the executives to understand the limitations of his seniors and problems of his juniors, improves communications thereby facilitating quality decision, helps employees in recognizing their strengths and weaknesses and also helps evaluate the impact of their decisions and so on. This would help the employees in overcoming the barriers emanating from their ignorance or poor knowledge in the field. It would also help the employees in designing their action plans for their overall development and acquiring greater competencies.

Training and Development: In virtually every market, customers are now demanding higher quality, lower costs and faster cycle time. To meet these requirements, the firms must continually improve their over all performance. Rapid advances in technology and improved processes have been important factors in helping businesses meet these challenges. However, the most important competitive advantage for any firm is its workforce—one must remain competent through continuous training and development efforts. However, successful organizations realize that well structured and significant employees training and Development correlate strongly with long-term success. Improved performances, the bottom-line purpose of Training and development. This leads the organizations into matured learning organizations. Employee training and development initiatives can transform organizations with providing extra skills to your employees to not only increase safety and productivity but training leads to higher job satisfaction, which shows up in better corporate performance.

Role Analysis: Role analysis is a participatory process which aims at defining the work content of a role in relation to all those with whom the role occupant has significant interaction in the performance of his job.

Job has to be analyzed for proper planning of work which is necessary for improving the efficiency. Such an analysis is known as task/job analysis. It is the very useful for semiskilled and skilled jobs. However, the nature of the managerial/supervisory job is more complex and interdependent on the performance and expectation of all those who are concerned with the accomplishment of the tasks in a work situation and thus one is judged not only on individual contribution but also on his 'role' in canalizing the willing cooperation and efforts of those who are concerned.

Career Planning: The business environment today is highly competitive and complex and there is a certain degree of ambiguity and uncertainty about the career development. Consequently, employees are also confused about their career development. Earlier the employees are enjoyed the job security by taking up a position in an organization. It is a psychological contract between the employee and the employer. In the then time, the loyalty and devotion, commitments were the factors for higher position in an organization. Now, contrastingly, career planning for an employee is very difficult. Career growth has already crossed the boundaries and has undergone a great change. Career planning is an ongoing process whereby an individual sets career goals and identifies the means to achieve them. Career planning should not concentrate only on advancement opportunities since the present work environment has reduced many of these opportunities. At some point of time, career planning should focus on achieving success that does not necessarily entail promotions. Career development is a formal approach used by the organization to ensure that the people with the proper qualifications and experiences are available when needed. Formal career development is important to maintain a motivated and committed workforce. Career development tools, which are specified during career planning and utilized in the career development program, most notably include various types of training and the application of organizational development techniques. Career planning and development benefit both the individual and the organization and must therefore be carefully considered by the both.

Job Rotation: An alternation to boredom in work place is the job rotation. Job rotation implies moving of employees from one job to another without any fundamental change in the nature of the job. The employees may be performing the different jobs that are the similar in nature. The advantage of job rotation may be reduced boredom, broadening of employee's knowledge and skill and making them competent in several jobs rather than only one. However, caution needs to be exercised while shifting people frequently from one job to another job, it may be caused interruption or the employee may feel alienated in a new jobs. Another factor is job rotation does not provide the employee any challenge may feel frustrated.

(*i*) Horizontal movement/expansion is job.
(*ii*) Lateral transfer of employees to various jobs to broaden their focus and increase their knowledge.
(*iii*) One answer to the problem of boredom is the job rotation.
(*iv*) Jobs remain unchanged–more or less jobs of nature).
(*v*) Improve interdepartmental cooperation.
(*vi*) Employees become more understanding of each others problem.
(*vii*) Range of skills give the management more flexibility in scheduling work, adapting to changes and as the training costs are increased, work is disrupted.

Quality Circles: Quality Circles (QC) are a small group of employees in a small work area doing similar kind of work who voluntarily meet regularly to resolve work-related problem. The main objectives of QC include the development and effective utilization of human resources, improve quality of products and services, cost reduction, satisfying workers urge for participation and involvement, improving the employee morale, improving the supervisory and leadership skills, resolving problems in work environment, resolving the conflicts and more importantly tapping the dormant creativity of the workers. The function of QC can be made effective if the members are made to realize that there is more than one way of resolving problems.

The objectives of the Quality Circle:

- To develop, enhance and utilize human resource management effectively.
- To satisfy the workers psychological needs to motivate them.
- To improve supervisory skills of the employees like leadership, inter-personnel and conflict resolution.
- To utilize the skills through participation, creating and work interest inculcating problem-solving techniques etc.

Reward System: A reward system is the complex set of formal and informal incentives that connect individual motivation, behaviour, performance, and ultimately results to the various forms of pay or compensation received in exchange. It includes not only how people are incensed and paid but also how the underlying philosophy and principles about people and their contributions and the goals of the organization are created and communicated, how each individual's contribution is aligned with and tied to organization results, and how performance is managed and appraised. Defines a reward system as any process within an organization that encourages, reinforces, or compensates people for taking a particular set of actions. The people element of organization design encompasses all things that have to do with having the best workforce and ensuring that the culture of the organization and the contract between workers and the company is mutually beneficial.

In research done on reward systems, several basic premises have emerged:

- Rewards do influence motivation and behaviour.
- Reward systems must focus on what is valued in the organization.
- There must be a clear connection between the valued behaviour/result and the reward.
- If there is a discrepancy between what is espoused as valued in behaviour and/or outcomes and what is rewarded, that which is rewarded will be the stronger influencer of behavioural choices.
- Reward systems must be comprised of thoughtfully and strategically integrated components in order for them to be effective.

Organizational Development (OD): Organization is organization wide, planned effort managed from the top, placing emphasis on making appropriate intervention in the ongoing activities of the organization. OD provides a normative framework within which changes in the climate and the culture of the organization towards harnessing the human capital for realization of organizational objectives is brought out. Thus, OD is a planned change strategy aimed at developing and revitalizing the adoptive capacities of organizations so as to enable them respond to their internal and external environments in a pre active manner. OD exercises include team building programme, inter-personnel sensitivity, role clarity, MBO and stress management. Organization development—the diagnosis and design of systems to assist an organization with planning change. OD activities include: change management, team building, learning organizations, management development, and quality of work life, management by objectives, strategic planning, and participative management. organizational restructuring, job redesign, job enrichment, centralization vs. decentralization, changes in the organization's reward structure, process consultation, executive development, action research, third party interventions, and more.

Human Resource Planning: Human resources planning is a process by which management determine how the organization should move from its current manpower position to its desired manpower position. Through planning, management strives to have the right number and the right kinds of people, at the right place, at the right time, doing things, which result in both organization and the individual receiving maximum long-run benefits.

Objectives of the Human resources planning

1. To ensure optimum use of human resources current employees.
2. To assess or forecast future skill requirement.
3. To provide control measures to ensure that necessary resources are available as when required.

4. A number of specified reasons for attaching importance to manpower planning and forecasting exercise are:
    - To link manpower planning with the organizational planning.
    - To determine recruitment levels.
    - To anticipate redundancies.
    - To determine optimum training levels.
    - To provide a basis for management development programs.
    - To cost the manpower.
    - To assist productivity bargaining.
    - To assess future accommodation requirement.
    - To study the cost of overheads and value of service functions.
    - To decide whether certain activity needs to be subcontracted, etc.

The HR forecasts in responsible for estimating number of people and the jobs needed by an organization to achieve its objectives and realize its plans are time in the most efficient and effective manner possible. An ideal human resources planning system should be:

- Holistic in its approach linked with strategies planning and budget process.
- Built around our service needs and skills required to deliver quality service.
- Responsive to change variables *i.e.*, economic, technological, political, environmental mandate.
- Supportive of continual learning and development concepts.
- Data driven that allow for scenario building because of changing assumptions for different desired out comes.

Recruitment, Selection and Placement: The hiring process consists of three activities: recruitment, selection, and orientation. The hiring process is filled with challenges. These include: 1. Determining which characteristics are most important to performance, 2. Measuring these characteristics. 3. Evaluating applicants' motivation, and 4. Deciding that should make hiring decisions. Meeting the challenges of effective staffing that because choosing the right person for a job can a tremendous positive effect on productivity and customer satisfaction, it is important that each step of the hiring process be managed carefully. The recruitment process should focus on attracting qualified candidates internally and/or externally. Recruitment efforts should be tied with HRP efforts. To ensure proper fit between hires and their jobs and to avoid legal problems, firms should conduct job analysis. Many selection tools are available. These include letters of recommendation, application form, ability test, personality test, psychological test, interviews, assessment centers, drug test, honesty test, reference checks, and hand writing analysis. The best (and foremost legally defensible) selection is both reliable and valid. The placement is the process of assigning the selected candidate with the most suitable job. It underlies the need for placing right men at the right job so that the best results could be obtained.

Quality of Work Life (QWL): The conditions under which the workers work and live, this is an important factor which influences workers satisfaction or otherwise and consequently the job satisfaction. In order to priorities, it comes next to the earnings of a worker in the Indian context. For an employee to be able to work at his best, it is necessary to understand that inadequate working and living conditions produce adverse mental and physical effect on the employee, ultimately causing decline in the efficiency.

The HRD system takes care of the employees' health and well being of their families by providing them with better working conditions which generally promote a healthy atmosphere of development and motivation.

HRD Process

"HRD has assumed prominence as a dynamic and creative, means to achieve increased productivity and profitability, improved moral, better industrial relations and career development of employees; all eventually leading to achieve overall goals of mega-sized organizations. In the process of HRD, many challenging issues like treatment of HRD expenses as capital expenditure or revenue expenditure, retention of the human resources developed in the HRD process of organization and resistance shown by the employees against HRD process are being experienced. Like in other organizations, HRD is also widely practiced in Indian banking sector.

This is mainly directed towards knowing the perceptions of employees with regard to the major contents of the HRD philosophy, the various elements of HRD climate, the major problems and difficulties in the management of HRD process and the process of resolving the pertinent challenges of HRD practices and measures. Moreover, the study covers the relationship between the levels of expectations and the levels of satisfaction as perceived by the employees from various HRD practices and measures. As such, the book will be very much useful to the practicing human resources managers looking after HRD in the banking world, as also to the researchers, policy framers and advance learners in the field of Human Resource Management."

Human Resource Development (HRD) is a process by which the staff of our institution is helped in a continuous and systematic way to acquire capabilities required to perform various functions associated with their expected roles. It helps to develop their general capabilities as individuals and discover their own potentials for the growth of the institution. It involves in developing culture in which teamwork, interface between programmes become strong and contribute to the professional well being and motivation of staff.

In terms of the scope of its impact, HRD could make its presence felt at different levels: In placement, to develop staff who are motivated and committed the interpersonal relationships with others or team, and interface for developing institutional culture. Hence HRD could be viewed as a system consisting of several interdependent and interrelated subsystems, which helps in integrating the growth and development of work force.

HRD is a continuous dynamic, proactive and planned process which lays emphasis on the individual, need and behaviours. It is human relation approach focuses on inter-personal relationships lays emphasis on motivation, job satisfaction and morale there by enhancing quality of life. It is concerned with providing learning experiences organized to bring 3 c's–competencies, culture and commitment.

The term OCTACPAC has been coined to denote the characteristics of HRD climate which the HRD process works that includes: openness, confrontation trust, autonomy, proaction, authenticity and collaboration.

Openness: The term openness refers to the freedom to express the ideas, opinions, views, frankness, outspoken, straightforwardness. If a team is to be effective, then its member needs to be able to express their views, their differences of opinion, interests and problems without fear of ridicule or retaliation. No team work is really effective if there is a 'cut-your-throat' or 'stabbing-in-the back' atmosphere, where the members are will to involve very less with themselves. The result is wastage of energy, effort, creativity etc.

Confrontation: The confrontation refers to 'conflict', 'encounter', and 'dispute' to evolve the effective and efficient suggestions and solutions to a given problem. There is a dire need to confront problems and issues rather than avoid them. In order to be effective, one should confront even delicate or unpleasant issues honestly and squarely instead of avoiding them.

Trust: Trust means 'belief', 'confidence', 'faith'. One cannot orders others to trust, it comes only through their experience. Organization employs people who come from different backgrounds, values and expectations and the perceptions of each of them are different from others and the work-life involves them in many complex relationships with others. The goals and objectives can be achieved only when we have an atmosphere of friendship, trust among the employees and the supportive tendency of each other. With trust people can talk freely about their fears and problems and receive from others the help which they need to be more effective. We should understand that trust takes a long time to achieve but it can be destroyed in a few seconds. So in order to be effective, continuous support and trust among employees should be inculcated and developed continuously.

Autonomy: The term means to 'freedom', 'independence'. Freedom to do a thing in the way that one wants tends to act as morale booster. Every individual has his own way of doing things; it is the job of his superior to ensure that creativity in the individual/group is not discouraged while working for achieving objectives.

Proaction: This refers to "planning in advance, lead from the front, 'state of alertness/preparedness'. As it is often said 'prevention is better than cure', the word proaction means that the leadership/ top management should be capable of forecasting, predicting, projecting, anticipating things well in advance and plan accordingly to meet any eventuality at any given point of time.

Authenticity: This refers to factual, genuine, actual etc. Every institution has a goal and various departments are used in the process to achieve the objectives through their varied and their specialized skills. The method of achieving the objectives is more important than that of extent of achievement. That means the management has to ensure that in the process of achieving objectives none of their employees/departments uses any illegitimate/unlawful/unethical procedures/methods which affect in varying degrees the reputation and status of the organization.

Collaboration: This refers to cooperation, participation, teamwork, association. Cooperation means working together. It implies that individuals are committed and willing to be involved in the work they do, and that they are ready to share their skills and information with the rest of the employees, knowing that the others will reciprocate. People find ways of being more helpful to each other and are ready to share their feelings, skills, there by achieving the objectives with less operational time and minimum cost.

Organizational effectiveness and HRD

More now than ever, companies today want to deliver products better, faster, and cheaper. At the same time, in the high-technology environment of the twenty-first century, nearly all organizations have found themselves building more and more complex products. Today, a single company usually does not develop all the components that compose a product. More commonly, some components are built in-house and some are acquired; then all the components are integrated into the final product. Organizations must be able to manage and control this complex product development and maintenance.

Organizational effectiveness

Organizational effectiveness has been defined as the ability of an organization to fulfill its mission through sound management, strong governance and a persistent rededication to achieving results. Effective nonprofits are mission-driven, adaptable, customer-focused, entrepreneurial, outcomes-oriented and sustainable. Organizational effectiveness is the central theme of organization theory. It is viable concept from the standpoint of management. It is very difficult to conceive a theory of organization that does not include the concept of effectiveness.

Organizational effectiveness has been defined as the ability of an organization to fulfill its mission through sound management, strong governance and a persistent rededication to achieving results. Effective nonprofits are mission-driven, adaptable, customer-focused, entrepreneurial, outcomes-oriented and sustainable.

Several assessment tools are available on this site to assess your organization's strengths and weaknesses in the above areas. A library of organizational effectiveness resources is also available to assist you in strengthening areas of weakness. A generic definition of organizational effectiveness or a set of criteria, rules, or attributes that would define an effective organization. The definition should be universal and apply equally to health care, not-for-profit, and for-profit environments. This is appropriate as profit, financial control, or effective budgeting and cash-flow management ensure the long-term survival of any organization. Yet other researchers argue that pursuing a single objective, such as profit or creation of shareholder wealth. Effectiveness is an organizational dynamic that haunts managers. The concept of effectiveness is hidden within the cloak of more popularized notions. Popular theories of Total Quality Management (TQM), Continuous Quality Improvement (CQI), and organizational efficiency are seen as ways to effectiveness. This model uses organizational survival and maximizing return as key variables of effectiveness along with self-regulation, which is responsible for orchestrating a balance between eight other minor variables including internal-external boundary permeability, sensitivity to status and change, contribution to constituents, transformation, promoting advantageous transactions, flexibility, adaptability, and efficiency.

The other model also choose Four selected indicators of organizational effectiveness including management experience, organizational structure, and political impact, board of directors' involvement, volunteer involvement, and internal communications.

The final academic model was used to compare for-profit and non-profit organizational effectiveness and is termed the competing value framework. This model used four quadrants representing

1. Human relations,
2. Open systems,
3. Rational goals and
4. Internal process.

1. The *human relations* side stressed participation, discussion, and openness as ways to improve morale and achieve commitment.
2. The *open system* side relates insight, innovation, and adaptation as a path toward external recognition, support, acquisition, and growth.
3. Finally, the *internal process* side sees internal processes as measurement, documentation, and information management as methods to achieve stability, control, and continuity.
4. The *rational goal* side seeks profit and productivity through direction and goals.

This model has been tested and validated more than the other three models in academic literature. It seems organizational effectiveness is about doing everything you know to do and doing it well. The universals of management—planning, organizing, leading, direction, and controlling have not changed. They are still important and executing them well remains challenging. Organizational effectiveness relates to the capacity of an organization to sustain the people, strategies, learning, infrastructure and resources it needs to continue to achieve its mission. It is a long-term outcome that some capacity building strategies may affect, while others may not (and this is acceptable in the continuum of management support service strategies needed to build capacity). There are many definitions and characterizations of effectiveness, taking into consideration elements such as organizational structure, culture, leadership, governance, strategy, human resources, etc. The various frameworks for measuring organizational effectiveness can be helpful in defining indicators for the success of capacity-building initiatives. Achieving organizational effectiveness is a constant and continuous struggle for each and every organization. Many efforts that involved a great amount of money are invested towards attaining this ultimate aim.

The HR function and its activities are being examined in microscopic detail in many large organizations. Human resource processes, especially those involving the collection and dissemination of information, are being computerized and automated, potentially eliminating routine clerical activities. HR information and knowledge is being linked and integrated with other information systems, breaking down departmental barriers. As HR processes become more easily measurable, the need for justification and the means to do so become more obvious. Concepts such as the high performance organization and knowledge management offer HR specialists the chance to push HRM to the fore. HR processes and their outcomes are central to these concepts and the introduction of technology allows more exact methods of determining whether or not human resource initiatives do affect the 'bottom line' and shareholder value.

The HRM function and HRD profession have undergone tremendous change over the past 20–30 years. Many years ago, large organizations looked to the "Personnel Department," mostly to manage the paperwork around hiring and paying people. More recently, organizations consider the "HR Department" as playing a major role in staffing, training and helping to manage people so that people and the organization are performing at maximum capability in a highly fulfilling manner. Note that some people distinguish a difference between HRM (a major management activity) and HRD (Human Resource Development, a profession). Those people might include HRM in HRD, explaining that HRD includes the broader range of activities to develop personnel inside of organizations, including, *e.g.,* career development, training, organization development, etc. The functions includes a variety of activities, and key among them is deciding what staffing needs you have and whether to use independent contractors or hire employees to fill these needs, recruiting and training the best employees, ensuring they are high performers, dealing with performance issues, and ensuring your personnel and management practices conform to various regulations. Activities also include managing your approach to employee benefits and compensation, employee records and personnel policies. Hence, HRD can become very important.

The HRD can play effective role in

- Optimizing the use of employees for the growth of organization.
- Enabling employees to grow with the organization.
- Helping in the congruence of individual aspirations and organizational expectations.

- Promoting collaborations and team spirit by establishing a climate of trust, openness and interdependence.
- Maximizing the effectiveness of the employees and organization.
- Maximizing the managerial effectiveness by having an involved committed and highly motivated team of managers.
- Building and acquiring the skills necessary to meet existing and long-term organizational needs.
- Providing a favourable work environment and consciously fostering an open, largely participative management style based on trust and cooperation.
- Achieving good employer-employee relations through regards for basic human values.
- Quality employees with a passion for their work and a level of satisfaction that leads to low turnover.
- Communication strategy with consistent and energizing messages.
- Clear practices, policies, and decisions.
- An environment accepting of change and innovation for new product development.
- Interdepartmental communication.
- Effective management of human resources—increased information sharing, extensive training, financial and non-financial rewards, appraisal and extensive feedback.
- Strategic choices about which markets to pursue and which opportunities to ignore but with flexibility to pursue experimentation.
- An ability to anticipate competitor reactions to strategic responses as well as anticipate employee responses.
- A strategy linked to organizational goals and reviews.
- All organizational levels participating in communicating core messages and communication flowing from top to bottom and bottom to top.
- Good external communication—from new releases, fact sheets, annual reports, supervision and leadership.
- Opportunities for employee advancement and growth.
- An emphasis on planning, training, and support.
- Adaptive organizational forms and structures.
- High levels of organizational trust—which minimize the potential for destructive conflict, unnecessary bureaucratic control, administrative expenditures, and expensive overhead.
- Consistency and congruency between words and actions.
- Effective Boards of Directors.
- Using information technology effectively.
- Integrating employees from different organizational units; particularly important in multinational organizations.
- An emphasis on ethics, the environment, and sustainability.
- Customer focus and ability to optimize customer value.
- Choosing the right partners and building trusting, durable relationships.
- Empowerment and delegation of real decision-making authority to those closest to the customers.
- Lean production and an emphasis on efficiency and efficient processes.
- Strong culture and mission.

Organizational Effectiveness and Essentials of Human Resource Development

The complexity and competitiveness of today's business environment requires that companies continuously raise the bar on their effectiveness. Top performance increasingly demands excellence in all areas, including leadership, productivity, and adaptation to change, process improvement, and capability enhancement (knowledge, skills, abilities, and competencies). It is no doubt, that improve Organizational Effectiveness (OE) is only way to lead business success. But how to improve OE and what are key factors affect OE is still no certain answer. According to research, there are some directions to improve organizational effectiveness. Typical organizational effectiveness projects include:

Process mapping and measurement; Process improvement; Expert facilitation of internal interventions; Productivity improvement; Monitoring and evaluation; Measuring and assessing climate and culture; Improving communication processes; Team building and team effectiveness improvement; cohering management teams and rationalizing the complexities of organizational structure. In those processes where manual intervention is necessary, the company's employees have a very important bearing on the output. The operators must be very flexible in their problem solving behaviour and very ingenious in using all sorts of available knowledge when applicable and their diagnostic performance increases with experience. Since multiple employees typically handle processes, the personnel and coordination dimensions refer to the training and management that are necessary for the process to achieve its desired result. Thus it includes issues such as: What are the process expertise requirements? How many individuals are required? How often should they meet? What criteria should be used to evaluate them? How should they be trained? For how long should employees be trained? How should they be co-coordinated? What development programs have been carried out and what are the results of these programs? Those questions are the key direction for this study.

10.2 PRINCIPLES OF SUCCESSFUL ORGANIZATION

According to Morley (1990), he has developed some principles of organization in doing total development work: Select cohesive teams, based on sentiments of mutual liking and respect for each other's expertise. Organize controlled convergence to solutions that everyone understands and everyone accepts. Organize vigilant information processing and encourage actively open-minded thinking. Avoid the facile, premature consensus. Maintain the best balance between individual and group work. Let individuals do the things that individuals do best for example, the initial generation of new concepts. The organization and leadership on the multifunctional product development team help to develop the successful practice of Morley's 10 principles. If these and the principles are practiced, then any of the three product-focused modes can be successful-heavyweight product manager or project execution team. Organized Effectiveness and Leadership Enterprises are a maze of explicit and implicit structures that make up organization culture. Good performance and organizational effectiveness can only occur when employees know the culture of their workplace. Both organizational effectiveness and leadership skills are required. Organizational effectiveness skills include the behaviours, attitudes and knowledge an employee needs to achieve success on the job both as an individual and as a member of an enterprise. Each employee uses these skills to adapt to organizational expectations, rules and regulations including expected job performance levels. They provide guidelines for establishing appropriate and effective interrelationships.

Organizational effectiveness skills are the building blocks for leadership. Without them, leadership can be misplaced or even be counter productive. At its most elementary level, leadership means that a person can influence others to act in a certain way. The employee may need at times to influence his work group and to provide a vision of what the organization as a whole or the specific task at hand requires. Leadership skills are necessary at every level of the enterprise from chief executive to the line worker. Organization and other education and training institutions will need to incorporate the teaching of these basic workplace skills in their curriculum to ensure that future labour market entrants are properly equipped for the world of work. Likewise enterprises need to teach these skills to their existing employees. Enterprises in the industrialized countries, particularly the larger ones, are undertaking such training. This research study of ten managers and twenty workers showed that they have expanded the scope and mission of training from merely upgrading the technical skills of their professional managers to ensuring that all their employees as well as key customers and suppliers understand the company's quality vision and develop the skills and competencies needed for success.

Knowledge management and Life long learning

Education and training are the other important factor for organizational effectiveness. In fact, training must be tied to the enterprise's strategic business requirements and maintain the organization's core competencies in every field at every level. Provide all levels of employees with opportunities for life-long learning will promote organizational effectiveness directly. Continuous training and retraining are provided to all levels of employees. Learning becomes a habitual activity instead of an occasional event. Require workers to be accountable for learning new skills. These companies have developed an individual training and development plan for each employee as a way to help employees be accountable for learning new skills. These plans are reviewed regularly to ensure responsiveness to the changing needs of the workplace and the marketplace as well as appropriateness of the type and the timing of the training. Extend training beyond internal employees to key members of the customer/supply chain. Training by these companies is extended throughout the customer and supply chains. They realized it is no longer enough to have their own well-trained employees. The success of the company depends on working with a core group of suppliers and customers to achieve its quality vision in the marketplace. Thus customers are not just taught how to use the company's products or services but also how to run their business successfully. They even reach out to schools to cultivate a commitment to quality and to promote thereby a highly qualified student force. Recruit well so that training can have the greatest impact on productivity. Many skills required of workers assume they also have a broad set of human traits such as persistence and initiative. Training must be considered only as one aspect of a process, which also includes recruiting employees with the appropriate attitudes and qualities.

Knowledge Management

Rapid changes in business and technology are forcing organizations to learn at an unprecedented rate. Many are realizing that unless knowledge collection and transfer occurs at an equally rapid rate, their competitiveness is affected, leading them to focus more intently on their knowledge assets. Though the full specification of the set of these assets is evolving, there seems to be a consensus that they include the organization's employees, structure, culture and processes. Of these, the Knowledge Management (KM) literature has tended to emphasize employee knowledge, particularly tacit knowledge, on the grounds that this is where the interesting knowledge resides. While this viewpoint is probably valid and useful, process knowledge is also an essential part of organizational knowledge and has tremendous significance from a knowledge management perspective. To begin with, organizations have a sizeable intellectual investment in the form of formalizations of processes. Descriptions of manufacturing processes, for instance, include the raw material and equipment used, the appropriate environmental conditions to be realized, the treatment times etc. These descriptions are essential to training employees, establishing standards and communicating best practices within the organization. But they are by no means static.

Conclusion

According to the analysis of the research data, there are seven factors effecting organizational effectiveness: 1. Personal characteristics, 2. Leadership styles, 3. Organizational culture, 4. Working environment, 5. Model of organizational operation, 6. Flexibility, 7. Organizational commitment. From the interview with managers, some suggestions for organizational improvement are indicated following:

1. **Vocational Education and Training:** Workers would need some vocational education and training to perform well in the workplaces of the future.
2. **Knowing How to Learn:** Learning is a part of working life with competitive pressures and changing technology. Furthermore the availability, amount and complexity of information has increased. Employers see the skill of knowing how to learn as the key to retraining efforts and continuing education. Most importantly the skill enables more efficient application of new knowledge to work thus greatly assisting the enterprise to meet its strategic goals and competitive challenges.
3. **Reading, Writing and Computation:** For traditional jobs working often involves going through a regularized process or repetitive interaction with machines. Illiteracy and innumeracy could be hidden or ignored. But today's workplace involves increasingly interaction with sophisticated computerized equipment, which requires good reading and computation skills. Higher mathematical skills are required with the introduction of approaches like statistical process controls. Writing is frequently the first step in communicating with customers, documenting competitive transactions or successfully moving new ideas into the workplace. Workers spend daily an average of one and one-half to two hours reading forms, charts, graphs, manuals, computer terminals etc. Writing remains the primary form of communicating policies, procedures and concepts. Computation is used daily to conduct inventories, report on production levels, measure machine parts or specifications etc. Deficiencies in these skills will result in productivity decline, increased accident rates and costly production errors. It will also be difficult to effect necessary job retraining. An employer's ability to meet strategic goals and to be competitive will be impaired.
4. **Communication is central to the smooth operation of an enterprise:** These skills are at the heart of winning and keeping customers. Pitching innovation, contributing to quality circles, resolving conflicts and providing meaningful feedback all hinge on effective communication skills. Workers spend most of their day in some form of communication. Success on the job is linked to good communication skills. In fact recent studies have shown that only job knowledge ranks above communication skills as a factor for workplace success. Business leaders estimate that deficiencies in these skills cost employers millions each year in lost productivity and errors.
5. **Adaptability Skills: Solving Problems and Thinking Creatively:** Enterprises are increasingly placing a premium on a worker who is both a problem solver and a creative thinker. As decision-making is decentralized to the point of actual production or service delivery, a company's competitive position may hinge on its workers' ability to solve problems quickly. Competitive advantage is frequently tied to a company's capacity to innovate quickly. This capacity rests in large part on the skills that employees have to free themselves from linear thinking in order to make the creative leap. Successful problem solving involves firstly skill in individual problem solving; secondly skill in-group problem solving and thirdly practical ability in combining individual and group skills. Cognitive skills, group interaction skills and

problem-processing skills are crucial to successful problem solving. Creative thinking is the ability to use different modes of thought, to come up with something new, to visualize, foresee or form new combinations of ideas to fulfill a need. In the workplace creative thinking is generally manifested as creative problem solving or creative innovation. Often a group activity, creative problem solving is characterized by effective teamwork, the examination of problems in a new way and the invention of new solutions to existing problems. On the other hand creative innovation is either an individual or group activity. It is the development of new activities that expand markets and improve such elements as productivity. An enterprise's ability to achieve its strategic objectives often depends on the problem solving and creative thinking skills of its workforce. Unresolved problems create dysfunctional relationships in the workplace, which can become impediments to dealing with strategic change in an open-ended and creative way. Creative solutions help the enterprise to move towards its strategic goals.

6. **Developmental Skills: Managing Personal and Professional-Growth:** Personal management skills are the building blocks for good morale, a focused work life and even organizational productivity. A strong foundation of skills self-esteem, motivation, goal setting and employability/career development influences the behaviour, attitudes and desires of workers and ultimately contributes to an enterprises' ability to carry out its mission and strategies. Today workers are increasingly called upon to make decisions at the point of production or at the point of sale and to display good interpersonal skills when they work in teams or with customers. A positive sense of self worth is important to success in these areas. For an employer to succeed in the market place, employees must be motivated. They must possess the ability to set and meet reasonable goals. Individual employee's lack of motivation or goal setting skills can produce repeated errors, absenteeism and quality problems or it can hinder change. Group Effectiveness, Interpersonal Skills, Teamwork and Negotiation Skills are the developmental skills. At work an employee constantly interacts with other people to perform work roles effectively requires good interpersonal, teamwork and negotiation skills. Interpersonal skills include the ability to judge and balance appropriate behaviour, cope with undesirable behaviour in others, absorb stress, deal with ambiguity, listen, inspire confidence in others, structure social interaction, share responsibility and interact easily with others. These skills are essential to successful negotiation of conflicts, which are a fact of work life. Negotiating skills include the ability to separate people from the problem, to focus on interests not positions, to work out compromises for mutual gain, to use objective criteria and an understanding of the approach demanded by the circumstance. Interpersonal and negotiation skills are the cornerstone of successful teamwork. Teams, which are increasingly being used, are organized in the workplace so that appropriate talents and skills can be pooled to accomplish vital tasks and goals. This pooling of resources requires team members to have an array of skills that individual or routine jobs do not demand. Quality teamwork results when team members know how to recognize and cope with the various and unique personalities and when each has a sense of the cultures and approaches that other team members represent. Team members also need an understanding of group dynamics which evolve and change as the team approaches its goals. Finally team members must be aware of the technical skills of fellow members and how these skills can be applied.
7. **Consider new employee orientation as a strategic process:** Many of the companies cover not just the policies and procedures for entry and exiting but also the vision, values and 'big picture' of the company in orientation for their new employees. Considered a gradual and strategic process than a one time event, the orientation is designed to help ensure all new

employees develop a firm foundation in the company's values, culture, traditions and philosophy of customer service as well as bond with the company and its quality vision.

8. **Design a training curriculum to stress corporate citizenship, contextual Framework and core competencies:** The purpose of training in corporate citizenship is to have workers who are knowledgeable about the history, culture, traditions and values of the company. The aim is to engender a strong feeling of belonging to the company. Training in contextual framework on the other hand is to provide a well-informed understanding of the company's 'big picture' and its products and services in the context of what competitors are offering and the best practices in the industry.

   The traditional classroom format is being supplemented by innovative techniques of learning in these companies. Experiential learning and company specific case studies in which the trainee, not the instructor takes the principal role are two examples of such techniques. Sustain the message of training with a system of employee recognition. Once an employee is trained to solve problems and deliver the company's vision, the next critical step pursued by a number of companies is to reinforce training through a systematic approach to recognition. When recognition is given consistently and regularly, the need for training can be reinforced throughout the enterprise. A company-wide system of recognition of individual and team accomplishments on the spot, monthly, quarterly and yearly supplements peer recognition of each other's achievement.

9. **Sharing employee success throughout the company:** Employees who have succeeded in redefining and enhancing their jobs must be encouraged to share their successes with other employees. Such sharing will improve the work of others. Simply publicizing them through newsletters and magazines is not enough. Employers must actively relate and cooperate in an attempt to learn from one another. Every organization is unique. The suggestions above may not fit for any organization. In other word, to improve organization effectiveness, manager must customize all of possible method to meet the specific requirements of the organization and situation. Every one who wants to promote organizational effectiveness must invest extra time to learn their business, to understand the need to align people's skills with business goals in an ever more competitive market. The best business strategy requires the best people strategy. The most important principle is: People drive an Organization's success.

The process of strategic HRD aligning is an important predictor for HRD effectiveness. The (perceived) HRD effectiveness is even extra positive, as the mean company score on the quality of HRD aligning is higher. The findings also indicate that no differences in perceived HRD effectiveness were observed for some contextual factors (*e.g.*, size and structure of the company, structure of the HRD function, transfer and evaluation conditions). On the other hand, the findings reveal some factors enhancing or impeding HRD effectiveness, because positive or negative correlation was found between contextual factors such as the quality of the HRD programme, HRD climate, the form the HRD programme takes, position of the HRD department, and perceived HRD effectiveness.

In summary, there are numerous benefits that accompany the integration of the HRD function with the organization's mission and strategic goals. These include:

- Optimum uses of the HRD function as a tool to increase organizational productivity.
- A sound rationale for the organization to invest in HRD programs and allocate resources according to priority needs.
- Visibility for how HRD supports other HR functions as well as other agency systems.

- Increased involvement of supervisors, line management, and executives in the training and development of their workforce.
- Orderly system of planning for current and future workforce needs.
- Mission-related standards and guidelines against which HRD activities can be evaluated.
- Increasingly responsive, results-driven, customer-driven HRD activities.
- Containment of costs as human resource services become inextricably linked to the business requirements of the agency.

Human resources, in the context of strategic HRD, are seen as a vital factor in business planning and survival. This means moving HRD from a series of fragmented activities to a situation where training and development is systematically linked to the agency master plan and overall tactical objectives.

To be successful in the current rapidly-changing world, we need to maximize the productivity of all of our resources–physical, financial, information, and human. How are we doing?

- **Physical resources:** We've made major investments in updating our physical equipment, so we can compete with state-of the-art production tools and facilities.
- **Financial resources:** Sure, we're really capital intensive. But that's the nature of our production businesses. The money will follow our ideas, our successes, and our productivity.
- **Information and knowledge resources:** That's one of our success stories. The paper industry is more open and cooperative than other manufacturing industries. But we have our work cut out for us—to continue attracting capital in competition with other industries, we need to be as good as they are in accessing the new world of information. It's time to join the Internet. But that's another story for another time.
- **Human resources:** This is the leverage point! Here's where we can make significant differences in our lives, our careers, and our organizations.

And our organizations and jobs will never be the same. Changes are based on the global economy, on changing technology, on our changing work force, on cultural and demographic changes, and on the changing nature of work itself. The changes are different this time. They are permanent, and will permanently affect the way our work and our lives are structured.

We need to learn new skills and develop new abilities, to respond to these changes in our lives, our careers, and our organizations. We can deal with these constructively, using change for our competitive advantage and as opportunities for personal and organizational growth, or we can be overwhelmed by them. Who is affected by change–you are! With all the downsizing, outsourcing and team building, responsibility and accountability are being downloaded to individuals. So everyone is now a manager. Everyone will need to acquire and/or increase their skills, knowledge and abilities to perform their jobs (and now, to perform other people's jobs too!). The goal of HRD is to improve the performance of our organizations by maximizing the efficiency and performance of our people. We are going to develop our knowledge and skills, our actions and standards, our motivation incentives, attitudes and work environment. HRD can give you the tools you need to manage and operate your organizations. Everything—production, management, marketing, sales, research and development, you-name-it—everything may be more productive, if your people are sufficiently motivated, trained, informed, managed, utilized and empowered, In future articles in this series, we're going to tell you how to do it. Stay tuned.

REFERENCES

1. Rao, T.V, *The HRD Missionary, Oxford and IBH*, New Delhi, 1990, p. 8. Megginson, C Leon, "*Personnel and Human Resources Administration*", 1977, p. 4.
2. Dayal, Eshawr, HRD in Practice: "*Some experience and Reflection*", 1977, p. 4.
3. Stout, D., "*Performance Analysis for Training*", Niagara Paper Company, Niagara, WI, 1995.
4. Gilbert, T., "*Performance Engineering*", *in What Works at Work: Lessons from the Masters,* Lakewood Books, Minneapolis, 1988, p. 20.
5. Brinkerhoff, R.O., *Achieving Results from Training*, Jossey-Bass Inc., San Francisco, 1987, pp. 40–47.
6. Brinkerhoff, R.O., *Achieving Results from Training*, Jossey-Bass Inc., San Francisco, 1987, p. 39.
7. Zemke, R., and Gunkler, J., "*Using Small Group Techniques for Needs Assessment, Data Gathering, and other Heinous Acts*", Seminar notes, American Society for Training and Development Southern Minnesota Chapter, Minneapolis, July 9, 1985.
8. Margolis, F.H., and Bell, C.R., *Understanding Training: Perspectives and Practices*, University Associates, San Diego, 1989, pp. 13–15.
9. Steadham, S.V., "*Learning to Select a Needs Assessment Strategy*", Training and Development Journal 30, Jan. 1980, American Society for Training and Development, pp. 56–61.
10. Benjamin Schneider and rover A. Snyder," *Some relationships between Job Satisfaction and Organizational Climate*, Journal of Applied Psychology, 60, No. 3, 1975, p. 318.
11. Argyris, C., and Schön, D. (1978), *Organisational learning: A theory of action perspective,* Reading, Mass: Addison Wesley.
12. Argyris, C. and Schön, D. (1996), *Organisational learning II: Theory, method,* leading, Mass: Addison Wesley.
13. Bohm, D., Factor, D. and Garrett, P. (1991), *'Dialogue-a proposal'*, *the informal education archives.*
14. Bolman, L.G. and Deal, T.E. (1997), *Reframing Organizations. Artistry, choice and leadership* 2e, San Francisco: Jossey-Bass. 450 pages.
15. Castells, M. (2001), '*Information technology and global capitalism*' in W. Hutton and A. Giddens (eds.) *On the Edge. Living with global capitalism*, London: Vintage.
16. Cohen, D. and Prusak, L. (2001), *In Good Company. How social capital makes organizations work*, Boston: Harvard Business School Press.
17. Dixon, N. (1994), *The organizational learning cycle. How we can learn collectively*, London: McGraw-Hill.
18. Easterby-Smith, M. and Araujo, L. '*Current debates and opportunities*' in M. Easterby-Smith, L. Araujo and J. Burgoyne (eds.) *Organizational Learning and the Learning Organization*, London: Sage.
19. Gradous, Deane B. (1989), *Systems theory applied to human resource development.* Theory-to-Practice Monograph. Alexandria VA, ASTD 191 p.
20. McLagan, Pat (1996), *Great ideas revisited. Training and development*, January 1996, pp. 60–65.
21. Nadler, L. and Z. Nadler (1989), *Developing human resources: Concepts and model*. 3rd ed. San Francisco, Jossey-Bass p. 328.

11

CHAPTER

TRAINING AND DEVELOPMENT

11.1 INTRODUCTION

Training refers to the teaching, learning activities carried on for the primary purpose of helping members of an organization to acquire and reply the knowledge, skills, and abilities and attitudes needed by that organization. It is the act of increasing the knowledge and skill of an employee for doing a particular job.

Employee training equips the employees with adequate skills and knowledge to contribute to the organization's efficiency and cope with the changes in the environment. There should be a continuous re-assessment of the managerial caliber and skills to cope with environmental changes. Technological changes make the skills obsolete, which necessitates training activities. As a brief review of terms, training involves an expert working with learners to transfer to them certain areas of knowledge or skills to improve in their current jobs. Development is a broad, ongoing multi-faceted set of activities (training activities among them) to bring someone or an organization up to another threshold of performance, often to perform some job or new role in the future.

Many organizations spend time and money on training efforts to teach new skills to employees who are using a small fraction of the skill developed in the past training. Efforts are made to develop employees and allowing those who want become more involved [which are most of them] usually will have much higher returns. An additional benefit is, they are then more valued employees whose change in attitude is reflected in their work.

Teaching people how to use relatively simple problems solving tools and techniques is the easy part of employee development. Usually after just a little training and experience with one or two work related problems the basic tools are mastered well enough for most to start using them on their own. Even high motivated employees need the necessary tools to do a good job. When placed in teams they are prepared to make use of the many specifics that only they know to improve products and work processes. Employee training and development initiatives can transform organizations with providing extra skills to your employees do not only increase safety and productivity but training leads to higher job satisfaction, which shows up in better corporate performance. Valuable training also includes situational training that provides personnel the skill sets that allow them to make timely, knowledgeable decisions that benefit both the customer and the company.

A positive environment for learning is always critical for success, whether it is the environment of a classroom or the environment of your organization. The learning environment provided by an organization is a function of the organizational culture. Organizational culture means the values, attitudes and beliefs reflected in the mission and goals, and practices of the organization.

Benefits from Employee Training and Development

Employee training and development initiatives can transform organizations with providing extra skills to your employees to not only increase safety and productivity but training leads to higher job satisfaction, which shows up in better corporate performance. Valuable training also includes situational training that provides personnel the skill sets that allow them to make timely, knowledgeable decisions that benefit both the customer and the company.

You can have the greatest business model in the world and the best systems, but if your people can't handle the growth, you're still toast. If your company isn't investing in training, think about all the companies you admire as models for doing business right. You'll not only find that they've got a good training program, but training is a part of their culture. If you ask them why they train, they probably would look at you like you were from Mars, because it's like asking them why they breathe. If you want to breathe some life into your operation, start by investing in your people.

Many companies provide some sort of introductory training or orientation for most of their new employees. It may take the form of an older employee assigned to show the new employee "the ropes." Or it may be left to the HR department or the individual's new supervisor to show them where the coffee pot is and how to apply for time off. Many organizations, especially in government and academia, have created new employee training that is designed, exclusively or primarily, to provide mandated safety familiarization. Yet some companies in highly competitive industries recognize the value in New Employee Orientation (NEO) that goes much farther. They require several weeks or even months of training to familiarize every new employee with the company, its products, its culture and policies, even its competition. The technology in the workplace is changing very rapidly and companies that can't keep up will drop out of competition. To survive and excel in the productivity and efficiency the training and development is seems to be inevitable.

There are numerous reasons for supervisors to conduct training among employees. These reasons include:

- Increased job satisfaction and morale among employees.
- Increased employee motivation.
- Increased efficiencies in processes, resulting in financial gain.
- Increased capacity to adopt new technologies and methods.
- Increased innovation in strategies and products.
- Reduced employee turnover.
- Enhanced company image, *e.g.,* conducting ethics training (not a good reason for ethics training!).

Reasons for emphasizing the growth and development of personnel include:

- Creating a pool of readily available and adequate replacements for personnel who may leave or move up in the organization.
- Enhancing the company's ability to adopt and use advances in technology because of a sufficiently knowledgeable staff.
- Building a more efficient, effective and highly motivated team, which enhances the company's competitive position and improves employee morale.
- Ensuring adequate human resources for expansion into new programs.

Research has shown specific benefits that a small business receives from training and developing its workers, including:

- Increased productivity.
- Reduced employee turnover.
- Increased efficiency resulting in financial gains.
- Decreased need for supervision.

Employees frequently develop a greater sense of self-worth, dignity and well-being as they become more valuable to the firm and to society. Generally they will receive a greater share of the material gains that result from their increased productivity. These factors give them a sense of satisfaction through the achievement of personal and company goals.

The pace of change has an impact on workplace learning. If you think of your current position you most likely have had to increase your competence in change management, fund raising, diversity management, and so on. In other words, you have had to consciously develop as an employee. "[Change] also put the spotlight on training and education as a means of equipping workers with the tools they need to adapt to changing skill requirements, organizational change and increasing complexity in the external environment."

In addition, employee training and development are part of good management practices and good risk management strategies. The following issues and changes in an organization many indicate the need for employee training and development:

- Employee's request
- Employee survey results
- Evaluation deficiencies
- Individual development plan
- Law and regulation changes
- Need to develop new leaders
- New employee
- New equipment
- New manager
- New program
- New technology
- Reassignment
- Safety issues

At the same time as the need for employee training and development is increasing, it can be argued that the time and money available in organizations for traditional forms of learning such as formal training courses has decreased. To meet this gap between the need for training and its accessibility, we've identified a variety of inexpensive methods for employee development can offer longer leaves than the law requires. Or, your policy can stipulate that employees will be paid while they are on leave have been identified. By using these methods in a deliberate and thoughtful way, performance of your employees and your organization can be improved.

This benefit highlights five major benefits of employee training. Let's take a look:

1. **Impact on bottom line:** Successful employee training delivers improvements in employee performance which, in turn, creates a better performing business and an improved bottom line.
2. **Staff retention:** Want to spend more training recruiting staff? Training increases staff retention which will save you money. Instead of paying recruitment fees, re-investing in training, loss of management time why not treat your people as your number one asset? Invest in their development and they will receive a return your investment many times over.
3. **Improved quality and productivity:** Training that meets both staff and employer needs can increase the quality and flexibility of a business's services by fostering:
   - Accuracy and efficiency.
   - Good work safety practices.
   - Great customer service.
4. **The flow-on effect:** The benefits of training in one area can flow through to all levels of an organization. Over time, training will boost the bottom line and reduce costs by decreasing:
   - Wasted time and materials.
   - Maintenance costs of machinery and equipment.
   - Workplace accidents, leading to lower insurance premiums.
   - Recruitment costs through the internal promotion of skilled staff.
   - Absenteeism.

   The benefit of this culture is a happy, innovative and successful workforce. A positive culture only comes through a respect for and an investment in your people. Start cultivating a progressive culture within your business today through employee training programmes and other forms of people investment.
5. **Remaining competitive:** Businesses must continually change their work practices and infrastructure to stay competitive in a global market. Technology, previously the main driver of competitive advantage, is progressively taking a back seat to people. As economies become progressively service orientated, it is the development of people that is providing successful businesses with long-term sustainable success. Training staff to manage the implementation of business strategies, improvements to procedures and customer service policies can also act as a benchmark for future recruitment and quality assurance practices. As well as impacting on business profit margins, training can improve:
   - Staff morale and satisfaction.
   - 'Soft skills' such as inter-staff communication and leadership.
   - Time management.
   - Customer satisfaction.

So there we are. Start thinking now about how investing in the skills of your people can benefit your business to make more money, save money or save time. Training programs should align with organizational values, goals, and objectives in order to be successful. Supervisors develop an effective training program by assessing training needs and designing training programs to meet those needs. If a gap is found in what is needed and what employees can do, training fills in the gap.

Definition of Training and Development

Training is an organized activity for increasing the knowledge and skills of the people for a definite purpose. It involves systematic procedures for transferring technical know how to the employees so as to increase their knowledge and skills for doing specific jobs with proficiency. In other words, the trainees acquire technical knowledge, skills and problem solving ability by undergoing the training programme.

According to Edwin B. Flippo, "Training is the act of increasing the knowledge and skills of an employee for doing a particular job". Training involves the department of skills that are usually necessary to perform a specific job. Its purpose to achieve a change in the behaviour of those trained and to enable them to do their jobs better. Training makes newly appointed workers fully productive in the minimum time. Training is equally necessary for the old employees whenever new machines and equipment are introduced and/or there is a change in the techniques of doing thinks. In fact, training is a continuous process. It does not stop any where. The managers are continuously engaged in training their subordinates. They should ensure that any training programme should attempt to bring about the positive change in the (*i*) Knowledge, (*ii*) Skills and (*iii*) Attitudes of the workers. "The purpose of training is to bring about the improvement in the performance of work. It includes the learning of such techniques as are required for the better performance of definite tasks".

McFarlane, defines the several concepts used in the development of human resources. Although training and education are closely related, theses concepts differ in crucial ways. While the "training" refers to imparting specific skills of specific objectives, the term "education" involves the development of the whole individual socially, intellectually and physically. Accordingly, training forms only a part of the entire educational process. Moreover, education is more a kin to the concepts of growth and development than training. The term "development" can be defined as the nature and direction of change taking place among personnel though educational and training processes. The relative amount of training and education changes with the nature of task and the responsibility in the organizational settings. As one goes upward in the organization, the amount of training usually declines and the amount of education enhances. Explicitly, non-managerial personnel require more job and trade related skills than managerial personnel demanding the generalized and conceptual skills and human relations insights. Accordingly, the difference in employee training and management development. So, training is related to non managerial workers, while the development is refers to managerial. The training is task oriented, where as development is more conceptual and career centered. As, development is applies to managerial which accomplish not merely skills in their present jobs but also helps to develop the competencies for prospective assignments of higher responsibilities.

However, Dunn and Stephens, do not limit the term "development" to the managerial personnel only. Training refers to the organizational efforts to improve an individual's ability to perform a job or organizational role, whereas development refers to the organization's efforts (and individual's own efforts) to enhance an individual's abilities to advance in his organization to perform additional duties. The training is always job oriented but the development is job related (broader in scope) this is implied that the management development is purporting to prepare managers for higher level positions. It enhances general knowledge related to a job as well as the ability to adopt to change. Thus training is narrow in scope and largely relates to the acquisition of skills, while development is a broader scope.

Fig. 11.1 Training Vs. Development

Training	*Development*
1. Training means learning skills and knowledge for doing a particular job. It increases job skill.	1. Development means the growth of an employee in all respects. It shapes attitudes.
2. The term "Training" is generally used to denote imparting specific skills among operative workers and employees.	2. The term "development" is associated with the over all growth of the executives.
3. Training is concerned with maintaining and improving current job performances. Thus, it has a short-term perspective.	3. Executive development seeks to develop competencies and skills for future performances. Thus, it has a long-term perspectives.
4. Training is job centered in nature.	4. Development is career centered in nature.
5. The role of trainer or supervisor is very important in training.	5. All development is "self-development". The executive has to be internally motivated for self-development.

Human Resource Development is major HRM function that consists not only of training and development but also individual career planning and development activities, organizational development and performance appraisal, an activity that emphasize training and development needs. Training and development is the heart of a continuous effort designed to improve the employee competency and organizational performance. Some managers use this term interchangeably. It prepares employees to keep pace with the organization's it changes and grows. Training and development activities have the potential to align a firm's employees with its corporate strategies.

In virtually every market, customers are now demanding higher quality, lower costs and faster cycle time. To meet these requirements, the firms must continually improve their over all performance. Rapid advances in technology and improved processes have been important factors in helping businesses meet these challenges. However, the most important competitive advantage for any firm is its workforce—one must remain competent through continuous training and development efforts. However, successful organizations realize that well structured and significant employees Training and Development correlate strongly with long-term success. Improved performances, the bottom-line purpose of training and development. This leads the organizations into matured learning organizations. It is important to note that formal training refers to training activities that is planned, structured and occurs when people are called away from their workstations to participate in it.

During the last one hundred years in the training development field, it has seen many rapidly changes and still continues experiencing them in its head long rush to keep up with the evolutionary process of adaptation to an ever changing world and its ever changing technology. With this comes the never-ending process of developing new learning process and methods to meet this changing technology. The word "Training" is an encompassing term, which is often used, in describing changes occurring in our behaviours because of an experience we have encountered at some point in our lives. We usually call it training. Webster dictionary defines "training" as, the act, process, or method of one that trains, the skill, knowledge, or experience acquired by one that trains, the state of being trained. And defines the word experience as a direct observation of or participation in events as a basis of knowledge, the fact or state of having been affected by or gained knowledge through direct observation or participation, practical knowledge, skill, or practice derived from direct observation of or participation in events or in a particular activity, the conscious events that make up an individual life and the events that make up the conscious past of a community or nation or mankind generally something personally encountered, undergone, or lived through the act or process of directly perceiving events or reality.

These encounter experiences we call often call learning are really changes in or modification of our behaviour because of an encounter of some kind in our lives, it caused us to change, modify or altar our behaviour because of these encounters, as a results we formed an image of these events storing them in our mind as an experience. The events or experiences which we store in our minds are from us seeing, feeling or hearing something or even thinking about something real or imaginary, whatever the event was, we will retain this as an experience or as a memory of that experience. This process of us experiencing and storing them as experiences in our memory banks is in essences how we learn. And because of all of this our behaviour has been changed and modified in some form, this is a constant never-ending process we all experience from the moment of birth to the day we die.

This acquisition of knowledge we humans receive from experiencing different events and encounters within our lives are often referred to as "learning behaviours" and have been the focus of studies for centuries trying to understand how we humans learn and acquire new knowledge about new things. And over those same centuries we have also seen the development of many different learning theories; some working and others have not. However, many of these fundamental learning theories used within the last century, have been either redefined and validated and categorized into different theories, such as, the Behaviourists, Cognitive, Constructist, Motivation, and Elaboration Theories, and many or a combination of them are currently in use today. Yes, there are more learning theories out there, but we're not going to go into them in any great depth because its well beyond the scope of things that we want to accomplish here today.

Many factors can and often do affect an individual ability to learn, but usually before any learning can really occur several things must be present. Maybe the foremost important factor in learning is the learners themselves and how receptive are they to learning. Yes. There is theory about that too, its called the "Conditions of Learning".

To plan and develop a successful training program and teach it effectively, an instructor needs to understand some of the basic in human learning behaviours to know what skills their students brings with them to use to learn with. The instructor who is knowledgeable about these learning behaviours can and often does apply this knowledge during the design phase of a training program and even during their interacting with learners during the actual training process itself. Most instructional designers are very knowledgeable when it comes to how we humans learn things and design their training programs around this information. They will use many different types of training models to develop training programs with this objective in mind realizing that no two individuals will learn the same way. A well-developed training program will the learners to use all or in combination any one of those skill set to learn the subject been taught.

One of the more generally used training model used in developing training programs which can achieve these objectives of reaching broad range of learners is a training model known as the "ADDIE" training system which consist of the following five element making up the ADDIE model:

- Assess
- Design
- Develop
- Implement
- Evaluate

We can use these five planning elements in the model when in the developmental and planning stages of a new training program to develop a very effective training program, and once all of the individual phases making up the model have been implemented. The model then closes the loop in the training developmental cycle by validating the effectives of the training program.

The evaluation and validation of any training process is a very important key element not to be overlooked or treated lightly in the development of any training development process. Why? Because it becomes the tool used to tell us if we reached our intended goals or objectives. The evaluation and validation data (testing results) will show us where and/or what is needs to be tweaked or changed in our training program to improve it. Training refers to the teaching, learning activities carried on for the primary purpose of helping members of an organization to acquire and reply the knowledge, skills, and abilities and attitudes needed by that the organization. It is the act of increasing the knowledge and skill of an employee for doing a particular job.

Employee training equips the employees with adequate skills and knowledge to contribute to the organization's efficiency and cope with the changes in the environment. There should be a continuous re-assessment of the managerial caliber and skills to cope with environmental changes. Technological changes make the skills obsolete, which necessitates training activities.

Typical Areas of Employee Training

1. **Communications:** The increasing diversity of today's workforce brings a wide variety of languages and customs.
2. **Computer skills:** Computer skills are becoming a necessity for conducting administrative and office tasks.
3. **Customer service:** Increased competition in today's global marketplace makes it critical that employees understand and meet the needs of customers.
4. **Diversity:** Diversity training usually includes explanation about how people have different perspectives and views, and includes techniques to value diversity.
5. **Ethics:** Today's society has increasing expectations about corporate social responsibility. Also, today's diverse workforce brings a wide variety of values and morals to the workplace.
6. **Human relations:** The increased stresses of today's workplace can include misunderstandings and conflict. Training can people to get along in the workplace.
7. **Quality initiatives:** Initiatives such as Total Quality Management, Quality Circles, Benchmarking, etc. require basic training about quality concepts, guidelines and standards for quality, etc.
8. **Safety:** Safety training is critical where working with heavy equipment, hazardous chemicals, repetitive activities, etc. but can also be useful with practical advice for avoiding assaults, etc.

9. **Sexual harassment:** Sexual harassment training usually includes careful description of the organization's policies about sexual harassment, especially about what are inappropriate behaviours.

Benefits of Training

You can have the greatest business model in the world and the best systems, but if your people can't handle the growth, you're still toast. If your company isn't investing in training, think about all the companies you admire as models for doing business right. You'll not only find that they've got a good training program, but training is a part of their culture. If you ask them why they train, they probably would look at you like you were from Mars, because it's like asking them why they breathe. If you want to breathe some life into your operation, start by investing in your people.

Employee training and development initiatives can transform organizations with providing extra skills to your employees do not only increase safety and productivity but training leads to higher job satisfaction, which shows up in better corporate performance. Valuable training also includes situational training that provides personnel the skill sets that allow them to make timely, knowledgeable decisions that benefit both the customer and the company. It may take the form of an older employee assigned to show the new employee "the ropes." Or it may be left to the HR department or the individual's new supervisor to show them where the coffee pot is and how to apply for time off.

There are numerous reasons for supervisors to conduct training among employees. These reasons include:

- Increased job satisfaction and morale among employees.
- Increased employee motivation.
- Increased efficiencies in processes, resulting in financial gain.
- Increased capacity to adopt new technologies and methods.
- Increased innovation in strategies and products.
- Reduced employee turnover.
- Enhanced company image, *e.g.,* conducting ethics training (not a good reason for ethics training!).
- Risk management, *e.g.,* training about sexual harassment, diversity training.

Training Needs Assessment

What, Why and How?

Are you charged with the task of having your employees trained but do not know where to start? Consider performing a training needs assessment first. You'll optimize the benefit to your employees while saving on the bottom line.

What is a training needs assessment?

A tool utilized to identify what educational courses or activities should be provided to employees to improve their work productivity.

Why conduct a training needs assessment?

- To pinpoint if training will make a difference in productivity and the bottom line.
- To decide what specific training each employee needs and what will improve their job performance.
- To differentiate between the need for training and organizational issues.

How is a training needs assessment performed?

There are several techniques that can be utilized individually or in combination with each other. More than one tool should be considered to get a better view of the big picture, however, which tools are used should be left up to company.

1. **Meet with management:** Since most supervisors are involved with the planning of projects and the future of the company, they know what will be needed. They should be able to communicate where their employee's current abilities lie and what is needed to get them to the next level for new projects on the horizon.
2. **Meet with employees:** Discuss what struggles they may be facing from day-to-day and what would make their job easier and more efficient. Remember to keep them focused on what they need rather than what they want.
3. **Conduct surveys:** Surveys are beneficial because many people can be polled in a short period of time. Additionally, surveys provide employees with the opportunity to confess a need on paper that they may be too embarrassed to admit needing in a face-to-face meeting. Surveys should take the form of a questionnaire and can include close-ended or open-ended questions, or a series of both. Close-ended questions require the respondent stay within certain perimeters set by the person who created the survey. Being that the answers are limited, tabulating the data is simple. Open-ended questions allow an employee to provide more feedback and introduce new ideas that may not have been considered initially, although tallying the results may be more difficult. A good option during the creation of a survey would be to include a combination of both close-ended and open-ended questions.
4. **Conduct focus groups:** Focus groups allow for small group interaction, allowing the assessor to uncover details about their target audience. Brainstorming is encouraged allowing for an exchange of new ideas and a revelation of what training may be needed. They should be at least ninety minutes long to initially break the ice and for participants to become comfortable enough to express their thoughts. Depending on time limits, focus groups can be held once or repeatedly.
5. **Review company goals and mission statement:** A brief review of the company's past and where they are headed for the future may reveal valuable information for training. A comparison should be made of what employees are currently doing and what will be expected of them as the company continues to grow and change.

Three things to consider

- Consider meeting with employees that are already successfully completing tasks. You may uncover useful techniques that can be taught during training to other employees.
- Keep surveys brief. More employees will be willing to complete them and tallying the results will be more manageable.
- Good hand-written notes should be taken during a focus group and consideration should be given to either audio taping or video taping the session allowing it to be reviewed later for any details initially missed.

Six Steps

Step 1: Sit down with a business partner to get their input on what they think their employees' needs are.

Step 2: Develop a survey to be passed out to employees. Include some questions using a Likert scale of 1 to 5 and some open-ended questions. For example, have you ever thought, "I could do this job faster and easier if I just…."

Step 3: Conduct a focus group.

Step 4: Hold a second meeting with the employer to review the data from the survey and the focus group.

Step 5: Develop a specific, customized training plan.

Step 6: Execute the training.

Identification of Training Needs

This training needs assessment works best in small to mid-sized organizations. It will give you a quick assessment of the training needs of an employee group. These training needs assessment helps find common training programs for a group of employees.

1. The facilitator gathers all employees who have the same job in a conference room with a white board or flip charts and markers.
2. Ask each employee to write down their ten most important training needs. Emphasize that the employees should write specific needs. Communication or team buildings are such broad training needs, as an example that you would need to do a second training needs assessment on each of these topics. How to give feedback to colleagues or how to resolve a conflict with a coworker are more specific training needs.
3. Then, ask each person to list their ten training needs. As they list the training needs, the facilitator captures the training needs on the white board or flip chart. Don't write down duplicates but do confirm by questioning that the training need that on the surface appears to be a duplicate, really is an exact duplicate.
4. When all training needs have been listed, use a weighted voting process to prioritize the training needs across the group. In a weighted voting process, you use sticky dots or numbers written in magic marker (not as much fun) to vote on and prioritize the list of training needs. Assign a large dot 25 points and smaller dots five points each. Distribute as many dots as you like. Tell needs assessment participants to place their dots on the chart to vote on their priorities.
5. List the training needs in order of importance, with the number of points assigned as votes determining priority, as determined by the sticky dot voting process. Make sure you have notes (best taken by someone on their laptop while the process is underway) or the flip chart pages to maintain a record of the training needs assessment session.
6. Take time, or schedule another session, to brainstorm the needed outcomes or goals from the first 3–5 training sessions identified in the needs assessment process. This will help as you seek and schedule training to meet the employees' needs. You can schedule more brainstorming later, but I generally find that you need to re-do the needs assessment process after the first few training sessions.
7. Training needs assessment can be, and often needs to be, much more complicated than this. But, this is a terrific process for a simple training needs assessment.
8. Make sure you keep the commitments generated by the training needs assessment process. Employees will expect to receive their key identified training sessions with the brainstormed objectives met.

The quality of employees and their development through training and education are major factors in determining long-term profitability of a small business. If you hire and keep good employees, it is good policy to invest in the development of their skills, so they can increase their productivity.

Training often is considered for new employees only. This is a mistake because ongoing training for current employees helps them adjust to rapidly changing job requirements.

The Training Process

The model below traces the steps necessary in the training process:

- Organizational Objectives
- Needs Assessment
- Is There a Gap?
- Training Objectives
- Select the Trainees
- Select the Training Methods and Mode
- Choose a Means of Evaluating
- Administer Training
- Evaluate the Training

Your business should have a clearly defined strategy and set of objectives that direct and drive all the decisions made especially for training decisions. Firms that plan their training process are more successful than those that do not. Most business owners want to succeed, but do not engage in training designs that promise to improve their chances of success. A well-conceived training program can help your firm succeed. A program structured with the company's strategy and objectives in mind has a high probability of improving productivity and other goals that are set in the training mission.

For any business, formulating a training strategy requires addressing a series of questions.

- Who are your customers? Why do they buy from you?
- Who are your competitors? How do they serve the market? What competitive advantages do they enjoy? What parts of the market have they ignored?
- What strengths does the company have? What weaknesses?
- What social trends are emerging that will affect the firm?

The purpose of formulating a training strategy is to answer two relatively simple but vitally important questions: 1. What is our business? and 2. What should our business be? Armed with the answers to these questions and a clear vision of its mission, strategy and objectives, a company can identify its training needs.

Training needs can be assessed by analyzing three major human resource areas:

- The organization as a whole,
- The job characteristics, and
- The needs of the individuals.

This analysis will provide answers to the following questions:

- Where is training needed?
- What specifically must an employee learn in order to be more productive?
- Who needs to be trained?

Begin by assessing the current status of the company how it does what it does best and the abilities of your employees to do these tasks. This analysis will provide some benchmarks against which the effectiveness of a training program can be evaluated. Your firm should know where it wants to be in five years from its long-range strategic plan. What you need is a training program to take your firm from here to there.

Second, consider whether the organization is financially committed to supporting the training efforts. If not, any attempt to develop a solid training program will fail.

Next, determine exactly where training is needed. It is foolish to implement a companywide training effort without concentrating resources where they are needed most. An internal audit will help to point out areas that may benefit from training. Also, a skills inventory can help determine the skills possessed by the employees in general. This inventory will help the organization determine what skills are available now and what skills are needed for future development.

Also, in today's market-driven economy, you would be remiss not to ask your customers what they like about your business and what areas they think should be improved. In summary, the analysis should focus on the total organization and should tell you : 1. Where training is needed, and 2. Where it will work within the organization.

Once you have determined where training is needed, concentrate on the content of the program. Analyze the characteristics of the job based on its description, the written narrative of what the employee actually does. Training based on job descriptions should go into detail about how the job is performed on a task-by-task basis. Actually doing the job will enable you to get a better feel for what is done.

Individual employees can be evaluated by comparing their current skill levels or performance to the organization's performance standards or anticipated needs. Any discrepancies between actual and anticipated skill levels identifies a training need.

Selection of Trainees

Once you have decided what training is necessary and where it is needed, the next decision is who should be trained? For a small business, this question is crucial. Training an employee is expensive, especially when he or she leaves your firm for a better job. Therefore, it is important to carefully select who will be trained.

Training programs should be designed to consider the ability of the employee to learn the material and to use it effectively, and to make the most efficient use of resources possible. It is also important that employees be motivated by the training experience. Employee failure in the program is not only damaging to the employee but a waste of money as well. Selecting the right trainees is important to the success of the program.

Training Goals

The goals of the training program should relate directly to the needs determined by the assessment process outlined above. Course objectives should clearly state what behaviour or skill will be changed as a result of the training and should relate to the mission and strategic plan of the company. Goals should include milestones to help take the employee from where he or she is today to where the firm wants him or her in the future. Setting goals helps to evaluate the training program and also to motivate employees. Allowing employees to participate in setting goals increases the probability of success.

Training Methods

There are two broad types of training available to the businesses: on-the-job and off-the-job techniques. Individual circumstances and the "who," "what" and "why" of your training program determine which method to use.

On-the-job training is delivered to employees while they perform their regular jobs. In this way, they do not lose time while they are learning. After a plan is developed for what should be taught, employees should be informed of the details. A time-table should be established with periodic evaluations to inform employees about their progress. On-the-job techniques include orientations, job instruction training, apprenticeships, internships and assistantships, job rotation and coaching.

Off-the-job techniques include lectures, special study, films, television conferences or discussions, case studies, role playing, simulation, programmed instruction and laboratory training. Most of these techniques can be used by small businesses although, some may be too costly.

Orientations are for new employees. The first several days on the job are crucial in the success of new employees. This point is illustrated by the fact that 60 per cent of all employees who quit do so in the first ten days. Orientation training should emphasize the following topics:

- The company's history and mission.
- The key members in the organization.
- The key members in the department, and how the department helps fulfill the mission of the company.
- Personnel rules and regulations.

Some companies use verbal presentations while others have written presentations. Many small businesses convey these topics in one-on-one orientations. No matter what method is used, it is important that the newcomer understand his or her new place of employment.

Lectures present training material verbally and are used when the goal is to present a great deal of material to many people. It is more cost effective to lecture to a group than to train people individually. Lecturing is one-way communication and as such may not be the most effective way to train. Also, it is hard to ensure that the entire audience understands a topic on the same level; by targeting the average attendee you may undertrain some and lose others. Despite these drawbacks, lecturing is the most cost-effective way of reaching large audiences.

Role playing and simulation are training techniques that attempt to bring realistic decision-making situations to the trainee. Likely problems and alternative solutions are presented for discussion. The adage there is no better trainer than experience is exemplified with this type of training. Experienced employees can describe real world experiences, and can help in and learn from developing the solutions to these simulations. This method is cost effective and is used in marketing and management training.

Audiovisual methods such as television, videotapes and films are the most effective means of providing real world conditions and situations in a short time. One advantage is that the presentation is the same no matter how many times it's played. This is not true with lectures, which can change as the speaker is changed or can be influenced by outside constraints. The major flaw with the audio-visual method is that it does not allow for questions and interactions with the speaker, nor does it allow for changes in the presentation for different audiences.

Job rotation involves moving an employee through a series of jobs so he or she can get a good feel for the tasks that are associated with different jobs. It is usually used in training for supervisory positions. The employee learns a little about everything. This is a good strategy for small businesses because of the many jobs an employee may be asked to do.

Apprenticeships develop employees who can do many different tasks. They usually involve several related groups of skills that allow the apprentice to practice a particular trade, and they take place over a long period of time in which the apprentice works for, and with, the senior skilled worker. Apprenticeships are especially appropriate for jobs requiring production skills.

Internships and assistantships are usually a combination of classroom and on-the-job training. They are often used to train prospective managers or marketing personnel.

Programmed learning, computer-aided instruction and interactive video all have one thing in common: they allow the trainee to learn at his or her own pace. Also, they allow material already learned to be bypassed in favour of material with which a trainee is having difficulty. After the introductory period, the instructor need not be present, and the trainee can learn as his or her time allows. These methods sound good, but may be beyond the resources of some small businesses.

Laboratory training is conducted for groups by skilled trainers. It usually is conducted at a neutral site and is used by upper and middle management trainees to develop a spirit of teamwork and an increased ability to deal with management and peers. It can be costly and usually is offered by larger small businesses.

Trainers

Who actually conducts the training depends on the type of training needed and who will be receiving it. On-the-job training is conducted mostly by supervisors; off-the-job training, by either in-house personnel or outside instructors.

In-house training is the daily responsibility of supervisors and employees. Supervisors are ultimately responsible for the productivity and, therefore, the training of their subordinates. These supervisors should be taught the techniques of good training. They must be aware of the knowledge and skills necessary to make a productive employee. Trainers should be taught to establish goals and objectives for their training and to determine how these objectives can be used to influence the productivity of their departments. They also must be aware of how adults learn and how best to communicate with adults. Small businesses need to develop their supervisors' training capabilities by sending them to courses on training methods. The investment will pay off in increased productivity.

There are several ways to select training personnel for off-the-job training programs. Many small businesses use in-house personnel to develop formal training programs to be delivered to employees off line from their normal work activities, during company meetings or individually at prearranged training sessions.

There are many outside training sources, including consultants, technical and vocational schools, continuing education programs, chambers of commerce and economic development groups. Selecting an outside source for training has advantages and disadvantages. The biggest advantage is that these organizations are well versed in training techniques, which is often not the case with in-house personnel.

The disadvantage of using outside training specialists is their limited knowledge of the company's product or service and customer needs. These trainers have a more general knowledge of customer satisfaction and needs. In many cases, the outside trainer can develop this knowledge quickly by immersing himself or herself in the company prior to training the employees. Another disadvantage of using outside trainers is the relatively high cost compared to in-house training, although the higher cost may be offset by the increased effectiveness of the training.

Whoever is selected to conduct the training, either outside or in-house trainers, it is important that the company's goals and values be carefully explained.

Training Administration

Having planned the training program properly, you must now administer the training to the selected employees. It is important to follow through to make sure the goals are being met. Questions to consider before training begins include:

- Location
- Facilities
- Accessibility
- Comfort
- Equipment
- Timing

Careful attention to these operational details will contribute to the success of the training program. An effective training program administrator should follow these steps:

- Define the organizational objectives.
- Determine the needs of the training program.
- Define training goals.
- Develop training methods.
- Decide whom to train.
- Decide who should do the training.
- Administer the training.
- Evaluate the training program.

Following these steps will help an administrator develop an effective training program to ensure that the firm keeps qualified employees who are productive, happy workers. This will contribute positively to the bottom line.

Evaluation of Training

Training should be evaluated several times during the process. Determine these milestones when you develop the training. Employees should be evaluated by comparing their newly acquired skills with the skills defined by the goals of the training program. Any discrepancies should be noted and adjustments made to the training program to enable it to meet specified goals. Many training programs fall short of their expectations simply because the administrator failed to evaluate its progress until it was too late. Timely evaluation will prevent the training from straying from its goals.

The realities that face non-profit organizations and their workforce today have led to a renewed and expanded interest in learning in the workplace. Often when people think about the learning opportunities provided by employers, they think of traditional classroom training. In recent years, learning at work has expanded to include both formal and informal methods for preparing employees for their current and future work. Employee training refers to providing an employee with the knowledge and skills do perform his or her current job well. Employee development can offer longer leaves than the law requires. Or, your policy can stipulate that employees will be paid while they are on leave is focused on preparing the employee for future positions.

Approaches to Evaluation of Training

Commonly used approaches to educational evaluation have their roots in systematic approaches to the design of training. They are typified by the Instructional System Development (ISD) methodologies, which emerged in the USA in the 1950s and 1960s and are represented in the works of Gagné and Briggs (1974), Goldstein (1993), and Mager (1962). Evaluation is traditionally represented as the final stage in a systematic approach with the purpose being to improve interventions (formative evaluation) or make a judgment about worth and effectiveness (summative evaluation) (Gustafson and Branch, 1997). More recent ISD models incorporate evaluation throughout the process (see, for example, Tennyson, 1999).

Six general approaches to educational evaluation can be identified (Bramley, 1991; Worthen and Sanders, 1987), as follows:

- Goal-based evaluation
- Goal-free evaluation
- Responsive evaluation
- Systems evaluation
- Professional review
- Quasi-legal

Goal-based and systems-based approaches are predominantly used in the evaluation of training (Philips, 1991). Various frameworks for evaluation of training programs have been proposed under the influence of these two approaches. The most influential framework has come from Kirkpatrick (Carnevale and Schulz, 1990; Dixon, 1996; Gordon, 1991; Philips, 1991, 1997). Kirkpatrick's work generated a great deal of subsequent work (Bramley, 1996; Hamblin, 1974; Warr *et.al.,* 1978). Kirkpatrick's model (1959) follows the goal-based evaluation approach and is based on four simple questions that translate into four levels of evaluation. These four levels are widely known as reaction, learning, behaviour, and results. On the other hand, under the systems approach, the most influential models include: Context, Input, Process, Product (CIPP) Model (Worthen and Sanders, 1987); Training Validation System (TVS) Approach (Fitz-Enz, 1994); and Input, Process, Output, Outcome (IPO) Model (Bushnell, 1990).

Table 1 presents a comparison of several system-based models (CIPP, IPO, and TVS) with a goal-based model (Kirkpatrick's). Goal-based models (such as Kirkpatrick's four levels) may help practitioners think about the purposes of evaluation ranging from purely technical to covertly political purpose. However, these models do not define the steps necessary to achieve purposes and do not address the ways to utilize results to improve training. The difficulty for practitioners following such models is in selecting and implementing appropriate evaluation methods (quantitative, qualitative, or mixed). Because of their apparent simplicity, "trainers jump feet first into using [such] model[s] without taking the time to assess their needs and resources or to determine how they'll apply the model and the results" (Bernthal, 1995, p. 41). Naturally, many organizations do not use the entire model, and training ends up being evaluated only at the reaction, or at best, at the learning level. As the level of evaluation goes up, the complexities involved increase. This may explain why only levels 1 and 2 are used.

Fig. 11.2. *Goal-based and Systems-based Approaches to Evaluation*

Kirkpatrick (1959)	*CIPP model (1987)*	*IPO model (1990)*	*TVS model (1994)*
1. **Reaction:** To gather data on participants reactions at the end of a training program	1. **Context:**Obtaining information about the situation to decide on educational needs and to establish program objectives	1. **Input:** Evaluation of system performance indicators such as trainee qualifications, availability of materials, appropriateness of training, etc.	1. **Situation:** Collecting pre-training data to ascertain current levels of performance within the organization and defining a desirable level of future performance
2. **Learning:** To assess whether the learning objectives for the program are met	2. **Input:** Identifying educational strategies most likely to achieve the desired result	2. **Process:** Embraces planning, design, development, and delivery of training programs	2. **Intervention:** Identifying the reason for the existence of the gap between the present and desirable performance to find out if training is the solution to the problem
3. **Behavior:** To assess whether job performance changes as a result of training	3. **Process:** Assessing the implementation of the educational program	3. **Output:** Gathering data resulting from the training interventions	3. **Impact:** Evaluating the difference between the pre-and post-training data
4. **Results:** To assess costs vs. benefits of training programs, *i.e.,* organizational impact in terms of reduced costs, improved quality of work, increased quantity of work, etc.	4. **Product:** Gathering information regarding the results of the educational intervention to interpret its worth and merit	4. **Outcomes:** Longer-term results associated with improvement in the corporation's bottom line its profitability, competitiveness, etc.	4. **Value:** Measuring differences in quality, productivity, service, or sales, all of which can be expressed in terms of dollars

On the other hand, systems-based models (*e.g.,* CIPP, IPO, and TVS) seem to be more useful in terms of thinking about the overall context and situation but they may not provide sufficient granularity. Systems-based models may not represent the dynamic interactions between the design and the evaluation of training. Few of these models provide detailed descriptions of the processes involved in each steps. None provide tools for evaluation. Furthermore, these models do not address the collaborative process of evaluation, that is, the different roles and responsibilities that people may play during an evaluation process.

Different approaches to evaluation of training discussed herein indicate that the activities involved in evaluation of training are complex and not always well-structured. Since evaluation activities in training situations involve multiple goals associated with multiple levels, evaluation should perhaps be viewed as a collaborative activity between training designers, training managers, trainers, floor managers, and possibly others.

There is a need for a unifying model for evaluation theory, research, and practice that will account for the collaborative nature of and complexities involved in the evaluation of training. None of the available models for training evaluation seem to account for these two aspects of evaluation. Existing models fall short in comprehensiveness and they fail to provide tools that guide organizations in their evaluation systems and procedures. Not surprisingly, organizations are experiencing problems with respect to developing consistent evaluation approaches. Only a small percentage of organizations succeed in establishing a sound evaluation process that feeds back into the training design process. Evaluation activities are limited to reaction sheets and student testing without proper revision of training materials based on evaluation results. Perhaps lack of experience in evaluation is one of the reasons for not consistently evaluating. In this case, the organization may consider hiring an external evaluator, but that will be costly and time consuming. Considering the need for the use of internal resources and personnel in organizations, expert system technology can be useful in providing expert support and guidance and increase the power and efficiency of evaluation. Such expert systems can be used by external evaluators as well.

Strong, completely automated systems offer apparent advantages, but their development and dissemination lack behind their conceptualization. Future research needs to focus on the barriers to evaluation of training, how training is being evaluated and integrated with the training design, how the collaborative process of evaluation is being managed and how they may be assisted. This will be helpful in guiding the efforts for both the unifying theory of evaluation and in developing automated evaluation systems.

11.2 MANAGEMENT DEVELOPMENT

Introduction

"Management development" has become the new mantra of the transforming economies of different countries. Having rapidly created the basic institutional infrastructure of a market economy and weathered a post-liberalization recession, the economies now faces new challenges—learning to cope with the requirements of production and managerial efficiency in a modern economy. Thus, full economic recovery depends not only upon the continued evolution of those businesses which survived the transition from a command to an open economy, but upon the establishment of new businesses which operate under the principles of modern management techniques.

Management development is usually defined as "the attempt to improve managerial effectiveness through a planned and deliberate learning process" (Mumford, 1995: 6). Management development in transforming economies may be viewed as an open-ended process, which not only involves managers themselves, but also prospective managers (that is, newcomers to the market of managerial positions) and the enterprises over which they exercise control. Governmental and non-governmental organizations also play an important role in management development by designing, regulating, supporting and performing a number of activities which favour management development.

Irrespective of the rising doubt as to the complete applicability of Western economic and managerial paradigms to the transforming economies of Central and Eastern Europe, the process of management development in these countries has already begun. So far, the chief characteristic of management development in Central and Eastern Europe has been rapid internationalization. The major international donor agencies which have provided financial support for management development in Central and Eastern Europe, naturally insisted that Western standards be applied to the content of such programmes—not only as a means of ensuring the programmes' cost efficiency, but as a prerequisite for the receipt of such aid. However, a second, and far more powerful catalyst behind the rapid internationalization of management development, is the opening of the formerly closed economies of Central and Eastern Europe to foreign competition, through trade liberalization and direct foreign investments. These have led to a fundamental transformation in the managerial culture of successful businesses, resulting in significant shifts in priorities and paradigms.

The experience of developed economies suggests that the massive transformation of management techniques and managerial culture will neither be easy nor quick. A recent survey of 160 large multinational companies revealed that a change in managerial initiatives required, on average, approximately four years. Moreover, the transformation of such crucial aspects of an enterprise as "training/development", "workforce composition", "leadership style" and "career development" may take as long as eight years or more (Carr *et al.,* 1996: 228). In the case of an economy undergoing transformation, managerial change is complicated by a general ambiguity about the direction of change, the agents of change and the objects of change.

In general, a successful transition to a market-based economy requires that a large number of people learn completely new commercial, financial and managerial skills. In transforming economies, millions of managers, entrepreneurs and administrators are restructuring enterprises, creating small businesses, operating new banks and transforming public finance and administration. This transformation has created an overwhelming need for managerial development as a means of filling the enormous and ever-increasing demand for managerial skills in many critical areas. Given these factors, it is impossible for a single study to encompass all of the peculiarities of management development in every area of a transforming economy. Therefore, the scope of this paper is limited to an evaluation of the trends in managerial development in enterprise management. These trends are illustrated by selected cases of best practices in management development.

Concept of the Executive Development

Executive or management development consists of all activities by which executives learn to improve their behaviour and performance. It designed to improve their behaviour and effectiveness of managers in their present jobs and to prepare them for higher jobs in future. It is the process by which managers acquire not only the skill and competency in their present jobs but also capabilities for future managerial tasks of increasing difficulty and scope. The executive development denotes the planned efforts to improve the current and future performance of the organization.

Executive or management development includes "all activities and programs which have substantial influence on changing the capacity of the individual to perform his present assignment better and in so doing are likely to increase his potential for future management assignments". Management development is planned, systematic and continuous process of learning and growth designed to include behavioural changes in individuals by cultivating their mental abilities and inherent qualities through the acquisitions, understanding and use of new knowledge, insights and skills as they are needed for effective managing. This learning process involves the implication of that there will be changed behaviour on the part of the individuals given the adequate training and education.

Development of the managers takes place not only by participating in informal courses of instructions drawn by the organizations, but also through the actual job experiences in the organization. It should be recognized that it is for the organization to provide the development opportunities for its managers and potential managers. But an equal, perhaps the most important concept in the whole programme of management development. The participants must have the interest and motivation to learn and to develop themselves.

Meaning of Executive Development

Executive or management development includes "all activities and programs which have substantial influence on changing the capacity of the individual to perform his present assignment better and in so doing are likely to increase his potential for future management assignments". Management development is planned, systematic and continuous process of learning and growth by which managerial personnel gain and apply, understanding and use of new knowledge, insights and skills as they are needed for effective managing.

According to Michael J. Jucious, "Executive development is a program by which executive capacities to achieve desired objectives are increased".

According to Edwin Flippo, "Management development includes the process by which the managers and executives acquire not only the skills and competency in their present jobs but also capabilities for the future managerial tasks of increasing difficulty and scope".

The executive development is a planned effort to improve current and future managerial performance. The executive program is needed for all levels of executive top, medium and lower levels, who direct, control and coordinate the various activities of the people and the organization.

Features of Executive Development

By analyzing the above meaning we reveal the following features of executive development:

- Executive development is a planned, organized and systematic process of learning.
- It is a continuous process throughout the executives' entire professional career because there is no end to learning.
- Managerial skills cannot be developed over night or in a one slot. It is along-term process.
- Executive development is guided self development.

Nature of Executive Development

(*a*) **Educational Process:** Development is more akin of education than it is to specific training in the skill. Thus a manager cannot be developed only by taking a course, attending the lectures, and conferences, job rotations, and the like. The processes of learning on an executives part has to be accepted as a discipline of self education. Management development implies the development of the people of different aptitudes, talents, aspirations, needs, and the motivation. Because of the individual differences among them, they should be provided an effective organizational climate to develop themselves.

(*b*) **Behavioural Changes:** Executive or Management development is a planned learning process and growth designed to bring behavioural change among the executives. It implies that there will be a change in knowledge and behaviour of the individuals undergoing development program. The individual will be able to perform his present assignment better and will increase his potential for future assignments.

(*c*) **Self-Development:** Manager develop them by participating in training organized by the organizations. They also make use of actual job experiences in learning new behaviour. The organizations can merely provide the facilities for development, but the real urge of the development should arise from within the individuals. That is why, it is often said all development is which development which implies that the individuals must be motivated to learn and develop their competencies.

(*d*) **Continuous Process:** Executive development is an on going or never ending exercise rather than a one-time affair. It continuous throughout the executives' career because there is no end to learning. It is long-term process as managerial skills cannot be developed over night.

Objectives

The main objectives of executive development are given below:

- To impart the basic knowledge to the new entrants so that their overall knowledge is increased and their conceptual and decision-making skills are improved.
- To improve the performance of the mangers at all levels in their present jobs by exposing them to the new concepts, techniques.
- To build up a second line competent managers.
- To develop and implement the latest management techniques in place of traditional systems in order to increase the productivity.
- To introduce the change in the organization by developing executive into change agents.
- To influence the behaviour of workers through the executives.
- To provide the opportunities to the mangers for their career advancement.

Necessity

Executive development is comparatively new concept. Before the World War II, the common belief was that the managers are born, not made. Now it has been replaced by the view that managers can be made by giving them proper opportunities for development. The assumptions that a man could acquire leadership, skills and management abilities by serving long-term have gone wrong. Every worker cannot be a good manager by his experience alone. For achieving the common objectives and managing people at work, certain abilities to lead and motivate the people are necessary which cannot be acquired without introducing systematic and organized executive development programs. The importance and need of the executive development program can be viewed as below:

1. **Managerial Obsolescence**: Advancements in the science, human psychology, anthropology etc. have thrown better light into the pattern of human behaviour and motivation and have developed better mathematical and/or tools for the benefits of managers. Those managers who have abreast with these advancements are able to update their knowledge and managerial skill. Such managers are in a position to apply better methods of taking decisions whose chances of success are more. If we don't update their managerial knowledge are likely to become obsolescence in their profession.
2. **Technological Obsolescence**: Contemporary period has shown unprecedents progress in technology. Technology has become a third and the most powerful dimension in industry, the other two being capital and labour. Technological breakthrough have changed the design of products, the existing production methods, the prevailing practices of storage and transportation, age-old methods of testing, servicing and maintains etc. Based on these, better machines are designed and new layouts of production lines have been developed. Information revolution and introduction of computers have introduced automated production lines. This has changed the working environment. Executive must be exposed to these changes to understand, appreciate and get them involved and become in the line with the modern setting.
3. **Conservation of Resources:** The most important task is the optimum utilization of the resources. Executive should be exposed new techniques to find better methods of utilization of resources. He should be new techniques to find better methods of utilization, preservation and conservation of the resources.
4. **Competitive Advantages:** Globalization and Liberalization has made the competition more severe. Managers must learn to take action for quality improvement, cost reductions techniques, better logistic, better after sales and services. The training on innovative management methods in the entire gamut of managerial activities.
5. **Quality of Life:** Improvement in quality of the life of the people is the national objectives of all nations. Business organizations cannot shirk their national responsibility. This leads to change in the very attitude of executives towards their shareholders, owners, workers, suppliers and consumers also. They should rethink and bring a new focus on consumers and society. They must have the knowledge on how they should satisfy the all segments of the people. Proper training and executive development of managers in such organizations will be great boon to improve the quality of life of people because all these services directly affect their life.

Executive Development Process

Contemporary organizations have realized the importance of human capital and increasingly finding its necessary to continuously train and develop human resources. The training and development needs of the employees cannot be looked at in isolation; any proactive organization has to view the individual training needs in the overall organizational context. The training and development processes are no longer adjunct to other departments but have become a part of organizational strategy and one of the key organizational objectives. The process of arriving at the developmental needs of the executives can be comprehensively viewed through the process given in Fig. 11.3.

Fig. 11.3 Executive Development Process

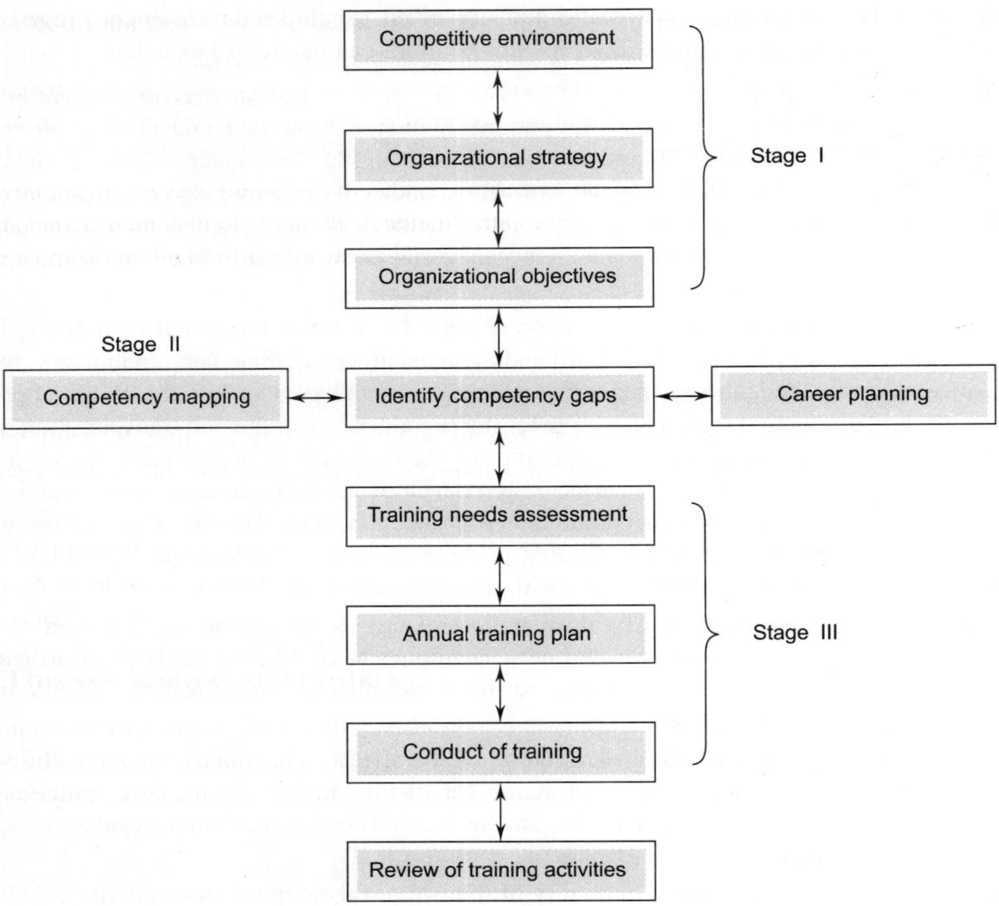

The Process of Executive Development

Stage I: In the Stage I, at the macro level, there are three key elements are considered as competitive advantage, organizational strategy and organizational objectives. The analysis of competitive environment helps the organization to decide its competitive positioning in the market place, based on which the organizational strategy is drawn out in an attempt to transform or reposition of the organization. The macro view is broken down into specific organizational objectives for further dissemination to functional/departmental, group, and individual levels.

Stage II: This stage is most important and crucial phase of executive development process. This stage deals analysis on the competency mapping, identification of competency gap and career planning. In the competency stage which helps to capture the competencies of all the employees of the organization which includes the capacities of the management also. In the second stage, the organizational requirements and competency gap to be analyzed. In the third phase, this deals with identifying and verifying the organizational needs, individual growth and along with career planning of the executives.

Stage III: This stage is consisting of three levels. The first level of this stage deals with the activities involving training need assessment of individuals and of all employees based on which Annual Training Plan (ATP) is drawn. Based on the annual training plan the employees are chosen to expose to either corporate training program, for internal training programs and external organizations. While deciding the venue and types and nature of the training program the personnel department and training facilitator should consider the various issues like no of executives, cost, outsourcing and availability of technical expertise in the organizations. In case of organizational development related exercises, the combination of internal and external training programs should be arranged for the all employee of the organization.

Though the money, infrastructure and finally the manpower to be utilized in the whole process keeping into this, the top management has to take decision in this regard. The training department, management and HR Department should work in union. It is a collective phenomenon, which is mostly initiatives, motives of the top management. If entire process of executive development is mostly determined by its efficacy and its effectiveness.

Factors Influencing Executive Development

The factors which influence the executive development process of the organization: which are described below:

- Failure to train the managers will lead to ineffective and inefficient managers who negatively affect the organization's performances.
- In the absence of training and development concept in an organization may lead negatively, unmotivated, frustrated that may lead severe losses to the organization.
- The organizational performances are affected by the degree of market share, lower sales and reduced profitability etc.
- The absence and shortage of trained executives, make it important for the organizations to have retention policy.
- The continuous pressures on the organizations are necessary to continuously develop, new products and better services and also the maintaining the quality of existing ones.
- Competitive environment is making it imperative for the organizations to continuously restructure and re-engineer and to embark upon these processes, it is essential for the organizations to retain the managers for the new organizational environment.

Executive Development: Methods and Techniques

Management development programs help in acquiring and developing managerial skills and knowledge. A variety of methods of management development have come into prominence these days. Different types of techniques are used to acquire and develop various types of managerial skills and knowledge as given in the table below:

Sl. No.	*Competency Development Area*	*Methods*
1.	Decion-making skill	In-basket, Business games, Case study
2.	Interpersonal skills	Role playing, Sensitivity Training
3.	Job Knowledge	On-the-Job experiences, Coaching, Understudy
4.	Organizational Knowledge	Job Rotation, Multiple Management
5.	General Knowledge	Special course, Special Meeting, Specific Reading
6.	Specific Individual Needs	Special Projects, Committee assignments.

Managerial Training/management Development: The following diagram shows the stages involved in the managerial training.

Fig. 11.4 Stagesof Managerial Training

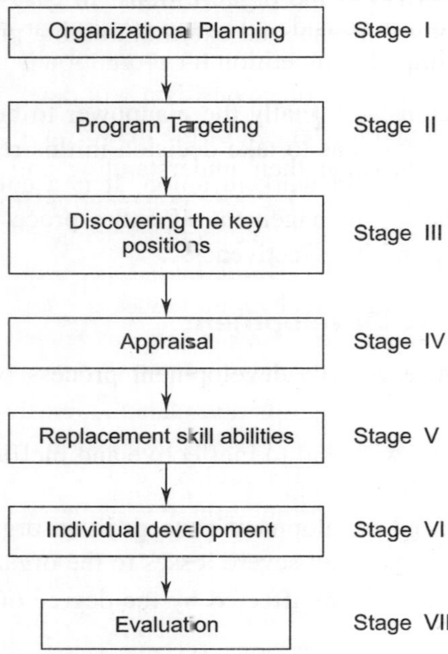

In all the above stages, we should satisfy the following essential aspects in order to make the programmes a success:

1. Policy Decisions
2. Acceptance.
3. Appreciation.
4. Support.
5. Conducive atmosphere.
6. Strong urge for learning.
7. Participation.
8. Identification of strength and weakness.
9. Involvement.
10. Self-development.

Tools/Methods and Techniques

(*a*) **Guided Experiences programme:** (It includes on the job training and coaching as assignment).

(*b*) **Learning on the job:** (It is learning by doing the job).

On-the-Job Coaching: (The immediate supervisor coaches the trainee on the job.).

Understudy: (In the case of the understudy, the executive trainee is prepared to work or fill the position of the higher level executive. He who at a future time will assume the duties and responsibilities of the position currently held by his immediate superior when the letter separates from the job because of transfer, promotion, resignation, retirement etc. It is quite similar to the coaching with a differences the manager can pick up one individual from the department to become his understudy. The understudy is developed to take over the superior's job. The major advantage of this method is that it ensures the ready supply of competent people whenever the vacancy arises due to promotion, demotion, transfer, retirement. This method is built in motivation because it is considered a step towards promotion of the trainee. This also has some demerits like feeling of competition for promotion is over, reduces the motivation for both executive and subordinates, act of favouritism will develop etc.).

Job Rotation: (It is the planned movement of the men from one of the job to another in order to develop their skills and broaden their understanding and experience). Job rotation is a systematic and coordinated effort to shifting the executive from one job to another job, one plant to another plant in a same level. The executive given all the normal duties and responsibilities which go along with the job to which he is transferred. This method helps in broaden the outlook of the executive in as much as he comes to appreciate the problem faced by the other functional managers, plant, departments etc. Job rotation serves to curb the feeling of superiority of one department over the others. By this inter-departmental cooperation will be enhanced. Job rotation increases the induction of new ideas into the departments. It is used a stepping stone for the career development of the employees. This will stimulate the attitude of more team-work in the organization. It not also free from obstacles. Work can suffer due to disruption caused by the changes and limitation to adjust with new work. It will be better if the span of job rotation will increase.

(*c*) **Assistant-to-position** (Here, learning takes place by experience. While observing and doing things, the learners gain the first hand information) **Conferences:** (these are discussions, in which the specialist starts with presentations, the line managers come to face and tries to help them to arrive at satisfactory solutions). **Corporate Conference**, a highly informative event bringing top international and regional executives to discuss current issues, challenges and trends in Corporate Communications. During the past few years, with the rapid growth of companies in the region, Corporate Communications has become one of the most important methods of marketing and building brand awareness. As competition in the region vastly increases, keeping up with the trends in communication is of major importance for your company's future growth and development. By creating motivational workforce and keeping them informed and learning to handle crisis situations, not only will you be in sync with your competitors, you will be one step ahead of them. Executive **Corporate Communications Conference** will help you overcome the challenges in organising your Corporate Communications department to ensure your communication strategy is delivering bottom line results.

Why Conferences

Discover present and pioneering international programmes:

- **Learn** about the latest technical developments.
- **Think** about current and future corporate communication and customer services needs.
- **Network** with industry key personnel.
- **Discuss** the right set of tools for your business needs.
- **Source** new companies in the market.
- **Benchmark** with experts from leading companies.

This will provide practical information and proven strategies on corporate communication that incorporates multiple types of experiences, providing organisations the information on how best to benefit from the positive impact of such processes.

(*d*) **Committee Assignment:** These are regular or ad hoc committees entrusted with some special objectives.

(*e*) **Critical Incident:** (Here, a particular incident is the pivot, around which the entire method revolves.

(*f*) **Multiple Management:** (It provides knowledge about the organization to the junior and middle managerial personnel. Here the members are exposed to all types of the decision taken at higher level).

(*g*) **Planned Reading Programme:** (It helps to broaden their intellectual and cultural interest).

Other tools, methods and techniques like:

- Audio-Visual Aids
- T-group/Sensitivity Training
- Case Studies
- Role Playing
- Simulation
- In-basket
- Transactional Analysis (TA)
- Group Discussions
- Seminars, Symposiums and MBO

These are also adopted during the managerial training programme.

To sum up, the managerial training is a challenge for organization to equip the managerial personnel to meet the ever advancing Technology and other Socio-economic and Political factors. It enriches and experiences of the managerial personnel to get maximum productivity in an organization.

Job Rotation

(*i*) Horizontal movement/expansion is job.

(*ii*) Lateral transfer of employees to various jobs to broaden their focus and increase their knowledge.

(*iii*) One answer to the problem of boredom is the job rotation.

(*iv*) Jobs remain unchanged more or less jobs of nature.

(*v*) Improve interdepartmental cooperation.

(*vi*) Employees become more understanding of each others problem.

(*vii*) Range of skills give the management more flexibility in scheduling work, adapting to changes and as the training costs are increased, work is disrupted.

Case Study

You will learn that decision-making is often a confrontational activity involving people with different points of view. Most important, you will learn how to work toward consensus while tolerating legitimate differences of opinion.

Decision-making is what managers do. The decisions of managers directly influence revenues, costs, and profits of an agribusiness firm. If you are to be successful in an agribusiness career, you must learn to be a good decision-maker. You must develop the ability to apply classroom training in business and economics to agribusiness problem solving so that you can learn how to: (1) make decision-making easier, (2) improve the analytical quality of decisions, (3) reduce the time required to make decisions, and (4) increase the frequency of correct decisions.

After completing a few case studies, you should find them an interesting and rewarding way to learn. You will soon discover, however, that case studies require an approach that is different from normal homework assignments. Each case can have more than one right answer depending on how the problem is defined and which assumptions are made. Students commonly spend several hours preparing the solution for a case assigned for classroom discussion. The time you spend working on case studies will be well spent because it will prepare you to confidently take on a position in agribusiness in which decision-making challenges face you each day. Success in your career will be the real reward for the work you do in preparing case studies.

The **case study** is one of several ways of doing social science research. Other ways include experiments, surveys, multiple histories, and analysis of archival information (Yin 2003).

Rather than using large samples and following a rigid protocol to examine a limited number of variables, case study methods involve an in-depth, longitudinal examination of a single instance or event: A case. They provide a systematic way of looking at events, collecting data, analyzing information, and reporting the results. As a result the researcher may gain a sharpened understanding of why the instance happened as it did, and what might become important to look at more extensively in future research. Case studies lend themselves to both generating and testing hypotheses (Flyvbjerg, 2006).

Yin, on the other hand, suggests that case study should be defined as a research strategy, an empirical inquiry that investigates a phenomenon within its real-life context. Case study research means single and multiple case studies, can include quantitative evidence, relies on multiple sources of evidence and benefits from the prior development of theoretical propositions. He notes that case studies should not be confused with qualitative research and points out that they can be based on any mix of quantitative and qualitative evidence (Yin, 2002). This is also supported and well-formulated in (Lamnek, 2005): "The case study is a research approach, situated between concrete data taking techniques and methodological paradigms".

The Seven Steps of Problem Analysis

Using an organized seven-stem approach in analyzing a case will make the entire process easier and can increase your learning benefits.

1. *Read the case thoroughly:* To understand fully what is happening in a case, it is necessary to read the case carefully and thoroughly. You may want to read the case rather quickly the first time to get an overview of the industry, the company, the people, and the situation. Read the case again more slowly, making notes as you go.
2. *Define the central issue:* Many cases will involve several issues or problems. Identify the most important problems and separate them from the more trivial issues. After identifying what appears to be a major underlying issue, examine related problems in the functional areas (for example, marketing, finance, personnel, and so on). Functional area problems may help you identify deep-rooted problems that are the responsibility of top management.

3. *Define the firm's goals:* Inconsistencies between a firm's goals and its performance may further highlight the problems discovered in step 2. At the very least, identifying the firm's goals will provide a guide for the remaining analysis.
4. *Identify the constraints to the problem:* The constraints may limit the solutions available to the firm. Typical constraints include limited finances, lack of additional production capacity, personnel limitations, strong competitors, relationships with suppliers and customers, and so on. Constraints have to be considered when suggesting a solution.
5. *Identify all the relevant alternatives:* The list should all the relevant alternatives that could solve the problem (*s*) that were identified earlier. Use your creativity in coming up with alternative solutions. Even when solutions are suggested in the case, you may be able to suggest better solutions.
6. *Select the best alternative:* Evaluate each alternative in light of the available information. If you have carefully taken the proceeding five steps, a good solution to the case should be apparent. Resist the temptation to jump to this step early in the case analysis. You will probably miss important facts, misunderstand the problem, or skip what may be the best alternative solution. You will also need to explain the logic you used to choose one alternative and reject the others.
7. *Develop an implementation plan:* The final step in the analysis is to develop a plan for effective implementation of your decision. Lack of an implementation plan even for a very good decision can lead to disaster for a firm and for you. Don't overlook this step. Your teacher will surely ask you or someone in the class to explain how to implement the decision.

By preparing solutions to cases studies, you will be exposed to a variety of management roles, and business situations. Your decision-making skills will be enhanced as you sift through large volumes of information to identify problems, determine corporate goals, define relevant alternatives, and develop plans to implement decisions. You will have your ability to apply analytical tools in true-to-life situations. By preparing reports, you will learn how to express yourself succinctly, both orally and in writing. You will also develop the ability to defend the logic of your analysis and conclusions. These are all valuable skills for a future agribusiness manager and will help you go a long way in a rewarding career.

Case (History) is a written description of a situation faced by a company.

It is applicable to all fields of the management.

Analysis of the case is for developing the broad range of skills.

Descriptions of real situations or work of fiction.

It is a simulated learning and provides practices in problem solving.

What skills do cases give to the managers (part of the training techniques)

(*a*) Analytical skills (convert assorted data to information—classify/Organize/Evaluate information).
(*b*) Application Skills (Applying the techniques).
(*c*) Creative Skills (Vital for alternative solutions).
(*d*) Communication skills (Present/convince/defend).
(*e*) Social skills (Interact/cooperate/guide/argue).
(*f*) Self-analysis skills (Self appraisal).

Learning from the Case

(*i*) Understanding the Situation
(*ii*) Diagnosing problem area
(*iii*) Creating alternative solutions
(*iv*) Predicting outcomes
(*v*) Evaluating alternatives
(*vi*) Communicating the analysis.

Transactional Analysis: (Eric Berne in the 1960's)

The analysis of transactions, socially between individuals and internally different parts of the self.

TA is used to promote understanding, change, and growth in individuals, organisations and within educational settings.

The goals of TA can be described as two fold:

1. To reach **autonomy** including the use of all the ego states in awareness; Ego states are described full later, however one simple way of thinking about ego states is to think of them as different states of the self.
2. Developing **intimacy** which in TA. Is described as the free exchange of strokes without ulterior transactions and allowing for spontaneity.
3. **(Parent-adult-Child: Complementary transactions-Crossed Transactions—Ulterior Transactions)**
4. **Games:** A repeated pattern of relating to others, which ends in dissatisfaction.
5. **Strokes:** Giving and receiving recognition, either positive or negative.
6. **Life Script:** The unconscious life plan which a person lives his/her life by:
   - TA is interactional in analyzing the transactions within their social context.
   - TA works with the affect, helping people let go of their 'old' feelings and expressing their emotions in the here and now.
   - TA is contractual in its approach. This contractual approach which Berne emphasized is one of the differentiating markers which define TA from other psychotherapy approaches.

Sensitivity Training/T-group Training (Group Training)

Welcome to the world of behaviour modification via a technique that has been perfected over the past 30 years— 'sensitivity training.' It is a technique developed steadily over the past fifty years that has proven successful in changing a person's world view, that is, his or her values, fundamental beliefs, and even religious convictions. Sensitivity training has been successfully employed by behavioural scientists over the past thirty years to implement radical curriculum of changes. Sensitivity training is based on research on human behaviour that came out of efforts during World War II to ascertain whether or not an enemy's core beliefs and behaviour could be modified by the application of certain psychological techniques. These techniques have been gradually perfected over the years by efforts of business and industry leaders to persuade people to buy products, including the radio and television industry to ascertain how an audience might be habituated to certain types of programming.

Kurt Lewin is credited with being the 'father' of sensitivity training in the United States. The techniques perfected by behavioural scientists to change our core beliefs aim at sowing confusion in the minds of those who would oppose such change. This confusion is created by presenting logical contradictions as equally plausible, valid, and actionable. Those without a strong belief system, be it empirical, scientific, religious, or logical are especially susceptible to the urgings of those who seek change. Those who have strong enough belief systems that enable them to challenge, refute, and oppose this change are coerced by small-group encounter techniques to conform to the 'majority' view as determined and sown by a 'facilitator' and supported by the core group of 'believers' plus the newly recruited 'sheep' who join the 'majority' group for fear of confrontation. If the challenger does not conform to the group pressure to adopt the 'consensus' view, he is further isolated from the group and/or discarded. He is never allowed to participate fully in the process thereafter.

Sensitivity to the circumstances and feelings of others is the cornerstone of human relationships. The seasons of sunshine and joy and alternatively the seasons of cold and suffering spare no mortal the desperate need for caring and understanding from his fellow human beings. It is important to note that sensitivity is not just an emotion; it must express itself in actions as well, especially when people we know are experiencing pain and difficulties.

(*i*) A kind of laboratory training as it is conducted under controlled conditions.
(*ii*) It means the development of awareness and sensitivity to behavioural patterns of oneself and others.
(*iii*) Help to understand how groups actually work and to discover how they are interpreted by the others.

Two major functions

1. To help its members learn how group works, and
2. To give each member of the group a chance to discover how other people interprets and is affected by his own behaviour.

(*i*) Group involves sitting around the table discussing for hours.
(*ii*) It is an important tool of helping managers win the cooperation of people working with them.
(*iii*) T-group is one of the most effective development strategies.
(*iv*) Sensitivity training can be used in the preparing as change agent, for implementing planned change in the organization.
(*v*) Increased self-awareness or insight about own behaviour and know how others perceive it.
(*vi*) Enhance ability to interpret accurately the emotional bases.
(*vii*) Increased insight into inter-group interactions

Role Playing

In most role-playing exercises, each student takes the role of a person affected by an issue and studies the impacts of the issues on human life and/or the effects of human activities on the world around us from the perspective of that person. More rarely, students take on the roles of some phenomena, such as part of an ecosystem, to demonstrate the lesson in an interesting and immediate manner. Role-playing is simultaneously interesting and useful to students because it emphasizes the "real-world" side of science. It challenges them to deal with complex problems with no single "right" answer and to use a variety of skills beyond those employed in a typical research project. In particular, role-playing presents the student a valuable opportunity to learn not just the course content, but other perspectives on it. The problem with teaching pure, undiluted information is that afterwards, the students, if they paid attention, will be left asking, "What is it for? What does it mean?" Role-playing enables them to start answering these questions and to start expanding them: "What does it mean to a farmer in Nigeria, to a coal miner in Ohio, to an oak population in the Balkans." Information, alone, rarely makes people change their minds, but personal experience often does. Role-playing, like any good inquiry approach, transforms the content of education from information into experience.

- The creative aspect of the exercise will make it seem more like play than like work.
- The pressure to solve a problem or to resolve a conflict for their character can motivate a student far more than the sort of pressure that they usually face preparing for an exam, and it is far more typical of the pressure that will be on them in real life.
- Role-playing exercises are particularly useful in courses for non-majors to emphasize the intersection between science and daily life. Popular geoscience role-playing scenarios generally deal with hazards and environmental issues that combine natural and social sciences.
- The primary purpose of role-playing exercises is to get students to look at the material they are learning in a new light. The instructor is persuading them to alter their mental maps of the world instead of just filling them in mind.
- Role-playing exercises show the world as a complex place with complicated problems that can only rarely be solved by a simple answer that the student has previously memorized.
- Additionally, the students learn that skills they learn separately (such as quantitative and communications skills) are often used together in order to accomplish many real-world tasks.
- Adding a sympathetic, generally human element to science is often encouraging to students with science and math anxiety. Lessons can use role-playing to emphasize the value of feelings and of creativity as well as of knowledge.
- Exercises emphasizing the importance of people and their viewpoints are important preparation for students who will go on in many professions, including business, academia, and politics.
- Students need to understand the needs and perspectives of the people around them to get through life, and to understand themselves.
- Role-playing exercises can be used to develop skills important inside and outside of science. The kind of skills needed to make learned information useful in the real world. Many of these are very difficult to teach using more traditional methods of instruction: self-awareness, problem solving, communication, initiative, teamwork.
- If an assignment includes research or problem solving, students are more likely to retain knowledge that they have constructed themselves more than that simply handed to them in lecture.
- Tried, with some success, to instil ethics in school children using role-playing.
- Accounting students from the University of Illinois had an easier time finding jobs after completing a curriculum that included role-playing than they did after the traditional curriculum.

Types of Role-Playing Exercises

Role-playing can be thought of as unstructured drama. In these exercises, a student looks at the topic from the perspective of a character, which will affect and be affected by the topic. The instructor provides the setting and the characters, but the students have to decide their characters' lines and directions. Generally, the executives will need to do some research to make informed decisions from their characters' perspectives. This research opportunity can easily become an inquiry element. Role-playing exercises teach skills that are often assumed to be learned outside of the classroom (and sometimes aren't), and how to use those skills to complement scientific knowledge. These exercises require the trainee to use imagination, background knowledge appropriate to the character being role-played, and communications skills.

Individual Role-Playing Exercises

The executives write about or present the issue being studied in a format appropriate to the character they've been assigned. The challenge for these exercises is for the trainee to "get into character", to accept and work in the role that they've been assigned, especially if their character is very different from them.

Interactive Role-Playing Exercises

These are group projects that range from simple brainstorming exercises or scripted demonstrations to in-character debates or problem-solving exercises dealing with organizational situation. These lessons may include individual assignments to prepare the executives for their roles and for the project as a whole. It is easier for executives to get into character and stay there with help from their mates, but keeping the debate friendly and productive.

(*a*) Like Sensitivity Training, role playing is also a technique of laboratory development.

(*b*) Role playing technique is used for human relations and leadership training. It gives an opportunity to learn human relations skills through practice and to develop insight into one's own behaviour and its effects on the other.

(*c*) A conflict situation is artificially constructed and two or more trainee is assigned different roles to play.

(*d*) The role players are given with written or oral description of the situation.

(*e*) Role they are to play.

(*f*) It provides opportunities for developing human relations understanding and skills.

(*g*) The proceedings are being recorded the trainees are given a chance to listen to their performance and note their strengths and weakness.

In-Basket method: The in-basket exercise has been successfully used for decades by a wide variety of organizations for selection and management development in both the public and private sector. It is now one of the most commonly used situational exercises, and is often used outside assessment center programs. However, because each candidate's responses to the in-basket items must be evaluated by trained assessors, the cost of using an in-basket exercise may discourage organizations from using it, despite its success in predicting performance in management jobs. If an easier-to-score in-basket exercise that still retained the situational test format of a traditional in-basket could be developed, organizations might make greater use of this well-established selection and management development tool.

The purpose of this study was to compare two methods for scoring an in-basket. The first method involved a traditional in-basket exercise during which participants wrote down the actions they would take on each item. The second method consisted of a multiple-choice in-basket test based on the same collection of in-basket materials.

The typical in-basket contains a collection of items of varying importance and priority that managers find in their in-baskets, such as phone messages, memos, and documents, and the candidate must indicate what action they would take on each item. Some of the items may be interrelated to add complexity, and there is also generally a time limit, which puts candidates under some time pressure to handle all of the items. It is a simulated work task designed to measure performance on work that managers typically do, so it has high face validity for candidates. The collection of items in the in-basket is usually targeted to a specific job or they can be made very general, including the kinds of items that any manager might deal with. Trained assessors score the exercise by coming to consensus on ratings on performance dimensions such as prioritization, decision-making, delegation, organization, and interpersonal skills, or on some overall measure of performance such as "exercise effectiveness." This approach reduced scoring time to less than 30 minutes per in-basket and increased scoring reliability to the 0.90 range. Subject matter experts specified "must dos," "nice to dos," and "should not dos" for each item, and each item was scored by comparing the responses to the expert judgments.'" None of these studies reported tests for adverse impact.

(*a*) This method is used for developing decision-making skills among the managers.

(*b*) In-basket training is structured around the familiar receptacles used for collecting incomings mail, memos and reports.

(*c*) Materials that require problem solving are put into an in-basket.

(*d*) The trainee the role of a manager responsible for solving the problems.

(*e*) The trainee is given the background information on the personalities and situations involved.

(*f*) The trainee is asked to take appropriate action within a short period of time.

(*g*) The in-basket method has been used mostly to learn about effective management and supervision.

(*h*) The technique simulates real-life situations.

(*i*) Using a time limit helps to create the tension inherent in everyday problem solving.

(*j*) He has to list priorities, make assumptions, and distribute work among subordinates and delegate authority.

(*k*) After the time is over, the trainee will meet the trainer who will evaluate the farmer's performances and suggest ways for the improvement.

Management Games/Business Games

Because of the recent upheaval in our economy, many companies have been forced or have opted to undergo internal restructuring and reorganization. This can be an exciting but often difficult process for all levels of employees in the company. Organizational change management is an important tool for many businesses. It allows for the stabilization and continued growth of a company which is currently experiencing a turbulent period. However, the management of change can often be a tricky and rocky process without the right tools and guides for this exciting journey. Specific strategies are necessary to maintain productivity, hold on to clients, and keep up morale in the work environment. Change management games can be a fun, interesting way to impart the skills and strategies needed to accomplish those goals. They can help keep management excited about the alterations within the company, and, in turn, this energy will encourage all of the employees that they manage.

We provide many different programs to serve just that purpose some of which may include PUSH for Change and Beyond Coaching. We also provide individual change management consultants to suit the varying needs and requests of a wide range of individual companies and leadership coaching to aid those in management to better lead through this time of transition.

Varieties of business and management games have been devised and are being used with the varying degree of success in the development programmes. A management game is classroom exercise in which a number of teams of trainees compete against each other to achieve certain objectives. The game is representation of close to real life situation. The executive trainee are given scope to take decision-making about the production, cost, R & D, inventories, sales etc. for a simulated organization. Since, they are divided into competitive teams as companies, experience also obtain in teamwork.

(*a*) Being used in management development programmes.

(*b*) A management games is a classroom exercise in which a number of teams of trainees compete against each other to achieve certain objectives.

(*c*) A close representation of the real-life situation.

(*d*) The trainees are asked to take decision about the production, cost, research and development, inventories, sales etc. for a simulated organization.

(*e*) They are often divided into teams as the competing companies; experience is also obtained in teamwork.

(*f*) Management game may be either simple or complex.

(*g*) The game can be continuous.

(*h*) Team receive all or part of the result of their decisions.

(*i*) The executives learn by analyzing problems by using some intuition.

(*j*) Making trial and error type of decisions.

(*k*) The error of an unsound decision could be disastrous in real business situation but in a game, an executive learns from his mistakes and has a chance of recoup his losses without harmful consequences.

Conclusion

The pace of change has an impact on workplace learning. If you think of your current position you most likely have had to increase your competence in change management, fund raising, diversity management, and so on. In other words, you have had to consciously develop as an employee. It explains the need to constantly learn and develop new skills has never been greater. "[Change] also put the spotlight on training and education as a means of equipping workers with the tools they need to adapt to changing skill requirements, organizational change and increasing complexity in the external environment." At the same time as the need for employee training and development is increasing, it can be argued that the time and money available in organizations for traditional forms of learning such as formal training courses has decreased. To meet this gap between the need for training and its accessibility, we've identified a variety of inexpensive methods for employee development can offer longer leaves than the law requires. Or, your policy can stipulate that employees will be paid while they are on leave have been identified. By using these methods in a deliberate and thoughtful way, performance of your employees and your organization can be improved. "It points out that development opportunities help to ensure that your organization is a desirable place to work. In the foreword to this report, it states that employee training and development programs also have a positive impact on performance: "Job quality affects worker morale, job satisfaction, and the scope workers have to apply their skills and abilities to the job, all key contributors to productivity performance."

After employees are selected, they enter an orientation program to be formally introduced to their jobs. A job is a specific position an employee holds in an organization. The orientation program expands on information received by the employee during the selection process. Orientation is a program that introduces new employees to the organization as a whole, their work unit and co-workers, and their job duties. Organizations are concerned with productivity. Productivity is output per unit of input, usually expressed as a ratio. Measurement of productivity helps supervisors examine critical aspects of production. It is usually determined by a single-factor index, such as output per hour of labour or output per amount of capital invested, or a combined-factor index which integrates different inputs into one overall measure.

An important influence on productivity is the quality of the work force. A major investment necessary to productivity is training. In order to meet new challenges, even the best-educated employees need to increase and adapt their skills. "*Training is absolutely the fundamental point of getting more productivity. The only way you could really improve anybody, other than improving the method of how they do the work, is to train them*". The success of your business is measured by the quality of services and products you provide to your customers. If employees are not properly trained to create or provide the services or product your organization specializes in, how will your company ever grow? Business researchers indicated in a recent Nation's Business article that at present, the average American business spends about one per cent of their payroll on employee training. To compete successfully in the 21st century, however, will require businesses to expend closer to three per cent of their payroll on training.

A positive environment for learning is always critical for success, whether it is the environment of a classroom or the environment of your organization. The learning environment provided by an organization is a function of the organizational culture. Organizational culture means the values, attitudes and beliefs reflected in the mission and goals, and practices of the organization.

CASE STUDY–I Measuring Return: Qualitative or Quantitatives

How to evaluate the return on investment in training is a question that is commonly asked of personnel at the American Society for Training and Development. The result—oriented business mentally places pressure to show that training offers a positive return on investment. The assumption, of course, is that the impact of training can and should be captured financially.

In stark contrast to this trend, Taco, Inc., a privately owned manufacturer of pumps and valves, takes a much more qualitative, if not philosophical, approach to measuring training effectiveness. The company offers impressive educational opportunities. More than six dozen courses are offered in an on-site learning center. The facility cost the company $250,000 to build and the education delivery amounts to $300,000 in annual direct expenses and lost productivity. Asked to place a dollar value on the return from the training, the chief executive simply points to the return in the form of employee attitude.

QUESTIONS

1. What do you think is the best or most appropriate measure of the return on investment for training? Why?

2. In what situations, if any would a financial measure of return be inappropriate?
3. Evaluate the Taco, Inc. approach to evaluating training effectiveness. Do you agree with their approach?
4. With your partner or team, develop an approach for evaluating the effectiveness of training from a customer perspective. You might want to start with the four levels of measurement presented in this chapter and apply them to a customer perspective.

CASE STUDY–2 Training and development: School Net India Ltd.

School Net India Ltd. is an initiative of Infrastructure and Financial Services (I and FS) recognized for its infrastructure and development activities? With a turnover of Rs. 2000 crores, School Net, which was founded in March 1999, is committed to bring about positive changes in the way the lessons are delivered to school children by integrating technology, content, and training. The activities include teacher training, content development (syllabus-based lessons), web-based learning, implementation of a programme at schools, etc. The cornerstone of School Net's K-10 programme is the concept of networked learning. It creates networks of like-minded schools, students, and teachers who exchange ideas, views, and learning resources. Net worked learning is founded on three major components, namely technology, content, and training. The impact of in-service training on school teachers' performance has been identified based on a survey pursued through primary data collection pertaining to the variables in the training aspects of school teachers. The survey was carried out through a questionnaire, clearly focusing on the current situation of training among school teachers and the present pitfalls in the existing training courses. The questionnaire also surveys the need for additional training for school teachers and other related determinants for school teacher training. Apart form questionnaire, general counseling and interviewing also helped to deduce the determining forces for the in-service teacher training. The schools covered were within the scope of Hyderabad.

Findings

The attitudes of many respondents towards the design of the training programme were based on the prescribed syllabus.

Modern sources of knowledge up gradation were not within the reach school teachers.

Many of the respondents put forth that there were hindrances from the management for making it convenient for the school teachers to attend the training programmes.

Most of the school teachers showed deep interest in envisaging a system that would assist in the implementation of new teaching skills.

Training programmes so far designed had been fabricated only aiming at horizontal coordination among school teachers.

A careful study of the syllabi, text, and examination papers at the school reveal that very little concentric development in the subject matter is learnt by a student.

There were very few organizations that dealt with coordination among different schools for proper integration of educational pursuits and goals. Student's caliber and efficiency is assessed by promotional examination, which makes learning monotonous.

Advanced technology usage is still stagnant. There is multi utilization of advanced educational resources.

Student's performance is directly linked with the length and coverage of the syllabus. An unnecessarily bulky syllabus retards skills and creativity both in the student and in the school teacher. Classroom teaching is generally based on the concept of passive learning.

Suggestions

The standard facts elucidated in the textbook need to be supplemented with adequate references. A more comprehensive and integrated study of teaching area should be adopted by the in-service teacher training centers.

Efforts should be channelized within the training centers to make the syllabus of the subject amenable to the future inclusions apart form being precise, brief, and informative. It is also a prerequisite, which fashions the syllabus that much of practical work should be attached for each topic.

The process of learning should be activity based, including experience, experiments, and teamwork.

Orientation learning with audiovisual aids can uplift the student's performance. So, the teacher may be trained to use these aids.

Within a training team, coordination among teachers should be given due importance. Primary-level teachers can coordinate with the middle-school teachers and, thereafter, senior secondary-level teachers for building up a common goal and purpose.

Organizations like School Net can help in organizing interschool cooperation among teachers. Additional material can be circulated among teachers. Quality circles of teachers may be organized to help the less talented teachers.

Critical teaching and creative teaching should be the basis corner stones for the application and realization of knowledge.

Question: Examine the relationships between findings and suggestions critically.

CASE STUDY–3 Training And Development: India Movie Corp. Limited

India Movie Corp. Limited (IMCL) is an entertainment company set up in 1995 by one of the top movie stars of Bollywood, *i.e.,* Mr. Manoj Mehta. An attempt towards establishing a full-fledged infrastructure, he was recruited a Vice President (HR). He has designed a full-fledged HR policy for recruitment, promotion, training, etc. The company is the following four divisions:

- Movie Production
- Movie Distribution
- TV Software Production
- Space Selling

Each of the divisions is headed by a Vice President and supported by a team of 50 experienced people from the areas. The company being a start-up company, it was essential for an organization to recruit experienced people along with youngsters from respective fields. The founder Mr. Mehta believes in growing through sincerity and dedication and he envisions that all employees of the organization also cherish these values and try to uphold them. In the initial two years, the movie production company has produced around two big-budget movies and two small-budget ones. The two big-budget movies, where Mr. Mehta himself was the lead star, bombed at the box office. One of the small-budget movies was an average money earner, while the other was a moderate hit. As regards the movie distribution, the rights of the movies purchased by the company for distribution did not do well at the box office. The morale of the employees was severely affected. The founder, who went for Initial Public Offering (IPO), was over subscribed but as the company did not do well, the stocks soon lost their sheen in the stock market. Mr. Mehta at this juncture felt it necessary for reviewing the state of affairs of the organization and engaged the services of a HR consultant and financial expert to review the matters and suggest remedies for a turnaround of the company.

The financial expert, after examining the financial matters, suggested the following remedies:

Restructure debt by reducing the high-interest borrowing from banks and financial institutions and replacing them with lower interest advances.

Co-produce the movies with renowned producers who are willing to take the financial burden.

Reduce the exposure of the company to production and distribution of movies and increase the focus on production and marketing of TV content, which is a low-risk area.

The HR expert, after examining the structure and profile of all the employees' vis-à-vis the pay scales, felt that the organization has not recruited the right personnel for the right job. It is anxiety to create the hype about the organization; it went about recruiting high-profile executives with astronomical salaries from the FMCG sector, who were not aware of the nuances of the business of the company. The HR expert suggested the following steps for organizational restructuring:

- Replace the key functionaries in the movie production and distribution divisions with personnel with exposure from respective areas.
- Recruit employees for the TV content business from other leading channels in the field.
- Create a full-fledged marketing department to aggressively market the TV software/content to various TV channels and ensure steady revenue streams of the company.
- Train the employees in movie production areas by making provisions for them to be associated with the leading directors.
- Train the financial team, who can keep an eye on the financial health and suggest suitable steps from time to time.
- Train the employees in the movie production and distribution divisions in creativity and innovative thinking.

QUESTIONS

1. Examine the HR strategies of HAL and the training approaches adopted by it to address the problems (Case Study 1).
2. Can training be a solution for larger organizational issues ? Examine it in the context of Case Study 2.
3. Do a role-play with your co-learners and prepare a turnaround strategy for IMCL (Case Study 4).

4. What steps has Coal India Limited (Case Study 2) taken to develop existing human resources and balance the need for technology with manpower growth ?
5. Critically examine the impact on improving the reach of Infrastructure and Financial Services to classrooms.

CASE STUDY–4 Training The First-Level Supervisors

A new year ago, the top executive of a well-managed Government Company dedicated to organize an early Management Awareness Program for first level supervisors. This company had long been in the forefront of management education and was quite ready to listen to the advice of management specialists concerning this subject. They surveyed their own experience only to find that many young people, professionally trained, were leaving the company for private employment, where the rewards were thought to be greater. This left the company with something less than the best qualified candidates for supervision; it also left it with a notably older group of supervisors.

A career development program was carefully worked out. The development of the candidates comprised:

1. A week of formal supervisory training.
2. Assignments to an establishment supervisor would act as a teacher and guide, advising the candidate on a course of reading and enrolment in college courses wherever available, discussing the theory and practice of management with the candidate and evaluating his or her progress.
3. Work on task-force assignments as available and appropriate. Frequently, candidates were appointed were appointed to supervisory positions before they finished their programs, if not, they would either stay within the program until assigned or resign form it to resume a technical career.

Several advantages emerged from this program. The candidates were pleased that their careers were a matter of interest and concern to the higher level executives; candidates could more easily bring themselves to the attention of their superiors; the company was provided with a group of youthful candidates for supervision. The brain drain from the company almost stopped. Gradually more vigor in management levels became evident and young men and women could establish a broader base of experience from which to decide whether they really wanted to be managers.

Certain disadvantages also became apparent. Many good candidates failed to apply for the program because they were not sure of their own career objectives, they did not want to move away from the places where they were originally domiciled or they felt too busy too undergo the training described (it was in addition to their full time positions). Some complained of inadequate counseling and many who had failed to apply were later disgruntled when they found themselves no longer among the candidates for supervisory appointments.

The company is now in a mood to reassess its experiences with the program.

QUESTIONS

1. Is this a good training program? Are there any missing elements ?
2. If you are asked to suggest improvements, what would you say?

CASE STUDY–5 Learning First Means Unlearning

Jim Sullivan, and operator of successful restaurants for nearly 30 years, has recently stated that the most critical step of adult education is not to learn but to unlearn. He contends that new behaviours will never be used until the old ones are unlearned. Many academic scholars agree with him.

As a simple example, let us say you are a restaurant manager and you want your wait staff to provide customers with a stand-up list of appetizers. You bring in the staff, tell them what you want them to do, and present a video covering the correct way to use stand-up menus.

No doubt, you have provided training. Why, then, are the staff not using the stand-up appetizer menus a week later? The answer is simple. The training did not cover what needed to be unlearned—the habit of initially interacting with customers by asking whether they are ready to order. The workers need to replace the ingrained behaviour with the new behaviour of providing the stand-up menu.

Changing a typical way of doing something is difficult. Unlearning and replacing with a new behavior works best if there is a motivating context. For example, the shift to providing stand-up menus might occur most quickly if the wait staff is made aware of the slim profits in selling entrees versus appetizers. Now the staff is more likely to get on board with this simple change.

DISCUSSION QUESTIONS

1. Do you think unlearning is an important step in learning? Why or why not?
2. How can unlearning be accomplished? If you were responsible for training people in a new way of doing things, how would you go about the "unlearning" phase?
3. Unlearning implies that trainees are not blank slates. However, most training programs do not take this into account. Describe a training program in which you could add the step of unlearning.

REFERENCES

1. Brethower, K.S. (1967), "Maintenance Systems: The Neglected Half of Behavior Change," in *Managing the Instructional Programming Effort* (Rummler, Yaney, and Schrader, Eds.). University of Michigan.
2. Dewey, John. (1910), *How We Think*. D.C. Heath.
3. Drucker, Peter F. (1959), *Landmarks for Tomorrow*. Harper and Row.
4. Drucker, Peter F. (1989), *The New Realities*. Harper and Row.
5. Edwin B. Flippo, "Principles of Personnel Management, McGraw-Hill, Tokyo, 1989, p. 209.
6. Kirkpatrick, Donald L. (1975), "Techniques for Evaluating Programs." Parts 1, 2, 3 and 4. *Evaluating Training Programs*. ASTD.
7. Nickols, Frederick W. (1982, April), "Training: a strategic view." *NSPI Journal*.
8. Nickols, Frederick W. (1983, October), "Half A Needs Assessment: What is in the world of work and working." *NSPI Journal.*
9. Reith, Jack (1975), 1969 "Miami Conference Evaluation Methods and Results." *Evaluating Training Programs*. ASTD.
10. Baldwin, T.T., and Ford, J.K. (1988), Transfer of training: A review and directions for future research. *Personnel Review*, 26 (3), 201–213.

11. Bassi, L.J., and van Buren, M.E. (1999), *1999 ASTD state of the industry report*. Alexandria, VA: The American Society for Training and Development.
12. Bramley, P. (1996), *Evaluating training effectiveness*. Maidenhead: McGraw-Hill.
13. Bernthal, P.R. (1995), Evaluation that goes the distance. *Training and Development Journal*, 49(9), 41–45.
14. Bunderson, C.V., Inouye, D.K., and Olsen, J.B. (1989), The four generations of computerized educational measurement. In R.L. Linn (Ed.). *Educational measurement* (3rd ed.) (pp. 367–407). New York: Macmillan.
15. Bushnell, D.S. (March, 1990), Input, process, output: A model for evaluating training. *Training and Development Journal, 44*(3), 41–43.
16. Carnevale, A.P., and Schulz, E.R. (July, 1990), Return on investment: Accounting for training. *Training and Development Journal, 44*(7), S1–S32.
17. Dixon, N.M. (1996), New routes to evaluation. *Training and Development*, 50(5), 82–86.
18. Donoghue, F. (1999), *Promoting added value through evaluation of training*. Dublin: European Commission Leonardo-PAVE Project.
19. Eseryel, D., Schuver-van Blanken, M., and Spector, J.M. (2001), Current practice in designing training for complex skills: Implications for design and evaluation of ADAPT-IT. In C. Montgomerie and J. Vitelli (Eds.), *Proceedings of ED-MEDIA 2001: World Conference on Educational Multimedia, Hypermedia, and Telecommunications* (pp. 474–479). Tampere, Finland: Association for Advancement of Computing in Education.
20. Eseryel, D., and Spector, J.M. (2000), Assessing adaptive instructional design tools and methods in ADAPT-IT. In M. Crawford and M. Simonson (Eds.), *Annual Proceedings of Selected Research and Development Papers Presented at the National Convention of the Association for Educational Communications and Technology* (Vol. 1) (pp. 121–129). Denver, CO: Association for Educational Communications and Technology.
21. Fitz-Enz, J. (July, 1994), Yes…you can weigh training's value. *Training*, 31(7), 54–58.
22. Gagné, R., and Briggs, L.J. (1974). *Principles of instructional design*. New York: Holton, Rinehart and Winston.
23. Goldstein, I. (1993), *Training in organizations: Needs assessment, development, and evaluation*. Monterey, CA: Brooks-Cole.
24. Gordon, J. (August, 1991), Measuring the "goodness" of training. *Training,* 28(8), 19–25.
25. Gustafson, K.L, and Branch, R.B. (1997), *Survey of instructional development models* (3rd ed.). Syracuse, NY: ERIC Clearinghouse on Information and Technology.
26. Hamblin, A.C. (1974), *Evaluation and control of training*. Maidenhead: McGraw-Hill.
27. Holcomb, J. (1993), *Make training worth every penny*. Del Mar, CA: Wharton.
28. Kirkpatrick, D.L. (1959), Techniques for evaluating training programs. *Journal of the American Society of Training Directors*, *13*, 3–26.
29. Mager, R.F. (1962), *Preparing objectives for programmed instruction*. San Francisco, CA: Fearon Publishers.
30. McEvoy, G.M., and Buller, P.F. (August, 1990), Five uneasy pieces in the training evaluation puzzle. *Training and Development Journal*, 44(8), 39–42.
31. McMahon, F.A., and Carter, E.M. A. (1990), *The great training robbery*. New York: The Falmer Press.
32. Phillips, J.J. (1991), *Handbook of training evaluation and measurement methods*. (2nd ed.). Houston, TX: Gulf.

33. Phillips, J.J. (July, 1997), A rational approach to evaluating training programs including calculating ROI. *Journal of Lending and Credit Risk Management,* 79(11), 43–50.
34. Rossi, P.H., Freeman, H.E., and Wright, S.R. (1979), *Evaluation: A systematic approach*. Beverly Hills, CA: Sage.
35. Ross, S.M., and Morrison, G.R. (1997), Measurement and evaluation approaches in instructional design: Historical roots and current perspectives. In R.D. Tennyson, F. Scott, N.M. Seel, and S. Dijkstra (Eds.), *Instructional design: Theory, research and models*. (Vol. 1) (pp. 327–351). Hillsdale, NJ: Lawrence Erlbaum.
36. Sadler-Smith, E., Down, S., and Field, J. (1999), Adding value to HRD: Evaluation, investors in people, and small firm training. *Human Resource Development*, 2(4), 369–390.
37. Spector, J.M., Polson, M.C., and Muraida, D.J. (1993) (Eds.), *Automating instructional design: Concepts and issues*. Englewood Cliffs, NJ: Educational Technology Publications, Inc.
38. Tennyson, R.D. (1999), Instructional development and ISD4 methodology. *Performance Improvement*, 38(6), 19–27.
39. Warr, P., Bird, M., and Rackcam, N. (1978), *Evaluation of management training*. London: Gower.
40. Worthen, B.R., and Sanders, J.R. (1987), *Educational evaluation*. New York: Longman.
41. P. Jyoti, D.N. Venkatesh, Human Resources Management, Oxford University Press, New Delhi, 2006.
42. T.N. Chhabra, Human Resource Management: Concepts and Issues, Dhanpat Rai and Co. (P) Ltd., New Delhi, 2002.
43. Edwin B. Flippo, "Principles of Personnel Management, McGraw-Hill, Tokyo, 1989, p. 209.

12 CHAPTER

COMPENSATION STRATEGY AND STRUCTURE

12.1 INTRODUCTION

In fast-paced, continuously changing, high performance organizations, the emphasis must be on finding the people who not only bring relevant skills, competencies, and experience but who are also willing and able to apply them in a variety of situations and projects. Here, flexibility and adaptability are essential, and people are viewed as resources whose abilities contribute to the core capabilities and overall performance of the organization.

The people element of organization design encompasses all things that have to do with having the best workforce and ensuring that the culture of the organization and the contract between workers and the company is mutually beneficial. It includes how and by what criteria people are recruited and hired to work at the company, how they develop and maintain the necessary skills and competencies, and how they are valued and managed. The key underlying principles of the people aspect of Organization Design have to do with designing a system that enables having the right people, at the right place, at the right time, encourages and enables all employees to make significant contributions that add value, and ensures that they be highly engaged, take initiative, and be involved in meaningful and motivating ways. **Compatibility with corporate culture becomes more important,** because an employee's ability to see what needs to be done and do it in an environment that has less stability and structure takes on added importance. Under these conditions, adaptive thinking, seeing and making a path where there was none and influencing others are critical success factors for the individual and the organization. The "how" of these capabilities is heavily influenced by company compensation policy and structure.

To develop a loyal and motivated workforce, companies of all sizes must create competitive compensation and benefits packages. This is particularly important when starting a shared service centre from scratch. In recent years, rising healthcare costs, proposed rulings concerning the expensing of stock options, pension schemes and shifting employee values have prompted many businesses to re-examine their compensation programmes and make adjustments designed to maximize their value while minimizing their costs. By monitoring emerging developments affecting pay and incentive programmes and responding accordingly, these firms have increased their ability to recruit and retain the most talented professionals. As the economy gains momentum and many organizations begin augmenting their staffing levels, this is an opportune time for companies to re-evaluate the effectiveness of their compensation and benefits programmes. The quality of a company's people is the greatest single factor determining its future.

A competitive compensation and benefits package is key to a company's ability to attract and retain top talent. As the economy shows increasing signs of improvement, employees at all levels are likely to have more career choices. Still, managers should not expect a wholesale return to the rewards and perks of the late 1990s. Market realities have shifted since that time and continue to shift. Companies need to establish compensation systems that take into account new market trends, worker demographics and employee priorities. By creating thoughtful strategies, businesses balance employee needs with bottom-line results. Regardless of the size of the shared service centre or who ultimately establishes the compensation and benefits strategy, every hiring manager should make an effort to understand the key elements involved. Full comprehension of a plan's components will aid employers in refining their recruitment strategies and approaches to salary negotiations.

Establishing an effective compensation programme for your company should starts with a pay philosophy closely linked to the firm's business strategy. This philosophy should reflect the organization's culture as well as its long-term goals. Companies must decide, for example, whether they want to set salaries on par with other firms in their area or if they want to position themselves as premium employers that will pay more for talent. Companies that feel they lack the ability to compete on salary alone may choose to distinguish themselves by offering unusual perks to employees. A carefully fashioned, strategically driven compensation philosophy should be at the heart of every salary decision. For at least a decade, companies have been establishing policies aimed at helping employees balance work and personal issues. Commonly referred to as work/life benefits, these include such accommodations as flexi-time, telecommuting, job sharing and permanent part-time arrangements. During the recent recession some businesses abandoned or de-emphasized their work/life programmes, as these benefits were no longer seen as necessary to attract top talent given increased competition for jobs. Offering work/life balance benefits not only helps firms attract and retain talent—it also may help improve staff productivity levels. By providing workers the flexibility to attend to personal priorities, many companies find their employees are more focused and driven on the job. In addition, programmes that result in reduced absenteeism, less turnover and decreases in overtime can represent significant cost-savings for a business, and sometimes these advantages are quantifiable. Today's firms face myriad challenges when developing their compensation and benefits programmes, and most of these issues will remain at the forefront.

12.2 COMPENSATION ISSUES

The power of an effective compensation program can be significant; the impact of an inadequate, short-sighted program can be debilitating. An organisation helpsto define design, and deploy compensation and reward strategies that drive organizational success. Whether part of reorganization, merger, acquisition, or launch of a new division, An organisation with a total compensation system that aligns employee motivation and productivity with defined roles and performance measures. **Compensation** is the **Human Resources Management** function that deals with the every type of **reward** individuals **receives** in the exchange for **performing organizational tasks**. It is the **major cost** of doing the business for many organizations. It is the chief reason why some individuals seek employment.

Financial compensation is either **direct or indirect**. The **direct financial** compensation consist of the person receives in the form of wages, salaries, bonuses or commissions etc. **Indirect compensation** consists of the like praise, self-esteem, recognitions, motivation, productivity, (Benefits and Welfare). In the present economic situation the major cash flow of the organization is more than 50% in financial and non-financial compensations. Pay is influenced by series of external and internal factors.

Compensation/Pay represents by far the most important and contentious element in the employment relationship, and is of equal interest to the employer, employee and government:

- to the employer because it represents a significant part of his costs, is increasingly important to his employees' performance and to competitiveness, and affects his ability to recruit and retain a labour force of quality;
- to the employee because it is fundamental to his standard of living and is a measure of the value of his services or performance;
- to the government because it affects aspects of macro-economic stability such as employment, inflation, purchasing power and socio-economic development in general.

While the basic wage or pay is the main component of compensation, fringe benefits and cash and non-cash benefits influence the level of wages or pay because the employer is concerned more about labour costs than wage rates *per se*. The tendency now is towards an increasing mix of fringe benefits, which therefore have an important impact on pay levels. In industrialized countries, and sometimes in countries with high personal tax rates, the non-pay element of executive compensation has substantially increased in recent years.

Compensation and HR Practices

Job candidates choose to work for particular companies for a number of reasons, including career development opportunities, training, the companies' reputation for being a good place to work, location, and compensation. Companies try to spark job candidates interest by communicating the positive features of the core and fringe compensation program.

Achieve their goals and measures your success. Depending on how you have moved towards accomplishing and surpassing the personnel goals and that you have set for yourself, the companies are ready to express their appreciation.

1. **Compensation and performance Appraisal:** Accurate performance appraisal is the key to effective merit pay program. For merit pay program to succeed, employee must know that their efforts toward meeting production quotas and quality standards may raise the pay of the employees. Moreover, the employees must have the strong relationships between attaining performance standards and receiving pay increases. Administering merit pay system requires a sound performance appraisal practices.
2. **Compensation and Training:** When training is well designed, employee should be able to learn the skills needed to increase their pay, as well as the skills necessary to each or coach other employees in the organization.

3. **Career Development:** Most employees expect to experience career development within their present companies. Employees career develops in two different ways *i.e.,* change their focus of the work and the second, other maintain their focus and more responsibility. This change exhibit advancement upward thorough the company's hierarchy, which leads to increase in the compensation.
4. **Compensation and labour-Management Relations:** Collective bargaining agreements describe the terms and conditions of employment where the compensation is the key issue. Unions always fight with management to raise the compensation of employees in the organization.

12.3 OBJECTIVE OF THE COMPENSATION

Pay determination may have one or more objectives, which may often be in conflict with each other. The objectives can be classified under four broad headings.

The first is equity, which may take several forms. They include income distribution through narrowing of inequalities, increasing the wages of the lowest paid employees, protecting real wages (purchasing power), the concept of equal pay for work of equal value. Even pay differentials based on differences in skills or contribution are all related to the concept of equity.

A second objective is efficiency, which is often closely related to equity because the two concepts are not antithetic. Efficiency objectives are reflected in attempts to link a part of wages to productivity or profit, group or individual performance, acquisition and application of skills and so on. Arrangements to achieve efficiency may be seen also as being equitable (if they fairly reward performance) or inequitable (if the reward is viewed as unfair).

A third objective is macro-economic stability through high employment levels and low inflation, for instance. An inordinately high minimum wage would have an adverse impact on levels of employment, though at what level this consequence would occur is a matter of much debate. Though pay and pay policies are only one of the factors which impinge on macro-economic stability, they do contribute to (or impede) balanced and sustainable economic development.

A fourth objective is the efficient allocation of labour in the labour market. This implies that employees would move to wherever they receive a net gain; such movement may be from one geographical location to another, or from one job to another (within or outside an enterprise). Such movement is caused by the provision or availability of financial incentives. For example, workers may move from a labour surplus or low wage area to a high wage area. They may acquire new skills to benefit from the higher wages paid for skills. When an employer's wages are below market rates employee turnover increases. When it is above market rates the employer attracts job applicants. When employees move from declining to growing industries, an efficient allocation of labour due to structural changes takes place.

The objective of the compensation **is to create the system of rewards** that **is equitable to the employers and employees alike**. The desired outcome of the employees is to attract the employees towards the tasks. And motivated to do the good job for the employer. The **compensation policy** depends on certain criteria below:

1. **Adequate**: Minimal Governmental, union and managerial levels should be met.
2. **Equitable**: Each person should be paid fairly, in the line with his or her effort, abilities and training.

3. **Balanced:** Pay, benefits and other rewards should provide a reasonable total rewards package.
4. **Cost-effective:** The pay should not be excessive, considering what the organization can afford to pay.
5. **Secure:** Pay should be enough to help employees feel secure and aid him or her in satisfying basic needs.
6. **Incentive providing:** Pay should motivate effective and productive work.
7. **Acceptable to the employee:** The employee should understand the pay system and feel it is a reasonable system for the enterprise and him or herself.

Fig. 12.1 *Compensation: An Overview*

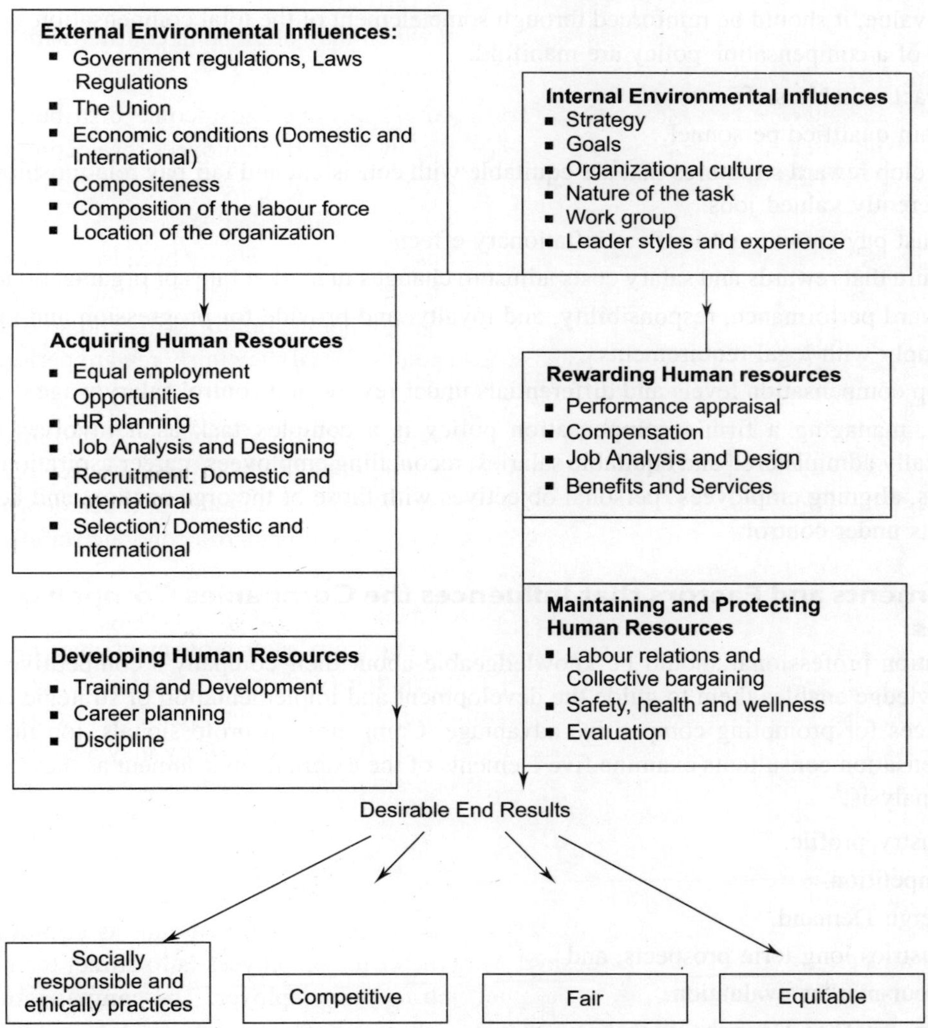

"What is compensation?" While there may be as many answers to this question as there are employees, we'll start with the following definition:

"Compensations the outcomes (rewards) employees receive in exchange for their work, or Pay is an exchange between the individual or group and the employer".

From a manager's perspective, the compensation package offered a firm's employees is important not only because it costs money, but because it's likely to be the primary reason the employees work for the firm. Compensation packages with good pay and benefits can help attract and retain the best employees. A quick survey of employees about compensation is likely to reveal an expectation that wages cover basic living expenses, keep up with inflation, leave some money for savings (perhaps for retirement) and leisure, increase over time, and are fair.

A firm's compensation policy also communicates a great deal about the firm's values and cultures. Employees are more likely to look at what a company pays rather than what it says. In many respects, people behave as they are rewarded. In sofar as this is true, a compensation scheme communicates to the employees what the firm's expectations are of them. Therefore, for example, if quality is an important value, it should be reinforced through some element of the total compensation system. The objectives of a compensation policy are manifold:

- Attract suitable staff.
- Retain qualified personnel.
- Develop reward structures that are equitable with consistent and fair pay relationships between differently valued jobs.
- Adjust pay structures to reflect inflationary effects.
- Ensure that rewards and salary costs adjust to changes in market rates or organizational change.
- Reward performance, responsibility, and loyalty, and provide for progression and increases.
- Comply with legal requirements.
- Keep compensation levels and differentials under review and control salary/wage costs.

Clearly, managing a firm's compensation policy is a complex task as it involves providing systematically administered and equitable salaries, reconciling employees' career aspirations in terms of earnings, aligning employees' personal objectives with those of the organization, and keeping the firm's costs under control.

Environments and Factors that Influences the Companies Compensation Practices

Compensation professional should be knowledgeable about their company's competitive situation. Such knowledge enables them to guide the development and implementation of strategic compensation practices for promoting competitive advantage. Compensation professionals, top management and compensation consultants examine five elements of the external environment as they conduct for strategic analysis.

- Industry profile.
- Competition.
- Foreign Demand.
- Industries long-term prospects, and
- Labour-market evaluation.

Industry profile: Describe such basic industry characteristics as sales volume, the impact of relevant government regulations and the impact of recent technological development on business activity. Compensation professionals use industry profile information to determine the kinds of compensation practices they should recommend to top management.

Competitions: Companies take the stock of competitors' business activities to help themselves in the market. Companies can distinguish themselves from the competition in different ways and they can achieve lowest-cost objectives in various ways. Compensation professionals play a role by recommending pay systems and setting pay levels that support differentiation or lowest-cost objectives.

Foreign Demand: Most companies are interested in foreign demand for their products or services because such demand is the indicator of additional sales revenue potential. This factor has the major impact on their compensation policy.

Industry long-term prospects: Long-term prospects set the backdrop for strategic planning because these prospects are the indicators of the company's future. Companies establish strategic plans that fit with their industries long-term prospects.

Labour market Assessment: This represent as key activities. The company should carefully evaluate labour market to determine the availability of talent employees. These labour force trend have direct implications for compensation practices of the company. In general, there will be more competition among the companies for fewer qualified individuals. Higher demand for labour relative to labour supply should lead to higher wages. Companies will have to increase their wages to get the best individuals to choose employment in their companies rather than their competitors companies.

Compensation professionals, top management and compensation consultants examine three elements of internal environment as they conduct for strategic analysis.

- Functional Capabilities
- Human Resources Application
- Financial Condition.

Functional Capabilities: Companies must determine with functional capabilities are the most crucial to maintaining competitive advantage. Functional capabilities include manufacturing, engineering, research and development, operations, management information system, human resources and marketing etc. The financial capabilities definitely contribute in company's compensation policy.

Human Resources Application: Research and development, manufacturing system and efficient marketing and distribution system cannot give competitive advantage unless there are motivated, knowledgeable and productive employees. Per for performance, merit-pay, and pay-for knowledge programs should be included in the company's compensation policy. Employee should know in advance that the reward increases with higher performance attainments as well as how much an employee will earn for achieving particular performance.

Financial Conditions: The companies' financial condition is the key factor in total compensation policy of the company. This factor determines the company's ability to pay. Sound financial conditions definitely contribute in higher compensation of the employees of an organization.

The several factors that influences the companies' competitive strategy and compensation tactics. These include:

National Culture: National culture refers to the set of shared norms and beliefs among the individuals within national boundaries which are indigenous to that area. National culture increasingly has become an important consideration in strategic compensation policy of the company and influences the effectiveness of various forms of pay as motivator of potential employee behaviour. Compensation experts maintain that understanding the normative expectations of different national cultures and also familiar with different national cultures and also understand how those differences may influences the effectiveness of different pay programs of the companies.

- **Power Distance:** A power distance is the extent to which people accept a hierarchical system or power structure in the companies. Status differentials between employees and employers are typical in high power distances culture. Culture that highly value power distances are likely to have the compensation strategies that reinforce status differentials among employees, perhaps using visible reward that project power.
- **Individualism-Collectivism:** Individualism-Collectivism is the extent to which individual's value personal independence or group membership's individualistic culture gives importance to personal goals, independence, privacy, whereas the collectivism culture favour social cohesiveness and loyalty to such social groups as co-workers and as families. The company should understand the degree of their cultures which favours the both in different extents. The individualistic cultures (US) adopt compensation strategies that reward individual performance, as well as acquisition of skills and knowledge. In collectivistic society (Japan), the compensation of employees on the basis of group performances and individual seniority to recognize the importance of employee affiliations with groups.
- **Uncertainty Avoidance:** This represents the methods by which a particular society deals with risk and the instability of their members. Fear of random events, value of stability and routines and the risk aversion are the hallmarks of high uncertainty avoidance (Italy, Greece etc.). On the other hand, welcoming random events, facing challenges and seeking risks characterize by the low uncertainty avoidance. Where the uncertainty avoidance is high employers probably use bureaucratic compensation policies emphasizing fixed pay is more important than variable pay. When the low uncertainty avoidance (Singapore and Denmark) employers probably use incentive pay programs.
- **Masculinity-Femininity:** It refers to whether masculine or feminine value is dominant in the society. "Masculinity" favours material possession. "Feminity" encourages caring and nurturing behaviour (Finland and Norway). The compensation policies of the company of masculine culture (German) are likely to contain pay policies that allow for inequities by gender, as well as paternalistic.

Organizational Culture: Although all the organizations have cultures, not all cultures have an equal impact on employees' behaviour and action. Strong Cultures-cultures in which the key values are deeply held and widely shared-have a greater influences on the employees than do weak cultures. The employees accept more than the key values and the greater their commitments to those values, the stronger the cultures are: Some organization does not make it clear what is most important, what is not; this lack of clarity is an example of the weak culture.

Characteristics of organizational Culture

- Individual Autonomy
- Structure
- Support
- Identity
- Performance-reward
- Conflict tolerances
- Risk tolerances.

Impact of culture on the modern organization

- Freedom (free to take the different actions)
- Equality (equal pay for the equal work)
- Security (japans life time employment)
- Opportunity (climate of providing the opportunities)
- Traditional Organizational Hierarchy
- Flatter Organizational Structure
- Team Orientation.

It is a shared value and believes which (includes above factors) produce a norm of behaviour which influences the company's compensation policy of an origination.

Organizational Product Life-Cycle: The companies behave (products and services) as people *i.e.,* born, grow, mature decline and die. The companies also adopts different compensation strategies during different point of time.

- **Growth:** Differentiation compensation strategy is the appropriate for the companies in the growth phase. Growth companies always tend to emphasize market competitive pay system over internally consistent pay systems.
- **Maturity:** Lowest-cost strategies are the most appropriate for mature companies. Products and services have fully evolved within the constraints of technology. Mature companies strive to maintain or gain market share. Efficient operations are the paramount to striking a balance between cost containment and offering the best possible quality products or services. Mature companies must have well structure internal (company's current labour force) labour market. By this time the employees are more skilled and make the greater contribution to attainment of company goals. Accordingly the compensation policy has to make such arrangement that will further help in develop skills with adequate compensation.
- **Decline**: In this situation, the company runs under poor performances. Business leaders can respond to decline in two different ways. Either allow to decline or make substantial change to reverse the decline. So the compensation policies are also changes accordingly. Differential strategies become the focus when the companies choose to redirect activities towards distinguishing themselves from the competition by modifying existing products and services in some creative way or by developing the new products or services. Low-cost strategies are the most appropriate when companies allow decline to continue to business closure.

Consequences of Pay/Compensation Dissatisfaction/Significance of Compensation

There are also clear consequences to neglecting a firm's compensation policy. The desire for more pay has the potential to lead to reduced productivity, increased levels of grievances, strikes, and the search for higher paying job. Further, organizational symptoms of pay dissatisfaction may include increased levels of absenteeism and job accidents, and psychological withdrawal. The financial compensation is of significance from the standpoints of the individual, the enterprises and the national economy. Actually, the compensation is the major source of purchasing power of individual, which reflects employees' standard of living, determinant of the status, prestige and worth of the employees in the social parlance. Thus, financial compensation is of great significance to the individuals.

As per the enterprise is concerned, the compensation seems to be the cost factor interacting with total revenue related to the success of the organization. Indeed, it is the crucial element in the cost of production. Accordingly, while attempts are made to pay high compensation as required to attract, motivate and maintain competent human resources, simultaneously, stress is laid to keep them as low as possible to earn profits adequate enough to attract new capital, expand productive capacity and satisfy customer needs. This reveals utmost significance of financial compensation from the stand point of the organization.

The national economy suffers a set back from frequent strikes and grievances arising from the compensation issues (dissatisfaction on compensation). Moreover, there exists a possibility of inflation if the compensation is increasing much faster rate than the production this also harm the national economy. Financial compensation is of importance from the standpoint of the national economy because it forms a major part of its income.

12.4 COMPENSATION FUNCTIONS

There is difference of opinions about the functions of compensation in an organization. As the compensation is provided for two reasons including as a reward for the past services and also stimulus to increased performance in the future. Accordingly, financial compensation has two functions—the equity function and the motivational function.

First financial compensation serves as a standard for evaluating the individual's past performances and current effectiveness. This necessitates that wages are linked with the ability and motivation with which the work has been performed in the past. Explicitly, compensation forms the reward for the past productive performances on the part of the employee. The equity function tends to be equality regarding the compensation is concerned. The rational of this function is that the individual tends to feel that the existing compensation system of the organization in the form salary, wages incentives and bonuses etc. provides them adequate compensation for the physical and mental efforts and contributions. In other words, the compensation is perceived as "equitable" leading to the formation of effective groups and reinforcement of desirable behaviour of the employees to attain organizational goals.

Second, the remuneration serves a motivator to the future initiatives. It has been presumed, that differential increase in the remuneration cause direct and proportional differential increases in efforts, that employee performs varies in the terms of the rewards obtained from the group and the management, and that the individual perceptions of "fairness" of their remuneration determines its motivational effects of performances. However, human motivation in as highly complex issue. It has been indicated that there is exist a multiplicity of motivational factors causing individual behaviour. Motivation interacts with several factors such as individual perception and social comparison. Moreover, it should be kept in mind that although financial compensation provides the "Mainsprings of Motivation" it exerts motivational effects depending on prevailing needs of the individuals.

12.5 COMPENSATION POLICY AND OBJECTIVES

An organization's total compensation philosophy includes both compensation and benefits values and is the driver for leading-edge compensation strategies that align with the overall strategic direction of the company. In today's environment of ever-rising benefit costs, it is imperative for organizations to communicate the value of a total compensation program approach to employees. We begin with the articulation of a clearly stated compensation strategy to ensure that compensation programs meet the organization's business and cultural needs through a clear process we:

- Identify project deliverables and success measures.
- Review organizational, human capital, and business information.
- Gather input from executives, managers, and employees.
- Test the market competitiveness of pay.
- Develop a total compensation strategy and a design "blueprint".

From this foundation, we design all aspects of employee pay programs, including:

- Systems that cover all elements of total direct compensation such as base, short-term incentives or bonuses, and long-term equity through stock or other accumulation plans.
- Job/role analysis.
- Market analysis.
- Job worth determination and evaluation.
- Performance/success-based pay systems.
- Job, incumbent, and team reward programs.

As part of the effort to develop and maintain a quality workforce, public sector organizations must position themselves as "employers of choice" and recognize the value of their human capital. The methods, by which employees are recruited, trained, retained, measured, and compensated are under scrutiny to ensure that goals can be accomplished and that future needs can be met. It is not enough to develop and implement programs to recruit, train, retain, measure and compensate—in the face of global competition, organizations must develop strategies to manage these important human resource functions. In today's market a number of organizations are continuously seeking new strategies to meet both organizational and employee needs. From a global perspective there are still substantial differences in the way people get paid. However, organizations are finding that their human resource strategy can be structured using similar philosophies to reward people regardless of where there are located. The logic of market-based economies suggests that the differences are narrowing as employers worldwide cope with similar pressures. All are affected by intense competition for Critical skills; or are influenced by global financial markets. Public sector organizations need to develop aggressive pay policies to compete successfully for well-qualified employees. Compensation levels must be high enough to attract a strong applicant pool and retain the best among current employees. Morale is enhanced if employees know they are being paid at least as much as comparable employees are being paid by other employers. Classification and compensation systems should therefore not only classify positions on the basis of uniform criteria, but also allocate positions to salary grades that reflect their relative worth and market value. An increasing number of organizations are trying to link pay to performance, through programs such as variable or incentive pay, where a percentage increase in pay depends on the employee's achievement of predetermined measurable goals; skill-based pay, where employees are paid for the number of skills they possess; and most recently, competency-based pay, in which an employee is paid for the range, depth and types of skills and knowledge he/she is capable of using in the job rather than for the position they hold. Strategies that are linked to organizational goals, as well as examine various pay systems and structures. Compensation and reward systems can become an important signal of an organization's culture and values. When considered from a strategic perspective, organizations could customize classification and compensation systems to help create a culture and attract a workforce that possesses the values, knowledge, skills, and abilities that support the organization's strategic goals and objectives. The guiding principles for a successful classification and compensation program should ensure that:

- Employees doing similar work should receive comparable wages.
- Variations in pay must be based on significant differences in responsibilities and required knowledge, skills, and abilities (KSAs) on salaries paid by other employers in the marketplace.
- The process for classifying and evaluating the relative worth of positions must be fair.
- In addition, a classification and compensation plan that is continuously maintained results in:
  - Fewer requests for reclassifications,
  - Fewer grievances arising out of disputed job requirements,
  - Fewer pay inequities and morale problems, and
  - A solid basis for evaluating work performance.

One of the most fundamental and difficult tasks in the management of any personnel system is determining the comparative worth of each position. Employees are acutely aware of what they are paid, how much responsibility they are assigned, and the "status" of their positions in relation to other positions. Perceived inequities in pay or status can be a source of intense dissatisfaction, which translates into declining morale, lost productivity, absenteeism, grievances, and chronic bickering. It is impossible to eliminate all feelings among employees that inequalities exist in the pay system, but every effort can be made to achieve fair job groupings and an equitable pay level for all positions in the workforce. In recent years, organizations have responded to changes in the economy and shortages of employees with specific skills by taking a short-term approach that addresses the immediate need. Changes made to increase the flexibility of current classification and pay systems have allowed organizations to be more responsive to the changes in the external climate and internal needs. The broadening of job classes, allowing for higher pay maximums, is just one way that flexibilities have been introduced. Those types of initiatives have been generally successful in the public.

The long-term pay strategies recognize the important role that compensation can play in achieving business objectives. Pay strategy looks at using pay to motivate employee behaviour towards the achievement of employer goals, and bases salary levels and salary increases on the value employees bring to their work.

There are five important elements that make up the foundation for pay strategy:

Pay Philosophy: The organization's concept of how employees will be compensated. It communicates the employer's direction and intent about Employee's salaries. An organization's pay philosophy must be simply stated, practical in its approach and application, and clearly communicated. It is a vitally important component in preparing management to understand and apply employee salaries and salary changes in ways and circumstances that consistently support the employer's strategic goals. Pay philosophy is the core element in developing a successful pay strategy.

Pay Competitiveness: Easy to understand but difficult to achieve and communicate. The main reason, for most public sector employers, is the general unpredictability of operating budgets, which often negatively impact the organization's ability to fund employee salary increases. Most employers address pay competitiveness issues from only a tactical perspective, focusing on the individual situation as the issue presents itself. However, most public sector employers will never achieve total salary competitiveness if they continue with a short-term approach. Employers focused on pay strategy, however, have a much better chance to succeed by managing and defining it on their terms. Competitiveness from the perspective of a pay strategy suggests that the organization prioritize based on both the position and the person. Salary us are directed to those positions most critical to the employer's operating mission(s) while also addressing retention of critically skilled employees and those employees performing at high levels. This approach to pay competitiveness, while unlike the approach typically taken in the public sector, can be very effective in achieving business results. Paying competitively also does not necessarily mean paying the market average. Pay strategy focuses on *total compensation (*salaries and benefits) and ranges of pay as opposed to specific pay levels to attract and retain employees.

Pay Delivery in the public sector has traditionally been through rigid and inflexible systems. Traditional pay structures with pre-determined pay steps and timing intervals are still common in many jurisdictions, and are the most frequently used structure for delivering base salary and salary increases to employees. High performing organizations are often those that recognize and reward achievement in as many ways and circumstances as possible. Allowing managers greater discretion in pay structure can be very beneficial in positioning the organization as an "employer of choice." Public sector employers who are able to use compensation to attract and retain high performers will experience the most success in the accomplishment of their business mission.

Pay Practices are the systems an organization uses to deliver pay and pay increases. Pay practices play an important role in the application of pay strategies in the public sector; from the way a pay increase is granted (*i.e.,* base pay or lump sum) to increases for special skills, job hazards or geographic work location. Public jurisdictions can maximize long-term pay strategies by adopting flexible and innovative pay structures and systems that integrate well with each other and accomplish their purpose.

Communication is an important, but often worst applied component of personnel system change. Typically, information is shared with employees on a "just in time" basis, and oftentimes knowledge is typically uneven throughout the management structure and messages and timing usually are out of Synchronization. Developing a strategic approach to communicating your pay strategy helps assure that the right messages are delivered and received in the right time and in the right manner. A well developed communications plan will support an important strategic objective of achieving employee understanding of the organization's compensation plan.

Management Compensation: Indian Scenario

One of the most vital factors for the motivation, retention and the morale amongst the employees is the compensation system, policies and review philosophies of any organization. While the bargainable employees generally have their unions to negotiate or review terms with the Management—which are governed by the Long-term Settlements—the terms of the Managerial employees are mostly seen to be at the sweet mercy or the goodwill of the organization or the top bosses, reviews of which may or may not be regular or timely, or often do not seem to meet the expectations or logic of such management staff.

The objective is to look back at the history and past practices of the progress of the managerial compensation system followed generally in prominent multi-national commercial organizations in India, and attempt to evolve some criteria best suited to the present competitive scenario.

The evolution of the management compensation system for the larger organizations came mostly from the pre-independence British companies, or from the Indian government system—which too was initiated by the British, and was generally paternalistic and protective. The system provided a 20–30 year grade scale of Basic Salary for each level of employees generally linked to age, with other fixed allowances for each grade. It was felt that with increasing age and the family size, their needs increased, which required consideration in the compensation. Annual increments were provided with increasing steps as one progressed through the salary scale, even though the increases were often adhoc. Festival, Puja or Annual Bonus was paid to meet the social needs—usually once a year, and was often linked to the profits of the Company. To meet the inflationary trends, a Dearness Allowance system was introduced during the World War II days in the early forties, but this was generally not applicable to management staff-Basic Salary remained the main component of compensation for them. Benefits frequently included provision of housing—often furnished partially or fully—or an allowance in lieu, annual leave travel expenses—generally quantum linked to the family size and fares to hometown or nearest hill station, use of Company transport or cars (from limited use to extensive, with or without driver-grade related), medical coverage or assistance, and retrial benefits. To encourage managers in social and sporting activities, either Company clubs existed, or financial assistance was given to join the local clubs depending on the level. Overall compensation increased with grade, age and service, with only very limited linkage to performance, and which was often adhoc at the discretion or pleasure of the boss. The company was usually quite actively concerned and involved with the managers social life and style of living, and strongly believed that the Company's image demanded this conforming discipline from the family members as well.

Most multinational companies operating in India had a fair number of expatriate staff—even as late as in the sixties—having vastly different terms and conditions of service as compared to the local staff at the same level. This continued partially out of necessity to attract them to overseas postings, and also due to past colonial and historical reasons. Excellent furnished housing was provided to them, and many other personal or social needs for them and their family members were mostly taken care of by the Company, including overseas education for their children, home leave and travel expenses etc. as well as protection of benefits available at the home country to their compatriots. Class distinctions existed even amongst the expatriates—they were generally separated as 'blue blood' at top positions, and 'commoners' at middle management positions! The local Indian Covenanted cadre managers identified for senior positions were often higher in hierarchy than the expatriate middle managers in rank, but their gross terms were generally lower. The junior management local staff were a class apart, and their terms were substantially lower, but were in line with the above philosophy, and therefore, while the cash component may have been low, the benefits of furnished housing, leave travel expenses, use of company vehicles etc. enabled the overall living standards during the service period remain at a good level. With limited opportunities, retention of management staff was not an issue at all those days. Revisions in overall terms were usually done after 3 to 5 years. The management salaries were considered to be a highly confidential topic, and any discussion on this subject was seriously frowned upon by the top brass. The management style did not inspire openness, and the lower levels were expected to follow orders rather than suggest any major changes. Participative style was not practiced or encouraged generally. Employee and Managerial costs were a small part of the total expenses, and profits were easily made by most of these large corporations having little competition in near monopoly conditions in India.

From the sixties onwards the salaries of bargainable workers increased phenomenally due to the successes of the Unions in negotiations—at times by pressure tactics. At the same time, the Government statutorily limited the Directors maximum Basic salary at a very low level—in line with the socialistic philosophy. This resulted in the need for creating other indirect compensation mainly through perquisites for the management staff due to the salary compression. These perquisites and benefits given to the management staff gradually started being valued by the authorities, and had to be included for tax purposes, thereby further compressing the "in hand post tax" compensation range drastically—with the junior or middle managers being affected most adversely. The marginal tax rates had also risen to very high levels, and so was the inflationary trend, requiring much larger increases to meet the employee expectations. The earlier 'taboo' regarding management salaries being a close subject for discussions was also reducing, and the top management started recognizing disparities that needed urgent attention. It started dawning on most progressive organizations that the compensation governance needed clear cut philosophy and policy, instead of the ad hoc solutions of the past, and that motivation and retention of capable managers was getting to be a very crucial need in the growing scenario in India. Some of the Personnel directors or Heads of major companies informally discussed these issues at regular intervals, and shared data and policies with each other, at what later became the Remuneration Clubs, to address this important subject.

Many companies had chosen to use somewhat 'shady' reimbursements or perquisite routes, in order to maximize the in-hand amounts or benefits, and contain the overall costs in the assumption of these being non-taxable, and therefore, meeting the compensation needs more easily, rather than the larger cost of taxable increases for the same net gain. The basic salary as the main component of overall compensation had also consequently become lower—with reduced indirect component costs that affected the retrial benefits substantially, often ignored by the company.

The above stated traditional system started being challenged during the last two decades by the "money for the job", "total cost to the company", "flexible package" and "variable performance pay or bonus" concepts followed by some of the well known large new organizations, with annual increases mostly linked to performance, results and inflation, rather than gradually increasing salaries with traditional 'grey hair' philosophy of age. The protective long term security of employment was shaken by these companies with easier hire and fire practices, with second raters and non performers not being acceptable or retained. This resulted in much larger compensation packages being suddenly available to young and confident managers without having to wait for years, as in the past. This so called "American" compensation strategy conflicted with the traditional (British) methodology, causing unexpected upheavals.

The government had in the meanwhile realized the futility of very high rates of taxation which encouraged tax evasion, and had also relaxed the compensation limits for the company directors in the meanwhile as well. This provided an opportunity for companies to realign their compensation philosophy to suit the organizational needs, and rectify tax irregularities, during the reviews. Many companies started moving away from the perquisite oriented style. They recognized the need for greater freedom to their managers to choose their own standard or style of living, with remuneration based on the market compensation trends. With liberalization came greater competition and new opportunities for jobs, and therefore both organizational excellence and retention of key managers became paramount. The need for an effective impartial performance appraisal and reward systems therefore became essential.

The Y2K era opened the floodgates for the Indian IT industry and personnel for lucrative overseas jobs, and easier to and fro movement, which created new paradigm for managing the aspirations of IT professionals—so very different to the traditional managers in Indian Industry. Job security, and long-term employment needs came much lower down for these people, and the international compensation based on declining exchange rates created newer benchmarks. The Retrial benefits were discarded as a major need by many of the young professionals. The distinction between manager and an entrepreneur faded in small start-up companies, as did compensation and profits through value addition for such people. Stock options suddenly became a part of the remuneration package despite tax implications, and international compensation systems influenced the Indian scenario substantially, which did not remain unique to the IT industry only. For such 'knowledge workers' in the organizations, changes in compensation strategies were needed that had to be extended to the traditional industry, which had become very competitive.

Management compensation therefore, now plays a very significant part along with the working style and environment, empowerment etc. in the organization's success strategy. While individual organizations may have differences in their methodologies based on factors best suited to their perceived needs, some general directions are evident, and are discussed below:

1. Salary, Basic Salary or Consolidated Salary continues to remain as the major component of compensation, though Salary Scales are often discarded these days, or used only as guides. Individual Salary is generally decided initially using the scale, but thereafter performance, contribution to targets or results generated determine the revisions periodically—which may vary widely from individual to individual. 'Salary broad banding' is therefore, getting recognition and acceptance.
2. Grade wise flat allowances are being consolidated generally, except where tax exemption benefits are still available, when they continue as separate components. Allowances may be linked to the salary as a percentage or by slabs, but preference is for flat amounts, which do not increase automatically, and therefore increases could be discretionary, and therefore controllable.
3. Reimbursements of expenses incurred on company work has become limited, and in line to conform to the tax laws. Being actual in most cases, they are not considered as a part of the compensation, unless it is provided towards personal benefits.
4. Annual payments: Bonus or Commission, and Leave Travel are common features–some tax relief does apply for the latter.
5. Benefits generally comprise of mostly unfurnished company owned or leased accommodation, use of company owned or leased vehicle, medical coverage, retrial benefits covering Provident Fund, Pension or Superannuation and Gratuity, post-retrial medical assistance, easy loan schemes at low or zero interest rates for house building, cars or vehicles, furniture or utility items etc. renting employee owned housing, club entrance fee reimbursement etc. Minor benefits could be provision of security, driver or gardening assistance, sale of products or assets at a concessional rate, relocation and transfer expenses including admission etc. fees for children, credit card fees, phones etc.
6. Employee stock option schemes—which have been popular in IT industry—is not extensively used yet, not being tax advantageous to other industries, nor seen as being very attractive with lesser growth trends for their share values, especially in the well established older companies.
7. The "Total cost to the company" concept is used as basis by most companies, as against earlier visible costs. Cost of most benefits are averaged or computed on actual basis, and included in the above. Greater openness is practiced, and some permit individual flexibility within the system of the overall cost, but with greater compliance to tax laws, this 'basket concept' is on the wane.

8. As mentioned earlier, retirement benefits are important to many, whilst the younger generation and specially IT professionals, do not consider it as an advantage, unless the benefit value is available to them on moving to a new job. This is a complex issue, and may require attention. Periodic improvement in pensions or a guaranteed grade minimum pension is practiced by some in recognition of the past external experience of pensioners, and to partly offset the inflation post retirement.
9. Against the past practice of modest gradual increases applicable to all, with only marginal additional to the good performer, the differential in performance is now being recognized through very substantial and varying increases during the review to the very good performer, and often a Salary freeze or loss of job is being used for poor performers! This strategy manages the rewards often within the same total cost.
10. While the salary increases in the past resulted in benefits continuing during the rest of the service period, now large amounts in once off (annual) Performance Bonus that do not increase future liability, is being given more and more as a recognition of results generated. Emphasis on Variable Performance Pay or Bonus as a reward is getting to be an important and growing component of the compensation system. It requires transparent, balanced and fair systems and benchmarks, and also agreed targets by the managers in advance during planning and review discussions.
11. From the earlier grade oriented compensation system within reasonable boundaries, compensation often has to be somewhat tailor made for specialists or key contributors to retain them in the very volatile job market. This has many repercussions, and therefore policies for such compensation need to be carefully built into the system in an open manner to avoid loss of credibility.
12. Compensation review periods have become annual generally and sometimes oftener, as compared to every three to five years earlier, in the fast changing market situation. The quantum of increases has jumped of late, and successful organizations need to not only keep pace, but have to be seen and reputed to be amongst the best to attract talent. The employee cost increases have to be set off through productivity and greater contribution from the resources. This requires constant market data on compensation practices and benchmarks, and very pragmatic analysis for determining strategy.
13. Retention strategies employed are generally the attractive interest free or at low rates for loans, on which market rate of interest may apply on early exit, renting employee owned property to set off repayment of loans, qualifying periods or attractive service benefits added to the retrial benefits or post retirement benefits etc. besides the terms, compensation and any special deals. Managers and teams having commitment require empowerment, lean and supportive structure, a healthy organizational climate—which are all great retention motivators, and also end up as a 'puller' from the external environment or the competition!

To conclude, the need to regularly carry out detailed compensation reviews both within and without, and with full support and commitment from the top is essential. The specific needs of the organization must be identified and addressed during such reviews. Openness and transparency are important to the managers in the very sensitive and personal issue of management remuneration, and therefore policies and practices should match the rhetoric. The remuneration and the systems have to be, and seen to be, fair and just, non bureaucratic and dynamic, and which are dealt with human feelings and necessary speed, and still remain competitively attractive, quite a management challenge in today tough and highly aggressive scenario!

12.6 DETERMINANTS OF COMPENSATION

Fair and adequate compensation is critical to motivating employees attracting high-potential employees, and retaining competent employees. Compensation has to be fair and equitable among all workers in the same company (internal equity). Internal equity can be achieved when pay is proportionate to the individual employee's qualifications and contributions to a company. On the other hand, compensation also has to be fair and equitable in comparison to the external market (external equity). If a company pays its employees below the market rate, it may lose competent employees. In determining adequate pay for employees, a manager must consider the three major factors: the labour market, the nature and scope of the job, and characteristics of the individual employee. Potential employees are recruited from a certain geographic area—the labour market. The actual boundary of a labour market varies depending on the type of job, company, and industry. Pay for a job even within the same labour market may vary widely because of many factors, such as the industry, type of job, cost of living, and location of the job. Compensation managers must be aware of these differences. To help compensation managers understand the market rate of labour, a compensation survey is conducted. A compensation survey obtains data regarding what other firms pay for specific jobs or job classes in a given geographic market. Large companies periodically conduct compensation surveys and review their compensation system to assure external equity. Several factors are generally considered in evaluating the market rate of a job. They include the cost of living of the area, union contracts, and broader economic conditions. Urban or metropolitan areas generally have a higher cost of living than rural areas. Usually, in calculating the real pay, a cost-of-living allowance (COLA) is added to the base wage or salary. Cost-of-living indexes are published periodically in major business journals. The characteristics of an individual employee are also important in determining compensation. An individual's job qualifications, abilities and skills, prior experiences, and even willingness to work in hardship conditions are determining factors. Within the reasonable range of a market rate, companies offer additional compensation to attract and retain competent employees.

In principle, compensation must be designed around the job, not the person. Person-based pay frequently results in discriminatory practices, which violates the legal preconditions. For job-based compensation, management must conduct a systematic job analysis, identifying and describing what is happening on the job. Each job must be carefully examined to list the necessary tasks and actions, identify skills and abilities required, and establish desirable behaviours for successful completion of the job.

With complete and comprehensive data about all the jobs, job analysts must conduct systematic comparisons of them and determine their relative worth. Numerous techniques have been developed for the analysis of relative worth, including the simple point method, job classification method, job ranking method, and the factor comparison method. Information resulting from the comprehensive job analysis will be used for establishing pay or wage grades. Once a manager, can identify fair and realistic wages of two or more jobs, desirably top and bottom ones, then all the rest can be prorated along the wage curve.

In order to simplify the administration of a wage structure, similar jobs in the approximate cluster are grouped together into a class or grade for pay purpose.

As the market becomes more dynamic and competitive, companies are trying harder to improve performance. Since companies cannot afford to continually increase wages by a certain percentage, they are introducing many innovative compensation plans tied to performance. Several of these plans are discussed in this section.

Incentive Compensation Plan: Incentive compensation pays proportionately to employee performance. Incentives are typically given in addition to the base wage; they can be paid on the basis of individual, group, or plant-wide performance. While individual incentive plans encourage competition among employees, group or plant-wide incentive plans encourage cooperation and direct the efforts of all employees toward achieving overall company performance.

Skill-Based or Knowledge-Based Compensation: Skill-based pay is a system that pays employees based on the skills they possess or master, not for the job they hold. Some managers believe that mastery of certain sets of skills leads to higher productivity and therefore want their employees to master a series of skill sets. As employees gain one skill and then another, their wage rate goes up until they have mastered all the skills. Similar to skill-based pay is knowledge-based pay. While skill-based pay evolved in the manufacturing sector, pay-for-knowledge developed in the service sector (Henderson, 1997). For example, public school teachers with a bachelor's degree receive the lowest rate of pay, those with a master's degree receive a higher rate, and those with a doctorate receive the highest.

Team-Based Compensation: As many companies introduce team-based management practices such as self-managed work teams, they begin to offer team-based pay. Recognizing the importance of close cooperation and mutual development in a work group, companies want to encourage employees to work as a team by offering pay based on the overall effectiveness of the team.

Performance-Based Compensation: In the traditional sense, pay is considered entitlement that employees deserve in exchange for showing up at work and doing well enough to avoid being fired. While base pay is given to employees regardless of performance, incentives and bonuses are extra rewards given in appreciation of their extra efforts. Pay-for-performance is a new movement away from this entitlement concept (Milkovich and Newman, 1996). A pay-for-performance plan increases even the base pay—so-called merit increases—to reflect how highly employees are rated on a performance evaluation. Other incentives and bonuses are calculated based on this new merit pay, resulting in substantially more total dollars for highly ranked employee performance. Frequently, employees also receive an end-of-year lump sum bonus that does not build into base pay.

12.7 COMPENSATION STRUCTURE

A company's pay structure is the method of administering its pay philosophy. The two leading types of pay structures are the *internal equity method*, which uses a tightly constructed grid to ensure that each job is compensated according to the jobs above and below it in a hierarchy, and *market pricing*, where each job in an organization is tied to the prevailing market rate. A company needs job descriptions for all its positions so that people know where they fall within the organization. A pay structure helps answer questions about who's who, what each person's role is, and why people are compensated differently. It also helps human resources personnel to fairly administer any given pay philosophy. For example, a company might want to pay everyone at market; or pay some people at market and some above it. Opportunities for incentives are also dealt within the pay structure.

What is pay structure?

A pay structure provides a framework within which an organization defines the different levels of pay for jobs or groups of jobs, on the basis of assessment of their relative internal value and external relativities (Market rates) this may be negotiated.

Most important types of the Pay Structure:

1. Graded Pay Structure.
2. Broad Band Pay Structure.
3. Job Family Structures.
4. Individual Pay Structures.
5. Benefit Grade Structures.
6. Pay Curves.
7. Spot Rate Structure.
8. Pay Spines.
9. Pay Structures for Manual Workers.
10. Integrated Pay Structure
11. Rate for age scales.

Graded Pay Structure: That consists of a sequence of job grades into which jobs of broadly equivalent value are slotted.

Broad Band Structure: That consist of far fewer and for wider "bands" than the grades in a conventional structure *i.e.,* is the compression of a hierarchy of pay grades or salary range into a small no. of wide bands.

Job Family Structure: Jobs that are related to one another in terms of the basic activities carried out and skills used, *i.e.,* in a group of jobs, their nature and purpose is similar but carried out at the different levels (specific work groups).

Individual Job Structure/Ranges: Where content and size of jobs is widely different.

Benefit Grade Structures: Superimpose benefits grade structure on the top of individual job range (benefit available).

Pay Curves: Maturity and progression on curve of job family structures rewarding people on performance, combination of its worth.

Spot Rate Structure: In its simplest form, a spot or individual job rates structure allocates a specific rate for a job. There is no scope for the basic rate for the job to progress through defined pay range.

Pay Spines: Pay spines consist of series of incremental points extending from the lowest to highest paid covered by the structures *i.e.,* Public sector.

Pay Structure for Manual Workers: The structure is similar to any other pay structure is that it incorporate pay differentials between jobs which reflect real and assumed differentials in skill and responsibility but are influenced by practice and by settlements reached between management and trade unions.

Integrated Pay Structure: An integrated structure may have one grading system, which includes all employees—managers, professionals, technical, and office and manual workers, all though such structures leave out senior management.

Rate for Age Scales: Rate for age scales provides for a specific rate of pay or a pay brackets to the linked to age for staff in certain cases.

Pay structures, also known as salary structures, set out the different levels of pay for jobs, or groups of jobs, by reference to:

- Their relative internal value, as established by job evaluation.
- External relativities, via market rate surveys.
- Where appropriate, negotiated rates for the job.

What are the main characteristics of Pay Structures?

- Indicate rates of pay for different jobs.
- Provide scope for pay progression via performance, competence, contribution, skill or service.
- Contain pay ranges for jobs grouped into grades, individual jobs or job families.

Why do organizations need pay structures?

- Establish a logically-designed framework within which equitable, fair and consistent reward policies can be implemented.
- Determine levels of pay for jobs and people.
- Basis for the effective management of relativities.
- Help monitor and control the implementation of pay practices.
- Communicate the pay opportunities available to employees.

Developing a pay Structures

Once the job evaluation is complete, the data generated become the basis for the development of company's pay structure. Which means the pay rates are established that is compatible to the ranks, classifications or points arrived at through job evaluation. The way the organization structures its compensation packages is primarily a mątter of organizational philosophy though the market trends play an important role. The company can choose several options available. It can be using a single rate structure in which all the employees perform the same work receive the same pay. Or the second method is tenure based, that is based on the time for which an individual has been associated with the organization. This can be a combination of seniority and tenure based plans also. At times, pay can be linked with performance or productivity. The job evaluation methods give us the inputs for developing an organizational over all pay structure. Besides that other sources of information can be utilized for above said purposes:

- Conduct of Surveys
- Reports
- Pay Commissions reports
- Reports of the Wage Boards
- Reports of the employee and employer
- Trade Union Journals etc.

Choice of the Structures

1. Types of the organization; size, complexity, culture and tradition.
2. Formal organizational structures and internal relativities.
3. Degree of knowledge workers.
4. Degree of Formalities.
5. Degree of growth of the company.

Standard Salary Structure

A standard base pay program offers fixed salary ranges for each position type for employees performing the standard duties of their jobs. Set up minimum and maximum levels within those pay ranges to account for variations in experience and skill levels. When setting the base pay structure, determine where your company falls within your own industry as well as competing industries that may also offer job opportunities for your employees. Set up your pay levels to be competitive, or else you risk losing employees. You can use the Internet to find industry-standard salary levels for specific jobs in specific geographical areas.

Once your base pay structure is in place, most companies then set up a merit pay program that will take the employee through the salary range for their position at a performance-driven speed. This comes into play when the employee's managers do **annual employee performance reviews**. The downside of this is that employees may begin to see it as a given that they will get a salary increase after each evaluation, and it ceases to be a motivation to perform better in their jobs. For this reason, more companies are moving toward more of a reward-based compensation style, also called **Incentive Compensation**.

Incentive Compensation

Incentive-based compensation is becoming much more common because of the increased emphasis on performance and competition for talent. This type of compensation structure significantly helps motivate employees to perform well. Hiring bonuses are also frequently used now, even for new college graduates. However, you might want to tie in a specific time period prior to the employee collecting this bonus—for example, one-half after six months and the remainder after one year of employment. Otherwise, you could run the risk of the employee departing after that first check, which would defeat your purpose. So does that mean incentive compensation is the way to go? May be so, if your business is in an industry where you really have to compete to get good employees.

Setting up an incentive-based compensation program requires the same research into your industry as the base pay program. You'll still establish base pay levels, but it may be slightly lower and you will build into that base the annual or quarterly (or any other interval) bonuses, commissions, or other types of shared cash compensation.

12.8 JOB EVALUATION SYSTEMS

Compensation management starts with the job evaluation. The job evaluation is a set of systematic procedures to determine the relative worth of jobs within the organization. The ultimate goal is the establishment of an hierarchical alignment of jobs based on a common set of criteria. These evaluation criteria are generally expressed in the form of "compensable factors":

Components of job content or work demands that are felt to provide the basis for compensation.

In general, most organizations use four broad categories of factors:

- Skill
- Effort
- Responsibility
- Working Conditions

Point-factor plans or factor comparison approaches typically employ similar sets of factors.

Some commonly used factors are:

- Knowledge Required

- Supervisory Controls
- Complexity
- Scope and Effect
- Personal Contacts
- Purpose of Contacts
- Guidelines
- Physical Demands
- Work Environment

There are, of course other factors, which also play a role in the establishment of a rational compensation policy:

- Scarcity of supply of skills or tightness of the labour market.
  - Labour mobility and market activity in response to pay differentials.
- Recruitment and retention.
  - Associated costs of moving-physical and psychological.
- Life style aspirations of current or prospective employees.
- Loyalty towards current employer.
  - Sense of security, willingness to face change.
  - Attraction of benefits, work relationships, organizational values.

Remuneration policy must embrace factors such as the firm's objectives, its finances, cash flow, profitability, government regulations on pay, and any company growth/contraction that may be expected.

Job Evaluations and Market Considerations

A firm can arrive at appropriate wages for positions in the firm on the basis of two main compensation management tools: 1. job evaluations (based on compensable factors such as effort, skill, working conditions, and responsibility), and 2. the going rate (or market value) of a job.

Job evaluation

Through job evaluations, jobs in the firm may be rated according to their relative "importance." Each job might be given its own rate, or jobs of comparable importance may be grouped into a single wage classification, or pay grades. Job evaluations compare positions in an organization with respect to such factors as effort, skill, working conditions, responsibility, and so on.

For the job evaluation to be useful, a detailed list of compensable factors needs to be articulated. To increase the utility of the job evaluation, workers may be asked to participate in the process of evaluating the firm's jobs. Employees can add valuable insight into the essential job attributes for various positions.

Job evaluations, then, reflect the relative value or contribution of different jobs to an organization. Once a job evaluation has been completed, market comparisons for a few key jobs need to be used as anchors for market reality. In theory, other jobs in the job evaluation can be adjusted correspondingly.

Market considerations

In practice, results of job evaluations are often compromised by market considerations. For example, no matter what the firm's job evaluation may indicate, it is unlikely that the firm will be able to pay wages drastically lower (or higher) than the going rate. Whereas the "market" clearly plays a role in the establishment of wages, the market is not totally free. Legal constraints such as pay equity schemes and minimum wage legislation clearly affect wages.

To establish external equity, employers need information about what other employers pay in the same labour market. Wage surveys of jobs in similar industries should describe jobs accurately, as positions may vary widely, even for jobs with the same title.

Job evaluations and market surveys

In setting wages, it is essential to reconcile market information and job evaluation results rather than to rely on only one or the other.

Job evaluation methodologies

A variety of methodologies may be used to arrive at the hierarchical alignment of jobs required for purposes of arriving at equitable wages.

Job ranking

In job ranking, each job is ranked subjectively according to its importance in comparison with other jobs in the organization. Unfortunately, overall rankings of jobs frequently fail to differentiate between the relative importance of the jobs. For example, a ranking system may fail to show that the value of a number two ranked job is essentially the same as that of the number one ranked job (and, consequently, worth almost as much in terms of compensation), whereas the number three ranked job may contribute not nearly as much value to the firm (and, consequently, be worth substantially less in terms of compensation).

Job grading

In the job grading method, each job is assigned a grade according to it's match with a standard description. Each job description is compared with the standard "grading" description.

Job grading example

JOB GRADE STANDARD DESCRIPTIONS

GRADE	STANDARD DESCRIPTION
I	Work is simple and highly repetitive; with close supervision, requiring minimal training and little responsibility or initiative.
II	Simple and repetitive work done under close supervision and requiring some training or skill. Employee is expected to assume responsibility or exhibit initiative only rarely.
III	Work is simple, with little variation; done under general supervision. Training or skill required. Employee has minimum responsibilities and must take some initiative to perform satisfactorily.

IV	Work is moderately complex, with some variation; done under general supervision. High level of skill required. Employee is responsible for equipment or safety; regularly exhibits initiative.
V	Work is complex, varied, done under general supervision. Advanced skill level required. Employee is responsible for equipment and safety; shows high degree of initiative.

Using the job grading system, all jobs falling into a particular category would receive the same compensation. In effect, they are assumed to be contributing equivalent "value" to the firm.

Factor comparison

The factor comparison methods requires jobs to be compared on critical job components.

Critical job components are those factors common to all jobs in the organization being evaluated. In general, these factors can be grouped into four broad categories:

- Skill
- Effort
  - Mental effort
  - Physical effort
- Responsibility
- Working conditions

A Step-by-Step Approach to Factor Comparison

Step 1.	**Determine the Critical Factors** • Determine which factors are common and important over a broad range of jobs. ▪ Involve employees using a variety of methodologies—interviews, questionnaires, brain-storming.
Step 2.	**Determine the Key Jobs** • Key jobs are common throughout the organization. • Key jobs are also common in the local labour market. ▪ A market price can thus be determined for these jobs.
Step 3.	**Apportion present wages for Key Jobs** • Allocate a part of each key job's wage rate to each critical factor. ▪ The allocation depends on the importance of that factor to the job in question.
Step 4.	**Place Key Jobs and Jobs to be Evaluated on Factor Comparison Chart** • Rows: key jobs. • Columns: critical factors.
Step 5.	**Evaluate Other Jobs** • Use Key Jobs as benchmarks. • Compare other jobs as the basis of critical factors. ▪ Assign dollars of the basis of this comparison.

Point system

The point system involves an evaluation of critical factors with an allocation of points instead of dollars to ascertain the relative worth of a variety of jobs to the firm.

Step

Step	
Step 1.	**Determine Critical Factors** • Brainstorm with department heads to determine which job factors are critical across a broad range of jobs within the organization.
Step 2. and Step 3.	**Determine Levels of Factors** • Extent of responsibility for factors varies from job to job. • Points allocated to various levels for each critical factor (*e.g.*, a total of 1000 points).

Job evaluations, gender bias, and pay equity

Job evaluation plans are the principal means for establishing the comparability of jobs and, as such, they are used in efforts to achieve greater pay equity. However, they remain controversial because they have often been found to contain gender biases.

For example, the selection of factors and factor weights in most job evaluations is designed to reflect market wage relationships. It is argued that a firm's wages must reflect "reality". However, the use of such factors and factor weights may serve to institutionalize gender biases contained in prevailing market rates. It cannot be assumed that market rates are free of bias.

Further, job evaluations are highly subjective in their application and gender biases may be introduced at any number of steps in the process.

12.9 PAY EQUITY

One consideration in the establishment of a compensation policy has to do with absolute versus relative levels of pay. Quite simply, absolute levels of pay provide for satisfaction of an employee's physiological and safety needs (see Maslow on the topic of motivation). On the other hand, relative pay levels address issues of satisfaction of social and esteem needs. Relative pay levels have to do with the comparisons employees make of pay within the organization, and deal with feelings of fairness or equity. Worker dissatisfaction is likely increase if either internal or external equity principles are violated.

Simply put, internal equity refers to the relative fairness of wages received by other employees in the same organization. External equity is fairness relative to wages outside the organization.

Employees will act to restore equity if they perceive an imbalance. In evaluating the fairness of their pay, employees balance the ratio of their inputs (*e.g.,* work effort, skills) and outcomes (*e.g.,* pay, privileges) against those of their coworkers. Workers may thus experience guilt if they feel over-compensated, or they may feel anger if they perceive that they are being under-compensated.

The greater the perceived disparity, the greater the tension. In order to relieve this tension, employees may seek balance in a number of ways:

1. Modify input or output (*e.g.*, if underpaid, a person may reduce his efforts or try to obtain a raise; if overpaid, he/she may increase efforts or work longer hours without additional compensation—although they are as likely to be able to rationalize their level of over-compensation);
2. Adjust the notion of what is fair (*e.g.*, if underpaid, a worker may think of himself as being the recipient of other benefits—such as doing interesting work; if overpaid, an employee may come to believe he deserves it);
3. Change source of equity comparison (*e.g.*, an employee who has compared himself with a promoted co-worker may begin to compare himself with another worker);
4. Attempt to change the input or output of others (*e.g.*, asking others not to work so hard or to work harder);
5. Withdraw (*e.g.*, through increased absenteeism, mental withdrawal or quitting);
6. Force others to withdraw (*e.g.*, trying to obtain a transfer for a co-worker or force him to quit).

Employees use a myriad of factors (both inputs and outputs) to arrive at their perceptions of fairness. As such, reward systems must compensate not only for levels of work done, but also for quality of performance, age, and length of service. The reward system is clearly an integral part of the motivational process. Further, the reward system also serves to protect employees against inflationary pressures.

12.10 EXECUTIVE COMPENSATION

The traditional view of executive remuneration or compensation is to attract and retain qualified personnel. While true in simple terms, this definition fails to consider the significance of compensation programs in the overall governance of organizations. For long-term investors, a much broader view of remuneration is required that encompasses proper alignment, incentives to pursue optimal capital allocation and good corporate governance. Investors have taken an increased interest and more active role in remuneration in recent years for several reasons. First and foremost, institutional investors have a fiduciary responsibility to act in the best interest of their beneficiaries, and executive remuneration is an important cornerstone.

Secondly, because remuneration programs have such a significant impact on the alignment and incentives of management, they are inexorably linked to the long-term viability of the company. Well designed remuneration programs have a demonstrable positive impact on the long-term performance of the company. Conversely, poorly designed or poorly executed compensation plans can have a serious negative impact on share holders value. In this regard, the opportunity for a significant principal/agent problem arises. Thus, investors have a clear economic interest in addition to a fiduciary interest in the design and implementation of remuneration plans. The combination of these drivers give owners, particularly long-term owners, a role in setting broad policies and guidelines related to executive remuneration and in overseeing the practices of companies in this area through such means as proxy voting and direct engagement. These guidelines are primarily addressed to companies and their non-executive or supervisory board members, and set out key remuneration principles which should be applied by companies regardless of their domicile. They cannot address every issue related to remuneration. Rather, they reflect the overall policy and philosophical approach to remuneration that leading institutional investors and their associations expect from companies. In this regard, the guidelines set out general principles that reflect best international practice. They should be applied pragmatically, taking into account the specific circumstances of each company and the economic and legal environment in which it operates.

Executive remuneration basically centers on factors such as job complexity, the companies ability to pay, and the executive human capital. Organizations decide the executive compensation packages consisting of basic pay, allowances, perquisites, and stock options, based on no. of factors. Some are also base on the accountability, problem-solving and know how. Some considered the following factors to determine the remuneration of the executives *i.e.,* education, experiences, scope of the activities, need to negotiate, and types of problem handled, decision-making authority, size of the unit managed, influence on the results, no. of people supervisied, and no. of reporting steps to the head of the unit. The Indian companies generally structure executive compensation based on the following factors: salary, bonus, commission, PF, family pension, medical reimbursement, pension fund, LTC, HRA, and other perquisites. In recent years, other types of the allowances including Stock Options and developmental initiatives have also been included.

Remuneration packages must be set to attract the best people for the job. But it is important that high pay at the top is linked effectively to performance. All remuneration should be related to the performance of individuals, teams or organizations as a whole or to permutations of these three. Yet at the most senior levels, executive pay and other remuneration continue to arouse controversy, particularly where increases are accompanied by weak corporate performance and/or pay restraint for other employees. Director's pay is not just an issue of the cost to the company, but also has serious implications for corporate performance. It must provide the right incentives to senior management, be linked to performance targets and have the desired effect on the morale and motivation of employees, customers and the public as a whole. Remuneration committees, mostly of non-executive directors, have been set up by big companies to control the executive pay spiral and protect shareholders' interests.

Executive remuneration: background

It has long been recognized in all but the most closely held owner-managed companies, that the powers delegated to the directors may enable them to serve their own interests at the expense of shareholders. In response to the need for direction and clarity over board issues, such as directors' pay, various committees were established over the 1990s. The background of the executive remuneration debate stems from the following reports:

- The report of the Committee on the Financial Aspects of Corporate Governance chaired by Sir Adrian Cadbury ("the Cadbury Report"), published in December 1992;
- The report of a Study Group on directors' remuneration chaired by Sir Richard Greenbury ("the Greenbury Report"), published in July 1995; and
- The report on the Committee on Corporate Governance chaired by Sir Ronald Hampel ("the Report") published in January 1998.

The first, the Cadbury Committee, issued a Code of Practice in 1992 on:

- The board's role and functions;
- Its composition, and appointment procedures for directors;
- Qualities required of a non-executive director;
- Executive directors' pay; and

- Duties of the board to present a balanced view of the company's performance, and maintain effective internal controls and relationships with auditors.

The code was directed to listed UK companies, but the Committee hoped that as many other companies as possible would aim to meet its requirements. In 1995, public outcry over very large pay increases awarded to directors of newly privatized companies led to the establishment of the Greenbury Committee. This elaborated on the work of Cadbury on executive director remuneration. In 1996, the Hampel Committee was established. Hampel's remit was to:

- Review the Cadbury Code and its implementation;
- Keep under review the role of directors (executive and non-executive);
- Review the Greenbury recommendations; and
- Address the roles of shareholders and auditors in corporate governance.

In particular, its more notable findings on remuneration were:

- Boards should set as their object the reduction of directors' contract periods to one year or less, although this cannot be achieved immediately. [Addressing this issue Sir Ronald Hampel stated that he did not believe that directors' service contracts could be reduced without compensation].
- Decisions on the remuneration packages of executive directors should be delegated to the remuneration committee; the broad framework and cost of executive remuneration should be a matter for the board on the advice of the remuneration committee. [The Committee agrees that shareholder approval should be sought for new long-term incentive plans, but does not favour obliging companies to seek shareholder approval for the remuneration report. In this respect the Committee has stated: 'To require shareholder approval for a single aspect of company policy would, in our view, be inappropriate.']

The purpose of the remuneration policy

Those responsible for remuneration need to be clear on:

- The purpose of the remuneration policy, the strategy and the objectives of the arrangements;
- Whether there should be a pay 'spine' and, if so, how long it should be; what the intervals are; whether it should be automatically adjusted or on some other basis;
- Whether jobs should be graded and, if so, how; whether each grade should have a money band; whether these should be sequential; what overlap there should be;
- The basis on which salaries are fixed within a band;
- The basis on which individuals progress through the bands—*e.g.,* automatically or on merit only;
- When to use non-recurrent, non-pensionable bonuses;
- Performance reviews—for training or for pay or for both; and
- The use of external comparators.

Special Features of Executive Compensation:

Executive remuneration had certain unique features:

1. Executive remuneration cannot be compared with ages and salary schemes meant for other employees in the organization. Simple comparisons rating may not be possible in these jobs as factors and variables involved are numerous.

2. Executive are denied the privileges of having unions. It is the workers who resort to strikes, slogan shouting etc. and if they succeed in their efforts, executives too benefit.
3. Secrecy is maintained in the respect of executive remuneration. Secrecy is maintained because no executives in the private sector, in the same grade, receive the same pay. Remuneration depends on such factors as competency, length of services and the loyalty to the founders.
4. Executive pay is not supposed to be based on individual performance because an executive's own performance is assumed to be rather directly reflected in the measure of unit and/or corporate performance.
5. Executive remuneration is subject to statutory ceiling. These ceilings however, do not apply to the private limited companies.

Executive Compensation Plan

Compensation plans generally consist of **four primary categories**: Cash and short-term incentives; equity and long-term incentives; retirement and post employment benefits and "other" compensation, such as perquisites.

Cash and Short-term Incentives: The cash component and short-term incentives should generally be tied to annual performance measures. Objectives should be set and recorded at the beginning of the performance period. Companies should disclose the circumstances in which short-term performance measures may be adjusted, including the process and timing of disclosure of these actions.

Equity and Long-term Incentive Tools: The equity and long-term incentive component should consist of an appropriate mix of equity and equity like tools, which may include options, restricted shares, stock appreciation rights, and other equity-like incentive structures for example. The companies should provide clear justification for the types of equity tools employed and the relative mix of these tools.

Companies should provide a clear plan (contained within the remuneration report or other disclosures) that details how these tools will be used including the target dilution levels, cumulative dilution to date, and projected run rates over a multi-year period and actual run rates over previous years. This justification should include the methodology by which companies will determine the appropriate dilution and run rate, and evaluate the effectiveness of the plan over time, including its impact on long-term value creation. The equity plan should also include a maximum annual limit on individual participation and the planed distribution of equity tools (In other words, distribution between the executive ranks and employee base including the rough percentage of the overall plan that will go to each group).

Performance-based Methodologies: It strongly supports the use of performance measures tied to the vesting of equity and equity like instruments. This may include indexing or premium pricing methodologies and other performance criteria such as key operational metrics. The ICGN does not support time accelerated vesting as a legitimate or desirable performance vesting methodology.

Performance targets associated with equity components should be consistent with long-term sustained superior performance. This means that performance goals should be constructed to measure sustained performance over long periods (including multiple accounting periods). Care should be taken to mitigate potential unintended negative incentives that may be associated with performance measures. For example, poorly constructed performance programs could provide an opportunity to manipulate short-term accounting measures to meet performance goals.

Post Employment and Other Benefits: Post employment and other benefits include retirement arrangements (both defined benefit and defined contribution plans), health care, and other benefits such as perquisites (both during and after employment). Should companies utilize any of these forms of remuneration, care should be taken to integrate these structures within the overall philosophy and structure of the total plan. Post employment and other benefits can entail significant liability for the company and may represent significant portions of the total value of the remuneration program. As such, the alignment and incentive characteristics of these elements of the remuneration plan can have a material impact on its overall effectiveness.

The main principles of the executive remuneration policy are

- To provide total remuneration which is competitive in structure and quantum with comparator companies' practices in the regions and markets within which the group operates;
- To achieve clear alignment between total remuneration and delivered business and personal performance, with particular emphasis on shareholder value creation and performance in the health, safety and environmental areas;
- To link variable elements of remuneration to the achievement of challenging performance criteria that are consistent with the best interests of the Group and shareholders over the short, medium and long-term;
- To provide an appropriate balance of fixed and variable remuneration; and
- To provide appropriate relativities between executives, in order to support executive placements to meet the needs;
- The composition of total remuneration packages for management, including the remuneration of the company secretaries, is designed to provide an appropriate balance between fixed and variable components. This is in line with stated objective of aligning total remuneration with personal and business performance.

Executive remuneration: a summary

Directors face a direct conflict of interest when setting their own remuneration. This has caused controversies over directors' pay in recent years. It is in shareholders' interests to see this issue dealt with satisfactorily if the integrity and reputation of business is not to be undermined.

Remuneration policy should reflect the requirements to attract, retain and motivate executives. The key principle must be the effective link of rewards to performance. However, financial rewards need to be seen in the context of the director's other terms and conditions, the company's culture and its aims and objectives.

Remuneration packages

1. Should be such as to enable people of appropriately high ability to be recruited, retained and motivated within levels of affordability.
2. Should be auditable and publicly defensible.
3. Require a clear statement of responsibilities to which achievement and reward can be related.
4. Should be transparent, fully disclosed and explained.
5. Should be structured to link rewards to corporate and individual performance.

When designing and implementing remuneration schemes it is necessary to:

1. Consider the extent to which remuneration really influences management's impact on corporate performance and the evidence available to support this.
2. Consider the activities and conditions of the business. Remuneration schemes are particular to the organization and the individual therein. They must fit its particular circumstances.
3. Review the existing reward process and determine areas for improvement.
4. Consider whether the advantages of management incentive schemes outweigh the disadvantages.

Do not underestimate the time and effort required creating and managing an effective executive remuneration policy. You need to, for example:

1. Review the executive remuneration structure, what is being paid and how, compared to the market.
2. Be able to audit performance levels against agreed personal tasks derived from the business plan and corporate objectives.
3. Assess the current management culture and decide the relativity that the organisation wishes to have between the remuneration of senior executives and that of other employees.
4. Be able to evaluate the apparent links between executive performance and corporate performance separating the reality from predetermined belief.
5. Test the schemes are not divisive and do not reward individuals for behaviour damaging to the overall position.
6. Avoid short-term expediency at the expense of performance growth and improvement in quality over the sustainable longer term.
7. Ensure that short-term rewards do not get incorporated into recurrent rewards unless justified by sustained performance improvement.

12.11 COMPENSATION TRENDS

How will employee compensation programs evolve during the 21st century? Predicting developments in this field is difficult for many of the same reasons that making economic predictions is difficult. We live in a vibrant economy that routinely outpaces our ability to understand it fully and in a world where outside factors often change a system before we can model it precisely.

Like the economy as a whole, the compensation field is affected by forces working in opposite directions. Employers seek to curb labour costs to remain competitive in supplying goods and services, but at the same time may need to upgrade compensation programs to attract and retain skilled workers. Additionally, an aging population, by placing increased demands on employer health care and retirement plans, may prompt employers to adopt cost containment measures. At the same time, however, a small supply of young workers may prompt employers to enhance compensation packages to compete for qualified staff.

These opposing forces will challenge efforts to maintain correct and relevant statistics on compensation in this new century. The voluntary nature of most data collection relies on the cooperation of employers and especially human resource professionals. As these individuals face the difficult task of developing competitive compensation packages while limiting costs, their ability to comply with requests for detailed data may be strained.

Three major trends characterized employee compensation in the last years of the 20th century, and these trends will probably shape employee compensation in the early years of the new century. As with the last century, however, it is unlikely that the ways employees are compensated will evolve along a straight path. Companies and governments will try many alternative programs; some will work and become the paradigms of the 21st century; others will not and will be discarded or will be adopted in only a few workplaces.

Aligning pay to organizational goals: The first of these three major compensation trends is aligning pay to organizational goals. As our Nation's economy becomes increasingly tied to world economic conditions, competitive pressures will prompt employers to seek ways to efficiently use their work-forces. Employee compensation, in this environment, will increasingly be viewed as a tool for promoting increased productivity and innovation among workers. Compensation programs are, thus, likely to be geared to employee performance or desired characteristics such as skills or knowledge. Examples of these compensation programs include variable pay schemes that tie pay to individual or group performance and salary plans that reflect the possession or acquisition of knowledge or skills deemed critical to the success of the organization. Compensation in the 21st century is also likely to evolve in ways that tie employee pay and benefits to corporate performance. Examples include stock options and profit-sharing plans.

Tailoring compensation to employee needs: The second major trend is tailoring compensation to employee needs. This is a way of efficiently delivering compensation to employees by giving them a choice in what they want or need, rather than providing a universal program that meets the needs of the average employee. Examples include choices among health care and within retirement savings plans, flexible work schedules and telecommunicating arrangements, and reimbursement accounts. Implicit in this flexibility is the increase of employee responsibility in making prudent choices. On the other hand, this flexibility may be constrained, particularly if significant numbers of employees make poor choices. Social policy concerns about the consequences of unwise choices, however, are less likely to stymie—than to shape—the evolution of this flexibility.

Reconfiguring employee benefit plans: The third major trend is reconfiguring employee benefit plans to provide for a defined level of employer contributions, rather than a defined level of ultimate benefit. This has been the trend in retirement plans over the 1980s and 1990s and may spread to other types of employee benefits plans. Examples include defined contribution employee health insurance plans, defined contribution retiree health insurance plans, and employer-funded reimbursement accounts. These arrangements give employers greater control over costs than in the past and greater ability to predict costs. On the other hand, employees are required to absorb more risks associated with insuring against future events than formerly. Coupled with the trend to charge employees with more responsibility for retirement savings and other benefits, the move towards defined contribution insurance arrangements may spur counter-measures to insulate employees from these risks. For example, a defined contribution health insurance plan might be required to include a core set of benefits that guards employees against catastrophic expenses.

In the 1990s these three major compensation trends were seen as helping to meet the needs of a mobile work-force. With the expected labour shortages of the early years of the new century, however, these trends are likely to be tempered in ways thought to increase employee incentives for remaining with the organization. Employer drives to increase efficiency and curb costs may have to be balanced with one of the traditional goals of compensation programs—to acquire and maintain an adequate supply of skilled labour.

Capturing and reporting data that adequately illuminate these major trends will be a challenge for the Bureau of Labour Statistics and others. The movement toward compensation that is based more on individual performance—and, thus, fewer standards—will require more data collection and innovative means of reporting results. No longer can pay be captured and reported as an hourly rate; all manner of pay such as individual bonuses, group bonuses, gain sharing, and stock options might need to be included in the new concept of pay.

The trend toward greater employee choice in compensation has already posed data collection and tabulation challenges; expansion of such choices will only compound the challenges. For example, where once employers offered only one health insurance plan, the often present choice of several plans means more data must be collected. And employee choice to substitute one benefit for another makes it more difficult to identify how much of a benefit cost is paid by the employer versus the employee. Additionally, flexibility in work hours (called flextime or flexitime) and work location (telecommuting or sometimes flexplace) make the traditional concept of compensation per hour less meaningful than before. Just as the 20th century saw an evolution in compensation statistics to address changes in the law and the growth of benefits, it is likely that statistics at the close of the 21st century will little resemble data available today.

Compensation Issues/Challenging issuers on employee compensation

It is important for small business owners to understand the difference between wages and salaries. A wage is based on hours worked. Employees who receive a wage are often called "non-exempt." A salary is an amount paid for a particular job, regardless of hours worked, and these employees are called "exempt." The difference between the two is carefully defined by the type of position and the kinds of tasks that employees perform. In general, exempt employees include executives, administrative and professional employees, and others as defined by the Fair Labour Standards Act of 1938. These groups are not covered by minimum wage provisions. Non-exempt employees are covered by minimum wage as well as other provisions.

It is important to pay careful attention to these definitions when determining whether an individual is to receive a wage or a salary. Improper classification of a position can not only pose legal problems, but often results in employee dissatisfaction, especially if the employee believes that execution of the responsibilities and duties of the position warrant greater compensation than is currently awarded.

When setting the level of an employee's monetary compensation, several factors must be considered. First and foremost, wages must be set high enough to motivate and attract good employees. They must also be equitable—that is, the wage must accurately reflect the value of the labour performed. In order to determine salaries or wages that are both equitable for employees and sustainable for companies, businesses must first make certain that they understand the responsibilities and requirements of the position under review. The next step is to review prevailing rates and classifications for similar jobs. This process requires research of the competitive rate for a particular job within a given geographical area. Wage surveys can be helpful in defining wage and salary structures, but these should be undertaken by a professional (when possible) to achieve the most accurate results. In addition, professional wage surveys can sometimes be found through local employment bureaus or in the pages of trade publications. Job analysis not only helps to set wages and salaries, but ties into several other Human Resource functions such as hiring, training, and performance appraisal. As the job is defined, a wage can be determined and the needs for hiring and training can be evaluated. The evaluation criteria for performance appraisal can also be constructed as the specific responsibilities of a position are defined.

Other factors to consider when settling on a salary for a position include:

- Availability of people capable of fulfilling the obligations and responsibilities of the job.
- Level of demand elsewhere in the community and/or industry for prospective employees.
- Cost of living in the area.
- Attractiveness of the community in which the company operates.
- Compensation levels already in existence elsewhere in the company.

Traditional compensation

For the most part, traditional methods of compensation involve set pay levels (wage or salary) with regular increases. Increases can be given for a variety of reasons, but are typically given for promotions, merit increases, or cost of living increases. The Hay Group points out that there is less distinction today between merit increases and cost of living increases: "Because of the low levels (3 to 4 per cent) of salary budget funding, most merit raises are perceived as little more than cost of living increases. Employees have come to expect them." This "base pay" system is one that most people are familiar with. Often, it includes a set salary or wage, a set schedule for merit increases, and a set benefits package.

Benefits

Benefits are an important part of an employee's total compensation package. Benefits packages became popular after World War II, when wage controls made it more difficult to give competitive salaries. Benefits were added to monetary compensation to attract, retain, and motivate employees, and they still perform that function today. They are not cash rewards, but they do have monetary value (for example, spiraling health care costs make health benefits particularly essential to today's families). Many of these benefits are nontaxable to the employee and deductible by the employer.

Many benefits are not required by law, but are nonetheless common in total compensation packages. These include health insurance, accidental death and dismemberment insurance, some form of retirement plan (including profit-sharing, stock option programs, 401(k) and employee stock ownership plans), vacation and holiday pay, and sick leave. Companies may also offer various services, such as day care, to employees, either free or at a reduced cost. It is also common to provide employees with discounted services or products offered by the company itself. In addition, there are also certain benefits that are required by either state or federal law. Federal law, for example, requires the employer to pay into Social Security, and unemployment insurance is mandated under OASDHI. State laws govern worker's compensation.

Changes in compensation systems

As businesses change their focus, their approach to compensation must change as well. Traditional compensation methods may hold a company back from adequately rewarding its best workers. When compensation is tied to a base salary and a position, there is little flexibility in the reward system. Some new compensation systems, on the other hand, focus on reward for skills and performance, with the work force sharing in company profit or loss. One core belief of new compensation policies is that as employees become employee owners, they are likely to work harder to ensure the success of the company. Indeed, programs that promote employee ownership—and thus employee responsibility and emotional investment—are becoming increasingly popular. Examples of these types of programs include gain sharing, in which employees earn bonuses by finding ways to save the company money; pay for knowledge, in which compensation is based on job knowledge and skill rather than on position (and in which employees can increase base pay by learning a variety of jobs); and incentive plans such as Employee Stock Options Plans (ESOPs).

Pay for Performance: Probably the most popular of the newer concepts in compensation is the easiest to understand—compensation based on performance. These programs, sometimes referred to as variable pay programs, generally offer compensation incentives based on employee performance or on the performance of a team. Pay for performance rewards high performance and does not reward mediocre or low performance, and is the definition of the "merit" system.

In a true merit based system, there are a few conditions which must be satisfied for it to be meaningful:

- Employees must have control over their performance. If employees are overly dependent on the actions and output of other employees or processes, they may have little control over their own performance.
- Differences in performance must mean something to the business. If there is little difference between a high performer and a mediocre one, merit pay won't work.
- Performance must be measured regularly and reliably. A clear system of performance appraisal, with defined criteria that are understood by the employee and regularly scheduled meetings must be in place.

Innovations in compensation systems

As the market becomes more dynamic and competitive, companies are trying harder to improve performance. Since companies cannot afford to continually increase wages by a certain percentage, they are introducing many innovative compensation plans tied to performance. Several of these plans are discussed in this section.

Incentive Compensation Plan: Incentive compensation pays proportionately to employee performance. Incentives are typically given in addition to the base wage; they can be paid on the basis of individual, group, or plant-wide performance. While individual incentive plans encourage competition among employees, group or plant-wide incentive plans encourage cooperation and direct the efforts of all employees toward achieving overall company performance.

Skill-based or Knowledge-based Compensation: Skill-based pay is a system that pays employees based on the skills they possess or master, not for the job they hold. Some managers believe that mastery of certain sets of skills leads to higher productivity and therefore want their employees to master a series of skill sets. As employees gain one skill and then another, their wage rate goes up until they have mastered all the skills. Similar to skill-based pay is knowledge-based pay. While skill-based pay evolved in the manufacturing sector, pay-for-knowledge developed in the service sector (Henderson, 1997). For example, public school teachers with a bachelor's degree receive the lowest rate of pay, those with a master's degree receive a higher rate, and those with a doctorate receive the highest.

Team-based compensation: As many companies introduce team-based management practices such as self-managed work teams, they begin to offer team-based pay. Recognizing the importance of close cooperation and mutual development in a work group, companies want to encourage employees to work as a team by offering pay based on the overall effectiveness of the team.

Performance-based compensation: In the traditional sense, pay is considered entitlement that employees deserve in exchange for showing up at work and doing well enough to avoid being fired. While base pay is given to employees regardless of performance, incentives and bonuses are extra rewards given in appreciation of their extra efforts. Pay-for-performance is a new movement away from this entitlement concept (Milkovich and Newman, 1996). A pay-for-performance plan increases even the base pay—so-called merit increases—to reflect how highly employees are rated on a performance evaluation. Other incentives and bonuses are calculated based on this new merit pay, resulting in substantially more total dollars for highly ranked employee performance. Frequently, employees also receive an end-of-year lump sum bonus that does not build into base pay.

Administering compensation programs

Compensation programs and policies must be communicated clearly and thoroughly to employees. Employees naturally want to have a clear understanding of what they can reasonably expect in terms of compensation (both in terms of monetary compensation and benefits) and performance appraisal. To ensure that this takes place, consultants urge business owners to detail all aspects of their compensation programs in writing. Taking this step not only helps reassure employees, but also provides the owner with additional legal protection from unfair labour practices accusations.

Conclusion

In exchange for job performance and commitment, an employer offers rewards to employees. Adequate rewards and compensations potentially attract a quality work force, maintain the satisfaction of existing employees, keep quality employees from leaving, and motivate them in the workplace. A proper design of reward and compensation systems requires careful review of the labour market, thorough analysis of jobs, and a systematic study of pay structures.

There are a number of ways of classifying rewards. A commonly discussed dichotomy is intrinsic versus extrinsic rewards. Intrinsic rewards are satisfactions one gets from the job itself, such as a feeling of achievement, responsibility, or autonomy. Extrinsic rewards include monetary compensation, promotion, and tangible benefits.

Compensation frequently refers to extrinsic, monetary rewards that employees receive in exchange for their work. Usually, compensation is composed of the base wage or salary, any incentives or bonuses, and other benefits. Base wage or salary is the hourly, weekly, or monthly pay that employees receive. Incentives or bonuses are rewards offered in addition to the base wage when employees achieve a high level of performance. Benefits are rewards offered for being a member of the company and can include paid vacation, health and life insurance, and retirement pension.

A company's compensation system must include policies, procedures, and rules that provide clear and unambiguous determination and administration of employee compensation. Otherwise, there can be confusion, diminished employee satisfaction, and potentially costly litigation. In fast-paced, continuously changing, high performance organizations, the emphasis must be on finding the people who not only bring relevant skills, competencies, and experience but who are also willing and able to apply them in a variety of situations and projects. Here, flexibility and adaptability are essential, and people are viewed as resources whose abilities contribute to the core capabilities and overall performance of the organization. To develop a loyal and motivated workforce, companies of all sizes must create competitive compensation and benefits packages. This is particularly important when starting a shared service centre from scratch. In recent years, rising healthcare costs, proposed rulings concerning the expensing of stock options, pension schemes and shifting employee values have prompted many businesses to re-examine their compensation programmes and make adjustments designed to maximize their value while minimizing their costs. By monitoring emerging developments affecting pay and incentive programmes and responding accordingly, these firms have increased their ability to recruit and retain the most talented professionals. As the economy gains momentum and many organizations begin augmenting their staffing levels, this is an opportune time for companies to re-evaluate the effectiveness of their compensation and benefits programmes. The quality of a company's people is the greatest single factor determining its future. A competitive compensation and benefits package is key to a company's ability to attract and retain top talent. As the economy shows increasing signs of improvement, employees at all levels are likely to have more career choices with fair compensation packages.

CASE STUDY–I Innovating consulting limited

Innovating Consulting Limited is a leading organization providing consulting services to the banking and financial sector in the country. The company was established by a team of six principal consultants who were working in various reputed consulting organizations and had a minimum experience of 20 years. Initially, the company obtained business because of the contacts of the principal consultants. During a brainstorming discussion, the six consultants decided to increase the scope of activities and cover other emerging sectors such as telecom, retailing, etc. Further, they also thought of increasing the headcount of the organization and decided to design the organizational structure as shown in the chart below.

After deciding on the organizational structure, the next issue was structuring the compensation package. After detailed deliberations the following compensation package were agreed upon.

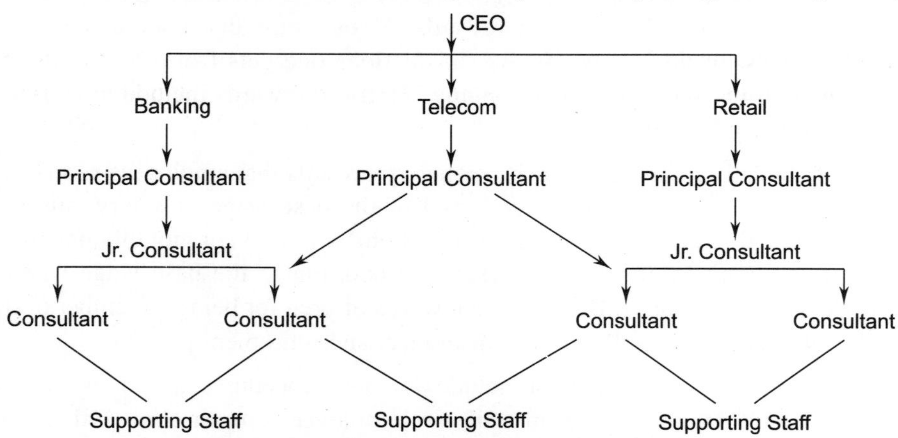

Organization Structure of Innovative Consulting

No.	*Designations*	*Pay-scale (per annum)*
1.	Chief Executive Officer	Rs. 22,00,000–Rs. 18,00,000
2.	Principal Consultants	Rs. 8,00,000–Rs. 5,00,000
3.	Jr. Consultants	Rs. 5,00,000–Rs. 3,00,000
4.	Supporting Staff	Rs. 2,00,000–Rs. 150,000

The next challenge faced while deciding the compensation structure was to provide the total figure to the concerned candidate and give the promotion to him or her to fix the break-up of the components or alternately to fix the break-up of the remuneration. The company initially decided to save expenditure on compensation by recruiting consultants and other staff from medium-sized consultants or beginners rather than internationally reputed consulting agencies. Another reason influencing this decision was that the company felt that high-fliers would not have any organizational loyalty but would try to execute their personal agendas. Accordingly, the company advertised for and recruited the required personnel. After functioning for over two years, it discovered that its revenue had become stagnant and, in fact, observed that apart from the banking and finance group, which included the founders and principal consultants, the other two areas, that is, the telecom and retailing group, were not growing at all. After reviewing the situation, the company decided to recruit high-fliers in these two areas, who could bring in more business because of their contacts. But thus the company was forced to offer higher compensation packages to the new employees. This led to discontent, and the existing employees began to deliberately delay the pace of work.

QUESTIONS

1. If you were the CEO, how would you manage the existing employees vis-à-vis the high-fliers.
2. Critically analyze the compensation structure vis-à-vis the organizational structure.
3. Can you suggest a better compensation structure for the organization ?
4. Should the organization attract a greater number of high-fliers and facilities the outflow of the existing employees ?

CASE STUDY–2 The search that went wrong

Today's economy is demanding more from business executives than ever before: creativity, judgment, motivational skills, and sometimes sheer courage. In these trying times, many CEOs are rediscovering the truth in their bland annual mantra that 'people are our most important asset'. But if having the right people is all important, how do you get them in the first place? The answer is long and involved, and you have probably he all before. So let us make it more interesting taking a look at an executive search that failed case study is based on a real incident. Online identifying details have been changed. The company was involved in processing agriculture products in western Canada. It was just become aware of a potential new market for one product line, so it asked our firm to help find a new sales executive who could exploit the market. The consultants tried to help but the organization made almost every mistake in the book.

As soon as the consultants sat down to discuss the job, they could see they might have trouble. The compensation package the company envisioned for its new sales executive was liberal by its own internal standards. But for a position that requires pioneering and personal risk, the outside marketplace paid more. The client, Harry, said increasing the compensation for this new person would disrupt his firm's entire salary structure—a decision with huge implications for attracting a top candidate. Obstacle No. 2: The consultants quickly determined that the combination of seniority and experience their client was looking for was extremely rare in Canada. 'So look in the States', said Harry. The consultants warned him it was not usually quite that easy.

First, the compensation gap would be an even bigger problem for US executives. And the consultants determined few potential candidates there who were interested in coming to Canada. One researcher compared it to someone in Toronto or Calgary being offered a job in Gander. For most of these executives, Canada was not even on their radar. Casting around again for possible Canadians, the consultants finally found one in Quebec. One problem: She did not wand to move her children outside the province. The consultants played up the concept of French immersion schools and asked Harry to call and use all his persuasion skills to tell her about the job's present and future rewards. Harry refused. 'I won't try to sell her on this job', he said, not realizing that is exactly what many organizations are doing these days to attract top talent.

The consultants found another candidate, who was introduced to Harry and his team. Unfortunately, he bonded only with Brad, Harry's youngest executive. Everyone else, he told the consultants later, seemed old enough to be his father. Worse, by the time the consultants could arrange another meeting, Brad had left the firm. Now there was no one in top management close to the candidate's age. The consultants tried to get Harry to bring another young manager to the meeting, to give the candidate someone to identify with, but is did not happen. The meeting went badly. Perhaps the consultants should have done more. For whatever reason, the consultant never filled the position. There were too many problems standing in the way. The client did not take his search seriously; he never made it a priority. He failed to offer sufficient incentive, taking into account the shortage of qualified candidates and the need to motivate them to make a gutsy move. He was unwilling to look at more junior candidates who might be attracted by the salary and see the opportunity as a step up. And it never occurred to him there might be people who did not want to move to his province, let alone Canada.

Finally, despite prompting, Harry never tried to understand what was going on in the candidates' minds. What would influence their decisions ? Harry paid no attention. And if you do not know what your best candidates want, you are unlikely to satisfy them when it comes to balancing opportunity versus risk. Many business people are afraid to admit they made a mistake. But we learn more from failure than from success.

QUESTIONS

1. Analyze the client's constraint in not accommodating the compensation demands of the would be recruits.
2. Critically analyze the parameters influencing in the client company.
3. Analyze the cross-cultural and inter-country compensation-related problems in shifting from the USA to Canada in the context of the case.
4. Analyze the recruitment practices vis-à-vis compensation practices in the company.

CASE STUDY–3 An academic question on compensation

Mountain States University is a medium-sized public university with 21,000 students and 1,200 faculty members. The College of Business Administration is the largest one on campus, with 8,000 students and 180 faculty members. For the past few years, the dean has had to deal with a large number of dissatisfied faculty who complain that they are underpaid relative to newly hired faculty. Many of the complainants are senior tenured professors who refuse to engage in committee activities beyond the minimum service requirements and who are seldom in their offices because they feel aggrieved. They teach six hours a week, spend two hours in the office, and then disappear from campus. Recently, the head of the college's faculty council compiled some statistics and sent these to the dean, demanding "prompt action to create more equity in the faculty pay structure. "The average salary statistics are shown in the table below.

	1986		*1992*	
Rank	**New Hires**	**Current**	**New Hires**	**Current**
Full Prof	$ 47000	$ 42000	$ 68000	$ 56000
Assot. Prof	$ 39000	$ 36000	$ 62000	$ 51000
Asst. Prof	$ 34000	$ 30000	$ 52000	$ 48000
	1998		*Now*	
	New Hires	**Current**	**New Hires**	**Current**
Full Prof	$ 79000	$ 62000	$ 86900	$ 66340
Assot. Prof	$ 73000	$ 61000	$ 80300	$ 65270
Asst. Prof	$ 61000	$ 59000	$ 71150	$ 63130

The dean replied that he has little choice but to make offers to new faculty that are competitive with the market and that the university will not give him enough funds to maintain equitable pay differences between new and current faculty or between higher and lower ranks.

QUESTIONS

1. Based on the data collected by the faculty council name three compensation problems that exist at Mountain States University.
2. Is the dean's explanation for decreased pay differences by rank and/or seniority justifiable?
3. How would you suggest the dean deal with senior faculty who feel underpaid?

GROUP LEARNING EXERCISE

4. A group of six faculty members has come to see the dean to express dissatisfaction with pay compression at the college. All six represent current faculty; two are assistant professors, two are associate professor, and two are full professors. Students divide into groups of seven and role-play this situation as the dean attempts to deal with the pay complaints raised by the faculty. The dean doesn't have the money to correct the pay-compression problem, yet he can't afford to alienate the faculty.

CASE STUDY–4 Management skills builder: Issues and exercises

Guarding Your Gold

In a free society employees can move from one firm to another in response to better compensation offers elsewhere. But this belief is increasingly being challenged by a so called "inevitable disclosure" doctrine that recognizes that certain employees carry in their memories invaluable proprietary information. It also assumes that such and employee, if hired by a competitor, will inevitably, even if inadvertently, disclose this information—to the first employer's detriment. This concern is becoming a hot issue in a knowledge-based economy where information technology is at the core of competitive advantage for many firms where the departure of even a few key employees can result in irreparable damage to the company.

Judges in more than a dozen states have issued orders prohibiting departing employees—including those who never signed none complete agreements and those who signed unenforceable—from accepting or continuing in new positions until the value of the confidential information in their minds has dissipated. (For instance, having to wait a full year before starting the new job). Judges relying on the doctrine have not required evidence of any actual disclosure. The rule has thrown a cloud of uncertainty over an employee's fundamental freedom to change employers. At the same time, companies do have a legitimate interest in protecting crucial assets such as secret formulas, confidential marketing plans, and closely guarded management strategy.

One example of this controversial trend is that of J.R. "Butch" Lockhardt, Jr., Firestone's Building Products' Vice President who was fired from the company after Firestone realized he had interviewed with a competitor, GAF Materials. Lockhardt went ahead anyway and accepted an offer from GAF, so Firestone used in federal court in Indianapolis to block his job change on the basis that "Lockhardt knew Firestone's strategic plans. He knew its key customers, and he was privy to confidential documents."

How do sought-after key employees keep from being ensnared? There is a better path than mere deterrence one founded on agreement and reward. At the time of hiring or later, the employer could ask a key employee to give it the right to engage him as a consultant for a limited time (let's say six months to a year) if he is terminated or resigns. As a consultant, he could not join a company that might benefit form learning the first company's trade secrets because that would pose a conflict of interest. A cousin to "golden parachutes" and "golden handcuffs," the concept might be dubbed a "golden muzzle." Although largely untested, this idea may become commonplace in the future.

Consider the Issues

1. Do firms have a proprietary right to the knowledge and training acquired by employees "on company time"? Explain.
2. How can the courts determine if the "proprietary" knowledge a worker has may cause irreparable damage to the employer if the employee is lured away by a competitor?
3. Do you agree that a "golden muzzle" is a better way to protect intellectual capital than restricting an employee's freedom to work for a competitor?

Take Action

4. Assume you were "Butch" Lockhart's supervisor. You learned of his interview and decided to take action. Assume further that Lockhart is seriously considering the new job. Would you handle the case differently than Firestone? Draft a proposal of actions you would take to handle the situation.
5. What compensation policies would you implement to reduce a company's "brain drain" to competitors? Create an outline of the policies.

6. Some firms have an informal compensation policy of matching external offers for selected employees to remove their incentive to join direct competitors. What are some of the pros and cons of this practice?

Do It Together

7. Divide the class into teams of here to five students. One set of teams will defend Lockhart's decision to leave Firestone. Another set of teams will defend Firestone's decision to penalize Lockhart for attempting to secure a job at GAF Materials. For the sake of discussion, assume that Firestone did not make an attempt to equalize GAF's compensation offer for fear of creating internal inequities, thereby promoting more exits.

REFERENCES

1. A. Rees and D. P. Jacobs, *Real Wages in Manufacturing, 1890–1914* (1961); E.H.P. Brown, *A Century of Pay* (1968); J.W. Wright, *The American Almanac of Jobs and Salaries* (serial).
2. Allen R.C. "The Great Divergence in European Wages and Prices from the Middle Ages to the First World War." *Explorations in Economic History* 38, No. 4 (October 2001): 411–448.
3. Brown, Henry Phelps, and Sheila V. Hopkins, *A Perspective of Wage and Prices.* London, 1981.
4. Campbell, B. "Agricultural Progress in Medieval England: Some Evidence from Eastern Norfolk." *Economic History Review* 36, No. 1 (February 1983): 26–46.
5. De Vries, J., and A. van der Woode. *The First Modern Economy: Success, Failure and Perseverance of the Dutch Economy,* 1500–1815. Cambridge, U.K., 1997.
6. Epstein, S. "Craft Guilds, Apprenticeship, and Technological Change in Preindustrial Europe." *Journal of Economic History* 58, No. 3 (September 1998): 684–713.
7. Grantham, G. "Contra Ricardo: On the Macroeconomics of Pre-industrial Economies." *European Review of Economic History* 3, No. 2 (August 1999): 199–232.
8. Hoffman, P.T. *Growth in a Traditional Society.* Princeton, 1998.
9. Hoffman, P.T., D. Jacks, and P. Lindert. "Real Inequality in Europe since 1500." *Journal of Economic History* 62, No. 2 (June 2002): 322–355.
10. Jones, E.L., *The European Miracle: Environments, Economies, and Geopolitics in the History of Europe and Asia.* 2nd ed. Cambridge, U.K., 1987.
11. Malthus, T.R., *An Essay on the Principle of Population.* 1798.
12. Mokyr, J., *The Lever of Riches: Technological Creativity and Economic Progress,* New York, 1990.
13. North, D.C. *Structure and Change in Economic History,* New York, 1981.
14. Ozmucur, S., and S. Pamuck., "Real Wages and Standards of Living in the Ottoman Empire 1489–1914." *Journal of Economic History* 62, No. 2 (June 2002): 293–321.
15. Reddy, W.M., *The Rise of Market Culture: The Textile Trade and French Society,* 1750–1900. Cambridge, U.K., 1984.
16. Van Zanden, J.L., "Rich and Poor before the Industrial Revolution: A Comparison between Java and the Netherlands at the Beginning of the Nineteenth Century." *Explorations in Economic History* 40, No. 1 (January 2001): 1–23.
17. Wrigley, E.A., *Continuity, Chance and Change: The Character of the Industrial Revolution in England.* Cambridge, U.K., 1988.
18. Wrigley, E.A., and R.S. Schofield., *The Population History of England* 1541–1871: *A Reconstruction,* Cambridge, Mass., 1981.

19. R.S. Dwivedi, Managing Human Resources: Personnel Management, Golgotia Publishing House, New Delhi, 2000.
20. Boyett, Joseph H., and Henry P. Conn, *Workplace 2000: The Revolution Reshaping American Business.*
21. Dauten, Dale A., *The Gifted Boss: How to Find, Create and Keep Great Employees.* Morrow, 1999.
22. Hay Group, *People, Performance,* and *Pay- Dynamic Compensation for Changing Organizations.*
23. Kinne, David W. "Employee Compensation: What Gets Rewarded is What Gets Done," *Compensation and Benefits Management.* Spring 2000.
24. Milkovich, George T., and Alexandra K. Wigdor. *Pay for Performance: Evaluating Performance Appraisal and Merit Pay.*
25. Parrott, Mark D., "Employee Compensation." *Do-It-Yourself Retailing,* January 2000.
26. Joseph J. Matrocchio, Strategic Compensation, Pearson Education, New Delhi, Third Edition, 2006.
27. Mejia, Balkin and Kardy, Human Resource Management, Pearson Education, New Delhi, Low priced Edition, 2005.
28. Sashi K Gupta and Rosy Joshi, Human Resource Management, Kalyani Publication, New Delhi, 2007.
29. R. wane Mondy, Robert M. Noe, Human Resource Management, Pearson Education, New Delhi, Ninth Edition, 2006.
30. N.G. Nair, Latha Nair, Personnel Management and Industrial Relations, S. Chand and Company, New Delhi, 2004.
31. P. Jyothi and D.N. Venkatesh, Human Resource Management, Oxford Publication, New Delhi, 2006.
32. T.N. Chahabra, Human Resources Management: Concept and Issues, Dhanpat Rai and Co., New Delhi, Third Edition, 2002.

13 CHAPTER

LABOUR-MANAGEMENT RELATIONSHIPS

13.1 INTRODUCTION

Labour and manpower are inter-related fields. Satisfied labour is the source of development and prosperity of people at large. Manpower management requires development of human resources through objective-oriented training and relations, so that external and internal labour markets are supplied qualified and trained labour to cater to the needs of the industry and have the sustained productive capacity to contribute uninterruptedly to the overall economic and industrial growth. This will pay dividends in the form of enhanced economic activity and creation of jobs to solve the unemployment problem. Efforts will be made for better manpower planning, extensive skilled labour training in trades prevalent in industry and also in highly specialized trades to prepare for the new technology. In addition measures will be taken for the provision of basic amenities to workers including housing accommodations, better wages, increased quantum of incentives, better schools for workers' children, consistent and sustainable social insurance schemes etc. All these efforts will be made through short and long-term planning (to be periodically reviewed for updating) to meet the present and future challenges of technology and economic and business objectives of the country. Government believes that in the realization of increased competitiveness, growth and employment in a globalized economy, a highly educated and skilled labour force has a critical and prominent role to play. The rich heritage of legislation, dating back to colonial British India, has been amended and revised over the years of legislation that is sometimes overlapping in its competence and coverage and anomalous in definition and scope. The variety and complexities of laws has contributed to a labour relations system which sometimes relies excessively on the judiciary and labour courts of resolving labour-management problems. The large number and complexity of labour laws with over-lapping provisions and multiple definitions of worker, employer, wages, establishment, industry, etc. have served no useful purpose and have complicated the industrial labour relations which have unfortunately led workers and employers to protracted litigation. Their present structure has also posed the smooth bilateral relationship of workers and employers, the objective consolidation and simplification of labour laws is one of the priority areas which the Government wants to concentrate in order to facilitate the understanding and implementation of these laws. The large number and complexity of labour laws with over-lapping provisions and multiple definitions of worker, employer, wages, establishment, industry, etc. have served useful purpose and have complicated the industrial labour relations machinery. Their present structure has also allowed for maximum bilateral relationship of workers and employers, the objective consolidation and simplification of labour laws is one of the priority areas which the Government wants to concentrate in order to facilitate the understanding and implementation of these laws.

Labour relations should be seen as an essential part of management systems and techniques, and not as a discipline or activity apart from management. Changes in labour relations within an organization are often affected by management practices. Therefore attitudes towards industrial relations should be understood in the background of theories and practices relating to the management of enterprises and organizational behaviour. The present trend in labour relations and human resource management is to place greater emphasis on employee involvement, harmonious employer-employee relations and mechanisms, and on practices which promote them. One of the important consequences of globalization and intense competition has been the pressure on firms to be flexible.

In recent times, industrial relations has been influenced by other social sciences such as organizational psychology and behaviour. Traditionally economics and law were two main influences on industrial relations, which led to a concentration on macro level industrial relations, and therefore on unions, government and collective bargaining. Organizational behaviour has been influenced by psychology which centres on the individual, and by social psychology which focuses on relationships between people and on group behaviour. It is easy to see, therefore, why human resource management has been influenced by organizational behaviour. Paradoxically industrial relations, though dealing with 'relation', has until recently largely ignored the social sciences relevant to behaviour and human relations. While labour problems are the result of imperfections in the employment relationship, industrial relations should be seen as the theories and methods which have been developed over time to address and correct these problems, in both the external and internal labour markets. A sound industrial relations system is one in which relationships between management and employees (and their representatives) on the one hand, and between them and the State on the other, are more harmonious and cooperative than conflictual and creates an environment conducive to economic efficiency and the motivation, productivity and development of the employee and generates employee loyalty and mutual trust. Industrial relations itself may again be described as being concerned with the rules, processes and mechanisms (and the results emanating there from) through which the relationship between employers and employees and their respective representatives, as well as between them on the one hand and the State and its agencies on the other, is regulated. Industrial relations seek to balance the economic efficiency of organizations with equity, justice and the development of the individual, to find ways of avoiding, minimizing and resolving disputes and conflict and to promote harmonious relations between and among the actors directly involved, and society as a whole. The rules, processes and mechanisms of an industrial relations system are found in sources such as laws (legislative, judicial, quasi-judicial), practices, customs, agreements and arrangements arrived at through a bipartite or tripartite process or through prescription by the State.

13.2 CONCEPT AND SCOPE OF INDUSTRIAL RELATIONS

Human Resource Management (HRM) and/or Personnel Management (PM) has become a very vital part of the management process in the twenty-first century, and is getting significant attention in management discussions, or in the business strategy of most organizations as compared to the past, more so post liberalization. The importance of this function for the success of an organization is highlighted in glowing terms with emphasis on Human Resource Development (HRD), knowledge management, empowerment, flat organization structure, motivated work groups etc. To some they sound as jargon, but to serious minded people they seem to make a lot of sense, even if there are differences of opinion. It also seems that even professional managers often differ in their understanding of the role differences between HRM and PM, if any at all. Many feel that it is the same old wine in a new bottle with a different label, or that HRM is only a more modern terminology. During the 1990's, the new demands of international competition and dramatic advances in technology—the forces of globalization—have changed substantially the nature and operation of the "market place", and how production is organized, in many industries across the world. Individual enterprises are now being required to innovate to provide "the right product, at the right price and time".

These requirements are placing considerable demands on employers and their enterprises to develop and implement new strategies, structures and processes. There is an increasingly strategic role for Industrial Relations (IR) within the enterprise, as much of what has to be done involves significant changes to traditional practices in this and the related area of Human Resource Management (HRM). The result has been that the nature of IR is changing in many enterprises. A new approach is emerging, relying on a broader concept of employment relations.

This new approach is based on a range of IR and HRM practices directed to improving the flexibility and skills of the workforce, within an environment which emphasizes communication, cooperation and trust between managers, workers and their representatives. Adoption of this approach, however, has been neither universal nor uniform. It has been particularly pronounced in industrialized countries, and is increasing in industrializing countries. But both the forms it has taken and its spread, has varied considerably within industries and across regions in the same country, and among countries and regions having different industrial relations policy, legal and institutional frameworks and traditions.

Much more than any other previous influence, globalization is emphasizing the importance of IR to industrialization and economic development in the region. It is creating new challenges for, as well as highlighting old tensions among, governments and the social partners. It has also brought with it a number of strategic opportunities, if the parties can take advantage of them, to improve the prospects of enterprises and workers and to position the region for a period of continuing strong economic growth and development into the twenty-first century.

Employers, as the force driving economic changes, and their organizations have to take the initiative to develop a reform agenda which can deliver these benefits. This will require a strategy directed to improving employment relations and which seeks changes in attitudes and behaviour in the workplace and addresses the key issues of skills development, compensation, work organization and flexibility, and cross-cultural management.

Industrial relations constitute one of the most delicate and complex problems of the modern society which is characterized by the rapid change, disputes, unrests, ideological conflicts in the national and international spheres. It is a dynamic concept which changes with the pattern of society and social order, economic system, and political set-up of a given country. It is an art of living together, for the purpose of production, productive efficiency, human well being and industrial progress. This comprises with the network of relations among the employees, employers and the involvement of the

State. The term industrial relations refers to all types of relationships between all the parties concerned with industry. The parties related to industry are the workers and the management representing the owners. Thus, industrial relation connotes a vast complex of relationships between management and union, management and employees, between union and employees, between employees and finally the relationships among the employees, employers and Government etc. which arise out of industrial activities. The area of industrial relations has been extended to relations among the State, employer and employees. Accordingly to Encyclopedia Britanica, "The subject of industrial relations includes individual relations and joint consultation between employers and workers at the place of work, collective relations between employers and their organizations and trade unions and part played by the State in the regulating these relations". In its wider connotation, it means the organization and practices of multipronged relationships between workers and management, unions and the workers and the unions and managements in an industry. Dale Yoder defines it is a "Whole field of relationships that exist because of the necessary collaboration of men and women in the employment process of an industry". It is the relationships between management and employees or among the employees and their organization that arise out of employment.

Tead and Metcalfe observe that "Industrial relations are the composite result of the attitudes and approaches of the employers and employees towards each other with regard to planning, supervising, directing and coordinating the activities of the organization with a minimum of human efforts and frictions with an animating spirit of cooperation and with proper regard for the genuine well being of all the members of the organization. According to Allan Flanders, the subject of industrial relations deals with certain regulated or institutionalized relationships in industry. Prof Clegg defines, industrial relations is the broadest terms as encompassing 'the rules governing employment together with the ways in which the rules are made and changed their interpretation and administration". Relations between management and workers, especially in manufacturing industries. Relations between the management of an industrial enterprise and its employees.

Industrial Relations or Labour Relations is an expression used not only for relationships between employers and Trade Unions, but also for those involving Government with the aim of defining policies, facing labour problems.

As Industrial Relations definition we can accept the concept of the outfit of:

- rules for employment management;
- methods defining those rules;
- typology of actors (both employers and workers organisations and representatives; but also state and institutional bodies);
- interaction processes between these entities.

"IR" may be defined as the means by which the various interests involved in the labour market are accommodated, primarily for the purpose of regulating employment relationships.

IR is essentially collectivist and pluralist in outlook. It is concerned with the relationships which arise at and out of the workplace (*i.e.,* relationships between individual workers, the relationships between them and their employer, the relationships employers and workers have with the organizations formed to promote and defend their respective interests, and the relations between those organizations, at all levels). Industrial relations also includes the processes through which these relationships are expressed (such as, collective bargaining; worker involvement in decision-making;

and grievance and dispute settlement), and the management of conflict between employers, workers and trade unions, when it arises.

These relationships and processes are influenced by the government and its agencies through policies, laws, institutions and programmes, and by the broader political, social, economic, technological and cultural characteristics of each country. The IR policy, legal and institutional framework in a particular country is developed through bipartite consultative processes (*i.e.,* between employer and worker representatives, and by them, individually, with government) and tripartite consultation and cooperation (involving government and the social partners).

IR outcomes are a series of rules which apply to work, setting down minimum (and other) wages and terms and conditions of employment for workers. These employment conditions can cover hours of work, leave, training, termination of employment and the like, as well as issues related to occupational safety and health, social security (sometimes), and conditions applying to special categories of workers. These rules also define the roles and responsibilities of the parties, individually and collectively (*e.g.,* through legislation; collective labour agreements; decisions by arbitrators and courts; and enterprise work rules).

IR processes or arrangements have traditionally been expressed through the individual employment relationship and collective bargaining, and have a meditative function. They are directed to achieving a compromise between "market forces" (which seek to set the price and quantity of labour) and intervention in the market place by employers, workers and their representatives (and by government and its agencies, for political and social reasons) which establishes the various types of rules (noted above) which govern the employment relationship.

The essential rationale for intervention is three-fold-firstly, the right of those involved and affected by decisions in the marketplace to participate in resolving employment relationship issues; secondly, the function of freedom of association and collective bargaining in redressing the balance of power between "capital" and "labour"; and, thirdly, to prevent labour exploitation (*e.g.,* sweated and child labour). The relative "balance" between the role of market forces and intervening IR arrangements in regulating employment relationships will vary between countries.

The four main parties who are actively associated with any industrial relations system are the workers, the managements, the organizations of workers and managements, and the state. Fundamentally, the term industrial relations refer to organized relationship between two organized parties representing employers and employees regarding matters of collective interests. But the scope of the industrial relations cannot merely be confined to common labour-management relations or employee—employer relations. It is a comprehensive and total concept embracing the sum total relationships that exist at various levels of the organizational structure. More specifically, it connotes relations among workers themselves within the class of employees, relations among the management within the class, and relations between the two distinct classes of workers and management. It involves the all types of inter-group and intra group relations within the industry, both formal and informal. It consists of a complex web of relationships that arise out of functional interdependence between workers and managements and between industrial organizations and society. Industrial relations is a social concept because it deals with social relationships in different walks of life. It is a relative concept because it grows and flourishes or stagnates and decays in accordance with socio-economic-political-cultural situations, the degree of science and technology operates in a country.

The purpose of industrial relations is to secure the highest possible level of mutual understanding and good will between the several interests which participate in production and service activities. This depend primarily on fair dealing and good working conditions, highest standard of living, a friendly atmosphere, spirit of working together for a common purpose must be developed. The main purpose of industrial relations is not just 'peace'. It is an art, the art of living together for the purpose of production and or services. It is derived from the principle of many disciplines; economics, law, human and industrial psychology, anthropology, sociology, social work etc. Industrial relations everywhere are undergoing a change due to the emergence of new trends and concepts. Employment flexibility, human resource management practices, increased labour—management cooperation, workers' participation and involvement in decision-making of their organizations are few new trends and concepts that draw on insights from economics, organizational behaviour and other disciplines. Internal control system is developed in modern industrial relations whereas traditional industrial relations rely on external control systems or traditional management styles. Structural changes that are taking place in the face of globalization of economies are leading to the adoption of modern and sophisticated management styles.

13.3 FUNCTIONS AND OBJECTIVES OF INDUSTRIAL RELATIONS

A sound industrial relations system is not capable of precise definition. Every industrial relations system has to take into account, and reflect, cultural factors. Systems cannot change culture, but only behaviour within a cultural environment. As such, one can only describe some of the elements which have generally come to be recognized as contributing to a sound industrial relations system. These elements would constitute a sort of 'check-list'. A relatively sound industrial relations system will exhibit some of these elements.

A sound industrial relations system is one in which relationships between management and employees (and their representatives) on the one hand, and between them and the State on the other, are more harmonious and cooperative than conflictual and creates an environment conducive to economic efficiency and the motivation, productivity and development of the employee and generates employee loyalty and mutual trust. Industrial relations itself may again be described as being concerned with the rules, processes and mechanisms (and the results emanating there from) through which the relationship between employers and employees and their respective representatives, as well as between them on the one hand and the State and its agencies on the other, is regulated. Industrial relations seek to balance the economic efficiency of organizations with equity, justice and the development of the individual, to find ways of avoiding, minimizing and resolving disputes and conflict and to promote harmonious relations between and among the actors directly involved, and society as a whole. The rules, processes and mechanisms of an industrial relations system are found in sources such as laws (legislative, judicial, quasi-judicial), practices, customs, agreements and arrangements arrived at through a bipartite or tripartite process or through prescription by the State.

Industrial relations operates at different levels—at the national level, at the level of the industry and at the enterprise level. The elements which reflect a sound industrial relations system at all these levels are not necessarily the same. At the national level industrial relations operates so as to formulate labour relations policy. In market economies this is usually done through a tripartite process involving government, employers and workers and their representative organizations. At the industry level industrial relations often takes the form of collective bargaining between employers' organizations and unions. This process may result in determining wages and other terms and conditions of employment for an industry or sector. It may also result in arrangements on issues which are of mutual concern such as training, ways of avoiding or settling disputes, etc. At the enterprise level the relationship between employers and workers is more direct, but the interests of workers may be represented by unions. Employers' organizations, however, are not usually involved (though sometimes they are when negotiations take place between them and unions in respect of enterprise issues) at the enterprise level in representing the employers' interests with workers or their union, but this does not mean that they do not have an important promotional role at this level. Sound industrial relations at the national level build trust and confidence between representatives of workers and employers. A sound relation at the enterprise level builds trust and confidence between workers and management, which is the point at which the system must ultimately be effective. Effectiveness at one level would naturally have some impact on the other.

A sound industrial relations system requires a Labour Management Relations Policy (LMRP). There are many specific objectives of such a policy, all of which go to make up the policy at the national level. The following are some of the objectives, the emphasis varying from country to country depending on the priorities and stage of development of each of them at any given point of time:

(*i*) Employment and job security and increased employment opportunities.

(*ii*) Raising living standards through improved terms and conditions of employment.

(*iii*) Productivity improvement which enables employers to be more competitive and to increase their financial capacity to raise the living standards of the employees.

Minimizing conflict, achieving harmonious relations, resolving conflicts through peaceful means and establishing stable social relationships. In western industrialized societies "harmony" and "harmonious relations" are not explicitly referred to either as an objective or as a means, though basically it represents an important objective in such societies. However, this concept is explicitly referred to in many Asian societies. Development has an economic and social dimension on the one hand and a cultural dimension on the other. The economic and social aspects involve guiding or influencing economic and social change in a desirable direction. This means not only economic development measured in terms of growth rates and per capita incomes, but also equity in terms of income distribution and employment opportunities, life expectancy, population growth rates, literacy, poverty alleviation, etc. As aptly stated by John Kenneth Galbraith: "It is one of the least advertised, and for the very affluent the least attractive, of economic truths that a reasonably equitable distribution of income throughout the society is highly functional."

A sound industrial relations climate in an enterprise is essential to a number of issues which are critical to employers, employees and the community. The efficient production of goods and services depends to an extent on the existence of a harmonious industrial relations climate. Efficiency and quality depend on a motivated workforce, for which a sound industrial relations climate is necessary. Productivity—a key consideration of profitability, the ability of enterprises to grant better terms and conditions of employment and for economic and social development-needs a sound labour relations base. Productivity does not depend on individual effort alone. Many mechanisms which contribute towards productivity gains are workable only where there is teamwork and cooperation *e.g.,* small group activities, joint consultation mechanisms. Therefore labour management relations should be geared to creating the climate appropriate to securing the cooperation necessary for productivity growth. Labour Management Relations (LMR) and Labour Management Cooperation (LMC) are also important to the creation of a culture which is oriented towards innovation, adaptable to and encourages change, where authority is decentralized and two-way communication, risk-taking and maximizing opportunities are encouraged, and where the output rather than the process is what matters. Changing attitudes, awareness and behaviour to move from counter-productivity to a productivity culture requires the appropriate labour management relations climate based on labour management cooperation.

Similar principles were recognized by the productivity movement in Europe. The underlying theme here relevant to the present discussion is that all three principles mentioned above form a part of labour management relations and cooperation.

Another important link between labour management relations and productivity has arisen in the context of recent events in many societies and major changes in industrial relations such as the move towards labour market flexibility. The latter involves the need for employers to adopt, in the interests of competitiveness, new working time and work arrangements, a typical contracts of employment, new methods of pay and remuneration, and control over the size of the labour force. These developments have partly resulted from intense competition, new technologies, shorter product life and so on, all of which require flexibility in the use of resources if an enterprise is to remain productive and competitive. These changes are more likely to achieve the objectives of increased productivity, if they are introduced through cooperation and consensus at the enterprise level. Therefore labour management relations and cooperation have a vital role to play in achieving, with the least possible conflict, the changes of the type referred to above which are critical to productivity and competitiveness in the modern enterprise.

A sound labour management relations system is important to the removal of one of the main objections of workers and unions to productivity drives by employers. Productivity increases have sometimes been opposed by workers and unions on the grounds that they do not result in equitable sharing of benefits to workers and that increased productivity may lead to redundancy. Developing understanding of basic productivity concepts and of the methods of increasing productivity, as well as of the formulation of equitable productivity gain-sharing schemes help to dispel such suspicions. This task is easier where there are mechanisms which provide for dialogue and two-way communication between management and workers. Labour management relations therefore play a crucial role in securing acceptance by workers and unions of the need for productivity improvement, and also in obtaining their commitment to achieving it.

Cooperation between management and workers or unions facilitates not only a settlement of disputes or disagreements but also the avoidance of disputes which may otherwise arise. At the industry level the relationship between employers' organizations and representatives of workers is a precondition to collective bargaining. Where collective bargaining takes place at the enterprise level, management workers/union relations determine to a great extent the success or otherwise of collective bargaining. At the national level a good relationship between representatives of employers and workers enables them to effectively participate in labour-management relations policy formulation and to arrive at a consensus.

Function: Industrial relations

Good industrial relations, while a recognizable and legitimate objective for an organization, are difficult to define since a good system of industrial relations involves complex relationships between:

(*a*) Workers (and their informal and formal groups, *i.e.,* trade union, organizations and their representatives);

(*b*) Employers (and their managers and formal organizations like trade and professional associations);

(*c*) The government and legislation and government agencies and 'independent' agencies like the Advisory Conciliation and Arbitration Service.

Oversimplified, work is a matter of managers giving instructions and workers following them—but (and even under slavery we recognize that different 'managing' produces very different results) the variety of 'forms' which have evolved to regulate the conduct of parties (*i.e.,* laws, custom and practice, observances, agreements) makes the giving and receipt of instructions far from simple. Two types of 'rule' have evolved:

- 'Substantive', determining basic pay and conditions of service (what rewards workers should receive).
- 'Procedural,' determining how workers should be treated and methods and procedures.
- Financial, policy and market constraints on the parties (*e.g.,* some unions do not have the finance to support industrial action, some have policies not to strike, some employers are more vulnerable than others to industrial action, some will not make changes unless worker agreement is made first, and rewards always ultimately reflect what the market will bear).
- The technology of production (the effect of a strike in newspaper production is immediate—it may be months before becoming effective in shipbuilding).
- The distribution of power within the community that tends to vary over time and with economic conditions workers (or unions) dominating in times of full employment and employers in times of recession.

Broadly in the Western style economies the parties (workers and employers) are free to make their own agreements and rules. This is called 'voluntarism'. But it does not mean there is total noninterference by the government. That is necessary to:

- Protect the weak (hence minimum wage).
- Outlaw discrimination (race or sex).
- Determine minimum standards of safety, health, hygiene and even important conditions of service.
- To try to prevent the abuse of power by either party.
- The Industrial Relations Commission conciliates and arbitrates to resolve industrial disputes, sets conditions of employment and fixes wages and salaries by making industrial awards, approves enterprise agreements and decides claims of unfair dismissal.

To provide a framework for the conduct of industrial relations that is fair and just:

- To promote efficiency and productivity in the economy of the state.
- To promote participation in industrial relations by employees and employers at an enterprise or workplace level.
- To encourage participation in industrial relations by representative bodies of employees and employers and to encourage the responsible management and democratic control of those bodies.
- To facilitate appropriate regulation of employment through awards, enterprise agreement and other industrial instruments.

- To prevent and eliminate discrimination in the workplace and in particular to ensure equal remuneration for men and women doing work of equal or comparable value.
- To provide for the resolution of industrial disputes by conciliation and, if necessary, by arbitration in a prompt and fair manner and with a minimum of legal technicality.
- To encourage and facilitate co-operative workplace reform and equitable, innovative and productive workplace relations.

Industrial Relations is concerned with the duties and obligations established by the employment relationship and the main functions of Industrial Relations Department include:

- Formulating Industrial Relations strategies and systems to support corporate priorities and strategic direction.
- Advising on the application and interpretation of industrial awards, agreements and the legislation which regulates aspects of employment.
- Liaising and negotiating with unions and with central agencies.
- To provide a framework for the conduct of industrial relations that is fair and just.
- To promote efficiency and productivity in the economy of the State.
- To promote participation in industrial relations by employees and employers at an enterprise or workplace level.
- To encourage participation in industrial relations by representative bodies of employees and employers and to encourage the responsible management and democratic control of those bodies.
- To facilitate appropriate regulation of employment through awards, enterprise agreement and other industrial instruments.
- To prevent and eliminate discrimination in the workplace and in particular to ensure equal remuneration for men and women doing work of equal or comparable value.
- To provide for the resolution of industrial disputes by conciliation and, if necessary, by arbitration in a prompt and fair manner and with a minimum of legal technicality.
- To encourage and facilitate co-operative workplace reform and equitable, innovative and productive workplace relations.

The volume of international business continues to expand dramatically from year to year. The advent of the Internet and e-commerce is further fuelling the flow of goods and services across the globe. Companies are organizing across the national borders. Even the more traditional industries have not only modernized their production lines and supply chains in the pursuit of the lean organization, but have developed the capacity to move products rapidly to different parts of the world in order to gain competitive advantage in terms of cost and speed of distribution.

As more and more companies operate internationally, the impact on various business functions becomes more pronounced. Professional managers in every function must develop the skills, knowledge, and experience in the international arena that will help their companies to succeed in this demanding and often volatile environment.

This is particularly true in the case of the human resources management, and industrial relations function. The implication is that globalization is a reality and that people management philosophy, hence, has to acknowledge this fact and operate within this framework and context. "There is a global concern about the new human resource policies and practices, and their impact on industrial relations. The broad trend towards decline in employment in the manufacturing sector, low union activity in sunrise sectors, decentralized collective bargaining, and direct communication with and involvement of workers can be seen as efforts at political restructuring of industrial relations." The analyses of kaleidoscopic developments in the sphere of industrial relations in India in the backdrop of the international scenario. The nation has to synchronize the national economic policy with the emerging trends in industrial relations—how each must mesh with the other.

Apart from the primary objective of bringing sound and healthy relations between employers and employees, industrial relations aim at:

- To facilitate production and productivity;
- To safe guard the rights and interest of both labour and management by enlisting their cooperation;
- To achieve a sound, harmonious, and mutually beneficial labour management relations;
- To avoid unhealthy atmosphere in the industry, especially work stoppages, go-slow gheraos, strikes, lockouts; and
- To establish and maintain industrial democracy.

Accordingly to Kirkaldy, industrial relations in a country are intimately connected with the form of its political government; and the objectives of an industrial organization may vary from purely economic to purely political ends. The objectives of the industrial relations can be divided into four categories:

- Improvement in the economic conditions of workers in the existing State of industrial management and political government;
- Control exercised by the state over industrial undertaking with a view to regulating production and promoting harmonious industrial relations;
- Socialization and rationalization of industries by making the sate itself a major employer; and
- Vesting of a proprietary interest of workers in the industries in which they are employed.

13.4 APPROACHES OF INDUSTRIAL RELATIONS

The term industrial relations is used to denote a specialist area of organizational management and study which is concerned with a particular set of phenomenon associated with regulating the human activity of employment. It is, however, difficult to define the boundaries of this set phenomenon, and therefore the term itself, in a precise and universally accepted way. The term may be used in a restrictive sense to include only the formal collective relationships between management and employees or in all inclusive sense to encompass all relationships associated with employment. However, it is doubtful whether the two approaches can or should be separated so easily—informal, interpersonal or group relationships are influenced by the formal collective relationships which exist within the industrial relations system and it may be argued, the formal collective relationships are themselves in part determined by the nature of individual relationships. The way we perceive the overall nature of this area of organizations study determines to a very large extent not only how we approach and analyze specific issues and situations within industrial relations but also how we expect others to behave, how we respond to their actual behaviour and means we adopt to influences or modify the behaviour in examining the different approaches it is useful to differentiate between those approaches which are concerned with the general nature of employment organizations and those which specially deal with the industrial relations system itself.

Fig. 13.1 *Approaches to Industrial Relations*

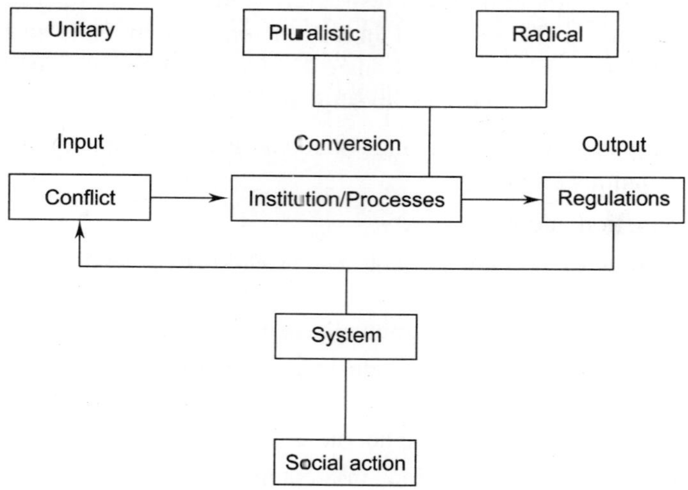

Systems approach

IR System of any given country is a mixture of traditions, customs and a web of actions, reactions and interactions between the parties operating in a social, technological, economic and political environment. IR system can conceived at the macro, micro level and intermediary level *i.e.,* workplace, the industry, regional and national levels. IR can be viewed from a system's angle. As a system, IR can be defined as compromising the totality of the power interactions of participants in the workplace, when these interactions involve industrial relations issues. It is viewed as an integral and non-separable part of the organizational structure and dynamics. The components of IR system are:

Participants: The duly recognized representatives of the parties interacting in several roles within the system.

Issues: The power interaction of the participants in a workplace creates IR problems. These issues and the consequences of the power interactions a find their expressions in a web of rules governing the behaviour of the parties at a workplace.

Structure: It consists of all form of institutional behaviour in system. The structure may include the collective procedures, grievance settlements practices etc. legal enactments relevant to power interactions may also be considered to be part of the structure.

Boundaries: In systems analysis, it is possible to find issues which one participants is totally indifferent to resolving while, at the same time, the other participants is highly concerned about resolution of the same. These issues may serve to delimit systems boundaries.

At least there are three marked features of this systems approach; (*i*) Interdisciplinary in character: some theorist regards the system approach to be universally applicable to all human relationships, in small or large units. Its flexibility of application in the behavioural sciences has been aptly demonstrated. (*ii*) Suitability to work organization and their sub-system: The adaptability of the systems approach to organization is also a frequently discussed trait. This springs from the fact of that organizations and to some extent their sub-systems, are rational and purposeful. (*iii*) Dynamic approach: A system approach is oriented towards the study of interactions and changing relations.

The following are the some of the contributors to the systems approach in industrial relations:

(*i*) **Robert Dubin:** He used the concept such as inter-group (Union-Management) power interactions, boundaries of the social system and functions performed by the system. According to him, union militancy is greatest when the union bargains for the minimum sources of attachment to work, such as wages, hours of work and working conditions.

(*ii*) **Robert Cox:** In his approach to a "Futurology of industrial relations" 1971, Cox enumerates the following system:

- The Peasant-Lord system (purely paternalistic):
- The primitive market system (where the first generation industrial workers migrating to urban areas from the rural);
- The small organized system (workers are getting organized, the Govt. wiling to intervene);
- The life time commitment system as in Japan;
- The bi-party system of which collective bargaining is the main function;
- The tri-party system where the Govt. also plays an important role as in India;
- The Corporatists-Bureaucratic system in countries where employers' and workers organizations are semi-autonomous as in UK;
- The mobilizing system, where the elite political power determines worker and the employer behaviour, as in communist countries at the initial stage;
- The socialist system where a contractual employment relationship is established between the parties.

(*iii*) **Kenneth Walker:** He proposed building of multi-dimensional, interactive models of industrial relations system. He argued that the basic manner to more useful theorizing has been the inadequacy of the Psychological models of human behaviour in work situation. He therefore, proposed a more adequate model which views man as; calculating and emotional; cooperative and conflicting and expressive and instrumental. Such model, according to Walker, tends to effective integration with the industrial relations theory and direct attention to many areas of needed research.

(*iv*) **Herbert Haneman:** His model (1960) contains stimulating insights concerning the components and variables to be included in a systems model of industrial relations. His main focus was on the workers and managers and their interaction at the workplace.

(*v*) **Richards Peterson:** His model shows that essentially managerial view of the function of industrial relations in different organizations.

(*vi*) **Jhon T. Dunlop:** He has laid down a generalized IR framework which, according to him, "is design to applicable at once to three broad areas of industrial relations experiences, namely: (*i*) industrial relations within an enterprise, industry or other segment of a country and a comparison among such sectors, (*ii*) IR within a country as a whole and a comparison among countries, and (*iii*) IR as a totality in the course of economic development. He defined IR System as; "An IR System at any one time in its development is regarded as comprised of certain actors, certain context, an ideology which binds the industrial relations system together, and a body of rules created to govern the actors at the workplace and work community. There are three sets of independent variables: The "actors", the "context" and the "ideology" of the system".

(*a*) **The actors in the system**

- Hierarchy of managers and their representatives in supervision (who issue instructions downward).

- A hierarchy of workers (non-managerial, who follows the instructions given by the managers and which may be organized into several complementary or competing units such as workers councils, unions and the parties.
- Specialized Governmental agencies (private agencies created by the first two actors) concerned with workers, enterprises and their relationships (which may override the hierarchies of mangers and workers) on almost all matters.

In other individual relations systems, the role of the specialized governmental agencies, at least for many purposes, may be minor or constricted.

(*b*) **The context of the system**

- The technological environment (place and nature of the work, methods of the work, layout and technology, the simplicity and complexity of the work, the work flow and job design etc.).
- The market and budgetary constraints (demand fluctuations, change in customary preferences, financial constraints on the organization, competition etc.).
- The locus and distribution of the power in the larger society (the distribution of power within the organization need not necessarily be exactly on the lines of its distribution in the outer environment, yet it is a pointer to the power equation and political equilibrium within the organization).

(*c*) **The ideology of the industrial system:** The set of the ideas and benefits commonly held by the actors help to bind or to integrate towards the system together as an entity.

Each IR System contains its ideology or shared understandings. The ideology defines the role and place of each actor and the ideas which each actor holds towards the lace and function of the others in the system. The ideology or philosophy of a stable system involves a congruence or compatibility among theses views and the rest of the system. Each of the actors in industrial relations systems may be said to each of its own ideology. An industrial relations system requires that these ideologies be sufficiently compatible and consistent so as to permit a common set of ideas which recognize an acceptable role for each other.

(*d*) **Establishment of Rules:** The actors in a given context frame rules for the conduct of their day-to-day relations. These rules are broadly grouped under three categories:

- Rules governing compensation in all its form
- The duties a performance expected from workers, including rules of disciplines for failure to achieve these standards, and
- Rules defining the rights and duties of workers.

In short, Dunlop's IR system is an analytical enquiry into the structure and process of the dynamics of relations between management, workers and the Government. The systems model provides a useful framework for classifying and describing the elements within any industrial relations system by focusing on 'output' or rules of the industrial relations systems, on their processes such as collective bargaining and the other types of rule making, and on their 'inputs' such as the actors involved in rule making.

(*vii*) **The Oxford approach:** This approach is based on the Donovan Commission (1965–68). According to this, the industrial relations system is a study of the institutions job regulations and the stress is on the substantive and procedural rules as Dunlop's model. Flanders, an exponent of this approach, considers every business enterprises as a social system of production and distribution, which has structured pattern of relationships.

The 'institution of the job regulation' is categorized by him as internal and external; the former being an internal part of the industrial relations system such as code of work rules, wage structures, and internal procedure of joint consultation, grievance procedures etc. He views trade unions as an external organization and excludes collective agreements from the sphere of internal regulation. He observes that the growth of external job regulation was in response to market forces, which could be controlled by the externally. Therefore, the union's concern was and is mainly external regulation. According to him, collective bargaining is the central to the IR System. The rule of the system are viewed as being determined through the rule making process of collective bargaining, which is regarded as a political institution, involving a power relationships between worker and the management.

The difference between the 'systems approach' and 'oxford approach' lies in the fact that where as the former emphasizes the role of wider influences on the rule making, the latter has stressed the process of rule making through the collective bargaining. The oxford approach to IR has influenced not only public policy in the field but also many of the younger generation of scholars in industrial relations.

(*viii*) **The Industrial Sociology Approach:** Mergenson hold the view of IR is the nature and development of the conflict itself. Conflict is the basic concept that should form the basis of the study of IR. According to this school of thought, there are two major conceptual levels of industrial relations. One is intra-plant level where as situational factors, such as job content, work task and technology, and interaction factors produce three types of conflict *i.e.*, distributive, structural and human relations. These conflicts are being resolved through collective bargaining, structural analysis of the socio-technical systems and management analysis respectively.

The second level is the outside the firm and, in the main, concern with the conflict not resolved at the intra-organizational level. However, this approach rejects the special emphasis given to rule determination by the 'systems and oxford models'. In its place, it suggests a method of inquiry, which attempts to develop sociological models of conflicts. However, the emphasis on the significance of conflict in IR is not new one. The nature and importance of industrial conflict was extensively studied in the 1950 and 1960s by number of writers.

(*ix*) **Action Theory Approach:** Like the systems approach, it takes the collective regulation of industrial labour as its focal point. The actor operates within a framework, which can at best be considered as a coalition relationships. This actor, it is claimed, agree in principle to cooperate in the resolution of the conflict their cooperation taking the form of bargaining. Thus, the action theory analysis of industrial relations focuses primarily on bargaining as a mechanism for the resolution of the conflicts. Where as the systems model of IR constitutes a more or less comprehensive approach, it is hardly possible to speak of one uniform action theory concept.

(*x*) **The Marxist Approach:** Marxism is essentially a method of social enquiry into the power relationships of society and a way of interpreting social equality. The application of Marxian theory as it relates to IR derives indirectly from the later Marxist scholars rather than directly from the works of Marx himself. Marxist Approach is primarily oriented towards the historical development of the power relationships between capital and labour. It is characterized by the class struggle of these classes to consolidate and strength their respective positions with a view to exerting greater influences on each other. In this approach, IR is equated with power-struggle. The prices payable to the labourers are determined by a confrontation between conflicting interests. The capitalist ownership of the enterprises endeavors to purchase labour at the lowest possible price in order to maximize their profits. The lower price paid by the owner of the means of production for the labour he employs, the greater is his profits. However, this analysis of IR is not a comprehensive approach as it takes into account only the relations between capital and labour. It is rather a general theory of society and social change, which has implications for the analysis of industrial relations within what Marxism would describe as capitalist societies.

(xi) **The Pluralistic Approach:** Clark Kerr, an important exponent of pluralism holds that the social environment is an important factor in industrial conflicts. The isolated masses of the workers are more strike prone as compared to dispersed groups. When industrial jobs are more pleasant and employees get more integrated into wider society, strikes will become less frequent. Ross and Hartman's cross national comparison of strikes postulates the declining incidence of strikes a societies industrialize and develop appropriate institutional framework. They claim that there has been a decline in strike activity all over the world in spite of an increase in union membership. The thecry of Flanders propounds that conflicts is inherent in the industrial system and highlighted the need for a formal system of collective bargaining as a method of conflict resolution. Industrial conflict is accepted by pluralists not only as being inevitable but also as required containment within the social mechanism of collective bargaining, conciliation and arbitration as different methods of settling industrial disputes. Robert Fox distinguishes the two aspects of IR, as first is a market relationship (essentially economic in nature) and second is participation of unions in joint decision-making. The major criticisms are this approach is the Marxists according to whom exploitation and wages and salaries will continue unabated in the institutional structure of pluralism.

(xii) **The Human Relations Approach:** The Elton Mayo, the proponent of HR School and later propagated by the Keith Davis, as "the integration of people into a work situation that motivates them to work together productively, cooperatively and with economic, psychological and social satisfaction". This highlights certain policies and techniques to improve employee morale, efficiency and job satisfaction. It encourages the small group to exercise considerable control over its environment and in the process helps to remove a major instinct in labour—management relations. There are lots of criticism from Marxist, Pluralist and others on the ground that it encourages dependency and discouraged individual development and ignored the importance of technology and culture in the industry. Taking a balanced view, however, it must be admitted that the human relations school has thrown a lot of light on certain aspects such as communication, management development, acceptance of workplace as a social system, group dynamics, participation in management etc.

(xiii) **The Gandhian Approach:** The faith in goodness of men the evils of the modern world have been brought by the wrong system but not the wrong people/individual. He insisted on recognizing each individual worker as a human being (trusteeship). Trusteeship has influence on the whole process of IR. In short, the theory of trusteeship is based on the view, that all forms of property and human accomplishments are gifts of the nature and as such, they belong not to any one but they are to society. This approach is totally different from other theories of IR. It aims to achieving economic equality and material development of the employees in a capitalist society by non-violence means. Gandhi gave a greater importance to change in the attitudes and to regard themselves as co-equals and co-partner in a joint venture. He recognizes the need for higher productivity and 'pleaded that the management should share with the workers the gains from higher productivity'. He also emphasize on the importance of job enrichment.

(*xiv*) **The Unitarist Approach:** Some theory has developed which views that there is no inherent contradiction between the interests of management and the workers. It refers to, 'HRM is the by product of organizational behaviour'. There are need not exist any conflict between the employer and his employees and that they have a common interest, in survival and growth of the organization. More specifically, this school advocates that "IR" is too sensitive a field to be left to be handled by trained specialists, and the management's initiatives in this regards should be driven by line management, it declares that "every manager is a human resource manager". This theory also emphasize that there is no need of trade union to consult with employer, can be handled directly in one-to-one basis. This school eliminates the role of trade unions and postulates the practices of non-trade union organization. In addition, it focuses on rewards to the total exclusion of punishment's 'soft' approaches to the exclusion of the need for self-assertion on the part of management according as the circumstances demand.

13.5 KEY ISSUES AND CRITICAL CHALLENGES IN INDUSTRIAL RELATIONS

The volume of international business continues to expand dramatically from year to year. The advent of the Internet and e-commerce is further fuelling the flow of goods and services across the globe. Companies are organising across the national borders. Even the more traditional industries have not only modernised their production lines and supply chains in the pursuit of the lean organisation, but have developed the capacity to move products rapidly to different parts of the world in order to gain competitive advantage in terms of cost and speed of distribution.

As more and more companies operate internationally, the impact on various business functions becomes more pronounced. Professional managers in every function must develop the skills, knowledge, and experience in the international arena that will help their companies to succeed in this demanding and often volatile environment.

This is particularly true in the case of the human resources management, and industrial relations function. The implication is that globalisation is a reality and that people management philosophy, hence, has to acknowledge this fact and operate within this framework and context. "There is a global concern about the new human resource policies and practices, and their impact on industrial relations. The broad trend towards decline in employment in the manufacturing sector, low union activity in sunrise sectors, decentralised collective bargaining, and direct communication with and involvement of workers can be seen as efforts at political restructuring of industrial relations."

- Intensified Competition
- The Deregulation of Public Markets
- The Control of Public Expenditure and the New Public Management
- Changes in the Structure of Competition
- The Structure and Strategy of International Companies
- New Managerial Theories, Policies and Techniques
- The Deregulation of Service Markets and Intensified
- Competition
- The Decentralization of Bargaining Structures
- The Emergence of Sophisticated Non-Union Models
- Challenges to Management

- Challenges to Trade Unions
- Conclusion.

From its inception, the Labour Relations Commission has been dealing with the consequences of the most profound set of changes in Irish industrial relations practice for more than half a century. Since the 1980s the middle ground, that had marked out adversarial principles of good industrial relations, has been giving way in the face of a series of challenges to established practice. Many of these challenges strike at the understanding of the adversarial system. In response to new challenges, a different or extended understanding of good industrial relations is in the process of being articulated. This new middle ground and its implications for dispute mediation and the strategic role of the Labour Relations Commission will be considered in subsequent chapters. This chapter examines the major challenges now being presented to adversarial industrial relations across a range of industries and in workplaces in the private and public sector.

Intensified Competition

The implications for industrial relations of intensified international competition in recent years are profound, particularly in an economy as dependent on international trade as Ireland's. The completion of the Single European Market has had a major impact on the liberalisation of trade in product and service markets. The collapse of the former Soviet Bloc and the integration of Eastern and Southern European countries into the international economy has added to competitive pressures. East Asian economies have also emerged over the past decade as competitors in a range of sophisticated product and service markets. The enlargement of the European Union and the completion of the Uruguay Round of GATT will further intensify international competition and lead to increased competition from Third-World countries. Domestically, the deregulation of industries such as financial and airline services have added a further impetus to competition.

Faced with intensified competitive pressure, companies have been forced to reassess their management systems and cost structures. Labour cost structures, productivity levels and associated industrial relations practices have been critically affected by the managerial response to the rising pace of competition. Issues that appeared to be agreed, or could be so treated, a decade ago are frequently no longer viewed as immutable. In consequence, a new industrial relations agenda has developed which has sought to address such issues as the boundaries between general operatives and crafts, deeply entrenched working practices, multi-union bargaining structures, the power of custom and practice, the 'cultures' or attitude climates characterising relations between companies and employees, recruitment channels, promotion paths and the balance between permanent full-time jobs and part-time, temporary and contract employment. Unionisation itself has come to be viewed as an option rather than an imperative by many companies opening green-field facilities.

The Deregulation of Public Markets

Similar pressures to those being felt in the private sector have begun to impact on hither to highly regulated or monopolistic product and service markets in the public domain. The process of European economic integration has led to the deregulation of industries long subject to high levels of government regulation. The airline industry was one of the first to be affected. More recently the European Union has sought to introduce competition into electricity utilities and telecommunications. These developments have had a profound impact on semi-state companies like Aer Lingus, ESB and

Telecom Eireann. Long protected by regulation or statutory monopoly, these companies now face competition. EU economic policies favouring trade liberalisation within the Union have also made it considerably more difficult for governments to subsidise uncompetitive public-sector companies. The revision of established industrial relations practice occupies a major place in the responses of semi-state companies to the new competitive environment. The opening up of the large public procurement market to competition across the European Union has also intensified competition within the public domain and among private sector companies depending on public contracts for a significant part of their business.

The Control of Public Spending and the New Public Management

Tighter fiscal discipline has been one of the policy imperatives facing Irish governments for about the past decade. It was indeed the social partners who agreed the need for tighter control of public spending and provided the parameters that were to guide fiscal policy under the tripartite programmes since 1987. The fiscal targets set out in the Maastricht process and in the timetable for European Monetary Union have reinforced financial discipline. The broad consensus across the political spectrum that taxes on employment and employees needed to be reduced has further bolstered the control of public spending. Tighter fiscal discipline has a number of implications for industrial relations. First, it has strengthened the Government's resolve to provide a clearer commercial mandate to semi-state companies at a time when their markets are facing competition for the first time in their history. Second, it has led to a focus on greater efficiency and higher productivity in the public services, resulting in reviews of public service pay determination, grading structures, employment contracts and working practices. Finally, it has provided added impetus to new approaches to public management such as the 'strategic management initiative' and devolved administrative budgeting. In stressing the importance of clearer objectives for service delivery, more accountability and flexibility in deploying resources and devolved authority to make management decisions, these new approaches to public management again inevitably cast a spotlight on established industrial relations practices in the public services, health, education and local authorities.

Changes in the Structure of Competition

International and domestic competition can be, and often is, focused mainly on product and service cost. However, competition can also be focused to varying degrees on quality, diversity or innovation in products or services. Where competition is focused strongly on these attributes of goods and services, competitive success may not be determined mainly by price or cost. Across a range of consumer markets the structure of competition has changed in this direction. In consumer markets as diverse as car manufacturing, food and financial services, product quality, product range, delivery time and customisation now assume considerable importance in defining the character or structure of competition.

So-called 'diversified quality production' may provide some degree of shelter from intense price competition. The industrial relations implications of building and defending a competitive posture around quality and product diversification are beginning to be understood. A growing body of international research indicates that such competitive postures require radical changes in traditional industrial relations practices. Flexibility and speed in deploying and redeploying human resources in response to possibly short product-cycles assumes considerable importance. The skill, commitment, enthusiasm and creativity of the workforce comes into play to a greater degree than in traditional mass production or uniform service markets. Significantly greater provision needs to be made for training and development. Providing for training, enlisting the support of the workforce for flexibility and gaining their co-operation with ongoing change in products and processes, requires that employment security be emphasised to the maximum degree consistent with competitive success.

Suppliers of components, services or finished goods to companies adopting competitive postures based on quality or innovation are required in turn to accept rigorous strictures of product quality and to apply industrial relations principles geared to their realisation.

A trend in public sector and public service markets, in many respects analogous to developments in private consumer markets, is the gathering pace of 'consumerism'. The advent of 'charters', setting out the service entitlements of various categories of public service users, points to an understanding of public service delivery focused on the needs and rights of the consumer rather than the convenience of service providers. Consumerist principles are now influencing public service delivery in a number of European countries and beyond, where they often guide the redesign of services to make them more accessible to the consumer and more responsive to consumers' needs. This often involves changing a range of industrial relations practices: for example, encouraging more fluid boundaries between professional occupations, developing team-based service delivery and changing reporting relationships and traditional career channels. The principles associated with public service consumerism have already begun to influence public service provision in Ireland and seem set to gain momentum in the years ahead, raising challenges to established industrial relations practices across a range of public services.

The Structure and Strategy of International Companies

The liberalisation of trade and the more intense competition between countries for mobile international capital have made it easier for multinational companies to manufacture or source products in different locations around the world. Global sourcing of components and the establishment of parallel manufacturing sites for the same finished products is strongly evident in industries like automotive components and personal computers. International companies are also frequently configured to permit inter-plant competition for business and ultimately for investment. The survival and development of plants in a given location may now depend critically on 'benchmarking' exercises in which plants in different locations are compared on a range of production and commercial criteria. Benchmarking is also used to drive the competitive restructuring of working practices in plants. Ireland has witnessed such competitive pressures in recent years in industries like computer hardware and software, automotive components, electronics and pharmaceuticals. The margin available in Ireland for plants to compete by cutting wages or intensifying work (for example by extending working hours) is limited. The burden must then fall to a greater degree on skill, work practices and the general features of industrial relations.

New Managerial Theories, Policies and Techniques

In response to the kinds of competitive pressures outlined above, management theory has undergone change. The challenges from without have evoked a series of challenges from within the corpus of managerial thinking itself. Companies have begun to develop 'mission-driven' business strategies in which competitive objectives are linked with carefully crafted policies in different functional areas, including industrial relations and human resource management. 'Transformational leadership' is replacing caution and prudence as the dominant understanding of the purpose of senior executives. These developments often mean that what comes to be seen as institutional and policy inertia will be tackled and working arrangements, long sanctioned by tradition, will no longer be acceptable.

A new genre of management thinking and writing from the mid 1980s, adopting 'excellence' as its rallying call, has made 'people issues' a major concern of senior executive and general management. This has to pre-mature functionat and middle managers to innovate and experiment with new approaches to industrial relations. Line and general managers have assumed added responsibilities in personnel management and have become a major force in collective bargaining. Often, to avoid being swept aside, personnel managers have been forced to redefine their role in more stridently managerial terms. The familiar personnel posture of mediating between the company and the workforce has lost credibility and is no longer viable. New techniques of production and service delivery, requiring new industrial relations practices, have been honed and copied: total quality management, lean production, just in time production are but a small number of recent additions to manufacturing strategy. So-called 'human resource policies' have captured the high ground in industrial relations innovation. Companies are now enjoined by management texts, consulting houses and business schools to combine excellent communications, performance with skill-based pay, team-based work organisation, employee empowerment and job security in order to develop the most effective outcomes in managing employees. Research indicates that the actual degree of coherence and impact of these innovations on the ground falls well short of the theory which inspires them. Nevertheless, they present a formidable challenge to established industrial relations practice.

The Deregulation of Service Markets and Intensified Competition

Over the past decade major changes have occurred in the regulation of markets for various services, particularly banking, insurance services, building societies and associated financial services. These changes, in combination with the liberalisation of international trade in services, have profoundly altered the competitive circumstances of firms in these industries and their employees. Competition, both nationally and internationally, has intensified; product ranges have diversified; the performance and skill of employees have assumed greater importance as sources of competitive advantage. Established relationships with trade unions have frequently come under strain as bargaining structures, organisational patterns and processes, established career paths and long-established traditions of employment security have become subject to change. These industrial relations concerns and strains show no sign of abating in the medium-term, as the competitive challenges with which they are associated will continue to work themselves out in long established service industries.

In the distributive services, domestic competition has also intensified while international competition, through local outlets of international chains, is also becoming a feature of the Irish retail market. In response to these trends, different firms have sought to subject their cost structures and employment practices to more careful scrutiny. Attempts to clarify competitive postures have been apparent, with firms in some instances appearing to opt to compete stridently on the basis of cost, while others attempt to compete on the basis of service quality. As competition is more aggressively engaged in the industry, established working hours, working practices, and contractual conditions have become issues of dispute. Traditional approaches to the conduct of industrial relations, in some instances, have proven ill-suited to the demands now being faced.

The Decentralization of Bargaining Structure

One of the apparent paradoxes of Irish industrial relations over the past decade is that pay bargaining has centralised while bargaining structures have decentralised. Under the tripartite programmes since 1987, periodic round increases in pay have been provided in three-year agreements negotiated centrally by unions employers and government. Many of the industrial and area-based bargaining units that dominated collective bargaining in Ireland for the greater part of the post-war period have collapsed.

While provision has been made for annual pay adjustments at central level, an upsurge of bargaining activity has occurred at the level of companies and workplaces. Bargaining at these levels frequently centres on pay structures and systems, working arrangements and organisational restructuring. The emergence of the company and the workplace as key bargaining levels in Irish industrial relations can be traced back to the 1970s. The return of decentralised pay rounds in the early 1980s saw these levels assume critical importance. The competitive and other challenges outlined have spurred the trend towards company and workplace bargaining in spite of the advent of centralised pay agreements. Much bargaining activity at these levels reflects the employer-driven change agenda discussed above. Negotiations have frequently centred around 'concession bargaining' in which unions and their members have been asked to accept drawbacks in pay and conditions in return for plant survival or greater employment security. In bargaining of this type complex issues of competitive position, inter-plant benchmarks, technology and work practices can be at issue. As the locus, and to some degree the character of bargaining activity has shifted in these ways, shop stewards and plant managers have often been forced to come to grips with negotiating agendas reflecting profound changes in competitive conditions. More is required of them in terms of understanding both business issues and industrial relations processes.

The Emergence of Sophisticated Non-union Models

From the vantage point of the 1960s and 1970s the dominant model of adversarial industrial relations, based on union recognition and active union representation, seemed set fair to win the support of incoming multinational companies. In fact, differences in styles and features of industrial relations practice, as between indigenous and foreign unionised companies, were becoming more pronounced. Sophisticated policies of 'union avoidance' or 'substitution' also became common in electronics and related industries. The companies which operate such policies influence general practice in a number of ways. First, they represent practical exemplars of new approaches to employee relations that appear viable in a highly unionised national environment. Second, they present a challenge to unionised models of industrial relations to match or surpass their performance, judged in terms of business success and employee pay and conditions. Third, they may suggest policy innovations capable of application within unionised models of industrial relations.

Challenges to Management

Management is now faced with a series of major challenges which necessitate a departure beyond established ways of managing employees and relations with trade unions. Employee commitment needs to be fostered and maintained, particularly where firms seek to adopt competitive strategies based on product and service quality and differentiation. Flexibility must also be developed and sustained—the particular form it takes varying with the demands placed on different firms, products and categories of employees. Above all, management is now faced with the challenge of adopting more numerous and more focused policies in the human resource and industrial relations fields, encompassing payment systems, selection, training and employment security, collective bargaining, employees and union involvement and work organisation.

Challenges to Trade Unions

From 1980 to the late 1980s trade unions in Ireland suffered their most serious membership losses since the 1920s. Since then membership and organisation have stabilised or experienced a moderate recovery. Unions remain an integral part of the fabric of Irish industrial relations: the level of unionisation in Ireland in 1993 was the 7th highest of 23 OECD countries. The response of Irish unions to the setbacks of the 1980s and to the new industrial relations challenges was three fold. First, membership losses and associated financial strains encouraged mergers and organisational rationalisation. Second, many unions sought to provide an extended range of services for members. Third, unions collectively, under the aegis of the Irish Congress of Trade Unions, began to review their approaches to representation. This review is continuing. The new policies and ways of representing members set out in the Congress documents, New Forms of Work Organization (1993) and "Managing Change" (1995) represent the most radical, and potentially the most far reaching, change in union methods in the history of the Irish trade union movement. Congress acknowledges the challenges presented by new managerial approaches and the forces which they reflect. There is an acceptance of the need to move beyond the adversarial model, subject to satisfactory assurances from employers in respect of union security and the pay and conditions of union members. The new policies endorsed by the ICTU are recent innovations. The level of support they are capable of attracting from unions in companies and workplaces has yet to be determined. The willingness of employers to work with unions on the basis of these policies also remains to be established.

Conclusion

This has identified a series of challenges to the established adversarial model of industrial relations in Ireland. In combination, these challenges comprise the most profound set of forces for change bearing on Irish industrial relations practice for nearly half a century. The trends involved are primarily long-run or secular in character and, as such, are unlikely to be reversed in the decades ahead. The implications of these trends on how 'good industrial relations' can now be understood will be considered in near future.

Management of Industrial Relations

(*a*) **Grievance Handling and Industrial Relations:** There is hardly any organization does not have any feeling of dissatisfaction/discontentment of one kind or other. The grievances are real or invalid, genuine or false. A grievance produces unhappiness, discontentment, indifferences, low morale, frustration etc. Ultimately; it affects the employees' concentration, efficiency and also productivity. A large no. of work stoppages, shop floor incidences, and strikes could be attributed to the faulty handling of grievances. In the maintenance of peace in the industrial units, a well defined and adequate grievance procedure for redressal of day-to-day grievances is an essential pre-requisite. Prompt and effective handling of grievances is the key to industrial peace. The Grievance is a claim initiated by an employee alleging his/her employment or productivity has been adversely affected by unfair applications of business policies and procedures, or illegal discrimination, and on which remedial action is desired. The grievance procedure is a process through which employees may bring their concerns to upper level management. The process requires that rules be followed strictly. Grievance procedures for the resolution of complaints of unlawful discrimination. Types of complaints:

- Discrimination complaint; a complaint resulting from an event or act which the complaint believes occurred because of discrimination on the basis of race, colour, national origin, religion, sex, age disability, sexual orientation, veteran status, or political affiliation.
- Non-discrimination complaint; a complaint regarding the terms or conditions of employment resulting from an event or act which the complaint believes is objectionable, but which the complaint does not identify a discrimination complaint.
- The Grievance Procedure really got a toe hold during World War II, when the War Labour Board was developed for the purpose of keeping steady employment, minus the threat and practice of strikes, for the purpose of keeping productivity at a peak during the war effort. It was during these years the Grievance Procedure reached its real recognition as means of preventing strikes and at the same time giving the worker an opportunity to air his differences with the employer. Employers must ensure that employees know the company rules, what will happen if they are ignored or disregarded, and what he/she should do. If they have a Grievance/complaint against their employer or another employee. Conflicts and disagreements between employees are inevitable. It is the policy of all businesses to resolve these disputes at the lowest possible level.

The cost of the grievance can be high in terms of time lost, poor work, damage to costly machines by neglect, employee resentment, poor customer services, resistance to change, union-management relationships/conflict and so on. Whatever the causes and factors of the grievances which are responsible for employee grievances, there is an urgent need to manage them by establishing efficient and effective grievance resolution machinery. Grievance redressal machinery permits employees to express their complaints without jeopardizing their jobs, and encourageous and facilitates the settlement of misunderstanding between management and labour. The very existence of this mechanism which will build the confidences among the employees, allow ventilating their discontents, enhancing their morale, satisfaction of being heard. It also acts as the communication to management regarding responses and reactions to its action and facilitates reviews and corrections. It enables the employees to develop faith in the organization and improve discipline. Thus the magnitude and nature of grievances indicates the state of organizational health, projects the shop floor culture and show the leadership quality, establishment of grievance redressal mechanism for managing them is of utmost importance in organizational setting. The managers should analyze the facts to reach a decision. The decision should be reached carefully because they will be precedents for future. The management should attempt to avoid these errors. Indeed, effective handling of grievances facilitates the integration of interests.

(*b*) **Industrial Disputes and Industrial Relations:** Industrial Peace and industrial harmony may have the same meaning; but we are inclined to think that the concept of industrial peace is somewhat negative and restrictive. It emphasis absence of strife and struggle. The concept of industrial harmony is positive and comprehensive and it postulates the existence of understanding cooperation and a sense of partnership between the employers and the employees. That is why we prefer to describe our approach as one is quest of industrial harmony.

Industrial Dispute means any dispute or difference between employer and employees, or between employer and workmen or between workmen and workmen, which is connected with the employment or non employment or the terms of employment or with the conditions of labour, or any person. The Scope the definition of Industrial Dispute is very wide. The words employment and non employment in the definition are of widest amplitude and have been but in juxtaposition to make the definition comprehensive. Any dispute concerned with employment or non-employment constitute the subject matter of one class or industrial disputes. The matters which can form subject matter industrial dispute are enumerated in Second, Third and Fourth Schedule given at the end of Industrial Dispute Act.

There are two types of Industrial Disputes-interest disputes and rights disputes. Interest disputes relate to determination of new wage level and other condition of employment while rights disputes on the other hand relate to interpretation and application of existing standards and usually involve and individual worker or group of workers. Under category of rights disputes, claim is made that the workmen have not been treated in accordance with the rules, individual contracts of employment, laws and regulations and as per collective agreements. Such disputes are also described as grievance disputes. Such grievances may be regarding retrenchment, dismissal, payment of wages, working time, overtime, demotion, promotion, transfer, seniority, job classification, work rules and fulfillment of obligation relating to safety and health laid down in an agreement. The definition of Industrial Dispute as given in the Act has a wide coverage. All disputes relating to employment or non-employment, or the terms of employment or with the condition of labour are covered under the definition.

Settlement means a settlement arrived at in the course of conciliation proceeding and included a written agreement between employer and workmen arrived at otherwise than in course conciliation proceeding where such agreement has been signed by the parties there to in such manner as may be prescribed and a copy thereof has been sent to the officer authorized in this behalf by the appropriate government and the conciliation officer. The definition envisage two categories of settlement.

(1) Settlement arrived at in the course of conciliation, and

(2) Settlement arrived at privately or otherwise than in the course of conciliation.

The settlement arrived at in the course of conciliation stand on a higher plane than the settlements arrived at otherwise than in the course of conciliation. The legal effect of both these settlements is not identical. The settlement arrived at otherwise than in the course conciliation binds only the parties to settlement and none else. In any case it does not stand on higher plane than the settlements arrived at in the conciliation and that makes the two distinct and different from each other.

Procedures for settling labour dispute: Collective Bargaining, Negotiation, Conciliation and Mediation, Arbitration and Adjudication are well known methods for settlement of industrial disputes.

Industrial adjudication has undoubtedly played a conclusive role in the settlement of industrial disputes and in ameliorating the working and living conditions of labour class. In this context the National Commission of Labour observed: the adjudicating machinery has exercised considerable influence on several aspects of conditions of work and labour management relations. Adjudication has been on of the instruments for the improvement of wages and working conditions and for securing allowances for maintaining real wages, bonus and introducing uniformity in benefits and amenities. It has also helped to avert many work stoppages by providing an acceptable alternative to direct action and to protect and promote the interest of the weaker sections of the working class, who were not well organized or were unable to bargain on an equal footing with the employer.

(*c*) **Trade Union and Industrial Relations:** "Any combination formed primarily for the purpose of regulating the relations between workmen and employers or workmen and workmen or employers and employers or for imposing restrictive conditions on the conduct of any trade or business and includes any federation of two or more trade unions."

From the above definition it is clear that Trade union is not just an association of the workmen of a factory or a trade or a business but also can be formed by officers and managers. **Trade union movement in India was started and led by philanthropists and social organizations and not by the workers.** Trade union is a direct product of industrialization and a very recent development. In India, the foundation of modern industry was laid between 1850 and 1870. Prior to that trade was confined to individuals and families like craftsmen and artisans. They had expertise and specialized skills which was inherited by their off springs. After industrial revolution, these people started losing their individual identities and had to join factories to earn their livelihood and compete with mass production. There was a psychological dislocation as they were losing their identities. Since the mid-1980s the practice of Human Resources Management (HRM) has significantly altered traditional union-management relations in the advanced sectors of production, notably in multinationals and other private firms. Since the economic reforms of 1991, some public sector firms have also incorporated modern HRM practices into their otherwise traditional labour-management relationship. Some of the essential characteristics of these HRM practices are: attempts at direct communication between managers and employees; individualized and/or contingency pay systems; modular organization of production through work teams with team leaders who often form part of the management structure; carefully designed and fairly implemented performance appraisal systems; and so on. While many would argue that modern HRM practices undercut union effectiveness at enterprise level, there is no clear evidence of this in India. Unions have a strong presence in the firms where modern HRM practices are implemented successfully, and it is only with cooperative union-management behaviour that this has been possible. But this applies mainly to the manufacturing sector.

With economic liberalization, competitive forces began to affect the structure of the union movement. In several private enterprises "independent" rank-and-file led unions came into existence and engaged in informed and militant bargaining, often with multinational employers, securing substantial wage and non-wage gains in the process. As these unions "traded off" increased wages against employment growth, and as employers shifted to "outsourcing" from non-union sites, the traditional party-based unions found their potential recruitment terrain both challenged and curtailed. More recently, since the liberalization process officially began in 1992, many of these centralized party-based unions have united under a common front to resist government attempts at privatization and decentralization in the public sector. However, the organized labour movement as a comprehensive organization continues to face a fractured and segmented constituency, divided by skill, region, industry and ethnicity. In addition, major labour law reform continues as an unfinished (and forever postponed) agenda.

Unions would need to consider the possible scenario that in the years to come the likelihood is that managements will look increasingly to HRM to enhance enterprise competitiveness. This is particularly so as enterprises come to depend on people—on their skills and productivity—as one critical factor in this regard. HRM is being increasingly taught as a part of management education, and this would perhaps increase resort to HRM by future managers. Besides, declarations of policy at national or central level may not necessarily affect what employees and unions may in fact be prepared to do at local level. Unions could opt to be involved in consultation mechanisms at workplace level at which new HRM initiatives are discussed. This implies that unions need to concentrate more on enterprise level problems and issues. It also implies massive training programmes for unions in HRM issues, if they are to be in a position to respond to and participate in HRM initiatives. The attitude of unions on productivity issues is likely to condition the willingness of employers to involve them in HRM initiatives. Perhaps most of all, unions which are able to take a long-term perspective on issues are most likely to be involved in or participate in change.

(*d*) **Role of State and Industrial Relations:** We are always must reluctant to put any interpretation upon labour legislation is likely to prejudice the rights or welfare of labour. We are fully conscious of the fact that our legislature has put labour legislation on the statue book primarily for the purpose of redressing the balance between employers and employees and that we would not, unless we are compelled to do so by the clear language used by the legislature put any construction upon any provision of labour legislation which will in any way prejudicially affect their rights.

State intervention in industrial relations is essentially a modern development. With the emergence of the concept of welfare state, new ideas of social philosophy, national economy and social justice sprang up with result that industrial relation no longer remains the concern of labour and management alone. Many countries realized that for general progress to be assured, economic progress was a must. In no country is a complete laissez faire attitude now adopted in the matter of labour management relations.

In all the countries, over a period of time, the state has assumed power to regulate industrial relations. It is the state which is now the most significant element in determining the legal environment within which industrial relations operate. Bean regarded state as an actor within industrial relations performing a number of distinct roles. The distinct role that state performs are broadly, categorized by him as five. Firstly, it acts as a third party regulator promoting a legal framework which establishes general ground rules for union-management inter-action, particularly in the procedure for collective bargaining. Secondly, and additionally, as a means of supporting and underpinning collective bargaining or as a supplement to it the law can be used establish minimum standards while collective bargaining exploits particular advantages to secure higher standards whenever it can is used. The third well established function in many countries is the provision of state service for conciliation, mediation and arbitration with a view to facilitating the settlement of industrial disputes. A fourth aspect of the role of the state that has become increasingly important is that of a direct and primary participation as a major employer in the public sector. In this respect, it influences the pattern of industrial relations by its own behaviour and example. A fifth role that the state has come to play in many countries is that of a regulator of incomes. As a result, direct and active state involvement in the industrial relations has become much more pronounced in recent years.

The concern of state in matters relating to labour is product of its obligations to protect the interest of industrial community, while at the same time fostering economic growth in almost all countries. State has assumed powers to regulate labour relations in some degree or the other. In some, has taken the form of laying down bare rules or observance by employers and workers; in others, the rules cover a wider area of these rules. So far as our country is concerned, State intervention in labour matter can be traced back to the enactment of the Employers and Workmen's Disputes Act 1860 which provided for the speedy disposal of the dispute relating to the wages of workmen engaged in railways, canals and other public works, by Magistrates. After World War-I however, State intervention in Dispute Resolution became more systematic and effective.

Industrial relations systems are founded on a framework of labour law which exerts an influence on the nature of the industrial relations system. However, recourse to the law and its potential to influence the resulting industrial relations system may sometimes be over-emphasized. It is useful, therefore, to examine, from three points of view, the role of the law in influencing an industrial relations system—what its objectives should be and the areas it should cover, as well as what the law cannot achieve.

In any working situation people need to cooperate with each other if there is to be maximum gain to themselves, to management and to society as a whole. Cooperation, however, is not easily obtained as people working together have conflicting interests. Employees are primarily concerned with the security of their jobs and what they can earn, and the employer with what he can produce as cheaply as possible to obtain the maximum profit. When these conflicting interests have taken definite form and shape, the State has often stepped into protect some of these interests through legal control. Labour law has amply demonstrated the sociological theory that contributes istablishing better employer-employer hardships.

Besides employers and employees, governments and institutional bodies have also become relevant actors in the Industrial Relations, with the aim to define policies related to new labours related problems. New information and communication technologies and their particular characters determine deep changes in industrial organisation and, in particular, in work organisation. Relevant consequences are arising with regard to traditional content of Industrial Relations, such as professional skills, future career perspectives, work satisfaction, working time, etc.

The role of public authorities is to broaden the range of choices, eliminating constraints and, sometimes, to guarantee procedures. In addition, old tools of unionist bargaining have to be updated and to assume a different character, trying to improve worker's autonomy. At a general level, it emerges a need of a more consistent industrial democracy in a socio-economic framework continuously evolving towards the so-called globalisation.

Technological innovations, linked to networked and multimedia work development, clearly emphasise meanings and forms of distance working. During these last years, at organizational level, telework has enlightened a need of a flexible and not centralized management of the workforce, asking for a precise individualization of formal relationship between parties, usually determined by national labour law.

(*e*) **Workers Participation in Management:** Workers Participation in Management (WPM) has come to stay in both developed and developing countries. Its efficacy as a system is no longer a question. The concept is an extension of political system to the work place. In a democracy, participation of the people in the political process is an essential ingredient of the system. WPM is an extension of the political process to workplace relations. Participation is an influencing process, it also affects employees terms and conditions of the employment. The structure of the WPM, content mostly depends on the political ideology and systems adopted by a particular society. The forms of WPM can be depends on the differences in the level of management, the subject matter of participation, the strength of the union and the pattern of industrial relations. The important forms of participation in management are collective bargaining, joint decision making, consultation and information sharing. WPM falls into the several categories. These are informative (sharing of information), consultative (consult on the matters of welfare) associative (council for solving a problem) administration (Joint decision bodies) and decisive (highest form of participation) participation.

The philosophy of WPM provides a sound basis for the economic and psychological involvement of workers in decision-making. It is a part of HRD strategy of enterprises. The pattern of participation largely depends upon the socio-cultural milieu of the society and the culture and ethos of the organization. However, necessary infrastructure of participative work culture is to be carefully built-up in the organization through such informal methods like small group activities, leadership styles, motivation patterns and communication system. It also calls for a change in the social and inter personnel skills on the part of the management as well workers. The institutional mechanism of participative management is to be geared to the interests of both the organization and its employees. Workers should be given all necessary facilities and encouragement to start small self-managed firms and also takeover of certain firms by organizing themselves into cooperative. Moreover, the growth of professionalism in industry, advent of democracy and development of principles of social justice, transformation of traditional labour management relations have added new dimensions to the concept of participative management. The philosophy underlying workers participation stresses: democratic participation in decision-making, maximum employer-employee relations, minimum state interventions, realization of greater measure of social justice, greater industrial efficiency and higher level of organizational health and effectiveness.

13.6 GLOBALIZATION AND INDUSTRIAL RELATIONS-ITS EMERGING TRENDS

"Globalization is the closer integration of the countries and peoples of the world..... brought about by the enormous reduction of costs of transportation and communication, and the breaking down of artificial barriers to the flows of goods, services, capital, knowledge, and people across borders."

—Joseph Stiglitz

An economist and winner of the Nobel Prize

Globalization is a newly emerging phenomenon. It has been defined as "a set of processes by which the world is rapidly being integrated into one economic space via increased international trade, the internationalization of production and financial markets; the internationalization of a commodity culture promoted by an increasingly networked global telecommunication system" **(Graham, 1996).**

Globalization transcends socio-economic and political barriers that the countries of the world are prone to build around themselves. It is not only a process "integrating just economy, but culture, technology and governance. It is giving rise to new markets, foreign exchange and capital markets linked globally, new tools, internet links, cellular phones, media network, new actors; the World Trade Organization with authority over national governments, the multi-national cooperation with more economic power than many states, new rules, multi-national agreements and intellectual property, multi-lateral agreements on trade" **(Human Development Report, 1999).**

Globalization is expected to have a positive influence on the volume, quality and spread of knowledge through increased interaction among the various states. 'In a globalized world, as technology becomes its main motor, knowledge assumes a powerful role in production, making its possession essential for nations, if they are successfully to pursue economic growth and competitiveness **(Stromquist, 2000).** Education, being the most potent instrument of creation, assimilation and transmission of knowledge, assumes a central role in the process.

In a market oriented competitive world, unleashed by the forces of globalization, education has to assume a somewhat different role. It cannot afford to be conventional, rigid and impervious to change. It has to keep abreast of the latest developments in various fields and be capable of creating, absorbing and transacting neo-technology and information systems that are sweeping across the countries of the world. There has also to be a paradigm shift in the contents of education with substantial emphasis on the productivity aspect of the curriculum. It would also call for adequate emphasis on research and development (R and D).

It is, however, necessary to guard against being swept off our feet by the new 'cult of technology', and consequently, 'the diminution of respect for spiritual and cultural values' **(Maugey, cited in Namer, 1999).** An unfettered and ruthless pursuit of economic goals, without regard to considerations of moral and social values is bound to be disastrous for the people, particularly in developing countries.

Globalization, as an effective instrument of international exchange of goods and services, has to have a human face, based on ethical considerations rather than on cut throat competition. It should play a positive role in reducing economic and social disparities within, and among, the nations. It should also be an effective tool for promoting sustainable development.

During the 1990s, the new demands of international competition and dramatic advances in technology—the forces of globalization—have changed substantially the nature and operation of the "market place", and how production is organised, in many industries across the world. Individual enterprises are now being required to innovate to provide "the right product, at the right price and time".

These requirements are placing considerable demands on employers and their enterprises to develop and implement new strategies, structures and processes. There is an increasingly strategic role for Industrial Relations (IR) within the enterprise, as much of what has to be done involves significant changes to traditional practices in this and the related area of Human Resource Management (HRM). The result has been that the nature of IR is changing in many enterprises. A new approach is emerging, relying on a broader concept of employment relations.

This new approach is based on a range of IR and HRM practices directed to improving the flexibility and skills of the workforce, within an environment which emphasises communication, cooperation and trust between managers, workers and their representatives. Adoption of this approach, however, has been neither universal nor uniform. It has been particularly pronounced in industrialised countries, and is increasing in industrialising countries. But both the forms it has taken and its spread, has varied considerably within industries and across regions in the same country, and among countries and regions having different industrial relations policy, legal and institutional frameworks and traditions.

Within this new economic and industrial environment, the situation in Asia and the Pacific presents a range of contrasts—from the generally strong but variable economic performance of the advanced countries in North, East and Southeast Asia and the Southwest Pacific, to the rapidly industrializing countries in Southeast Asia, the accelerating growth in South Asia, and the special situations of the countries in transition and the island states of the South Pacific.

Much more than any other previous influence, globalization is emphasising the importance of IR to industrialization and economic development in the region. It is creating new challenges for, as well as highlighting old tensions among, governments and the social partners. It has also brought with it a number of strategic opportunities, if the parties can take advantage of them, to improve the prospects of enterprises and workers and to position the region for a period of continuing strong economic growth and development into the twenty-first century. Employers, as the force driving economic changes, and their organizations have to take the initiative to develop a reform agenda which can deliver these benefits. This will require a strategy directed to improving employment relations and which seeks changes in attitudes and behaviour in the workplace and addresses the key issues of skills development, compensation, work organization and flexibility, and cross-cultural management.

Increasing international economic interdependence has disturbed traditional IR arrangements in several broad ways. Firstly, such arrangements have normally been confined to the circumstances created by national markets; but globalization has fundamentally changed, and considerably expanded, the boundaries of the market place. In this respect, the extent of information flows made possible by new technology is building inter-enterprise networks around the world, is calling into question the traditional boundaries of the enterprise and is eroding current IR arrangements.

MNCs are the primary driving force for change. They are organizations that engage in FDI and own or control productive assets in more than one country (Frenkel and Royal 1996–7). They are creating very complex international production networks which distinguish globalization from the simpler forms of international business integration in earlier periods. As producers of global goods and services (notably, in the area of mass communications), centres of networks and large employers, MNCs have an impact extending far beyond urban centres in the countries in which they are located. In addition to the activities of MNCs, many locally-based enterprises, of varying sizes, in many countries are using information technology to focus on the demands of international (and domestic) "niche" markets in a way which is contributing to a growing individualization and decollectivism of work.

Secondly, globalization has disturbed the status quo between 'capital' and 'labour' in each country, in the sense that capital is significantly more mobile in an open international environment, while labour remains relatively immobile (here it should be noted that, under globalization, international labour migration is continuing, but, proportionately to the rate in the 1970s, has not increased—see World Bank 1995: 53). This can place 'labour' at a relative disadvantage, in that capital can now employ labour in different countries, at lower cost and on a basis which can prejudice the continuing employment of workers in the originating country.

Thirdly, globalization is having a contradictory impact on IR. It is accelerating economic interdependence between countries on an intra-and inter-regional basis and encouraging similarities in approach by individual enterprises in competitive markets. This may lead to some convergence in industrial relations arrangements around the world. At the same time, there is clear evidence of resistance towards convergence, based on particular national and regional circumstances (*e.g.,* in Europe and Asia).

The scope of IR must now be viewed as extending to all aspects of work-related activities which are the subject of interaction between managers, workers and their representatives, including those which concern enterprise performance. But issues which are critical to the manner in which an enterprise operates—such as job design, work organization, skills development, employment flexibility and job security, the range of issues emerging around HRM, and cross-cultural management issues—have not until recently been considered as part of labour-management relations; and, in many cases, they have not previously been made the subject of collective bargaining or labour-management consultation. But this situation is changing, and has been particularly noticeable in Western industrialized countries.

A broader approach to IR would seek to harmonize IR and HRM, by expanding the boundaries of both fields. In particular, IR will need to address, much more than it does currently, workplace relations-and people-centred-issues, and recognise that it can no longer focus only on collective relations. Given the range of issues which should now be the subject of labour-management exchange at enterprise level, it may be that a different, more all embracing expression (for example, "employment relations") might be used to describe these relations. To these developments must be added other changes which have been taking place to the IR environment in many countries, and as a result of broader societal changes. The impact and the pace of these changes has varied from country to country, and will have varying impact in the Asia and Pacific region. They include the continuing shift in employment from manufacturing to service-oriented industries, accompanied by a shift from traditional manual occupations to various forms of "white-collar" employment. Also, public sector employment (in both line Ministries and state-owned enterprises) continues to decline in most countries. Broad social developments in many countries have also witnessed the increasing incidence of women in the labour force. This has been combined with growing demand for atypical forms of employment (*e.g.,* part-time, temporary and casual employment; and home work, in the form of certain kinds of process work and, increasingly, telework).

All of these changes have affected IR, and are likely to continue, to a greater or lesser extent, in individual countries. The manufacturing and public sectors in many countries have been the traditional base of support for trade unions. They are now experiencing considerable difficulties in maintaining and increasing membership, as the source of growth in many economies is increasingly coming from a services sector whose workers have demonstrated a reluctance to join unions.

The changing nature of IR

IR is not a self-contained area of activity. It can only be understood clearly by reference to the persons, groups, institutions and broader structures with which it interrelates (including, for example, changing product markets, the processes of labour market regulation, and the education and training system) within a particular country, as well as to influences arising from beyond its borders.

The development of global enterprises, the changes occurring in the course of industrialization and the impact of new management systems (particularly, HRM) require a broader perspective to be taken on employment relationships.

The scope of IR must now be viewed as extending to all aspects of work-related activities which are the subject of interaction between managers, workers and their representatives, including those which concern enterprise performance. But issues which are critical to the manner in which an enterprise operates—such as job design, work organization, skills development, employment flexibility and job security, the range of issues emerging around HRM, and cross-cultural management issues—have not until recently been considered as part of labour-management relations; and, in many cases, they have not previously been made the subject of collective bargaining or labour-management consultation. But this situation is changing, and has been particularly noticeable in Western industrialized countries.

A broader approach to IR would seek to harmonize IR and HRM, by expanding the boundaries of both fields. In particular, IR will need to address, much more than it does currently, workplace relations-and people-centered-issues, and recognise that it can no longer focus only on collective relations. Given the range of issues which should now be the subject of labour-management exchange at enterprise level, it may be that a different, more all embracing expression (for example, "employment relations") might be used to describe these relations. IR policies and those supporting industrialization for economic development. The impact of globalization is requiring IR systems in Asia and the Pacific to adapt to ensure improved economic competitiveness, flexibility and overall efficiency to respond to changing international market circumstances.

Individual enterprises, whether domestically or internationally-based and organized, are in "the frontline" of these changes. Employers and their organizations therefore have the most important role in generating the responses needed to take advantage of these new and emerging circumstances. But while globalization is a significant factor, it is not the only factor, driving IR changes in the region. Factors internal to each country—some of traditional IR concern, others instigated or exacerbated by liberalization—are prompting similar changes.

In addition to helping to achieve the improved efficiency and productivity which is driving enterprises in responding to a more competitive business and trading environment, the changes required to IR arrangements must provide stability in relations between managers and workers and ensure equitable participation by workers in the benefits of increased enterprise development and growth. That is, the essential challenge for each country is how to achieve a stable and flexible IR system which balances "efficiency" with "equity".

In this endeavour, attention must be given to traditional and emerging areas of IR concern (which together should constitute a broader focus for action than previously, based on the concept of "employment relations"). This will require action in the areas of policy, legislation, institutions, workplace practices and associated capacity building. A re-examination of the roles of government and the social partners and of the relevance and scope of IR laws and other rules and institutions will be necessary to acknowledge the realities of a more decentralized IR environment, and the need for the norms of the system to move away from a regulatory, to an increasingly facilitative, role, while still providing appropriate protections for workers. A renewed commitment to tripartite action and a greater emphasis on bilateral relations will be critical in realizing these changes.

In all of these areas, employers—as the generators of economic development and growth—and, through them, their organizations, have a clear set of priorities and strategies to address the factors, both internal and external to the enterprise, which will affect their capacity to harness employment relations as a key element in improving enterprise competitiveness and performance. The diverse IR situations across the region make it unrealistic to predict, with any degree of certainty, the future course of IR in the region. While globalization emphasizes convergence between economic and related systems, and this is occurring to some extent in Asia and the Pacific, IR are ultimately determined by a complex range of factors within individual countries, reflecting particular national, cultural and institutional circumstances.

13.7 CONCLUSION

To understand the range of Industrial Relations (IR) challenges that employers and their organizations are likely to face in Asia and the Pacific during the next decade, it is necessary to appreciate the current as well as historical factors which have shaped and are shaping such relations in the region. Much more than any other previous influence, globalization is emphasising the importance of IR to industrialization and economic development in the region. It is creating new challenges for, as well as highlighting old tensions among, governments and the social partners. It has also brought with it a number of strategic opportunities, if the parties can take advantage of them, to improve the prospects of enterprises and workers and to position the region for a period of continuing strong economic growth and development into the twenty-first century. Labour-management relations policy formulation is one of the significant tasks at the national level, and its successful formulation and implementation can influence the labour relations climate at the industry and enterprise levels. Such policy formulation, however, can be formulated not only at the national level through a tripartite process, but also at the industry level on a bipartite basis as between employers' and workers' organizations. Whether bipartite policy formulation becomes a part of national policy depends largely on the respective strengths of employers' and workers' organizations. In some of the industrialized market economies there is a greater likelihood than in developing countries of bipartite policy formulations being reflected in national policies due to the strength of the employers' and workers' organizations.

CASE STUDY–I Industrial Relations Amazon Textiles

Amazon Textiles is a textile industry located in the old industrial district of Mumbai. The company was established in 1870 and has seen several ups and downs. It suffered extensively on account of the export and import policy of British regime, whose main aim was to discourage the growth of the textile industry in India and use the country as a supplier of material for the textile industry in Manchester, UK. The promoter of the company, Mr. Manoj Birla, was a patriot and was closely associated with the independence movement and its various phases. He was a liberal man and had a paternalistic approach towards the employees. The growth of trade unions during his period (1870–1930) was minimal, since the trade union leaders were also co-leaders in the independence movement.

After the demise of Mr. Manoj Birla, Mr. Sanjay Birla took over as chairman of the company. He shifted the focus of the company from pure silk to other categories of textile goods such as cotton, polyester, etc. During he process, the modernized the looms and the machinery. In order to increase productivity, he did not increase the wages of the employees over a period of one decade, during which the productivity of the company rose by 20%. However, the trade union leaders could see through the ploy of chairman and became vociferous and demanding. There were two violent agitations and strikes by the two trade unions, who were also supported by the leaders of the independence movement. In order to improve his business prospects, Mr. Sanjay Birla sided with the Britishers, much to the annoyance of the leaders of the independence movement. In order to improve his business prospectus, Mr. Sanjay Birla died in an air crash in 1946. At this juncture, Mr. Sanjay Birla's younger brother Mr. Yash Birla took over as Chairman of the Company. He was the true son of his father and a loyal patriot who strongly supported the independence movement. His style of management was paternalistic and caring, and he was proactive in wage revision of the employees. The situation was peaceful till the 1970s until Mr. Mohan Samant, a powerful trade union leader in Mumbai industrial circles arrived on the scene. The latter believed in adopting a confrontationist attitude towards the management, irrespective of whether or not it was just. He tried to influence the trade union leaders in the company, but with little success. During the mid 1980s, there was a serious crisis in the textile industry and Amazon Textiles was not an exception. There was a sharp decline in exports as well as in domestic sales, which led to a sharp drop in profits, and, ultimately, losses over a continuous period of four years. The banks and financial institutions refused to refinance the sick company and Mr. Yash Birla began to scout for an opportunity to turn around its fortunes. At this juncture, he could foresee that the denim market would expand in a big way over the next 10 years and immediately set up modern textile mills in Ahmedabad to exclusively manufacture branded and generic denim.

The modern units in Ahmedabad flourished while the sick units in Mumbai could not be turned around since the cost of modernizing them was prohibitive. After detailed discussions with the trade unions, Mr. Yash Birla convinced them that it was best to close down the sick mills in Mumbai. Those desirous were relocated to the new units in Ahmedabad and the option of VRS was given to the other workers.

QUESTIONS

1. Examine the sociopolitical influence of the growth and development of trade unions on the company.
2. Analyze the interrelationship between the approach of the management and trade union activism.
3. Do a role-play based on the case study.

CASE STUDY–2 Industrial Relations Super Spinning Mills

Super Spinning Mills Limited was established in 1920 in Coimbatore for manufacturing yarn and supplying it to the cotton mills in and around the city. The company was initially founded with limited capacity and over a period of one decade, it grew to become one of the largest yarn mills in Coimbatore. The founder of the company, Shri Murali Iyengar, was a follower of Gandhian philosophy and believed in a paternalistic approach towards the employees, because of which there was little scope for grievance. But after some time, owing to the influence of politicians and freedom fighters, the trade union movement picked up in Coimbatore. Due to pressure from the workers of other units, two trade unions were formed in Super Spinning Mills, one with the support of the communists and the other with the support of the Indian National Congress. The leaders of these unions were very keen to increase the membership. To do so, they began to rouse the anger of the employees against the 'injustice' being done to them. Shri Iyer, in spite of his best efforts, could not convince the unions to maintain harmonious industrial relations. The union leaders, to meet their own selfish ends, started to create industrial unrest on the most minor issues, leading to loss of production. There were strikes lasting from five days to one month over a span of two years. On each of these occasions, the management took the help of leading freedom fighters for conciliation and arbitration, and were able to reduce industrial unrest.

QUESTIONS

Critically analyze the above case and identify the problems faced by the management.

Do you think that the management was right in redressing the grievances of the employees?

What could have been the best approach of the management towards proactively addressing the industrial unrest?

Do you suggest any other approaches for resolving the problems?

CASE STUDY–3 IR Andhra Pradesh State Road Transport Corporation (APSRTC)

Andhra Pradesh State Road Transport Corporation (APSRTC), the autonomous body providing public transport services in the state of Andhra Pradesh, was established in the early nineteenth century as a part of the erstwhile United Railways and Road Transport Corporation. The company was started by the then Nizam of Hyderabad, with a fleet of around 10 buses in the twin cities of Hyderabad and Secunderabad. In the early 1950s, after independence and the formation of the state of Andhra Pradesh, in independent road transport organization (APSRTC) was set up. The corporation is now one of the largest road transport undertakings in the country with a fleet of over 20000 buses and an employee strength of more than one and half lakh. The organization has two major trade unions, namely Employees Union (EU) and Bharatiya Mazdoor Sangh (BMS). The corporation has a record of peaceful industrial relations and the elections to the unions lead to one of them coming to power on an alternate basis. Liberalization and privatization meant that private road transporters were allowed to operate, leading to severe competition. The organization, which has a record of employee welfare, has to compete with the private players, who do not adhere to statutory obligations. Further, the organization also suffers on account of certain welfare policy measures, which have been announced by the State Government, such as concessional and free bus passes to a certain segment of citizens. In addition, it has to pay Motor Vehicle Tax to the State Government at a high rate, leading to serve losses. Further, there have also been rumours that the corporation would soon be privatized on account of the accumulated losses. The trade unions felt it was their responsibility to safeguard the existence of the corporation. For this purpose, they placed the following demands before the management as well as the State Government:

- Waive of Motor Vehicle Tax.
- Provide budgetary support from the State Government to offset the losses on account of concessions being announced by the State Government.
- Stop privatization/outstanding of private buses, improve maintenance operations, and purchase more buses.
- Reduce the administrative staff and streamline the purchase procedures.

Based on these demands, the unions had prolonged discussions with the management. However, the management could not respond to the major demands and referred the matter to the State Government. The State Government, on account of the severe financial crunch, refused to accept the major demands of the unions, following which the unions went on a strike for 20 days. This led to severe losses to the corporation and the government encouraged the private players to run additional services in order to weaken the position of the unions. Further, the State Government also persuaded once of the unions to withdraw from the strike, which led to the partial restoration of bus services. The employees of the other union put pressure on the union leaders to stop the strike. The other union leaders had negotiations with the State Government and agreed to stop the strike on the following conditions:

- The management should not initiate any disciplinary action against the employees.
- Participation in the strike should not be a ground for disqualification from the timely release of increments.
- The State Government would consider the waiver of the Motor Vehicle Tax and also provide partial budgetary support to the corporation.

QUESTIONS

1. Critically analyze the above case study.
2. Do you think that the unions were right in going on strike ?
3. What could have been a better strategy adopted by the unions to protect the interest of the corporation ?
4. Do you think the management had any role in preventing industrial unrest.

REFERENCES

1. Encyclopedia Britanica, Vol. 12, London, 1961, p. 297.
2. Dale Yoder, Personnel Management and Industrial Relations, pp. 5–6.
3. Tead and Metcalfe, Personnel Administration, p. 2.
4. Flanders A., Industrial Relations: What is wrong with the system? Faber, 1965, p. 10.
5. Clegg H.A. The System of industrial relations in Great Britain, Blackwell, 1970, p. 1
6. Kirkaldy, H.S., The Spirit of Industrial Relations, pp. *viii*–ix.
7. Jhon T. Dunlop, Industrial Relation System, Southern Illinois University Press, 1958. p. 7.
8. Sharma, A.M., Industrial Relations: Conceptual and legal Framework, Himalaya Publishing House, 2002, p. 4–5.
9. Venkata Ratnam, C.S., Industrial Relations, Oxford University Press, 2006, p. 25.
10. Pigou, A.C., Economics of Welfare, London, UK 1948.
11. Richardson, J.H., An Introduction to the study of Industrial Relations, George Allen and Unwin Ltd., London, UK pp. 18-20.
12. A. Fox, "Industrial Sociology and Industrial Relations", Royal Commission Research; Paper No. 3, HMSO, 1966. p. 2.
13. A. Clegg, "Pluralism in industrial relations, British Journal of Industrial Relations, Vol. *xiii*, 1975, p. 301.
14. M. Jackson, Industrial Relations (IInd Edition) Groom Helm, 1982, p. 20.
15. S.R. de Silva, Senior Specialist in Employers' Activities, East Asia Multidisciplinary Advisory Team, I.L.O., Bangkok.
16. Ahadeo Dhandu Jadhav vs. Labour Appellate Tribunal [1956], 1 LLJ 252, 254 (Bom.) R. Bean, Comparative Industrial Relations: An Introduction to Cross-National Perspectives, 100 (1985).
17. *Ibid.*
18. All modern states try to fix the rules of the game by, at a minimum, specifying tactics which are not permitted and by facilitating the coming-together of the parties for negotiation.
19. H.A. Clegg, Trade Unionism under, Collective Bargaining: A Theory based on Comparisons of Six Countries, 101 (1976).
20. Government of India Gazette (1969), Report of the National Commission on Labour p. 307.
21. Isaacs J, Jumbuna Coalmine, No liability vs. Victoria Coalminer's Association 6 CLR 309, 370 (High Court of Australia).
22. Supra Note 6, page 53. Section 2 (K) of Industrial Dispute Act.
23. What Every Body should know about Labour Law by H.L. Kumar (Universal Publishing) p. 104. Section 2(p) of Industrial Dispute Act.

24. Jagannatha Shetty J. Karnal Leather Karamchari Sanhathan vs. Liberty Foot Wear Co. 1990, Lab I C 301, 307, (SC).
25. The Law of Industrial dispute volume I page 9 O.P. Malhotra. 2004 ed.
26. K. Alexander, Collective Bargaining in Industrial Labour in India, compiled by V.B. Singh, 1963 Edn, pp. 384–85.
27. E.A. Ramaswamy, Trade Unions, Rule Making and Industrial Relations, (1985) 20 Economic and Political Weekly 524.
28. Beaumont, P.B. (1995), The Future of Employment Relations, Sage, London.
29. Deery, S. and Mitchell, R.J. (1993), Labour Law and Relations in Asia-Eight Country Studies, Longman Cheshire, Melbourne.
30. de Silva, S. (1996), Employers' Organizations in Asia in the Twenty-first Century, ILO Bureau for Employers' Activities, Geneva.
31. Frenkel, S. (1993), Organized Labour in the Asia-Pacific Region-A Comparative Study of Trade Unionism in Nine Countries, ILR Press, Ithaca.
32. Frenkel, S. (1995), "Workplace relations in the global corporation: A comparative analysis of subsidiaries in Malaysia and Taiwan," in Frenkel, S. and Harrod, J. (eds) (1995)- Industrialization and Labour Relations-Contemporary Research in Seven Countries, ILR Press, Ithaca.
33. Frenkel, S. and Royal, C. (1996), Globalization and Employment Relations (paper prepared for ILO/EASMAT, Bangkok; published under authorization as Centre for Corporate Change Paper No. 63, University of New South Wales, Sydney).
34. ILO (1995), Ozaki, M. Industrial Relations (paper prepared for ILO/World Bank Mission on Labour Market Policies for Higher Employment), Geneva.
35. ILO (1996c), "Industrial Relations: Towards a Negotiated Compromise between Democracy and the Market"—Background Document by the ILO Task Force on Industrial Relations (unpublished paper), Geneva.
36. ILO/JIL Network of National Institutes for Labour Studies in Asia and the Pacific (1996), The Impact of Globalization and the World of Work, ILO Regional Office for Asia and the Pacific, Bangkok.
37. International Industrial Relations Association (IIRA), 3rd Asian Regional Conference, Taipei, 1996, Record of Proceedings (Vol. 1—The Transformation of Industrial Relations under Democratization; Vol. 2—The Impact of Globalization on Industrial Relations; and Vol.4—The Perspectives of Industrial Relations in the 21st Century).

INDEX

A

Abilities 279
Absenteeism 90, 333
Accounting techniques 234
Action theory approach 383
Addie model 288
Adjudication 393
Administration 396
Analytical skills 310
Annual bonus 338
Application skills 310
Apprenticeships 295
Approaches 41, 219, 297, 379
As HR processes 253, 179
Assessment centers 141, 152
Associative 396
Attitudes 171, 254, 261, 282
Attrition 7, 9
Audiovisual methods 294
Audit 217
Autonomy 311

B

Behaviour event interviewing 141
Behaviour modification 311
Behaviourally anchored rating scales 119
Beliefs 254
Benchmarking 206, 207, 209, 288
Benchmarking objective 212
Benchmarks 293, 307
Benefits 221, 339, 359
Benefits of HRD 259
Bilateral relationship 369
Bonus 341
Broad band 102, 344
Business environment 62, 185
Business goals 195
Business integration 399
Business plans 218
Business strategies 28, 31, 32, 195

C

Campus recruitment 70
Capability enhancement 274
Career 5
Career coaches 150
Career decisions 193
Career development 187, 300
Career goals 13
Career growth 187, 231, 265
Career management 7, 13, 25, 151
Career paths 5, 188
Career planning 188, 253, 262, 265
Career planning programs 190
Career development, performance appraisals 218
Case studies 308
Case-study analysis 154
Cash 327
Centralized vs. Decentralized recruitment 65
Challenges in industrial relations 385
Challenges of recruitment 74
Change 213, 274, 283, 316
Changes in the structure of competition 387
Characteristics of pay structures 345
Choice 345
Climate 260
Coaching 109, 195, 315
Collective bargaining 11, 373, 391

Common matric questionnaire 159
Communication 148
Communication skills 310
Comparative 219
Compensable factors 346
Compensation 26, 29, 87, 143, 223, 232, 326, 327, 334
Compensation administration 218
Compensation philosophy 326
Compensation policy 334
Compensation systems 335
Compensation tactics 331
Competence 316
Competence-related pay 110
Competence and competencies 2, 102, 109, 130, 253, 304, 325
Competency analysis 142
Competency assessment 141, 181, 186
Competency management 232
Competency mapping 138
Competency-based pay 335
Competency-based systems 142
Competition 6
Competitive advantages 6, 14, 211, 218, 228, 303
Competitive benchmarking 209
Competitive compensation 325, 326
Compliance 219
Concept mapping 140
Conciliation 378, 393, 395
Conditions of learning 287
Consequences 333
Consultants 70
Consultative 396
Content analysis 156
Continuous learning 208
Continuous quality improvement (CQI) 271
Contribution-related pay 110
Control of public spending 387
Controlling 272
Core competencies 143, 148, 186, 211
Corporate citizenship 278
Corporate culture 260
Corporate governance 351
Corporate integrity 113
Corporate productivity 171
Corporate responsibility 113
Corporate social responsibility 107
Corporate strategies 5, 286
Cost benefit analysis 221
Cost-of-living allowance 342
Cost-of-living indexes 342
Creative skills 310
Critical incident technique (CIT) 155
Critical incidents 119, 155
Critical success factors 211, 325
Cross-cultural management 399
Cultural shock 91
Culture 107, 236
Customer satisfaction 284

D

Data 229
Data banks 71
Decision-making 236, 310, 397
Decisive 396
Definition 285
Delphi technique 52
Demand analysis 48
Demand and supply analysis 46
Demotion 86
Demotion policy 86
Deregulation 19, 31, 386
Description 89
Developing a pay structures 345
Development 26, 253, 281, 285
Development of human resource 29
Development, succession planning, 187
Differentiating competencies 142
Dimensions of HRD 260
Direct financial 327
Direct financial compensation 327

Direct foreign investments 300
Dismissal 92
Disputes 11
Distinguished performance 122
Diversification 24, 37
Diversity 9, 252
Diversity management 283, 316
Division of labour 10, 37
Domestic competition 389
Downsizing 33, 187
Due diligence 151
Dynamic 269

E

E-HR 33
E-learning 33
Economic environment 13
Education 285
Effectiveness 397
Employee commitment 390
Employee competencies 254, 286
Employee development 20, 197, 281
Employee performance 101, 357
Employee potential 171
Employee selection 26
Employee stock option schemes 340
Employee stock ownership 359
Employee training 12
Employee welfare 31
Employer-employee relations 397
Employment interviewers 115
Employment relations 401
Employment security 391
Empowerment 22, 32
Engagement 204
Enterprise level 374
Environment 3, 262
Environmental challenges 21
Environmental changes 31
Equity function 334
ESOPS 9
Essential competencies 142
Evaluation of training 296, 299
Executive compensation 351, 353
Executive development 10
Executive or management development 300
Exit interviews 93, 220
Expectancy model 115

F

Factor comparison 349
Factor comparison method 342
Factors 305
Factors affecting recruitment 66
Factors that influences companies compensation 330
Features 301, 353
Feedback 118
Flexible package 339
Flexible work 9
Forces of globalization 398
Forecasting 39, 49, 51, 226
Forecasts 38
Fringe benefits 327
Function: Industrial relations 376
Functions 231, 312, 374

G

Games 311
Gandhian approach 384
Gap analysis 46, 49, 51
Global citizens 10
Globalization 4, 12, 19, 31, 32, 399, 401
Goal of HRD 279
Goal setting 277
Goal-based 297
Goals 292
Golden handcuffs 77
Grade structures 344
Graphic rating scales 119
Grievance 391

Grievance handling 12, 391

Gross national product 45

Group discussions 308

Group think 52

H

Halo 124

Hard skills 172

Headhunters 76

Hiring strategies 62

Holistic 107, 205

HR 226

HR accounting 234

HR accounting 241

HR activities 218, 239

HR applications 138

HR audit 218, 219

HR audit report 225

HR audit review 227

HR audit systems 227

HR challenges 21

HR competencies 161

HR effectiveness 62

HR expenditure 239

HR function 5, 51, 153, 194, 206, 215, 223, 234, 237, 252, 272

HR information 227, 232, 259, 272

HR measurement 204

HR models 26

HR planning 39, 46, 223, 226

HR policies 215, 218

HR practices 4, 205, 225, 226

HR processes 60, 138, 145, 226, 272

HR research 255

HR role 7

HR service 145, 235

HR strategies 9, 22, 27, 239

HR system 30, 161, 229

HR utilization 39

HR value 237

HRD climate 261, 278

HRD competencies 256

HRD culture 260

HRD effectiveness 278

HRD function 278

HRD interventions 261

HRD matrix 262

HRD mechanisms 258

HRD outcome 263

HRD philosophy 255, 269

HRD process 269

HRD roles 255

HRD strategy 261, 397

HRD system 253

HRD techniques 253

HRIS 227, 230

HRM function 28

HRM objectives 23

HRM practices 25, 228, 259

HRM strategy 9

HRP at the macro level 40

Human capital 18, 43, 204, 228, 234

Human capital management 46

Human relations approach 384

Human resource accounting 234

Human resource information system 224

Human resource measurement intervention 205

Human resource planning 13, 25, 29

Human resource policies 105, 389

Human resource strategy 5

Human resource valuation 215

Human resources 1, 3, 4, 18, 27

Human resources development 251

Human resources information system 264

Human resources management 29

Human resources outcomes 204

Human resources planning 37

Human resources strategies 204

Human resources valuation 242

I

ICT 228

In-basket 141, 154, 183, 308

In-basket method 314

In-house 295

Inbreeding 69

Incentive 112, 343

Incentive compensation 346

Indirect 327

Indirect compensation 327

Individual 22

Individual career planning 189

Individual challenges 22

Individual job structure 344

Individual role-playing 314

Individual traits 116

Individualism-collectivism 332

Induction 91

Induction programme 91

Industrial disputes 392

Industrial environment 398

Industrial relations 12, 370, 374, 379

Industrial relations strategies 378

Industrial sociology approach 383

Industry 374

Information 229

Information technology 32

Informative 396

Ingredients 214

Innovation 13

Intellectual assets 234

Intellectual capital 4, 18, 237

Intensified competition 386

Interactive role-playing 314

Internal audit 293

Internal environment 331

Internal equity method 343

International companies 388

International competition 389

International HRM 5

Internships and assistantships 295

Interpersonal skills 277

Intervention 239, 255

Interview format 72

Interview techniques 157

Interviewers 115

Interviews 71, 183

Intimacy 311

Inventory analysis 159

J

Job abandonment 92

Job accidents 333

Job analysis 140, 153, 218, 342

Job classification method 342

Job description 89, 122, 130, 167, 293

Job design 399

Job enrichment 87

Job evaluation 12, 139, 148, 346

Job evaluation methodologies 348

Job families 145, 344

Job grading 348

Job knowledge 119, 171, 276

Job performance 118, 274

Job ranking 348

Job ranking method 342

Job redesign 267

Job rotation 13, 87, 266, 295, 307

Job satisfaction 9, 22, 262

Job security 339, 399

Job specifications 61, 89

Job standards 189

Job structure, job design 83

Job training 5

K

Knowledge 279

Knowledge management 275

Knowledge occupation 230

Knowledge workers 9

Knowledge; wisdom 229
KRAS 9
KSAS 143, 181, 186, 336

L

Laboratory training 295
Labour market 66
Labour turnover 90
Labour welfare 12
Labour-management relations 399
Lay off 92, 118, 187
Layout 123
Leadership 274
Leadership coaching 315
Leadership enterprises 274
Leadership skills 275
Leadership styles 276
Learners 281
Learning 13, 110, 275, 299
Learning organization 6
Learning process 300, 301
Learning theories 287
Lectures 294
Leniency 124
Levels 374
Levels of evaluation 297
Liberalizations 12, 64, 300 , 389
Life script 311
Loyalty 90, 124

M

Macro 370
Man-power planning 19
Management 2, 3
Management development 285, 299, 300
Management games/business games 315
Management remuneration 341
Management techniques 299
Managerial obsolescence 303
Managing change 391
Managing for results 180
Manpower 38
Manpower planning 37
Manpower requirement approach 45
Market pricing 343
Masculinity-femininity 332
MBO 122, 219, 267
Meaning of executive development 301
Measurable 139
Measurement 209
Measurement of productivity 317
Measurement strategies 203
Measurements 242
Mechanisms 255
Method 180
Methods and techniques 305
Methods of competency mapping 152
Minimum age 11
MIS 230
Mixed model 114
MNCS 399
Mobility 9, 83
Modern appraisal 104
Monetary benefits 43
Monetary value 235
Morale 84, 221, 258, 277
Morale and satisfaction 284
Motivate 237
Motivated workforce 325
Motivation 8, 63, 115, 258, 277
Motivational function 334
Multinational companies 388
Multiperson comparisons 120
Multiple management 308

N

National level 374
Nature 258, 302
Nature of job 9
Necessity 302

Need pay structures 345
Negotiated performance appraisal 103
Negotiating skills 277
Network benchmarking 209
Nominal group technique 52
Non-cash benefits 327
Non-monetary benefits 44

O

Objectives 26, 230, 239, 302, 374
Objectives of succession planning 192
OCTACPAC 261, 269
OD 261
Off-the-job techniques 294
On-the-job coaching 306
On-the-job training 294
Organisational performance 105
Organization design 325
Organizational audit 4
Organizational behaviour 370
Organizational career planning 188
Organizational challenges 21
Organizational change 126, 316
Organizational climate 261
Organizational culture 282, 332
Organizational design 166
Organizational development 107, 190, 253, 267
Organizational development techniques 266
Organizational effectiveness 227, 259, 271
Organizational effectiveness skills 274
Organizational environment 40
Organizational exit 55
Organizational goals 39, 166
Organizational health 397
Organizational leader 148
Organizational objectives 22, 303, 304
Organizational planning 189, 190
Organizational strategies 233, 259, 304
Organizational structures 1, 26
Organization's culture 77
Organization's culture and values 335
Organization's performance 206
Orientation program 317
Orientations 294

P

Participation 395, 396
Pay 110
Pay competitiveness 336
Pay curves 344
Pay equity 350
Pay for performance 360
Pay levels 350
Pay philosophy 336
Pay spines 344
Pay structure 336, 343
Pay structure for manual workers 344
Pay system 130
Payroll 230, 233
Peers 117
Pension schemes 325
Perception 125
Performance 8, 101
Performance appraisal 13, 25, 101, 167, 253
Performance appraisal, potential appraisal, 264
Performance coaching 106
Performance evaluation 114
Performance excellences 138
Performance management 101, 126, 232
Performance management process 126
Performance planning 106
Performance-based 343
Performance-rating 111
Performance-related pay 110
Perquisites 339
Personnel administration 12, 19
Personnel research 30
Physiological needs 3
Placement 84, 88, 235, 260
Planned process 269

Planning 213, 272
Pluralistic approach 384
Poaching 8
Point method 342
Position analysis questionnaire 159
Potential 197, 221, 235
Potential appraisal 169, 197, 253
Potential assessment 197
Potential employees 118
Potential gaps 160
Power distance 332
Practices 207, 370
Principles 355
Privatization 31
Proactive 269
Problem solving 276
Problem-solving processes 260
Process 181, 222, 303
Process improvement 274
Process mapping 274
Production transfer 87
Productivity 19, 37, 104, 172, 233, 257, 276, 292, 357
Productivity bargaining 38
Profits sharing 12, 359
Programmed learning 295
Promotion 39, 83, 84, 240, 260, 306
Promotional policies 75
Psychological contract 265
Psychological withdrawal 333
Purchasing power 333
Purpose 114, 217, 353
Purpose of training 285

Q

Quality 257
Quality circles 13, 190, 266, 288
Quality of life 259, 303
Quality of work life (QWL) 268
Questionnaires 159

R

Ranking approach 120
Rate of return approach 44
Rating scale 121, 171
Ratio analysis 52
Real wages 393
Recruitment 9, 39, 47, 63, 65, 218
Redeployment 40
Redundancies 32, 38, 40
Reengineering 4
Regulator 395
Reinforce 143
Reinforcement 111
Reliability 124
Remedial transfers 87
Remuneration 341
Remuneration policy 347, 353, 355
Replacement charts 53
Replacement transfers 87
Resignation 93
Restructuring 187
Retaining employees 234
Retention 9, 39, 47, 187, 237, 339
Retention strategies 341
Retrenchment 393
Reward management 20
Reward system, job enrichment 13, 25, 262
Rewards 104, 327, 264
Rights disputes 393
Rightsizing 187
Role analysis 265
Role of state 395
Role playing 294, 308, 312
Role-plays 141

S

Safety 288
Salary 9, 234
Salary administration 19
Scientific management 12

Scope 218, 285
Selection 29, 218
Self-analysis skills 310
Self-esteem 151, 277
Self-evaluation 117
Seminars, symposiums and MBO 308
Sensitivity training 190, 311
Separations 92
Several categories 396
Sickness 239
Significance 258
Similarity errors 124
Simulation 141, 153, 294, 308
Simulation interview 183
Skill-based 343
Skills 279
Skills development 227
Smarter 124
Social demand approach 41
Social goals 22
Social justice 395, 397
Social needs 3
Social policy 357
Social skills 310
Socialization 82
Socialization process 83, 94
Societal objectives 23
Soft benefits 173
Spot rate structure 344
Spreadsheet 155
Staffing 10
Staffing process 223
Standard of living 333
Standard salary structure 345
State intervention 395
Steps in benchmarking 210
Stock option programs 359
Stock options 325
Strategic 5, 14
Strategic benchmarking 209
Strategic competencies 143
Strategic HRD 279
Strategic human resources development 251
Strategic plan 293
Strategic planning 160, 267
Strategic process 277
Strategies 234, 237, 272
Strengths and weaknesses 265
Stress management 267
Strokes 311
Subsystems 253
Subsystems of the HRD 264
Succession planning 53, 191, 193
Succession plans 232
Succession process 194, 196
Succession savvy 196
Supply analysis 48, 49
Supply of labour 48
Supporting 395
Sustainability 113
Sustainable 172
SWOT 50, 160
System 241
Systematic development 252
Systems 205
Systems approach 380

T

T-group/sensitivity training 308
Talent 187
Talent management 108, 193
Tangible 241
Tangible asset 234
Task analysis 184
Team building 190
Team building, learning organizations, 267
Team performance 110
Team work 269
Team-based 343, 360
Team-based pay 110

Teams 110
Teamwork 277, 316
Technical and generic competencies 194
Technical skills 277
Technique 155, 241, 311
Techniques of recruitment 69
Technological changes 6
Terms of employment 392
The challenges of HR 6
The marxist approach 383
The self-assessment 189
Theories 370
Time management 284
Tools 219
Total quality management 223, 224, 288
TQM 117, 271
Trade union 68, 71, 391, 394
Traditional performance appraisal 103
Training 4, 8, 26, 187, 203, 264, 281, 287, 293
Training and development 29, 223, 265
Training design 299
Training design process 299
Training needs 153
Training needs assessment 290
Training, OD 253
Training program 292
Training/development 300
Traits 151
Transactional analysis (TA) 308
Transfer 83
Transfer policy 88
Transfers 87
Trend analysis 51
Trends 356
Turnover 52, 84
Turnover, absenteeism 218
Type 327
Type of appraisal 123
Types of industrial disputes-interest disputes 393
Types of role-playing 313
Types of training models 287

U

Uncertainty avoidance 332
Union 391
Utilization of HR 39

V

Valuation 215
Valuation models 239
Values 254, 282
Variable performance pay 341
Versatility transfer 87
Voluntarism 377

W

Wages 10, 11, 393
Weighted checklist 121
Whole-person 122
Work culture 260
Work environment 221, 279
Workbooks 124
Workers participation in management 396
Workforce 19, 83, 193, 220, 254, 262, 288, 398
Workforce composition 300
Workforce diversity 32
Workforce management 173
Working environment 239, 276
Workplace 288, 372
Workplace learning 283
Workplace planning 47
Workshops 125